WODEN
A HISTORICAL COMPANION

WODEN
A HISTORICAL
COMPANION

STEPHEN POLLINGTON

UPPSALA BOOKS

London

UPPSALA BOOKS

London

www.uppsalabooks.com

Copyright © Uppsala Books 2024

ISBN 978-1-961361-06-5 Hardback

ISBN 978-1-961361-07-2 Paperback

ISBN 978-1-961361-08-9 eBook

CONTENTS

Illustrations i

Foreword..iii

    Glossary.. vii

CHAPTER 1

INTRODUCTION...1

    Background to the study 2

        Models of Transmission 4

    Outline of Scholarship 7

        Archaeology 17

        Iconography, Sceattas and Bracteates 19

        Place-Name Evidence... 25

        Of Heathens and Heroes.. 30

    The Name 'Woden' 33

CHAPTER 2

IN THE BEGINNING 39

    The Three Divine Brothers... 41

    The Ribe Skull Fragment Text 42

    From Wóden to Óðinn 43

    Textus Roffensis - East Anglian Kinglist...................... 44

    Divine Threes.. 47

    Old Saxon Baptismal Vow – The Saxon Triad 50

        The East Saxon Kinglist 51

    The Svear Triad... 54

    Divine Duos 55

CHAPTER 3

FROM IRON-AGE WARLORD

TO MEDIEVAL RULER 59

    2nd century BC 60

        Glasbacka Mount.. 60

        Negau Helmet B 61

    1st - 3rd century AD 62

        Tacitus: *Germania*.. 62

        Mercurius Hranno 75

        Local Mercury Cults 78

        Mars Halamarðus 79

4th – 5th century AD 81

    The Vindelev Bracteates 81

6th – 7th century AD 87

    The Nordendorf Brooch 88

    The Strängnäs Runestone 90

    The Sutton Hoo Treasure 91

    The Hellvi Helmet 106

    Uppland Helmets 108

    The Åker Buckle 110

    The Torslunda Dies 113

    The Finglesham Buckle 117

    The Fen Drayton Die 119

    The Eggjum Stone 124

    The Uppåkra Complex 125

    Jordanes: *Getica* 126

    Jonas of Bobbio: *Vita Columbani* 128

    The Lombard Sources I 131

8th – 9th Century 135

    Bede: *Historia Ecclesiastica Gentis Anglorum* 135

    Anglo-Saxon (Old English) Glossaries 156

    Eddius Stephanus: *Vita Sancti Wilfrithi* 157

    Beowulf 158

    Indiculus Superstitionum et Paganiarum 170

The Lombard Sources II 173

    Paul the Deacon: *Historia Langobardorum* 173

    Versus Pauli ad Carolum 177

Gotland Picture Stones 178

Runestones 185

    The Rök Runestone 186

9th – 10th century AD 189

    The Lejre Figurine 189

    The Tissø Pendant 190

    Anglo-Saxon (Anglian) Kinglists and the *Chronicle* 190

    Nennius: *Historia Brittonum* 196

Old High German Sources 198

    Second Merseburg Charm 198

Oseberg Tapestries 200

10th – 11th century AD 202

    Thorwald's Cross 202

    Ledberg Runestone 203

    Kirklevington Cross 203

    Saltfleetby Spindlewhorl 204

    Ælfric of Eynsham: *De Falsis Deis* 205

    Exeter Book 206

    Lacnunga Manuscript 215

    Solomon and Saturn 225

    The Old English Rune Poem 226

    Adam of Bremen: *Gesta Hammaburgensis* 228

    Thietmar of Merseburg: *Chronicon Thietmari* 233

    Orderic Vitalis: *Historia Ecclesiastica* 234

12th – 14th century AD 235

    Church Carvings 236

    Skog Tapestry Fragments 237

    Bergen Runic Wand 238

    Passio et Vita Waldevi Comitis 239

    Symeon of Durham: *Libellus de Primo Saxonum*

    uel Normannorum Adventu 239

    Henry of Huntingdon: *Historia Anglorum* 240

    Walter Map: *De Nugis Curialium* 240

    Saxo Grammaticus: *Gesta Danorum* 241

    Sturla Þórðarson: *Sturlunga Saga* 244

    Egils saga Skalla-Grímssonar 244

    Laxdæla Saga 249

    Orkneyinga Saga 249

    Bárðar Saga Snæfellsáss 250

    Oddr Snorrason: *Ólafs saga Tryggvasonar* 250

    Qrvar-Odds Saga 251

    Ólafs saga Tryggvasonar en Mesta 252

    Snorri Sturluson: *Heimskringla* 253

    Snorri Sturluson: *Prose Edda* 265

    The Poetic Edda 273

    Baldrs draumar 299

    Hyndliuljóð 303

    Úlfr Uggason: *Húsdrapa* 304

    Eiríksmál 304

    Eyvindr Finnsson: *Hákonarmál* 305

    Þjóðolfr of Hvinir: *Haustlǫng* 305

    Ágrip af Nóregskonungasǫgum 305

    Íslendingabók 306

    Hervarar Saga ok Heiðreks 306

    Vǫlsunga Saga 310

    Skjǫldunga Saga 311

    Hrólfs Saga Kraka 312

    Styrbjarnar þáttr Svíakappa 313

    Gautreks saga 313

15th – 16th century AD 317

    Harðar Saga ok Hólmverja 317

    Hálfs Saga ok Hálfsrekka 318

    Icelandic Rune Poem 318

CHAPTER 4

LORD OF THE MEAD HALL 323

Lordship 325

Divine Ancestors 326

Lord and Lady 327

The Drink of Transformation 330

Sharing of the Drink 333

    Leaders of the Rites 334

    Ale, Beer, Mead 337

    The Drink of Inspiration I: Theft & Deceit 339

    The Drink of Inspiration II: Exchange & Pledge 344

    Óðhrérir 349

    The Meaning of Mead 350

    The Serving and Drinking Vessels 351

CHAPTER 5

LORD OF THE DEAD 353

Cemetery Evidence 358

    Diversity in Death 360

    King Eadmund's Fate 361

God-Posts 367

God of the Hanged 371

    Suffering and Death on the World Tree 375

Gaut, Gapt, Geat 384
   Choosers of the Slain 388
Leader of the Wild Hunt... 390
The Warrior Brotherhood 393
Einherjar 397
Berserkir 398

CHAPTER 6
LORD OF INSPIRATION.. 403
   Poetic Inspiration in the Hall 405
   The Whispering God.. 407
Quest for Knowledge.. 408
   Hliðskalf... 409
   Huginn and Muninn.. 409
   Geri and Freki 411
   Gaining the Runes on the World Tree............................ 412
   Óðinn's 'Missing' Eye.. 418

CHAPTER 7
WORKER OF MAGIC, READER OF RUNES 429
Gods in the Runes.. 430
Initiation 432
   The Separable Soul.. 436
   Seiðr 437
Initiation Rites 442
   Boy.. 445
   Youth 446
   Man 447
   Elder 448
Loki 448
Animal Transformations 452
   Animal Motifs 452

CHAPTER 8
WARLORD 455
Woden's Offspring.. 456
Games, Luck and Strategy 457
Battle-Magic.. 460
Binding and Loosing... 464
   First Merseburg Charm 465

Gungnir – Spear of Victory.. 469

CHAPTER 9

HEALER 473

Contra Vermes 474

Wuldortanas 475

Gandr... 476

Healer Iconography 479

CHAPTER 10

CONCLUSION 483

'The Roman Interpretation'?.. 483

Masks and Iconography 485

Successor States 488

A Scandinavian View.. 490

Dark Light In A Bright Age 491

The Way Ahead 495

Appendix I: Divine Threes.. 497

Appendix II: Óðinsheiti – The Bynames of Óðinn 498

Bibliography... 511

Index.. 555

ILLUSTRATIONS

1. Vindelev bracteate (IK738) with horse and rider figure, runic text
2. The large gold buckle from Sutton Hoo Mound 1 with interlaced serpents, birds and quadrupeds
3. Rider figures on *pressblech* plates
4. Rider figure from Sutton Hoo Mound 1
5. Hornhausen stone with rider figure above a lattice of fabulous beasts
6. Dancing warriors with horned headgear, wielding swords and spears
7. The original stone from Sutton Hoo Mound 1 (above) with Brian Ansell's copy being checked for accuracy before final finishing
8. Schematic of the stone with ring and stag fittings
9. Face from the lower end of the stone showing modified eye
10. The gold-plated bird figure from the Sutton Hoo Mound 1 shield (replica)
11. Ornate belt buckle from Åker, Norway
12. *Pressblech* dies from Torslunda, Sweden
13. Warrior and monstrous assailant on the helmet plate from Vendel Mound 1
14. Die from Gutenstein, Germany, showing a wolf-coated warrior with spear and sheathed sword
15. Gilt-bronze buckle from Finglesham, Kent, with dancing warrior
16. The Fen Drayton die with wolf-warrior
17. Gilt-bronze appliqué from Cambridgeshire with horned headgear and two spears
18. Ardre VIII stone Gotland, with detail of the upper scene in which a bearded figure rides an eight-legged horse
19. Tjängvide Stone with detail of the female figure
20. The sacrifice scene on Lärbro Stora Hammars I stone

21. Lärbro Stora Hammars III stone

22. The Hunninge picture stone depicting a battle scene with a horse-man, sword-wielding warriors, a hound and a lady with a drinking horn (perhaps a valkyrja)

23. The Snoldelev runestone (DR248) and the three-horns motif

24. Silver Valkyrie pendant from Wickham Market, Suffolk, England

25. Scabbard chape with mask and flanking birds, from Micheldever, Hampshire

26. Scabbard mount from Chessel Down, Isle of Wight

27. Spearshafts with incised knotwork designs carved into the wooden surface

28. Strap-end from Würtemburg, Germany, with zoomorphic knot-work motifs

29. Bronze *pressblech* die from Icklingham, Suffolk England

30. Reconstruction of the dense interlace panel from the outer face of the shield, Sutton Hoo Mound 1

31. The Undley bracteate with helmeted head, wolf-and-twins motif and runic text

FOREWORD

The inspiration for this book lies in the extensive research projects undertaken in connection with several of my earlier publications: the history of runes and runic studies; the traditions of healing and the application of medicinal substances; the use of alcoholic drinks in social ceremonies and initiations; the developing military culture of early Germanic Europe; the details of art styles and material culture and what the evolution of these styles may have meant to the societies which used them.

The book is also in part a reaction to a long-term trend in popular culture which sees 'Odin' as a simple alpha-male, a testosterone-fuelled 'Viking' – with all that image entails in terms of machismo, arrogance, destructiveness and sociopathic attitudes. Axes, beer and studded leather figure heavily, too. Proponents of this view in my experience have generally not read many of the sources even in translation and often rely on poor or antiquated derivative texts and a raft of secondary material, much of which plays to adolescent power fantasies. The genuine student and interested reader deserves better than that.[1]

The story of Óðinn and his cognates (Woden, Wuotan, Godan, etc.) is infinitely more interesting than such facile, superficial and narrow readings might suggest. The source of these modern notions of the god lies, at least in part, in the 'science fiction' and 'superhero' stories which glamourize aspects of ancient cultures, while also cramming characters drawn from genuine myth into a modern 'superhero' stereotype with restricted moral and social attitudes (Jakobsson, 2011). That Óðinn was not himself restrained by the moral codes of the societies of his worshippers is often overlooked:

---

[1] I have called this book '*A Historical Companion*'; my initial thought was to call it '*A Restitution of Decayed Intelligence*', after Richard Verstegan's work of 1605 in which he tried to bring together as much as might be discovered or inferred in his day about the origins of the Anglo-Saxons, although his motives were rather more in line with 17th century monarchical and republican politics than he put into the title of his book.

for example, Norse society in the Viking age was firmly patriarchal and homophobic, yet the principal god was non-normative in his sexuality.

Most modern interpretations of heathen religion – usually demoted to the status of 'cult' – use as their primary sources the various works of Snorri Sturluson, Saxo Grammaticus and sundry other medieval writers whose output comprised or included stories of the pre-Christian gods. The tales thus recorded are interesting and sometimes encompass details which can be related to the archaeological survivals from the pre-Christian period. But it is a cardinal error to regard a document such as *Hávamál* 'The Sayings of the High One' as the explicit and definitive guide to appropriate and correct behaviour in pre-Christian society. Even a cursory familiarity with the subject should make the reader aware that Germanic religion in antiquity was never based on a fixed body of scripture: there were never any heathen 'holy books' in a preliterate society. Snorri's writings are a medieval Christian's interpretation of the beliefs and practices of his forefathers; they do not constitute 'holy writ', since such a static, monolithic and inflexible notion could not stand at the core of an evolving, amorphous, dynamic and multivalent religious tradition. Snorri knew more than he wrote – much that we wish he had recorded – but his society had already been exposed to notions of 'kingship' and 'divinity' drawn from the Mediterranean world for more than a millennium – considerably more if the Baltic amber trade in the Bronze Age had been a vector for new ideas. There were as many ways of understanding the gods as there were worshippers and dissenters.

Óðinn in the medieval sources is untrustworthy and transgressive; many aspects of his cult are hard to determine and there are few constants. Motifs such as the 'missing eye' and the horned headdress are puzzles on which I hope to shine light in these pages, as also the continued interest in his cult even after Christianity had displaced local traditions as the official ideology across northern Europe.

My long association with Paul Mortimer, Matt Bunker, Maria Legg and others in connection with the important royal site of Sutton Hoo in East Anglia, has led to some lengthy conversations on the nature of kingship in early England, the meaning of the various symbols in Anglo-Saxon art and the foundations of authority, both secular and religious. Extensive study of the Sutton Hoo Mound I remains and their analogues elsewhere in northern Europe and beyond has led me to focus on specific topics for further investigation, which we (Paul and I) have both explored in various media and encouraged others to take up. Visits to relevant sites across northern Europe have only whetted my appetite for deeper inquiry into the subject. The friendship and advice of Neil Price, Frans Herschend, Jon Ljungkvist and others at Uppsala have been invaluable.

My more recent research with Dr Sam Newton and Professor Leonard Neidorf has brought home to me how important it is to approach these matters with an open mind. As much as the archaeology of northern Europe can point us towards physical evidence for the god's worship, the old texts are still by no means exhausted in respect of what they can say to us about human attitudes and the notions which surround the figures in mythology. Although the corpus of texts has been pored over for centuries, fresh insights are still possible – and it may happen that a modern scholar's revelatory intuition was already published (and later dismissed) a century before.

The present book represents a selection of the ideas thrown up by this research. It is not exhaustive, and does not aim to be. There are already a number of fine editions of (particularly Icelandic) texts and many capable translations. The quantity and accessibility of such material can overshadow the less well-known and less frequently cited texts. Likewise, in terms of iconography, there are more instances of horned-headed dancers than I could hope to include within these pages. Improved familiarity with both the archaeology of Iron Age Europe and the various relevant literary remains provides fuel for more wide-ranging treatments: all conclusions are necessarily *provisional*. For example, the discovery and publication of the Vindelev bracteate early in 2023 entailed some hefty rewriting of the text just when it was close to completion, but I am thankful that it was made known in time to avoid an immediate second edition.

My thanks are due to Suzanne Rance, Stephanie Paull, Lindsay Kerr and Ross Harvey, who read drafts of the text and offered valuable suggestions. The present work builds on several of my previous studies, including *Elder Gods*, *Runes: Literacy in the Germanic Iron Age* and *Wayland's Work*. I have refined and revised my opinions where it seemed right to do so.

Steve Pollington,
Essex, November 2023

GLOSSARY

Adam of Bremen	12th c. writer on the history of the Hamburg bishopric, incorporating some interesting side-lights on pre-Christian religious beliefs
Ælfric of Eynsham	Anglo-Saxon 10th-11th c. cleric who wrote homilies concerning standards of behaviour among the Anglo-Danish population
æþeling	OE, nobleman, prince, member of a ruling family
ASC	*Anglo-Saxon Chronicle*
Bede	Northumbrian cleric who in the early 8th c wrote *Historia Ecclesiastica Gentis Anglorum,* abbreviated to *HEGA,* a history of the conversion of the Anglo-Saxons to Christianity
Beowulf	OE, extensive epic poem concerning the history of southern Scandinavia in the 6th c.
comitatus	Latin, band of warriors sworn to the service of a leader
deuterotheme	second word in a compound e.g., *-way* in *pathway*
dísir	ON, female divinities or spirits who required sacrificial offerings from humankind
Elder Edda	See *Poetic Edda*
Eote	a people of northern Jutland (now Denmark) called by Bede *Iutae* and usually written 'Jutes' in modern English
euhemerization	process by which gods are demoted to the status of legendary human characters and their myths become adventure stories or folktales
Fredegar	author of *Chronicon,* a 7th c. legendary history of the Lombards
Germania	work by C. Publius Tacitus detailing current (late 1st c. AD) Roman opinion of the tribes living beyond the Rhine frontier

Gesta Hammabur-gensis Ecclesiae Pontificum	work by Adam of Bremen on the history of the bishopric of Hamburg, Germany
Gylfaginning	ON '*The Deluding of Gylfi*', a prose account of the Scandinavian pantheon, composed by Snorri Sturluson
Hávamál	ON, '*Sayings of the High One*', a series of verses attributed to Óðinn, recorded as a section of the *Poetic Edda* but originally a separate work
Historia Ecclesiastica Gentis Anglorum	Bede's 8th c. history of the early church in England
Nennius	Putative 9th c. author of the *Historia Brittonum*, a compilation of legendary and historical material about early Britain
IRP	*Icelandic Rune Poem*
Íslendingabók	ON, '*The Book of Icelanders*'
Jonas of Bobbio	author of the *Vita Columbani* describing the saint's missionary work among the Lombards and others
jǫtnar	ON, giants, enemies of the gods
Jordanes	Gothic historian who wrote *Getica*, a partly legendary history of the Goths
limes	Latin, borderland of the Roman Empire
Migration Period	Age after the fall of Rome, often dated from the Vandals' crossing of the frozen Rhine in 406 AD, and lasting until the late 7th c.
MLG	Middle Low German
NRP	*Norwegian Rune Poem*
OCS	Old Church Slavonic
Óðinsheiti	byname of the god Óðinn
OE	Old English
OERP	*Old English Rune Poem*
OHG	Old High German
OIr	Old Irish
ON	Old Norse

OS	Old Saxon
Other World	The world of supernatural beings, gods, elves, etc. as distinct from the everyday world of human existence. There may be more than one realm involved, but collectively they are understood to constitute an order of existence separate from that of mankind
PAS	*Portable Antiquity Scheme*; UK-based body which records archaeological finds made by the public, by chance or with metal-detecting equipment
Paul the Deacon	author of an 8th c. legendary history of the Lombards, *Historia Langobardorum*
Poetic Edda	also *Elder Edda* or *Sæmundar Edda*; compendium of mythological poems and accompanying explanations in the *Codex Regius* manuscript, produced in the later 13th c. in Iceland from earlier material
Prose Edda	Snorri's compilation of mythic tales designed to explain obscure references in poetry
Proto-Germanic	(abbreviated to PGmc) reconstructed (hypothetical) language ancestral to all the recorded languages of the Germanic group; such reconstructed forms are marked with an asterisk, e.g., **wodenaz*
prototheme	first element in a compound e.g., *path-* in *pathway*
regin	ON, holy powers, gods
Rothari	king of the Lombards and promulgator of their first lawcode in 643 AD
Saxo Grammaticus	Danish churchman of the 12th c. who composed a Latin summary of the Norse myths, presented as legendary history
Snorri Sturluson	Icelandic statesman of the 13th c. who composed lengthy texts explaining the mythological references in Norse verse
Southumbrian	Pertaining to the Anglo-Saxon kingdoms south of the River Humber (i.e., not Northumbrian)
Sturla Þórðarson	Snorri Sturluson's nephew, who wrote about the early history of Iceland

Tacitus	C. Publius Tacitus, Roman patrician of the late 1st c. AD who wrote a survey of the Germanic lands and peoples
Textus Roffensis	*Textus de Ecclesia Roffensi per Ernulphum episcopum* 'The Book of the Church of Rochester up to Bishop Ernulf', a compilation of Kentish historical documents written in the 1120's
valkyrja	ON (pl. *valkyrjur*), supernatural female emissaries of Óðinn
vǫlva	ON (pl. *vǫlur*), seeress, woman with prophetic powers

In these pages, Old Norse-Icelandic texts are given with the spelling conventions of the stated editions, so for example that the pronoun 'I' may appear as '*ek*' or '*ec*', according to the custom of the editor and the source manuscript(s). I have not attempted to standardise such variations.

Runic forms are cited in bold type, e.g., **wigiþonar**. Bind-runes are marked with the symbol '=', e.g., '**h=a**' denotes **h** and **a** sharing a common stave.

Phonemic forms are cited between slashes, stressed syllables prefixed with ' and long vowels marked with a colon, e.g., /'wo:den/.

The Middle English character *yogh* is transliterated with '*3*' as in *fol3i* 'I follow'.

Beowulf is cited throughout from the fourth edition of Klaeber (Fulk et al., 2008); other Old English poems are cited throughout from their respective editions in the *Anglo-Saxon Poetic Records* (Krapp & Dobbie, 1931-1953).

All translations are my own unless otherwise stated.

CHAPTER 1

INTRODUCTION

Mythology, n. The body of a primitive people's beliefs concerning its origin, early history, heroes, deities and so forth, as distinguished from the true accounts which it invents later.

Bierce, The Devil's Dictionary

The subject of this book is the enigmatic deity known variously as Woden, Uuotan, Godan, Uþin, Óðinn, etc. who inspired many kings, poets and leaders in the post-Roman and early medieval worlds. To avoid endless repetition of the litany of variant names, I shall use the term 'Woden' generally and when referring to the earlier (Anglo-Saxon and other) manifestations of the god and 'Óðinn' when referring to the specifically Scandinavian character for whom the literary records are more copious. References to the god are not necessarily confined to these etymologically cognate terms, as the listing of Óðinn's poetic names (in Appendix II: *Óðinsheiti – The Bynames of Óðinn*) shows, so the form 'Woden/Óðinn' appears as a shorthand term to cover all possibilities (e.g., Hár, Yggr, Grímnir, Grim, etc.). Inconvenient as this may be, it saves the reader the trouble of endlessly repeated lists and caveats.

Texts dealing with the god are quite sparse until the Middle Ages, although perhaps not so rare as is often supposed. The date at which a manuscript is thought to have been written cannot be assumed to coincide with the inception of the story it records. Skaldic verse, for example, may date from a time of composition in the 9th century yet not survive in a written form older than the 13th. All we can reasonably infer is that, at the date of the manuscript's production, such ideas were already current in the society which produced it. How long they had been current is a matter for detailed research.

BACKGROUND TO THE STUDY

For decades, it has been the methodical approach to perform a study of the deity Ódinn by collecting all of the sources concerning him and to analyze them together to form a composite picture, such as was done in E.O.G. Turville-Petre's *Myth and Religion of the North*. This approach has merit in that it provides one with multiple perspectives and a wealth of material from which to draw conclusions. It has limitations in that it implicitly assumes that composite image to represent a holistic reality rather than a series of perspectives strewn across vast planes of time and space; further, it runs the risk of fixating on the content of each source in ignorance of their underlying context.

Levin, *Hlǫðskviða and Wīdsīð:*
A Comparative Analysis of Oral-Literate Networks
and Medieval Memory of the Migration Period

Levin's warning, cited above, is worth considering before any discussion of the subject can proceed. It is unwise to select individual data from the sources and to use these as if they represent the whole; where our sources diverge in time by more than a millennium, smaller or larger adjustments in attitude and context must have taken place multiple times – perhaps with every successive generation. Of course, any study that relies solely on one set of sources (e.g., skaldic poetry, or Saxo's Latin prose) is bound to present a distorted image or, at best, a snapshot drawn from a single culture and time-period. There is much that is now largely irrecoverable, and no amount of research and conjecture will enable us to recapture it. But it is nevertheless worth the effort to bring together familiar material (e.g., mythic tales), enigmatic material (e.g., the inscriptions on the Rök runestone) and newly discovered material (e.g., the Vindelev bracteates) in an attempt to provide the basis for a synthesis, a study which takes into account as much as we can safely say on the subject.

Dedicated and detailed studies of Woden/Óðinn and his cult published in English are not plentiful, and discussion of the cult of Woden in England or Godan in Italy has not been so fruitful as for the Scandinavian god, Óðinn. Yet some of the Anglo-Saxon material is among the earliest recorded and needs to be reappraised in the light of more recent archaeological evidence from both Britain and Scandinavia. In this respect, the interpretation of the grave-goods from Sutton Hoo (Suffolk), the finds from Hellvi (Gotland), the Vindelev (Denmark) bracteate and Professor Neidorf's work on *Widsith* (Neidorf, 2022a) have proven highly instructive.

As Lassen noted in her recent summary of the Scandinavian documentary material: 'There is almost nothing [to say] that has not already been said about Odin, and the majority of it has also been rebutted' (Lassen, 2022, p.1). The search for the pre-Christian figure of Óðinn in the mythological poems and tales which have come down to us has to take into account the fact that *all* the Icelandic sources are products of a Christian society in search of its past. Pre-Christian religion was perhaps still on the edge of memory, but it no longer formed the dominant ideology for the bulk of the population, even in distant Iceland. The figure of Óðinn in the Icelandic texts reflects traditions which were often already centuries old, but no longer fully understood (Karnitz, 2022, p.4).

Scholarship must operate in the margins between what is known or can be reasonably inferred, and what the researcher would really like to know. To generalise somewhat, early discussions operated on the assumption that evidence for Óðinn in Scandinavia can be taken at face value and given weight as evidence for the same god in England, Germany, eastern Europe, northern Italy and elsewhere. Subsequently, more nuanced critical assessments of the sources – particularly Snorri Sturluson's writings – have undermined faith in the accuracy and relevance of those works for an understanding of the god's cult in pre-Christian northern Europe. As so often happens in scholarship, the pendulum of opinion swings to the extremes and any reasoned, well-argued median position is ignored or derided as 'out-of-date', which usually means little more than 'temporarily unfashionable'. In fact, Scandinavian evidence does often have a bearing on that from other contexts, but it is important to establish from the outset the extent to which there may be a genuine cultural continuum and close connection among the various societies involved before any such evidential weight can be accepted. In other words, the relevance of Christian-period Icelandic evidence for earlier periods and other cultural areas must be demonstrated and constantly verified in order to avoid circular reasoning or acceptance of unwarranted assumptions.

If a good case can be made for the worship of a particular deity (with similar names and attributes) in societies linked by more-or-less close geographical and cultural ties, it is perverse to discard such evidence from one society, region or period in discussion of the evidence from another, especially where so little evidence of any kind is available. But this does not mean *automatic* acceptance that, e.g., the Anglo-Saxon concept must be identical to the Lombardic, Danish, Saxon or Icelandic one, even to the limited extent that such narrow notions can be determined.

It is also important to note that the date of composition of a manuscript marks the point at which the oral material develops a parallel set of traditions which appear in writing. This has two important corollaries: first, that the date of the manuscript's composition is not the date when the story was devised (it must *already* have existed in order to be thought worth recording in writing); second, that the written tradition at that point might develop a trajectory of its own, divergent from its oral-culture origins and no longer dependant on them. Woden in the *Exeter Book* poem *Maxims I* became a literary figure, but oral tales of the Woden-character did not cease being told with the creation of that literary reference. The two versions of the single persona existed side-by-side, serving different purposes and among different sets of people.

MODELS OF TRANSMISSION

One mechanism for the transmission of ideas, including religious ones, among North-Sea-based communities should never be dismissed – the role of fosterage and the patronage of outsiders. As a general rule, Germanic societies across northern and western Europe used fosterage widely and on a scale which it is difficult for us to imagine. Examples are legion of a child from a middle-rank or noble family raised in the hall of an ally, kinsman or neighbour – whether we look to the works of Gregory of Tours, Bede, Saxo, Snorri or others. The routine nature of the process is commemorated in appellatives such as *Aðalsteinsfóstri* ('Athelstan's foster-son') for King Hákon I of Norway who spent part of his youth at King Athelstan's court in England and learnt much there which he tried to implement back home when he came to his father's throne.[2]

Beyond fosterage in the narrow sense (accepting a child as a fictive member of the household) is the related custom of young males on the brink of manhood setting off with a group of companions in order to win fame and fortune in the wider world, often ending up in military service to a foreign leader for a defined period (e.g., Waldere among the Huns, Beowulf's stay with Hroðgar at the Danish court, Egil Skallagrímsson's adventures in Norway and England, and countless other examples). 'Setting off' implies an act of free will, which may not always have been the case, since the custom of banishing those who found themselves on the losing side of a struggle was also firmly established in those societies.

Exogamy seems to have been widely practiced at the upper end of the hierarchy, with brides married to eligible men in distant communities which were likely to make useful allies. What the brides thought about such matches is not recorded, although it might never

---

[2] The name is given in *Ynglinga saga* ch.11 (trans. Hollander, 1964). Contemporary English sources do not mention Hákon but the circumstances of his rise to power in Norway indicate that he had been raised in a Christian, western European society. He gained a reputation among Christian writers for apostasy, because he had to accept the continuation of heathen observances. His half-brother and predecessor as king, Eirík Blood-axe, fled to the Orkney islands and later to York where he ruled for a while but was eventually overthrown and killed alongside his son, Hærik. This was recorded in a contemporary poem, *Eiríksmál*.

have been their expectation to avoid marriage; and, given the generally short life-span of the élite males, it may not have been a long-term burden. Status, authority and wealth could be the rewards for a few years of responsibility and child-bearing among strangers.

The employment of youthful foreign warriors who stayed with an established leader in order to 'win their spurs' was entrenched in the military culture of the age. Likewise, the custom whereby the sons of leading men were removed from their family at around seven years old to receive military training and induction from the household of a kinsman or friend of the father, may account for the close similarity of weapon-types and other aspects of military culture across northern Europe at this time (Nørgård-Jørgensen cited in Hårdh, 2000, p.646; Holst et al., 2017, item 39a [Anglo-Saxon sword pommel from Tissø]; Pollington, 2002, p.79). This exchange of military and other ideas between Anglo-Saxon England, Scandinavia and the Merovingian world led to various innovations in technology and organisation, as well as the spread of material culture into distant areas, e.g., evidence of Langobard culture in Anglo-Saxon England (as exemplified by some details of the goods in the burial mound at Prittlewell, Essex), or the close ties between the nobility of Kent and those of both Norway and Francia (Welch, 2007; Blackmore et al., 2019).

Prisoners captured in war and held for ransom and also *gislas* (men held as hostages to ensure the compliance of their families) are likewise a factor. In one notable instance, a group of defeated Gepid captives mocked Alboin, the victorious Langobard prince who had overcome them, because he wore his traditional costume with white hose - one prisoner even compared him to a mare with white 'stockings' on its lower legs (Bóna, 1976; Pohl, 2006, p.137). This hostage-taking custom extended into the 10th c. at least, as we see in the listing of characters present at the battle fought at Northey Island (Essex) in August 991 and commemorated in the poem *The Battle of Maldon*. It included one Æscferð who was the son of a Northumbrian leader (text from Scragg, 1981):

Him se gysel ongan   geornlice fylstan;

he wæs on Norðhymbron   heardes cynnes,

Ecglafes bearn,   him wæs Æscferð nama.

He ne wandode na   æt þam wigplegan

ac he fysde forð   flan genehe

The Battle of Maldon, ll.265–9

'The hostage began to support him [Byrhtnoð] eagerly: he was from a stout kindred in Northumbria, his name was Æscferð, the son of Ecglaf – he did not weaken at all at the war-play but rather he sped forth many arrows…'

Such examples demonstrate that intimate relations and interactions among members of disparate communities could be commonplace. In such environments, especially where long-term fosterage was involved, the exchange and development of shared social customs and religious ideas would be quite natural. Such a system would also explain how literacy was kept at a low level of incidence (if the archaeological record is any guide) but retained a strong uniformity in its detailed practice (Pollington, 2011, p.174; 2016, p.362).

OUTLINE OF SCHOLARSHIP

Since, by definition, all historical research must deal with more or less loose presumptions, such as eyewitnesses' subjective accounts, with the consequences of actions and the interpretation of motives, and since consequently historical research can only result in hypothesis, it appears that, at least sometimes, the baby is thrown out with the bath [sic] for the sake of the method – that it is more important to demonstrate "modern" methods than to evaluate all available sources without prejudice…

Rausing, *Beowulf, Ynglingatal and the Ynglinga saga - Fiction or History?*

The history of published research in English into the nature and origins of Woden shows that such work has not infrequently been both meagre and sensationalist, driven by the intellectual fashions of the day. One such fashion is structuralism, which searches for (or perhaps 'imposes') oppositions within an overall scheme, most often expressed as binary pairs with a third, 'neutralised' entity completing the set. So, for example, in Norse myth the gods (*Æsir*) are in structural opposition to the giants (*jǫtnar*), and Loki is the mediator (neutralisation) between these two groups by virtue of his genetic background among the giant-kin and his blood-brotherhood with Óðinn (Liberman, 2016, pp.23-7). Another structuralist approach is that of Kozák (2021, p.1) who compares the stories of the theft of the mead of inspiration and that of the god's hanging on the tree to win the runes, and finds in them 'a series of oppositions: simple–complex, static–dynamic, passive–active, etc. Their contrast is so pronounced that it paradoxically seems to point to their deeper connection'.

Structuralist ideas have influenced the study of mythology since the mid-20th century, with the emphasis firmly on the system as a whole, rather than the individual elements within it. Dumézil is often considered the primary structuralist in the sphere of mythological studies, although there have been many others. Failure to deal adequately with diachronic developments and synchronic anomalies has called the usefulness of the structuralist approach into question, despite the obvious attractions of its methodological neatness and regularity.[3] Establishing useful parallels as well as discriminating between these and random congruences is at the heart of the enquiry: 'The burning of the ring Draupnir on Baldr's funeral pyre has an analogue in Ossetian epic poetry… Since this observation leads nowhere, it matters little whether we register it or not' (Liberman, 2016,

---

[3] Frakes (2002) deals at length with the anomalous position of Loki, whose ambiguous character defies all attempts to slot it into the tripartite structure. This failure calls into question the relevance of Dumézil's tripartition for the Scandinavian myths.

p.198). Simply piling up an impressive quantity of data serves only to confuse study rather than to elucidate it. Price has usefully summarised the 20th c. research into Óðinn in his 2002 work *The Viking Way: Religion and War in Late Iron Age Scandinavia* (updated and reissued in 2019).

Attempts at 'defining' or explaining Óðinn have often been reductive: a death-bringing spirit (Unwerth, 1914), a patron of trade (Wissowa, 1916) or a sorcerer (von der Leyen, 1902) were among the early favourites in the 20th c. (Liberman, 2016, pp.32-4 and references there): as late as 1941, a correspondent with the initials 'B.C.' was moved to ask 'How came the more or less subordinate god Mercury to be identified with Woden, the chief god of the Teutons? Caesar refers it to Mercury's being the inventor of all arts, the conductor of travellers, a mighty power in money getting. But do the functions and attributes of Woden correspond with this?' (*Notes and Queries*, March 8, 1941, p.171).

Early treatments often placed 'Odin' in the role of 'king of the gods' and looked no further than the adjacent classical (Graeco-Roman) model for a context. Odin could then be regarded as a version – and a poor one, at that – of Roman Jupiter, the stern and rather distant father of the divine family– although a more fruitful comparison might be with the Greek Zeus, who shares the Germanic god's tastes for deceit, seduction, vengefulness, shape-shifting and capriciousness. H.M. Chadwick's 1899 essay *The Cult of Othin* assembled as much as could then be determined of the background to the god's worship from literary sources with full consideration of the philological exegesis surrounding them, then applied these data to the archaeological record. The study took in Scandinavian, OE and OHG sources. The result was something of a breakthrough in the historiography of the god's worship, in that it demonstrated that the literary sources are not mere fictions but reflections of actual practices. Building on Chadwick's work, de Vries published an interesting examination of the god's role in the matters of warfare and death (1931).

Chadwick's approach inspired Hilda Ellis Davidson, G.N. Garmonsway and others to delve into the subject of early Norse society (Ellis Davidson, 1971; Garmonsway, 1928): '*The precise nature of the relationship between Wodan, the god of the early Germanic tribes, and the later Scandinavian deity Odin is not perhaps as simple as we tend to assume*,' wrote Ellis Davidson in 1971 with great prescience, and the exploration of the development from the one to the other has occupied many scholars' waking hours ever since.

In his monumental work *Teutonic Mythology* (*Deutsche Mythologie*, trans. Stallybrass) Jacob Grimm saw in the god a personification of 'wish' (*Wünsch*) as an appeal to the benevolence of the deity and his ability to deliver favourable outcomes to those whose will is up to the task of making their wishes come true (Tatar, 2021). While interesting, this observation does not appear to lead anywhere.

An origin for Woden in some eastern or Asiatic religion has often been proposed. This may be assigned to the Goths or their Eastern Germanic neighbours (Gepids, Vandals, etc.) or, more precisely, it may be ascribed to the period when Attila held sway over a large part of Europe and aspects of religious cult might then have been influenced by the contemporary Hunnic religious practice. This has been argued more recently by Lotte Hedeager (2011). Kaliff and Sundqvist (2004) saw a source - or at least a strong influence - from the cult of Mithras which was very widely practised among Roman troops along the imperial frontier, and they suggest that it is the worship of Mithras by military men which was responsible for the specifically martial aspects of the Óðinn persona.

The study of the gods of Ásgarð and their complex relationships has yielded some interesting results. The Swedish historian of religion, Folke Ström, proposed that Óðinn and Loki were originally a single deity (Ström, 1956). However, exactly when this situation might have existed is (almost) impossible to determine, and in turn it does not preclude the possibility that the period of Óðinn-Loki unity might have resulted from the fusion of two earlier separate characters (Schjødt, 2019, p.71). Schjødt has analysed published research into pre-Christian religion in northern Europe and divides it into 'strands' or principal subject areas which comprise: (1) historical – examination of historical sources; (2) literary or philological – focusing on ancient and medieval texts and the forms of words used in them; (3) structuralist-comparative – researching the nature of myths in the wider sense and applying this knowledge to the records; (4) other structuralist schools – similar to (3) but not confined to the comparative method (Lassen, 2022, pp.30-1).

The structuralist-comparative scholar Dumézil is famed for his development of the *idéologie tripartie* and his detection of this tripartite structure in the early stories of many cultures in Europe and Asia. The mythological and religious aspects of the 'three functions' have been rehearsed and debated at length, and the rigidity of Dumézil's systemic categorisation has invited criticism (Dumézil, 1973; Dillmann, 1979; Liberman, 2016, pp.23-5, 80-3). For example, the second function figure (the warrior) is clearly important in the cult of Óðinn; likewise, the first function figure (the ruler or leader) is present, whether secular (king) or sacral (priest), both of which appear to have a bearing on the Norse myths. Dumézil further developed the idea of the 'dark' side of Óðinn, his role as an inciter of discord and stirrer of strife (Schjødt, 2019, p.64). It is hardly to be doubted that some facets of a similar god (or gods) were already present in the Indo-European background. However, such theories have not won universal acceptance (Liberman, 2016, p.19):

'Experience shows that the mythologist should beware of opening too many doors with one key. Nature mythology, solar mythology, a dogmatically euhemeristic approach to the gods, and so forth failed miserably despite the fact that some of their proponents were great scholars. In similar fashion, I have no enthusiasm for the application of Georges Dumézil's scheme to the Germanic gods. Guided by common sense, rather than grand theories, Jacob Grimm's book has aged gracefully, whereas many endeavours of later mythologists are often devoid of even historical interest… The more convoluted structuralist experiments are, the more useless they appear to be. The objectivity of a structure imposed by the researcher on the material is an illusion.'

wrote Liberman in the introduction to his important collection of papers on Germanic myth.

The usefulness of reconstructed Indo-European data in elucidating the Germanic past is often questioned, partly because so few of the 'standard' ideas (such as tripartition) fit the Germanic evidence neatly, and partly because the Indo-European picture is itself a jigsaw puzzle with most of the pieces missing, having to be filled in by the researcher's own imagination. Where Germanic evidence can be brought to bear on an Indo-European issue it can be very helpful, but its relevance is seldom beyond dispute (Lincoln, 2018, ch.1).

Ryan's essay 'Othin in England: Evidence from the Poetry for a Cult of Woden in Anglo-Saxon England' opened with the statement (Ryan, 1963):

> It is a commonplace in the criticism of Old English literature to state that the whole poetic technique was a heritage from Germanic heathendom. It is, similarly, widely admitted that the ideas, which were given heathen dress, meant a great deal – in some vague way – to the minds of the early English. It is not so generally agreed that a close analysis of this received material may still yield us some knowledge of the ways in which our ancestors regarded their deities.

The paper appeared at a time when this 'commonplace' was no longer universally accepted in English academic establishments and the subsequent two and more decades saw attempts at wholesale rebuttal of the notion that anything substantive derived from the pre-Christian past could have permeated the Christian Anglo-Saxon tradition. Ryan's treatment included the observation that cult animals associated with the god continued to appear as emblems in even quite late OE verse, the 'beasts of battle' such as the wolf, eagle and raven; the same traditions underlie the later traditional poems *Twa*

Corbies and *Three Ravens*, and even the 13ᵗʰ c. *The Owl and the Night-ingale* which includes the owl's claim that (text from Cartlidge, 2001):

> Þar aȝte men boþ in worre,
>
> An fareþ boþe ner an forre,
>
> An oueruareþ fele þode,
>
> An doþ bi niȝte gode node,
>
> Ich folȝi þan aȝte manne,
>
> An flo bi niȝte in hore banne.'

> "Where bold men go to war and travel near and far while they overrun many peoples, and do good service at night, then I follow those valiant men and fly at night in their company."

An Indo-European heritage for Woden was explored at great length by Kershaw (2000), who traced the god's functions and several aspects of his cult to very early traditions concerning Rudra, an Indian god with many qualities overlapping those of Woden, not least his healing and protective abilities which are foregrounded in, e.g., the *Nine Herbs Charm* or the *Second Merseburg Charm*. One such aspect is the association with warfare and specifically the men who practice it – a notion which was developed by Enright and others (Enright, 1996, pp.217-8 and references there) in relation to the post-Roman 'warband' or *comitatus* motif which informed so many early European societies. Here, the etymologically related Old Irish terms *confad* 'rabies' and *confadach* 'rabid' point to the meaning of *furor* as a state of unthinking, uncontrolled aggression. But Enright's work displays a progressive 'certainty-creep' whereby an initial vague suggestion develops into a possibility early in the text, then becomes a probability, and eventually a conviction and a self-evident truth. Enright utilizes the idea of the human warlord as the prototype for the role of Woden – in the context of European Iron Age societies speaking both Celtic and Germanic languages (Enright, 1996; Schjødt, 2019, p.65). This development took place along the Rhine frontier, which was already a culturally and linguistically diverse area into which the Roman Empire intruded in the last century BC, bringing Mediterranean ideas and practices. The cult of Mithras played its part here too. There was already a god of 'Odinic type' among the local Rhinelanders, Enright maintained, but contact with the Roman military developed both the warrior aspects of the cult and its association with leadership as reflected in the later role of Woden as founder of dynasties, for example. There is broad agreement that the expansion of dedicated warbands around the 1st c. BC-AD and the attendant ritualised aspects of gift-giving, feasting, prognostication, verse-making and much else were all influential in promoting the god's cult.

Hilda Ellis Davidson wrote widely on various Norse and Germanic mythological subjects, often from a folklore perspective (Ellis Davidson, 1964, 1971). Many of her essays are invaluable for their breadth of scholarship and the range of evidence she was able to adduce. *Gods and Myths of Northern Europe*, published in 1964, is a masterly overview of the subject of Germanic mythology from Roman-period references through to the medieval sources, compressing a vast amount of erudition into a few pages. Each of her other works – *The Road to Hel, The Battle-God of the Vikings, Pagan Scandinavia* and the rest – introduces new ideas and fresh interpretations.

E.G. Stanley took the wholly uncompromising view that all references to the gods and heroes of the Germanic past in Anglo-Saxon literature were condemnations of these characters as 'unsaved', i.e., not redeemed by submission to the Christian saviour (Stanley, 1964). 'Beowulf is damned' he wrote in one paper (Stanley, 1987), a view which contrasts strongly with many contemporary interpretations where Beowulf is himself considered as an allegory of Christ (e.g., Bloomfield, 1963; Cabaniss,1963; MacNamee, 1963).

David Wilson published *Anglo-Saxon Paganism* in 1992, in which he sought to remove discussion of the religion of the pre-Christian Anglo-Saxons from its prevalent context of literary evidence, mainly drawn from Scandinavian sources, specifically Snorri and Saxo (Wilson, 1992). Anglo-Saxon literary references were likewise excluded from consideration because of the difficulty for modern readers in grasping exactly what such texts were understood to mean by their medieval readership. Having thus discounted all the potentially relevant comparanda, Wilson's study proceeded to a discussion of the structure of graves and their inclusions as a means of understanding the religious behaviour of the Anglo-Saxons unmediated by linguistic and textual filters. Unsurprisingly with such a reductive approach, his conclusions are entirely negative, relying on the precarious assumption that the structure and contents of graves are primarily informed by the religious attitudes of their creators.

Iconographic evidence is likewise fraught with pitfalls. Kathryn Starkey reacted against the work of Karl Hauck, whose extensive study of the evidence of bracteate iconography is invaluable for an understanding of the topic, but whose interpretations often exceed the bounds of the probable (Starkey, 1999; cf. Neiss, 2007). Hauck assumed *á priori* that a fully-formed cult of Óðinn existed in the period of bracteate production (broadly, the 6th c. AD) and that the scenes presented on these discs must therefore represent episodes from the myths of the gods who later appear in Snorri's works. Hauck further supposed that bracteates were a 'pan-Germanic' cultural phenomenon, common to all Germanic-speaking groups, while in fact they were limited to communities surrounding the North Sea with outliers in the Baltic region. Bracteates do not appear to have played any part in the rituals and traditions of the Franks, for example, nor the Ostrogoths, Visigoths, Burgundians and many other powerful nations of the post-Roman world. Among the peoples of Denmark, southern Sweden, the coastal Netherlands and eastern England they were an important but short-lived cultural phenomenon (Gaimster, 1992, 1998, 2001; Wicker, 1994, 2005, 2006, 2008, 2011, 2014; Starkey, 1999; Axboe, 1993, 1999, 2001; Suzuki, 2006; Bursche, 2008; Austin, n.d.). Yet, while Hauck perhaps over-interpreted the bracteate evidence, he correctly surmised that the notion of the god's worship having begun further back than the 'Viking age' is supported through their iconography (Price & Mortimer, 2013).

Philip Shaw's 2002 study *Uses of Wodan: The Development of his Cult and of Medieval Literary Responses to It* concentrated on the Anglo-Saxon evidence for Woden as a royal ancestor and sought to separate the Anglo-Saxon from the Scandinavian tradition by positing two homophonic proto-forms of the name, each with a different sphere of interest (Shaw, 2002; cf. Pollington, 2011, p.174). Shaw suggested that Christian missionaries were simultaneously (i) attempting to convert the northern peoples to Christianity and (ii) forcing a remodelling of their ideas about their heathen gods into a format closer to the Graeco-Roman one in which the various deities form a heavenly family. Such a project would have been ambitious, to say the least, involving wholesale changes in social attitudes, hierarchies, place-names and other aspects of daily life. Quite why a Christian zealot would want to revise popular opinion about a god which he must have deemed pernicious, false and an emanation of Satan was never made clear. Shaw's study retains much useful discussion but fails to convince.

One of the longest-running disputes concerns the context of the god within the narrative tradition. 'Is he a latecomer (perhaps no earlier than the beginning of the Germanic Iron Age) in Scandinavia or has he been there since the Indo-European migrants arrived (probably towards the beginning of the Bronze Age) – or something in between?' (Kershaw, 2000, pp.1-9; cf. Schjødt, 2019, p.59) As Schjødt notes, the problem hinges upon the development of ideas about Óðinn and since we have so little early evidence to use for comparison (so few early instances of the god's name, for example) we immediately confront a methodological problem: comparison of Wotan, Woden, Mercury and Gaut involves decisions about what constitutes 'sameness' and what 'difference'. To what extent can Roman Mercury or Anglian Woden be considered a direct ancestral form of the Scandinavian Óðinn? What was the god's original nature and function? Various proposals have been made: god of death, psychopomp, god of warfare, god of the winds, god of magic – the list goes on.

ARCHAEOLOGY

The search for Woden's place in early Anglo-Saxon social, ideological and mythic structures is not primarily an archaeological matter, although archaeological evidence must play its part in the investigation. It should come as no surprise that physical remains taken in isolation can tell us little about gods and their myths: without taking the literary data into account, it is all but impossible to say anything meaningful about the Anglo-Saxon past.

As a rule, when dealing with pre-literate or proto-literate societies, the greater the remove from the first historical records, the greater must be our caution. This book cites studies into Germanic culture which refer to northern European societies and languages of the Iron Age, beginning in perhaps the 5th c. BC or a little earlier. The evidence for Germanic society and culture drawn from linguistics is impressive, but attempts to relate these language-based data to archaeology are less certain and often fiercely debated: there are many vested interests in archaeological and linguistic research, as well as national pride and foundation myths to defend. The further back in time we project, the greater the uncertainty (Liberman, 2016, ch1).

An attempt to relate archaeologically-derived iconography to the underlying belief system is that of Nicolay (2017), who examined the iconography of a set of square-headed bow-brooches found in the southern coastal zone of the North Sea, mainly Friesland. A remarkable find of such an item was made in 2012 and 2015: the brooch was broken into two fragments, resting at a depth of 10-25cm in the topsoil and about 20 metres apart. The site was a *terp* or artificially raised 'mound' in a salt marsh on the former estuary of a river which had been an important political boundary in earlier times. Coin and other evidence found locally suggests that the site was inhabited from Roman times into the later Middle Ages. The brooch was parcel-gilt silver with chip-carved decoration and niello filling, with zoomorphic and geometric ornament on the headplate which may be interpreted as a mask or human face; tellingly, the left

eye is shown much smaller than the right. The decoration is executed in so-called Animal Style I Phase A. The brooch belongs to
the 'Jutlandic group', which is found in Kent (England), in Friesland
and in Denmark (e.g., at Gudme). The earlier-dated finds relate to
the period 460-520 AD and are called 'type Engers', while the later
ones of 'type Tournai' date to the period 480-550 AD. The Frisian
brooch is in some respects like another brooch from Bifrons, Kent,
which bears similar decoration and dates from the same period,
probably made around 550 AD. The brooch was not recovered from
a grave but apparently had been deposited in the settlement itself.

Nicolay surmised (2017, p.508) that the bearded head placed between animals which appears on the Jutlandic brooches can be
related to a similar head with a bird-head finial to the hair, a motif
which occurs in bracteates of Types A and C. A human face placed
between animals or birds is a recurrent theme in early Germanic art
(Pollington, 2010, pp.444-8), which he then related to Óðinn with
his spirit-helpers in the guise of wolves or ravens. Nicolay further
linked the large brooch-type as seen in the find at Wijnaldum to the
references in Þrymskviða to the Brísingamen, the resplendent jewel
which forms part of the outfit of the goddess Freyja, and from this
he deduced that the brooch was part of the cult costume of the goddess.

The leaders of tribes settled in the Frisian areas formed part of
the continuum of non-Christian societies which extended north
into Scandinavia; this is confirmed by the close relations maintained
between Frisia and Jutland in the early 6th c. when groups of Jutland
emigrés escaped the centralising power of the Danes in Zealand and
left to serve the Frisian king Finn (Tolkien, 1982; Shippey, 2022).

Óðinn's power rested, in this scheme, on creating and maintaining political alliances through gift-giving, gaining wisdom through
access to the supernatural world by means of runes, and through the
preservation of cosmological knowledge in traditional tales (Nicolay,
2017, p.509). The 'Scandinavian phase' of the Frisian coast can be
linked to movement of southern Scandinavians (e.g., Angles and

Eote among others) moving westwards to establish settlements in Britain and elsewhere.

ICONOGRAPHY, SCEATTAS AND BRACTEATES

The search for Woden has often led investigators into murky corners where surprises await them – and disappointments.

There is a source of putative 'Woden iconography' which must be discounted immediately. A series of very early Anglo-Saxon coins called *sceattas* features on the obverse a full-face male mask with looped hair framing the face and a zoomorph on the reverse; these have been known as 'Woden-head sceattas' in the specialist literature since the 19th c. on no basis whatsoever (Shaw, 2002, p.27; Gannon, 2003; Abramson, 2006). The use of a facing mask on coins dates to ancient times (at least the 5th century BC) and has no particular relevance for the cult of any god or hero; likewise, many coins bear a highly stylized 'monster' or animal on the reverse. The designs on the obverse and reverse faces of early coins seldom have any significance: for English hammered coinage, one face may bear the name of the king and the other the name of the moneyer and his mint, but any repetition of these will be due to an overlap in the time of striking the coins rather than to a thematic link between these design elements. The mechanical nature of the process by which coins were produced makes random congruences of this sort almost inevitable.

A more nuanced treatment is necessary when discussing bracteates. The Latin term *bractea* 'thin plate' has been used for a variety of struck (or, rarely, cast) thin metal items such as medallions and amuletic pendants (Smith, 1923, p.86; Bakka, 1981; Hatch Wicker, 1992, p.149; MacGregor & Bolick, 1993, pp.154-5; Simek, 1993, s.v. *bracteates;* Axboe, 1994, 2005; Hauck, 1994; MacGregor et al., 1997, pp.57-8, 87-8; Hinton, 2005, p.33; Franceschi, Jorn & Magnus, 2005a, pp.42-5; Wicker, 2005; Suzuki, 2006; Imer & Vasshus, 2023). For present purposes, 'bracteates' comprise thin metal foils into which a design has been impressed from a master or die, often known by the German term *Pressblech* which refers to the matrix from which the bracteates were struck. There are around a thousand examples known from Scandinavia and the North Sea rim, dating from the 5th to 7th c. The designs on them are of four main types, although there does not seem to be any chronological significance to the variation: all four designs were in use simultaneously, it appears (Imer & Vasshus, 2023, p.61).[4] Similar dies and techniques were also used to produce decorative plates for helmets (e.g., Sutton Hoo, Vendel, Valsgärde, etc.), drinking horn mounts, shield fittings and various other kinds of display items. Bracteates were worn at the neck by high-status females, suspended on a chain or a braided thong; some had been in use long enough to have worn away part of the suspension loop (Gaimster, 1992, p.12; Axboe, 2001, p.120; Schutz, 2001, p.190; Leahy, 2003, p.157; Owen Crocker, 2004, p.88).

The Anglo-Saxon examples are crucial to understanding how bracteates were used, since they are mostly found in graves whereas the Scandinavian examples are more usually from deposited hoards (Hines, 1989, p.197ff; Gaimster, 1992, p.2; Wicker, 2005).[5] Generally, they appear on the chest or at the throat of persons with female grave-goods, sometimes accompanied by beads (Wicker, 2005, p.52).[6] Many examples are heavily worn and degraded, even after reinforcement with an additional gold panel at the reverse of the

---

[4] Probably the type 'M', a close copy of a Roman medallion, should be considered to have been produced earlier than the other designs which are its variants.

[5] The southern Scandinavian finds are almost all from hoards, while in Germany, England and elsewhere grave-finds are usual, and on Gotland both locations may occur.

[6] Two examples from Gotland were found in graves with male grave-goods (weapons), but in neither case was there a suspension loop on the disc and it is possible that the item was a keepsake for a female relative. Only one complete bracteate was found with a male, in a grave at Monkton (Kent) where it was not worn prominently on the chest but instead had been concealed. All the known supposedly-male bracteate burials are in peripheral areas to the main bracteate-using culture.

loop. It therefore seems likely that bracteates were sometimes in use for a long period (long enough to start to wear through at the suspension hole) and were probably passed from one generation to the next if they were not selected for burial with the last owner. The suspension cords never survive, which suggests that they were made from an organic material or had been removed prior to burial.

While the iconography of the discs references a male figure, the users were female (in Anglo-Saxon England at least, and where grave-goods correlate with gender) (Gaimster, 1998, 214ff.).[7] The central character often appears to be a profile figure in the guise of healer and user of magic, less often associated directly with rulership or warfare (Franceschi, Jorn & Magnus, 2005a, pp.46-7).[8] The Anglo-Saxon women who were buried with these items are all accompanied by other high-status objects and were portrayed at the time of burial as the most respected females in their communities, probably wielding considerable power in the legitimation of control or 'kingship' (Magnus, 1997, p.194; Hawkes, 2000; Gaimster, 1992, p.17; 2001, p.152).

Researchers have held differing opinions about the chronology of bracteate production and use, but a date-range in the Migration Period is generally agreed, the 5th-6th c. (Imer & Vasshus, 2023, p.61). Since bracteates appear as grave-goods, this may indicate that they were instrumental in creating and symbolising marriage and kinship ties among North Sea communities, and were 'retired' on the death of the brides who bore them. These items were not mere showy dress accessories – rather, they were highly charged symbols in themselves with (probably mythological) figural scenes displayed

---

[7] In Anglo-Saxon England, Continental Germany and Norway, the bracteates always occur in female graves but in Denmark and southern Sweden there are occasional finds from male graves (4 cases out of 70). This may indicate that the meaning of the pendants differed in peripheral societies from that of the originating area. It is also possible that their use as grave-goods indicates that they were intended as payment to the guardians of the Otherworld, like Charon's *obol* in Classical Greece.

[8] However, there are other interpretations of some of the iconography.

prominently on their surfaces (Gaimster, 1992, p.12).[9] They bear runic characters in some cases, seldom with an obvious meaning (Haughton & Powlesland, 1998; Pollington, 2016, pp.156-78).

Bracteates served no mundane purpose, unlike brooches and clasps, and therefore 'may be considered a vehicle used primarily to convey status and belief' (Wicker, 2005, p.57). A bracteate would be prominently displayed on a woman's costume, worn among beads of glass, crystal and amber – part of the adornment of such a figure as the *goldhroden cwēn* 'gold-adorned queen' of *Beowulf*. Only close inspection would reveal the iconography embossed on the obverse, so only viewers already initiated into the appropriate religious and social mysteries would be able to read the messages of ethnicity, status and identity conveyed on them. The pendants also possibly functioned as *donatives*, symbolic gifts from a ruler which signified the initiation of a personal relationship with the recipient – a bond of trust and loyalty. The standard iconography of the original later-Roman products shows the Emperor as a divine and impressive figure in his benign aspect. This style was adopted and developed in post-Roman contexts, so that the religious attributes were emphasised: the 'Emperor-God' became the 'King of the Gods' (Hauck, 1994).

Politically, bracteates were part of a cultural assemblage which was used by southern Scandinavians to bind together societies on the eastern, western and southern edges of the North Sea into a single cultural continuum, with a key 'magical' figure, possibly a 'Woden the healer', at its centre (Franceschi, Jorn & Magnus, 2005a, p.500; Schjødt, 2020b, p.1135) although the text on the Vindelev find calls this identification into question.

The artefact typology has long been established, divided into seven classes; the work of Karl Hauck has been instrumental in understanding the series and their relations (7 volumes, 1985-9). The probably earliest group, Type M, is a local copy of an imperial Roman medallion, depicting the Emperor (understood as a 'king', lawgiver or warlord in the Germanic cultural context). Type A features

---

[9] McLeod & Mees (2006, p.21) describe them as 'belt-hangings'.

a human head in profile, sometimes with profile animals around it; this head has been said to represent Woden. Type B shows one to three standing figures, one raising a T-shaped sceptre, called the 'three-gods' type; a link to the legend of Baldur is sometimes proposed. A profile bust above a horse (sometimes with crescent horns on the brow) features on Type C; runic text is most common on this series. Type D features a stylised animal reduced to its outline. It is found only on Gotland in the Baltic. Type E features a triskele beneath a D-shaped mask; these are mostly struck in bronze rather than gold. Type F features an animal in profile similar to that on Type C, but without the male bust; a link to the healing of Baldur's foal (*Second Merseburg Charm*) has been suggested (Imer & Vasshus, 2023, p.61).

Bracteate studies are very much a work-in-progress as new finds come to light, and the typology is still evolving (Shepherd, 1998, p.9; Imer & Vasshus, 2023). Some problems of dating have been tackled through art-historical assessments, with varying success and little agreement among the experts. The animal forms partake of stylistic elements from both Styles I and II: they are disjointed in the manner of Style I beasts, but they may also include ribbon-like bodies and interlace in the manner of Style II (Pollington, Kerr & Hammond, 2010, pp.281-8). Salin regarded them as forming a transition from the earlier to the later style, encouraging the development of classic Style II forms.

Hauck's interpretations of the iconography have been very influential. He proposed that some figures can be interpreted as Woden in his magic-working and ecstatic states, evidenced by their various poses and gestures (Kershaw, 2000, p.6-7; Neiss, 2007, p.83).[10] He published several exhaustive studies of the bracteate material illustrating his interpretations of the iconography in terms of Snorri's Icelandic myths which he believed were inherited from the Migration Period

---

[10] The posture with the thumb raised to the lips or chin seems to have had some special significance relating to the acquisition of knowledge (Nicolay, 2017, p.508).

(Franceschi, Jorn & Magnus, 2005a, p.46). While the basic premise seems sound – that the iconography represents current religious motifs – the small size of the pieces and the manner of their execution excludes any fine detailing which might assist with identification and interpretation. The runic texts are seldom helpful, the stories which the scenes might represent are largely unknown and it is by no means certain whether the scenes are meant to show gods enacting myths or human worshippers enacting rituals. In the light of these uncertainties, it has been difficult to determine how the evidence of bracteate iconography can advance our knowledge of the religion of the societies which produced them.

However, in 2023 a metal-detector find close to the Danish royal site at Jelling caused a revision of opinion when a hoard of bracteates was published, one bearing the retrograde runic sequence ...**wodnasweraz**... (i.e., 'Woden's man'). The bracteate is of Type C and the find sheds a new light on the iconography, since it rather suggests that the rider figure should not be seen as the god himself but rather the 'man' – a devotee, follower or worshipper. It is also the earliest unambiguous example of the *wodanaz* name in any medium so far discovered.

Taking a long step back in time, we may look for evidence of the spear-wielding god in the Bronze Age rock carvings of Bohuslän, Sweden where indeed just such a figure appears ('an early representation of the sky god who ruled over the battlefield as well as the rain and thunder, bringing fruitfulness to the earth' wrote Ellis Davidson) and on the Vitlyckehäll stone near Tanumshede, in Västra Götaland (Ellis Davidson, 1972; Kershaw, 2000, p.7; Schjødt, 2019, p.74). But the rock carvings are famously difficult to explain. Many show scenes of conflict with spearmen and axe-men wielding their weapons, and seafaring vessels, waggons and other objects placed around these scenes. There is little to identify the figures as either human or divine and, if the latter, to put any kind of interpretation to them.

One late image was found in a stave church at Hegge, Norway of 13th c. date (dendrochronolgy puts some timbers at 1215 AD); a male face is carved inside at the top of one of the staves, shown with one eye, a crooked mouth and protruding tongue. Interpretations of the image have ranged from 'Óðinn' to a 'hanged man' – these two themes are not mutually exclusive, of course, and the hanged god may have been in the carver's mind when he made the image (Kershaw, 2000, p.7).

PLACE-NAME EVIDENCE

Place-name evidence for the cult of Woden is not plentiful in the modern English landscape and may never have been so. Likewise, in Scandinavia, sites named for the god are few, and in Iceland entirely absent. This may be taken as evidence that the god was not worshipped there, or that original theophoric place-names were later changed for reasons of tabu or religious orthodoxy. Further, it might be thought likely that most place-names were given by the locals – farmers and traders and craftsmen – for whom the god of warfare and arcane knowledge was largely irrelevant (Schjødt, 2019, p.68). The Scandinavian toponyms referring to Óðinn are situated in the south, where settlement was denser and social centralisation came earlier (Schjødt, 2020, p.1133)

Places in modern Denmark which retain an *Odin-* or *Oden-* name include the city of *Odense* on Funen (Odin's lake); *Onsholt* on Jutland (Odin's wood) near Viby (settlement by the *vê*). In Norway, the island *Óðinsøy* in Ostfold is an outlier of the group. Sweden has an *Onslunda* (Odin's stand of trees), *Odensåker* (Odin's field), *Odensvi* (Odin's *vê*) and several examples of *Odensjö* or *Onsjö* (Odin's lake). (Finland's *Odensö* is probably a corruption of a previous Finnish toponym.) Germany has both a *Godeberg* and a *Gudensberg*, both originally *Wuodenesberg* 'Wotan's mountain' and a *Godensholt* (from *Wodensholt* 'Wotan's grove'). The Netherlands has both a *Woensdrecht* (Woden's portage) and a *Woensel* (Woden's hall) (Mitchell, 2020).

The antiquity of these names is often conjectural and there remains the possibility that some are rationalisations or folk-etymologies, but they do appear in many cases to be of at least medieval date and therefore may plausibly have been given when the worship of the god was still in public memory. The renaming of salient landscape features in early modern times is known – *Kung Björns Hög* or *Hågahögen* at Uppsala, Sweden; *Björn Järnsidas Hög* on Munsö; *Onsbjerg/Odinsbjerg* on Samsø. These new, archaistic names have been applied with reference to an imagined distant past, perhaps to add drama and romance to the landscape, and to explain an otherwise puzzling place-name (Mitchell, 2020, p.284-93). However, the 'Odin Stone' or 'Wodden Stone' at Stenness on Orkney was a megalith erected in the Neolithic period (around 3000 BC): it stood about 2.5 metres (8 feet) high and was pierced by a single large hole which presumably prompted the association with the one-eyed god. The stone featured prominently in local folk-tradition: children were passed through the hole to ensure their health; after circling the stone nine times at midnight, an observer could look through the hole and see the realm of the elves, *Hildaland*; a fair was held in the kirk nearby every New Year's Day at which betrothals took place, and the marriage oath was sworn with the man and woman holding their right hands through the stone's hole; all oaths and contracts similarly sworn were held to be inviolable. Some of these traditions were recorded in the 18th c. (attributed to Principal Gordon of the Scots College in Paris '*Remarks made in a Journey to the Orkney Islands*' in *Archaeologica Scotica*, vol. I, 1792, p.263) and appeared in the literature and popular ballads of the time, including the detail in the traditional ballad *The Play o 'de Lathie Odivere* (Traill Dennison, 1893) that one young suitor '*swore bae him dat hang on tree to marry her*' which immediately recalls the image of Óðinn on the World-Tree as well as Christ on Calvary. The stone was toppled and destroyed in the 19th c. by the landowner, who resented the damage to his crops that the many visitors caused.

English toponymic evidence for the Woden is quite widespread (Branston, 1957, p.18, 41ff; Owen, 1981, p.9; Welch, 2007, p.192, 218, 235; Wilson, 1992, p.11): *Wednesbury* (Staffs), *Wednesfield* (Staffs), *Woodnesborough* (Kent), *Wormhill* (Kent), *Wenslow* (Beds), *Wensley* (Beds) and *Wensley* (Derbyshire) are among those which have survived into modern times.

Both Woodnesborough and the Neolithic chamber-grave and mound now called 'Adam's Grave' (Wiltshire) bore the name *Wodnesbeorh* 'Woden's hill' while Wenslow is *Wodnes hlaw* 'Woden's burial mound' (Ellis Davidson & Webster, 1967; Meaney, 1966, p.105).[11] Field-names such as *Wodnesfeld* (Gloucs)[12], *Wodnesfeld* (Essex) and *Wednesfeld* (Essex) occur in older records and point to the god's worship in open country (OE *feld*) as well as on hills, while Wensley is *Wodnes leah* 'Woden's glade'.

The Wansdyke, a large linear earthwork in Wiltshire, is probably *Wodnes dic* 'Woden's ditch' and elsewhere in the same county was a *Wodnes dene* 'Woden's vale' (Meaney, 1966, pp.106-9).[13] The group of Staffordshire Woden-names has been associated in the popular imagination with the rise of Penda as king of Mercia; these sites are not close to known heathen-period Mercian cemeteries and their location on the western edge of Mercia may even have been an act of deliberate defiance against the Christian British to the west.

It does not follow that every place-name bearing the prototheme *Woden-* was necessarily a temple or place of worship, and it may have been some association with other aspects of the god's cult which prompted the name (Neidorf, 2022b). It is notable that the *beorh* and

---

[11] The *beorh* need not have been a simple geological 'hill' feature but rather a *burh* or (Iron Age) hill-fort. If so, the military associations of such a site would not have been lost on the Anglo-Saxons.

[12] *Wodenesfeld* is the named site of the battle of Tettenhall in 910, a Danish raid into the heart of Mercia which turned into a military disaster once they could not get back to their ships on the River Severn.

[13] Whether all three elements (valley, ditch and hill) were separately named from a concentration of reverence for Woden in this area, or whether the hill served as a cult site from which the ditch and valley were named, is not known. As the ditch was the site of some military activity, it is reasonable to suspect that a notable victory was ascribed to the god's intervention and prompted the naming of the hill and the ditch; see Neidorf, 2022b and references there. The barrow was later renamed 'Adam's Grave' probably because the position of apical ancestor of the West Saxon kings was changed from Woden to Adam under Christian influence. (S. Newton, pers.comm.)

dic names imply artificial constructions with defensive or military purposes, so it may be that *Wodnes dic* was originally an earthwork
believed to have been created under the inspiration or supervision of
the god rather than a site of his worship.

A word of caution may be appropriate. The evidence of place-
names is often cited in discussion of the cults of the gods, whose worship had to take place somewhere in the landscape. But the survival
of place-names is governed by many factors, in which chance and
personal preference may figure large. The dominant religious and intellectual climate will also play a part.

That worship took place at specified sites from time immemorial is
beyond dispute. The need for worshippers to come together to enact
their rites means that any place selected for this purpose must have been
known to a great many people. Important sites with a larger catchment
area would be known to a greater number of people than minor shrines
with only local importance. The major 'temple' of Uppsala (eastern
Sweden) was known as a centre for heathen ceremonies in the 11th c.
as far away as Bremen (northern Germany). Furthermore, the absence
of any Óðinn place-names in Iceland has been cited as evidence that
the god's worship was already waning by the time of the island's settlement in the 10th c. (Lassen, 2022, pp.2-3). However, the settlement was
carried out largely by free-born landowners with a preference for Þórr
and Freyr – and the lack of any hereditary aristocratic élite among the
settlers may have made the worship of Óðinn almost obsolete.

Starkey dismisses the place-name evidence for Óðinn in Scandinavia on the grounds that the name appears rarely: 'cult place-names
based on the name Odin do not even amount to 10 percent of the
theophorous place-names, and none based on or containing the
name Odin is found in Iceland at all' from which she concludes that
'the veneration of Odin was comparatively young in Scandinavia'
(Starkey, 1999, p.378). It hardly needs stating that place-name evidence is not easy to interpret quantitively because the survival of any
name is often accidental (Pollington, 2011, p.31). Place-names based
on the name of a heathen god are probably less likely to survive in

a rigorously Christian context than any other type of toponym, especially if the society has experienced a strong Protestant or Lutheran phase.[14] Furthermore, Snorri's listing of alternative names for the god Óðinn has to be based on something other than his own imagination: the names are drawn from stories and poems known to him, even if they are largely lost to us. It is not unreasonable to assume that the god was invoked by a different name or set of names in every cult group (regional, class-based or occupation-based), and that these various terms reflected different aspects of his character. It is a moot point at what stage it becomes necessary to speak of a 'different' god, rather than a 'variant' of Óðinn: if the people of an area called their one-eyed god of war and magic *Yggr* 'the fearsome one' or *Grimr* 'the masked one', does that mean that they did not recognise Óðinn (cf. Kershaw, 2000, p.1)?

Natural features may attract legends which amplify their importance. The prominent conical hill now known as Roseberry Topping (Yorkshire) was called *Othinsborg* in the 12th c. and was allegedly used as a holy site by the local (by then, Anglo-Danish) population in the 10th c. but neither toponymics nor archaeology has so far provided any clues as to the site's use in earlier Anglian religion (Smith, 1956 s.v. *topping*; Ellis Davidson, 1993, p.57).

Shaw (2002, p.33) contends that English place-names such as *Wodnesdic* 'Wansdyke, Woden's ditch' could be given in Christian-period contexts to mark out ancient, pre-Christian features and to indicate their antiquity; this would avoid any specific traditional or religious element in the name. It seems *á priori* unlikely that a pious Christian community would invent a name commemorating a being regarded as an emanation of Satan, but the wide occurrence of names such as *Devil's Dyke, Devil's Punchbowl, Hell's Kitchen* and others shows that such names can occur. Perhaps the names of heathen

---

[14] The matter of slow development in society versus sudden transformation is discussed in Härke & Belinskij, 2015. Gradual change over a long period of time is a normal function of human societies, but sudden developments are often easier to detect archaeologically.

gods were sometimes genuinely associated with these sites from heathen times and remained attached to them because they inspired awe and fear, and thus discouraged devout Christian people from venturing to them.

While theophoric personal names such as Þórolf, Ingolf, Þórir, Ingeld, (H)Inguar and the like appear to have been common throughout the Viking period, there is only one plausible name based on Óðin – the female name on a runestone in Vestmanland, Sweden: **utintisa**, transliterated as ON Óðindís (Schjødt, 2020b, p.1133).

OF HEATHENS AND HEROES

[*Beowulf*] has also been taken for a romance, composed in a monastery by aristocratic monks, men with a thorough knowledge of their families' early history in pagan times. However, the Christian references are limited to a small number of passages which could, conceivably, have been transubstantiated into a Christian form from a pagan one. Changing but a few words would turn *Beowulf* into a thoroughly pagan poem.

Rausing, *Beowulf, Ynglingatal and the Ynglinga saga*
- Fiction or History?

It may be surprising that any references at all to pre-Christian deities can be found in medieval literature, given that literary composition was largely the preserve of the church and that those members of the laity who acquired the skill had to conform to the restrictive ideology of the clergy. There was certainly a nervousness among churchmen about discussing the gods of old, even those from classical antiquity. Ælfric, writing in the 11th c., attacked interest in the literary sources circulating in his day devoted to Hercules (text from Papahagi, 2002):

Oððe hwylc halignyss wæs on þam hetelan ercule þæm ormetan ente þe ealle acwealde his nehgeburas and forbærnde hine sylfne swa cucenne on fyre siððan he acweald hæfde men and þa leon and þa micelan næddran?

'Or what holiness was in that hateful Hercules, the huge ent who killed all his neighbours and burnt himself alive in a fire once he had killed men and the lion and the great serpent?'

We know that monastic communities were celebrating the performance of secular heroic verse in the 8th c. because the cleric Alcuin railed against it in his famous rhetorical question: *Quid enim Hinieldus cum Christo? Angusta est domus; utrosque tenere non poterit* 'What has Ingeld to do with Christ? The house is narrow, it cannot hold both' (Bullough, 1993; Neidorf, 2022c, pp.115-8). Tales of the heroes of old were evidently considered a threat to the authority of the church, because they dealt for the most part with the human struggle: violence and vengeance, monsters overcome and wrongs righted – and all without the involvement or intervention of the church. The association of heroic tales and heathen worship was strong: in *Widsith* the narrator says [*ic wæs*] *mid hæðnum and mid hælepum* '[I was] with heathens and with heroes' (Papahagi, 2002, p.76).[15] One way out of this conundrum was to recount the stories in a quasi-historical setting before Christianity imposed itself in the north – e.g., the world of Beowulf and his mythic battles, set in an imagined 6th century milieu (Shippey, 2022).[16]

Early Anglo-Saxon kings often regarded themselves as successors to the ancestral powers who had established human societies on earth, whether the kings were heathen or Christian. As Moisl remarked, 'belief in descent from a god was an important ideological principle in the ordering of society among the early Germans' (Moisl, 1981, p.217). To be a 'scion of Woden' was to claim membership of the

---

[15] Neidorf (2013) notes of the scribe of the *Exeter Book* that '[these] common nouns were most likely introduced by scribes who did not recognize the peoples known elsewhere as the Heiðnir, Hærepas...' so that the original reference was to two tribes (in a lengthy poem cataloguing the tribes of northern Europe and elsewhere) with names which coincidentally developed into OE forms close to *hæþenas, hæleðas*.

[16] Shippey, 2022, pp.7-9. The only closely datable event in the poem is the death of Hygelac in a raid on Frisia which can be associated with Frankish records relating to ca. 525 AD or a little later.

clan of the god. Such membership conferred benefits which might include access to some of the god's secret wisdom, access to potent stratagems and tactics of warfare, and possibly acceptance by the god's own kindred in death (Yorke, 2015).

The tales of the old gods and heroes were presented (and preserved) in verse, and many of our oldest vernacular sources of myth have at least an element of verse in the record: the *Nine Herbs Charm*, for instance, or the *Wið Færstice* charm both contain a long poetic text with a prose beginning and ending – a format which also appears in some Norse material (Lindow, 2016, pp.115-6).

Through fosterage between Anglo-Saxon and Scandinavian dynasties, traditions of Woden as a royal ancestor probably influenced the Scandinavian cult of Óðinn (North, 1997, p.130). But Scandinavian traditions developed on their own trajectories, albeit retaining traditional stories and recasting them according to the author's agenda. The character of the god, as described in our sources, changes with the nature of the text (Lassen, 2022, p.1). In the *Prose Edda* with its focus on the practical, metrical needs of poets, Óðinn is shown as the god with a particular relevance for skalds. In the early sections of *Heimskringla* dealing with the establishment of kingship in Scandinavia, the god figures as a successful and powerful chieftain. In the pages of Saxo's account of Danish history, he is the patron of the Danes above all others. In the sagas concerning two Norwegian kings, Olaf Tryggvason and St Olaf, both associated with Christian missionary efforts, he is presented as an emanation of Satan. The early tales of the settlement of Iceland have little to say about him, preferring Þórr and Freyr. In short, the nature of the god is affected – even determined – by the type of story being presented. On this basis it would be impossible to say anything definitive about the god.

Icelandic custom appears to have separated the praxis of heathen religion from the mythic content, and as long as heathen worship was deprecated there was no objection to the rehearsal of mythic themes for entertainment and in the formal verse for which Scandinavian poets were famed. Indeed, myth is enmeshed in verse, and much Norse poetry cannot be understood without a knowledge of the mythic tales to which it alludes. Poetry itself was called 'Óðinn's mead' in reference to the tale of the winning of the powerful mind-expanding drink from the giant Suttungr by that god, and later *Hárs lið* 'the high-one's strong drink' (10ᵗʰ c.) and *Alfǫður brim* 'all-father's surf' (11ᵗʰ c.) (Lindow, 2016, p.116-7). Without a fairly detailed knowledge of the store of tales which underlie the dense imagery, it would be quite impossible to extract the poet's meaning.

THE NAME 'WODEN'

The etymology of the god's name may offer a clue as to his origin, just as, e.g., an abstract noun of feminine gender *sjafni* meaning 'love' inspired the goddess *Sjǫfn* who was believed to be helpful in the sphere of love and marriage (Simek, 1993, s.v. *Sjǫfn*). The basis of the Norse name 'Óðinn' is the adjective *óðr* 'furious, raging, vehement, etc.' and the nouns *óðr* 'song, verse' and *œði* 'rage, fury', the verb *œða* 'to rave' and its reflexive form *œðask* 'to grow furious, to become frantic' (Orel, 2013 s.v. *wōðaz, *wōðīn, *wōðjanan*). The OE words in the same etymological group include the adjectives *wōd* and *wōdlic* 'mad, frenzied, raging' (glossing Latin *rabidus vel insanus*) and the derived verb *wēdan* 'rave, rage, go mad'; the corresponding noun *wōd* means 'madness, lunacy, raving' with a derivative *wōda* 'madman, one possessed'. Interesting compounds include *wōddor* 'mouth, the gate of speech' implying that *wōd* here is not mere babble or meaningless raving but 'inspired speech'. *Wōddrēam* glosses '*demonium*' while *wōdendrēam* is again 'madness' or 'fury, *furor animi*'. 'Ravenous' is glossed *wōdfrec* where the second element means 'greedy, savage'. OHG has the terms *wuot* 'rage, fury', *wuotnissa* 'dementia' (Ebbinghaus, 1994, s.v. *wuot*). Looking further back, we may cite Gothic *wóþs* 'possessed by demons'.

Both ON Óðinn and OE Woden are derived from a PGmc word *wódanaz* formed on the PIE root *wet- and the very productive 'lordly suffix' *-no- or *-Hno- (Jackson, 2012, p.57-8; Pinault, 2000; Kershaw, 2000, p.74-7). This root is often rendered 'see' (Latin *videre*) or 'know' (OE *witan*). The semantics of the derivatives of *wet- in languages of the Celtic and Germanic groups involve specific qualities such as 'watchfulness', 'prophecy', 'poetic wisdom', and 'frenzy' or 'ecstasy' (Hyllested, 2010, p.110). The latter quality appears in the previously cited Gothic term *woþs* glossing Greek *daimonisthei* (Kershaw, 2000, p.71, 80). The god is the embodiment of the *furor Teutonicus* and of the *ekstasis* of the youthful warrior; like Dionysos, he can imbue his followers with mindless rage expressed in savagery, or with a divine rapture.

The adjectival forms are based on *wōð- and its nouns *wōðaz (masculine) and *wōðō (feminine), the first of which is possibly cognate with the Latin noun *vates* 'seer, prophet' and Old Irish *fáith* with the same general meaning. Chadwick (1899, p.67) and Kershaw (2000, p.69) reject the notion that the Latin word might be a borrowing from Celtic while Koch (2020, p.140) supports it; Liberman (2016, p.48, 75) regards the connection as 'irrelevant', and proposes instead that the name means 'the unstoppable [one]' (2016, p.51).

The derived verb *wōðjanan means 'to be *wōðaz, to rage, to be possessed'. It was once considered likely that *woðen* could be the passive participle of the verb *wēdan* with the meaning 'enraged', substantivized as 'the one who is enraged' but this has been generally rejected since the early 20th c. (Liberman, 2016, p.38, 41). Older scholarship invoked the IE. background, citing Sanskrit *vāta-* and Latin *ventus,* both 'wind' (Chadwick, 1899, p.66). This agrees broadly with the assumed origin of the god in the tradition of the Wild Hunt also called '*Odens jagt*' (Odin's hunt) in Sweden, but it ignores other evidence, e.g., Adam of Bremen's phrase '*Wodan, id est furor*'.

An Iron Age brooch from Gårdlösa (Sweden) bears the enigmatic text **ekunwodz** which is evidently linked to the adjective *wod-* (/woːð/) and the divine name *Woden*. The text can be read as *ek unwodz with the first word the pronoun *ek 'I' and the second a strong adjective compounded from *un- 'not' and *wod(a)z 'raging, inspired, ecstatic' (Antonsen, 2002, p.217). Antonsen translates this as 'calm one', i.e., 'not raging'. The prefix *un- in early Germanic idiom does not always provide a negative or contradiction of the noun or adjective to which it is appended, but can be a pejorative modifier, e.g., OE *weder* 'weather', *unweder* 'storm, bad weather' (Quirk & Wrenn, 1955, p.112). It is therefore possible that **unwodz** means something akin to 'fiercely raging' or 'madly inspired'.

The root sense of **wōd-* seems to be 'inspired, excited, mentally aroused' (Kershaw, 2000, p.69; Liberman, 2016, p.36-51). The Roman writer Vergil accepted the equation of *vates* 'soothsayer' with Greek *poeta* 'one who speaks in verse [inspired by a god]' (Kershaw, 2000, p.70). While the notion of raving, raging and madness is strong in this group there is enough overlap with words for 'speech', 'song', 'verse' and the like to posit the idea that **wōd-* originally meant something like 'possession; loss of personal control; inspiration by an outside power' and that the Latin and Old Irish words derive from this in the sense of 'one imbued with prophetic power due to possession by a god'. In his discussion of the terms *óðr, wōd* and so on, Liberman rejected de Vries's assertion that the god was associated principally with intellectual and spiritual power on the basis that 'no primitive deity had such a lofty function. We can imagine that a demon whose name contained the root *óð-* would make people lose their sanity rather than controlling their intellectual activities' (Liberman, 2016, p.36; see also ibid., p.42, 47, 48). However, this assumes that possession by the *wōd*-god necessarily leads to impaired mental functions, whereas his association with poetry, music, inspiration and clairvoyance rather suggests a heightening of awareness and raising of creative powers. Adam of Bremen's phrase *Wodan, id est furor* 'Woden, that is fury' mentioned above (p.34) should perhaps be read as an example of a Christian and Latin-language interpretation of the name, and the cleric's trustworthiness in this and other matters is not beyond dispute. Nor is it clear exactly what Adam meant by *furor*: 'fury' or 'madness' is possible in the sense of 'loss of control', but perhaps also 'vehemence', 'ecstasy' or 'inspiration' (Liberman, 2016, p.37, 43, 69).

The sense in which *furor* 'rage, raving, insanity' can be interpreted here is probably that of 'unrestrained behaviour' – which might as well encompass great deeds on the battlefield, composition of music and verse, or the kinds of deprecated behaviour that will lead to lasting shame (Liberman, 2016, p.51). This aspect of the god's character is often foregrounded in the Scandinavian material – his championing of leaders and warriors who lead dishonourable and dissolute lives, for example – and is also encoded in some of the Anglo-Saxon traditions.

The PGmc title *woðenaz which gave rise to the recorded forms Woden, Uþin, Óðinn and the rest, is constructed as the root *wōð- and suffix –in- denoting 'mastery' (Benveniste, 1973, pp.245-6 ; Kershaw, 2000, p.11; Libermann. 2016, p.38-9, 41-4;):[17]

term	meaning	construction	root
Latin			
dominus	master of a household	dom -in -us	*domus* 'household'
tribunus	master of a tribe	trib -un -us	*tribus* 'tribe'
Germanic			
Gothic *þiudans*	master of a tribe	þeud -in -az	*þiud* 'tribe'
Gothic *kindins*	master of a kindred	kind -in -az	*kind* 'family'
OE *dryhten*	master of a warband	druht -in -az	*druht* 'warband'
ON *herjann*	master of an army	harj -in -az	*hari* 'military force'

All these words made with the suffix –inaz (and the Latin with its cognate –inus, -unus) meaning 'lord, master' have as their root a word for a group of people, for whom the nominated individual was

---

[17] See also Pinault, 2000 and Clackson & Olsen, 2004, p.229 for a discussion of the 'Hoffmann suffix' in the formation of Germanic theonyms.

the master or leader.[18] Therefore, logically we should be looking at a Germanic word *wōða, *wōðu as the thing of which *wōðenaz is the leader, and this *woða should be a group of people characterized by *woð-, i.e., 'excitement, rage, inspiration'. This group might be the 'warband' or the 'Wild Hunt', the 'raging ones', the *ghost riders in the sky*, or perhaps even a band of musicians and poets given over to inspired verbal and musical performances, soothsaying and possession by the spirit of the music. However, the formation of the term appears to be late (Iron Age?) in date and restricted to Western Indo-European (Germanic, Italic, Celtic). If wider Indo-European parallels are sought, the implication of a 'group-leader' is less certain, as *Neptunus* is simply 'lord of waters' and *Ouranos* is 'lord of rain' (Kershaw, 2000, p.11; Tolley, 2009, p.102); the god *Neptunus* is merely the embodiment or personification of water.

Another factor in the puzzle is the figure named Óðr who is said to be the absent husband of Freyja for whom she continuously searches, which gives rise to the tradition that she weeps tears of gold. This tale is alluded to in *Gylfaginning* and was evidently known to Saxo, who relates that Othinus was accustomed to making long trips (Kershaw, 2000, p.72).

---

[18] Liberman, 2016, p.42 discusses recent scholarship regarding the *-ono-* suffix, denoting 'belonging to' rather than 'mastery over'.

CHAPTER 2

IN THE BEGINNING

> The attempt to gain knowledge of the past is also a journey into the world of the dead.
>
> Walter Benjamin, *On the Concept of History*

> The question about the age of the Óðinn cult in Scandinavia is bound to remain unresolved. Óðinn appeared there early enough to be included in the story of the creation of the world and become the giant's kin.
>
> Anatoly Liberman, *Óðinn's Path to Greatness* in *In Prayer and Laughter. Essays on Medieval Scandinavian and Germanic Mythology, Literature, and Culture*

We begin our investigation into the history and prehistory of the god of inspiration with an apparently secondary matter which brings into focus a number of the issues to be explored in detail in these pages. The *Prose Edda* records that (text from Faulkes, 1998):

> ... Sá heitir Alfǫðr at váru máli ... Lifir hann of allar aldir ok stjórnar ǫllu ríki sínu og ræðr ǫllum hlutum, stórum ok smám ... Hann smíðaði himinn ok jǫrð ok lopt ok alla eign þeira ... Óðinn er œztr ok elztr Ásanna. Hann ræðr ǫllum hlutum, ok svá sem ǫnnur guðin eru máttug, þá þjóna honum ǫll, svá sem bǫrn fǫður

> 'He is called "All-father" in our language... He lives forever and rules all his kingdom and controls all outcomes, great and small... He created heaven and earth and the air and all their properties... Óðinn is the highest and the eldest of the gods... he controls all

outcomes and even as the other gods are mighty, they all obey him as children do their father.'

This image of the almighty creator is familiar from both Christian notions of the patriarchal god, and from parallels in the classical world (Zeus, Jupiter, etc.). It is a vision of the creator-god as a single omnipotent deity, from whom a number of lesser entities derive their strength and potency. Such a vision as equivalent to or identifiable with Óðinn requires some clarification.

Our investigation concerns Snorri's notion that the chief creator-god did not act alone: he was one of three brothers named Óðinn, Vili and Vé: 'lord of inspiration', 'will' and 'holy one'. Snorri, writing in the 13th c. in the relatively young society of medieval Iceland, included these names in the *Prose Edda* text - but where did he get them from? They do not appear as a trio in any of the other known sources – Adam of Bremen, for example, wrote of *Uoden, Thor* and *Fricco* as the three gods revered by the Swedes in their great temple at Uppsala. The Continental Saxons were required to renounce three of their traditional gods upon baptism, but these were named *Uuoden, Thunær* and *Sahsginot*. The notion of a triad of gods seems sound, but the companions of Woden had different names. Vili and Vé play no leading part in the myths that Snorri recorded,[19] the names do not appear epigraphically and there appears to be little further evidence in support of the existence of these characters (Simek, 1993, p.362).[20] How then can we be confident that Snorri did not just make the names up?

---

[19] In *Lokasenna*, Loki insults Óðinn by suggesting that Vili and Vé had slept with his wife, Frigg: 'Þegi þv, Frigg! þu ert Fiorgyns mer oc hefir e vergiorn veriþ, er þa Vea oc Vilia leztv þer, Viþris qven, bada i badm vm tekit' (Be quiet, Frigg! you are Fjorgynn's daughter and have always been lustful since you, the wife of Viðrir, took Vé and Vili both to your bosom).

[20] They appear together in *Gylfaginning* as sons of Borr who take part in creation; in *Ynglinga saga* as princes who assume rule when Óðinn is absent; Vili is named separately in two poems: *Ynglingatal* and *Sonatorrek*.

There are two reasons to accept that Snorri's information – whatever its source may have been – was founded in tradition: one etymological and one literary.

THE THREE DIVINE BROTHERS

The three god-names appear in their Norse forms (Óðinn, Vili and Vé), pre-dating Snorri's document by an unknown (but considerable) length of time. Examination of the etymological evidence shows that originally all three names began similarly, and it is the various processes of linguistic evolution that have brought about the divergence apparent in Snorri's spelling.

The three names, if taken back to their prehistoric, Proto-Germanic forms, would be *Wōdenaz, *Weljōn, *Wīhaz, i.e., all three names with initial *w-* forming an alliterative group.[21] Such naming schemes were traditional in early Germanic societies: King Alfred the Great, for example, was the youngest of five brothers with alliterating names: Æðelbald, Æðelberht, Æðelræd, Æðelstan and Ælfræd (Alfred) himself – all sons of Æðelwulf. We may assume that Snorri was aware of the tradition of alliteration in the names of nobles and would have applied it to the trio of euhemerised gods if he were inventing them himself - but if so, it is difficult to account for his choices, given that two names begin with *v-* while the third and most prominent one begins with a vowel (*ó-*). If Snorri had concocted the names of the two less-known brothers, it would surely have been more reasonable to make them alliterate with the name of the better-known and more prominent Óðinn.

An indication of the date at which the *w-* of the god's name disappeared in Scandinavia lies in two early references, both in archaeological

---

[21] Orel, 2003, s.v. *wōðanaz, weljón, wíxaz*. The *Wóðanaz name may also be reconstructed as *Wōðinaz, i.e., the vowel of the suffix may either be reconstructed as *-a-* or *-i-*; in the latter case, it would cause i-mutation of the preceding vowel, whence such OE forms as *Wédnesbeorg*, etc. *Vili* is a 'weak' or *n*-stem noun in contrast to the other two strong nouns.

rather than literary contexts, which are rare in contemporary manuscripts and are therefore liable to errors of copying.

One of these instances occurs outside Scandinavia and far from
the area where memory of Óðinn's cult might have lingered into
Snorri's time, on the reverse of the Nordendorf brooch, an Alemannic dress item of late 6th or 7th c. date. An earlier date (5th century)
can be assigned to the Vindelev bracteate which is currently the first
known epigraphic example of the god's name; the item was found
close to Jelling in Jutland.

The presumption of an initial *W-* in the deity's name is well
founded in both the English material (Anglian Kinglists) and the
corresponding German evidence (Nordendorf brooch); in Scandinavia, the *W-* was present in the 5th c. (Vindelev bracteate) but was
deleted at some later date in accordance with the development of
North Germanic dialects. A date-range for the loss of *W-* in the
north can be inferred.

THE RIBE SKULL FRAGMENT TEXT

When did the name Woden lose its initial *W-*? The best evidence is
a portion of human skull found at Ribe (Denmark) which bears a
text in runes, the lines curled to conform to the outer edge of the
fragment (Moltke, 1976, p.287; Stoklund, 1996; Nielsen, 2000,
p.257, 263; McKinnell & Simek, 2004, p.17, 50; Spurkland, 2005,
pp.72-4; Bishop, 2007, p.36; Mitchell, 2008):

ulfuRAukuþinAukHutiuR'HiAlbburiisuiþR

þAiMAuiArkiAuktuirkunin

buur

This may be transcribed into normalised Old Norse as:

UlfR auk Óðinn / auk HótýR / hialp Buri es / viðr þæima:
værki auk dværgynni. Bur.

'Ulf and Odin / and High-Tyr, help is for Bur against these: pain and dwarf-stroke. Bur [made this]'

The text came from a context dated to the 720s in the town's marketplace.[22] Ribe lies about 30 miles north of the present German border, close to the North Sea; it was probably part of the 7th c. network of emporia which included Quentovic (Northern France), Dorestad (Frisia) and Ipswich, Canterbury, London and Southampton (southern England). The runes show signs of the ongoing development from the Elder to the Younger Fuþark, which indicates that the onset of these runic changes must therefore logically predate this text (Barnes, 2012, p.61). The phonemes /h/ and /m/ are represented by ᚻ (transliterated H) and ᛗ (transliterated M), while the star-rune ᚼ apparently has the value /a/ (transliterated A) (Spurkland, 2005, pp.72-4). The narrow dating of this text to around 720 AD pinpoints the development of *woden to *óðinn in this area.

FROM WÓDEN TO ÓÐINN

The Ribe text is most helpful in recording the name **uþin,** i.e., Óðinn, with its initial vowel after deletion of the *w*- (Stoklund, 1996, p.204). The archaeological evidence indicates that in the Jelling area of Jutland around 400 AD, the god's name had a phonemic shape which could be recorded in runes as **wodinas** (genitive singular, the nominative perhaps **wodin** /woːdin/) on the Vindelev bracteate while four centuries later and 70 kilometres to the southwest at Ribe, the *w*- had been elided and the name remodelled to **uþin** (perhaps /oːðin/). The loss of *w*- in that area (the eastern shore of the North Sea) must therefore have been completed before the deposition of the skull fragment in the Ribe marketplace.

The early Old English manuscript texts (e.g., *Textus Roffensis* and the other kinglists) naming the god, of which the earliest date from the 8th c., routinely use the form 'Woden'. The later *Old Saxon Baptismal Vow* still records the form *Uuoden,* i.e., /woːden/, retaining

---

[22] Søvsø (2013) assigns the text to the period 725-750.

the initial *w-*. The vow is probably of 9th c. date or a little earlier, but likely influenced by the Anglo-Saxon ecclesiastical tradition brought by missionaries, and thus it may not represent the Continental Saxon form(s) of the god's name. (Furthermore, it is possible that the Saxons did not use the name 'Woden' for the principal god, but rather 'Grim'.)

The god's name was recorded without the *w-* in 11th c. England, when Ælfric wrote about a figure known among the Danes as *Oðon*. The dental fricative (/ð/ in *Óðinn* rather than the dental stop /d/ of *Woden*) suggests that his informant knew the name from a genuine North Germanic tradition. He presumably also knew of the worship of a heathen deity called *Oðon* by contemporary Scandinavians in England and Ireland. The churchman does not appear to have connected this figure with the *Woden* of the Anglo-Saxon kinglists, or perhaps he chose to remain silent on this matter.

Ari Þorgilsson, the 12th c. author of the *Íslendingabók* understood the correspondence (text from Jónsson, 1930):

Voden, þann köllum vér Óðin. Frá honum eru komnar flestar konunga ættir í norðr hálfu heimsins

'Voden, whom we call Óðinn: from him are descended most of the families of kings in the northern half of the world.'

Saxo Grammaticus, writing in Denmark in the 12th c., names the god as *Othinus* in his Latin text, again with *-th-* to represent the North Germanic /ð/.

TEXTUS ROFFENSIS - EAST ANGLIAN KINGLIST

More literary evidence for the triad **Wódenaz, * Weljón, *Wíhaz* (i.e., precursors of Snorri's set of creator-gods) comes from the western shores of the North Sea, specifically the kingdom of East Anglia. A kinglist for that polity is recorded in the *Textus Roffensis*, starting with the contemporary ruler Alfwald (who died in 749 AD) and

extending back through the generations to the primal ancestor, Woden.[23] The sequence includes the name of each king and the name
of his predecessor (often his putative father) with the associative suffix -*ing* (text from Sawyer, 1962):

> Alfwald Aldwulfing / Aldwulf Æðelricing / Æþelric Ening / Eni
> Tytling / Tytla Wuffing / Wuffa Wehhing / Wehh Wilhelming
> / Wilhelm Hrypping / Hryp Hroðmunding / Hroðmund
> Trigling / Trygil Tytmaning / Tytman Casering / Caser
> Wodning / Woden Frealafing.

The names from Alfwald back to Wuffa may be regarded as 'historical', in the sense that they were plausibly borne by rulers *(cyningas,
þeodnas, drihtnas)* of the people who later called themselves *eastengle*
'East Angles'. Wuffa himself, his name based on *wulf* 'wolf', may
bear a name which is symbolic since the royal family were designated
Wuffingas 'wolf-folk' but that does not in itself preclude him from
having been a historical person (perhaps bearing a dithematic name
with *Wulf-* as the prototheme?).

Wuffa's father, Tytla, bears the anglicised form (<*tutila) of the
name of a famed Ostrogothic king, Totila, which may have achieved
some currency among the rulers of Germanic Europe in the middle
of the 6th c. Neidorf demonstrates that there was a strong tradition
of naming aristocratic children after heroes of legend, which lasted
down to the 8th c. in England (Neidorf, 2013). Tytla's name stands
above that of Eni (*Eni Tytling*), who is regarded from other evidence
(i.e., Bede's *Historia Ecclesiastica Gentis Anglorum* [Colgrave & Mynors, 1969]) as the brother of King Rædwald; this king is usually

---

[23] The manuscript is dated to the first quarter of the 12th c. containing material
of which the earliest might be 500 years old at the time of compilation. It
begins with the earliest surviving English law-code, issued by King Æthelberht
of Kent, dating from circa 600 AD, followed by those of two Kentish successors,
the joint-kings Hlothere and Eadric, circa 679–685, and King Wihtred of 695.
The manuscript is the only surviving source for these law-codes, though the
last is based on or influenced by the laws of the contemporary West-Saxon
King Ine (Liebermann, 1903, p.15–25; Treharne, 2012).

identified with the occupant of the treasure-filled ship-burial in Mound 1 at Sutton Hoo, Suffolk, dating from the first third of the 7th c. Rædwald's reign then probably extends from circa 600 to 625 AD, and Tytla's reign therefore likely belongs to the latter end of the 6th c. and Wuffa's to earlier in that century.[24]

In the upper reaches of the *Textus Roffensis* list we find Woden, the ancestor of all Anglo-Saxon kingly families, other than the East Saxon line. Above Wuffa is the enigmatic name *Wehh* which appears to be a variant spelling (for the pronunciation /wex/) of the OE word *wéoh* 'holy; holy place, shrine, temple', cognate with the ON *vé* 'holy one; sacred space'. Above *Wehh* is *Wilhelm*, whose name's prototheme, *Wil-*, is likewise cognate with the ON *vili* 'will'. In the East Anglian kinglist we thus may have a (distant and distorted) memory of the Anglian holy triad: *Wōden, Wila, Wēoh*.

The Anglian series of kinglists survive in four manuscripts, but the sequence of names is of unknown antiquity. The *Textus Roffensis* is the earliest manuscript to include them and, since this may have been compiled in the early or mid-8th c., the genealogical information therein may plausibly date back to Tytla's reign. How much earlier than the late 500s its composition may be is debatable. Furthermore, there are other Anglian traditions regarding Woden as the apical ancestor of their ruling line.

It is remarkable that the kinglists show no agreement beyond their common source at Woden – especially if, as seems likely, the Anglian genealogy was dominant – whereby Offa of Angeln or his grandson Eomer might have been a suitable candidate for progenitor

---

[24] King Totila came to power among the Ostrogoths in 541 AD and died in 552 at the Battle of Busta Gallorum attempting to repulse a Byzantine invasion force under the general Narses. With his defeat and death, Ostrogothic power in Italy was broken and the remainder of that people were absorbed into the Langobards or took the path of exile and carved out a new identity elsewhere. Tytla's name may well have been known a generation later (circa 575) as that of a famous figure in heroic tales, and the East Anglian *æþeling* could be thus named for him.

(Woolf, 2017, pp.4-5). As Woolf notes (2017, p.5) 'Instead, the latest common ancestor in each case (save that of the West Saxons who seem to have borrowed the upper portion of the Bernician pedigree) is Woden Frealafing, upon whom the English had no special claim. This evidence might even tempt us to imagine that this schema presupposed the existence of a pan-Germanic sense of identity of the sort that is viewed with extreme scepticism by many scholars today.'

The Wuffings' association with Woden and his cult is also referenced in the archaeology of their kingdom – a subject to which we shall return below (p.93, 361).

DIVINE THREES

On the Ribe skull fragment, the sequence **HutiuR** for *Há Týr* 'High Tyr' is an early (8th c.) record of that god's name. At this time the word *týr* still designated 'god, deity (in general)' rather than the specific character 'Týr' who appears occasionally as the one-handed god of justice. The skull's text invokes 'Ulf and Odin and High-Tyr' in yet another iteration of the three-god formula which is found in most records of the myths, even though the identity of *Ulfr* 'the wolf' remains a mystery.[25] Yet Óðinn sometimes has two companions on his missions: for example, Hœnir and Loki in *Reginsmál* and *Skáldskaparmál*. He is also accompanied by his two ravens, Huginn and Muninn.

In Snorri's origin tale, the three divine brothers (Óðinn, Vili and Vé, sons of Bor) slew Ymir the primordial giant and created the world from his dismembered carcass; this first act of creation has an echo in the Greek tale whereby the brothers Zeus, Poseidon, and Hades overcame and dismembered the Titans. It is a story told to

---

[25] It is tempting to cite this *Ulfr* 'wolf' in discussion of the historicity of *Wuffa* of the East Angles, but to do more than note the congruity of names would be mere speculation. Male personal names with the element '*Wulf-*' or '*-wulf*' and its cognates are numerous.

account for the imagined similarities between things in the environment and parts of the human body (e.g., grass: hair, stones: bones,
stars: eyes, etc.) (Lincoln 1986, ch.1).

In the prose text *Gylfaginning*, three gods acted in concert to give
mankind rationality and senses. To the first human pair, Askr and
Embla,[26] Óðinn gave 'soul' and 'life;' Vili gave 'wit' and 'sense of
touch'; Vé gave 'form' and 'features', 'speech', 'hearing' and
'sight'.[27] The same story is alluded to in *Vǫluspá*, where it is two
'minor' gods, Hœnir and Lóðurr, who assisted Óðinn (text from
Dronke, 1997):

> Unz þrír kvómo
>
> ór því liði
>
> ǫflgir ok ástgir
>
> æsir at húsi.
>
> Fundo á landi
>
> lítt megandi
>
> Ask ok Emblo
>
> ørlǫglausa.
>
> Ǫnd þau né átto,
>
> óð þau né hǫfðo,
>
> lá né læti
>
> né lito góða.

---

[26] Usually taken to be the trees named 'ash' and 'elm' but other suggestions
have been proposed.

[27] Liberman (2016, p.48–51) argues for different meanings for these gifts. *Ǫnd*
he accepts as 'breath' with the developed senses 'spirit' and 'life'. *Litr* might be
'genitals'. *Óðr* is sometimes translated 'voice', as a developed sense of the more
usual meaning 'metrical speech, verse', but it might rather be 'power of movement'.

Ǫnd gaf Óðinn,

óð gaf Hœnir,

lá gaf Lóðurr

ok lito góða.

Vǫluspá, v.17–8

'Until three came from their meeting into the world, mighty and good-hearted Æsir. Askr and Embla they found on the earth of little might, lacking *ǫrlǫg*: breath they owned not, 'sense' they had not, [nor] blood nor willpower, nor good form. Breath gave Odin, 'sense' gave Hœnir, blood gave Lóðurr, and good form.'

The same episode is alluded to in Snorri's *Prose Edda* where he writes (text from Faulkes, 2005):

Þá er þeir Bors synir gengu með sævarstrǫndu, fundu þeir tré tvau, ok tóku upp tréin ok skǫpuðu af menn. Gaf hinn fyrsti ǫnd ok líf, annarr vit ok hrœring, þriði ásjónu, málit ok heyrn ok sjón; gáfu þeim klæði ok nǫfn. Hét karlmaðrinn Askr en konan Embla, ok ólusk þaðan af mannkindin, þeim er bygðin var gefin undir Miðgarði.

'When Borr's sons were walking along the seashore, they found two trees, and they took up the trees and shaped men from [them]. The first gave them spirit and life; the second, wit and feeling; the third, form, speech, hearing, and sight. They gave them clothing and names: the male was called Askr and the female Embla, and from them mankind sprang, to whom a dwelling was given beneath [in] Midgard.'

The gods are not named individually but referred to as 'Borr's sons', who were previously named in that work as Óðinn, Vili and Vé but then are called elliptically 'the first', 'the second' and 'the third' (Dronke, 1997, p.11). This sequential or numeric triad recalls in turn the enigmatic group who appear at the beginning of *Gylfaginning* named only as *Hár, Jafnhár* and *Þriði* 'High One', 'Just-as-High One' and 'Third One'.

The divine names Hœnir and Lóðurr are displayed elsewhere in Snorri's works. In *Ynglinga saga*, Hœnir and Mímir were sent to the Vanir as hostages to seal a truce after the war in heaven (Oosten, 1985). Hœnir relied on Mímir in all matters of judgement and was otherwise silent, so that the Vanir soon came to despise him. Lóðurr may appear epigraphically in the runic **logaþore** of the Nordendorf brooch text. Some sources link this name to Loki, who occasionally appears as a companion of Hœnir and Óðinn (e.g., the Edda story concerning Þjazi) (Paxson, 2017, p.101).[28]

It is interesting that in the *Vǫluspá* verse it was the god Hœnir who gave *óð* – here translated as 'sense', but transparently the word *óðr* from which Óðinn takes his name (North, 1991, p.44; Liberman, 2016, p.49). Perhaps 'inspiration' or 'intoxication' would be a more accurate translation, relating to an older version of the story (Kershaw, 2000, p.73).

OLD SAXON BAPTISMAL VOW - THE SAXON TRIAD

The Continental Saxons appear to have worshipped a trio of deities distinct from those of the Angles. The Angles were on the fringe of Scandinavia in Jutland/Schleswig-Holstein and may have shared cultural traits with communities extending north and east as far as Uppland in Sweden, while the Saxons were more firmly linked into the culture of the southern North Sea.

A 9th c. Old Saxon 'baptismal formula', 'renunciation oath' or 'vow' is recorded in the same manuscript (Codex Palatinus Latinus 577) as *Indiculus Superstitionum et Paganiarum*, a Latin-language collection of superstitious practices and beliefs probably compiled during the forced

---

[28] Liberman (2016, p.179) mentions Axel Olrik's idea that *Loki* might be a diminutive of Lóðurr on the basis of Icelandic naming practice. Lóðurr, in turn, has been connected to an original **lohaþuraz* which gives rise to OE *logeþor* 'cunning'. Yet the fact that no other god has such a diminutive form of his or her name makes this implausible.

conversion of the Old Saxons by Charlemagne in the later 8th c. The text refers to a god named *Saxnot*, whom the new Christian convert had to repudiate while reciting the following verbal formula (Pertz, 1835; Simek, 1993, s.v. *Saxon Baptismal Vow, Saxnot;* Green, 1998, pp.344-5; Shaw, 2002, p.82ff; Kay, 2013, p.17; text from Gallee, 1864):[29]

> ec forsacho allum dioboles uuercum and uuordum, Thunaer ende Uuöden ende Saxnote ende allum them unholdum the hira genötas sint.

> 'I forsake all the devil's works and words, Þunor and Woden and Saxnot and all the unholy (ones) who are their companions.'

The gods *Thunaer* and *Uuoden* are manifestly Þunor and Woden, while *Saxnot* is not clearly defined according to the taxonomy set up by Snorri. The 'missing' member of the trio is presumably Fricco / Freyr, but the name *Saxnot* is not linked (etymologically or thematically) to that of the god of the Vanir. It has been suggested that originally all Saxon kinglists began with *Saxnot*, and that the move to accommodate (Anglian) Woden for the West Saxons was inspired by the politics of the Middle Saxon period (Cronan, 2014).

THE EAST SAXON KINGLIST

There is a further 'Saxon' link for the name, however. A figure named *Seaxneat* is recorded as an ancestor of the rulers in the East Saxon kinglist, where his primary position indicates his status as a

---

[29] Hall (2007, p.73) notes that the vow is probably based on an OE original, and that this may be due to the part played by Anglo-Saxon missionaries in the conversion of Continental Germany. Shaw (2002, p.84) likewise points to the use of *hira* 'their' instead of standard OHG *ira*; this is closer to OE *heora* with the initial *h*- and supports an association with the Anglo-Saxon mission to the Saxons based in Fulda. The point is that the oath-taker did not have to deny the existence or objective reality of the gods and their associates, only to repudiate them.

(probable) heathen god and founder-ancestor – the position occupied by Woden in Anglian-influenced kinglists (North, 1997, p.13). The manuscript is *BL Additional MS 23211*, probably compiled during Alfred's reign (text from Cockayne, 1866, p.444):

> De regibus orientalium seaxonum, offa sighering, sighere sigberhting, sigberht s[aweard]ing, saweard saberhting, saberht sledding. sle[dd] æscwining, æscwine offing, offa bedcing, bedca [sigefugling], sigefugl swæpping, swæppa antsecging, ants[ecg] gesecging, gesecg seaxneating.

> 'Concerning the kings of the East Saxons: Offa son of Sigehere, son of Sigeberht, son of Sæweard, son of Saberht, son of Sledd, son of Æscwine, son of Offa, son of Bedca, son of Sigefugl, son of Swæppa, son of Andsecg, son of Gesecg, son of Seaxneat.'

The *Seax-* element may refer to the knife (*seax*) or more probably to the people (*Seaxe*, Saxons) who used it. The deuterotheme *-neat, nyten* often means 'cattle' but the term *geneat* refers to a class of minor noble or freeman, and it must be this sense which is intended here. (The alternative OS spelling *Sahs-ginot* supports this, as *ginot* is apparently cognate with WSax *geneat* 'companion, brother-in-arms'.) If, as both Ellis Davidson and Dumézil suggested, the name signifies 'sword-companion, comrade in arms' then it may be relevant that Tacitus mentions the performance of sword-dances by young men as part of the ceremonies or entertainment at Germanic feasts (Ellis Davidson, 1964, p.60). North further suggested that Saxnot might have been the first ancestor of the Saxons, referred to as the 'great god' or *Irmingot* to whom the *Hirminsuul* was dedicated, the mighty pillar which sustained the world (North, 1997, p.113).

While for the East Saxons, Seaxneat occupies the apical kinglist position which elsewhere belongs to Woden, his presence alongside *Uuoden* in the Old Saxon text above (p.50) contradicts any suggestion that the two are identical. Modern commentators have taken Seaxneat to be a byname for either Tiw, Frea or Ingwe, but it remains most likely that he was envisaged as a separate divine being, whose tales were later melded with those of the other gods (Polomé, 1989, pp.81-2). The fact that Seaxneat was named alongside Uuoden and Thunaer led Polomé to suggest that he might be a third-function god, associated with farmers, fishers, workmen and merchants, and that he was thus among the top tier of deities (Polomé, 1989, p.82).

Perhaps the character of Freyr in the existing tales misleads us, and there was once a tradition concerning that god in which his *seax* played an important part. If so, it is hard to resist an association with the 'magical' sword which could fight on its own, also associated with Freyr who had such a weapon. It was lent by him to his servant, Skírnir, in order to ensure his help in consummating his desire for the giant-maid, Gerðr. It was the one and only remarkable sword among all the treasures of the Æsir and Vanir in Snorri's accounts.

Moreover, the deuterotheme -*neat* in the god's name might equally be related to the word *nett* 'net' (from PIE *ned- 'bind, tie up') and therefore refer to the binding of the sword or *seax* in military service associated with Woden and the *herfjoturr*, or even the binding of the cosmic wolf (a tale attributed to Týr).

The reasons for the retention of this deity name (Seaxneat) among the Saxons of Essex (but not of Wessex or Sussex) are unexplained, but not beyond conjecture. It is likely that Woden was the Anglian name for the war-god, and that the dominance of (Anglian) Mercia in the period when kinglists began to be recorded invited or required other kingdoms' lists to show conformity with the Anglian tradition for reasons of prestige. The South Saxons' beliefs are unrecorded, largely overshadowed by the dominance of neighbouring Wessex and by the kingdom's late conversion to Christianity (circa 674 AD) which may have entailed loss or deprecation of much traditional lore.

It may be that the East Saxons, sandwiched between the Jutish-Frankish folk of Kent and the Angles of East and Middle Anglia, felt a greater need to align and associate themselves with a traditional ancestral figure of some antiquity in order to mark their separate identity. Undeniably, the East Saxons were closely linked economically and politically with the rich and powerful kingdom of Kent, but their rulers were not mere clients or puppets of Canterbury, and perhaps they used their descent from Saxnot to affirm this. East Saxon kings at times actually wielded power in west Kent (Welch, 2007, p.193, 209, 230).

THE SVEAR TRIAD

Adam of Bremen's later 11ᵗʰ c. account in *Gesta Hammaburgensis Ecclesiae Pontificum* of the temple or *triclinium* at *Ubsola* (Uppsala) includes mention of three gods whose images stood there: *Thor, Wodan, Fricco*. Thor's image was placed in the centre and wielded a sceptre (*Mjǫlnir?*), Wodan stood to one side of him and was shown in armour, while Fricco's statue included an erect penis (Schjødt, 2020b, p.1177). Adam's record adds the information that the Uppsala people also worshipped gods who were once men, and who had become immortal because of their famous deeds. This assertion agrees very well with other evidence (e.g., Jordanes, *Getica*, ch.78) indicating that the gods of the Germanic peoples were often 'deified ancestors' who had come to take a prominent place in the legends and myths of the societies they once led (Pollington, 2011, s.v. *Ese*; van Nuffelen & van Hoof, 2020).

Adam also notes that each of the three gods has a dedicated priest whose function is to offer sacrifices from the people and to intercede with the gods. In the event of famine or plague, a sacrifice would be made to Thor; if there were to be war, a sacrifice would be made to Wodan; if a marriage were to be celebrated, then a sacrifice would be made to Fricco. The account adds the important information that on every ninth year a communal festival of every province in Sweden was held in *Ubsola* (Uppsala); Christians were allowed to buy themselves out of observing these ceremonies.

The name *Wodan* given by Adam reflects his German-language interpretation of the god's title (based on contemporary references to *Wotan?*), since other evidence (e.g., the Ribe skull fragment) suggests that by the later 11ᵗʰ c. the form *Óðinn* or similar should have been in use in Scandinavia.

DIVINE DUOS

Aside from the triads of gods enumerated above, there is also a strong
tradition of pairs of gods who take part in some very specific stories,
mainly concerning the coming of the dawn and the establishment
of human societies. These are sometimes called the 'Divine Twins'
although in Germanic tradition the couples are more often presented
as pairs (groups of two unrelated beings) rather than twins. They
appear in the foundation stories of many of the historical peoples of
early medieval Europe: among the Angles, the most famous pair is
Hengest and Horsa mentioned by Bede in the *Historia Ecclesiastica
Gentis Anglorum* Book I ch.15, one of the earliest literary sources for
information on the traditions of the Germanic kingly families in
England (Shaw, 2002, p.97). Both Hengest and his brother Horsa
were understood to be the sons of *Uictgilsus* (Wihtgils), sons of *Uitta*
(Witta), sons of *Uecta* (Wehta), sons of *Woden*; they were therefore
'Woden-sprung' and partly divine, although Bede does not mention
this aspect of their ancestry and simply notes that many royal families
share this apical figure (Chambers, 1912, p.33; Ellis Davidson, 1964,
pp.169-71; Moisl, 1981, p.235; Shaw, 2002, p.97ff.).[30]

It is quite possible that the names Hengest and Horsa (stallion
and horse, or horseman?) were traditional titles given to adventurer-
princes and that the two bore different given-names; the fact that
Hengest's family in Kent knew the figure of *Æsc* or *Oisc* as their
progenitor may reinforce this suggestion (Welch, 2007, p.190).[31]
Oisc had a kinsman (brother?) named Octa who was allegedly the

---

[30] Curiously, the names above the two brothers are all apparently based on the
element *Wiht-* which is perhaps derived from *Vectis* or *Vecta*, the Isle of Wight
(Rivet & Smith, 1979, s.v. *Vectis*). The archaeology of Wight in the post-Roman era is linked quite closely to that of east Kent, where the tomb of Horsa
is supposed to have stood. Since the name *Vecta* predates the Kentish royal
genealogy of Bede by many centuries, it cannot be a case of the island having
been named from a Germanic claimant to the territory.

[31] Shaw, 2002, p.100ff sees the W-alliterating line and link to Woden as a later
insertion, with the real ancestral figure for the Kentish kings as Oisc, from
whom the title *Oiscingas* derives.

father of Irminric of Kent, with whom the historical records of the kingdom begin: Irminric was the father of Æþelberht, the Kentish king who secured his alliance with the Franks by marrying into the Merovingian family.

Brothers who share the kingship are a feature of some early Germanic societies - for example, the joint-kings Hlothere and Eadric who shared rule in Kent in the later 7th c. and several examples among the East Saxons, including the three sons of King Sæberht (Bede's *Historia Ecclesiastica Gentis Anglorum* ch.5; Kelly, 2021, p.7; Rippon, 2022, p.18).

The 'divine twins' or brother-gods were certainly known among some early Germanic peoples. The cult of the Alcis is mentioned by Tacitus (*Germania*, ch. 43) in connection with the tribe called Naharvali. He says that in a grove 'a priest decorated like a woman' (*sacerdos muliebri ornatu*) conducts religious services which 'call to mind Castor and Pollux in the Roman understanding' (*sed deos interpretatione romane Castorem Pollusemque memorant*) (Polomé, 1989, p.78; Motz, 1995, p.84).[32] They are called the *Alcis* and they have 'no images' (*nulla simulacra*) but they are venerated as youths and brothers and are not remnants of the beliefs of foreign wanderers (by which he means that the cult has not been introduced through outside influence). The Alcis are not stated to be twins (*Gemini*) but the reference to *Castor* and *Pollux* indicates that he intends the Roman reflex of the Divine Twins (Ward, 1968, ch.IV; Simek, 1993, s.v. *dioscuri*; Stone, 1997, pp.113-6; Härdh, 2006).[33]

---

[32] Gunnell (1995, p.51) associates this account with a small figure on the Gallehus horn, who wears a long robe and holds a horn but has a beard. These attributes are typically female (except the beard), which Gunnell thinks may mean that the figure is a transvestite priest. While intriguing, this would be more convincing if the horn were not a facsimile of a lost original: we cannot discount the possibility of copying errors.

[33] The reference to 'no images' must mean that there are no anthropomorphic likenesses of the gods of the classical type, but there is evidence that posts or stakes formed part of their cult.

It is very interesting that the names *Hengst und Horst* have been given to the gable-posts of timber-framed houses in Schleswig-Holstein, implying a link with the English tradition of the two leaders, Hengest and Horsa. These gable posts were traditionally carved with horse-heads (Yorke, 1993, p.46; Simek, 1993, s.v. *Hengist and Horsa*; Schutz, 2001, p.26).[34] Given the details of the Hengest story in the *ASC* – two brothers with equine links arrive by sea with military aid for a failed leader in distress – the link to the Germanic 'Twinned Gods' seems self-evident (Ward, 1968, p.55; Grigsby, 2005, p.126).[35] It may be that, even if Hengest and Horsa were not known as 'gods' among the Angles, there were nevertheless analogues of the twin gods in the pantheon of the East Angles which gave rise to the pairs of dancing youths on the Sutton Hoo helmet (Bruce-Mitford, 1978, ch.III; Neuman de Vegvar, 1999, p.265). Here the figures appear in a vigorous or 'dancing' pose in a prominent place on the front of the helmet's bowl (Pollington, 2011, pp.246-50). There are similar pairs in the Scandinavian tradition, but they are usually shown fighting each other, as on the helmets from Vendel, barrows XII and XIV (Mortimer, 2011, p.28, 30-35). Such combat scenes may show a duel or, perhaps more likely in the context of the helmets' Woden imagery, a ritual contest, part of the military initiation process (Arent, 1969, p.136). In these scenes no warrior wears a helmet or rides a horse, both these attributes being emblems of 'elder' status – so the implication is plausible that these are youths attaining full adulthood.

However, there is no firm association of such paired divinities with traditions concerning Woden, although paired 'ancestor-gods'

---

[34] Some post-medieval northern German houses have crossed gables terminating in horse-heads, which are believed to protect against the Wild Hunt.

[35] In one version of the story (in *Historia Regum Britanniae* by Geoffrey of Monmouth), Hengest gives his daughter, Rowena, in marriage to Vortigern, the British leader, in exchange for a parcel of land on which to settle.

are found among many Germanic cultural groups, such as the Lombardic duo of Ibor and Agio, probably to be interpreted as 'boar' and 'sharp tusk' (Ward, 1968, p.51).

CHAPTER 3

FROM IRON-AGE WARLORD
TO MEDIEVAL RULER

The Óðinn figure, as we meet him in the medieval sources, mainly from
Iceland, is surely a multifaceted god and a very complex figure.
Jens Peter Schjødt, *Mercury – Wotan – Óðinn:*
One or Many?

The career of Woden mirrors the historical expansion of Germanic military activity and prestige. At the outset, the god was
associated most closely with male initiatory groups – and this connection may reach back into the Bronze Age or further, giving it
several thousand years of developmental history in Eurasia (Kershaw,
2000). By the Iron Age, from about 500 BC onwards, a period of
rapid technological change mirrored an expansion of ambition: the
Amber Road into northern Europe from the Black Sea and eastern
Mediterranean allowed wealth, goods and ideas to flow in both directions. The chiefs who controlled this trade-route expanded their
political and economic power - and it is at about this time that the
god's role may have broadened from bringing poetry and inspiration,
for example - language-based skills - into the areas of commerce and
negotiation which likewise rely on careful and precise use of language.

Later, centuries of trade and conflict with the Roman Empire
introduced new ideas, again often military and commercial in nature.
With Rome's decline in the west and the increased reliance on out-
sourced manpower for the military, another aspect of the god's character was developed: he became the winner of a writing system. In

post-Roman Europe, the old god of youthful warbands adapted again to the role of kingmaker, tactician and diplomat.

Rome's influence was neither entirely nurturing nor benevolent, but it had been decisive at a time when the societies on its north-eastern borders were transforming into organised kingdoms. Roman sources largely have next to nothing to say about Germanic religion and all discussion must take into account the evidence of the text *De Origine et Situ Germanorum* (usually abbreviated to the *Germania*) (Anderson, 1997; Rives, 1999).

The following are the principal primary sources of information about the god in roughly chronological order according to the date of composition of the texts.

2ND CENTURY BC

GLASBACKA MOUNT

This bronze figure is arguably the earliest evidence for a one-eyed aviform character from Scandinavia. It is formed as the hollow finial to a staff or sceptre, and has two basal loops (perhaps arms, if not part of the mounting mechanism) below a head which is beaked like a bird of prey, with domed eyes one of which is significantly flatter than the other. The findspot is assigned to Glasbacka in Halland (Sweden). The possible association with Óðinn arises from the possibility that the motif is both one-eyed and shaped like a raven, hawk or eagle (Schjødt, 2020b, pp.1134-5).

The casting has not been closely dated since its find-context is unknown – estimates based in the Late Bronze Age put it in the range 1000-500 BC, while an Early or Middle Iron Age date has also been suggested, around 500 BC- 400 AD. Needless to say, the identification with Óðinn is contentious, but it remains quite possible that a deity with the power to transform into a bird might have roots in the traditions of the Bronze Age.

NEGAU HELMET B

For the sake of completeness it is worth recording here the earliest known text in a Germanic language: the epigraphic legend *harigasti teiwa*. In 1812, a cache of 26 bronze military helmets was found at Ženjak, near Negau in the southern Alps. This area was the ancient borderland of territories which would later become Roman provinces: Pannonia and Noricum. The helmets may have been made in the 5th c. BC but they were inscribed in the 2nd c. BC, and were probably battlefield loot when they were placed in the ground (Schjødt, 2020c, p.250). Markey (2001, p.124) suggests they were a votive deposit at an open-air temple site – they were already ancient heirlooms and were perhaps revered because of this.

Seven of the helmets were inscribed, two of them in North Italic script, one (Helmet A) with the names of three successive owners and the other (Helmet B) with the words *harigasti teiwa ///IP*. This graffito has been interpreted as a votive inscription '[to the] god Harigast' expressed in an early language of the Germanic group (Elliott, 1958, pp.9-10; Markey, 2001; McKinnell & Simek, 2004, p.11). It demonstrates that speakers of a Germanic language were present in the southern Alps in the last centuries BC, and that they were familiar enough with the local script to make an inscription in their own language.

The name *Harigast* 'military guest' or perhaps 'outsider who serves in the military' suggests the kind of wandering adventurer that appears in the later Norse stories of Óðinn and Heimdallr, among others. Furthermore, the word *teiwa* or *teiva* is taken to be the accusative singular of **teiwaz*, the reconstructed Proto-Germanic word for 'deity'. The interpretation may then be rendered as 'for the god who has a host (of dead warriors) as guest' (Mees, 2023, p.29).

It is admittedly unlikely (but not impossible) that the reference here is genuinely to an early iteration of Woden-Óðinn. Moreover, this transliteration of the text is not universally accepted, nor even the language in which it was written (Blomfield, 1945; Simek, 1993, s.v. *Harigast*; Nedoma, 1995; Mees, 2023, p.27-30).

1ˢᵀ – 3ᴿᴰ CENTURY AD

Information from this period is scant. Tacitus names only two deities among the Germani of his day: *Germania* ch.2 states that *carmina antiqua* 'ancient songs' are their only records for revered tales, which presumably includes origin tales and the deeds of the gods and human ancestors (who are sometimes the same figures) including Tuisto (or, in one manuscript, Tuisco) and Mannus. The former is *terra editum* 'produced from the earth' and may be related to later traditions concerning Ymir who was freed from the primal ice. An intriguing inscription from the Roman *limes* provides a possible reference, but no further information.

TACITUS: GERMANIA

This work, completed in 98 AD, is the source of a great deal of information about the Germanic peoples of the 1ˢᵗ c. AD (Rives, 1999, pp.21-5).[36] It appears to have been compiled following the standard Roman model for such 'ethnographic treatises' with notes on the various tribes and their customs. We do not know in detail what source(s) Tacitus used, but it is assumed that he had earlier Roman (and Greek?) works available to him, as well as at least one personal informant. The treatise is not a work of modern scientific study, and Tacitus has received unwarranted criticism for not producing such a text: it is an educated Roman's view of the peoples beyond the Rhine, with a heavy dash of moralising – contrasting the virtuous savages of the north with the corruption and decadence of civilised men, while also mocking the barbarous customs and naïve beliefs of his subjects. Tacitus, it seems, was a rather supercilious and haughty character who was happy to share his low opinion of both Germanic and Roman societies alike. However, where it can be

---

[36] The Germani were regularly subsumed within the Celts and/or Scythians in classical works until the 1ˢᵗ c. BC when the Cimbri tribe became known to Roman writers, and through Caesar's remarks in *De Bello Gallico* concerning the Suebi.

checked against archaeological evidence, the text appears to be generally reliable (Thurston, 2001, p.45).

Surprisingly for a work on a foreign people, it contains almost no examples of their language(s). One Germanic word - *framea* - appears, the name for a type of spear. The only other non-Latin terms in the text are the names of the tribes themselves and of a few gods (e.g., *Mannus*) and persons (e.g., *Veleda*). The tribal names are not always easy to interpret, but they have often proved to be quite accurate where they can be tested against other sources. The text's *Aestii*, for example, who appear to be a Baltic people, make an appearance in King Alfred's 9th c. geographical supplement to Orosius as the *Estas,* among whom his informant, the shipmaster Wulfstan, spent some time (Bately & Englert, 2007).

RELIGION: PRAXIS

Concerning Germanic religious beliefs and practices, Tacitus has little of substance to say. Sadly, due to the *interpretatio Romana* – the habit of interpreting foreign gods purely in terms of the Roman pantheon – the text contains just a few names of deities or officiants, and it describes religion in a rather cursory manner. He remarks in *Germania* (ch.2) on the oral traditions of the Germanic tribes of his day (text from Anderson, 1997):

> Celebrant carminibus antiquis, quod unum apud illos memoriae et annalium genus est, Tuisconem deum terra editum. Ei filium Mannum originem gentis conditoremque Manno tris folios assignant e quorum nominibus proximi oceano Ingaevones, medii Herminones, ceteri Istaevones vocantur. Quidam ut in licentia vetustatis pluris deo ortos plurisque gentis appellationes, Marsos Gambrivios Suebos Vandilios affirmant eaque vera et antique nomina.

> 'They celebrate with ancient songs, which are the only kind of memorial and record for them, a god, Tuisco, born from the ground. They assign him a son, Mannus, the source and founder of their kind, and to Mannus they assign three sons, from whose

names those near the ocean are called Ingaevones, those in the middle Herminones, the rest Istaevones. Some, due to the laxity of the olden times, claim more sons from the god and more names of peoples – Marsi, Gambrivii, Suebi and Vandili – and that these are true and ancient names.'

This material is both genealogical and religious in content and may imply that among the Germanic peoples there was no firm division between 'illustrious ancestor' and 'divinity' – a theme to which we will return below. It bears the stamp of authentic tradition in this regard.

Furthermore, a traditional succession order 1:1:3 can be found here in Tuisco : Mannus : Ingwe / Istæ / Ermin. This pattern recurs elsewhere - in Snorri's sequence Buri : Bor : Óðinn / Vili / Vé.[37] It appears to be nothing more than a template for the background to kingship, in the same manner as the three social 'functions' in myth. This scheme appears more consistent with a situation in which Teiwaz was the apical and pre-eminent deity, as were his cognates Jupiter and Zeus (Pollington, 2011, pp.167-8). Mannus, the human progenitor, shares that role with Woden, but his name 'Man' is transparently connected to human rather than divine status.

'RULER OF ALL'

Tacitus's account includes a reference to worship of a deity styled *regnator omnium deus* 'god, ruler of all' (*Germania*, ch.39) which recalls the *Óðinnsheiti* term *Alfǫðr* 'father of all' (text from Anderson, 1997):

Vetustissimos se nobilissimosque Sueborum Semnones memorant; fides antiquitatis religione firmatur. Stato tempore in silvam auguriis patrum et prisca formidine sacram omnes eiusdem sanguinis populi legationibus coeunt caesoque publice homine celebrant barbari ritus horrenda primordia. Est et alia luco reverentia: nemo nisi vinculo ligatus ingreditur, ut minor et

---

[37] A similar succession is supplemented by a further generation in *Beowulf's* Scyld: Beow: Healfdene: Heorogar / Hroðgar / Halga (Niles, 2007, p.258ff).

potestatem numinis prae se ferens. Si forte prolapsus est, attolli et insurgere haud licitum: per humum evolvuntur. Eoque omnis superstitio respicit, tamquam inde initia gentis, ibi regnator omnium deus, cetera subiecta atque parentia.

'The Semnones believe themselves to be the most ancient and noblest of the Suebi; their belief is strengthened by religious faith. At a certain time, all the various peoples of the same stock gather in a wood, hallowed by the worship of their forefathers and by religious awe in olden times. By publicly sacrificing a man in that place, they begin the fearsome observance of their worship. To this wood another sort of respect is paid. No one may enter it otherwise than tied with bonds, admitting his service and low status, and the authority of the god there. If he should fall down, he may not rise or be lifted, but must roll along upon the ground. Of all their beliefs, this is the understanding: that from this place the whole folk began, that here a god, the supreme ruler of all, resides, and that all things are subject to him and bound to obey him.'

The notion of binding and applying boundaries is found frequently in Germanic culture, especially in relation to death (Lindow, 2020, p.107).[38] This is the first evidence we have for Germanic sacrifice in a woodland setting, and the offering of a man's life may be a ritual re-enactment of the creation tale whereby a primordial being was slain and hacked apart to create the world.[39] The religious dimension to the Semnones' belief in their pre-eminence is explained by Tacitus in the next clause:

Adicit auctoritatem fortuna Semnonum: centum pagi iis habitantur magnoque corpore efficitur ut se Sueborum caput credant.

---

[38] Bauschatz, 1982, ch.2. The 'Angel of Death' at the Rus funeral on the Volga described by Ibn Fadlan causes the immolated slave girl to be strangled with a cord and stabbed with a dagger simultaneously (Lunde & Stone, 2012, p.52-3).

[39] Tolley, 2009, p.352. The notion of a primordial being whose death gives rise to the world is of Indo-European or greater antiquity.

'The luck of the Semnones adds to their authority: they inhabit a hundred lands and due to this large size, they believe themselves to be the head of the Suebi.'

Possession of the grove of the god brings the god's power to their cause, and they therefore enjoy great luck, expressed in a swelling population which brings them prestige (Moisl, 1981, pp.218-9).

MERCURY

Tacitus names the god *Mercurius* as the pre-eminent deity among the Germanic peoples, but since he does not offer the corresponding vernacular name(s) it is impossible to know with certainty which deity he had heard about, or in which way(s) he was thought to resemble the Roman Mercury (Liberman, 2016, p.31; Schjødt, 2019, p.65).[40] Centuries later, Paul the Deacon equated the Lombard ancestor figure *Godan* with Mercury and Jonas of Bobbio likewise *Vodan* with the same Roman god, so it is usually assumed that an earlier form of Woden may have been in Tacitus's mind when he made the statement (text from Waitz, 1878; Kershaw, 2000, p.65):

Deorum maxime Mercurium colunt cui certis diebus humanis quoque hostiis litare fas habent.

'Of the gods, they mainly worship Mercury, whom on certain days they think it right to appease with human offerings.'

It is possible that Tacitus was echoing what Julius Caesar had written about the Gauls of his day, more than a century earlier, in *De Bello Gallico* when describing the Gallic attitude towards Mercury in precisely the same words: *deorum maxime Mercurium colunt*.[41] Worship of Mercury may therefore have been a literary *topos* of ethnographic

---

[40] However, Helm (1948, p.8) considers the whole passage a trite, formulaic and conventional depiction of 'barbarian' society.

[41] Tacitus did not follow Caesar's later comments about the god as inventor of all arts, the patron of commerce; his immediate source may be Herodotus's remark about the kings of the Thracians who believed themselves descended from Hermes (Kershaw, 2000, p.65).

discourse when writing about the 'barbarians' of Europe. Yet it might still be an accurate record of Roman opinion at the time of writing. Relations between speakers of Germanic and Celtic languages (in that case, Gaulish) must often have been close; in the 1st c. BC, there were contingents of Germanic Suevi operating as supporters of the Gauls in their struggle with the Romans (Enright, 1996; North, 1997, p.79; Pollington, 2011, p.68). A specifically Gaulish but highly prestigious military cult might have been adopted by their allies, while both societies already shared many common (late western Indo-European) traditions.

Mercury was not one of the more important or influential Roman gods. He had no great temple in the city itself, and he played no crucial role in the older stories. His skill was in negotiation and the accumulation of wealth, which he achieved through venturing into distant lands – hence his images bear a wide-brimmed traveller's hat (*petasos,* adopted from the cult of the Greek Hermes) and a purse for coins (*marsupium*). He was also a healer and teacher, carrying the *caduceus* staff with snakes entwined about it. He invented writing and passed the secret on to mankind, as did his Greek counterpart Hermes (Birkett, 2019, pp.152-3). Some aspects of his appearance and character must have been recognisable in a Germanic and Gallic deity – the later Irish god Lug with his clairvoyant raven might be adduced here, for example (Enright, 1994, pp.223-8; Liberman, 2016, p.35; Schjødt, 2019, p.65, 76).

When we look for Mercury's correspondences to figures in Germanic myth, the evidence is not plentiful. The *petasos* or broad-brimmed hat is a feature which recurs in Óðinn's name *síðhǫttr* 'wide hat' but it was a common kind of headgear used by travellers and those working outdoors to keep both sun and rain off. Nor is the *caduceus* a close parallel for Óðinn's preferred implement, his spear *Gungnir* 'shaker'. Sometimes Óðinn adopts the guise of a humble wayfarer – for example, Bǫlverkr in the story of the theft of the mead from Suttungr – but he also appears as a youthful prince on a fine horse, or a wise king leading an army (Liberman, 2016, p.33). Perhaps the most fruitful correspondences with Mercury lie in the fact that both gods were deeply versed in lore and knew many secrets, both were notably eloquent, and both were known for their associations with death and the ancestral dead (Kershaw, 2000, p.67; Schjødt, 2019, pp.66-7).[42] Mercury was especially invoked for commercial negotiations, voluntary agreements and the transport of goods, while one of Óðinn's bynames is *Farmatýr* 'cargo-god, freight-god' (Orel, 2013, s.v. *farma*; cf. Neidorf & Xu, 2022).

It is not necessary to accept the simple equation *Mercurius = *Wodenaz* as invariable.[43] In the absence of detailed information, it is not possible to say for sure which Germanic god was intended when the name *Mercurius* was recorded in a Latin-language text, and it is not certain that it was always the same Germanic god (Schjødt, 2019, p.65). Indeed, given that the figure of Óðinn in medieval sources appears to be a composite of several types of deity (gods of battle, of magic, of initiation, of commerce, of literacy, of poetry, of inspiration, of death), there is a strong probability that a number of older gods and their attributes have coalesced into a single complex figure.

HUMAN SACRIFICE

Tacitus's statement about appeasing Mercurius with human sacrifice may seem jarring, sensationalist or perhaps ill-informed – a cultured Roman's mistaken assessment of travellers' tales that he did not fully understand. Yet the idea of large-scale human sacrifice in a god's honour recurs in the traditions of the Roman Empire, Germanic lands and elsewhere. It is not merely a late or 'invented' idea put about to cause revulsion among medieval Christian congregations.

---

[42] Hermes derives his name from the *herma*, a pile of stones used as a boundary marker, and later a stele supplied with a human mask and male genitals (Kershaw, 2000, p.67). Such a pile of stones corresponds to the ON *hǫrgr* and OE *hearg*, a cult-site with a cairn as its focus.

[43] The name *Wodenaz* refers to the reconstructed PGmc ancestral form underlying later recorded forms such as 'Woden', 'Godan', etc. It is used here because this form should be appropriate for the period in which the interaction is thought to have taken place, say, 1st century BC-1st century AD.

As mentioned above (p.65), Tacitus noted that the Germani thought it right to worship their god with human victims on certain days. Livy noted (*Periochae*, 67) that two armies of Cimbri and Teutones overcame a Roman force at Arausio in 14 BC and then killed 80,000 soldiers and 40,000 servants and camp-followers. These numbers may have been overstated, but the notion of total destruction of a defeated military force, including its weapons and equipment, is no mere literary convention: the bog-deposits at Thorsberg, Nydam, Illerup and elsewhere demonstrate that large quantities of material could indeed end up put beyond use in the liminal marshlands (Engelhardt, 1863; Ilkjaer, 1990, 1996, 2001; Bemmann, 1998; Düwel, Marold & Zimmermann (eds.), 2000).

Tacitus elsewhere mentions (*Annals*, I) that, following the defeat of three Roman legions by the Cheruscian leader Arminius in 9 AD, a later Roman expedition under Germanicus visited the site where the conflict took place: the soldiers' bones remained in the forest in heaps along with those of their horses, their weapons were scattered and the skulls of some of the men nailed to the trees (Furneaux, 1904; Murdoch, 2006; McNally & Dennis, 2011; Abdale, 2016). In a nearby grove stood the altars where the centurions and chief Romans had been executed.

Forty years later, a battle took place between the Chatti and the Hermunduri over possession of a holy site.[44] The Chatti had vowed to sacrifice the entire enemy army – including weapons and horses – to the gods Mars and Mercury in exchange for victory. In the event, they lost the battle and the Hermunduri did likewise with the Chatti (text from Fisher, 1963):

> Eadem aestate inter Hermunduros Chattosque certatum magno proelio, dum flumen gignendo sale fecundum et conterminum vi trahunt, super libidinem cuncta armis agendi religione insita, eos maxime locos propinquare caelo precesque mortalium a deis nusquam propius audiri. inde indulgentia numinum illo in amne

---

[44] Ellis Davidson (1971, p.2) identifies the territory as 'a holy place on the river Saale, N.W. Germany, where salt was obtained'.

illisque silvis [s]alem provenire, non ut alias apud gentes eluvie
maris arescente, sed unda super ardentem arborum struem fusa
ex contrariis inter se elementis, igne atque aquis, concretum. sed
bellum Hermunduris prosperum, Chattis exitiosius fuit, quia
victores diversam aciem Marti ac Mercurio sacravere, quo voto
equi viri, cuncta viva occidioni dantur. et minae quidem hostiles
in ipsos vertebant.

Tacitus, Annals, ch.57

'That same summer a great battle was fought between the
Hermunduri and the Chatti, both laying claim to a river which
passed by their lands and which was rich in salt. They had the
custom of settling every dispute by fighting, and also a belief that
such sites are near to heaven, and that there the gods hear men's
prayers. They think that through the kindness of the deities salt
is produced in that river and in those woods, not as elsewhere by
the drying up of seawater, but by the mixture of two opposing
elements, fire and water, when poured over a burning pile of
wood. The war turned out well for the Hermunduri and was the
harsher for the Chatti because they had offered the enemy's army
to Mars and Mercury if they achieved victory, an oath which
would send the horses, men and everything else on the defeated
side to destruction. Thus this deadly threat rebounded on
themselves.'

Again, Tacitus does not state the vernacular names of the gods who
were invoked for victory, giving only the Latin names Mars and
Mercury, but it is likely enough that one or other of these was *Wodenaz* and the other *Teiwaz*. We find the Winniles making similar
petitions in the 5th century to *Godan*.

The lethal dedication of captives and defeated foes is later associated with the 'Saxones', although the references are distant in time
and cannot refer to the same group(s) of people. Liudger, the Frisian
missionary who undertook the conversion of the Saxons in the area
of Münster, mentions the slaughter of captives during his lifetime, the

later 8th to early 9th c. (Diekamp, 1881). Earlier, the Gallo-Roman writer Sidonius Apollinaris notes that the Saxons of his day (mid to late 5th c.) sacrificed to their gods for a safe sea-passage home after raiding Gallia by throwing one in ten of their captives overboard (Dalton, 1915).[45]

Wholesale slaughter is linked with the Saxons in England, in the aftermath of the victory of Ælle over the inhabitants of *Anderida*, a Saxon Shore fort, in 491 AD which is recorded thus in the *ASC* MS E (text from Thorpe, 1861):

> Her Ęlle 7 Cissa ymbsæton Andredescester 7 ofslogon alle þa þe þærinne eardedon; ne wearþ þær forþon an Bret to lafe.

> 'Here Ælle and Cissa besieged Anderida-fort (Pevensey) and slew all those who dwelt inside; whereby there was not one Briton left as a survivor.'

Physical evidence of human sacrifice is not absent from the archaeological record. There are certainly several burials in Scandinavia for which this seems to be a reasonable inference, where a second body has been placed in the grave at or close to the time of initial deposition, suggesting that one person chose (or was selected) to follow the other into the Otherworld (Gardeła, 2014, p.72). The often-cited example is Grave FII from the Stengade II cemetery (Denmark, 11th c.) in which an exceptionally tall younger (25 years old) and an older (35 years old) man were placed side-by-side in a chamber; the older man's feet and hands were bound and his head was severed

---

[45] Letter VI to Namatius: 'Moreover, when the Saxons are setting sail from the continent, and are about to drag their firm-holding anchors from an enemy's shore, it is their usage, thus homeward bound, to abandon every tenth captive to the slow agony of a watery end, casting lots with perfect equity among the doomed crowd in execution of this iniquitous sentence of death. This custom is all the more deplorable in that it is prompted by honest superstition. These men are bound by vows which have to be paid in victims, they conceive it a religious act to perpetrate this horrible slaughter, and to take anguish from the prisoner in place of ransom; this polluting sacrilege is in their eyes an absolving sacrifice.'

and replaced above the collarbone (Taylor, 2014, p.170 and references there). A spear with lateral wings on the shank – unusual in Scandinavian contexts – was placed over the pair. Whether this weapon should be given symbolic meaning is uncertain, but an association with Óðinn would not be too far-fetched in this case as a visual reference to *Gungnir*, the god's powerful war-spear.

Likewise in Anglo-Saxon England there are occasional examples of unusual burials which have been characterised as those of 'outcasts' placed away from the customary communal burial sites or treated in some exceptional manner, such as having large stones placed on the chest; this practice continued from the pre-Christian into the Christian period and was thus not confined to 'religious outsiders' (Reynolds, 2009). It appears to have become more widely followed (or perhaps to have become more easily detected archaeologically) with the rise of formal *cwealmstowa* - places of legal execution, many of which were prominently sited at crossroads and by other landmarks.

WODEN'S DAY

The association 'Mercury: Woden' is strengthened by the equation of day-names: Latin *Mercurii dies* (day of Mercury) and, e.g., OE *Wodnesdæg* (day of Woden), each for the fourth day of the seven-day week. Yet this equation is partly misleading. The seven-day week is not a Germanic, nor even a European idea. It derives ultimately from the Judaic notion that every seventh day should be set aside for rest, and that the series of six ordinary days and the following holy day can be repeated in a cycle independently of the solar and lunar calendars (Green, 1998, pp.236-43; Shaw, 2002, p.94ff; Kay, 2013, p.16; Lindow, 2016). This was an innovation in the ancient world, where societies often used moon-phases and the like to measure time.

The seven-day week was adopted by Greek-speaking Jewish communities, then more widely in the Greek world and from there it spread with the early Christian cults to Rome. The resultant Greek and Roman weekdays were named for the more popular gods. The 'classical' gods were at about this time (1st c. AD) being increasingly identified with the visible planets due to a renewed interest in Chaldean astrology under the Emperor Augustus. Some early Christian sects reacted against this practice and used a more neutral system in which only the 'special' day (Sabbath) was named, the others being referred to as 'second day', 'third day' and so on. The Goths adopted this system from the Greeks on their conversion.

Traditionally, Germanic time was measured by nights rather than days, as Tacitus stated (*Germania*, ch.11), which can still be found in expressions such as 'fortnight' (fourteen nights), 'Christmas Eve' (night before Christmas) and so on. West Germanic-speaking tribes were not significantly touched by Christianity at this time but they had considerable dealings with Rome in the fields of politics, commerce, military activity and diplomacy. With their adoption of the Roman week, day-names were devised with suitable Germanic deities substituted for the Roman ones (Rausing, 1995).[46] Were the West Germanic peoples using astrological terms or god-names when they devised their words for the days of the week? The case of English 'Saturday' from OE *Sæternesdæg* is instructive, as this is clearly adopted direct from Latin *Saturni dies* 'day of Saturn'. Saturn was not a Germanic, but rather an Etrusco-Roman god: the term seems to have been used in place of the Judaeo-Christian *sabbatum* 'Sabbath' (Green, 1998, p.245; cf. Shaw, 2007; Kay, 2013, p.16). Therefore, the relationship between Germanic and Roman gods in the day-names has been coloured by the requirements of later religious observance.

---

[46] A three-way division evolved among Germanic-speaking communities. The Gothic day-names were translations from the Greek, and these were adopted by the Bajuwari and Alemanni in southern and central Germany. The Franks and Visigoths adopted the Latin day-names of their Catholic Christian subjects, based in part on practices devised under the cult of *Sol Invictus*. The North Sea peoples and Scandinavians translated the Roman terms into their own languages.

THE ROMAN INTERPRETATION

Roman *Mercurius* is himself not a straightforward deity. His name appears to be cognate with Latin *merx* 'trade, commerce' and more widely with Gmc **markan*, **markjan* 'border' (Orel, 2003, s.v. **markan*). He took on aspects of the Etruscan god *Turms*, and under the Hellenising influence of the Roman state he also acquired traits associated with Greek *Hermes* such as the roles of messenger, magician and guide of souls to the Underworld. His physical attributes in religious iconographic contexts include the broad hat (*petasos*), the serpent-staff (*caduceus*) and the pouch or bag of coins (*marsupium*) (Gardenstone, 2011, p.9ff). His images sometimes show the winged sandals previously associated with Hermes which confer both speed and the power of flight, but this is exceptional. He was credited with the invention of writing and passing it onto his human worshippers (Bremmer, 1991).

Evidence for the worship of Mercury is quite strongly associated with *Gallia*, *Britannia* and the Rhineland frontier provinces – the same areas, in fact, where worship of the *matronae* (maternal goddess figures) also seems to have flourished. If the god's help was called upon in such contexts as negotiating deals for commercial gain, then it would seem reasonable to suggest that it was this aspect which was foregrounded when the Roman empire set up diplomatic and trade contacts beyond its borders, and that such deals were sanctified by the god of commerce (Gardenstone, 2011, p.21; Liberman, 2016, pp.31-5). If so, then Mercury may have been the main Roman god invoked in the context of such contacts between Germanic and Roman societies, and the Romans may have imputed a similar character to whichever of the various Germanic gods was invoked by the Germani on these occasions.

An aspect of Roman Mercury that does not appear to be ancient is that of *psychopomp*, leader of souls into the Otherworld. This is another of the traits taken over from Greek Hermes; it may never have formed part of the Roman conception outside purely literary contexts. Indeed, there is little evidence that the Romans thought the departing soul needed a guide. This *psychopomp* notion feeds into the later Scandinavian idea of the *valkyrjur* who were later deemed to have been responsible for escorting the valiant slain to *Valhǫll*, but this is a (probably) late accretion to the myths, and more likely results from a separate tradition of female battle-spirits.

Mercurius Hranno

In Nordrhein-Westfalen, Germany, in the early 1980s, a heavily damaged stone figure was ploughed up and left unnoticed on the edge of the field where it had emerged; subsequently, carvings and an inscription were spotted by the landowner and it was handed over to the Rheinisches Landesmuseum in Bonn for research (Enright, 1996, pp.253-4; Liberman, 2016, p.35). The limestone statue dates from the 2nd-3rd century AD and is furnished with a socle pedestal bearing a short inscription, but the body is broken away at the middle of its lower legs, at a height of 79 cm. The reverse of the base is damaged but was once worked to a smooth finish, while on each of the lateral faces a vessel is displayed with s-shaped handles and ornamental foliage. Its catalogue reference is: inschrift / HD009212.

The figure represents Mercury with a turtle at his feet, and possibly a cockerel whose tail-feathers are still visible on the lower left leg. Between his legs rests the lower shaft of a spear. Comparison with other similar finds from the Bornheim area suggests that there was once a sanctuary to a local cult of Mercury in this region, althhough this statue was found at nearby Hemmerich.

On the front face of the base, an inscription in six lines was carved in capitals:

MERCVRIO
HRANNONI
NIGRINIA
TITVLA EX

VISV MONITA

L M

'I, Nigrinia Titula, dedicate [this] to Mercurius Hranno, having taken notice of a warning, gladly and deservedly.'

The dedicator was a female, and her clan-name Nigrinius/Nigrinia is largely restricted to the provinces of *Germania* and *Gallia Belgica*. She would have been a local woman of some wealth and social standing. The interest of the inscription for the present project lies in the cognomen attributed to Mercury: *Hrannoni* (dative singular from a nominative *Hranno*) with the characteristic development of **kr-* to **xr-* spelled 'HR-' in Roman epigraphic orthography.

In the medieval *Hrólfs saga kraka*, a character with the name *Hrani* appears; the name means 'blusterer, braggart, reveller' or 'brawler, troublemaker' and denotes a rough labourer or farmworker (see Appendix II *Óðinsheiti*). It turns out that *Hrani*, the one-eyed farmer, is Óðinn in disguise and he sets a challenge for Hrolf and his men *en route* to the great Swedish sacrificial site at Uppsala. On Hrolf's return journey, Hrani offers him weapons which the king refuses, and this costs him his life (Schjødt, 2020e, p.577).

The sense of 'rough' for *Hron-* may have derived from an older usage since a tribe called *Hronas* appears in *Widsith* (1.63) (text from Chambers, 1912):

Mid Hronum ic wæs ond mid Deanum ond mid Heaðoreamum.

'I was among the Hronas and the Deanas and the Battle-Reamas.'

These other peoples may be traceable: the *Deanas* may be the same folk as appear in the southern Scandinavian section of Ptolemy's *Geography* with the name *Daukiones* (Δαυκίωνες), while the *Heaþoreamas* are in *Beowulf* (1.518):

...   Þa hine on morgentid

on Heaþoræmas   holm up ætbær.

'Then, in the morning-time, the sea cast him up among the Battle-Reamas.'

This *Heaþoræmas* group were located in southern Scandinavia, since the prelude to this casting-up was the swimming contest between Beowulf and Breca, which must have taken place – to the extent that it is historical – in the Oslofjord area of the western Baltic Sea. Chambers (1912, p.210) says that they dwelt 'near the modern Christiania', i.e., Oslo; their kingdom was known as *Raumariki*, modern Romerike.

Returning to the statue's text: 'Hranno', then, is a plausible epithet for a local cult of Mercury and it is an n-stem noun like ON *Hrani*, but the evidence from *Hronum* in *Widsith* is unclear: the dative plural would be *Hronum* whether the nominative plural were *Hronas* or *Hronan*. (The noun *hron* 'small whale' is probably unrelated.)

It seems likely that there was once a cult of a god identified as Mercury by *Interpretatio Romana* among the folk of this area, who are believed to have been the Ubii; Enright (1998, p.254) insisted that this people must be 'Gallo-Roman' or 'Romanized Celto-Germanic' because he wanted this god to be the consort of Rosmerta, a Gallo-Roman goddess. This local version of Mercury was characterised as 'Hranno', so possibly 'boisterous' or 'troublesome' like Hrani in the saga – both certainly attributes of Óðinn.

It would have been instructive to see the statue in pristine condition, to determine whether there was anything unusual about the face, since in the mid-1st century the rebel leader Julius Civilis was active in this area; his promotion of local deities such as Hercules Magusanus, was a policy of his encouraging the break from Roman rule. Civilis was one-eyed.

LOCAL MERCURY CULTS

The statue and dedication to *Mercurius Hranno* is not unique: there are a few local Mercury figures whose names have been deduced from epigraphic evidence, mostly dating from the later 1st or 2nd century AD. Unfortunately, we do not know in detail what prompted the creation of these monuments, nor by whom they were erected: this lack of context reduces their usefulness as evidence for religious behaviour. In the following, I have relied on Simek's collation of data (1993, pp.212-4) and cite the *Corpus Inscriptionum Latinarum* (CIL) reference. Among the candidates are:

> *Mercurius Arvernorix*, whose name was discovered on a hill near Würzburg (Germany) and *Mercurius Arvernus*, which appears in seven separate instances in the Rhineland area. Both epithets, *Arvernorix* and *Arvernus*, imply dedication by members of the Arverni tribe, who are believed to have been Celtic-speaking and settled in south-west France.

> *Mercurius Cimbrianus* appears in five inscriptions (CIL XIII 6604, 6605, 6402, 6742) in the Heidelberg, Mainz and Würzburg areas, the latter next to the dedication to *Mercurius Arvernorix*. The name implies a dedication to the god of the Cimbri, a tribe located in the Jutland peninsula.

> *Mercurius Dumatius* appears in the same site as *Mercurius Arvernus* but its dedicator came from the Puy de Dôme area of southern France. *Mercurius [Fr]iausus* is one reconstruction of an inscription (CIL XIII 8726) found at Ubbergen, near Nijmegen, Netherlands. The text is fragmentary, and the reading very uncertain. *Mercurius Gebrinius* appears on ten votive stones from the Bonn area. The attempt to explain this name as related to ON *gífr* 'monster' is tendentious; many of the images include a ram, so derivation from the Celtic word *gabros seems more likely.

As with the Arverni inscriptions, all these dedications appear distant from the presumed homeland of those who erected the monument, which probably means that each statue was an object of veneration for travellers, traders or soldiers far from home, in much the same way that a Batavian inscription (RIB 1593) to *Mars Thincsus* and the *Alaisiagae* appears on a shrine at *Vercovium* near Hadrian's Wall in northern England (Grundy, 2014, pp.59-60).

> *Mercurius Leud[isius]* is one possible reading of an inscription (CIL XIII 7559) from Weisweiler, which has been related to a supposed verb **leudisjan* 'govern, rule' from the root **leudi-* 'people, group'. However, the adjective may rather refer to the Latin name of the nearby settlement of *Leudicum* (modern Lüttich).

More convincing are the agent-noun epithets applied to the god in various dedications including:

> *Mercurius Nundinator* 'Mercury the trader' appears on an inscription found near Wiesbaden (CIL XIII 7569) and the similar *Mercurius Negotiator* 'Mercury the dealer' from Heddenheim (CIL XIII 7360). The commercial association is also evident in the name *Mercurius Mercator* 'Mercury the businessman' on a votive stone from Metz (CIL XIII 4308).

> *Mercurius Rex* 'King Mercury' on an inscription (CIL XIII 1326) from the area of Nijmegen, Netherlands. Such an epithet would be very unusual in a Roman context since Mercury was not among the prominent deities. It seems like that this is *interpretatio Romana* at work, and the dedicatee was a local Germanic god who was both a ruler (*rex*) and a healer, inspirer of poetry, etc.

MARS HALAMARÐUS

An inscribed sandstone block intended as a statue-base was later included in the wall of St. Martinus's church at Horn, Netherlands. It dates from the first half of the 1st c. AD and is now in the National Museum's collection at Leiden. The dedicatory text is carved in clear capitals (Simek, 1993, s.v. Mars Halamarðus; Mees 2023, p.50):

MARTI

HALAMARÐ[I]

SACRVM

T[ITVS] DOMIT[IVS] VINDEX

Ɔ LEG[IONIS] XX V[ALERIAE] V[ICTRIX]

V[OTVM] S[OLVIT] L[IBENS] M[ERITO]

'Dedicated to Mars Halamarðus. Titus Domitius Vindex, a centurion of the 20th Legion Valeria Victrix, fulfilled his vow willingly [and] deservedly'.

The inscription records the stone's dedication to a god named by *interpretatio Romana* as 'Mars Halamarðus', of which the meaning was initially understood as 'man-slayer' but is now regarded as 'he who has dead heroes (as guests)', i.e., two elements cognate with OE *hæleþ* 'hero' and *morþ* 'death, dead'. The inscription includes the character 'Ð' (*Tau gallicum*, 'Gaulish T') which was adapted from Greek theta (θ) with its crossbar, indicating an assibilated or fricative form of 'T' (so probably /θ/ or /ts/).

The legion Valeria Victrix was raised by Augustus in 31 BC and served with distinction in several campaigns, including the one launched against the Marcomanni in 6 AD under Tiberius. After the slaughter of Varus's three legions in 9 AD (Strassmeir & Gagelmann, 2009; Abdale, 2016), the 20th legion was moved into *Germania Inferior* and later took part in the Claudian invasion of Britain in 43 AD; in the mid-century, it was based at *Camulodunum* (Colchester) where it took part in the suppression of the aftermath of the Boudiccan revolt (61 AD), and later in the construction of Hadrian's Wall. The 20th legion was probably still stationed in Britain when Roman rule was withdrawn in 407 AD. Its recruits in the early 1st c. were drawn from the area of the Tungri tribe (modern Tongeren, Netherlands) although Titus Domitius Vindex may have been a Batavian (Mees, 2023, p.51). If so, he may also have been among the early creators or users of the runic script (Pollington, 2016, pp.376-88). The Batavi were known to be an aggressive, militarised society with a fearsome god named *Hercules Magusanus* (Birley, 2011; Pollington, 2016, p.381; Mees, 2023, p.54) and several Matronae deities.

The stone erected by Titus, a centurion active early in the 1st c. AD, was dedicated to a local syncretic deity – a war-god (Mars) who hosts fallen heroes. In the context of the later history of the Batavi and their role in the development of the *comitatus* structure and plausibly in the spread of runic script, this fact appears to be rather significant (Pollington, 2016, p.85). The same attributes of the god reappear in the tales of Óðinn current in 13th c. Iceland (p.266, 288).

4TH-5TH CENTURY AD

This period was formative in the development of the cult of the god Woden, and it is likely that many of the characteristics later associated with him have their origins in this time, perhaps by the accretion of existing cult-figures and forms of worship. The first secure mention of the god's name appears on a bracteate from Vindelev. It is possible that the helmet found at Hellvi on Gotland was first made at this time too, but in its present modified form it probably belongs to the 6th c.

THE VINDELEV BRACTEATES

A great many bracteates bear figural ornament which has been interpreted in terms of the myths told about Woden/Óðinn – 'the noble horseman', 'the ruler with weapons', 'the healer of Baldur's foal', and other themes. All these are suppositions based solely on the iconography: none of the images names the god directly, so there has always been room for doubt as to the identity of the figures shown. That changed with the discovery of the Vindelev bracteate.

A gold hoard was found by two metal-detectorists in a field about 5 miles (8km) from Jelling (Jutland, Denmark) and reported in *Forskerzonen* (The Research-Zone) on the website Videnskab.dk by the runologists Lisbeth Imer of Copenhagen and Krister Vasshus of Bergen University (8th March 2023). The findspot had been a central place in the Iron Age, the residence of a wealthy chieftain – or perhaps an early 'king', given the later history of the Jelling area as a royal seat. The trove, now known as the 'Vindelev hoard', comprised about 800 grams of gold and included thirteen bracteates, four Roman medallions, a gold scabbard mount and a gold pendant (Imer & Vasshus, 2023, p.61). It was among the largest finds of hoarded gold ever made on Danish soil.

Fig. 1 Vindelev bracteate (IK738) with horse and rider figure, runic text. (Source: Arnold Mikkelsen / AP)

The Vindelev bracteates are unusually heavy and large for the type, and six of the thirteen bore some runic writing – three were texts already known from other finds while the others were unique. Bracteates are far from unknown at such important sites, and more than 1,000 examples have been found across northern Europe, of which more than 200 bear an inscription; [47] most of these legends

---

[47] Imer and Vasshus (2023, p.63) note that in March 2023 the corpus of bracteates stood at 1149 examples from 715 different dies; those with inscriptions total 272 from 182 dies.

are one-word 'identifiers' which resist clear interpretation and seldom have any obvious relation to the scene or design in the centre of the tondo. Some longer texts are hard to interpret simply because the runes' shapes are different from the standard fuþark forms, which makes accurate identification of the intended characters uncertain (Pollington, 2016, pp.156-78, fig. 36). Also relevant is the small size of the carved characters on the matrices (usually 2-3mm in height) which were used to impress the inscriptions. The finds are referenced with an 'IK' number in the academic literature, from Hauck's standard edition with the German title *Ikonographischer Katalog.*

Dating the Vindelev hoard focuses immediately on the 5th-6th c., but arriving at a more precise timeframe is contentious (Imer & Vasshus, 2023, pp.62-3); the date-range 450–490 AD was proposed by Morten Axboe, but Elisabeth Barford Carlsen more cautiously suggested '5th to mid-6th century AD'. Four of the Vindelev runic bracteates can be dated confidently to the 5th c. but two (IK737, 739) are probably later (early 6th c.). Three of the runic finds are close copies of types known from elsewhere in Fyn, which implies either diplomatic exchange between groups, or internal distribution within a single society. The quality of the gold used for impressions from the same die varies, which indicates that they were probably not all made in the same place or on the same occasion (Imer & Vasshus, 2023, p.74). From the distribution of known finds, it seems that links between the area around Odense in the north of Funen and the middle region of Jutland (Jelling, Vindelev) were at one time very close.

One bracteate (IK731) bears the unusual iconography of a male head with a smaller figure in front of him and a 'horse' beneath, derived from a Roman iconographic source in which the Emperor stands holding up a statue of Victoria (i.e., the smaller figure on the bracteate) (Imer & Vasshus, 2023, p.62, 86). It is an A-Type, similar to another found at Kristianslund (IK691) but not a perfect die duplicate. Its runic text is enigmatic, and even the division of characters is uncertain; Imer hesitantly transcribes it: (**u**)(**i**)(**u**)?(**u**)**za**(**s**)**ag**(**u**). It probably comprises two words because the medial sequence -uz appears to mark the nominative singular inflection of a noun (ᛉ 'z' as a grammatical marker should only occur in word-final position).

A bracteate from the hoard with a simpler design is numbered IK735 and shows a profile bust with pellets and crescents forming an elaborate hairstyle; below is a triskele with pellet finials, a T-shaped hammer with a ring finial and two runes: ᚠ 'a' and ᛏ 't', both inverted (Imer & Vasshus, 2023, p.89). It may be that this bracteate displays symbols or ciphers for the Æsir gods: t for Tīw/Týr; a hammer for Þunor/Þórr; a for the leading god, Wōden/Óðinn. But the character represented by the triskele remains unknown (Frigg? Heimdall? or perhaps one of the Vanir?).

Another bracteate (IK737) is a duplicate of a well-known C-Type find from Fyn (IK58) with a number of runic words embedded within the image in three separate sequences (Pollington, 2016, fig.34; Imer & Vasshus, 2023, pp.64-70, 94). Beneath the horse's muzzle is the sequence **laþu** and above the man's head in retrograde (s)u(l)i(t)a which may form part of the same text as **laþu**, which means 'invitation', or perhaps 'invocation, summoning' (Pollington, 2016, pp.331-2). Several interpretations of the retrograde text have been suggested, including a diminutive ending -ita of the word for a female pig *sū-, i.e., 'little sow' (Imer & Vasshus, 2023, p.94).[48] Between these two texts is the sequence **aarpaa**, which is noteworthy since it also appears on a runic stone unearthed at Hogganvik, Norway, in 2009 (Knirk, 2009) and likewise on other bracteates (e.g., IK145, IK41). Its meaning is unknown, but the recurrence of the exact sequence suggests that it was a recognised and traditional formula. Above the male head three runes are written: **al(u)**; the third rune is an unusual shape for **u** but this may be due to poor

---

Looijenga (2003, pp.204-5) offers an entirely different interpretation of this inscription based on the evident presence of mirror-runes in the text; she reads **aeraa=liu[s]** 'Aurelius' taken to be the name of the 'king' or worshipper derived from that of the emperor whose medallion formed the model for the design.

copying (for a discussion of **alu** see Pollington, 2016, pp.317-25). Another bracteate from the same hoard (IK739) bears the text **aul** which is likely a transcription error for **alu**; this erroneous or encrypted form appears also on the Tønder bracteate (IK353). Five runes placed between the horse's foreleg and its head read **horaz**; this sequence appears more clearly here than on IK58 and disproves the old suggestion that the reading should be **houaz**, a posited early form of the word *hár* which appears as a pseudonym of Óðinn in *Gylfaginning* (Pollington, 2016, pp.168-9; Imer & Vasshus, 2023, p.69, 92, 94).[49] The word **horaz** is cognate with Latin *carus* meaning 'cherished, beloved' and probably refers to the horse.

The most significant of the Vindelev bracteates for the history of Woden is IK738, a C-Type with a profile bust above a horse within concentric rings of rosette, pellet-in-triangle and horseshoe/crescent motifs. It bears a long runic text of 34 well-formed characters, although usage-wear has blurred some of the detail. It is considered probably an early example, since it shares stylistic features with Type A. The workmanship which produced both the die and its impression is highly accomplished, and the skill shown indicates that the production of clear and legible texts was within the scope of such runemakers; subsequent degeneration shown in copying errors, evident on many runic objects, should alert researchers to the likelihood that their makers were illiterate (Imer & Vasshus, 2023, p.91, 94).

Nevertheless, the initial interpretation is promising. The text is read as follows, with the author's own word-divisions (cf. Imer & Vasshus, 2023, p.71):

hos(t)i(-) he(l=p)u ufar fata=i jag=a iz wod(n)as
we=(r)az

---

[49] The sequence **houaz** is in any case hard to reconcile with the standard ON word *hár*. It is likely that this association was made in the belief that the horse-and-rider image must depict Woden. The Vindelev find clarifies the reading and removes a false trail in the search for early instances of Woden iconography.

This may be compared with the legends on another C-bracteate pair from Bolbro (IK31,2)[50] each with an abraded text to the border which probably reads:

ho(s)ti(a)z hetu u(f)(f)? (i)k u?-?-(i)z (þ)o(w)(a) ...-e-az

where the sequence -þow- may stand for -woþ- by confusion of the stave-and-bow shapes ᛈ 'w' and ᚦ 'þ' (Imer & Vasshus, 2023, pp.72-4, p.77, 91). The inscriber of IK31 was less careful than the one who worked on IK32 and his text is partly garbled because of this (e.g., **hetu** for **hel=pu**).

The first word in the Vindelev legend, read here as **hostiaz**, may be an agent noun derived from the verb *hwōstejan* 'cough' but Imer and Vasshus reject this in favour of the reading **hostioz**, a feminine nominative plural noun ultimately derived from Latin *hostia* 'sacrifice, animal offering' and likely borrowed into a Germanic dialect at an early date, perhaps the 2nd c. AD (Imer & Vasshus, 2023, p.78-9, 90). The use of an imported word for 'offering' may in itself indicate a practice adopted from contact with the Roman-dominated south. The sequence read as **hetu** on IK31 is more probably to be read, as on IK32, as **hel=pu**, a verbal 1st sing. pres. indic. meaning 'I help' (with the pronoun *ek* omitted). The sequence **ufar** is seemingly a preposition meaning 'above', although it is a non-standard form for North Germanic (where *ubir* might be expected) (Imer & Vasshus, 2023, pp.79-80). Its function in the semantics of the sentence is not entirely clear, but it may mean 'from above' or something similar.

The form **fatai** is probably the dative singular of a noun, governed by the verb **helpu** which often takes that case. Its derivation is likely from the verb *fat(t)ōn* 'fetch, catch, grasp' (Orel, 2003, s.v. *fatjanan*; Kroonen, 2013, s.v. *fat(t)ōn*) and it should mean 'catcher'.

---

[50] IK31 is a small disc with a beaded border and an applied ribbed suspension loop. The diameter of IK32 is about twice that of IK31 with the same design at the centre and the outer flan decorated with concentric rings and a band of guilloche ornament. Its suspension loop is also ribbed but with applied filigree and granulation.

The texts of IK 31 and IK32 both contain a sequence to be read as **iz wodanas weraz** which presumably means '(he/who) is Woden's man' with the preceding characters **jaga** denoting a personal name in the nominative (the hunter? cf. Kroonen, 2013, s.v. **jakk/gōn* 'rush, chase'). Plausibly, with the initial i- of **iz** also to be read as the final rune of the preceding word (a runic convention noted elsewhere) the form here may be **jagai**, a dative singular in apposition with **fatai**: **helpu ufar fatai Jagai* 'I help from above the catcher/huntsman Jaga'. The sequence **wodnas** is a standard genitive singular (= **wōdanas* with ellipsis of the unstressed medial vowel) from the nominative **wōdanaz*, differing in its stem vowel from the form **wōdinaz* which gives rise to the OE genitive *Wēdnes* and to **wodinz** on the Strängnäs runestone. The word **weraz** is a common noun meaning 'man, adult male', also nominative singular (Orel, 2003, s.v. **wiraz*).

The legend thus seems to mean 'Sacrifices. I help (from above) the catcher. (The) hunter is Woden's man' (adapted from the range of possibilities discussed in Imer & Vasshus, 2023, pp.83-4). It appears that this new inscription identifies the bracteate's profile figure as the 'worshipper' (**weraz**) rather than the god himself, as has often been argued in discussion of the many personal names which appear on the C-bracteates, although this then raises questions of interpretation regarding the surrounding symbols and the other elements of the design (Imer & Vasshus, 2023, p.92).

6TH - 7TH CENTURY AD

The period beginning around 500 AD and extending for about two centuries has proved to be quite productive for the evidence it can provide for the history of Woden as a named entity. The runic text on the Nordendorf Brooch can be dated to the 6th-7th century on stylistic grounds, as can the Strängnäs runestone.

The authorship of Fredegar's *Chronicon* may be dated to circa 658 AD, the year in which the entries cease, and the *Edictus Rothari* was completed in 643 AD. These are discussed below in the context of the works of the other Lombard sources and the works of Paul the Deacon.

As regards the acquisition of specific strategic knowledge, a god corresponding to Woden still appears to be the best candidate for the mythic initiator. And it may be that one group – the Angles and their neighbours in Jutland – formed an alliance of peoples responsible for elevating Woden from the status of war-god to the prime position in the pantheon, and the apical name in the Anglian kinglists. This change of emphasis cannot have been universal in Germanic societies – there is less evidence for it among the Goths, for example – but it came to be one characteristic of some élite groups who shared in the task of rebuilding Western European society after the collapse of Roman authority.

The wider region of southern Scandinavia was noted for its worship of Ingwe, a fertility god whose cult was connected to the ritual procession of a waggon (as the *OERP* relates), and probably to a period of *friþ* 'ritual temporary peace' during which weapons were put away, if Tacitus's description of the Nerthus-cult is a reliable guide here (Halsall, 1981; Pollington, 2011, pp.252-5). The rivalry between worshippers of the two families of gods is recalled in the opening of *Beowulf* and has been characterised as 'a triumph of Óðinn and the ravens of bloodshed for its own sake, over the gods of corn and fruitfulness' (Tolkien, 2016, p.330).

THE NORDENDORF BROOCH

The divine name appears epigraphically on the reverse of the 'Nordendorf brooch', an Alemannic dress item of late 6th or 7th c. date, in the form **wodan** (Simek, 2006, p.59; Liberman, 2016, p.43; Imer & Vasshus, 2023, p.92). The brooch was recovered from a grave where it had lain undisturbed for more than a thousand years, and the inscription had not been evident even when the item was worn. It had two runic texts scratched into the reverse:[51]

logaþore / wodan / wigiþonar

awa leubwini

The language is a West Germanic dialect (not North Germanic or Proto-Norse) but pre-OHG (i.e., before the Second Sound Shift which would result in the forms *wuotan, *-donar).[52] The second word is evidently the divine name *wodan*.[53] The third word is usually agreed to be a compound with -*þonar* as its deuterotheme (i.e., the god later called Þunor, Donar, Þórr) and the first element either 'battle' or 'hallower'. The first word is more contentious, with some scholars taking it to mean 'warlocks, deceivers, tricksters', while others see it as a reference to either (i) the god known in Norse as Loki, or (ii) the enigmatic god Lóðurr (Schwab, 1981, pp.42-4; Antonsen, 2002, p.38; Looijenga, 2003, pp.249-51; Fischer, 2005, p.174). An attractive comparandum is the OE word *logþor, logeþer* found in glossaries where it translates Greek *kakomikanos* 'mischief-making, scheming' and, once (Cotton MS Cleopatra A III) Latin *marsius*

---

[51] Schwab (1981, p.38) suggests a 6th c. date, while others have dated it to the 7th or even 8th c. The brooch was recovered in 1843 from a grave – a location which should exclude a date later than the late 6th or very early 7th c. when the use of grave-goods fell out of favour, after the conversion of this area to Christianity. Stylistically, an early 6th c. date for the brooch appears likely, but it is repaired and was probably already old at the time of deposition (cf. Roth, 1986, p.64). Perhaps a date of manufacture in the period 525–550 would be correct, with deposition around 575–610.

[52] Nedoma (2006, p.140-1) implies that the rune **d** no longer stood for /d/ but had necessarily changed to /t/ after the Second Sound Shift since its name had evolved to *tag* <*dagaz*. This inference is not wholly reliable. The form *Vodan* (also pre-OHG) occurs in the *Vita Columbani* of Jonas of Bobbio; Columbanus died circa 615 AD, but the existing manuscript dates from no earlier than the 9th c. The same text also gives the Alemannic word for a beer-vessel *cupa*, in its pre-OHG form which later appears as *chufa* /xuːfa/ in Notker.

[53] Gardenstone, 2011, p.113, 120-4; but see the Strängnäs Runestone below.

'snake-charmer, sorceror' (Schwab, 1981, p.42).[54] 'Troublemaker' is one interpretation of the epigraphic name Mercurius Hranno.

Unfortunately, we do not know exactly which dialect the inscription represents, and it therefore cannot be certain whether the brooch's text is evidence for the presence of Woden-worshippers among the Alemanni, or else for an immigrant female – perhaps won in an exogamous marriage – with no connection to the Nordendorf area other than through her burial in the gravefield of her husband's kindred.

For the sake of completeness, we may note that Menghin (2007, item VII.40.22) published a late 6th c. radiate-headed bow-brooch with the inscribed text to the reverse **Wödini.Jailag**, i.e., **wodini hailag** 'holy to Woden' with the star-rune **J** showing the value /h/. This text is generally considered a forgery.

THE STRÄNGNÄS RUNESTONE

A fragment of a runestone discovered at Strängnäs (Sweden) bears the Elder Fuþark text **(e)rilaz:wodinz** which appears to confirm the existence of both the divine name *Woden* and the office of *erilaz* in Sweden in the 5th- 6th century. The forms of the runes suggest a date in Phase I, i.e., before the development of a specifically Scandinavian fuþark.[55]

The dressed sandstone fragment has sometimes been dismissed as a fake since its discovery in 1962, although more recent investigation into its runic and archaeological context indicates that this assessment may have been unduly hasty (Kitzler Ahfeldt, 2007; Gustavson & Swantesson, 2011). Likewise, linguistic evaluation has not

---

[54] Looijenga (2003, p.250) links the *marsi* reference to the OE gloss *wyrmgaleras* 'snakecharmers' and regards this as a reference to Loki. Yet several gods have links to the serpent in early Germanic tradition including both Woden (who kills the snake in the OE *Nine Herbs Charm*) and Þunor – Þórr who is *orms einbani* (sole-slayer of the snake) in Norse tradition.

[55] Reference Sö ALLHSÖDERM; 77 U in the skaldic database.

detected any reasonable grounds for dismissing the artefact out of hand (Rau & Nedoma, 2013; Mees, 2023, p.146).[56] If it is a modern fake, the gifted maker was adept in the detailed history of ON phonology and in replicating medieval stone-working techniques. The more cautious scholars are still inclined to suspend judgement on the stone's authenticity pending the results of ongoing research.

THE SUTTON HOO TREASURE

How similar any Anglo-Saxon cult of Woden was to the cult of Odin in Scandinavia is not an easy question to answer, and it is, I would suggest, a question that cannot simply be dismissed in favour of an assumption that Odin's characteristics must also have been Woden's characteristics, and vice versa ...

Shaw, *Pagan Goddesses in the Early Germanic World:*
Eostre, Hreda and the Cult of Matrons

The material found in Mound 1 at Sutton Hoo (Suffolk) is taken here as a starting point for a wider discussion of some archaeological evidence pertaining to the cult of Woden. There are several visual references to a practice called 'eye modification' among the artefacts, as well as design elements which appear to refer to tales of the god recorded in manuscripts from centuries later. In other words, the Sutton Hoo material provides evidence that elements presented in tales known mainly from the writings of Snorri Sturluson in the 13th c. actually appear in the iconography of the 7th c. (Pollington, 2011, p.183; Price & Mortimer, 2014, passim).

---

[56] The spelling **wodinz** thus has to be taken as a nominative singular with syncopation of the stem vowel (Mees, 2023, p.171 note 18) (<*wodinaz*). The two nouns in sequence and both in the nominative are difficult to resolve as parts of a grammatically correct sentence, but the legend may have been intended as a simple declarative.

Fig. 2 The large gold buckle from Sutton Hoo Mound 1 with interlaced serpents, birds and quadrupeds. (Image: Lindsay Kerr)

The importance of Woden in Anglo-Saxon society has often been underestimated, partly because of the supposed lack of any literary evidence connecting early kings to the god and partly due to a perceived lack of archaeological evidence for Woden's worship. The few surviving place-names (e.g., Wednesbury) and the week-day-name 'Wednesday' are often dismissed from consideration without a framework of supporting literary and physical evidence (Stanley, 1964; Rausing, 1995; Shaw, 2002). That said, some recent archaeological discoveries and consequent re-evaluations of familiar material have cast new light on the topic. This is nowhere truer than in respect of the royal regalia recovered from Mound I at Sutton Hoo.

The site (which is still only partially excavated) includes a rather complex combination of burial mounds and satellite graves holding a wide range of interesting treasures. The most famous burial is Mound 1, which contained a 93' long wooden ship with a newly-built chamber amidships packed with wargear and feasting tableware. Mound 2, less well known, originally contained a similar ship and assemblage but was pillaged, probably in the early modern period (Carver, 1992; 2005). A total of fifteen (or possibly more?) other mounds stood on the site, alongside satellite burials and an extensive lower-status inhumation cemetery some distance off (Williamson, 2008).

The Scandinavian connections of the Mound 1 material were noticed immediately, especially in the details of the helmet, shield and cloisonné work for which close parallels were found in the rich Swedish ship-burials of Vendel and Valsgärde, and the huge mounds at Gamla Uppsala (Newton, 1993; Carver, 2017). What this resemblance might be taken to mean has proved contentious: a group of rich Swedes imposing their rule on the population of East Anglia, for example, or a shared 'Wuffing' identity encompassing parts of eastern Britain, Swedish Uppland and elsewhere and expressed in ornament, material culture and burial rites? Carver, the excavator of the site in the late 20th c., has argued for a 'complex and poetic web of aspiration, allusion, emulation and competition between the Scandinavian petty kingdoms and their English cousins' (cited in Price & Mortimer, 2014, p.2).

The Mound 1 assemblage is conventionally dated to circa 625 AD. This date refers to the (probable) year of the death of the East Anglian king, Rædwald, who is considered to be the most likely occupant of the ship-burial. Aside from the lack of direct evidence for the true identity of the buried king, the question remains open as to whether the assemblage was really ever the property of one man or even one family (it may have been collected for the purpose of the funeral), and how long it had been in circulation prior to its eventual inclusion in the burial. There is no compelling reason to accept the 625 AD dating for Mound 1 – but neither is there any evidence that it is radically inaccurate. The only closely datable items in the assemblage are the Byzantine dish, issued under the authority of Emperor Anastasius, and the coins. The dish must have been made during the reign of that emperor; he died in 518 AD, so that provides a neat start-date: the burial must have taken place when the dish already existed. The coins are less helpful since they do not bear dates, regnal years or even the names of issuing rulers, but numismatists have determined that they are of specific Merovingian types and probably belong to a period before circa 640 AD (this end-date is challenged periodically in the light of new numismatic interpretations, but it is generally considered reliable). An early 7th c. date of deposition is thus uncontroversial.

Several elements of the regalia from Mound 1 include visual references to stories about Woden which can be inferred from the later Norse material relating to Óðinn. These include the helmet, the purse, the stone and the shield.

HELMET

The helmet is made of iron and covered with plates of tinned bronze which provided a glittery silvery surface (Bruce-Mitford, 1978, p. 138-225; Mortimer, 2011, pp.23-8; Marzinzik, 2014). It was excavated in many hundreds of fragments of varying sizes, and there is no reason to believe that all the elements of the helmet survived in the soil in a state which would allow them to be recovered, or even identified. The present reconstruction is better than a mere 'best guess' but still lacks many details which, if present, might affect our understanding of its construction and decoration.[57]

It might have been made decades before the date of the ship-burial, as it had already seen service and had been repaired when it was buried (Bruce-Mitford, 1978). In the current reconstruction of the multitude of fragments, it is formed from five principal elements: the bowl, the mask, the two cheek-protectors and the neck-guard. The crown of the helmet is surmounted by a bronze D-section tube with inlaid silver wire, and gilt bronze bird-head terminals; this may be the element called in Old English the *walu* which elsewhere means a 'ridge' or 'crest'.

The bronze plates covering the helmet's surface had been stamped with repoussé interlace designs and figural scenes (Schjødt, 2020b, pp.1136-7). The face-mask (OE *grima*) is decorated with an ambiguous set of elements - human facial features which form the

---

[57] P. Mortimer, pers. comm. There are, for example, several blank areas on the reconstructed bowl and neck-guard due to lack of evidence for their decoration. See Mortimer, 2011, fig.H44 p.62-63 for detailed overview.

body and outstretched wings of a bird of prey. The eyebrows/wings terminate in boar-head finials and there is a line of inset cloisonné garnets beneath each brow. In common with the 4000+ other garnets in the Sutton Hoo assemblage (and high-status garnet jewellery generally in England, Merovingian Francia and Scandinavia), these were each set into a purpose-made cell with a small, stamped gold-foil reflective panel behind to give lustre to the stone (Arrhenius, 1985). There is however one exception to this rule: the 23 garnets of the (proper) right eyebrow are backed with such foils while the 25 of the left one do not have this feature (Bruce-Mitford, 1978, p. 169).[58] The decision not to include foils above one eye apparently was important to the designer of the piece, who also applied it to the cabochon garnet eye of the bird-head terminal sitting between the eyebrows (Bruce-Mitford, 1978, p.160). Clearly there was something different about the wearer's left eye which required commemoration in the design of the helmet while it served as the king's headgear. This modified eye is one of many such references to the story of the god's loss (or rather, surrendering) of an eye to Mímir.

The varied treatment of the eyebrows – which on this helmet must stand for the eyes of the wearer – indicates that the designer and/or maker of the piece wished to emphasise the fact that the eyes were different in some important way.[59] The same technique was used by the Swedish craftsman who made the shield found in grave 12 at Vendel (Sweden) dating to around 600 AD, where the animal-head terminal on the shield's grip has a cross-hatched foil behind the left eye but none on the right (Price & Mortimer, 2014, p.523). The dancing warriors of the Sutton Hoo plates were identified by Herbert Maryon as a close stylistic parallel to the (then unpublished)

---

[58] Marzinzik (2014) ascribed this to a repair, but close examination has revealed that the superficial similarity of the eyebrows disguises detailed differences in manufacture.

[59] Price & Mortimer (2014) note that the difference may not have been obvious in an outdoor setting but would more probably have been noticeable within a fire-lit hall.

images on the helmet from grave 7 excavated in 1933 (Lanz, 2021, p.12).

Such an interpretation of the 'modified eye' motif has been challenged: most recently by Matthias Friedrich (2023) who largely rejects the notion that archaeological discoveries can throw light on information gleaned from literary and other sources. He argues (p.17) that

> 'there can be no 'purely archaeological' perspective on sacral kingship – the concept itself stems from sundry historical and literary evidence in nexus with a focus on the "Germanic". It is not viable to substantiate kingship 'merely' from an archaeological point of view, let alone a sacral one. Accordingly, the reasoning presented by Price and Mortimer [2014] is highly permeated by notions of the "Germanic", limiting their study on 'the wider Germanic world', the "Germanic North", or the "Germanic culture area".'

While the notion of sacral kingship has not gone unchallenged, the broader point – that certain elements in the archaeological record can support details in the literary record – seems to have been discarded here. The differences in the treatment of the eyebrows are dismissed as 'speculation based on slender evidence' (p.19), alongside the other Swedish helmets and the Hellvi cavalryman's mask. The relationship of Woden to Óðinn is also rejected as a 'tenuous house of cards' (p.23) because the notion of a "Germanic' culture area' is questionable, in Friedrich's estimation. While the terminology may need refining (in which senses can Scandinavia be considered 'Germanic'? but, if not 'Germanic', what else may it be?) the essential similarity of artistic design in the 6th - 7th c. across a swathe of territory from the Baltic to Britain and southern Germany and southwards beyond the Alps is surely a fact capable of empirical verification. Friedrich's own personal unease with the notions of 'Germanic' culture and 'Germanic' peoples seems to be at the heart of the issue: 'I will firmly argue the need to disestablish the use of 'Germanic' when exploring and investigating the early Middle Ages and its visual culture in the future' (p.8).

The wider context of the helmet must be explored. The iconography of the *Pressbleche* elsewhere on the helmet's surface may be relevant, given that the dancers and their horned headgear have echoes elsewhere in contemporary culture. Likewise, the horseman figure from the Sutton Hoo helmet appears elsewhere (Vendel, Valsgårde, Pliezhausen, etc.) (Mortimer, 2010; Schjødt, 2020b, p.1136).

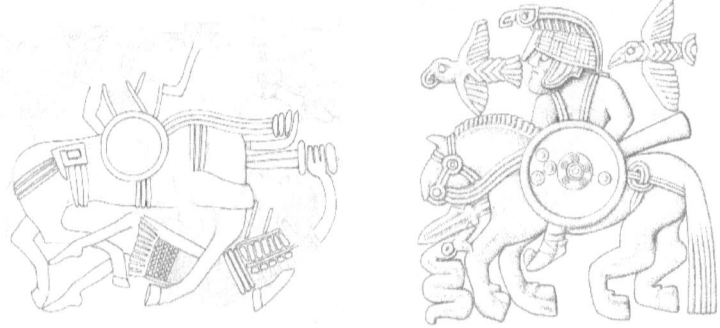

Fig. 3 Rider figures on pressblech plates. Left: Pliezhause (Germany), Right: Vendel, Grave 1. (Images: Lindsay Kerr)

Fig. 4 Rider figure from Sutton Hoo Mound 1. (Image: Lindsay Kerr)

Fig. 5 Hornhausen stone with rider figure above a lattice of fabulous beasts (Image: Lindsay Kerr)

Shepherd noted that early Scandinavian metalwork routinely depicts 'dancing' figures, in a vigorous pose with one foot placed at an acute angle as if walking or hopping (Shepherd, 1998, pp.64-7, citing work by Holmqvist). These images appear on items bearing Style I decoration, and are carried through into the Style II phase (e.g., the Sutton Hoo helmet plates) (Bruce-Mitford, 1978, pp.186-9; Pollington, Kerr & Hammond, 2010, fig. 13.49). (The 'hopping man' motif was seemingly abandoned with the adoption of Christianity as no examples later than the mid-7th c. are known.)

This horned dancer figure often accompanies the beast-man (wolf-warrior, bear-warrior) motif, and it is possible that the two concepts are linked in some way, e.g., the die from Torslunda, Öland, referenced as 'D' (Pollington, Kerr & Hammond, 2010, fig.6.05). Perhaps the dancer is the same person who then appears transformed into the man-beast – a spirit-healer whose journeys to other worlds are undertaken within the form of an animal. Gunnell rather saw the dancing figures – man and beast – as examples of cult rituals and processions which were of great symbolic importance in the life of the warrior, and which were commemorated on his wargear (Gunnell, 1995, p.70). The man-between-beasts and wolf-warrior figures he would regard as examples of such processions.

Furthermore, the dancer in his animal guise (as on Torslunda D and the Fen Drayton die [Pollington, Kerr & Hammond, 2010, fig.8.56]) may be the psychopomp, the figure who leads the soul of the dead person off to the Otherworld (Paulsen, 1967). The paired dancing warriors on the Sutton Hoo helmet have drawn swords in their inner hands, and two downward-pointing spears in their outer hands, with a further spear or stake behind them (Bruce-Mitford, 1978, pp.186-9). These additional spears are set up at an angle as if they should form part of a barrier or backdrop display. The fact that they cross at waist-height may indicate that they form part of a frame, either for dancing around, for leaping over or perhaps for supporting some cult objects.[60] The youths wear a form of headgear with curved panels or horns extending from the cheeks and a pair of crescent horns above terminating in birds' heads. Figures with similar headgear feature on several medallions from Anglo-Saxon England and elsewhere (Helmbrecht, 2008; Lanz, 2021).

Fig. 6 Dancing warriors with horned headgear, wielding swords and spears. (Image: Lindsay Kerr)

---

[60] Bruce-Mitford (1978, p.188) notes that the crossed spears do not occur on the parallel scene from the Valsgärde 7 helmet, and he interprets them as lying on the ground between the dancers, perhaps like the crossed claymores of a Scottish sword-dance.

A link might be proposed between the 'dancing man' on the helmet and what we know of Germanic military customs. One 6th c. king, Totila of the Ostrogoths, is said to have worn a splendid set of purple and gold armour while processing onto the battlefield in order to impress his foes, and then changed into more practical war-gear for the fighting (Halsall, 2003, p.175). Whilst arrayed in all his finery, he performed a number of intimidating acrobatic riding feats in full sight of his enemies before the battle of Busta Gallorum in 552 AD. In the light of this display of riding prowess and weapon-skill, the helmet figures in their raven-headed helmets brandishing spears and swords may have been intended to invoke the patronage of the war-god.

As noted above, the helmet features a man's face which is also the image of a bird, formed from the facial elements of the moustache (tail), nose (body), eyebrows (outstretched wings) and a bird's head between the eyebrows extending upwards across the forehead. This bird is placed in opposition to a serpent forming the helmet's *walu* crest which runs from brow to brim across the apex of the bowl. The helmet thus features a design in which a bird and a serpent figure prominently – a visual reference to the tale of the winning of the mead of inspiration. The helmet also features *pressblech* panels with a range of dense interlaced (Style II) designs which probably represent serpents.

A second type of figural panel appears at the sides of the helmet and features a horse-riding scene with a mounted warrior brandishing a spear and attacking a fallen foe, with a smaller figure grasping the rear end of his spear; this is also found on a similar helmet from Sweden on the Valsgärde graves 7 and 8 helmet plates, and repeated on a disc brooch from Pliezhausen (Germany) (Kühn, 1956, p.15; Bruce-Mitford, 1974, pp.38-9; 1978, ch.III; Holmqvist, 1977; Ament, 1980, p.57; Speidel, 2004, fig.17.5; Lanz, 2021, p.15).[61] Only

---

[61] The Pliezhausen warrior is in the same general stance as the Sutton Hoo rider figure, but the iconography differs in some important respects. The Pliezhausen rider's spear ends not in a spear-tip but in an eagle's head, which may signify

at Valsgärde is the figure behind the rider shown as a 'Dancing Warrior' with helmet and belt. One pragmatic interpretation of the scene
is that the smaller figure is a *cniht*, a youth who assists and supports
the rider, and that the figure gripping the Swedish rider's spear is
actually passing a replacement weapon to the warrior (Hawkes,
1965). Alternatively, he may be a supernatural helper guiding the
spear to its mark or, as Hauck believed, a character in a snake-helmet
who assisted the rider by casting a *Sieg- und Fluchspeer* 'spear of victory and cursing' referred to in the story of the war in heaven in
which Óðinn threw his spear over the enemy army (Lanz, 2021,
p.17).[62]

The rider is not necessarily triumphant in these scenes. Ellis Davidson suggested that the presence of the supernatural figure in the
horned helmet indicates that the warrior is a follower of Woden and
that he is thus doomed to die in battle (Ellis Davidson, 1965; Speidel,
2004, fig.11.5). A similar relationship is implied for the hunter on
the Vindelev bracteate, denominated as 'Woden's man'. This would
put the helmeted figure in the position occupied in later Norse literature by the *valkyrjur* (valkyries) who select the bravest and noblest
men for death in battle and then take them to Óðinn. Often in these
helmet-plate scenes, the rider's horse is being stabbed by a prostrate
figure – signalling disaster for the horseman. The fickle nature of the
battle-god is a main feature of the literary evidence regarding his
followers.

---

that the horseman is Woden, or a human invested with Woden's power. Above
the spear, a pair of quadrupeds is shown confronted, their open jaws forming a
lozenge. This may be nothing more than a motif from Roman funerary art
adopted into the Germanic iconographic tradition, but not without some new
symbolic content.

[62] This was in 1954; Hauck later changed his mind about the nature of the
helmets and the weapon-dancer figure.

PURSE

The purse or sporran from Mound 1 held a collection of Merovingian gold coins and small ingots, which has been interpreted in various ways (the king as guardian of the tribe's gold and wealth? the king as taker of tribute in victory? the king as dispenser of rewards for loyal service?). The decoration of the rigid lid (which was absent, so likely made from an organic substance) includes several gold panels with inlaid garnet and millefiori detailing, of which two are in the form of a facing humanoid figure with his arms raised and flanked on each side by an animal (horse? wolf?) with its muzzle placed against the sides of his head. These faces or masks have inset garnet eyes, of which one has been removed with sufficient force to leave a mark in the gold surface (Price & Mortimer, 2014, p.528ff). It is thus possible that the figure has had one of its eyes ritually altered – as if there were religious reasons for performing a ceremony involving the modification of one eye.

A similar motif (one-eyed man between beasts) is found on the textiles in the Högom grave (Sweden) dating to around 500 AD (Ramqvist, 1988; 1991).

STONE

The large carved stone object (sometimes called a 'whetstone', although it is ill-suited to this purpose) bears eight imposing masks carved in high relief (Mortimer & Pollington, 2013, passim.). One of these masks (numbered B1 in Bruce-Mitford's report) was modified by having the left eye struck out (Mortimer & Pollington, 2013; Price & Mortimer, 2014). The hardness of the stone (greywacke) makes accidental damage highly unlikely, as does the situation of the eye sheltered by the overhanging brow and the nose. Deliberate modification of the eye seems the only plausible answer to the question of how it was achieved; as to why, this is simply another example of eye-modification in the Sutton Hoo material.

The purpose of the stone has been much discussed, but it seems very probable that it represents a symbol of authority and is an object of veneration – probably an 'idol' in some sense, although it serves as a means of permanently encoding information as well (Pollington, Kerr & Hammond, 2010, p.319). The modified eye would only have been visible to an observer at very close quarters – and, like the Torslunda die, the alteration would probably only have been meaningful to someone with detailed knowledge of the god's myths and forms of worship.

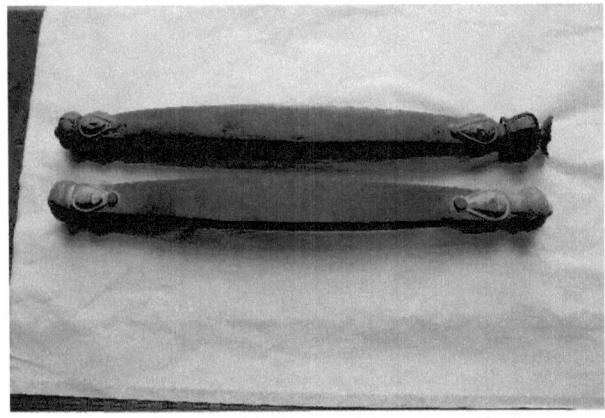

Fig. 7 The original stone from Sutton Hoo Mound 1 (above) with Brian Ansell's copy being checked for accuracy before final finishing. (Image: Paul Mortimer)

Fig. 8 Schematic of the stone with ring and stag fittings. (Image: Lindsay Kerr)

Woden was the principal god of the Anglian élite up to and even beyond conversion to Christianity – he stands at the head of all but one kinglist as the divine ancestor. It is of course highly probable that there were other gods whose standing was as important – Ingwe, for example (North, 1997).[63] It is therefore not possible to say with certainty whether the eight faces on the stone (one of which we can reasonably identify as Woden) represent eight deities of the Anglian pantheon, or else Woden and seven other ancestors of the royal kindred. It is equally possible that there was no contemporary distinction, and that the names below Woden in the kinglists were regarded as both legendary and divine. This semi-divine quality of charismatic leaders has been noted in regard to the Goths whose traditions may have influenced those of the East Angles (Woolf, 2017).

Fig. 9 Face from the lower end of the stone showing modified eye. (Image: Hannah Symons)

SHIELD

The shield features two gilt-bronze plaques, one depicting a bird of prey with curled talons, and the other a curious serpentine beast or 'dragon' with folded 'wings' or legs along the sides of the body (Pollington, Kerr & Hammond, 2010, pl.39, 40). The meaning of

---

[63] This god is named in the *OERP* and must have retained a central importance in folk tradition for some generations beyond the conversion to Christianity.

these creatures has been puzzled over since their discovery in 1939. It is certainly possible to read in them an artistic expression of a symbolic opposition: the dragon or serpent is a being of the earth and the bird is a being of the sky. Thus we may see here the opposition of the two notions of the Otherworld and the afterlife: the principal means of disposing of the dead by burial in the earth (Underworld, serpent) and by burning and converting the body to a column of smoke (Overworld, bird).

But the symbolism with echoes of tales recorded of Óðinn is not confined to this opposition. In one of the tales concerning how Óðinn gained wisdom, the god has to steal the mead of inspiration from Suttungr who has locked it in a cave beneath a mountain. He undertakes this task by means of three physical transformations: (a) changing from human form into a snake in order to crawl down a narrow bored hole to reach the chamber where the mead is stored; (b) changing from a snake to a handsome young man in order to trick the watchful maiden, Gunnlǫð, into surrendering herself and the precious drink which she is supposed to guard; then, (c) having drunk the liquid in three draughts, changing into a powerful bird in order to escape (cf. Kvilhaug, 2004, p.25 for god-animal transformation in Norse sources). The helmet combines the three transformations of bird (mask), serpent (crest) and human male (mask) in one object just as the god embodied them. Likewise on the shield we have the opposition of bird and snake drawn from the mead-stealing episode. The bird appliqué has an unusual feature on its hip – a facing male mask, the very same face as appears elsewhere on the material from this tomb, indicating that the 'bird' is to be recognised as a shapeshifted male god.

Fig. 10 The gold-plated bird figure from the Sutton Hoo Mound 1 shield (replica). (Image: Damir Radic)

THE HELLVI HELMET

The Baltic island of Gotland occupies a crucial position as a crossroads for traffic in that area, with its port of Visby recognised as a marketplace and supply-base for maritime travellers. The island has many unique features in its material culture in the early medieval period, such as specific types of brooch and bracteate which are seldom found elsewhere (MacGregor, 1997, p.22, 28, 35 etc.; Gaimster, 1992).

In 2011 the bronze face-plate of a Roman cavalry helmet was reported, having been discovered and dug up some time before by a metal-detectorist who had kept the find a secret (Price & Mortimer, 2014, p.525ff). This only came to light on his death, when his family had to dispose of his property. It is understood that the helmet had been recovered from the site of an Iron Age longhouse at a site called Hellvi. The object-type is well evidenced from antiquity: a form of Roman lightweight bronze helmet used in equestrian sports by members of the officer class (Travis & Travis, 2016). Some of these appear to have been manufactured as a portrait of the owner, while others represent a stylised face of Alexander the Great. The Hellvi helmet is of this type, and dates to the later 2nd c. It is possibly connected to the popularity of the legends of Hercules in Roman élite circles during the reign of Commodus (176-192 AD). The Hellvi helmet is the second find of this kind of helmet from Scandinavia – the other was recovered from the bog-deposit at Thorsberg (Denmark) (Matešić, 2015, p.196ff). A quantity of helmet-parts and other items have been recovered from the area of this site over a period of many decades: an 'eyebrow' was donated to the museum as far back as 1880 (Nerman, 1969).

An interesting feature of the helmet is the treatment of the eyes. Roman helmets of this type have voids or openings corresponding to where the wearer's eyes are placed; some have the additional protective feature of a cast ring for the 'iris'. It is this form of eye-hole that was used on the Hellvi mask, but at some date after its manufacture a separate panel representing the left eye was made and attached with brass rivets into the empty socket. The new 'eye' was fabricated with a bronze baseplate for the 'white' and an iris of silvered bronze bearing a central oxidised silver pin forming a darker pupil.

The modifications to the helmet took place at some time between its original manufacture (late 2nd c.) and the date of its deposition around 550 AD. Thus modified, the helmet could no longer function as a practical piece of wargear, confirmed by a series of nails placed pointing inwards around the neck: the helmet appeared to have been attached to a supporting post by these. Investigation of the findspot revealed a large building of three aisles with wooden roof supports, of a type known throughout the Baltic and believed to be a hall-dwelling. The exact spot where the helmet had been found was the site of some more remarkable finds including four Roman drinking horns (dismantled), a dress pin, a neck ring (broken), some buckles and several mounts alongside a silver bracteate. The collection appears to have been mounted and displayed on the stone wall of the building, and to have been dispersed when the wall collapsed. At the base of a roofpost about 2m from where the helmet fell was found the helmet's other eye-insert. It is likely that this 'eye' was deliberately detached from the mask at some point – that the eyeless Roman helmet had been altered to include new shiny 'eyes', and that one of these had later been removed to make the mask one-eyed; the extracted eye had been buried in the floor close to the niche where the ritual mask was displayed.

UPPLAND HELMETS

The region known as Uppland, Sweden, in which Stockholm is situated, was a very wealthy and productive area from the 6th c. onwards. The material culture of the region bears striking similarities to that of East Anglia at the same time, which led to the notion that the Sutton Hoo treasures might have been made in Uppland and brought in with an élite take-over in the early 7th c. This is no longer considered plausible, since there are far greater quantities of such items known from England than from Scandinavia, especially since the discovery of the Staffordshire Hoard (Fern et al., 2019). But the fact remains that a closely similar iconography was in use in both societies contemporaneously and this cannot be a mere accident (see Shippey, 2022, pp.116-7).

The principal sites are Vendel (near Uppsala) and Valsgärde in the same area (Mortimer, 2011, pp.23-38). The iconographic helmets bear panels of *pressblech* decoration while others feature openwork sections, presumably revealing a brightly-coloured leather cap worn beneath. The greater part of the repoussé ornament comprises knotwork and highly stylised animals similar to the panels on the Sutton Hoo helmet – and, again, like Sutton Hoo, there are figural panels displayed prominently. These mostly show martial scenes – warriors and horsemen – which are drawn from the military culture of the age, inspired by the gods of warfare.

VALSGÄRDE MOUND 7

This shows a procession of warriors on foot each with a prominent boar-crest on his helmet and his spear held before him (Mortimer, 2011, p.53a–e, 75). Above this band is another with panels showing a horseman in profile brandishing a spear with a fallen warrior beneath his horse's hooves and a smaller figure on the animal's rump. A scene with a man between beasts appears at the top beside the crest. Flanking the crest is a design of two dancing warriors brandishing spears and swords, wearing horned helmets. Its crest terminates in a beast-head with the 'beak' extending between the eyebrows.

VALSGÄRDE MOUND 8

The helmet has a band of panels running around the crown, each a horseman in profile brandishing a spear with a fallen warrior beneath his horse's hooves and a smaller figure on the animal's rump (Mortimer, 2011, p.53h, I, 78-80). The helmet's crest terminates in beast-heads.

VENDEL MOUND 1

A cap with provision for a mail aventail, it features another horseman scene, this time advancing and flanked by two birds in flight (Mortimer, 2011, p.30, 54). A warrior standing beside a chained beast is also present – perhaps a reference to Týr and Fenrir? Its crest ends in beast-heads and below, situated between the wearer's own eyes, is a small male mask with pointed features.

VENDEL MOUND 12

This helmet was recovered in very poor condition and the details of its construction and decoration are largely lost. It appears to have been similar in most details to the helmet from Vendel Mound 1, but was rather small and perhaps made for a youngster, although the damage and degradation it has suffered may have affected its shape (Mortimer, 2011, p.30, 70-1). The 'duellists' scene on the helmet from Vendel Mound 14 is included above the left eye – perhaps a replacement due to battle-damage.

VENDEL MOUND 14

This is an unusual helmet in many ways with few comparable pieces known (an example from Broa, Gotland being the closest). The skull of the helmet does not have a raised crest, but an applied fillet fulfils the function of separating the panels of the two halves and providing the opportunity to include a beast-head finial. It also has a prominent hinged face-guard and five iron strips hinged on the lower rim (Mortimer, 2011, p.28). The iconography of the *pressblech* plates includes two panels above the eyebrows each featuring two 'duellists' – warriors facing each other armed with a spear and shield in one hand and a drawn sword in the other (Mortimer, 2011, p.55) and a procession of armed warriors around the brow (Mortimer, 2011, pp.66-7).

THE ÅKER BUCKLE

This enigmatic item was removed from a rich burial mound at Åker, Norway and passed to the national collection in the late 19th c. The buckle, like the rest of the grave's contents, dates to the later 6th c. AD, although the settlement probably began in the 3rd c. and is located at a crossroads on the old north-south and east-west highways (Martens, 2013, p.329). The name Åker is considered likely to indicate a pre-Christian religious site in a landscape with many such names: *Vang* 'assembly field', *Vidarshov* 'temple of Viðar', *Torshov* 'temple of Þórr', *Disen* 'place of the Dísir'. The farm belonged to the royal family in the 9th c. and was the probable location for the regional assembly (*Eidsivating*) where King Magnus and Háraldr Harðráða were reconciled in 1046 AD (Martens, 2013, p.330).

The grave's contents were dug up piecemeal by local amateurs, and their context is not recorded. It has been suggested that the finds were possibly ritual deposits at the holy site, although the nature of the finds (weapons and strap-fittings) is consistent with the likely contents of a high-status male grave that would be recoverable by an untrained 'explorer' (Martens, 2013, p.330).

The buckle is made of gilt-bronze with silver and niello detailing and inset garnet cabochons. In form it conforms to the type with a triangular plate and three prominent bosses, a scallop-shaped shield at the rear of the tongue and a broad loop (i.e., similar to the finds from Sutton Hoo Mound 1, Prittlewell and many Merovingian finds). The decoration is spectacular and intriguing, but the density of the ornament makes accurate determination of the elements rather difficult. The central item is the facing figure of a male with large eyes in a tongue-shaped face with a broad crescent moustache, close-cropped beard, narrow nose and neat hair parted in the middle of the forehead. His hands are raised to his ears and the sleeves of his tunic are finished with broad cuffs. His lower body develops into two curved legs or 'bows' which extend outwards to become profile boar's heads with fierce tusks. Opposing the boars are two profile eagle-heads whose eyes are surrounded by filigree collars, and above each of these is a curved panel (the shoulder of the buckle) with a stylised beast-head motif. The fan-shaped shield is covered by a geometric design in garnet cloisonné. The loop is divided by the hinged attachment to the plate and by the couch for the tongue, at each side a narrow band with garnet cloisonné decorates the neck which develops to a profile bird-head flanking the couch (Ellis Davidson, 1969, p.47).

Fig. 11 Ornate belt buckle from Åker, Norway. (Image: Lindsay Kerr)

The imagery is highly symbolic, for here we see a male being (a man or a god?) transforming into a beast – the boars' heads at his lower body are surely indicative of such a transmutation. Such tales are widespread in myth in legend: 'in some ancient traditions, the creation of half-human, half-animal beings served to explore and acknowledge the paradox of similarity and difference between humankind and the world of beasts: animals are 'other' but, at the same time, they share a great deal in common with people' (Aldhouse Green, 2001, pp.204-26). In fact, the result of such a transformation is displayed on the shield from Sutton Hoo Mound 1 – the appliqué eagle motif has a small piriform plaque on its hip with a facing mask picked out in garnet cloisonné.

Is this being in the process of shape-shifting to be identified with Woden/Óðinn? That is one possibility, although the god does not transform into a boar in any of the stories recorded by Saxo or Snorri. In Norse tradition, some people were credited with being able to change their shape or appearance through manipulation of their *hamingja*, their 'changed outward form' but which may derive from *ham-gengja* 'shape-walker', i.e., someone whose soul can enter a different body (Orton, 2005).

The buckle's iconography is almost unique but clearly embedded in a tradition of human: animal transformation, such as was undertaken by many of the Æsir and Vanir gods in the later literature.

THE TORSLUNDA DIES

Four metal dies were found in 1870[64] at Torslunda (i.e., Thor's woodland)[65] on the Baltic island of Öland, dating from the 5th - 6th c. (Ellis Davidson, 1969, p.37, 91).They were used in the production of metal foils with symbolic or mythical designs: (A) a man between bears(?); (B) a man with an axe holding a rope attached to an animal (bear?); (C) two warriors with spears in procession; (D) a horned, dancing warrior leading a warrior in a wolfskin with a spear (Bruce-Mitford, 1974, p.215; Gunnell, 1995, pp.66-76; Kershaw, 2000, p.7; Ustinova, 2002, p.114). Die (B) was in a fresh condition on excavation, while (D) was heavily worn, and had not even been finished to a high standard originally. The site from which the dies were recovered had once held a structure, possibly a workshop. Two of the four dies were considered by Axboe to be secondary casts from previous *Pressbleche* (Alkemade, 1991, pp.291-2); in other words, the primary dies had been broken or abraded beyond repair and had to be re-fashioned by casting from a mould taken from an impression. This suggests that they had seen heavy service.

The dies were used in the production of low-relief foil panels (*Pressbleche*) displaying narrative scenes, mostly apparently relating to the ceremonies and mythic events; they were rectangular in form, intended to be applied to helmets (Pollington, Kerr & Hammond, 2011, p.146). The interpretation of such figural scenes has led to some useful insights into the world of both northern mythology and warrior rituals (Arent, 1969; Gaimster, 1998, p.13ff; Ustinova, 2002, provides Sarmatian and Iranian parallels). The corpus of *pressblech* plates and

---

[64] Oscar Montelius was the first to publish the dies in 1872, which he declared had been found some two years before in a cairn near Björnhovda (Lanz, 2021, p.7). Association of the bearskin-clad warrior on (D) with the figure on the Gutenstein scabbard mount was immediately seized upon for the light it was hoped it might shed on the *berserkir* and their cult.

[65] Lanz (2021, p.31) notes that other than the name *Torslunda* (Thor's woodland) there is nothing in the records to associate the site with Þórr or any other deity. The local archaeology does not offer any assistance in that regard.

dies includes finds from Vendel, Valsgärde and Torslunda in Sweden, Pliezhausen, Gutenstein (Banghard & Stauch, 2021, p.243; Lanz, 2021, p.15) and Obrigheim (Banghard & Stauch, 2021, passim; Lanz, 2021, p.15) in Germany; Sutton Hoo, Asthall, Fen Drayton and Caenby in England (Smith, 1923, pp.86-7; Kühn, 1956, pl.15; Bruce-Mitford, 1974, pp.38-9; Ament, 1980, p.57, 67; Haseloff, 1986; Gunnell, 1995, pp.66-76; Menghin, 1995, p.10, fig.6; Bertram, 2007). A Lombard plate from Cividale (Italy) bears a simplified design of a spear-wielding horseman (Smith, 1923, pp.86-7; Kühn, 1956, pl.15; Bruce-Mitford, 1974, pp.38-9; Ament, 1980, p.57, 67; Haseloff, 1986; Gunnell, 1995, pp.66-76; Menghin, 1995, p.10, fig.6).

The figures appearing in these scenes are usually interpreted as gods or heroes from the early legends. An origin in ritual, of which the Germanic sword-dance performed by young men was an important part, seems plausible for some of the imagery such as the dancing warriors (on C and D) and the wolf-warriors (on D).[66]

Of particular relevance here is the treatment of die D, the 'helmeted' dancer followed by the wolf-coated warrior, armed with two spears and a sword in its scabbard slung from a baldric over his right shoulder (Bruce-Mitford, 1974, ch.10; Gunnell, 1995, pp.66-76). Crucially, one of the figure's eyes, which were perfectly cast, has been modified by removing it – a clear indication that the helmeted figure is to be identified with the one-eyed god (Price, 2003, p.372; 2007; Price & Mortimer, 2014, p.524).[67] The figure was originally made with two eyes, and at some point one of these was removed – a process with implications for the purpose and significance of the piece. Yet the tiny scale of the modification could never have been evident when the helmet was in use: it formed part of a body of

---

[66] Arent, 1969, p.133. The comparable examples are drawn from the works of Ammianus Marcelinus, Procopius and Tacitus.

[67] Since die D was one of those which had been re-cast from an impression, it is uncertain whether the modification to the eye was actually present on the original or only on the copy.

'secret lore' which could only have been known to a handful or observers – presumably those who were also initiates into the mysteries of the cult of Woden.

The 'helmeted' figure is followed by a human warrior shown in the act of drawing a sword; he wears a wolf's pelt of which the head-section forms a mask while the body and tail hang down behind him. He is armed with a large spear held point-down and with the shaft resting on his shoulder, as well as a sword suspended high under the left arm. These elements mark him out as a leader or professional/dedicated fighter. The wolfskin mantle characterises the *ulfheðnar* (wolf-capes), a body of warrior-initiates to be discussed below. A connection with the mythic career of the thrice-blessed and thrice-cursed warrior-hero, Starkaðr, has also been proposed for this image (Dumézil, 1983, p.43). Hauck, following Oxenstierna, interpreted the scene as a ritual enactment of Óðinn's fight with the wolf Fenrir during the climactic battle of Ragnarǫk, (Hauck, 1954, cited in Lanz, 2021, p.13) which he believed was also present in the iconography of the *pressblech* from Obrigheim (Germany) showing a wolf-coated warrior grasping a vertical, scabbarded sword while a horned figure stands behind it (Banghard & Stauch, 2021). Hauck's interpretation later switched to a 'combat initiation ritual' with the horned figure representing Hagen/Högni versus the wolfskin-wearing opponent as Hetel/Heðinn (Lanz, 2021, pp.14-5).

Bronze die from Torslunda, Sweden, showing a dancing man and wolf warrior. 6th-7th c.

Bronze die from Torslunda, Sweden, showing two boar-crested warriors. 6th-7th c.

Bronze die showing a 'beast tamer'. From
Björnhofda (Parish of Torslunda), Öland,
Sweden. 6th-7th c.

Fig. 12 Pressblech dies from Torslunda, Sweden. (Image: Lindsay Kerr)

*Fig. 13 Warrior and monstrous assailant on the helmet plate from Vendel
Mound 1. (Image: Lindsay Kerr)*

*Fig. 14 Die from Gutenstein, Germany, showing a wolf-coated warrior
with spear and sheathed sword. (Image: Lindsay Kerr)*

THE FINGLESHAM BUCKLE

The Finglesham buckle came to light in the 1965 excavations at the Anglo-Saxon cemetery at Finglesham (Kent)(Hawkes, 1965; Ellis Davidson, 1965; Webster & Backhouse, 1991, fig.2; Price, 2003, p.386; Hinton, 2005, p.66; Hawkes & Grainger, 2006, pp.78-81, 264; Welch, 2007, p.192; Lanz, 2021, p.182), at the waist of a male skeleton in a grave (no.95) containing shoe buckles, lace-tags, a spearhead, a knife, a bronze-mounted wooden container, a bucket and a red ceramic bottle. It is 8cm long and made of heavily gilded bronze which accounts for its good state of preservation. It is of the standard three-bossed triangular design with a shield-shaped extension to the hinged tongue and loop.

Fig. 15 Gilt-bronze buckle from Finglesham, Kent, with dancing warrior. (Image: Lindsay Kerr)

The buckle-plate features figural ornament cast in low relief: a naked male, his legs slightly flexed, gripping a spear in each hand. His facing head is capped by a domed headdress from the sides of which spring two 'horns' terminating in opposed birds' heads meeting above the centre (Ellis Davidson, 1969, p.39). His only other attribute is a belt round his waist fastened with a kidney-shaped buckle. The proportions of the figure are slightly distorted to fit the field, with an over-large head and small shins and feet, and without forearms. The Finglesham figure is vigorous in attitude and naturalistic in design, with antecedents in Scandinavia and elsewhere;[68] contemporary and later Frankish anthropomorphs, deriving their designs from Late Roman and Christian iconography, are generally stylised and stiff, lacking the free expression of the Kentish artist.

The buckle is unique in Anglo-Saxon England in a number of ways: for example, the 'dancing man with horned helmet' motif and the moulded relief technique have no close parallels among Anglo-Saxon buckles (Marzinzik, 2003, p.52, 62, 86).[69] The overall design is fairly typical of Kentish types from the 7th c., which more usually feature Style II zoomorphs in moulded bands and gold filigree (e.g., the great buckle from Sutton Hoo Mound 1). A less exuberant style appears later in the 7th c. in which smooth, shiny surfaces are preferred to glittery ones. The Finglesham grave-goods suggest a mid-7th c. date for the burial, at the end of the period when accompanied inhumation was still fashionable.

Interestingly, in the same cemetery a female grave contained a small copper alloy pendant in the form of a human head wearing a helmet with conjoined horns, similar to the face shown on the buckle (Price & Mortimer, 2014, p.524).[70] The mount was worn in a small leather bag at the throat, and the wearer also had a rather magnificent necklace which included glass beads, silver rings, two scutiform pendants and a millefiori glass pendant in a bronze mount. The horned-head pendant had two rivets and traces of tooled leather

---

[68] S.C. Hawkes (1965, p.20) notes '… the art of the Uppland helmet-makers was the culmination of a long native tradition of pictorial ornament of a heathen religious character.'

[69] There are few Anglo-Saxon representations of the whole human form from this period.

[70] Horned masks of similar type are now a recognised motif in the archaeology of the early Anglo-Saxon period with many examples recovered by metal-detectorists and as casual finds.

on the reverse, as if it had originally been mounted on a strap (or perhaps a shield?) (Hawkes & Grainger, 2006, pp.98-100, 279).

What lies behind the iconography of the dancing spearman? The horned headgear with its opposed bird-heads surely points towards some cult figure – either a deity or a worshipper. It is likely enough (though beyond proof) that Woden was the leader of the weapon-dance, inasmuch as a figure with special headgear was the cult leader and sword-dances of various kinds persisted in folklore down to modern times, although the swords are sometimes replaced by staves or rods. One of the bronze dies from Torslunda (D, p.115) shows the helmeted dancing figure armed with two spears and a sword in its scabbard slung from a baldric over his right shoulder (Bruce-Mitford, 1974, ch.10; Gunnell, 1995, pp.66-76). Unlike the Finglesham design, his helmet has cheek-guards and he carries his spears (one long, and a shorter throwing-spear) point-down, details of presentation which may reflect merely the design preferences of the craftsman. The Finglesham dancer has not been subjected to eye-modification, so it seems likely that he is a worshipper rather than a deity.

THE FEN DRAYTON DIE

A die for the manufacture of *pressblech* panels found at Fen Drayton (Cambridgeshire) shows the familiar profile figure of a wolf-headed man with a spear in his right hand and a scabbarded sword in his left (Leahy, 2006).[71] The wolf's head is shown in profile with a large eye and prominent teeth. The lower part of the body is flared and decorated with angled lines, perhaps originally a 'diamond' pattern representing (quilted?) armour. A tail hangs behind the warrior's thin legs. A beaded border is present on the right edge behind the

---

[71] While the clearest English evidence for the 'wolf-warrior and spear-dancer' motif is on the helmet plates from Sutton Hoo, the similar fragment found at Caenby (Lincolnshire) indicates that it was not confined to East Anglia, and the presence of a die implies production of these motifs in England.

figure but does not appear to continue around the periphery, from which it is uncertain whether the design is complete or only partial – the surviving fragment of an originally larger scene.

The best parallel to this is Torslunda die 'D' where a similar figure follows the weapon-dancer, although the Fen Drayton warrior carries his spear with the point raised, which is unusual for such motifs. The sub-triangular shape of the die suggests that it may have been used for the manufacture of vandykes for drinking horns, although this does not preclude its having started out as a larger piece.

Fig. 16 The Fen Drayton die with wolf-warrior. (Image: Lindsay Kerr)

HORNED HELMETS AND DANCING WARRIORS

The motif of a 'dancing man in horned headgear' is known from Swedish and Anglo-Saxon finds with outliers in the Baltic and elsewhere.[72] They form a subset of the group of figures with crescent

---

[72] Lanz (2021) includes a catalogue of the known examples of these figures dating from the Later Iron Age (Scandinavia) or Early Medieval Period (Britain and Western Europe), broadly 400-1050 AD. They often appear in the popular literature with attribution to 'Oden' as in the find from Levide, Gotland, Sweden reported on 2nd June 2014 in *Helagotland.se* as *Sensationellt fynd i Levide* 'A Sensational Find in Levide' describing the item as 'an approximately four centimetre long metal pendant that depicts the god Odin with an arc over his

projections attached to their heads, but the abstract nature of the depictions makes a precise definition impossible (Ellis Davidson, 1969, pp.35-9).

An Anglo-Saxon example such as the Finglesham buckle is not likely to have arrived in Kent on the belt of a Scandinavian visitor or settler, because from typological evidence it was probably made locally (Welch, 2007, p.192).[73] The closest parallels to the Finglesham dancer are figures on the repoussé *pressblech* plates attached to the 'kingly' helmets found at Vendel and Valsgärde, where it is supposed that such figures must represent warlords, mortal heroes or gods, and the leading figure on the Torslunda die which was used to create such plates. The notion of 'dancing' is supported by the twisted attitude of the legs and feet which appear to hover above rather than touch the ground (Kershaw, 2000, pp.84-5).

In a female grave at Birka (Sweden, grave Bj.571) a small amuletic figure of a man in a 'horned helmet' was found, wearing a kaftan or mailcoat and carrying a sheathed sword in his left hand, a spear or staff in his right (Price, 2003, p.385). A similar example from Ekhammar (Sweden, gravefield 4, grave 6) shares the 'horned helm' but wears a belted tunic, carries a sword in his right hand and two spears or staves crossed in his left (Price, 2003, p.386).[74] There are parallels in the designs on the Oseberg tapestries, one of which

---

head … (with) holes on the sides, which suggests that it has been used as a pendant.' The possibility that the piece might be anything other than *Oden* (e.g., a worshipper) is not discussed.

[73] The three-bossed sub-triangular buckle is common in south-east England and rare in Scandinavia at this time. Therefore, there is a paradox: either the buckle is a Scandinavian rarity with common decoration, or it is a common Kentish form with almost-unique decoration. Copying of a religious motif onto a locally-made buckle seems probable. S.C. Hawkes (1965, p.22) suggests that the lord of the buried warrior might have had 'Sutton Hoo–class' wargear from Scandinavia and this was the source of the inspiration for the buckle decoration.

[74] The crossed spears more closely resemble those with the Sutton Hoo Mound 1 helmet's dancing warriors.

has some form of dangling decoration attached to the sleeve of his jacket; further parallels are found in the circumpolar traditions where 'shamans' often have long fringes and other dangling effects on their coats (Gunnell, 1995, pp.60-6).

A small cast bronze finial excavated from grave 161 at Dover Buckland, Kent, is interesting in that it comprises a balustered shaft topped by a head with bearded face and a helmet with tapering neck-guard; fixed to the upper face of the helmet is a large crescent terminating in opposed bird-heads (Evison, 1987). Heads with horned headgear are now a recognised class of metal-detector find — cf. 'Out of the Ordinary Odin', a cosmetic item found in East York-shire (*The Searcher*, April, 2022 p.14) or the horned-helmet mount from the Essex-Suffolk border ('Unearthing Woden', *Treasure Hunting*, November, 2018, p.8).

A religious significance is usually assumed for the scenes on these treasures, which may have functioned as ritual headgear or as 'combat equipment'. Religious iconography can be deeply conservative and this, in conjunction with the manufacturing technique, would tend to replicate and emphasise certain stock characters — prominent among whom is the figure with the 'horned helmet'[75] and two spears (Lanz, 2021, pp.162-4).[76] Lanz has shown that most depictions are 'relatively naturalistic, more abstract mask-like images and

---

[75] The term 'horned' here means 'provided with two tapering curved projections which meet above the centre of the headgear' and forming a tapering loop. The actual nature of the projections does not appear to be actual bovine horns attached to headgear — and the headgear is not always a 'helmet' of any kind. Often the terminals are shaped as avian heads, for example, and the projections are decorated with stripes or other detailing; where the figure is modelled in the half-round, the horns often appear to be flat in section.

[76] The technique here involves creating a master or die onto which thin sheet metal was carefully hammered to mould it to the shape (D. Roper, pers.comm.). This technique would therefore lend itself to producing many plates of the same design. There is evidence for reuse of a single die to make smaller plates showing only part of the design, and of partial repeats of a small design on larger plates. This is evident, for example on the scabbard-plates from the Gutenstein (Germany) sword where the design has clearly been trimmed and

puzzle pictures being almost exclusively restricted to Anglo-Saxon England'.

The horned figure is usually shown facing the viewer. Some examples are shown one-eyed, but it should not be overlooked that the dancer on the Torslunda die was originally cast with two eyes, of which one was subsequently struck out; likewise the mask on face B1 of the stone from Sutton Hoo Mound 1. From this we may infer that a figure originally made with two eyes was at some subsequent point modified by the removal of one of them.

The paired dancers were interpreted by Hauck as *Dioskouroi*, while single instances were assumed to refer to Woden. He states (cited in Lanz, 2021): 'According to the Ölandic mould [i.e., the Torslunda die], even though the piece of evidence only originates in the 6th century, the one-eyed god of war is to be discussed as the archetype of the Germanic *Cornuti* in the Roman army' (Lanz's translation). The *Cornuti* or 'horned ones' were a Gaulish motif taken over into Roman military culture: horned figures are featured among the shield designs of the *Notitia Dignitatum* and elsewhere and have been taken to represent members of a military cult, or as badges of such (Kershaw, 2000, p.85; Seeck, 2019). Tacitus's remarks about the sword-dances performed by Germanic youths (*Germania*, ch.24) have also been adduced in support of this idea (Kershaw, 2000, p.87).

War-dances (vigorous rhythmic body movements) were used alongside fasting to induce ecstasy in early warrior-groups; they feature in Saxo's tale of Uffo and his victory over two Saxons, both as part of the preparations for the fight and as part of the celebrations of the king's victory (Kershaw, 2000, pp.83-5).[77]

---

manipulated to fit a shape and area for which it was not originally intended (Lanz, 2021, pp.13-14).

[77] Saxo's 'Uffo' is none other than the Anglian hero, Offa, who agreed to fight two enemies single-handedly and won a great victory, thereby fixing the boundary between the two tribes. This story is alluded to in *Widsith*, 1.35-44.

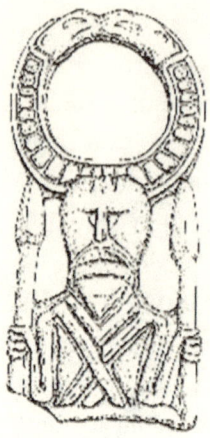

Fig. 17 Gilt-bronze appliqué from Cambridgeshire with horned headgear and two spears. (Image: Lindsay Kerr)

THE EGGJUM STONE

This monument (also called 'the Eggja stone'), found at Sogn, Norway in 1917, is listed as N KJ101 in the *Rundata* catalog and is conventionally dated to the period 650–700 AD on the basis of its runic inscriptions: with over 200 runes carved into its surface, it is the most extensive epigraphic monument of the period. The runes are a mix of Elder Fuþark (Phase I) forms and some more recent Phase II characters. The text is apparently metrical, but partly undecipherable due to its weathering and the deterioration of the stone, so that there is uncertainty in some places over the actual runes present and their transliteration, and consequently a good deal of disagreement among scholars as to the correct reading (Nielsen, 2000, p.75, pp.97-8, 223-4; Spurkland, 2005, p.54-71). The legend is in separate panels; Panel 2 includes the sequence:

huwᴀrob / kạmhᴀr[ss]ạhiạlạtgotnᴀ

which has been interpreted as:

hvaʀ of kom hẹráss á / hí á land gotna?

This appears to be a verse in *Galdralag* metre, translatable as:

'Whence came the army-god here, into the land of men?'

where *heráss* is one of the *Óðinsheiti* discussed below in Appendix II.

THE UPPÅKRA COMPLEX

At Uppåkra in southern Sweden, several years of detailed archaeological investigation have revealed extensive traces of a large and long-lived settlement complex dated to the late Iron Age. It was a 'central place', to use the anodyne terminology of the archaeological report – an important site where meetings were convened, under the auspices of a chieftain or regional magnate. It was both a marketplace and a cult-site (Thurston, 2001; Larsson, 2005).

One of the many buildings (House 2/House 14 in the schematic of Larsson & Lenntorp, 2004, p.7) was repeatedly rebuilt over several centuries and has been interpreted as a 'building having cultic functions' (Larsson, 2004) in other words a 'site of religious observance', a 'temple', in which it resembles the contemporary site at Gudme, Denmark, and several other probable religious centres (Hårdh & Larsson, 2007; Holst et al., 2017; Sørensen, 2022). Close to the building were many deposits of weapons – mainly spears and shields – and a right-side ocular and eyebrow from a helmet, similar to the types found at Sutton Hoo, Valsgärde and Vendel (Helgesson, 2004, p.223). This helmet-part can be interpreted, in the context of the wargear and the temple, as forming a fragment of an offering for religious purposes (Price & Mortimer, 2014, p.523).[78]

A notable figurine cast in bronze was excavated at the site, depicting a slender male with his arms hanging at his sides, wearing a tunic which terminates around the level of the knees (the lower portion of the figure is absent so this is not certain), with traces of incised transverse lines indicating a belt; the head is of an elongated

---

[78] A similar gilt-bronze ocular (eye-protector) from a helmet of similar date was found at the settlement at Gevninge, near Roskilde (Denmark).

piriform shape with large pellet eyes in shallow sockets, a long vertical nose and a small scaphoid mouth with the suggestion of a moustache; above the head is the remains of a crescent feature, usually considered to be paired horns. The true right eye has been struck out (Mortimer, 2018).

The weapons found close to the cult-house had been damaged and put beyond use. They were distributed in a deliberate manner, not randomly dispersed across the site. The spearheads especially were left in pairs and clusters, while other items were carefully deposited nearby. The interpretation of the material is still in progress but it seems clear that the deposits imply an active involvement in warfare for those who dwelt on the site: the fact of weapons having been put beyond use suggests that these belonged to a defeated foe rather than being the property of the local landowner, and that they had been collected and transported to the house of worship in order to form part of some celebratory rites (Helgesson, 2004, p.232).

JORDANES: GETICA

The *Getica* was written in Latin by the Gothic historian Jordanes sometime around 550 AD (van Nuffelen & van Hoof, 2020). It is specifically stated to be based on authoritative earlier works including what the author could remember of a history by Cassiodorus (now lost). The early sections of the narrative tell of the Goths' journeying from Scandia (probably Skaane, now southern Sweden) into eastern Europe and the lands of the Scythians; combined with such apparently genuine traditions are tales of derring-do, including encounters with Agamemnon and Egyptian Pharaohs. The more sober later portion of the work deals with the 3rd-4th c. contacts of the Ostrogoths and Visigoths with Rome and Byzantium, culminating in the Gothic defeat by Belisarius.

The Goths recognised that kings and leaders could be promoted to the authority of demi-gods, if their luck and skill were such that they won many victories. This is recorded by Jordanes (*Getica*, ch.78) where their foremost men were called '*ansis*' in the Latin ('half-gods') glossing the Gothic term *Anses* (Griffiths, 1996, pp.26-7; North, 1997, p.136; Lindow, 2016, p.21; Tolley, 2009, p.209; Pollington, 2011, pp.77-8; van Nuffelen & van Hoof, 2020; text from Mommsen, 1882):

> Tum Gothi haut segnes reperti arma capessunt primoque conflictu mox Romanos devincunt, Fuscoque duce exstincto, divitias de castris militum spoliant, magnaque potiti per loca victoria, jam proceres suos, quorum quasi fortuna vincebant, non puros homines, sed semideos, id est Ansis, vocaverunt. Quorum genealogia ut paucis percurram, vel quis quo parente genitus est, aut unde origo coepta, ubi finem effecit absque invidia qui legis vera dicentam ausculta: Horum ergo heroum ut ipsi suis in fabulis referent, primus fuit Gaut...

> 'Once the Goths were aware, they took their weapons and soon overcame the Romans in the first clash, they slew Fuscus, the commander, and looted the treasure from the camp of the army; because of the great victory they had gained in this region, they thereafter called their foremost men, through whose luck they had won, not mere men, but demigods, that is, 'Ansis'. Their lineage, as I shall briefly say, or who was born from which parent, and where [the lineage] had its beginning and ending, to this they listen attentively when it is spoken. Of these heroes the first was Gaut, as they tell in their own stories ...'

Here it is only the leading men, those blessed with great luck and famous achievements, who can qualify for the status of 'divine offspring'. An interesting point is the name 'Gaut' which recurs in later literature dealing with Woden and Óðinn.

A detail in *Getica* ch.39 concerning the prelude to the Battle of the Catalunian Plain shows Attila, leader of the Hunnic and Gothic forces, urging his men on to the fight with a resounding speech including the phrase (text from Mommsen, 1882; see Levin, 2020):

Non fallor eventu: hic campus est, quem nobis tot prospera promiserunt. Primus in hoste tela coiciam. Si quis potuerit Attila pugnante otio ferre, sepultus est.

'I make no mistake regarding the outcome: this is the battlefield which so many successes have promised to us. I shall throw a spear at the enemy first. Anyone who will have been able to rest while Attila fights, is [dead and] buried'.

The act which initiates war is the spear-cast; this need not be 'mythic', nor even legendary, but based on actual battlefield practice: some deed has to set the battle in motion. It is a motif which recurs in Norse tales.

JONAS OF BOBBIO: VITA COLUMBANI

The notion that *Mercurius* in Roman sources could be glossed with *Vodan* in Germanic ones appears to make its earliest appearance in northern Italy, in the writings of the ecclesiastic Jonas of Bobbio who lived in the early 7th c. Drinking bouts in celebration of gods and ancestors were evidently associated with Germanic 'paganism' in continental sources and were highly objectionable to Christian sentiment – so much so that efforts were made to expunge the practice.

Jonas of Bobbio's work *Vita Columbani* (*Life of St. Columbanus*) records that the missionary, Columbanus, while travelling to Brigantia (Bregenz, Austria), noticed some men about to drink beer in honour of Vodan / Mercury from a large vessel. The saint blew on it and destroyed it (Wood, 1995, p.259; Green, 1998, p.248; Shaw, 2002, pp.117-26; Nelson, 2005, pp.94-6, 161; Gardenstone, 2011, p.70; Liberman, 2016, p.43) (text from Migne, 1844-64):

Sunt etenim inibi vicinae nationes Suaevorum. Quo cum moraretur et inter habitatores loci illius progrederetur, repperit eos sacrificium profanum litare velle, vasque magnum, quem vulgo cupam vocant, qui XX modia amplius minusve capiebat, cervisa plenum in medio positum. Ad quem vir Dei accessit sciscitaturque, quid de illo fieri vellint. Illi aiunt se Deo suo Vodano nomine, quem Mercurium, ut alii aiunt, autumant, velle litare. Ille pestiferum opus audiens vas insufflat, miroque modo vas cum fragore dissolvitur et per frustra dividitur, visque rapida cum ligore cervisae prorumpit; manifesteque datur intellegi diabolum in eo vase fuisse occultatum, qui per profanum ligorem caperet animas sacrificantum.

'For in that vicinity are nations of the Swabians. While he remains with [them] and travels about among the inhabitants of that place, he learns of their intention to perform a profane sacrifice and a large vessel, which they commonly call a '*cupa*' [barrel], which held about twenty *modia* [measures of corn] was set up in the middle filled with beer. Thereat the man of god approached and asked what they meant to do with that. They said that they meant to sacrifice to a god of theirs, by name Vodan, whom others call Mercurius. Hearing of this deplorable matter, he blew into the vat and miraculously the vessel split into fragments and was shattered, and the force of the beer flowing out broke it apart; and he was visibly given the knowledge that a devil was hidden in that vessel who, through the unholy liquid, would seize the souls of the participants'.

Jonas recounts a similar story of Vedastis (St. Vaast) among the heathen Franks, who made the sign of the cross over a vat of beer which promptly emptied itself onto the floor (Nelson, 2005, p.96).[79] It is hard to be sure whether this means that Jonas used the 'vessel of drink' episode as a stock miracle for the holy men in his narratives, or whether the text's reference to 'Vodan' rather strengthens the case for a genuine tradition.[80] In any event, Jonas does not seem to have borrowed this event as a literary *topos* from any earlier writer.

---

[79] Nelson (2005, p.96) also recounts a similar tale of Athairne in Ireland. The 'bursting barrel' motif may have a prosaic explanation in the build-up of carbon dioxide during the fermentation process.

[80] Wood (2013, p.4) suggests that the episode need not have a religious dimension since 'we are scarcely dealing with active pagan cult, but rather with social

This may be the earliest surviving text (8th c.) to link the name Woden specifically with Mercury, an association which proved very long-lived in medieval tradition. The fact that the remark is parenthetical has been used to dismiss the information as unreliable,[81] but in fact Jonas is quite clear in stating that their god named *Vodan* (*Deo suo Vodano nomine*) is called by others *Mercurius*.

Communal meals held in celebration or commemoration of the gods relied on food and drink, and both these products were under the care of the gods of abundance. Without the ripening wheat there was no cereal crop, without corn or barley no bread and no beer; indeed, without the *hlaf* 'loaf' there was no *hlaford* 'lord' and no social hierarchy to maintain (North, 1997, p.16). It is notable that the missionary thought that the drinkers would lose their souls *per profanum ligorem* 'through the unholy liquid' indicating his understanding that the taking of strong drink was a rite of 'communion' parallel to the Christian acceptance of the blood and body of Christ by ingesting a solid and a liquid.

Of greater importance than food to the religious aspect of the occasion was mead – or its substitutes such as ale, wine, beer, cider and the like. Such substances were all able to induce 'transformations' and the sensations these drinks offered were highly prized and sought after. If the episode at the opening of *Beowulf* where Scyld Scefing takes away the meadbenches from his enemies is emblematic of his new political dominance, we may have another example of a mythic 'mead-theft' (Shaw, 2002, p.185). Shaw is certainly correct to stress

---

practices which may once have been religious, but now constituted part of the ritual of aristocratic feasting, and which would have been familiar to many supposedly orthodox Christians.' Yet we must doubt that even the most generous orthodox Christians would have accepted '*Deo suo Vodano nomine*' (their god named Vodan) as an appropriate dedicatee for a ceremonial feast.

[81] Gardenstone, 2011, p.70ff. The spelling *Vodan* is apparently West Germanic and predates the Second Sound Shift which gave rise to OHG *Wuotan*; this does not in itself entail that the name had been recently introduced by Anglo-Saxon missionaries into the tale, nor that a Wodan-god was unknown in Italy in Jonas's day.

the centrality of drink-distribution to Germanic heroic life, as also the hierarchical structure manifested in customary seating positions. Far more than just offering scenes of abandon and merrymaking to contrast with the grim fighting to come, the sharing of alcoholic drink in a structured and formalised manner was an important aspect of the story's *milieu*. Perhaps on such a momentous occasion the drink was shared in silence except for the solemn, ritual speech-acts – words of thanks, oaths of deeds to be performed, prayers to the gods.

THE LOMBARD SOURCES I

The Lombards' early history is quite opaque but, in outline, their first appearance is on the lower River Elbe in 5 AD in connection with Tiberius's military campaign, and they are mentioned by Tacitus (*Germania*, ch.40) as a small tribe who keep their larger neighbours at bay through their willingness to risk all in battle (Kershaw, 2000, p.143); they then appear in 167 AD in modern Lower Austria, whence they pass to Pannonia (Hungary) under the leadership of Audoin and to Italy in 568 AD under their king Alboin (Green, 2009, p.174).

Tradition has it that they were originally called *Vinnili* but changed their name to *Langobardi* 'long-beards': this may have coincided with a change in the dominant religious culture, since in ON sources *Langbarðr* 'long-beard' is one of the bynames of Óðinn, and the god *Godan* is specified as the author of this new identity. Strabo (*Geographia*, ch.vii) places them ($\Lambda\alpha\gamma\kappa\acute{o}\beta\alpha\rho\delta o\iota$) to the north of the Suevi or Swabians; Ptolemy mentions two groups – the *Lacco-Bardi* and the *Suebi Langobardi*.[82] Their home on the lower River Elbe was known in medieval times as the Bardengau (district of the Bards) and their name appears twice (with different prefixes) in the listing of northern European peoples in *Widsith* (text from Chambers, 1912):

---

[82] *Lacco-Bardi* is presumably an error for $\Lambda\alpha\gamma\gamma\acute{o}\beta\alpha\rho\delta o\iota$ (*Laggobardoi*) with the Greek - $\gamma\gamma$- spelling of the nasal in *Lango-*; the prefix *Suebi-* refers to the larger political grouping into which the Langobards were subsumed.

l.49 forheowan æt Heorote   Heaðo-Beardna þrym.

'they cut down the forces of the Battle-Bards at Heorot.'

l.80 Mid Lidwicingum ic wæs ond mid Leonum ond mid Longbeardum.

'I was among the Lid-Vikings and among the Leons and among the Longbeards.'

Chambers thought that the *Lidwicingas* could be identified as the *Letavici* or the Armoricans of the area which later became known as Brittany (sometimes called in OE *Lidwiccas*) but Malone identified them as the *Liðungar* of the Oslo region of Norway; the *Leons* are perhaps the *Ljónar*, a tribe of southern Sweden (Chambers, 1912, pp.213-4; Malone, 1962, pp.180-2). These two references to southern Scandinavia suggest that such was the homeland of the tribes in the poet's original listing.

Widsith's *Langobeardan* are often identified with the *Beardan* who played an important part in the action of *Beowulf*, since they were responsible for the burning down of the great hall, Heorot (ll.83-5) (Shippey, 2022, p.40). Their move away from the Elbe region caused a power-vacuum which brought the Angles in Jutland and Schleswig and the Swabians to the south into direct contact and soon led to border disputes. This situation was resolved by the action of the semi-legendary King Offa who fixed the common boundary at the River Eider (*Widsith*, ll.43-4; text from Chambers, 1912):

> ...   heoldon forð siþþan
>
> Engle ond Swæfe,   swa hit Offa geslog.
>
> 'The Angles and Swabians kept it afterwards as Offa marked it out.'

The *Beardan* and the *Geatas* were both enemies of the Danes, and their downfall had implications for the balance of power in northern Europe which played out for centuries to come.

EDICTUS ROTHARI

This document, completed in 643 AD, is the first compilation of Lombard legal statutes into a written form; previously, laws had been maintained only in human memory. The text is in late Vulgar Latin but includes a number of Lombard words for which no suitable Latin equivalent was current. The laws deal mainly with everyday matters such as the rules governing the conduct of duels, the calculation and payment of *wergeld*, and rights of inheritance. They were intended to strengthen the position of the king (i.e., King Rothari, the promulgator of the code) and to constrain the behaviour of his noblemen (Tosi, 1982).

The main text of the document is in Latin but some key legal terms are given in Langobardic, such as *aldius* 'half-free man', *faida* 'feud', *thinc* 'assembly', *gairethinx* 'spear-assembly; gift made at a public meeting' and many others. It is often difficult to isolate Langobardic words from those introduced into Italy by the Franks or the Ostrogoths (see Green, 2009, pp.175-7) but fortunately the Langobardic language was subject to the Second Sound Shift which it shares with Old High German. This makes it possible to isolate the word *gair-* 'spear' in *gairethinx* as neither Gothic (where it would appear as **gais-*) nor Frankish (where it would appear as *gêr-*). *Gair-* has a later history as the prototheme in, e.g., the name *Garibaldi* '(he who is) bold with a spear' (Green, 2009, p.183).

The *Edictus* refers to an ancestral figure called *Gauzo*, which may be the Langobardic form of the word which appears as *Gautr* in ON and *Geat* in Old English. Green (2009, p.197) lists **gauta* as 'man, stallion, mythical hero of procreation' in his summary vocabulary of the Langobardic language.

ORIGO GENTIS LANGOBARDUM

The earliest known extensive tale of Woden (i.e., one in which the god figures as an active participant) occurs in the 7th c. anonymous *Origo Gentis Langobardum* (Origin of the Lombard Nation) which was adapted by Paulus Diaconus (Paul the Deacon) for his work,

Historia Langobardorum. The tale of the seeress Gambara (discussed below, p.173) appears in this document.

FREDEGAR: CHRONICON

A similar tale to Paul the Deacon's concerning the acquisition of the Langobard name and the gift of victory is related in Fredegar's *Chronicon*, dating from the middle decades of the 7th c., in which the writer describes the emigration of the Langobards from Scandinavia and their entering the territory of the Huns, where a ruse gives rise to the folk-name (text from Collins, 2007):

> At ille mulieris eorum praecipunt comam capitis ad maxellas et mentum legarint, quo pocius virorum habitum simulantes plurima multitudine hostium ostenderint, eo quod erant mulierum coma circa maxellas et mentum ad instar barbae valde longa. Fertur desuper uterque falangiae vox dixisse: 'Haec sunt Langobardi', quod ab his gentibus fertur eorum deo fuisse locutum, quem fanatice nominant Wodano. Tunc Langobardi clamassent: 'Qui instituerat nomen, concidere victoriam'. Hoc prilio Chunus superant, partem Pannoniae invadunt.

> 'But they asked their women to stretch the hair from their heads to their jaws and chins, so that the few men seemed to their enemies to be many, because the hair around their jaws and chins appeared to be very long beards. It is said that a voice from above on both wings of the army said: "These are [the] Langobards" which was understood by these people to be a god speaking whom they zealously name 'Wodan'. Then the Langobards cried out: "May he who bestowed the name grant victory". In this battle they overran the Huns and entered part of Pannonia.'

This version of the tale has the virtue of explaining the face-covering motif as a military stratagem to make the Winniles' army appear more numerous than it was in reality (Kershaw, 2000, p.143; Shaw, 2002, pp.112-4). It sounds like a later rationalisation of an obscure episode which was no longer understood. The form *Wodan* is, of course, not specifically Lombardic and the origin of the story is un-known, but the inclusion of an etymological basis for the tribal name is nevertheless suggestive of genuine tradition.

8ᵀᴴ -9ᵀᴴ CENTURY

The Ribe skull fragment dates to the first quarter of the 8ᵗʰ century and the *Textus Roffensis* to the last quarter. The manuscript of the *Old Saxon Baptismal Formula* belongs to the 9ᵗʰ c. and the East Saxon Kinglist likewise. The discussion of the Gotland picture stones is included here since the bulk of the pictorial examples appear to be-long to the period 700–1100 AD.

BEDE: HISTORIA ECCLESIASTICA GENTIS ANGLORUM

Bede's *Historia Ecclesiastica Gentis Anglorum* (*Ecclesiastical History of the English Nation*) is one of the earliest (early 8ᵗʰ c.) literary sources for information on the traditions of the Germanic kingly families in Britain, but the cleric has little to say about the earlier origins of the people (Colgrave & Mynors, 1969). He appears to have been una-ware of Tacitus's work. Bede could not discuss the conversion of the Angles to the Christian faith without saying a little about their previous practices, if only to deride them. It seems probable that pre-Christian attitudes to the link between kingship and the super-natural powers were closer to those displayed by the Lombards in their accounts of Godan (Woden) being induced to give them vic-tory by a ruse (Yorke, 2015, p.168).

KING EDWIN AND THE MYSTERIOUS VISITOR

In his early life, Edwin was a nobleman in exile (if not actually 'on the run'), the throne of Northumbria having passed to Æþelfriþ, then the mightiest king in Britain. Edwin spent some time at the court of the Kentish king, Æþelberht, but had to leave there; he next came to the court of the East Angles, where Rædwald was at that time the king. Bede reserved a particular dislike for Rædwald

who had been baptised a Christian when a visitor at the Kentish
court, but reverted to the old religion when he returned to his own
land (Colgrave & Mynors, 1969, p148). A benighted heathen was
bad enough as a king, but one who had been shown the light of
Christian salvation and repudiated it was beyond Bede's sympathy.

Edwin (in Northumbrian, Aeduuini) was a scion of the old Bernician kingly family, and a particular favourite of Bede, who adapted
the tale of Edwin's life to fit his narrative of the inexorable rise of
the Christian faith. When Æþelfriþ found out where Edwin had fled,
he offered bribes and threats to secure his rival's murder. Then a
'mysterious visitor' intervened on behalf of the exile (Bede's *Historia
Ecclesiastica Gentis Anglorum*, Book II, ch.9; text from Miller, 1890):[83]

Midþy hine ehte Æðefrið se ðe ær him cyning wæs, 7 þurh
missenlice stowe he monigra geara tide flyma wæs, ða gesohte he
æt nyhstan 7 cwom to Rædwolde Eastengla cyninge; 7 hine bæd
þæt he his lif gescylde wið swa micles ehteres sætingum, 7 him
feorhyrde wære. Ond he lustlice hine onfeng 7 him geheht, þæt
he swa don wolde swa he hine bæd. Æfter þon þa Æþelfrið se
cyning hine þær geahsode, þæt he mid Rædwold þone cyning
wæs, þa sende he sona ærendwrecan to him 7 micel feoh, wið
þon þe he hine ofsloge oðþe him to cwale agefe; ne hwæþre
owiht on þon fromade.

Sende he eft æfteran siðe ærendwrecan; synde þriddan siðe, 7
maran gife micle 7 feoh, þonne he him ær sende, wið his cwale
ond het eac him onbeodan, þæt he hine wolde mid fyrde to
gefeohte gesecan, gif he his word 7 his gife forhogode. Þa wæs
his mod æghwæðer ge mid þæm beotungum gebreged ge mid
þæm geofum gewemmed, þæt he geþafode þæs cyninges bene 7
gehet, þæt he Eadwine ofsloge oðþe feondum to cwale gefe.

Þa wæs sum cyninges þegn his freond se getreowesta, þe þas þing
gehyrde 7 onget. þa eode he to his inne, þær he hine restan wolde

---

[83] For clarity I have amended the many masculine pronouns (*he, hine, his*) by
substituting the name of the referent in square brackets.

– wæs foreweard niht – 7 hine acegde ut 7 him sægde 7 cyðde, hu him mon emb don wolde. Cwæð him þa gyt to: 'Gif ðu wilt in þas seolfan tid, ic þe alædo of þisse mægðe, 7 in þa stowe alæde, þær þe næfre Rædwald ne Æðelfrið gemetan magon.' Cwæð he to him: 'On þonce me synd þin word 7 þin lufo, 7 hwæþre ne maeg ic þæt don, þæet þu me lærest, þæt ic ærest þa wære forlaete, þe ic to swa miclum cyninge nom, mid þy he me noht yfeles dyde ne laðes æteawde. Ac gif ic deað þrowian sceal, leofre me is, þæt he mec to deaðe sylle þonne unæðelra mon. Oðþe la hwider mæg ic nu leng fleon? Monigra geara tida ofer ealle Breotone ic flyma wæs, þæt ic me his hete bearh 7 warenode.' þa eode se his freond onweg from him, 7 he Eadwini ana þær ute gewunade; saet swiðe unrot on stane beforan þære healle, 7 ongon mid monegum hætum his geþohta swenced beon: 7 ne wiste hwider he eode oðþe hwæt him selest to donne wære.

Mid þy he þa longe swigendum nearonissum his modes 7 mid þy blindan fyre soden wæs, þa geseah he semninga on midre niht sumne mon wið his gongan uncuþes ondwlitan 7 uncuðes gegyrlan. Þa he ða to him cwom, þa wæs he forht geworden. Þa eode he to him, grette hine 7 frægn, for hwon he in þære tide, þe oðre men slepon 7 reston, ana swa unrot on stane wæccende sæte. Ða fraegn he hine, hwæt þæs to him lumpe, hwæþer he wacode oþþe slepe, 7 hwæþer he þe ute þe inne wære. Ða ondswarade he 7 him to cwæð: 'Ne tala þu me, þæt ic ne cunne þone intingan þinre unrotnisse 7 þinre wæcene 7 onslæpnesse þines seðles. Ac ic cuþlice wat, ge hwæt þu eart ge for hwon þu gnornast, 7 hwylc toweard yfel þu þe in neahnesse forhtast. Ac gesaga me hwylce mede þu wille syllan þam men, gif hwylc sy, þætte þec from þissum nearonessum alyse ond Rædwalde on mod beswape, þæt he noht laðes ne gedo ne þec þinum feondum to cwale agife?' Þa ondswarede 7 cwæð, þæt he ealle ða god þe he meahte for mede þislicre fremsumnesse syllan wolde. Ða ætecte he þa gyt his gesprec 7 cwæð: '7 nu gif he þe eac, adwaesctum þinum feondum, in soðe toweard cynerice gehateð,

swa þæt nales þæt an ealle þine yldran, ac ealle cyningas, þa þe in
Breotone wæron ær, þu in meahte 7 in rice feor oferstigest?'

Þa wæs he Eadwine baldra geworden in þære frignesse, 7 sona
gehet, se ðe him swa micle fremsumnesse forgefe, þæt he him
þæs wolde wyrþlice þoncunce don. Cwæð he þriddan siðe to
him, se þe him wið spraec: Ono, gif se mon, se ðe þyslice gife 7
swa micle soðlice þe towearde forecwið, ond eac swylce
geþeahte þinre hælo 7 betran lifes 7 nyttran þe æteawan mæg,
þonne ænig þinra maga oððe yldrena æfre gehyrde – cwist þu
hwæðer þu his þa halwendan monunge onfon wille 7 him
hearsum beon'

Þa ne elde he Eadwini owiht ac sona gehet þæt he wolde in
eallum þingum him hearsum beon 7 his lare lustlice onfon, se þe
hine from swa monegum ermþum 7 teonum generede 7 to
heanisse cynerices forðgelædde. Þa he þa þisse ondsware onfeng,
se þe mid hine spræc, þa instaepe sette he mid þa swiðron hond
him on þæt heafod 7 þus cwæð: 'Ðonne þis tacen þislic þe
tocyme, þonne gemyne þu þas tide uncres gespreces 7 ne yld þu
þæt þu þa þing gefylle, þe þu me nu gehete. Þa he ða þas word
spræc, þa ne wiste he semninga hwær he cwom; wolde þæt he
in þon ongete, þæt þæt mon ne wæs, se þe him æteawde, ac
þætte þæt gast wæs.

'Æþelfriþ, who was king before [Edwin], persecuted him and he
was an exile for many years in various places; [Edwin] sought out
and came at last to Rædwald, king of the East Angles, and asked
him to protect his life against the ambushes of so mighty an
oppressor and to become the guardian of his spirit. And [Rædwald]
eagerly received him and promised him that he would do just as
he asked. Afterwards, when King Æþelfriþ heard that [Edwin] was
there with King Rædwald, he straightaway sent a herald and a
large amount of wealth in order that [Rædwald] should kill him
or surrender him to his death. However, Rædwald would do

nothing of the sort. [Æþelfriþ] sent heralds on a second occasion, and on a third greater gifts and wealth than he had sent to him before in exchange for Edwin's murder, and also bade him bear in mind that [Æþelfriþ] would come against him with an army if Rædwald were to ignore his words and his gifts. Then [Rædwald's] mind was both overawed by the threats and enticed by the gifts, so that he accepted the king's request and promised that he would either slay Edwin or surrender him to his enemies to be put to death.

When one of the king's most loyal friends heard of these matters and understood [them], early in the night he went to the building in which [Edwin] intended to sleep and called to him to come outside, and explained and made known to him what they meant to do to him. He said to [Edwin] "If you wish it, I will bring you out of here at this very time and into a place where neither Rædwald nor Æþelfriþ will ever find you." Edwin said to him: "I am thankful for your words and your friendship, yet I cannot do what you suggest to me – that I should be the first to break the agreement that I undertook with so great a king, since he has done me nothing malicious nor exposed me to anything hateful. But if I must suffer death, it is more agreeable to me that [Rædwald] should bring me my death than a less noble man. Or else, indeed, where can I flee anymore? For many years I have been an exile in all parts of Britain, so that I have had to protect myself and take care against [Æþelfriþ's] malice." Then his friend went away from Edwin and he remained there alone: he sat down in despair on a stone in front of the hall and began to be troubled by many overwhelming surges in his thoughts and did not know where he might go or what it would be best for him to do.

[Edwin] was seething for a long while in his mind then with silent brooding and with secret anguish, when suddenly in the middle of the night he saw a man approaching with an unfamiliar appearance and strange garments. When he came towards him, [Edwin] became afraid; then [the figure] came to him, greeted him and asked why, at a time when other men were sleeping and resting, he was sitting alone on a stone so troubled and watchful. Then [Edwin] asked him what business it was of his whether he was awake or asleep and whether he was inside or outside. Then [the figure] answered him and said: "Do not judge me, [thinking] that I may not know the cause of your despair and of your wakefulness and of your sleepless vigil. But I evidently know both who you are and why you are troubled, and which coming evil you fear as immanent. But tell me what reward you would give to a man – if any such there may be - who might free you from this distress and change the mind of Rædwald so that he would do nothing hateful to you, nor hand you over to your enemies to your death?" Then [Edwin] answered and said that he would give all the goods that he could as a reward for such a benefit; then [the figure] added further to what he had already stated and said "And now, if he were to promise you a true future kingdom purged of your enemies so that you might outdo in might and power not only your own ancestors but all the kings who were in Britain before?"

Then Edwin grew bolder in that questioning, and straightaway promised that he would show honourable gratitude for it to whomever might provide so great a benefit for him. Then the figure who was speaking with him said for a third time: "Lo! if the man who foretells for you truly of such and of so great a gift in the future, and can show you such care for your welfare and a better and more useful life than any of your ancestors or kinsmen have ever heard about – do you say that you will accept his warning and be obedient to him?" Then Edwin did not delay at all but straightaway promised that he would be obedient to him in all things and gladly receive guidance from the one who saved him from so many hardships and hurts, and who led him on to the heights of kingship. When he who was speaking with him received this answer, he immediately set his right hand on [Edwin's] head and spoke thus: "When this sign comes to you in this manner, then remember this time of our speaking together and do not hesitate in fulfilling those things which you have promised me." Once he had spoken these words, [Edwin] did not know where [the visitor] had gone; he was inclined to suppose that it was not a man who appeared to him, but that it was a ghost.'

The mysterious nocturnal visitor who already knows the name and circumstances of the man he addresses, is perhaps a familiar figure: he arrives at the opportune moment when his words are able to turn the course of events in favour of his unfortunate protégé. A similar reversal of fortune happens to Cædmon at Streoneshalh, as we shall see.

Bede, of course, wants the reader to understand that the nameless visitor is an angel or emanation of the Christian powers, whose authority will later be brought to the fore under Edwin's rule. But the story does not read like a standard Christian hagiographic incident – it has rather the quality of a secular narrative where the king's future wellbeing is secured by a *gast* 'spirit, unearthly agent'. Which deity might have been the original patron-god of the kings and leaders of the Northumbrians? There are clues in other tales connected to their rise to power.

KING EDWIN AND THE HEATHEN PRIEST

The story of the repudiation of the old religion by Coifi, the heathen priest of the Northumbrians, is told at length by Bede. Once King Edwin heard of the Christian faith from a bishop, Paulinus, he was inclined to accept it (especially after his nocturnal visitor's warning) but realized that he would need the support of his close friends and advisers to carry through the conversion of the whole court (Pollington, 2011, pp.122-5). He asked for the bishop's forbearance and tact in handling the matter (text from Miller, 1890):

Þa se cyning þa þas word gehyrde þa ondswarode he him ond cwæð þæt he æghwæþer ge wolde ge scolde þam geleafan onfon þe he lærde; cwæð hwæþere þæt he wolde mid his freondum ond mid his wytum gesprec ond geþeaht habban þæt gif hi mid hine þæt geþafian woldan, þæt hi ealle ætsomne on lifes willan, criste, gehalgade wæran. Þa dyde se cyning swaswa he cwæð ond se biscop þæt geþafade.

Þa hæfde he gesprec ond geþeaht mid his witum ond syndriglice wæs fram him eallum frignende, hwylc him þuhte ond gesawen wære þeos niwe lar, ond þære godcundnesse bigong þe þær læred wæs. Him þa ondswarode his ealdorbisceop, Cefi was haten 'Geseoh þu, cyning, hwelc þeos lar sie þe us nu bodad is. Ic þe soðlice ondette þæt ic cuðlice geleornod hæbbe, þæt eallinge nawiht mægenes ne nyttnesse hafað sio æfæstnes þe we oð ðis hæfdon ond beeodon.' Forþon nænig þinra þegna neodlicor ne gelustfullicor hine sylfne underþeodde to ura goda bigange þonne ic; ond nohtþonlæs monige syndon þa þe maran gyfe ond fremsumnesse æt þe onfengon þonne ic ond on eallum þingum maran gesynto hæfdon. Hwæt! Ic wat, gif ure godo ænige mihte hæfdon, þonne woldon hie me ma fultumian forþon ic him geornlicor þeodde ond hyrde. Forðon me þynceð wislic gif þu geseo þa þing beteran ond strangran þe us niwan bodad syndon, þæt we þam onfon.

Þæs wordum oþer cyninges wita 7 ealdormann geþafunge sealde 7 to þære spræce feng 7 þus cwæð: 'Þyslic me is gesewen, þu cyning, þis andwearde lif manna on eorðan to wiðmetenesse þære tide þe us uncuð is: swylc swa þu æt swæsendum sitte mid þinum ealdormannum 7 þegnum on wintertide 7 sie fyr onæled 7 þin heall gewyrmed 7 hit rine 7 sniwe 7 styrme ute; cume an spearwa 7 hrædlice þæt hus þurhfleo, cume þurh oþre duru in, þurh oþre ut gewite. Hwæt, he on þa tid þe he inne bið ne bið hrinen mid þy storme þæs winters; ac þæt bið an eagan bryhtm 7 þæt læsste fæc, ac he sona of wintra on þone winter eft cymeð. Swa ðonne þis monna lif to medmiclum fæce ætyweð, hwæt þær foregange oððe hwæt þæt æfterfylige we ne cunnun. Forþon gif þeos niwe lar owiht cuðlicre ond gerisenlicre brenge heo þæs wyrþe is þæt we þære fylgen.' Þeossum wordum gelicum oðre aldormen ond ðæs cyninges geþeahteras spræcan.

Þagen toætyhte Cefi ond cwæð þæt he wolde Paulinus þone
bisceop geornlicor gehyran be þam gode sprecende þam þe he
bodade. Þa het se cyning swa don. Þa he þa his word gehyrde þa
clypose he ond þus cwæð: 'Geare ic þæt ongeat þæt ðæt nowiht
wæs þæt we beeodan; forþon swa micle swa ic geornlicor on
þam bigange þæt sylfe soð sohte swa ic hit læs mette. Nu þonne
ic openlice ondette þæt on þysse lare þæt sylfe soð scineð þæt us
mæg þa gyfe syllan ecre eadignesse ond eces lifes hælo. Forþon
ic þonne nu lære, cyning, þæt þæt templ ond þa wigbedo, þaðe
we buton wæstmum ænigre nytnisse halgodon þæt we þa hraþe
forleosen ond fyre forbærne.'

Ono hwæt he þa wæs se cyning openlice ondettende þam bioscope
ond him eallum þæt he wolde fæstlice þam deofolgildum wiðsacan
ond cristes geleafan onfon.

Midþyþe he þa se cyning from þæm foresprecenan biscope sohte
ond ahsode heora halignesse þe heo ær bieodon, hwa ða wigbed
ond þa hergas þara deofolgilda mid heora hegum, þe heo
ymbsette wæron, heo ærest aidligan ond toweaorpan scolde, þa
andswarode he: 'Efne ic! Hwa mæg þa nu eað þe ic longe mid
dysignysse beeode to bysene oðerra manna gerisenlecor
toweorpan þonne ic seolfa þurh þa snyttro þe ic fram þæm soðan
gode onfeng?' Ond he ða sona fram him awearp þa idlan
dysignesse þe he ær beeode ond þone cyning bæd þæt he him
wæpen sealde, ond stodhors þæt he meahte on cuman ond
deofolgyld towearpan, forþon þam bisceope heora halignesse ne
wæs alyfed þæt he moste wæpen wegan ne elcor buton on myran
ridan. Þa sealde se cyning him sweord þæt he hine mid gyrde
ond nom his spere on hond ond hleop on þæs cyninges stedan
ond to þæm deofolgeldum ferde. Þa ðæt folc hine þa geseah swa
gescyrpedne, þa wendon heo þæt he teola ne wiste ac þæt he
wedde. Sona þæsþe he nealehte to þæm herige þa sceat he mid
þy spere þæt hit sticode fæste on þæm herige ond wæs swiðe
gefeonde þære nytenesse þæs soðam godes bigonges ond he ða
heht his geferan toweorpan ealne þone herig ond þa getimbro

ond forbærnan. Is seo stow gyt ateawed gu ðara deofulgylda noht feor east from Eoforwicceastre begeondan Deorwentan þære ea ond gen todæg is nemned Godmundingaham, þær se bisceop þurh þæs soðam godes inbryrdnesse towearp ond fordyde þa wigbed þe he seolfa ær gehalgode.

'When the king heard these [the bishop's] words, he answered them and said that he both ought to and wanted to receive that faith which he taught; he said, however, that he wished to have deliberation and discussion with his friends and advisers so that if they would consent to that with him, then they would all be hallowed in Christ together in the fountain of life. Then the king did as he had said, and the bishop acceded to that.

Then he undertook discussion and deliberation with his advisers and he started to ask each of them separately how this new learning seemed to him, and should be viewed, and the religious behaviour which had been taught there. Then his elder-bishop answered him, who was called Cefi:[84] "See now, king, what this new lore is that is now preached to us. I truly confess to you what I have clearly learnt, that the observance which we had undertaken till this time has no power nor usefulness. Because none of your servants more rigorously nor willingly subjected himself to our gods' worship than I, yet nonetheless they are many who received more gifts and favours from you than I, and in all things had greater luck. Lo! I know that if our gods had any power, then they would have favoured me more, because I served and obeyed them the more readily. Thus, if you see those things which are preached to us anew as better and stronger, it seems to me wise that we should accept them."

To that one's words another adviser and elder of the king gave consent, and took up the discussion and spoke thus: "It seems to

---

[84] The name is given as Coifi in the Latin version of the text.

me thus, O king, this present life of men on earth as measured against the time which is unknown to us: as if you were sitting at a banquet with your ealdormen and thanes in wintertime, and a fire has been lit and your hall warmed, and outside there is rain and snow and storm; a sparrow comes and quickly flies through the house – he comes in through one door, and goes out through the other. Lo, for the time that he is inside he is not touched by the winter's storm, but that is one eye's blink and the least space of time, yet from the winter he straightaway goes back to the winter. So then, this life of men shows as a brief space of time: what precedes it or what follows it, we do not know. For this reason if the new lore may bring something more certain and more fitting, it is worthy that we should follow it." The other elders and the king's advisers spoke words of this kind.

Cefi still continued and said that he wanted rather to hear Paulinus the bishop speaking about that god of which he preached. Then the king ordered that such be done. When he heard those words, then he called out and spoke thus: "Readily I have understood it, that it was nothing which we used to worship, for the more I sought the truth itself in that worship, so much less did I find it. Thus I now openly confess that the truth itself shines in this lore, which can give us the gift of eternal blessings and the fortune of eternal life. Therefore I now advise, O king, that the temple and the altars – which we hallowed without benefits of any value – that we swiftly destroy them and let fire burn them up." Behold, then the king began to openly confess to the bishop and to them all that he wished definitely to forsake idol-worship and to receive Christ's faith.

While the king asked and enquired from the aforesaid bishop of the religion which they previously worshipped, as to who should render useless and throw down their idols with their boundaries within which they were set up – [Cefi] then answered "I, indeed! Who may then more readily and more fittingly than I throw down that which I worshipped for so long in error, as an example for other men through the wisdom which I received from the true god?" And he straightaway threw off from himself the empty folly which he previously worshipped and asked the king that he should hand him a weapon and a stallion so that he could get onto it and overthrow the idols, because for the bishop of their religion it was not allowed that he might brandish a weapon nor ride on any (horse) but a mare. Then the king handed him a sword so that he might bind it on himself and he took his spear in his hand and leapt onto the king's steed and travelled to the idol-shrine. When the people saw him so passionate, they then surmised that he was not in his right mind, but rather that he was raving. As soon as he approached the sanctuary, he lunged with the spear so that it stuck fast in the sanctuary and he was rejoicing greatly in the efficacy of the true god's worship, and he asked his companions to overthrow all that sanctuary and the buildings, and to burn them up. The place of the former idol-shrine is still visible, not far east from York city beyond the river Derwent and today it is named "Godmundingaham", where the bishop, through the inspiration of the true god, threw down and destroyed the altar which he himself previously revered.'

The OE text calls Cefi (i.e., Coifi) an *ealdorbisceop* 'elder-bishop' presumably to give the impression that he is a man of some substance within the heathen social structure. Wood (1995, p.258) noted that the Old Saxon *Heliand* describes Caiaphas as a *biscop* as there was no suitable word for 'heathen religious leader' in Old Saxon.[85]

North (1997, pp.333-5) made an interesting suggestion about the name 'Coifi': starting with Bede's Latin form *Coifi*, Alcuin's *Coefi* and the West Saxon *Cefi* as common (not proper) nouns, he proposed that they were derived from Latin *cofium* (or *cofia*) a kind of hood or head-covering. In late Latin it was soldiers' slang for a helmet, and it

---

[85] Perhaps the heathen word would have been too closely associated with the recent Æsir-cult and thus would not have had appropriate resonances for a biblical story.

is the origin of the word 'coif', a mail hood.[86] From this reference to a heathen priest who is characterized by the use of a hood, North made an association with the term *síðhǫttr* 'broad-hat' or perhaps 'long-hood' used of Óðinn in *Grímnismál*. He then related this to the tale of King Edwin above (p.135), and deduced that (i) the king might have made an oath to Woden earlier in his career (cf. the 'mysterious visitor' episode), and then (ii) have taken the female-attired Christian priesthood as a reminder that Woden expected him to make good his promise, while (iii) Paulinus may have worn a *cofia*, and gained the name *Coifi* from that garment, so that (iv) his appearance was described as 'frightening' by a contemporary, Abbot Deda. Whether Edwin really succumbed to the uncertainties of his age and took Paulinus's arrival as a sign that he should convert to the new ways from his heathen past we shall never know. North assembled some impressive evidence, and a movement of religious sentiment away from Ingui towards Woden (and then to Christ) does seem to have taken place in his lifetime. Edwin, as we saw, had already been warned by a stranger in unusual clothing to look out for a sign (his right hand placed on his head) and to heed the advice of the bearer of that omen.

Bede's tale is the best evidence available for a dedicated Germanic priesthood in the early middle ages; in the tales of missionary activity on the continent with its tree-hewing, idol-overthrowing and temple-burning undertaken by men of God, it seems that they were unopposed by any officiants or ministers of the heathen religion (Wilson, 1992, pp.30-1; Wood, 1995, p.257). While Bede is unlikely to have invented the story of Coifi out of his imagination, and because of the mention of tabus on stallions and weapons, it has the ring of truth but sadly, there is little else to corroborate the tale. North cautioned against taking anything Bede had to say at face value, and saw the story of the destruction of the heathen *hearh* as a necessary narrative prelude to the construction of the new church in York, to achieve a balanced tale of destruction of the old customs

---

[86] OE has the derivative term *cuffie* for a snood or head-covering.

and institution of the new faith (North, 1997, pp.12-3). Yet there are strong reasons to give credence to the story of Coifi, whose practical arguments in favour of the new religion seem odd in the mouth of a newly-converted Christian: his speech sounds like the words of a man used to leading the rites in a warrior society in which victory and the rewards which flow from it were of great importance (Tolley, 1995a).[87] Coifi's spear-cast was probably meant to recall the Woden rite in which a spear was launched over an enemy to consign him to destruction – a suitably symbolic gesture for a Woden-priest to make in destroying his own temple (North, 1997, p.330, 339).[88] In *Vǫluspá* (verse 24) the seeress says (text from Dronke, 1997):

Fleygði Óðinn

ok í fólk um skaut –

þat var enn fólkvíg

fyrst í heimi.

'Óðinn threw [the spear] and into the folk he cast [it] – that was the first folk-war in the world.'

It is worth recalling that Bede's Coifi, as a heathen priest, was denied the use of a spear and stallion: this may be seen as a form of ritual or symbolic denial of masculinity, an adoption of emblematic femininity (Hines, 1997, p.380; North, 1997, p.11, pp.330-3).[89] Bede was

---

[87] Bauschatz (1982, ch.5) argued that Coifi's easy acceptance of Christianity was due to the exploratory, receptive, enquiring nature of the Germanic world-view which constantly sought more information about the past in order better to understand the present (the non-past, the past in formation). Coifi's view does not require acceptance of the divinity or eternal nature of Christ, but rather the greater practical utility of accepting biblical doctrine in order to gain more wisdom and deeper insight.

[88] Possibly Edwin owned sacred herds of horses which were housed in Deira, just as Hrafnkel is said to have shared his herd with Freyr in the Icelandic *Hrafnkelssaga*.

[89] The absence of a recognizable heathen priesthood is otherwise assumed, and it may be that Coifi was merely a *seiðmann* or 'wizard'. Grigsby (2005, p.193)

probably not aware in detail of the Roman institution of the *flamen dialis* 'priest of Jupiter' whose life was hedged about with tabus, including prohibitions against riding or even touching horses; looking at an army outside the city walls; sleeping out of his own bed for more than one night; appearing in public without his headdress; wearing rings; having a knot in any of his clothing; touching a dog or bread or flour, and many other aspects of daily life (West, 2007, p.419; Woodard, 2013, p.113). It would be too much to claim that Bede invented Coifi on the basis of the *flamen*, since these two institutions likely derive from a common ancestral attitude, a feeling that the priest must be worthy of meeting his gods and must therefore be properly prepared and untainted for this purpose.

However this is not the only occasion when male 'effeminacy' (lack of male attributes) was associated with supernatural power. The earliest Roman Christian mission to the English under Augustine met with a hostile reaction because the newly-arrived Christian priests were dressed in long, flowing robes (*albæ*), an old Roman male fashion which had since fallen out of use for laymen, but was retained for the clergy. The Kentish king, Æþelberht, is said to have feared them as wizards, which may have been prompted by his association of their 'female' attire with male magicians.[90] A decade previously, Gregory of Tours noted that a Frankish nobleman insinuated that Christian priests wore long robes because, he believed, they were homosexual transvestites, perhaps like the

---

rather placed him among the Vanir priests since he had forsaken his gender-attributes and was forbidden to shed blood or use a male horse.

[90] King Æþelberht had already been married to a Christian Frankish princess for some years before the mission to Kent. Rather than seeing this as a reason to disregard Bede's story on the grounds that the king must have known about Christianity in detail and thus could not have held such a naïve belief about the priesthood, we might perhaps consider that the Frankish bishop, Liudhard, had cultivated an image of menacing supernatural power in order to raise his stature among the heathens of Kent.

later Norse *seiðmenn* (North, 1997, pp.316-7; Price, 2003, pp.212-4).[91] Christian priests in Iceland were considered effeminate and gender-transgressive due to their clothing, and Bishop Friðrekr was accused in a scorn-poem of having given birth to nine children; the alleged 'father' of these children killed the composers of the verse.

Is there literary evidence for Germanic priestly gender-transgression? The priests of the *Naharvali* (or *Nahanarvali*, the texts differ on the spelling) were said by Tacitus (*Germania*, ch.43) to be *muliebri ornatu* – 'ornamented like a woman' or 'decorated like a woman'. There have been many attempts to explain this curious phrase, most of which focus on the hair (Tolley, 2009, p.165). Long and abundant hair was an attribute of female beauty, but it is notable that some male individuals sported long hair: specifically, some of the kings and warriors, the most markedly masculine figures (Kershaw, 2000, p.81). The royal family of the Vandals was called the *Asdingi*, 'the people of the (long) hair', related to the Gothic word *hazd* 'head of hair' with cognates in other Germanic languages (Ward, 1968, p.42, 73-5; Dumézil, 1973; Gunnell, 1995, pp.49-53; Price, 2003, p. 210ff; Grigsby, 2005, p.90).[92] The rider on the Sutton Hoo helmet plates sports a fine head of thick, shoulder-length hair which was carefully depicted – indicating its importance to the figure.

Moreover, the hairstyle or headdress may not be what is intended here. The Latin phrase can mean broadly 'decorated or decked out like a woman': the most notable feature of Germanic female dress is

---

[91] Tolley (2009, p.148) notes that transvestitism was a feature of the shamans of several Asiatic peoples, including the Scythians with whom the early Germanic communities of eastern Europe had close contact.

[92] It is nevertheless possible that a male priest with some symbolic female attributes was part of the fertility rituals. There are enough incidents involving cross-dressing heroes (e.g., Hadding) and gods (e.g., Þórr) to suggest that the idea is indeed very ancient. It may be that in the case of Þórr, it was the adornment of the god's wooden idol with female decorations or attributes which is referred to. Tolley (2009, p.89) notes that in some Asiatic societies the shaman-healer could be male or female but had to be able to merge with the spirits of men, women, birds and beasts.

the richness of their jewellery. Female graves of all Germanic cultural groups typically contain brooches, beads, rings and decorated belts, while males often have little more than a belt-buckle and a knife. The various items of jewellery were glittery, reflective and showy. It therefore seems plausible that what Tacitus meant was that priests of this Germanic tribe were accustomed to wear golden ornaments, similar to those which women wear. Priestly regalia as such has not been recognized in the archaeological record so far, other than possibly in the neck-ring from Pietroasa (Rumania) (Harhoiu, 1977; Pollington, 1995, p.13; Oanţă-Marghitu, 2022), but there are several graves where the skeletal sex appears to be male while the grave-goods include one or more brooches. In an analysis of some Anglo-Saxon archaeological evidence, Knüsel & Ripley (2000) noted that osteologically-male skeletons occurred with female grave-goods with some regularity: Portway (3%); Dover Buckland (4%); Sewerby (6%); Norton (10%).[93] We should not overlook the fact that any kind of ritual garb or insignia is most likely to be curated or handed on in a heathen context, and to be destroyed in a Christian one – only exceptionally would it find its way into a grave.

It has been suggested that Óðinn belonged to a separate, third 'gender' which enabled him to both seduce females and to master the female sorcery, *seiðr*, which it was considered shameful for men to pursue (Glosecki, 1989, pp.96-7; Du Bois, 1999, pp.53-4; Price, 2003, pp.216, 302-5 ; Schjødt, 2008, p.212 ; Tolley, 2009, p.89).[94]

---

[93] There is however a fundamental problem in identifying the gender of the deceased from skeletal material alone. Confidence levels of 96% or greater are achievable when the pelvis and skull are intact; without these indicators, confidence falls sharply away. This factor will affect the basis for gender assignment and, therefore, the evidence for gender transgression (Pollington, Kerr & Hammond, 2010, pp.478-83).

[94] One problem with creating a 'third gender' is that there appears to be only one member of this class: Óðinn. Loki, likewise, must have been considered to have worked this form of magic as he is accused of various kinds of sexual depravity and is the mother of several destructive creatures. That aside, in many Siberian cultures such figures are regarded as a separate gender because the

'Sorcerers' were inherently transgressive or deviant characters who made it their business to ignore social boundaries. Hall saw the situation rather differently: gender-transgression in matters of appearance, he posited, was a characteristic of the 'ritual specialist', the priest, while a man or woman with attributes of the other gender was considered powerful, just as the gods and Otherworld beings who transgressed gender were empowered by the act (Hall, 2007, p.154, pp.159-61).[95] In the Otherworld, magic could be the province of males possessed of ethereal beauty and seductiveness (*ylfe* 'elves'), while warfare could be carried out by loud, weapon-bearing females (*hægtessan* 'witches').

WODEN, HENGEST AND HORSA

Bede does record one fragment of information concerning the position of Woden in establishing the Angles in Britain (Book I, ch.XV text from Colgrave & Mynors, 1969, p.50; cf. Miller, 1890):

> Duces fuisse perhibentur eorum primi duo fratres Hengist et Horsa; e quibus Horsa postea occisus in bello a Brettonibus, hactenus in orientalibus Cantiae partibus monumentum habet suo nomine insigne. Erant autem filii Uictgilsi, cuius pater Uitta, cuius pater Uecta, cuius pater Uoden, de cuius stirpe multarum prouinciarum regium genus originem duxit.

> 'Two brothers are said to have been their first leaders, Hengist and Horsa, [one] of whom, Horsa, was afterwards killed in battle against the Britons, and has a monument in the eastern part of Kent bearing his name to this day. They were furthermore sons of Uihtgilsus, whose father [was] Uitta, whose father [was] Uecta,

---

process of becoming a shaman causes first the destruction of the self, then its reforging, and during this process the old male : female polarity is transcended and finally negated.

[95] ON may have had two conceptual 'genders' - *hvatr* 'bold' and *blauðr* 'soft' - which correspond only approximately to 'male' and 'female'.

whose father [was] Uoden, from whose line the royal family of many 'provinces' is drawn.'

Both Hengest and his brother Horsa were thought to be Woden-sprung and partly divine, although Bede does not mention this aspect of their ancestry and simply notes that many royal families share this ancestral figure (Chambers, 1912, p.33; Ellis Davidson, 1964, pp.169-71; Moisl, 1981, p.235; Shaw, 2002, p.97ff.).[96] Yorke (2015, p.168) notes that the association of a pair of supernatural brothers with the establishment of an ordered society may have been encouraged by iconography relating to Romulus and Remus, which evidently played an important part in the development of kingship in East Anglia. The later 9th c. OE translation of the text follows this model (text from Miller, 1890):

Of Engle comon Eastengle and Middelengle and Mierce and eall Norðhymbra cynn; is þæt land ðe Angulus is genemned, betwuh Geatum and Seaxum; and is sægd of ðære tide þe hie ðanon gewiton oð todæge þæt hit weste wunige. Wæron ærest heora latteowas and heretogan twegen gebroðru, Hengest and Horsa. Hie wæron Wihtgilses suna, þæs fæder wæs Woden nemned, of ðæs strynde monigra mægða cyningcynn fruman lædde.

'From the Angles came the East Angles and Middle Angles and Mercians and all the Northumbrian nation; the land that is called 'Angulus' is between the Geatas and the Saxons, and it is said that from the time when they left until today it remains a wasteland. At first their leaders and warlords were two brothers, Hengest and Horsa. They were Wihtgils's sons, whose father was called Woden, from whose offspring the royal line of many nations traced its origin.'

---

[96] Shaw (2002, p.101) sees the repeated *Wiht-* element as a memory of an ancestral figure who gained the Isle of Wight, in much the same way as a Saxon trio of Port, Stuf and Wihtgar were supposed to have seized the West Saxon territory: Port is clearly a back-formation from *Portesmuða* 'Portsmouth'.

Notably only Wihtgils and Woden are mentioned in this version of the tale. The wording indicates that the two brothers were the first leaders of the Angles, associating the divine name of Woden with Bede's own nation.

CÆDMON

Bede's story of Cædmon centres on the miraculous poetic inspiration which he gained after an evening drinking beer in the communal hall at the Jarrow monastery in Northumbria. Cædmon, a humble layman whose duties included care of the cattle, lacked confidence in his ability to entertain his fellows at the nightly *gebeorscipe* 'drinks party' in the hall where it was the custom for the harp to be passed round among the drinkers for the amusement of the company. Cædmon took to leaving the hall before the harp reached him, wishing that he had the skill and eloquence to join in the entertainment but not wishing to embarrass himself by a poor performance. The OE translation of Bede's Latin original relates the story thus (text from Miller, 1890):[97]

> Þa he þæt þa sumre tide dyde, þæt he forlet þæt hus þæs gebeorscipes, 7 ut wæs gongende to neata scipene, þara heord him wæs þære neahte beboden þa he ða þær in gelimplicre tide his leomu on reste gesette 7 onslepte, þa stod him sum mon æt þurh swefn 7 hine halette 7 grette 7 hine be his noman nemnde:
>
> 'Cedmon, sing me hwæthwugu.'
>
> Þa ondswarede he 7 cwæð: 'Ne con ic noht singan; 7 ic forþon of þeossum gebeorscipe ut eode, 7 hider gewat, forþon ic naht singan ne cuðe.'
>
> Eft he cwæð, se ðe mid hine sprecende wæs: 'Hwæðre þu mcaht singan.'
>
> Þa cwæð he: 'Hwæt sceal ic singan?'

---

[97] The name *Cædmon*, although superficially in agreement with OE rules of word construction, appears to be a British form, *Catumanus*, which may imply that Cædmon's family were of mixed descent.

Cwæð he: 'Sing me frumsceaft.'

Þa he ða þas andsware onfeng, þa ongon he sona singan in herenesse Godes Scyppendes þa fers 7 þa word þe he næfre gehyrde, þara endebyrdnes þis is:

'Nu sculon herigean heofonrices Weard, / Meotodes meahte 7 his modgeþanc, / weorc Wuldorfæder, swa he wundra gehwæs, / ece Drihten, or onstealde. / He ærest sceop eorðan bearnum / heofon to hrofe halig Scyppend; / þa middangeard monncynnes Weard, / ece Drihten, æfter teode / firum foldan, Frea ælmihtig.'

One time when he did that – he left the house of the beer-drinking and started to go out to the shed with the cattle whose care was assigned to him for that night – he laid his body into rest at the appropriate time and fell asleep, then a certain man stood by him in his dream, and hailed and greeted him and named him by his name.

"Cædmon, sing something to me."

Then he answered and said "I cannot sing anything, and I went out from this beer-drinking and came here because I did not know how to sing anything."

He who spoke with him said again: "Yet you are able to sing."

Then he said: "What must I sing?"

He said: "Sing the original creation to me."

When he received this answer, he began straightaway to sing in praise of God the Creator those verses and those words which he had never heard before, of which this is the arrangement:

"Now we must praise the Keeper of heaven, / the Measurer's might and his mind's thought, / the Glory-father's work as for each wonder he, / the everlasting Lord, set the beginning. / He first made the earth for men, / heaven as a roof – the holy shaper – / then Middle-earth mankind's keeper, / the everlasting Lord made thereafter, / the world for men – the almighty Lord."

The events described in this tale would have taken place towards the end of the 7th century, among people who grew up in predominantly pre-Christian communities. The verse shows no specifically Christian features, since all the names and kennings for 'God' are plausibly drawn from pre-Christian tradition: 'keeper of the kingdom of heaven', 'holy creator', 'measurer', etc. The unnamed supernatural visitor was able to inspire Cædmon with the power of verse composition, one of the attributes of Óðinn in Norse tradition (cf. the portion which was lost when Óðinn won it from Suttungr). Like Edwin's mysterious visitor who turned his life around, Cædmon's inquisitor induced a change of fortune for the lay brother.

ANGLO-SAXON (OLD ENGLISH) GLOSSARIES

The 8th c. Anglo-Saxon *Corpus Glossary* (Corpus Christi College Cambridge MS144) – a listing of Latin words with their OE equivalents - gives the equation *mercurium : woden*; this term is not found in the *Épinal-Erfurt Glosses* which are the likely sources of much of the *Corpus* document (Pheifer, 1974; Sweet, 1978, p.61; see also Shaw, 2002, p.92).[98] That the Latin *mercurium* (acc.sing.) could be glossed by OE *woden* suggests that similarities between these figures were already apparent at this time, or perhaps somewhat earlier if the *Corpus* document represents the concatenation of the *Épinal-Erfurt* material with glosses drawn from other documents, no longer extant. However, the inspiration for the gloss may yet be found in the pre-existing correlation between the respective day-names (*dies Mercurii* – *Wednesdæg*) (p.72).

---

[98] But Erfurt (item 383) includes the word *uuoda* glossing *ep[h]ilenticus* 'madman' and (388) *woediberge* for *elleborus* 'hellebore' in the sense of 'maddening berry'.

EDDIUS STEPHANUS: VITA SANCTI WILFRITHI

The *Life of St. Wilfrid* is included in a compendium of sources relating to the early history of the Northumbrian church which also incorporates works on St. Cuthbert and St. Columba and Bede's *Ecclesiastical History of the English Nation*. It is found in two manuscripts: Cotton Vespasian D.vi. in the British Library, and the Bodleian's Fell vol. III 34a-56b; both are 11th-12th c. documents. Authorship is attributed to 'Stephanus, presbyter' or 'Stephen of Ripon'. Bede states that the saint brought a singing teacher from Kent to Ripon named Æddi Stephanus, whence the two instances of the name 'Stephen' have usually been assumed to refer to the same man although this is far from certain.

Wilfrith's (or Wilfrid's) turbulent and colourful life is described in the text, written shortly after his death in 709 AD. The work is a rare contemporary source to that of Bede, who used parts of it when writing about Wilfrid himself, but which offers a different view of the events surrounding the Synod of Whitby in 664 AD and other matters (text from Colgrave, 1927; cf. Webb, 1965). It contains remarkably few of the stock miraculous incidents of early medieval hagiography but does offer an insight into the politics of the Northumbrian court in the later 7th and early 8th centuries.

One incident has some relevance to the matter of Woden. In ch.13, Wilfrid was returning to Britain from Gaul with a group of clerics when bad weather drove them onto the coast of Sussex (*Australium Saxonum*), which was at that time not yet Christian-dominated. Once the ship had run aground on a tidal beach, the locals came out to salvage the wreck and seize the travellers, who numbered 120. Wilfrid took charge and led a spirited opposition to this attack. The chief heathen priest (*princeps sacerdotum idolatriae*) climbed onto the top of a barrow in order to 'curse God's people and to bind their hands with his magical skills' (*maledicere populum dei et suis magicis artibus manus eorum alligare*), but one of Wilfred's men threw a stone at the priest's head and killed him. The Christians were rescued from further distress by the unnaturally early arrival of the incoming tide which refloated their ship and allowed them to escape.

The episode is peppered with biblical references in the Latin text (Balaam, Pharaoh, Goliath, etc.) and appears to have little to say in detail about the religion of the South Saxons except for the notion that the nameless priest was using his powers to bind the limbs of the travellers – a magical act associated with Woden-Óðinn in other sources (p.371, 409). It is also significant that he ascended a high mound or barrow (*in tumulo excelsio*) to achieve this – prominent high places and especially burial mounds form a large part of the milieu for Woden's magic.

BEOWULF

The manuscript in which the single surviving text of *Beowulf* survives – the Nowell Codex – was copied at some date around 1000 – 1010 AD (Neidorf, 2016; contra Chase, 1981). The scribes who undertook this project worked from an existing (thus, older) manuscript which was a copy – probably itself a copy of an unknown series of copies – with a date of original composition in the early 8th century AD. As Neidorf (2014, p.1) notes: 'Scholarship on the dating of *Beowulf* is markedly uneven in quality: alongside sober and thoughtful argumentation, there has been a great deal of improbable hypothesizing about the author of the poem or the milieu in which it was composed.'

The story of Beowulf is important because it is the only surviving complete example in Old English of an epic poem but, frustratingly, the poet assumes in the audience a detailed knowledge of the events he relates and the political and social milieu in which they took place. The deficiency lies, of course, more in the surviving evidence and the modern reader's understanding of it than in the poet's presentation. Clearly the stories alluded in *Beowulf* were part of a lively and very rich oral tradition which was shared by Anglo-Saxon and Scandinavian societies, drawing on a store of legends and folktales of which only a little is known to survive (Neidorf, 2017b, p.439).

The presence of pre-Christian ideas and practices in the poem has long been known. The absences of churches, clergy, coinage, taxation and literacy all argue for a setting in the pre-Christian period, while details such as ring-hilted and pattern-welded swords imply a date at the end of that era – so, the 5th-7th c. The single datable event in the poem – the Geatish raid on the Frisian coast which took place around 520 AD – fits rather neatly with the historical documentation (Chambers, 1963, pp.2-4, 269; Neidorf, 2014, pp.41-3; Shippey, 2022, pp.7-9).[99]

One aspect of Beowulf's story which the poet refers to without comment is his prodigious size and strength: this is remarked upon when the hero first steps ashore in Denmark (ll.286-9), and periodically thereafter. He has the strength of thirty men (text from Fulk et al., 2008, ll.379-81)

> ...   þæt hē þrītiges
>
> manna mægencræft   on his mundgripe
>
> heaþorōf hæbbe.

'... that he, active in warfare, may have thirty men's might in his hand-grip'

He is furthermore described as *æðele 7 ēacen* in l.198, where *ēacen* means 'enlarged, increased in size; augmented' with a suggestion of some supernatural quality (Kershaw, 2000, p.82).[100] Yet for all his size, he is no lumbering brute and he manages to impress the Danes as much with his courteous manners and skilful speech as with his prowess at fighting (Neidorf, 2022c).

---

[99] Some scholars believe that the actual date may be put a little later, perhaps closer to 530 AD.

[100] The Irish hero, Cú Chulainn, is similarly prodigious and furthermore undergoes a physical transformation which renders him both hot to the touch and grotesque.

THE OLD SPEAR-FIGHTER

The presence in the poem of a transgressive Woden-like (or Woden-inspired) figure has been noted by a few commentators, not always in overt terms (Neidorf, 2022c). The character is simply referred to as *eald æscwiga* 'an old warrior' or more properly 'an old man with a spear'. The context is the so-called 'Tale of Ingeld' which forms one of the poem's digressions, but it is not narrated as a simple story with the salient events in the expected sequential order (Malone, 1959, pp.2-62). Rather, the reader must piece together the evidence from a mix of loose allusions. The sequence appears to be as follows (I rely here on the discussions of Tolkien [2014, pp.324-50] and Shippey [2022, pp.38-43]):

The king of the Danes at the time of Beowulf's visit is Hroþgar, with his younger brother Halga as co-regent; they are both sons of the late king, Healfdene. Hroþgar has two sons, Hreðric and Hroðmund, both still quite young, while also at Hroþgar's court at the Danes' major cult-site, Hleðra, is Hroþwulf, the son of Halga, already a grown man. (An elder brother, Heorugar, does not figure in this tale.) The Danes inhabit the region of Skåne in (modern) southwest Sweden and the adjacent islands including Zealand. To the south of the Danish lands are many rival tribes, including Saxons in the Elbe-Weser coastal region, and Beardan (or Heaðobeardan) who inhabit the Bardowiek area, the Ilmenau valley near the River Elbe. The Beardan once controlled the offshore cult-site at Hleðra (Lejre) on Zealand until Healfdene seized it as part of his Danish expansion. The king of the Heaðobeardan at that time was Froda, named after a mythic or legendary ancestor.

A long-lasting rivalry had thus developed between the Danes and the Beardan. After the death of King Healfdene, the Beardan attacked Hleðra and regained it temporarily; King Froda was killed in this foray. Froda's son, Ingeld, then held a personal grudge against Hroþgar whom he blamed for his father's death and the diminution of his authority. Meanwhile, Hroþgar prospered and decided to build a large feasting hall, in keeping with his ambitious nature. At some point, Ingeld visited the hall (named Heorot) and, despite his desire for vengeance, fell for the gracious Danish princess, Freawaru. Whether Ingeld's attitude towards Hroþgar softened then, or whether the old king saw a chance to capitalise on the prince's change of heart, a betrothal was arranged between Ingeld and Freawaru. The wedding ceremony was to take place at the court of the Beardan. Freawaru and a troop of Danes travelled to Bardowiek to formalise the wedding. The ceremony went ahead, but the king's good intentions were thwarted by an *eald æscwiga* 'old warrior with a spear'. The event was initially peaceful, but old resentments were simmering on both sides. Beowulf later reports this to his lord, Hygelac, with a deal of scepticism about the likelihood of success:

Weorod wæs on wynne;   ne seah ic wīdan feorh

under heofones hwealf   healsittendra

medudrēam māran.   Hwīlum mǣru cwēn,

friðusibb folca   flet eall geondhwearf,

bǣdde byre geonge;   oft hīo bēahwriðan

secge (sealde)   ǣr hīe tō setle gēong.

Hwīlum for (d)uguðe   dohtor Hrōðgāres

eorlum on ende   ealuwǣge bær;

þā ic Frēaware   fletsittende

nemnan hȳrde,   þǣr hīo (næ)gled sinc

hæleðum sealde.   Sīo gehāten (is),

geong, goldhroden   gladum suna Frōdan;

(h)afað þæs geworden   wine Scyldinga,

rīces hyrde,   ond þæt rǣd talað,

þæt hē mid ðȳ wife   wælfǣhða dǣl,

sæcca gesette.   Oft seldan hwǣr

æfter lēodhryre   lȳtle hwīle

bongār būgeð,   þēah sēo brȳd duge.

Beowulf, ll.2014-31

'The troop was joyous. I have not seen in my long life under the vault of heaven a greater mead-bliss among hall-dwellers. At times the remarkable lady, the peace-pledge of the nations, passed through the whole floor of the hall and urged on a youngster; often she gave a braided arm-ring to a retainer before she returned to her seat. The daughter of Hroðgar bore to the warriors in turn a goblet of ale for the veterans.

I heard a hall-companion name her 'Freawaru' when she gave a riveted jewel to some worthy warriors. She is promised – young and gold-adorned – to the lucky son of Froda. The lord of the Scyldings – the keeper of the kingdom – has brought this about and reckons it good advice, so that through the woman he may settle a deal of feuding and of fighting. Generally, it seldom happens that the deadly spear rests for even a short while after the fall of a leader, even though the bride may be fitting.'

Beowulf foresees trouble arising from such a match, due to the need for men to share drink in a hall together when they were, till recently, deadly foes on the battlefield.

Mæg þæs þonne ofþyncan   ðēoden Heaðo-Beardna

ond þegna gehwām   þāra lēoda,

þonne hē mid fǣmnan   on flett gǣð,

dryhtbearn Dena,   duguða biwenede.

On him gladiað   gomelra lāfe,

heard ond hringmǣl   Heaða-Bear[d]na gestrēon,

þenden hīe ðām wǣpnum   wealdan mōston –

oð ðæt hīe forlǣddan   tō ðām lindplegan

swǣse gesīðas   ond hyra sylfra feorh.

Þonne cwið æt bēore   sē ðe bēah gesyhð,

eald æscwiga,   sē ðe eall ge(man),

gārcwealm gumena   – him bið grim (se)fa –

onginneð geōmormōd   geong(um) cempan

þurh hreðra gehygd   higes cunnian,

wīgbealu weccean,   ond þæt word ācwyð:

"Meaht ðū, mīn wine,   mēce gecnāwan,

þone þīn fæder   tō gefeohte bær

under heregrīman   hindeman sīðe,

dȳre īren,   þǣr hyne Dene slōgon,

wēoldon wælstōwe,   syððan Wiðergyld læg,

æfter hæleþa hryre,   hwate Scyldungas?

Nū hēr þāra banena   byre nāthwylces

frætwum hrēmig   on flet gǣð,

morðres gylpe(ð),   ond þone māðþum byreð,

þone þe ðū mid rihte   rǣdan sceoldest."

Manað swā ond myndgað   mǣla gehwylce

sārum wordum,   oð ðæt sǣl cymeð

þæt se fǣmnan þegn   fore fæder dǣdum

æfter billes bite   blōdfāg swefeð,

ealdres scyldig;   him se ōðer þonan

losað (li)figende,   con him land geare.

þonne bīoð (āb)rocene   on bā healfe

āðsweord eorla;   (syð)ðan Ingelde

weallað wælnīðas,   ond him wīflufan

æfter cearwælmum   cōlran weorðað.

Þȳ ic Heaðo-Beardna   hyldo ne telge.

Beowulf, ll.2032-67

'This then may offend the lord of the Heaðobeards and many a thane of both those nations, when a noble scion of the Danes walks across the hall-floor with the maiden, surrounded by warriors on whom glitter the heirloom weapons of their own ancestors, the hard and ring-adorned treasures which belonged to the Heaðobards while they could wield their weapons - until they brought their beloved companions to ruin in the shield-play, and their own lives.

Then one who spots a ring speaks over his beer - an old spear-fighter who remembers well the war-death of fighters; his mood is grim. With a cruel heart he begins to test the courage of a young warrior, to reawaken war-hatred through his mind's cunning thought, so he speaks these words: "My friend, are you able to recognise that sword - that precious weapon – which your father wearing his war-mask bore to battle for the last time, where those Danes slew him? They had rule of the battlefield once Wiþergield the brave Scylding lay dead after the fall of the heroes. Now the son of one of them strides here on the hall-floor, proud in his prized belongings; he boasts of the murder and carries that heirloom which by rights you should possess." He eggs him on then and reminds him of it in every conversation with painful words, until the time comes that the lady's retainer shall die soaked in blood after the sword's stroke because of his father's deeds – he pays with his life; the other one gets away alive from there as he knows the land well. Then the oaths sworn by leaders shall be broken by both sides, once deadly hatred wells up in Ingeld and his love for his wife becomes the cooler after that surge of sorrow. Hence I do not count on the good faith of the Heaðobards.'

Matters get out of hand, which leads Ingeld to set aside his wife and mount an armed attack on his father-in-law's stronghold. The attack fails, and Ingeld dies in the fighting.

An early reference to this appears in *Widsith*. The action takes place at Heorot and involves Ingeld's attack which Hroðgar and Hroþwulf, his nephew, manage to repel. (Hroðgar's own sons were at this time too young to play a decisive role in the fighting.)

> Hrōþwulf ond Hrōðgār   hēoldon lengest
>
> sibbe ætsomne   suhtorfædran,
>
> siþþan hȳ forwrǣcon   Wīcinga cynn
>
> ond Ingeldes   ord forbīgdan,
>
> forhēowan aet Heorote   Heaðo-Beardna þrym.

Widsith ll.45-9

'Hroðulf and Hroðgar held the peace together, uncle and nephew, for the longest time once they drove off the kin of the Wick-men [=Beardan] and felled Ingeld's vanguard, cut down the Heaðobards' forces at Heorot.'

The role of the *eald æscwiga* in fomenting hatred where there should be peace and friendship is certainly characteristic of Woden in the legends (Neidorf, 2011, pp.8-9). In Saxo's account of the story of Ingellus (Ingeld), this disruptive figure is identified as Starcatherus (i.e., ON Starkaðr), a noted trouble-maker who was a favourite of Óðinn but a foe of Þórr. He was granted a triple life-span by his patron, during which time he travelled widely and met many great leaders, inciting strife between friends and kinsmen. Ingeld is urged on by his follower to turn against his in-laws and attempt to bring about their downfall; this rebounds on him and he meets an early and inglorious death as a result. The resonances with the careers and fates other Woden-favoured champions are obvious.

UNFERÞ THE ÞYLE

The text of *Beowulf* also refers to an important court functionary called in OE a *þyle* – this is the office ascribed to the character Unferþ, who challenges the Geatish hero on his arrival at the Danish court (Neidorf, 2017a, p.439; 2022, p.9). The poet has only a little to say about Unferþ, and what he does say has proved difficult for the modern reader to interpret (Liberman, 2016, pp.386-94; Neidorf, 2017a, p.440). Unferth embodies both positive and negative qualities in a way which defies attempts at simple characterisation:[101] 'sneering evil counsellor', for example, or 'pompous and overbearing court official' or 'bragging henchman' but also 'champion and guardian of the king's reputation'. From his capacity to speak for King Hroþgar at the Danish court, it is evident that Unferþ has an important position and uses this prestige to belittle Beowulf's previous misadventure, yet we learn from the hero's riposte that Unferþ (i) has no cause to boast since he has failed to stop Grendel and (ii) is widely known to have done away with his own brothers (*þeah ðu þinum broðrum to banan wurde* (l.587) 'though you became the killer of your brothers'). There are also dark suggestions about his role in later internecine strife at the court. These negative indications have to be set beside (i) the evident favour that he receives from King Hroþgar (...*Unferþ þyle æt fotum sæt frean Scyldinga* (ll.1165-6) 'Unferth the þyle sat at the feet of the lord of the Scyldings'); (ii) his ownership of a famous and trusty sword, Hrunting, suitable for a hero; (iii) his chivalrous decision to yield at Beowulf's retort; and (iv) his later to offer to lend the sword to Beowulf.

Kin-slaying was evidently regarded as a heinous sin in both Christian and pre-Christian tradition; the slaying of Abel by his brother Cain is cited by the poet as the source of all monsters in the

---

[101] Attempts have been made to treat Unferþ as a cypher, a 'standard baddy', whose character is signalled by the association of his name with the noun *unfriþ* 'discord, hostility'. Yet his name is drawn from tradition and evidently ancient, despite being modified by one or more scribes to *Hunferþ* (Neidorf, 2017a, p.442) perhaps by association with a famed sword named *Hunlafing* (l.1143).

world (l.108). Yet elsewhere in early Germanic literature, it may happen that a man is put into a position where he must make such a choice – Hildebrand is called upon to fight his own son Hadubrand, for example, in the OHG poem *Hildebrandslied* (Harris, 1988). In historical tradition, the *ASC* MS 'A' entry for the year 755 sets out in some detail the mini-saga relating to the struggle between King Cynewulf of the West Saxons and his kinsman Cyneheard, and the decisions of their respective retinues to join them in death rather than abandon their friends or leader. Later, Harold Godwineson's brother, Tostig, raised a coalition of enemies in 1066 AD against his brother in an attempt to seize the throne. Gregory of Tours's *Historia Francorum* is replete with tales of murderous kinsmen in the Merovingian royal family. There is no shortage of similar examples, from which we may conclude that storytellers were rather taken with the theme of a situation from which a hero could not escape with both his honour and his life, and in which the need to kill a trusted friend or relative was part of his dilemma (Neidorf, 2022c, ch.1).

That Unferþ had behaved dishonourably towards kinsmen who trusted him appears to conflict with Hroþgar's evident reliance upon him. It is clear that some backstory was attached to his name, and the frequent references to his father Ecglaf strengthen this (Neidorf, 2022c, p.44). The charge of fratricide was apparently well-founded, but Unferþ was not a minor character nor a negligible one: his annoyance at the arrival of the Geatish hero (ll.501-5) suggests that he was accustomed to being accorded the greatest respect, and saw the newcomer as a threat, someone likely to overshadow and outdo him. Unferþ's sword is explicitly praised because *næfre hit æt hilde ne swac* (l.1460) 'it never failed in battle' and *næs þæt forma sið þæt hit ellenweorc æfnan scolde* (ll.1463-4) 'that was not the first time when it had to accomplish a deed of valour' with the implication that its present owner was capable of performing such deeds. Beowulf's superiority to Unferþ in both physical strength and in moral judgement is included to highlight the hero's unparalleled worth rather than the failings of his challenger. Unferþ, we may conclude, was put in a position whereby his oath of service entailed his killing of kinsmen, and this was the effect of having sworn loyalty to a lord without being able to foresee the consequences. By killing his brothers, Unferþ both fulfilled an overriding commitment and overturned the moral order of ordinary members of society. The pre-Christian hero might be expected to choose between alternatives which were both or all highly unpalatable and disreputable, while the Christian tradition only offered a choice between the simple binary 'good' and 'evil' (Neidorf, 2022c, p.45). Thus, Unferþ may be seen in the light of the 'transgressive hero' figure – the very type of follower who might be associated with Woden.

ÞYLE – RITUAL SPECIALIST?

The OE word *þyle* glosses Latin terms such as *orator* 'spokesman' and *scurra* 'satirist' (Liberman, 2016, p.390). Our only detailed evidence for the duties of a *þyle* is the behaviour of Unferþ at Hroðgar's court, where he appears as a kind of 'prosecutor' whose function it is to query and question the applicant's credentials and motives (Bauschatz, 1982, ch.4; Enright, 1996; Herschend, 1998). Verbal duelling is a commonplace of heroic narrative in many cultures, but Unferþ appears also to have an authority which might derive ultimately from a role in cult worship, making the *þyle* also the leader of group rituals (Baird, *Unferth the Þyle* cited in Gardner, 1975). The office of *þyle* can be perhaps interpreted as 'priest of Woden' and thus ritual spokesman for the group. The Scandinavian equivalent term, *þulr* 'storyteller, lore-keeper, ritual specialist', certainly denotes an association with religious tales and gnomic wisdom. The basic sense seems to be the Germanic root **þul-* 'mumble, talk, sing, intone, chant'; a *þyle* could be an orator or a leader of rituals, but he might also be an entertainer or 'user of words' for specific purposes (Glosecki, 1989, p.49; Brink, 1996).

All things considered, the figure of the *þyle* must thus be taken as more than a 'champion' or 'master of ceremonies', though combining elements of both these functions. Hroþgar's *þyle* had something of the air of a 'priest' about him, a devotee of the war-god who lived for his reputation, but knew he would have to lose it to a better man in later life when his powers began to fail. He may have been a 'ritual specialist' who knew all the appropriate verbal formulas and was perhaps involved in the initiation of youngsters into the cult of Woden (Sundqvist, 2015, p.133) and in acquiring the skills and knowledge which he would need to succeed in the world of strategy and statecraft (Pollington, 2016, p.251).[102] The cognate ON term *þulr* certainly has echoes of such duties, as well as an ongoing role of confidante and adviser to the leader. An association with induction into knowledge and worship of the gods does not seem fanciful in this context. Interestingly, a Roman-period place-name in modern Lower Saxony is mentioned by Ptolemy; called *Tulifurdum*, presumably **Þulifurðan* / **-furðuz* 'ford of the sage', a passage over the River Leine named for a *þyle* (Mees, 2023, p.55).

Story, verse and song were important in a preliterate society as the means of recalling the past in order to interpret the present, of orienting society in harmony with the flow of events, of contextualising and commemorating great deeds. Thus, famous names outlived their owners, great men and women overcame the limits of their own mortality.

In early Anglo-Saxon society, the position of *scop* 'poet, storyteller' might also be bound up with religious practices and the poet's words were charged with oracular power – especially if he had been in communion with the gods through the use of alcohol or other entheogens (Glosecki, 1989, p.69ff). Cædmon, for example, had to withdraw from the beer-hall because he could not sing appropriately – this may mean that the verbal art of composition was accompanied by some traditional musical techniques (e.g., rhythmic strumming or tapping) which induced trance-like states of concentration in the participants.

Formal speech had a numinous quality: it could bind present deeds into the past, as much as it could bring the past into active contact

---

[102] The Brussels Codex glosses the term *rethorica* (i.e., rhetoric, motivating or persuasive speech) with *þelcræft* (i.e., *þylcræft*, the special skill of the *þyle*).

with the present. Often, individuals are referenced by ancestral kinsmen – *Ecgðeowes sunu* 'son of Ecgðeo' is mentioned alongside the
personal name Beowulf – in order to situate the speaker in the context
of the past of his kindred and their deeds and obligations. Terms such
as *gielpword* 'tale of success' and *beotword* 'tale of an oath fulfilled' imply
a happy outcome, a worthy deed successfully achieved. Both represent the positive interface of 'word and deed' (Bauschatz, 1982, ch.4).

Also worth noting is the poet's use of the *stæf* – a staff, a term
which can describe a pole or stick when it is used as a support or
weapon, but which also denotes a 'stave', a unit of verse. OE rec-
ognizes several kinds of *stafas* 'staves' including *runstafas* 'rune-staves,
runic letters', *bocstafas* 'book-staves, written letters', *gliwstafas* 'glee-
staves, melodies, incantations, charms' (Glosecki, 1989, pp.88-9) –
as well as *fācenstafas* 'deeds of treachery'. Like the modern 'rod, pole
or perch' it was also presumably a unit of measurement and may be
related to the *sceaftmund* or fixed unit of layout for building construction (Mortimer & Pollington, 2013, p.119). Verse was
constructed from *stafas* just like masonry or brickwork.

INDICULUS SUPERSTITIONUM ET PAGANIARUM

The late 8th or 9th c. manuscript (Codex Palatinus Latinus 577) of
this text, 'A Small Index of Superstitions and Pagan Practices' also
contains the *Old Saxon Baptismal Vow* (Gallee, 1864; Pertz, 1835;
McNeill & Gamer, 1938, pp.419-21). The text was discovered in
the 17th c. by Bishop Ferdinand von Fürstenburg of Paderborn in
the Vatican library and published in *Monumenta Paderbornensia* at
Amsterdam in 1672. The manuscript is written in a late 8th c. insular
continental hand, but some folios (1 recto to 73 recto) are in an
insular Anglo-Saxon hand.

The work is a collection of superstitious practices and beliefs
summarised in Latin and was perhaps compiled to assist missionaries
in detecting aberrant or sacrilegious beliefs and customs among the
rural population, with a view to correcting them. The early association of the text with the forced conversion of the Old Saxons by

Charlemagne in the late 8th c. has been controversial and is still disputed; an alternative interpretation connects it with the missionary work of the English missionary Boniface who was active in the first half of the 8th c. (Kolner, 2018).

The list includes some terms which are difficult to interpret, for example the second item (text from Pertz, 1835):

De sacrilegio super defunctos id est 'dadsisas'

'concerning sacreligious acts over the dead, which is "dadsisas".'

What are these practices connected to the dead? Some have taken them to be graveside feasts or communal meals in celebration of the life of the dead person – a common practice in pre-Christian times, for which there is sometimes archaeological evidence in the form of the remains of joints of meat in the grave-cut, etc. The word *dadsisas* appears to comprise *dad* 'dead; a corpse' and an element perhaps related to *sess*- 'settle, lay to rest'. Alternatively, it might refer to the singing of a eulogy over the corpse in praise of the life now extinguished – here we may think of the phrase in *Beowulf* (l.1117) at the funeral of Hnæf where his sister, Hildeburh, laid both her brother and her son on the same funeral pyre:

... Ides gnornode,

geōmrode giddum.   ...

'the lady mourned, lamented with songs.'

Similar practices occurred at the erecting of the memorial grave-mound over Beowulf himself (ll.3150-2):

swylce giōmorgyd   (Gē)at(isc) meowle

(æfter Bīowulfe   b)undenheorde

(sang) sorgcearig   ...

'likewise a Geatish maiden with her hair bound up sorrowfully sang a lament for Beowulf.'

A formal declaration of sorrow and loss is a fitting part of a leader's funeral ceremony. Item 6 on the list is:

De sacris silvarum quae nimidas vocant

'Concerning holy [things/acts] of the woods which are called "nimidas"'

The Old Saxon word *nimid* is related to the Celtic *nemeton* 'holy ground' and evidently refers to the stands of sacred trees which were venerated by the ancients (Green, 1998, p.26; Pollington, 2011, p.212). This element evokes Tacitus's statement about the sacred woodland of the Semnones and the creator-god who was thought to reside there. The *Indiculus's* eighth item relates specifically to veneration of the gods:

De sacris Mercurii vel Iovis

'Concerning the sacred rites of Mercury or of Jove.'

Here we must assume that Mercury stands for Wotan and Jove (Jupiter) either for Ziu (Tiw, Týr) or perhaps Donar (Þunor, Þórr) but we have no indication of what these holy rites may have been, although item 20 relates to

De feriis quae faciunt Iovi vel Mercurio

'Concerning the festival days which they make for Jove or Mercury.'

The Latin *feria* can mean 'weekday' but also has the extended meaning 'festival, celebration', implying a time set aside for religious observances and perhaps for social gatherings. Also potentially relevant is the tenth item:

De filacteriis et ligaturis

'Concerning amulets and knots.'

Knots have been used as a form of supernatural protection for millennia. The obvious association is with Woden's power to bind and loose his enemies, called in ON the *herfjǫturr*. Beyond this, interlace and braiding are recurrent motifs in pre-Christian Germanic art and clearly had great symbolic importance (Pollington, 2011, pp.432-3).

THE LOMBARD SOURCES II

PAUL THE DEACON: HISTORIA LANGOBARDORUM

Paul the Deacon's *Historia Langobardorum* (History of the Lombards) was written in the last years of the 8th century (probably completed by 796 AD), in which the cleric ties Godan (Woden) into the early history of his tribe (Malone, 1959, pp.86-107; Turville-Petre, 1964, p.72; Shaw, 2002, p.74; Ausenda, Delogu & Wickham, 2009; Kay, 2013, p.16) (text from Waitz, 1878):

> Refert hoc loco antiquitas ridiculam fabulam: quod accedentes Wandali ad Godan victoriam de Winnilis postulaverint, illeque respondit, se illis victoriam daturum quos primum oriente sole conspexisset. Tunc accessisse Gambara ad Fream, uxorem Godan, et Winnilis victoriam postulasse, Freaque consilium dedisse, ut Winnilorum mulieres solutos crines erga faciem ad barbae similitudinem conponerent maneque primo cum viris adessent seseque Godan videndas pariter e regione, qua ille per fenestram orientem versus erat solitus aspicere, conlocarent. Atque ita factum fuisse. Quas cum Godan oriente sole conspiceret, dixisse: 'Qui sunt isti longibarbi?' Tunc Frea subiunxisse, ut quibus nomen tribuerat victoriam condonaret. Sicque Winnilis Godan victoriam concessisse. Haec risui digna sunt et pro nihilo habenda. Victoria enim non potestati est adtributa hominum, sed de caelo potius ministratur.

> 'Antiquity at this point relates a laughable tale: that the Vandals, approaching Godan, asked [him] for victory over the Winniles and he replied that he would give victory to those whom he saw first at sunrise. Then Gambara approached Frea, Godan's wife, and [separately] asked for victory for the Winniles, and Frea gave [her] advice that the women of the Winniles should put their

unbound hair before their faces in the likeness of beards and should be present in the morning with their menfolk and should assemble in that place where Godan would look out from his window to the east. This was carried out so. When Godan saw them at sunrise, he said: "Who are these 'long-beards'?" Then Frea interjected that to those to whom he had attributed a name, he should allocate victory [as a naming-gift]. With this, Godan granted victory to the Winniles. These claims are ridiculous and should be counted for naught. Victory should not be attributed to men, therefore, but is administered from heaven.'

Paul, a pious Christian cleric, could not endorse the tale of a victory-bringing heathen god, but the tradition was important enough to the Lombards to be worth recording at some length. Godan is depicted here as a typical Germanic nobleman with a wife, Frea, and a dwelling with at least one window looking to the east; by reminding the reader that the narrative is ridiculous because 'men' cannot bestow victory, only the Christian god, Paul was framing the story as a simple folktale of no seriousness.[103] Paul claimed to have derived his tale from a Lombard tradition, which appears in the *Origo Gentis Langobardum* (Malone, 1959, pp.86-107; Shaw, 2002, p.114) where the Vandal leaders are named as Ambri and Assi, and the Lombards are saved by the quick thinking of the seeress Gambara and her two sons, Ybor and Agio.[104] Frea agrees to help them and turns the bed of her husband, Wodan, round to face the east; when Wodan wakes he does not realise the stratagem, but immediately asks about the identity of those 'longbeards' he can see from his window and is then honour-bound to supply a gift (victory) to accompany the newly-bestowed name.

---

[103] The tradition whereby the god and his wife are advocates of opposed human characters is repeated in the Norse tale of Agnar and Geirrøðr in *Grímnismál*.

[104] 'Gambara' is usually interpreted as from *gand-* 'wand, staff' and *bera* 'bearer', so 'the lady with the wand'. 'Ybor' is from *eburaz* 'boar', often used as a synonym for 'hardy warrior'. 'Agio' appears to be from *agjō* 'edge, blade' used of a sword (Orel, 2003). These names all seem to relate to the Vanir.

In the *Historia* (ch.5) the text states that *Audoin ex genere fuit Gausus* '(King) Audoin was of the kindred of Gausus'. The exact connection is disputed between this Langobardic *Gausus,* the mythic ancestor, and Gothic *Gapt,* OE *Geat* and other related forms. While *Gautr* surely appears as a byname of Óðinn in Norse tradition, it seems likely that we are dealing here with an originally separate deity who was later subsumed in the cult of the main war-god.

Paul's own background was aristocratic – he was born with the given personal name Winifrid, a son of a nobleman called Warnefrid – and he may well have learned the traditional stories of his people before accepting his religious calling. But as a deacon, Paul felt obliged to add further information in order to distance his story from Christian lore (text from Dümmler, 1881, *XIV Versus Pauli Diaconi*; Robinson, 1992, pp.224-5; Shaw, 2002, pp.77-8; cf. Kay, 2013, p.17):

> Certum tamen est, Langobardos ab intactae ferro barbae longitudine, cum primitus Winili dicti fuerint, ita postmodum appellatos. Nam iuxta illorum linguam lang longam, bard barbam significat. Wotan sane, quem adiecta littera Godan dixerunt, ipse est qui apud Romanos Mercurius dicitur et ab universis Germaniae gentibus ut deus adoratur; qui non circa haec tempora, sed longe anterius, nec in Germania, sed in Grecia fuisse perhibetur.

> 'Moreover it is certain, that the Langobards, who were first called Winniles,[105] were later named thus due to the length of their beards untouched by iron. Because according to their speech 'lang' means 'long' and 'bart' 'beard'. In truth Wotan, whom they called 'Godan' with the addition of one letter, is the same one as is called Mercurius among the Romans and is worshipped

---

[105] The name is explained by reference to the modern German word *winnig* 'howling (with rage)' by which logic the Winniles are 'the howling (men)' (Kershaw, 2000, p.142-3). Elsewhere in the work of Paul, there is a tradition of *cynocephali* 'dog-headed men' among the Langobards, which may recall some traditional character with a wolf-mask – for instance, the wolf-coated figure on the (English) Fen Drayton die or the (Swedish) Torslunda die.

as a god among all the peoples of Germania, who is understood
to have lived not in those times nor in Germania, but in Greece
long before.'[106]

It is worth stressing that Paul ascribes the tale to 'antiquity' which
presumably means traditional knowledge among the Lombard élite,
because no classical or patristic source knows this tradition. It is not
necessary to regard the setting for the tale as anywhere in the Italian
peninsula – indeed, with the chiefs petitioning a goddess, the setting
must be considered legendary or mythic in nature. Therefore, the
story may have formed part of the Lombard hoard of traditional tales
for some time (even centuries?) before it was reduced to writing. It
follows that it need not provide evidence for the active worship of
the god among the Lombards while they dominated Italy (Gardenstone, 2011, p.93).

The notion that Godan is equivalent to Wotan, explained by
Paul as *adiecta littera* 'the addition of a single letter', is probably a
description of phoneme substitution. The semi-vowel *w-* was present in Proto-Germanic and retained in some of the later dialects
(e.g., Gothic, OE) but transformed in various ways in others (e.g.,
in OS, OHG, ON). Substitution of initial *g-* (/g^w-/) for *w-* (/w-/)
occurs in several dialects, e.g., the Frankish name *Willhelm* is spelt
Guillelmus (William) on the Bayeux Tapestry just as the Lombard
word *wahtāri, wahteri* is still found in Italian as *guattero* 'guard, watchman' (Hutterer, 1975, p.341).[107]

It is interesting that Paul claims that Wotan was worshipped by all
the nations of *Germania*, since our knowledge of Langobardic culture

---

[106] An uncut beard was the symbol of a youth who had not proved himself in
war. It may then be the case that the 'long-beards' were the strikeforce of the
Winnili, their aggressive young warriors eager to achieve a higher status
through acts of bravado (Kershaw, 2000, p.144). They may yet all have been
warriors consecrated to the war-god and displaying this status in their appearance.

[107] The *w-/gu-* substitution accounts for modern English word-pairs such as
ward/guard, wage/gage, warranty/guarantee, war/guerr(illa), wise/guide, etc.

is incomplete and this statement helps to situate Wotan/Woden as a pan-Germanic deity - in Paul's view, at least. Exactly what the cleric understood by the term *Germania* is not as clear-cut as one might hope – the classical Roman concept included all the territories east of the Rhine and north of the Danube, but of course by the 8th century the name may have acquired a rather different meaning. It is not impossible that many linguistically separate groups could have used a common name for one of their most important gods, but it seems inherently more likely that each tribe would have had its own name and set of traditions relating to the deities. Perhaps the remark should be viewed in the context of missionary activities in northern and western Europe in Paul's day, whereby contact was established between religious communities in Italy, Francia, Alemannia, England, Ireland and elsewhere. The realisation that an Anglo-Saxon cleric used the term *Woden* where a German used *Wuotan* and a Lombard *Godan* might have prompted the observation about the god's worship across the Germanic language community.

VERSUS PAULI AD CAROLUM

Elsewhere, in a poem dedicated to Charlemagne, Paul remarks of King Sigifrid of the Danes *adveniat manibus post terga revinctis, nec illi auxilio Thonar et Waten erunt* '[he] should arrive with his hands bound behind his back, nor may Thunor and Waten be of help to him' (Shaw, 2002, p.78; Pollington, 2011, p.380).[108] Binding and loosing were particular activities associated with Óðinn in Norse tradition, but here the reference may be to the proper humility to be shown on a solemn occasion. Nevertheless, something of the Semnones' *Regnator Omnium Dies* is recalled in this passage with its binding motif.

---

[108] The Lombard form of the god's name was *Godan*, and the wider (pan-Germanic) version Paul spells *Wotan*, but *Waten* is clearly from a specifically Old High German dialect with the effects of the Second Sound Shift (-d- > -t-) in evidence.

GOTLAND PICTURE STONES

The Baltic island of Gotland has a unique archaeological history in many ways: styles of dress and decoration are found there which are absent from the rest of Scandinavia and the Baltic area: female 'box brooches', for example, and the famous 'picture stones' of which around 400 are known. These stele display geometric and symbolic motifs ('sunwheels', knotwork bands, guilloche bands, spirals), illustrate important aspects of life and death (livestock, seafaring, feasting, warfare), and include elements of religious iconography such as a rider on an eight-legged horse (e.g., the Tjängvide and Ardre stones, below) or a rider being welcomed by a standing figure (Lundin, 2006). The dating of the stones is contentious but they appear to extend from the 7th to the 12th c. (Vendel to Later Viking Periods) and they are conventionally subdivided into chronological and stylistic groups based on their shape and the ornament displayed (Nylén & Lamm, 1981, 1988; Guber, 2011; Karnell (ed.), 2012; Spears, 2016; Andersson, 2020, pp.73-84).

At first they were placed in gravefields but later examples were used to mark roads, bridges and other important landscape features. Many of them have been removed from their original locations, either for use in constructing churches or bridges, or more recently re-housed in the Swedish national collection in Stockholm.

Their exact significance cannot be determined although they certainly appear to have a memorial or commemorative function; the imagery is formulaic but may well relate to details of incidents known to the society which erected them. An á priori case for representations of Óðinn can often be accepted as probable, although there is a large element of inference based on attributes such as the eight-legged horse (Schjødt, 2020b, p.1134, 1137).

Fig. 18 Ardre VIII stone Gotland, with detail of the upper scene in which a bearded figure rides an eight-legged horse. (Source: Wikimedia Commons Museum number SHM11118)

Fig. 19 Tjängvide Stone with detail of the female figure. (Source: Wikimedia Commons Tjängvide.jpg)

TJÄNGVIDE STONE An important example is the Tjängvide stone (G110 in the Rundata database), a limestone slab about 1.7 metres high with a reserved design on a red field (Schjødt, 2020b, p.1138). The border is formed with loose loops within a continuous linear frame, and with a median bar of denser knotwork. The lower panel is roughly rectangular and is filled by the image of a ship with a high prow and stern formed as a coil: a broad sail covered with a chequer pattern which might represent a mesh of ropes used to control it; a crew of nine armed men, one of whom is steering from a seated position in the stern; and a thick mast and yardarm. The upper panel is damaged but includes a hall(?) with figures beneath and a dog; a prostrate figure, taken to be a warrior slain in battle; a female in a floor-length gown with carefully braided hair offering a drinking horn in her extended hands; a bearded rider holding a cup in one hand and the reins of his horse in the other, the horse being the largest element in the design and shown with eight legs – two sets of two angled forwards, one pair of hindlegs angled to the rear, and one pair of forelegs bent round as if galloping or leaping – with two serpentine coiled creatures between them (Ellis Davidson, 1969, p.46).

The stone bears a damaged runic inscription which is in two sections:[109]

(A) fuorkhn... ...fuþr-...

(B) ...(r)aisti   stainin   aft   iurulf   bruþur   sin   ÷
sikuif(i)r(t)(u)(a)(n)k(i)sifil

The standard reading is as follows:

(A) Fuþork hn[ias]...fuþ[o]r[k]...

(B) ... ræisti stæininn æftiR Hiorulf/Iorulf, broður sinn ...

translated as (the latter part of (B) being too uncertain for a reading to be possible):

---

[109] The text is discussed in the RUNES Projekt database at: www.runesdb.eu/en/find-list/d/fa/q////6/f/4975

(A) [the rune-row, partly repeated]

(B) [x] raised the stone after his brother, Jorulfr ...

Interpretations of the upper scene vary, but they hinge on the identity of the rider: is this Óðinn on his eight-legged horse Sleipnir? Or
a sovereign coming in triumph to his hall (Lundin, 2006)? Alternatively, the rider might be Sigurðr on his horse Grani meeting his
partner, Brynhild (Staecker, 2006)? Or is it a slain warrior being
welcomed to Valhǫll, having been brought there by the god's steed?
The evidence of the inscription tells in favour of the latter – the
commemorated dead man, Jórulfr or Hjorulfr, was thought so de-
serving of special treatment that his imagined and hoped-for journey
to the Otherworld and welcome from a valkyrie had to be recorded
on his stone.

Spears (2016) argues from an analysis of the variables (types of object or person depicted) on six picture stones that the juxtaposition of
the eight-legged horse and the welcoming valkyrie figure point to the
rider-figure as the god himself (Spears, 2016, pp.53-4):

> The variable of Odin will depend on the presence of one or more
> other variables for its accurate identification. The primary figure
> which could be interpreted as Odin will be a single mounted male
> rider. If this rider is present with ravens, Sleipnir, or Valknuts, a
> three-pronged multi-triangular symbol which has traditionally
> been associated to represent a religious symbol then it could be
> Odin (Nylén 1988:62). The religious symbol in this stone shows
> a sacrifice, and it was common to give sacrifices to Odin so it shall
> be defined as Odin. If this Variable is also present with the variable
> of a Valkyrie ... then possible identification can be made as well.

Identification of the rider is made possible by reference to Icelandic
sources which are however known not to be contemporary with the
creation of the stones (p.50):

> The variables related to myth are some of the most important
> ones in this discussion. Odin, Valknut, Sleipnir, Valkyrie, Raven,
> and Eagle variables are based upon of knowledge from the Sagas

in the majority of studies. The study and discussion of the Sagas are extremely useful for this interpretation due to the difference in dates for when the stones were made and when the Sagas were written down.

Corroboration of the rider's identity is based also on bracteate imagery (p.52):

These two facts, the rider on horseback and the ravens, correspond with what the Sagas say of Odin riding into a battle and having two ravens.

And further (p.81):

A Formula for Odin. Odin is a symbol which can only be identified when in conjunction with other symbols. The following observations can be made based on that premise to make up a formula for an Odinnic presence: Odin always appears with Sleipnir and a Valkyrie, but Sleipnir and Valkyries can appear without Odin. Ravens and Valknuts always appear together, but never appear with Odin.

These observations tell me that Sleipnir is the only variable which can positively identify Odin, which is corroborated by the presence of a Valkyrie greeting him with a drinking horn.

So, to clarify (pp.98-9):

A larger motif for the stones is that seen in the Odinic Formula. Odin is a god of death, associated with battles and Valhalla. He is shown riding Sleipnir greeted by a Valkyrie offering a drinking horn, a Welcome Scene. The two different Welcome Scenes were a motif analyzed to have a shared interpretation of a Valkyrie welcoming warriors, or a warrior, to Valhalla, a heaven realm for the Vikings, after they died. Valkyries are death related imagery because of their association with Odin, but also because of their association with battles and the dead. Sleipnir is a death related image because of his association with Odin, the god of the fallen. Together Odin, Sleipnir, and Valkyries make up a formula for identifying Odin on the stones, and thus giving the stones an association with death.

These conclusions about the meaning of the images and motifs come together to assign the stones a meaning as death related due to their iconography. That which is shown on monuments represents what the meaning of it is. For the Gotland picture stones that meaning/purpose is death.

The reasoning here is circular: only by identifying the rider with the god can the combination of elements be said to support that identification. It seems safer to note the *possibility* that Óðinn is depicted on the Gotland stones, while following the runic text and regarding the rider as more probably representing the dead man whose memory is affirmed in the imagery.

LÄRBRO STORA HAMMARS I STONE displays a more complex scene comprising: at left, a tree with either a hanged man attached beneath or possibly a warrior holding a shield; a large *valknútr* is placed at the end of the branch with a bird in flight above and a small figure below leaning forwards; to the right a high-seat or structure is presented with a small figure placed awkwardly across it by a tall figure with a large spear; next is another bird, perching with its wings folded and held by the first of the next group of four men armed with shields and brandishing their swords. It is possible that the scene depicts a funeral with the small figure representing the corpse flanked by a priest with his spear and a helper, while the armed warriors beat their swords on their shields - many of these details appear in the account of the Rus funeral given by Ibn Fadlan (Ellis Davidson, 1969, pp.34-5; Lunde & Stone, 2012, pp.52-3). The prominent *valknutr* points to a connection to Óðinn.

Fig. 20 The sacrifice scene on Lärbro Stora Hammars I stone. (Source: Wikimedia Commons)

Fig. 21 Lärbro Stora Hammars III stone. The scene has been interpreted as a visual reference to Óðinn and Gunnlaug, with Suttungr in bird-form. (Source: Wikimedia Commons)

Fig. 22 The Hunninge picture stone depicting a battle scene with a horse-man, sword-wielding warriors, a hound and a lady with a drinking horn (perhaps a valkyrja). (Harald Faith-Ell, Public domain, via Wikimedia Commons)

LÄRBRO STORA HAMMARS III STONE shows a large bird in flight approaching two human figures: the first is a noble female wearing an ankle-length dress and holding out a horn towards the bird; behind her is a bearded male brandishing a knife or small sword. The elements of the imagery suggest that the winning of the Mead of Inspiration is the allusion here.

KLINTE, HUNNINGE. This is one of the largest of the Gotland monuments. Its face is divided into four panels: at the curved top, a battle scene with a horseman, sword-wielding warriors, hound and lady with a drinking horn (perhaps a *valkyrja*); below this, a ship under sail with seven armed men on board; a small rectangular scene is inset below, a supine figure surrounded by snakes and a female entering through the end-wall; at the base, an enclosure with an ox and houses defenced by two bowmen against an attacking force accompanied by an eagle in flight and another horn-bearer. The combination of combat, a bird of prey, a horn-bearing *valkyrja* and a grave may be thought to invite associations with the god who presides over these matters (Ellis Davidson, 1969, p.41)

RUNESTONES

The majority of Scandinavian runestones date from the late 10th-12th century and were erected in the context of wealthy societies wishing to leave a permanent memorial in the landscape. (The Strängnäs runestone was discussed above: it does not seem to have been an object for public display in the manner of most Swedish and Norwegian examples.) These runestones are large, emphatic memorials, often dedicated to a named individual and with the name of the person who erected the monument included for posterity. The name of the god is notably absent from these monuments (Schjødt, 2020b, p.1133). The art-style most commonly used on them is Ringerike Style – sinuous serpent forms which loop and coil around the face of the stone, with runic text carved using the edges of the serpent's body as the upper and lower margins for the display of the script. This style is conventionally dated to the 11th c. (Graham-Campbell, 2013) and the stones are thus a product of the emergent medieval societies and very rarely contain any overt references to pre-Christian belief or thought.

THE RÖK RUNESTONE

This impressive monument (reference Ög136) stands beside the 12th c. church in Östergötland, Sweden to a height of 2.4m (8 feet); as with many of the larger runestones, it had been taken down and used in the construction of the local church. It was removed and re-erected in the 19th c. and now stands beneath a protective wooden canopy.

The stone features an extensive text (or texts: opinions vary) executed in a mixture of Elder Fuþark runes (Phase I, so up to the 8th c. in date) and later short-twig Swedish runes that came into use in the 8th-9th c. which makes a date of carving in the early 9th c. most likely; Nielsen puts it at ca. 825 on linguistic grounds (Nielsen, 2000, p.100, 261). The inscriptions cover all five visible surfaces, and include some enigmatic 'tent-runes', an encoded script. It is the longest known pre-Christian runic text, about 760 characters in all – but some damaged areas make an exact count impossible. The text shows no punctuation or even word-divisions, which leaves the reader to decide which words are present and in which form (number, person and tense of verbs, for example). It is considered 'not only the most impressive monument ever raised in Sweden to commemorate a dead kinsman – it also stands as the great memorial of Swedish literature in antiquity' (Jansson, 1987, p.31). The text has many of the characteristics of the riddling tradition – a very 'Odinic' context – reinforced by its enigmatic allusions and the multiple encoding techniques used in setting out the inscription (Harris, 2020; Levin, 2020, p.30).

Unsurprisingly, interpretations of the text vary markedly, but most agree that the dedicator of the stone was called Varinn (Warinn), that he was a wealthy local magnate and possibly a *þulr* or ritual specialist, while the dedicatee was his late son, Vémóðr (Wǣmōðr) (Jansson, 1987, pp.32-7; MacLeod, 2002; Harris, 2020; Levin, 2020). The inscription comprises the initial dedication and then refers to the following stories, often in question-and-answer format:

> The fall of King Theodoric (**þiaurikR hin þurmuþi** 'Theodoric the brave') of the Ostrogoths (**hraiþkutum**), who died circa 526 AD – around three centuries before the inscription was carved – which the inscription says occurred 'nine generations' before (**niu aldum**). Part of the text is in the verse metre called *fornyrðislag*, used in the *Edda* poems.

> A battle in which twenty kings (**kunukaR tuaiR tikiR**) died, who were from four kindred-groups; this is often considered to be the battle of Brávellir, fought circa 770 AD in the same area, between the Swedes from Uppland under King Sigurðr hringr and the local Gautar under the Danish king, Háraldr hilditǫnn, whose rule then extended into Östergötland. Sigurðr's forces included the famed Woden-blessed warrior, Starkaðr, according to Saxo Grammaticus's lively account (*Gesta Danorum*).

> Twenty kings occupied Zealand for four winters.

> Descendants of 'Inguld' (**igoldiga**) whose vengeance was fulfilled when his wife made a sacrifice (**hosli**).

> A man called Vilinn, born to a warrior, 'who knew how to crush an *etinn*' (**uilin is þat + knuą knati iatun**). Part of this text is written with the value of each rune offset by one position in the rune-row, i.e., **airfb** is to be read **sakum** 'I say' or 'I tell'.

> A man called Sibbi of Vé who begot a son at the age of ninety (**ul niruþR sibi uiauari**). Þórr also receives a citation here, perhaps as the sanctifying deity who made Sibbi's fatherhood so late in life possible. This text is encoded in tent-runes, but the group-numeration is in reverse order (i.e., the *ætt* numbered '3' here is the traditional first *ætt*: **fuþąrk**).

Clearly the text was compiled for the local population, to whom these tales were familiar, but the points of most of the allusions are now lost - yet not entirely beyond conjecture, hence the lively on-going debates concerning the identities of the people named.

There is a possibility that the Rök inscription was created by a society which had been traumatised by a significant downturn in the climate (Axboe, 1999; Holmberg, Gräslund & Williams, 2018); given that Scandinavia was always marginal territory for an agricultural way of life, a few unproductive summers spelt disaster for crops and livestock alike. This happened in the year 536 AD, and several more times in the decade afterwards (Shippey, 2022, pp.76-80; Ljungkvist, 2022). The initial remedy for this bad luck involved enhanced displays of devotion to the gods through elaborate deposits of gold symbolic items: *guldgubbar* and the like. But the supply of gold from Rome and Byzantium also dwindled at this time, threatening the economy of prestige goods on which many local potentates relied for their status and ability to support a retinue (Levin, 2020, p.38; Shippey, 2022, p.98).

Naturally, the reference to **niu aldum** 'nine lives [of men], generations' can be stretched or compressed to fit any date in a wide range, especially since the actual date of the stone's completion is not known.

The potential relevance of the Rök inscription for the story of Óðinn lies in the centrality of the riddles to its presentation, and in the stories of battle and the fall of heroes (Price, 2019, p.5). The god's role as guardian of knowledge and stirrer of strife probably lies behind these tales, but not one of them is presented in a straightforward narrative. Just like the allusions in *Hávamál* or *Vǫluspá*, these stories draw on centuries of traditional knowledge and lore.

9ᵀᴴ - 10ᵀᴴ CENTURY AD

The *Old Saxon Baptismal Formula* belongs to the 9ᵗʰ century, as does *BL Additional MS 23211* (the East Saxon kinglist). Here also should be included the *Second Merseburg Charm* of probable 10ᵗʰ century date.

THE LEJRE FIGURINE

In 2009, during Roskilde Museum excavations at the village of Gammel Lejre, a small figurine was unearthed inside a hall structure dating to around 900 AD (Christensen, 2009; Holst et al., 2017, pp.76-7); the hall measured 60m (197') long, the largest Viking-period building known in Denmark. Close to it was another 50-metre long hall of similar date, excavated in the 1980s, suggesting a very high-status settlement with multiple large social spaces in use concurrently.

The piece is 18mm (3/4") in height, cast in silver with niello detailing and some evidence of gilding. It depicts a throne or high-seat, square in plan with addorsed horse (or seal?)-heads on the corners of the backrest, hooked or curved finials on the four corners, two birds perched on the arm-rests and a seated figure wearing a floor-length robe, a separate ornamented apron, four tiered bead necklaces, a collar or neck-ring, a cloak open at the front and a cap or small hat (Holst et al., 2017, p.76).

The purpose of the figure is unclear – as an object of veneration (an idol) it is rather small for any kind of public display and even as a private religious icon it lacks presence, although it also seems rather over-elaborate for a gaming piece (Kozák, 2017, p.183).

Immediately, the figure was popularly identified as that of Óðinn on his high-seat, *Hliðskjálf*, a view promoted on the museum's own website. However, this suggestion disregards the fact that the figure's costume is entirely consistent with what we know of high-status female attire, and that it has two large circular eyes. Subsequent appraisals usually regard the seated figure as Frigg or possibly Freyja, or even as a human *vǫlva* (seeress).

THE TISSØ PENDANT

A silver pendant was discovered in excavations at Tissø, Denmark, a lake with a large settlement and several halls, and a separate hill-top assembly area which was probably a cult site. It came to importance around 550 AD and remained in use, with phases of rebuilding, until the mid–11th c.

The item is a long 'teardrop' with two bulging eyes, a prominent pointed beard and the suspension loop ribbed so as to appear to be part of the hair. It has carved panels on the cheeks with triquetra ornamentation, which has prompted an identification with 'Odin' (Holst et al., 2017, p.58). The context of the find was likely a ritual deposition. But is the image necessarily of Óðinn rather than, e.g., Freyr, Ullr, or any of the other deities? The name 'Tissø' probably derives from *tīwes ahwa 'lake of Tīw, Týr' (Holst et al., 2017, p.107) and it is perhaps more likely to be the mask of Týr that is commemorated here.

ANGLO-SAXON (ANGLIAN) KINGLISTS AND THE CHRONICLE

There are many references to the name Woden in the kinglists preserved in the various *ASC* manuscripts, and this is presumably not merely in deference to the authority of Bede. The name usually appears near the end (i.e., chronologically distant from the time of the text's composition), meaning that Woden was considered an ancestral figure from the past (North, 1997, pp.12-3, 111ff; Shaw, 2002, p.101). An example appears in the *ASC*, MS 'A' (9th century?) where the text gives the genealogy of Offa of Mercia (text from Thorpe, 1861, the *Parker Chronicle*, s.a. 755):

> Se Offa wæs Þincgferþing Þincgferþ Eanwulfing, Eanwulf Osmoding, Osmod Eawing, Eawa Pybing, Pybba Creoding, Creoda Cynewalding, Cynewald Cnebing, Cnebba Iceling, Icel Eomæring, Eomær Angelþowing, Angelþeow Offing, Offa Wærmunding, Wærmund Wyhtlæging, Wihtlæg Wodening.

'This Offa was the son of Þingferþ, son of Eanwulf, son of Osmod, son of Eawa, son of Pybba, son of Creoda, son of Cynewald, son of Cnebba, son of Icel, son of Eomær, son of Angelþeow, son of Offa, son of Wærmund, son of Wihtlæg, son of Woden.'

An alternative tradition for Æþelred, son of King Penda of Mercia, is recorded in the 10th century document Corpus Christi College, Cambridge, MS183:

Æðelred Pending, Penda, Pybbing, Pybba Creoding, Creoda Cynewalding, Cynewald Cnebbing, Cnebba Icling, Icel Eomæring, Eomær Angengeoting, Angengiot Offing, Offa Wærmunding, Wærmund Wihtlæging, Wihtlæg Wioþelgioting, Weoþelgiot Wodning, Woden Frealafing.

'Æðelred son of Penda, son of Pybba, son of Creoda, son of Cynewald, son of Cnebba, son of Icel, son of Eomær, son of Angengeot, son of Offa, son of Wærmund, son of Wihtlæg, son of Weoþelgeot, son of Woden, son of Frealaf.'

Many of these names are tantalizing in as much as they echo forms found in other documents – names which were well-known at the time of composition, but which are now consigned to the dimly-lit margins of history. The East Anglian version based on Alfwald was given above.

It is notable that this insistence on descent from Woden – perhaps to legitimise kinship – is heavily represented among the Anglo-Saxons but is almost absent elsewhere: *Ynglinga saga* (ch.8) states that from the union of Óðinn and Skaði came the line of the Jarls of Hlaðir in Norway (Schjødt, 2020b, p.1145).

The form 'Woden' may have originally designated an Anglian ancestor-god whose domain spread with Northumbrian and later Mercian Anglian dominance of the Southumbrian kingdoms. North suggested that the East Saxons' resistance to the Woden cult may shed some light on the process by which Woden came to head up so many genealogical documents (North, 1997, pp.113-4). Sæberht was the first East Saxon king to accept the Christian faith in order to comply with the religious preferences of his sometime overlord, King Æðelberht of

Kent; according to Bede (*Historia Ecclesiastica Gentis Anglorum* II ch.5), this conversion took place in 604 AD. On Sæberht's death in circa 616, his three sons expelled the bishop, Mellitus, from the city of London, the East Saxons' major emporium, and reverted to heathen worship which remained in force until the political ascendancy of Wulfhere of Mercia forced the East Saxon kings to accept Christ again in 659 AD. An outbreak of plague in 664 saw at least part of the East Saxon kingdom repudiate Christ and revert to the worship of the old gods (*Historia Ecclesiastica Gentis Anglorum* II. ch.30; Kelly, 2021, p.9). Since the East Saxons were able to maintain their links to their Saxon tribal ancestor, Seaxneat – uniquely among Anglo-Saxon kingdoms – it seems likely that the Woden cult must have flourished among Anglian kings as a political tool expressing domination at some point after Sæberht's conversion (604 AD), and before Wulfhere's accession (659 AD). The fact that Wulfhere did not insist on the adoption of a Woden-derived ancestry for the East Saxons under his sway implies that in his day adherence to the Anglian cult of Woden was no longer such an important aspect of accepting Mercian (and Christian) hegemony.

Woolf refers to the so-called 'Gothic Horizon' in Anglo-Saxon royal kinglists – names which appear to have been borne by individuals living at or just after the interface of the legendary and historical eras (Woolf, 2017, p.10). By this he means the names in the kinglists which occur at about the point where obviously mythological names (e.g., Woden, Geat) give way to more plausibly historical ones. At least three of the surviving pedigrees feature plausibly Gothic names at this point: in Kent, the father of King Æþelberht, who died around 560, bears the name Irminric (Searle, 1897, p.232); in East Anglia, Ine and Rædwald are both sons of Tyttla (Searle, 1897, p.463); in Bernicia, King Æðelfriþ has a father named Æþelric (Searle, 1897, p.48)[110] and an uncle called Þeodric (Searle, 1897, p.444). All these men were prominent in the last third of the 6th century and were thus probably born around the middle of that century. They have names which are rare or unique in the Anglo-Saxon corpus, but which do appear (in

---

[110] This name is quite well attested into the 11th c.

modified spelling) in the Ostrogothic dynasty in Italy. Irminric or Eormanric is the OE form of Ermanaric (*Airmanareiks), the ruler of the Gothic Greutingi who appears in the work of Jordanes. Tyttla is the anglicised form of Totila (from *Tutila with i-mutation and geminated consonant, confirmed by the Greek spelling *Toutilás*). Þeodric corresponds to Theodoric (*Þiudareiks) and Æþelric to his heir Athalaric (*Aþalareiks). That this phenomenon is not confined purely to Gothic names is confirmed by the tale of Eadwine and Ælfwine in *Widsith*, both Langobard rulers (Audoin, Alboin), again from the later 6th c. (Shippey, 2022a).

The 'Gothic Horizon' corresponds to a period in which the names of heroic figures from legend or folktale were commemorated in personal names of living persons (Shippey, 2014). It has sometimes been argued that these 'old-fashioned' names were inserted in order to give verisimilitude to the listings, to make them appear plausibly ancient because they contain forms and theme-combinations associated with recognised legends (Hoc, Hnæf, Wiþergyld and others). But this line of reasoning stems mainly from the work of Tolkien, who had his own reasons for promoting the notion of fantastical material – and who nevertheless took the historicity of sources very seriously.[111]

There is an interesting entry towards the end of the Laud Manuscript (MS 'E') which indicates a popular tradition concerning the Wild Hunt which was seen in England in 1127 AD (text from Thorpe, 1861):

> … Ne þince man na sellice þæt we soð seggen for hit wæs ful cuð ofer eall land þæt swa radlice swa he þær com þæt wæs þes Sunendæies þæt man singað *EXURGE QUARE O. D.* þa son þær æfter þa sægon 7 herdon fela men feole huntes hunten. Ða huntes wæron swarte 7 micele 7 ladlice. 7 here hundes ealle swarte 7 bradegede 7 ladlice. 7 hi ridone on swarte hors 7 on swarte bucces. Þis wæs segon on þe selue derfald in þa tune on Burch 7 on ealle þa wudes ða wæron fram þa selua tune to

---

[111] Tolkien's work on Finn and Hengest, edited by Bliss (1982), confirms this.

Stanforde. 7 þa muneces herdon ða horn blawen þæt hi blewen on nihtes. Soðfestemen heom kepten on nihtes. sæidon þes þe heom þuhte þæt þær mihte wel ben abuton twenti oðer þritti hornblaweres. Þis wæs sægon 7 herd fram þæt he þider com eall þæt lentedtid on an to Eastren. Þis was his ingang. of his utgang ne cunne we iett noht seggon. God scawe fore.

'… Let no man think strange what we truly tell, since it was well known through all the land that as soon as he [Abbot Henry] came there – that was the Sunday when one sings "Exurge quare O.D." – then soon thereafter many men saw and heard many hunters hunting. The hunters were black and large and ugly, and their hounds all black and big-eyed and ugly and they rode on black horses and on black goats. This was seen on the deer-park itself in the estate at Peterborough and in all the woods which extended from that same estate to Stamford, and the monks heard blowing the horns which they blew at night. Truthful men [who] kept watch at night said this: that it seemed to them that there might well be around twenty or thirty horn-blowers. This was seen and heard from the time he came there all through Lent, on up to Easter. This was his arrival; of his departure we cannot yet speak. May God provide!'

The horse- and goat-riding huntsmen here are practising some nightly ritual designed to frighten and disquiet the local populace as a protest against an unpopular Norman cleric, Abbot Henry. The form that their display of opposition took has strong overtones of the Wild Hunt and the terrifying spectacle of the nocturnal attacks of the *Harii*.

FREALAF

Woden is sometimes mentioned below the name Frealaf in Anglian lists, but this need not mean that Woden was held to be his son or successor. Rather, the compilers of kinglists had a more-or-less fixed series of names back to Woden, and when it became necessary to join one series to others (e.g., with biblical authority), they had no choice but to add the new material above the traditional starting point of the list. This probably happened in the time of Offa in the later 8th c. when the notion of Woden as 'legendary ancestor' had already usurped his position as 'supernatural power' (Meaney, 1966, p.110). Bede's *Historia Ecclesiastica Gentis Anglorum* (Book I ch.15) records the tradition of royal descent from Woden without mentioning the idea that this was a god; perhaps in his day, the cult of Woden had receded from official circles to such an extent that he did not feel it necessary to condemn those who had accepted Woden as a divinity.

Some pedigrees appear to have a numerical structure, in which Woden occupies a position based on the number nine or fourteen (Newton, 1993). Woden is, for example, the ninth 'father' (paternal ancestor) of Cerdic of the West Saxons in the *Parker Chronicle* manuscript s.a. 552, 597. The idea central to this pattern seems to be that the great men of old were superior to those around today (i.e., at the time of writing the manuscript), and that the further one goes back, the greater and nobler were the men (Hill, 1988).

Shaw (2002, p.34) has suggested that by the time of the compilation of the kinglists the name of Woden was regarded as 'an important and prestigious ancestor, but only a human king, not a god'. This same euhemeristic approach appears to have been adopted in Scandinavia where the oldest surviving list, the *Ynglingatal* of ca. 890 AD shows divine names in the earliest part, beginning with Fjǫlnir a grandson of Óðinn (Faulkes, 1978, p.5). Inserting Woden into the realm of 'the kings of old' does not conflict with the kinglist evidence but does fail to capture the special nature of the name and its relation to kingship.

However, there can be little doubt that the name Woden was recognisable to Anglo-Saxon audiences as that of a supernatural power worshipped in days of old (Neidorf, 2022b). His association with military earthworks is evidence that his name was still current in the early Christian period and down to at least 903 AD when King Edward the Elder refreshed a grant of land previously made by his grandfather, Æþelwulf (839–858) with reference to the fortification called *Wodnes dic* (Woden's dyke, now 'Wansdyke') (Neidorf, 2022b).[112]

NENNIUS: HISTORIA BRITTONUM

The *Historia Brittonum* (History of the Britons) is a spurious history of the post-Roman British peoples, possibly written around 828 AD. It survives in several versions, dating from the 11th c. or later. The text is attributed to Nennius, because some recensions have a preface bearing this name as that of the author. Most scholars have dismissed the preface as a later addition (or an outright forgery), preferring to view the work as an anonymous compilation of pre-existing material.

Its relevance to this project is the inclusion of 'Woden' and some genealogical information, relating to the kings of the 'Saxons'. Chapter 31 recounts the tale of Hengest and Horsa and their landing in Kent in the territory of Vortigern, tracing their line back to Woden and beyond. Chapter 57 gives the genealogy of the kings of Bernicia, 59 that of East Anglia, 60 that of the Mercian kings, 61 that of the kings of Deira; all these lines are also said to start with Woden. In the following, the Bernician listing, the OE names are given in brackets in my translation where these can be plausibly identified (text from Mommsen, 1898):

> Chapter 57 Woden genuit Beldeg genuit Beornec genuit Gechbrond genuit Aluson genuit Inguec genuit Aedibrith genuit Ossa genuit Eobba genuit Ida. Ida autem duodecim filios habuit quorum nomina sunt Adda Aedldric Decdric Edric Deothere Osmer et unam reginam Bearnoch. Ealric Ealdric genuit Aelfret

---

[112] Two later references include both East and West Wansdyke, as well as *eald dic* (the old dyke) which might be either of these; the same documents refer to *Wodnes beorg* (Woden's barrow or hill) and *Wodnes geat* (Woden's gap or path) which strengthens the case for a Woden-based nomenclature in the local landscape, as also the nearby *Wodnes denu* (Woden's dene).

ipse est Aedlfred Fleasur nam et ipse habuit filios septem quorum
nomina sunt Anfrid Osguald Osbiu Osgudu Oslapf Offa Osguid
genuit Alcfrid et Aelfguin et Echfird. Echfrid ipse est qui fecit
bellum contra fratruelem suum, qui erat rex Pictorum nomine
Birdei et ibi corruit cum omni robore exercitus sui et Picti cum
rege suo victores extiterunt et numquam addiderunt Saxones
ambronum ut a Pictis vectigal exigerunt. a tempore istius belli
vocature Gueith Lin Garan. Osguid autem habuit duas uxores,
quarum una vocabatur Riemmelth filia Royth filii Rum et alter
vocabatur Eanfled filia Eadguin filii Alli.

'Woden fathered Beldeg [Bældæg] fathered Beornec fathered
Gechgrond fathered Aluson fathered Inguec [Ingwe] fathered
Aedibrith [Æþelberht] fathered Ossa fathered Eobba fathered Ida.
Ida in turn had twelve sons of whom the names are Adda [Odda?]
Aedldric [Æþelric] Decdric [Þeodric] Edric [Eadric] Deothere
[Þeodhere] Osmer [Osmær] and one queen, Bearnoch. Ealric
fathered Aelfret, that is Aedlfred [Æþelfriþ] Fleasur and that one
had seven sons of whom the names are Anfrid [Eanfriþ], Osguald
[Oswald], Osbiu [Oswiu], Osgudu [Osgod], Oslapf [Oslaf], Offa.
Osguid fathered Alcfrid [Ealhfriþ] and Aelfguin [Ælfwine] and
Echfird [Ecgfriþ]. He is that Echfird who made war against his
own cousin, who was a king of the Picts named Birdei, and there
he fell with all the strength of his force and the Picts with their
king gained the victory and never thereafter did the Saxons
overcome the Picts so as to exact tribute. Since the time of this
war it is called Gueith Lin Garan.[113] But Osguid had two wives,
Riemmelth, the daughter of Royth, son of Rum; and another
called Eanfled, the daughter of Edguin [Eadwine], son of Alli
[Ælle].'

The *Historia Brittonum* is far from a reliable source and, while elements
of its narrative are probably founded on ancient tradition, the text is

---

[113] This event is usually identified as the battle of *Nechtansmere*, near Dunnichen,
Angus, Scotland or possibly Dunachton, Badenoch.

sometimes difficult to interpret. One version of it naming Nennius formed the basis for a translation into Irish around 1070 AD (Dumville, 1990).

OLD HIGH GERMAN SOURCES

References to *Wuotan* in OHG texts are sparse indeed. The runic text on the Nordendorf brooch surely falls within the relevant cultural area, but its early date means that the Second Sound Shift (which separates Old High German and Lombardic from the other West Germanic languages) had not yet taken place where and when the text was carved. It is therefore not clear what its owner's relationship may be to the OHG language community. Even the evidence of day-names does not assist since the form *Woutenestac* 'Woden's day' was replaced by the more innocuous *mittawecha* (*Mittwoch*, mid-week), a calque on the medieval Latin term *media hebdomas* (Simek, 1993, s.v. *Wodan;* Green, 1998, pp.242-3, 251). The only substantive reference is the *Second Merseburg Charm.*

Later sources in Middle High German occasionally make a passing reference to the god. Notable is the 14th c. exorcism ritual in which hanged men and those subjected to execution by breaking on the wheel are called *Wûtanes her und alle sine man* 'Wotan's troop and all his men' (Simek, 1993, s.v. *Wild Hunt*). Elsewhere the term *Wuotanes her* refers to the Wild Hunt, a concept which is strongly associated with the 'raging, frenzied' god who leads it.

SECOND MERSEBURG CHARM

A rare medieval German verse now known as the *Second Merseburg Charm* (Merseburg Cathedral Library MS 136, fol.85r) mentions Uuodan alongside Balder, Volla, Frige and Sunna (the sun) as well as the enigmatic figures Sinthgunt and Phol (Branston, 1957, p.49-50; Northcott, 1959; Ellis Davidson, 1964, p.183; Turville-Petre, 1964, p.73; Simek, 1993, s.v. *Second Merseburg Charm, Sinthgunt, Sunna;* North, 1997, pp.83-5; Pollington, 2000, p.506; Shaw, 2002, p.150ff; Mallory & Adams, 2006, p.117; Tolley, 2009, p.448; Lindow, 2016, p.115; text from Steinmeyer, 1916):[114]

Phol ende Uuodan vuoron zi holza

nu uuart demo Balderes volon sin vuoz birenkit

thu biguol en Sinthgunt Sunna era suister

thu biguol en Friia Volla era suister

thu biguol en Uuodan so he uuola conda

sose benrenki, sose bluotrenki, sose lidirenki,

ben zi bena, bluot zi bluoda,

lid zi geliden sose gelimida sin.

'Phol and Wodan went to a wood. Now Balder's foal wrenched its foot. Sinthgunt charmed it, Sunna's sister; Frija charmed it, Volla's sister; Woden charmed it as he well knew how: as bone-wrench, so blood-wrench, so limb-wrench; bone to bone, blood to blood, limb to limb, so they may be joined.'

Similar restorative charms are found in many Indo-European traditions, specifying by name all the parts which need to be rejoined: bone, blood and limb (Lincoln, 1986, ch.5; Watkins, 1995, pp.527-8; Pollington, 2000, p.444; Schjødt, 2020b, p.1130).[115] The text is performative, involving a rehearsal of myth in sacred time to effect a cure in quotidian time, just as seems to be the case for the Woden-section of the *Nine Herbs Charm*. The English *Lacnunga* manuscript is medical and curative in content, whereas the Merseburg document is mainly theological.

---

[114] The MS spelling is *Sinhtgunt*, and the name is unexplained, but the deuterotheme *-gunt* 'battle' recalls the type of name associated with Valkyries.

[115] There are parallels from Vedic tradition and elsewhere which suggest that charms of this kind were part of the folklore medicine of the Indo-European past.

The Charm uses the form *Uuodan* for the god's name, instead of the form *Wotan* expected for an OHG document. This spelling may indicate influence from outside the OHG speech community, if not original composition in a language not subject to the sound shift; but internal evidence (such as the words *suister* 'sister', *conda* 'knew' and *bluot* 'blood') shows that this text must be regarded as substantially OHG.

OSEBERG TAPESTRIES

The famous burial at Oseberg, Vestfold, Norway was discovered in 1903 by the landowner digging into an earth-mound and being confronted by wooden planks which appeared to be structural – the remains of a ship buried beneath the ground (Ellis Davidson, 1969, p.45; Christensen et al., 1992). It was identified as a Viking-period ship-burial by the experts from Oslo Museum, and a controlled excavation was planned and undertaken. The mound was found to contain a huge quantity of remarkable finds including a four-wheeled cart or waggon, four sleds, an iron-bound wooden chest, some wooden domestic items and the remains of sacrificed animals as well as two human females. Also among the grave-goods were some lavish textiles and the tools used in their production: five large looms, a tablet-weaving loom, a spindle and distaff, a yarn-winder, needles, scissors and other items. It is likely that the burial chamber was lined with a series of woven tapestries; there were pillows, blankets, mats, curtains and tents, the ship's sails and some decorative textile bands. Most of the fabric was a coarse woollen cloth with geometric patterns, mainly lozenges; these were probably the linings for the grave and may have been normal domestic furnishings. Rather more unusual were the ornamented textile bands, although their preservation was poor: the woollen warp had survived but the weft (probably linen) had largely decayed.

The imagery on one of the bands included a group of figures all facing left with horsemen and waggons, but the presence of some enigmatic figures alerted the museum staff to the probability that the image represented a religious procession. The leading figure (top left) is dressed in a tight-fitting shirt and baggy trousers reaching below the knee – a fashion also favoured by most of the weapon-bearing figures and thus probably representing contemporary male costume. His arms are both raised and in his left hand he carries a short sword (probably in its scabbard); his right hand is empty and shown with the fingers splayed. On his head he wears a conical cap or helmet, with curved horns above. This 'leader' character was immediately identified as Óðinn because of his headgear and his position at the front of the procession. Behind the 'leader' is a slightly smaller figure in similar costume with one arm raised, holding a spear or staff; there is a four-way knot motif above, which may have been the finial of the staff, but there are other instances of this motif in the scene and many are free-standing. Behind this 'staff-bearer' are placed eight more figures, shown at reduced size to fit in around the horse-rider and the upper waggon; four of these wear a floor-length robe which trails slightly to the rear, and the other four wear the shirt-and-baggy-trousers costume of the leader and staff-bearer.

There are many small and indistinct details in the tapestries, but recurrent motifs are spears and birds (related to the cult of Óðinn) and statuesque females (related to Freyja), some with boar-head hoods or masks. One scene shows a stylised tree with six figures dangling from the branches – reminiscent of the description of the Uppsala temple by Adam of Bremen with the great tree and the hanged men (Price, 2019, p.115). Beneath the tree are women with their hands raised, brandishing swords.

Aside from the wealth of grave-goods and textiles contained in the burial, there is great interest in the possible symbolic role of some of the items, since they may be associated with *seiðr*, and one or other of the bodies may be that of a *vǫlva* (Price, 2019, pp.115-8). The place-name Oseberg was initially interpreted as 'barrow of Åse', a semi-legendary queen, but more recent research suggests *ásaberg* 'hill of the Æsir' with the obvious implication of a cult-site.

The case for Oseberg as the burial of a wealthy female with links to the Otherworld and to religious authority is certainly strong. But the detailed identification of images with figures from Norse myth is fraught with uncertainty, and it would be worthwhile to bear in mind that 20th c. scholarship largely accepted the identification of the profile figure on bracteates with Óðinn, only to see this severely weakened by the evidence of the Vindelev inscription. The horned character may well have been Óðinn; he appears on the Torslunda dies and elsewhere, and is so frequently depicted that a central place in the worship of the gods must be assigned to him. But the symbolism of the Oseberg grave as a whole is much more closely allied to the cult of the Vanir and the *vǫlva* seeress (Price, 2019, p.118).

10TH-11TH CENTURY AD

Some written works of the late Anglo-Saxon period can be dated to the end of the 10th century or shortly thereafter. Here also should be placed the *OERP*, although the verse style may be characterised as 'archaistic' if its composition truly dates from the 11th c. A good many small pendants, brooches, amulets and other items from the Viking period probably had religious content, although it is not always possible to determine this for sure (Grundvad et al., 2017, p.35, 93-105).

THORWALD'S CROSS

A number of carved stone crosses erected on the Isle of Man in the 10th-11th c. bear iconography which reflects the narrative traditions of the mixed Manx-Norse population of the area (Ellis Davidson, 1969, p.104, 123). Most notable in this respect is the fragmentary 'Þorwald's cross' (Andreas 128), which resides in the churchyard at Andreas and is dated to circa 940 AD or later. The attribution to Þorwald is due to his name (**þurualtr**) carved into the surface of the lateral edge in Manx runes (Wilson, 2008, fig.39).

One face of the cross-shaft shows what may be the Ragnarǫk, when Óðinn is eaten by the wolf Fenrir. The god is shown in profile with a raven on his shoulder and his spear in his hand, point down-ward; his right leg is in the jaws of a wolf which attacks him from below while the god's left hand is gripping its muzzle. The god's single eye (he is shown in profile) is emphasised. He stands beside the reserved plaque which forms the central cruciform motif with knot-work ornament; on the reverse are also placed a figure with a book, a fish and a serpent – all standard Christian symbols which were also part of local tradition at the time of the monument's creation.

A later cross erected at Gosforth (Cumbria) may show a similar scene including a spearman placing his foot into the jaws of a monstrous wolf's head and pushing the upper jaw with his hand – interpreted as Víðarr breaking open the jaws of Fenrir to release Óðinn.

LEDBERG RUNESTONE

An irregular stone monument erected at Ledberg, Sweden, in the 11th c. depicts a man with his foot on the mouth of a quadruped; a helmeted figure is shown below, gripping the animal's hindlegs. This is usually interpreted as Víðarr freeing Óðinn from the belly of the wolf. The accompanying runic inscription refers to the sponsor 'Bisi' who raised the stone in memory of his father Þorgautr. A second text is an enigmatic 'spliced' sequence of runes 'þmk:iii:sss:ttt:iii:lll' which resolves into the words for 'thistle', 'mistletoe' and 'casket' (Pollington, 2016, p.292).

KIRKLEVINGTON CROSS

A sandstone cross-shaft was found in the course of church restora-tion in 1882 at Kirklevington, Yorkshire, dating from the 10th century. Between two panels of high-relief knotwork is a squat fig-ure carved in the half-round, standing wearing a knee-length cloak and pointed cap, and with a bird on each shoulder. An identification with Óðinn has been made on the assumption that these are ravens, although there are other possible interpretations drawn from Chris-tian iconography (Graham Campbell, 1981, p.93).

SALTFLEETBY SPINDLEWHORL

A lead spindle whorl found at Saltfleetby (Lincolnshire, England) in 2010 was incised with a short text in the Younger Fuþark (PAS reference LIN-D92A22). The object does not appear to be a Scandinavian import but rather a locally-made piece, of probably 11th c. date. The text around the side of the whorl reads:

.oþen.ok.einmtalr.ok.þalfa.þeir

and on the base:

ielba.þeruolflt.ok.kiriuesf

which has been interpreted as *Óðinn ok Heimdallr ok Þalfa þeir* 'Óðinn and Heimdallr and Þalfa they' and *hjalpe þér Úlfljót* ... '[may] help thee, Ulfljot ...'.[116] *Þalfa* is an unrecorded name but a masculine *Þjalfi* appears as the servant and companion of Þórr in some tales, e.g., the *Prose Edda* account of the god's journey to the hall of Útgarða-Loki. This may be the only reference to Heimdallr by name in a runic text presently known. The final eight runes have not been interpreted successfully.

Jesch has suggested that this interpretation is misleading and that the item – or rather its inscription - should be dated to the 12th century and set in the context of Christian-era Norse inscriptions (Jesch, 2020). A parallel is found in the Bergen inscription N B380 – a rune-stick dated circa 1185.

Norwegian merchants were active in the Humberside area in the 12th c. and King Henry II issued a writ enforcing the right of the reeves in Lincoln to impose tolls on them. Awareness of the old gods did not fade among Christian Scandinavians – witness Snorri's and Saxo's re-counting of their myths – and there does not seem to have been any firm prohibition against naming them.

---

[116] Hines's interpretation published on the PAS site reads 'Óðinn and Heimdallr and Þjálfa, they help thee, Úlfljótr', which presents a few syntactic problems. The last two words **ok.kiriuesf** are uninterpreted although **ok** is unproblematic for 'and' - but does it augment the subject or the object?

ÆLFRIC OF EYNSHAM: DE FALSIS DEIS

It is likely that some knowledge of Scandinavian Óðinn was imported into England by the settlers of the Viking age (mid-9th - 11th c.), although how firmly rooted it may have become is debatable (Meaney, 1966; cf. Heanley, 1898; Clemoes, 1997; Godden, 2000; Shaw, 2002, p.134, 145ff).[117] The Danes appear to have readily adopted Christianity as their dominant ideology once they were settled among the English. Ælfric, the 10th-11th c. West Saxon homilist, wrote in *De Falsis Deis* (Concerning False Gods) of *Mercurius*, a deceitful man whom the heathens in their folly worshipped as a god: *he is Óðon gehaten oðrum naman on Denisc* 'he is called by another name, Óðon, in Danish'. Other Christian texts dealing with the worship of false gods routinely equate Jove with Þórr and Mercurius with Óðinn (*Óðon*) which implies that a knowledge of contemporary heathen customs was part of the standard background information for a preacher and homilist in the later Anglo-Saxon period. Perhaps knowledge of current Scandinavian traditions about Óðinn affected what contemporary Christians thought about the god's heathen worshippers.

But the situation may rather be reversed: through continued links of marriage and fosterage between Anglo-Saxon and Scandinavian dynasties, the early insular traditions of Woden as a royal ancestor may have influenced the later Scandinavian cult of Óðinn (North, 1997, p.13). In other words, the notion of Óðinn as *alfǫðr* 'father of all' may have derived from the Anglo-Saxon concept of Woden as the apical divine ancestor, the founder of the kingly lines, the holy forebear of the leading kindreds.

Ælfric's work enjoyed some status in early medieval England and was disseminated widely. The cleric's equation of *Mercurius* with *Óðon* may be based in turn on Jonas of Bobbio's writings, on the day-name equation (*Mercurii dies* = *Wednesdæg*) or even on another (lost) source.

---

[117] Another eight manuscripts dealing with classical and heathen gods were composed by Ælfric after *De Falsis Deis*.

EXETER BOOK

The *Exeter Book* is an impressive manuscript of OE verse, gifted to the cathedral at Exeter (Devon) by its first bishop, Leofric, in 1072 when it was already perhaps a century old (Krapp & Dobbie, 1936). The contents are a miscellany of poems covering Christian religious themes (*Christ I, II and III; Juliana, Judgement Day* and others), legendary material (*Widsith, Deor* and others), heroic and elegiac themes (*The Seafarer, The Wanderer*), many riddles and a few poems which defy categorisation (*Wulf and Eadwacer, The Husband's Message*). There are references in some of these texts to tales which must once have been widely known, but which can no longer be reconstructed with confidence - *Wulf & Eadwacer* is one such, although its references to 'Eadwacer' have suggested a link to the tale of Odoacer, the Germanic leader who deposed the last Western Roman Emperor Romulus Augustulus and became 'king' of Italy in 476 AD (Harris, 1988). Likewise, there are metrical lines and phrases buried in these verses which may be presumed already to have formed part of the poetic tradition for centuries when the *Exeter Book* texts were compiled (Muir, 1994).

WIDSITH

The poem with the modern title *Widsith* ('Wide-Traveller') is an example of a 'catalogue poem' of wisdom and experience (Chambers, 1912; Malone, 1962; Shippey, 1972, p.82; Hill, 2009, pp.14-7). It is framed as a journey, told in the first person, among the peoples of northern Europe and further afield, as well as a listing of tribes and rulers augmented by some biblical and other lore (Neidorf, 2022a).[118] The context tells us that the narrator, 'Widsith', is a *scop* or poet who has been present at the courts of some of the leading rulers of the post-Roman period, as well as among many less well-known – and, indeed, some downright obscure – nations of that time. Widsith claims to

---

[118] Here, as in much else, I am especially indebted to the studies of Professor Leonard Neidorf and Dr Sam Newton.

have visited both Ermanaric of the Goths, who died in 375 AD, and Alboin of the Langobards who died two centuries later (572 AD) so the 19th c. notion that the poem describes the wanderings of a genuine human troubadour is clearly impossible. It has been supposed that an originally accurate or plausible verse narrative had been expanded to include additional characters, to the extent that it became implausible (or even farcical) due to the tampering of later poets (Chambers, 1912, pp.215-6). Subsequently, explanations based on a supposed metaphorical dimension to the text were proposed: the Widsith poet thus would be channelling the immaterial personhood of all poets, so standing as the epitome of poetic tradition and the archetype of the poetic class. As Neidorf notes, the poem has baffled modern critics who have tended to regard it as 'an arbitrary assemblage of heroic-legendary lore clumsily placed into the mouth of a wandering poet' (Neidorf, 2022a, p.14). There are clues in the text to its context and background.

As far back as 1931, Maragaret Schlauch took a different approach to its interpretation.[119] Basing her study on the observation that Widsith's supernaturally long life and interaction with kings and champions are paralleled by the Norse tales of Óðinn's favoured heroes, who likewise live for many generations of men[120] and have dealings with the most famous names of the post-Roman and early medieval periods in various disguises and under different names, Schlauch compared our poet with a handful of named figures with 'Odinic' qualities such as Gestr and Tóki Tókason in *Ólafs saga hins helga*, Víðfǫrull in *Rémundar saga Keisarasonar*, and (another) Víðfǫrull in *Mágus saga jarls*.

Taking one example, the character named 'Nornagestr' is cited as a parallel case, appearing in *Ólafs saga Tryggvasonar* where he claims to

---

[119] Schlauch (1931) is a wide-ranging review of the 'transgressive hero' figure in Germanic literature. Neidorf (2022, p.4) noted that Benjamin Thorpe had previously related the name 'Widsith' to various Odin bynames, and Henry Sweet had also suggested possible identification with the god.

[120] The long life of Starkaðr, for example, is laid upon him by Óðinn in *Gautreks saga*, while Thor counters this gift with the fate that he must commit a shameful act in each lifetime.

have spent time with Sigurðr the Vǫlsung, Ragnar Lóðbrok's sons, Haraldr Hárfagr and several other great names from antiquity, having taken part in their mighty struggles and been rewarded by them. The tradition centres on a solitary figure, tall and bearded, advanced in years, wearing a traveller's cloak and hat, wandering under an assumed name ('guest of the Nornir'): many of these bynames appear as *Óðinsheiti* 'aliases of Óðinn' elsewhere (e.g., Gestr in *Vafþrúðnismál*). Evidently Óðinn appears as a traveller, and his list of *noms de voyage* includes various kennings and paraphrases of 'wanderer' such Gangleri, Gangráðr, Vegtamr and others (see Appendix II); here we may venture to include *wīdsīð* 'wide-traveller' as well. Sometimes the itinerant character reveals himself to be the war-god, while in other instances his identity is left undisclosed (Neidorf, 2022a, p.13ff.).[121]

In *Nornagestsþáttr*, the hero Nornagestr attributes his long life to the strange fate he bears: that he cannot die until a candle, which was lit at the time of his birth, has burnt out; eventually, wearying of his protracted lifespan, he has himself baptised and shortly afterwards lights the fateful candle in order to attain a peaceful end (Schlauch, 1931, p.971; Tolley, 2009, pp.132-3).[122] This quiet acceptance of death is at odds with the notion of a heroic demise which should normally be a warrior's preference, the climax of his career.

The focus of the *Widsith* poem is on specific episodes relating to the 'big names' of Germanic history embedded in the catalogue sections citing many (possibly less interesting) rulers and their peoples (*Ætla weold Hunum, Eormanric Gotum, Becca Baningum Burgendum Gifica…* [ll.18-9] 'Attila ruled the Huns, Eormanric the Goths, Becca the Banings, Gifica the Burgundians…'). The first of these episodes (ll.5-9) is the poet's disclosure that he travelled from Angeln with the

---

[121] The disparity in dates of first recording for the OE and ON sources is sometimes offered as a barrier to such an interpretation. *Widsith* survives in a late 10th c. manuscript while the Icelandic material is mainly attributable to the 13th c or later. The OE poem was probably composed in the 7th c. and the original Norse verses, on which Snorri based his stories, perhaps by the 9th c.

[122] A similar motif is related in Greek myth of Meleager, who cannot die until a piece of wood in his hearth has burnt away.

lady Ealhhild, who was, in this tradition, betrothed to Eormanric the Gothic king who later repudiated her. She may be the princess known elsewhere as Swanhild or Suanilda, who was betrothed to that king and later put to death by him; this betrayal set in motion a series of violent actions and reactions which finally resulted in the king's violent downfall at the hands of his late wife's kinsmen. It follows, then, that Ealhhild's and Widsith's arrival at Eormanric's court coincide with the beginning of his ruination and demise. The king had previously been one of the god's favoured mortal followers and was rewarded for his loyalty by a sudden reversal of fortune and an untimely death – a motif which is associated strongly with Óðinn in his many guises.

A similar theme runs through the next section (ll.64-7), in which the poet receives a ring from the hands of King Guðhere of the Burgundians – better known today as Gunnar, or Gunther from the *Nibelungenlied* and elsewhere - who in history fell in battle against a Hunnic army, but whose story was transmuted into a tale of treachery and magic involving Attila and his family. The poet next appears among the Langobards (ll.70-4) whose king, Ælfwine (Alboin) died at the hands of his wife after having enticed her father to a feast, killed him and fashioned a cup from his skull which he then forced his queen to drink from. She could not tolerate this insult to her family and took steps to make sure the king paid for it with his life.

These three kings (Eormanric, Guðhere, Ælfwine) all met untimely deaths, but only after the itinerant poet had visited their courts and enjoyed their hospitality. Widsith did not receive such favourable treatment from another figure in the poem, Offa of Angeln, about whom the episode has little to say beyond recounting his martial skills (ll.35-44). The three kings who demonstrate bloodthirsty and transgressive behaviour (miserliness, betrayal of kinsmen, etc.) are singled out for the war-god's favour and subsequent betrayal, while the one who behaves responsibly (Offa) is rejected by him. Indeed, Neidorf shows that the 'Offa episode' functions as an opportunity for the wanderer to offer an assessment of the merits of great men of the past: in this instance, as much as Offa's rival Alewih was *modgast ealra* 'bravest of all' he was not better than Offa who achieved his greatness at a young age – *cnihtwesende* 'being yet a youth'.

The Danish legendary figures Hroþwulf and his uncle, King Hroþgar, appear in a brief allusion (ll.45-9) to their joint enterprise: the attempted destruction of the Danes' hereditary foes, the Heaðobeardan, under their king, Froda. The Danish king then attempted to heal the resulting feud by offering his daughter in marriage to the Heaðobeard prince, Ingeld, but this plan backfired when a fight broke out at the wedding feast. Some leading warriors died, so Ingeld was moved (or forced) to repudiate his bride and resume hostilities against the man who was now his father-in-law.[123] The poem does not specify who incited the fight – it is ascribed to an *eald æscwiga* 'old spearman', a bitter, eloquent, spear-wielding figure – who is understood from Norse parallels concerning Ingjaldr (equivalent to OE Ingeld) to be the monstrous warrior Starkaðr, almost an embodiment of the god himself. Nevertheless, the victorious Danes soon fell victim to the god's wiles in a continuation of their internecine strife which took the life of Hroþgar and of young Heoruweard, the king's successor – a later version of this tale forms the core of *Hrólfs saga Kraka*.

Wherever bloodshed and battle were in the offing, there Widsith travelled. The bitter struggle between the Goths and the Huns forms the background to another episode (ll.119-22) which is related elsewhere in Norse literature (e.g., *Hervararsaga*) as a family feud which spills over into pitched battle (Malone, 1925). Indeed, the poem's line 128 refers to the *giellende gar* 'screaming spear' which is launched against the enemy, recalling the practice of casting a spear over the enemy army before battle which Styrr-Bjǫrn, a devotee of Óðinn, undertook before battle (*Styrbjarnar þáttr* cited in Lassen, 2022, p.91).

---

[123] The story of Ingeld (Ingjaldr) related in Saxo's *Gesta Danorum* has Starkaðr encourage Ingjald to repudiate his bride and her family and to seek vengeance while in *Beowulf*, the nameless old warrior fulfils a similar role (l.2042): Ingeld is prompted to wage war against his wife's kindred in order to avenge his father, and he dies in the process.

The purpose of the listing of kings and heroes is partly a means for the poet to display his verse-making talent and prodigious memory for the tales of old. Catalogues and lists formed a recognised genre in ancient verse, hence the recital of the names of dwarves in *Dvergatal* and the uses of runes in *Rúnatal*. The OE tradition has its own catalogues, of course: the *Maxims* poems, or the *Fates of Men*. That there should be an age-old fund of tales – recounted in verse, as was traditional – relating to the interaction of the war-god and his notable human followers seems entirely reasonable; indeed, it would be perverse to claim that no such tradition existed.

Beyond that, if the association of Widsith with the war-god is accepted,[124] then the kings and heroes who fell at Óðinn's instigation were destined to form his personal following – the *Einherjar* – and the poem thus functions as a listing of the great warriors who were summoned to fight beneath the god's war-banner.

MAXIMS I

In lines 62-3 of the *Exeter Book* poem with the modern title *Maxims I* the words *Woden* and *wuldor* appear in close association (Watkins, 1995, p.426; text from Muir, 1994):

> Woden worhte weos,   wuldor alwalda
>
> rume roderas.
>
> 'Woden made idols, the All-ruler (made) glory, the broad heavens.'

It may be that the poet used *alwalda* 'ruler of all' in apposition to Woden so that the sense should be that 'Woden made holy places [and as] the ruler of all he [also] made the heavens'. *Wuldor* is the OE form of

---

[124] It would be a mistake to conclude that there is a simple equation here: Widsith = Woden. It is surely more fruitful to see in the enigmatic figure of Widsith a character sharing some attributes with Woden, an avatar or physical embodiment of the god. The ambiguity is rather the point, and the poet's skill in framing the riddle is to be greatly admired.

the word which appears in ON as *Ullr*, a god of the Æsir (Pollington, 2011, pp.283-6).

The *weos* (singular *weoh*) are 'holy places', probably with images of the gods (Markey, 1972; Neidorf, 2023).[125] The name occurs in modern place-names such as Wye (Kent) and elsewhere from Sussex (Patchway) to Lincolnshire (Wyham) and from Worcestershire (Weoley) to Essex (Weeley) (Stenton, 1941; Branston, 1957, p.43; Wilson, 1992, pp.8-10; Campbell, 2007, p.69; Semple, 2010, pp.39-40). *Weoh* is never found in conjunction with a specific god's name in English toponymy, so it must have been generic term for 'holy site' in place-names, perhaps similar in concept to the 'place closest to heaven' (*maxime locos propinquare caelo*) over which the Cimbri and Hermunduri fought.[126]

In translations of biblical texts, *wēoh* denotes various forms of idol (North, 1997, p.97; Green, 1998, p.28). The Norse *véstalli* (in which *vé* is cognate with *wēoh*) denotes a kind of wooden frame at which worship took place, perhaps the same kind of framed and covered object as the *heargtræf* of *Beowulf* l.175 (Simek, 1993, s.v. *altar*; Pollington, 2011, p.105). There is some archaeological evidence for such structures comprising four upright posts with beams on top, decorated with representations of horns (e.g., at Bangeroosterveld) (Simek, 2014).

The PIE root **weik-* gives rise to OE *wēoh* as well as Gothic *weihan* 'consecrate', *weihs* 'holy' (Lehmann, 1986, s.v. *weihs*). The underlying notion is of something 'divided' or 'separated' from the mundane world; once it had been cut off, it could be sanctified, rendered 'other' (Mallory & Adams, 2006, p.412). Latin *victima* 'thing or person sacrificed' is another derivative of this root (Lehmann, 1986, s.v. *weihs*).

---

[125] Markey takes the original meaning 'holy site' to have been expanded to include images, but the term *weoh* is etymologically related to Greek *(w)eikon* 'religious image, ikon' which thus seems to have been the earlier sense of the word.

[126] Simek (1993, s.v. *vé*) shows that in Sweden and Norway the term is used with Ullr, Skaði, Freyr, Óðinn and Þórr, but in Denmark only Óðinn has such names. There are none in Iceland.

The noun *wīh, wēoh* 'idol, shrine' from PGmc **wíha* is likewise cognate with Greek [*w*]*eikon* 'icon, religious image, idol' (Mallory & Adams, 2006, p.326).

RIDDLE 60

The character of Woden as one-eyed (or better, with one normal and one abnormal eye) is well-founded in England, as the Sutton Hoo Mound 1 evidence demonstrates. A vague later memory of the tradition may be found in the *Exeter Book* riddle (no.60, Krapp & Dobbie no.85) where we read:

> Wiht cwom gongan   þær weras sæton
>
> monige on mæðle,   mode snottre,
>
> hæfde an eage   ond earan twa
>
> ond ii fet   xii hund heafda
>
> hrycg ond wombe   ond honda twa
>
> earmas ond eaxle,   anne sweoran
>
> ond sidan twa.   Saga hwæt ic hatte

Exeter Book Riddle no.60

'A being came walking where many men sat in a meeting, wise in mind; it had one eye and two ears, two feet and twelve hundred heads, a back and a belly and two hands, arms and shoulders, one neck and two sides. Say what I am called.'

The bizarre but usual solution to this riddle is 'a one-eyed garlic seller', where the puzzle lies in the description of a normal human being with one eye who has a string of 1200 'heads' (garlic bulbs) around his neck. It is assumed that the riddle is derived from Symphosius's short Latin *enigma* concerning the *luscus alium vendens* 'one-eyed man selling garlic' (Bitterli, 2009, pp.68-9):

> Cernere iam fas est quod vix tibi credere fas est:
>
> Unus inest oculus, capitum sed milia multa

Qui quod habet vendit, quod non habet unde parabit?

Symphosius's *Ænigma* no.95

'Now you may see what it is hard for you to believe: one eye is within but many thousands of heads. Where may he who sells what he has acquire what he does not have?'

The OE riddle enumerates the body parts in order to provide the audience with an excess of information, thus multiplying the quantity of potential clues to be sifted through. A similar approach is adopted in some other Anglo-Saxon riddles in Latin, such as Aldhelm's four-liner about a woman giving birth to twins (based on Symphosius's *Mulier quae geminos pariebat*) (*Epistola ad Acircium* no.90).

The two riddles (*Exeter Book* and Symphosius's) are not alike, nor even parallel in most of their content. They share only the features 'one eye' (*an eage, unus ... oculus*) and many 'heads' (*xii hund heafda, capitum ... milia*); they are otherwise entirely dissimilar. The Latin text uses the simple disparity in quantities of body parts to confuse the reader, whereas the OE riddle provides a full setting in which men (*weras*) who are wise (*snottre*) are assembled in a meeting or discussion (*mæðle*), at which a 'being' (*wiht*) approaches on foot (*gongan*). It hardly needs stating that there may be an echo of Woden here, however feint, even if the ultimate inspiration was the Latin *enigma*, and the poet has gone to some trouble to incorporate details such as the wise men and the formal discussion which immediately evoke thoughts of *rædboran* and *sittan to rune*. The riddle-maker was playing with the expectations of an Anglo-Saxon leisured audience in constructing his scene.[127]

---

[127] I am indebted to Linden Currie for pointing out the disparity between the Latin and OE texts.

LACNUNGA MANUSCRIPT

The *Lacnunga* manuscript is now housed in the British Library (MS Harley 585) (Cockayne, 1864; Pollington, 2000, p.72). It comprises a miscellany of medical texts, mostly translations from Latin including the *Pseudo-Apuleius Herbarium*, Pseudo-Dioscorides's *De herbis femininis* and *Curae herbarum*, the *Medicina de quadrupedibus*, the *Lacnunga* (curative treatments) and various marginal notes, all in a 13th c. hand. Of particular interest is the four-part section now called the *Nine Herbs Charm* and the charm *Wið Færsticce* 'against a sudden stitch'.

THE NINE HERBS CHARM

This verse – one section of a longer text – is one of the most intensively studied Old English verse charms. It is numbered as sections 79 to 83 in modern editions of the *Lacnunga* manuscript (Cockayne, 1864; Lindow, 2016, pp.114-5). The charm is intended to harness the power of the nine herbs or plants named within the verse against nine 'poisons' or diseases, each of which is associated with a specific colour. The text of the charm is slightly defective (scribal copying error is most likely), so that one of the colours is attributed twice while another is a *hapax legomenon*, but the structural principle seems clear.[128] The correspondence has been noted between yellow-flowering plants used against the yellowing effects of jaundice, as also purple and white against demons and red for disorders of the head (Barley, 1973). Thus a symbolic use of, e.g., yellow-flowering plants against diseases characterised by yellow colouration seems to be at work (Price, 2019, p.293).

The text is a complex spell, one of several recorded in the manuscript. The author conceptualises disease and infection as something invisible projected by an unseen opponent; an appeal is made to Woden for help against this unseen threat: *ða genam woden viiii wuldortanas ... witig drihten, halig on heofenum þa he hongode, sette & sænde on vii worolde* 'then Woden took up nine rods of glory ... the wise lord, holy in

---

[128] But see Biggam, 1997 for the process of establishing a tentative meaning.

the heavens while he was hanged, [he] set and sent out [chervil and fennel] into the seven worlds'.

The text and translation are given here, the four enumerated sections of the manuscript. The 'charm' proper is numbered LXXX (80) (text from Cockayne, 1864; translation based on Pollington, 2000):

LXXVIII + Gemyne ðu mucgwyrt hwæt þu ameldodest / hwæt þu renadest æt regenmelde / una þu hattest yldost wyrta /þu miht wið iii & wið xxx /þu miht wiþ attre & wið onflyge / þu miht wiþ þa laþan ðe geond lond fereð. / + Ond þu wegbrade wyrta modor / eastan openo, innan mihtigu / ofer ðe crætu curran, ofer ðe cwene reodan, / ofer ðe bryde bryodedon, ofer þe fearras fnærdon, / eallum þu þonne wiðstode & wiðstunedst / swa ðu wiðstonde attre & onflyge / & þæm laðan þe geond lond fereð. / Stune hatte þeos wyrt, heo on stane geweox, / Sondeð heo wið attre, stunað heo wærce. / Stiðe heo hatte, wiðstunað heo attre / Wreceð heo wraðan, werpeð ut attor. / + Þis is seo wyrt seo wið wyrm gefeaht / þeos mæg wið attre, heo mæg wið onflyge / heo mæg wið ða laþan ðe geond lond feraþ. / Fleoh þu nu attorlaþe, seo læsse ða maran, / seo mare þa læssan oððæt him beigra bot sy. / Gemyne þu mægðe, hwæt þu ameldodest, / hwæt ðu geændodest æt alorforda / þæt næfre foe gefloge feorh ne gesealde / syþðan him mon mægðan to mete gegyrede. / Þis is seo wyrt ðe wergulu hatte / ðas onsænde seolh ofer sæs hrygc / ondan attres oþres to bote.

LXXX Ðas viiii ongan wið nygon attrum. / + Wyrm com snican, toslat he nan / ða genam woden viiii wuldortanas / sloh ða þa næddran þæt heo on viiii tofleah / þær geændode æppel & attor / þæt heo næfre ne wolde on hus bugan. / + Fille & finule felamihtiga twa / þa wyrte gesceop witig drihten, / halig on heofenum þa he hongode / sette & sænde on vii worolde / earmum & eadigum eallum to bote. / Stondeð heo wið wærce, stunað heo wið attre / seo mæg wið iii & wið xxx / wið feondes hond & wið heabregde / wið malscrunge minra wihta. / + Nu magon þas viiii wyrta wið nygon wuldorgeflogenum / wið viii attrum & wið nygon onflygnum / wið ðy readan attre, wið ðy runlan attre, / wið ðy hwitan attre, wið ðy hæwenan attre, / wið ðy geolwan attre, wið ðy grenan attre, / wið ðy wonnan attre, wið ðy wedenan attre, / wið ðy brunan attre, wið ðy basewan attre, /

LXXXI Wið wyrmgeblæd, wið wætergeblæd / wið þorngeblæd, wið þystelgeblæd / wið ysgeblæd, wið attorgeblæd / gif ænig attor eactan fleogan / oððe ænig norðan genægan cume / oððe ænig westan ofer werðeode. / + Crist stod ofer alde ængancunde: / Ic ana wat ea rinnende / & þa nygon nædran nu behealdað / motan ealle weoda nu wyrtum aspringan / sæs toslupan eal sealt wæter / ðonne ic þis attor of ðe geblawe.

LXXXII Mugcwyrt, wegbrade þe eastan open sy, lombes cyrse, attorlaðan, mageðan, netelan, wudusuræppel, fille & finul, ealde sapan; gewyrc to duste, mænge wiþ þa sapan & wiþ þa sapan & wiþ þæs æpples wos; wyrc slypan of wætere & of axsan, genim finol, wyl on þære slppan & beþe mid ðan gemonge þonne he þa sealfe ondo ge ær ge æfter. Sing þæt galdor on ælcre þara wyrta, iii ær he hy wyrce, & on þone æppel eal swa, ond singe þon men in þone muð & in þa earan buta & on ða wunde þæt ilce gealdor ær he þa sealfe ondo.

'79.[129] Remember, mugwort, what you revealed, what you set out in mighty revelation – 'una' you are called, eldest of plants, you have might against three and against thirty; you have might against poison and against infection; you have might against the evil that travels around the land. And you, waybread, mother of plants, open to the east, mighty within: carts ran over you, ladies rode over you, brides cried over you, bulls snorted over you; you withstood all then, and

---

[129] The numbering is that of Grattan and Singer, but most editors agree that leechdoms 79, 80, 81 and 82 belong together as a single entry. The overlap in plants named in all four is too great to be mere chance, and it is evident that similar verses addressed to chervil and fennel are absent.

you were crushed, so may you withstand poison and infection and the evil that travels round the land. This plant is called cress, it grew on a stone, it stands against poison, it attacks against pain. [This] is called nettle, it attacks against poison, it drives off harmful things, casts out poison: this is the plant that fought against the serpent; this one has might against poison, it has might against infection, it has might against the evil that travels round the land. Now, 'atterlothe' (betony? black nightshade?) – the lesser shall drive out the greater, (and) the greater the lesser until the cure for both be with him. Be mindful now, 'maythe' (chamomile?), of what you made known, of what you finished at elder-tree ford so that he never should give up his life for disease once maythe was prepared for his food. This is the plant which is called 'crab apple': a seal sent this forth across the sea's back as a cure for the bite of another poison.

80. [130] These nine spikes against nine poisons. A worm came crawling, he tore a man apart,[131] then Woden took up nine glory-rods, struck the adder then so it flew apart into nine [pieces], there apple ended it and its poison so that it would never [slither] into a house. Chervil and fennel, two of great might, the wise lord shaped these plants while he was hanging, holy in the heavens: he set them and sent them into the seven worlds for poor and for wealthy, as a cure for all. It stands against pain, it attacks against poison, it has might against three and against thirty, against foeman's hand and against lordly sleight, against bewitching of harmful beings. Now these nine plants have might against nine powerful diseases, against nine poisons and against nine infections, against the red poison, against the running poison, against the white poison, against the

---

[130] Grattan and Singer name this section 'Lay of the Nine Twigs of Woden' although, as noted above, it clearly forms part of the preceding section. See Watkins, 1995, ch.43.

[131] Turville-Petre (1964, p.70-1) reads this passage as *toslat he nan* 'it killed noth-ing' and begins the next phrase with 'For Woden took...' which implies that the disease-bringing worm was ineffective against the god's power, but the OE text merely says *Þa genam Woden* 'Then Woden took...'.

grey poison, against the yellow poison, against the green poison, against the pale poison, against the mauve poison, against the bright poison, against the purple poison.

81. Against worm-blister, against water-blister, against thorn-blister, against thistle-blister, against ice-blister, against poison-blister: if any poison flying from the east or any from the north should come, or any from the west over the tribe of men. "Christ stood over the ancient malevolent race; I alone know the running rivers and they enclose nine adders, all weeds may now spring up as herbs, seas slide apart, all salt water while I blow this poison from you."[132]

82. Mugwort, waybread which has opened from the east, lamb's cress, attorlothe, maythe, nettle, wood sourapple, chervil and fennel, old soap; work the herbs to a powder, mix them with the soap, and with the apple's juice; make a paste from water and from ashes; take fennel, boil it in the paste and warm it with the mixture when he puts on the salve, both before and after; sing the charm on each of the herbs thrice before they will be used, and on the apple likewise; and sing the same charm into the man's mouth and into both ears and onto the wound before he puts on the salve.'

The charm has been identified as probably performative, involving a ceremonial rehearsal of myth in sacred time in order to effect a cure in quotidian time. It is related thematically to some other texts, especially the *Second Merseburg Charm* although the *Lacnunga* manuscript is medical and curative in all its content, whereas the Merseburg document is mainly theological and ecclesiastical. The overall form of the charm is found in many Indo-European traditions and involves specifying all the parts which need to be cured: bone, blood and limb (Watkins, 1995; Pollington, 2000).

The healing aspect of Woden appears where he bears arms against the *wyrm*, portrayed as the disease-bringing serpent, the enemy of man. Hence Woden is linked to both the prevention of illness and its cure

---

[132] See Glosecki, 1989 ch.4. The reference may be to sucking out poison from a wound.

(Grendon, 1909; Branston, 1957, p.97; Meaney, 1966, pp.110-1; Pollington, 2000, pp.501-2). It is interesting that Woden bears *wuldortanas* 'rods (or twigs) of glory'. He uses them as a weapon against the nine illnesses, and the rods are drawn from the nine powerful, magical plants which the god had previously charmed (Glosecki, 1989, p.121). These rods might be considered the prototype of the staff or spear, *Gungnir*, which Óðinn uses on his travels. The *wuldortanas* perhaps evoke a memory of Mercury's *caduceus*, or of the *thyrsos* (fennel stalk) of Dionysos, being a symbolic plant-stem used by a god as both an emblem and a weapon.[133]

WIÐ FÆRSTICE

This text appears as sections 134-5 in the same manuscript as the *Nine Herbs Charm*. While it does not specifically name Woden, it does offer some close parallels to what may be surmised of the god's traditional cult, e.g., *esa gescot* 'the shooting of the Æsir' and the riding of supernatural females over a burial mound (valkyries, dead ancestors, etc.) (Price, 2019, pp.293-4). The charm is aimed at curing *færstice* 'sudden stitch'[134] conceived as the result of having been shot with a *lytel spere* 'little spear' by *mihtig wif* 'mighty women' (text from Cockayne, 1864; see Storms, 1948; cf. Pollington, 2000, p.238):

CXXXIIII. Wið færstice: feferfuige & seo reade netele ðe þurh ærn inwyxð & wegbræde, wyll in buteran.

CXXXV Hlude wæron hy la hlude ða hy ofer þone hlæw ridan / wæran anmode ða hy ofer land ridan. / Scyld ðu ðe nu þu ðysne nið genesan mote / Ut lytel spere gif her inne sie. / Stod under linde under leohtum scylde / þær ða mihtigan wif hyra mægen beræddon / & hy gyllende garas sændan / ic him oðerne

---

[133] The *thyrsos* is associated with the followers of Dionysos in Euripides's play *The Bacchae* as part of the ritual garb of the god's followers. *Thyrsoi* were converted to weapons when the god provided them with iron tips.

[134] *Fær* can mean 'sudden' but has other meanings including 'dangerous' and 'intense'. Likewise, *stice* can mean 'stitch, pain in the side' but further 'puncture', 'stab wound'. Cf. Bosworth & Toller s.v. *fær*, *stice*.

eft wille sændan / fleogende flanae forane togeanes. / Ut lytel
spere gif hit herinne sy. / Sæt smið sloh seax / lytel iserna wund
swiðe / Ut lytel spere gif herinne sy. / Syx smiðas sætan wælspera
worhtan / Ut spere, næs in spere. / Gif herinne sy isenes dæl /
hægtessan geweorc hit sceal gemyltan / gyf ðu wære on fell
scoten, oððe wære on flæsc scoten / oððe wære on blod scoten
[oððe wære on ban scoten]¹³⁵ / oððe wære on lið scoten næfre
ne sy ðin lif atæsed / gif hit wære esa gescot, oððe hit wære ylfa
gescot / oððe hit wære hægtessan gescot nu ic wille ðin helpan:
/ þis ðe to bote esa gescotes, ðis ðe to bote ylfa gescotes / ðis ðe
to bote hægtessan gescotes, ic ðin wille helpan. / Fleah þær on
fyrgenholt, fyrtst ne hæfde / hal westu nu, helpe ðin drihten. /
Nim þonne þæt seax, ado on wætan.

'134. Against a sudden stitch: feverfew and the red nettle which
grows in through a building and waybread; boil in butter.

135¹³⁶ "Loud were they, lo! loud as they rode over the barrow,
they were daring as they rode over the land. Shield yourself now,
so you may escape this attack. Out, little spear, if it be in here.
[I] stood under linden, under a light shield, where the mighty
women made known their force and yelling they sent spears.
Back to them I wish to send another, a flying dart in opposition.
Out little spear, if it be in here. A smith sat [and] hammered a
knife, a small weapon, a serious wound. Out, little spear, if it be
in here. Six smiths sat [and] wrought slaughter-spears. Out, spear,
be not in, spear. If there be in here a piece of iron, the work of
witches, it must melt away. If you were shot in the skin, or you
were shot in the flesh or were shot in the blood, [or were shot
in the bone] or were shot in the limb, may your life never be

---

¹³⁵ This phrase, a merism of a standard kind in magical charms, is not in the
original text and was supplied by Jacob Grimm to complete both the verse line
and the formula.
¹³⁶ Again, the numbering used follows Grattan and Singer, although clearly the
charm here numbered 135 is part of the same leechdom as the prefatory remarks under 134. The charm is in verse of an almost 'heroic' type.

threatened; if it were the gods'[137] shot, or it were the elves' shot, or it were the witches' shot, I will now help you. This as a cure to you for the gods' shot, this as a cure to you for the elves' shot, this as a cure to you for the witches' shot, I wish to help you. There it fled to the mountain [wood, no rest] did have. Whole be you now, may the Lord help you." Then take the knife, put it into the liquid.'

This short verse and its accompanying ritual have been regarded as among the oldest and best-preserved evidence of English pre-Christian thought. The text opens with the words *wið færstice* 'against sudden stitch' and part (i) then lists three 'ingredients' and their preparation – 'feverfew, the red nettle which grows in through a building, and waybread' – and closes with the ritual enactment 'then take the knife, put it into [the] liquid' (part [iv]). The metrical charm proper (lines 3 to 28) describes the attack of *þa mihtigan wif* 'the mighty women' and contains the command *ut lytel spere* 'out, little spear' repeated several times. Enigmatic references to 'a smith' and 'six smiths', to gods, elves and witches, loud and fierce riders, a burial mound, a light shield and a deadly spear all appear to be drawn from a rich body of traditional lore.

The text's interpretation has long been contentious, with most scholars proceeding from the assumption that the charm rehearses

---

[137] The OE *esa* here is presumed to be the genitive plural (gen.pl.) of the word *os* found in personal names (e.g., *Oshere* on the Coppergate Helmet) and in the *OE Rune Poem*. In philological terms, *esa* is not the expected form, since the gen.pl. should reflect the same vowel as the nominative singular (*os: osa*) – *boc* 'book' is a good parallel example with nominative plural *bec* and genitive plural *boca*. It is possible that the word *os* was no longer familiar at the time of writing the charm down, and the vowel *e-* was levelled throughout the plural forms. A similar process is found in, e.g., *stæf* 'staff', plural *stafas* where *-æ-* has been levelled from the singular to the plural in the modern language (*staff, staffs*) and *-a-* has been levelled from the plural to the singular (*stave, staves*). The word *os* denotes a pre-Christian god (from Germanic **ansuz, *ansiz*). While the phonological correspondence is not exact, the balance of probabilities favours this identification in a context where witches (*hægtessan*) and elves (*ylfe*) are also invoked.

one or more themes from Anglo-Saxon mythology or folklore. Can
the smith be identified with Weland? Are the mighty women to be
regarded as *wælcyrigean* (valkyries) or *hægtessan* witches? Are the 'loud
riders' the valkyries or the Wild Hunt? The *færstice* has been seen as
rheumatism or lumbago, although it might be wiser to regard the
'sudden stitch' as any sharp, unexpected pain (Grundy, 2014, p.54).
The phrase *ylfa gescot* (shot of the elves) is probably traditional, a
means of accounting for unexpected, sudden pain. Elves were
neither totally hostile nor especially friendly towards man, but a race
of fellow creatures pursuing their own aims and ambitions without
reference to the human world.

Glosecki (1989) sees the whole poem as an integrated performance, a healer's means of contacting the otherworldly cause of the
pain – *þa mihtigan wif* – and to deal with it through sympathetic
magic. The prose 'envelope' (parts [i] and [iv]) is usually treated
separately from the verse charm itself, but he regards the two elements as equally important aspects of the curative whole, the healing
performance, each relying on the other for full effect. He further
views the *ut lytel spere* refrain as an exorcism, the healer's therapeutic
song of command addressed to the immediate source of pain (the
spear) directly, in a purely animistic manner.

The probable sources of attack are addressed directly in lines 23–
26a, using significant words (*esa, ylfa, hægtessan*) which would lend
potency to his speech. The *læce* pursues his adversaries in ecstatic
flight to the otherworld and sends the spear back to the mountain
(line 27 *fleoh þær ... on fyrgenheafde*) from which they shot it.[138] The
strongly rhythmic litany might be intended to soothe the patient –
lines 24b and 26b are variations on *ic ðin wille helpan* 'I intend to help

---

[138] The hurling back of an enemy's weapon is known from Anglo-Saxon warfare and described in *The Battle of Maldon* 1.155 (*Wulfstanes beam, Wulfmær se
geonga / forlet forheardne faran eft ongean*); in later Norse literature it was one the
feats of the hero to catch a spear in flight and hurl it back at the attacker. Óðinn
in the *Hávamál* claims to know how to stop a speeding spear, if he can but see
it.

you' – and the imagery would provide a focus for his auto-suggestive healing powers. The healer's approach is directly confrontational and assertive, and intended to inspire confidence in his patient.

The four sections of the text over which various editors have argued are (i) herbal recipe – lines 1 and 2; (ii) mythic context – lines 3, 4, 7–9; (iii) exorcism – lines 5, 6, 10–28; (iv) performative act – line 29. The healer re-enacts the mythic context – through verse and probably other aspects of his performance – in order to open the gateway to the Otherworld, to allow the passage of the spear (the cause of pain) back to its source. The healer is himself protected by the figurative shield – *stod ic under linde, under leohtum scilde* 'I stood behind lindenwood, behind a light shield' (line 7) – from the power of the mighty women, who may be *wælcyrigean* (the *valkyrjur* of Norse tradition). Arguably the *hægtesse*[139] 'hag, witch', if not a human being, is a figure like one of the Norse *Nornir* or *dísir*.

Significantly, there is little in the wording of the charm which is overtly Christian.[140] For example, (i) traditional vocabulary for supernatural beings (*esa, ylfa, hægtessan*); (ii) martial imagery connected to protection from disease (*stod under linde under leohtum scylde*); (iii) weapon imagery (*lytel spere*) for the attack of supernatural enemies; these taken together strongly suggest a narrative which has come down from a time when such ideas were part of current symbolism.

---

[139] It is interesting that both *esa* and *ylfa* are (genitive) plural while *hægtessan* is (genitive) singular. The implication is that the 'gods' and 'elves' are groups, while the 'hag' is a single individual.

[140] The only possible Christian element is *helpe ðin drihten* 'may the lord help thee' – which avoids any specifically religious content since the 'lord' is not named. Jolly (1996) cautions that the wording does not prove that the charm is evidence of pre-Christian Germanic tradition and it may be part of the bulk of 'areligious folk healing' which readily transfers itself from one religious system to another.

SOLOMON AND SATURN

Solomon and Saturn is the name given to four Old English texts (two in verse and two prose) which present a dialogue between 'Solomon', the king of Israel, and 'Saternus', identified in the poems as a prince of the Chaldeans (Pollington, 1995; Anlezark, 2009). The two verse texts, *Solomon and Saturn I* and *Solomon and Saturn II*, have sometimes been treated as a single poem recorded in two manuscripts: Corpus Christi College, Cambridge MS 422 (known as MS.A) and MS 41 (known as MS.B). (In MS A there is a sequence of runic ciphers in addition to the Roman characters.) These are considered some of the most enigmatic verse in Old English due to the many unexplained allusions in the exchange of questions and answers.

In each case the whole text is a kind of challenge–dialogue between two competitive wisdom-figures, *Saternus* (whose background is in the classical pagan world) and *Soloman* (who is firmly Judaeo-Christian in his outlook). A runic element in the contest is brought into play when Saternus refers to *se gepalmtwigoda Pater Noster* 'the palm-twigged Pater Noster' (l.12) and Soloman goes on to set out the virtues of the various characters which spell the words, whereby these act as friendly warriors who mete out painful punishment to the 'foe' i.e., Satan. A similar 'knowledge challenge' format appears in Norse literature, for example in the poems *Vafþrúðnismál, Alvíssmál* and elsewhere (Pollington, 2016, p.243, 321).

The relevance of the text to the present study lies in the question in the *Prose Dialogue of Solomon and Saturn* where Saturnus asks a series of questions and Solomon answers each time. Exchange 58 in one manuscript runs (text from Cross & Hill, 1982, p. 34):[141]

---

[141] The other MS's exchange 16 is parallel: *Saga me hwa wrat bocstafas ærest. Ic þe secge, Mercurius se gigant.* (Say to me who wrote bookstaves first. I say to thee, Mercury the giant.)

Saga me hwa ærost bocstafas sette. Ic þe secge, Mercurius se gygand.

'Say to me who first set down bookstaves? I say to thee, Mercury the giant.'

Given that Mercury is often the classical reflex of Woden (e.g., *dies Mercurii* = *Wodnesdæg*) a link to a long-lived Anglo-Saxon tradition is at least possible in such a context of arcane lore. Mercury was also credited with the devising of writing in classical belief (Birkett, 2019, p.153), but there, it is a minor achievement of the god whose talents are more often deployed in the areas of commerce, medicine and negotiation.

THE OLD ENGLISH RUNE POEM

The *Old English Rune Poem* (*OERP*) was published for the first time in George Hickes's *Linguarum Veterum Septentrionalium Thesaurus* ('treasury of the languages of the old north'), a printed book of 1705 (Halsall, 1981; Page, 1999, p.63; Pollington, 1995, pp.45-51). The source from which Hickes took the text is unknown and is not thought to have survived; it was presumably a handwritten vellum leaf from a miscellany or verse compendium (e.g., on the model of the *Exeter Book*). The poem is set out with the verses in separate paragraphs, each preceded by its neatly serifed runic character. The runes' names appear to have been originally added as a marginal gloss to an existing verse manuscript, in which only the runic characters were originally given; Hickes transcribed both the rune and the marginal name. Although it is difficult to be sure without the original manuscript's evidence, the metrical regularity of the verse suggests either an early date for the poem's composition (e.g., ninth century or earlier) or a skilfully archaistic poem of somewhat later date.

The *OE Rune Poem* is important because it is the earliest complete version of this mnemonic device, which was at one time common across several different Germanic cultures (Halsall, 1981, p.3; Osborn, 1981; Pollington, 2016, pp.185-6; cf. Grimm,

1821).[142] The English poem's verses have a strong riddling aspect which appears less well developed in the later Norwegian and Icelandic versions. The verse for the fourth rune states:

ᚠ [os] byþ ordfruma   ælcre spræce

wisdomes wraþu   and witena frofur

and eorla gehwam   eadnys and tohiht.

'[god] is the origin of all language, wisdom's foundation and wise men's comfort, and to every hero a blessing and hope.'

The names of the runes stated in Hickes's printed text offer a fuller listing than appears in other rune poems because the Anglo-Saxon tradition retained the original runes, sometimes with a change of value, supplemented by new characters and a reassignment of phonemes to graphemes. The poem has extended the meaning of the name ōs (plural ēse) by implicating the Latin homonym os (mouth). The OE word ōs might refer to any of the ēse gods but most likely to Woden, closest associated with eloquence and prophecy, in the cleverly worded verse (Halsall, 1981, pp.109-11; Polomé, 1991, p.431). The rune ᚠ continued in fourth place in the fuþorc sequence even though a character with the original shape (æ) remained in use with a different sound value (/æ/). This suggests that the runes were remembered mainly by their names (not their shape-sequence), and that ōs continued to occupy the position of its predecessor *ansuz despite having a different form and phonemic value.

The IRP (Page, 1998) is more explicit in its identification (text from Halsall, 1981):

[142] The Abecedarium Nordmannicum (AN) in the 9th-century Codex Sangallensis 878, is arguably of similar date but features only the Scandinavian fuþark (Pollington, 1995, pp.51-2; Pollington, 2023). The AN verses do not have any obvious relevance to the wider runic tradition.

Óss er aldingautr ok ásgarðs jǫfurr ok valhallar vísi

'god is the originator of old and the prince of Ásgarð and the leader of Valhǫll.'

It points specifically to Óðinn as the 'creator-god', the 'prince' (literally 'boar' or protector) of the kingdom of the Æsir and 'the one who guides and directs in Valhalla' (Turville-Petre, 1964, p.71).

With the close connection of Woden/Óðinn to the winning and teaching of literacy, it is improbable that a reference to the god would be omitted from the mnemonic verses which promulgated their use. If the profile-bust images on bracteates and elsewhere are symbols of the god, this strengthens the case for his presence in symbolic contexts (but see the remarks on bracteate IK735 above, p.84). It is likely that the fourth rune was originally named for the god of secret knowledge, and that the deviser(s) of the fuþark needed only to mention him with the allusive name *ansuz 'the god', much as the theonym Týr became a synonym for '(any) deity' in later Norse.

ADAM OF BREMEN: GESTA HAMMABURGENSIS

The 11th c. bishop of the northern German diocese of Bremen wrote a monumental work on the history of his see, *Gesta Hammaburgensis Ecclesiae Pontificum*, in which he described the great temple or hall at which the Swedes worshipped in his day, i.e., around 1070 AD (Kay, 2013, p.14; Lassen, 2002, pp.52-3; Schjødt, 2020b, p.1138; text based on G. Waitz, 1876):

> Nunc de supersticione Sueonum pauca dicemus. Nobilissimum illa gens templum habet, quod Ubsola dicitur, non longe positum ab Sictona civitate. In hoc templo, quod totum ex auro paratum est, statuas trium deorum veneratur populus, ita ut potentissimus eorum Thor in medio solium habeat triclinio; hinc et inde locum possident Wodan et Fricco. Quorum significationes eiusmodi sunt: 'Thor', inquiunt, 'praesidet in aere, qui tonitrus et fulmina, ventos ymbresque, serena et fruges gubernat. Alter Wodan, id est furor, bella gerit, hominique ministrat virtutem contra inimicos.

Tertius est Fricco, pacem voluptatemque largiens mortalibus'.
Cuius etiam simulacrum fingunt cum ingenti priapo. Wodanem
vero sculpunt armatum, sicut nostri Martem solent; Thor autem
cum sceptro Iovem simulare videtur. Colunt et deos ex hominibus
factos, quos pro ingentibus factis immortalitate donant, sicut in
Vita sancti Anscarii leguntur Hericum regem fecisse.

Gesta Hammaburgensis Ecclesiae Pontificum, Chapter 26

'We now shall say a little of the superstitions of the Sweones.
That nation has a most remarkable temple which is called Ubsola,
sited not far from the town of Sigtuna. In this temple, which is
completely constructed with gold, three statues of gods are
worshipped by the people, so that Thor, the mightiest of them,
has its place in the middle of the hall, and also Wodan and Fricco
to the sides. Their meanings are of this kind: 'Thor' they say 'rules
over the sky and governs thunder and lightning, winds and storms,
good weather and crops. The second, Wodan – that is, 'rage' –
carries out warfare and gives men strength against enemies. The
third is Frikko, (who) brings peace and pleasure to mortals. His
likeness they also make with an exceptional phallus. Wodan they
display armed, as our (people) show Mars. Thor with his sceptre
is seen to resemble Jove. They also worship men made into gods,
to whom they ascribe immortality because of their remarkable
exploits, as it can be read in the *Vita* of Saint Ansgar that they did
in the case of King Eric.'

The remark '*Wodan, id est furor*' is very telling: the god's name was
associated with rage, fury, mental disturbance and the like. The worship of the gods is detailed in the following chapter:

Omnibus itaque diis suis attributos habent sacerdotes, qui
sacrificia populi offerant. Si pestis et famis imminet, Thorydolo
lybatur, si bellum, Wodani, si nuptiae celebrandae sunt, Fricconi.
Solet quoque post novem annos communis omnium Sueoniae
provintiarum sollempnitas in Ubsola celebrari. Ad quam
videlicet sollempnitatem nulli praestatur immunitas. Reges et

populi, omnes et singuli sua dona transmittunt ad Ubsolam, et quod omni poena crudelius est, illi qui iam induerunt christianitatem, ab illis se redimunt cerimoniis. Sacrificium itaque tale est. Ex omni animante, quod masculinum est, novem capita offeruntur, quorum sanguine deos placari mos est. Corpora autem suspenduntur in lucum, qui proximus est templo. Is enim lucus tam sacer est gentilibus, ut singulae arbores eius ex morte vel tabo immolatorum divinae credantur. Ibi etiam canes et equi pendent cum hominibus, quorum corpora mixtim suspensa narravit mihi aliquis christianorum LXXII vidisse. Ceterum neniae, quae in eiusmodi ritu libationis fieri solent, multiplices et inhonestae ideoque melius reticendae.

Gesta Hammaburgensis Ecclesiae Pontificum, Chapter 27

'All their gods have selected priests to offer sacrifices on behalf of the people. If plague and famine are near, a libation is poured to the idol Thor; if war, to Wodan; if weddings are to be celebrated, to Fricco. It is customary also after nine years to hold in Uppsala a common feast of all the provinces of the Swedes. None is exempt from attendance at this festival. Kings and people jointly and piecemeal send their gifts to Uppsala and, what is harsher than any punishment, those who have already accepted Christianity redeem themselves with these ceremonies. The sacrifice is thus: of every kind of living thing that is male, they offer nine heads with the blood of which it is usual to please gods of this sort. The bodies are hung in the grove that is close to the temple. Now this grove is so sacred to the heathen that each tree in it they consider divine because of the death or rotting of the victims. Even dogs and horses hang there with men, of which a Christian told me that he had seen seventy-two bodies suspended together. Moreover, the songs which are usually sung in the ritual of a sacrifice of this kind are many and shameful so it is better to keep silent about them.'

Here the number nine is foregrounded in the nine male heads and the nine-year cycle of sacrifice, with echoes in the later tradition, e.g., of Óðinn hanging for nine nights on the World Tree (Kay, 2013, p.14). The emphasis on 'nine' is supported by the runic text on the Stentof-ten stone which refers to the sacrifice of nine each of stags and stallions (Holst et al., 2017, pp.38, 53-5). The *scholion* continues:

> Prope illud templum est arbor maxima late ramos extendens, semper viridis in hieme et aestate; cuius illa generis sit, nemo scit. Ibi etiam est fons, ubi sacrificia paganorum solent exerceri et homo vivus immergi. Qui dum non invenitur, ratum erit votum populi. Catena aurea templum illud circumdat pendens supra domus fastigia, lateque rutilans advenientibus, eo quod ipsum delubrum in planitie situm montes in circuitu habeat positos ad instar theatri.

> 'Near this temple stands a very large tree with spreading branches, always green in winter and in summer, of whatever kind it may be nobody knows. There is also a well where the pagans make their sacrifices and plunge a live man into it. If he is then not found, the people's wish will be granted. A golden chain goes round the temple, hanging over the gable of the building and shining far off to those who approach, because the shrine stands in a plain with hills all about it like a theatre.'

The proximity of the well and the great tree to the temple is presumably not an accident: the spot had been chosen for the combination of appropriate features there (Bauschatz, 1982; Kay, 2013, pp.22-4). The *montes* 'hills' are the huge burial mounds which still dominate the landscape at this site, and which form a backdrop to the flat, boggy area of the hall-temple which stood on the site of the present cathedral.

The water from the well may have been used in rites of suste-nance and libation as well as for drowning victims, which in turn may have inspired the reference in *Vǫluspá* to the Nornir sprinkling *Yggdrasill* with the *aurr* 'mud, clay, silt' (text from·Dronke, 1997):[143]

> 19 Ask veit ek standa,
>
> heitir Yggdrasill,
>
> hár baðmr, ausinn
>
> hvítaauri.
>
> Þaðan koma dǫggvar,
>
> þærs í dala falla.
>
> Stendr æ yfir, grœnn
>
> Urðar brunni.
>
> 20 Þaðan koma meyiar,
>
> margs vitandi,
>
> þriar, ór þeim sæ,
>
> er und þolli stendr;
>
> Urð héto eina,
>
> aðra Verðandi –
>
> – skáro á skíði –
>
> Skuld in þriðio.
>
> Þær lǫg lǫgðo,
>
> þar líf kuro
>
> alda bǫrnom,
>
> ørlǫg seggia.

---

[143] A very similar description is given in *Gylfaginning* (16), framed in slightly more archaic language than in *The Poetic Edda* manuscript, e.g., the relative particle *es* instead of standard OIc *er*.

Vǫluspá, v.19-20

'I know an ash stands, it is called Yggdrasill, a mighty tree, moistened with loam whence come dews where they fall in [the] dales. It stands always green above [the] well of Urðr. Thence come maidens, knowing many things - three from the lake which stands beneath the tree; Urð one is called, the second Verðandi - they scored on the billet – Skuld the third; laws they laid down there, lives they chose there for sons of men, men's fates.'

THIETMAR OF MERSEBURG: CHRONICON THIETMARI

This work, which was completed in 1012 AD by the prince-bishop, relates to the history of modern eastern Germany around the millennium. Thietmar was of noble stock, and his family had been embroiled in the politics of imperial succession in the late 10th c. His chronicle, written in eight volumes, is a valuable source for early Slavic history as well as the support it provides for Adam of Bremen's account of heathen sacrificial rites in Denmark (text from Holtzmann, 2007; see Tolley, 2009):

> Sed quia ego de hostiis eorundem antiquis mira audivi, haec indiscussa preterire nolo. Est unus in his partibus locus, caput istius regni, Lederun nomine, in pago qui Selon dicitur ubi post viiii annos mense Ianuario post hoc tempus quo nos theophaniam Domini celebramus, omnes convenerunt et ibi diis suimet lxxxx et viiii homines et totidem equos cum canibus et gallis pro acciptribus oblatis, immolant pro certo ut predixi, putantes hos eisdem erga inferos servituros et commissa crimina apud eosdem placaturos.

'But as I heard marvellous tales of their ancient sacrifices, I do not want to pass them over without reference [to them]. In that region there is one place which is the kingdom's centre, Lederun (Hleiðre) by name, in the district which is called Selon (Zealand) where every nine years in the month of January when we celebrate the coming of the Lord they all gathered and to the gods they sacrifice ninety-nine men and the same amount of horses, with dogs and hens in place of birds of prey, as I said before, thinking for sure that they should be of service to those below and would buy peace for them regarding the offences they had committed.'

ORDERIC VITALIS: HISTORIA ECCLESIASTICA

Orderic was a Benedictine monk, born in 1075 AD, who compiled an *Ecclesiastical History* which he completed in 1141 AD or shortly thereafter. He was still alive the following year and able to make some additional notes, but probably died soon thereafter.

His interest to the present study is in his tale in Book VIII ch.xvii of a priest called Gualchelm who encountered the Wild Hunt in 1091 AD, which he believed to be a company of damned souls emanating from hell. Gualchelm (OE Wealhelm?) was an English cleric but his experience took place in Normandy. Orderic's text gives the priest's report of his terrifying vision, which ends thus (text from Malone, 1959):

> Hæc sine dubio familia Herlechini est; a multis eam olim visam audivi; sed incredulus relationes derisi, quia certa indicia nunquam de talibus vidi. Nunc vero manes mortuorum veraciter video; sed nemo mihi credet, cum visa retulero, nisi certum specimen terrigenis exhibuero.

> 'Without a doubt, this is the company of Herlechin; I have heard from many that it was seen at one time, but I laughed at those unbelievable tales because I had never seen secure evidence of such a thing. Yet now I truly do see the ghosts of the dead, but none will believe me when I speak of my vision unless I provide a definite sample of the soil.'

The *familia Herlechini* was the 'rabble' or 'host' of King Herla, the Wild Hunt, dealt with under the writings of Walter Map, below (p.240). The notion clearly had some currency at this time since

Peter of Blois, an Anglo-French cleric, wrote in 1175 AD denouncing the Anglo-Norman court as *milites Herlewini* 'troop of Herlewin' – a rhetorical expression which nevertheless shows familiarity with the idea of the Hunt and its leader as a threat to orderly life. The name *Herlewin* may be a conflation of *Herlechin* (= *Herla cyng*) and 'Herluin' which Malone postulated to be derived from *Herlan wine* 'followers of Herla' (Malone, 1959, pp.194-5).

12ᵀᴴ – 14ᵀᴴ CENTURY AD

The 12th and 13th c. material relevant to the study of Woden/Óðinn comprises the great bulk of Norse material recorded by Snorri Sturluson and the less well-known Danish traditions recorded in Latin by Saxo Grammaticus. The information so recorded is at once both invaluable for what it tells us of the myths and legends associated with the god, and disappointingly mixed with medieval notions concerning the foolishness of non-Christian beliefs, patronising attitudes to females, and the like (Schjødt, 2020b, p.1142). However, the manuscripts in which the sagas are found are often much later than the original compositions, and the contents redacted (where this can be verified by comparison of different texts) although the dates of the changes are seldom to be determined with accuracy (Lassen, 2022, pp.71-3).

References to Óðinn in skaldic verse are confined to the poems composed before or during the conversion to Christianity – *Húsdrapa, Haustlǫng, Eiríksmál,* and *Hákonarmál* (Lassen, 2022, p.112). The milieu for these poems is the Otherworld, removed from the world of men, and the poets are mainly Norwegians.

There are occasional references to Óðinn in stories which do not actual relate anything substantive about him: his name is given in a stock phrase relating to death, for example. These instances have not been included here for reasons of space. Óðinn appears only occasionally in the *Riddarasögur* 'courtly romances', mainly translations of French *chansons de geste* or Icelandic tales based on the same genre (Lassen, 2022, p.81). The god plays no important part in any of these tales, where he is portrayed as a magician and wearer of disguises. However, in the *konungasögur* 'kings' sagas' he often appears in disguise, usually attempting to divert or thwart the missionary efforts of the Norwegian kings. Several of the *fornaldar-sögur* 'legendary sagas' offer stories in which the god plays a major part (Schjødt, 2020b, pp.1142-3). Often, his intervention causes a clan to rise to power and his later withdrawal of support results in a calamitous fall. I have included summaries of the major texts, which fall more within the sphere of conventional medieval literature than of ancient myths and legends.

14th century texts are not numerous, but the oldest version of *Ǫrvar-Odds Saga* is usually considered to date from around 1300 AD.

The manuscript of *Textus Roffensis* (Rochester Cathedral Library MS A.3.5) with the kinglist for East Anglia dates from the 12th c. although the material is evidently considerably older.

CHURCH CARVINGS

From the 11th c. onwards with the rise of Christian usages in Scandinavia and the erection − or is that rededication? − of stave-built temples, there was a tendency to inclusion of motifs relating to the traditional stories alongside the new fables of saints and monsters. The same impetus may lie behind some unusual elements of church architecture elsewhere (e.g., rural England). There is little doubt that the Manx tradition honoured the old ways alongside the new religion: it may well be the case that such hybrid ideas were common elsewhere, and it is merely the choice of durable materials and their remote locations that have allowed these monuments to survive in some places.

HEGGE

The stave church at Hegge, Norway, with its carved and painted grotesque one-eyed face, has been dated to the period 1215-6 by dendrochronology (Ellis Davidson, 1969, p.112). It is adorned with a runic inscription naming the carver as 'Erlingr Arnason'. Whether

the face is that of the god or of a hanged human is still open to interpretation.

TORPO

A carved wooden bench-end dated to the 12ᵗʰ c. in the stave church
at Torpo, Norway, features a bearded male with his head and shoulders inside the jaws of a huge canine: this may be interpreted as a
reference to Óðinn's fate, his devouring by Fenrir at the Ragnarǫk
(Ellis Davidson, 1969, p.116)

GREAT CANFIELD

There are a number of carved wall and door-jamb elements in the
12ᵗʰ c. church at Great Canfield, Essex, which have been assumed
to recall a supposed Danish presence in the area in the 10ᵗʰ century.
A stern male face with a pelleted band beneath is alleged to refer to
the legend of Þórr and the serpent Jormungandr; a pillar in the south
porch depicts a bearded male face flanked by two birds and with a
band of swastikas carved in relief to the side. The quality of the
workmanship is competent rather than exceptional, and it may well
have been completed by a local provincial craftsman.

The carvings are intriguing and clearly had some religious significance. It is rather a leap to see in them a determined effort to
keep alive belief in the chief of the Old Gods. Humbler entities may
slip down the cracks and remain on the edges of public knowledge,
but the blatant display of Woden-symbolism in a 10ᵗʰ c. church
seems improbable. Yet if this is not Woden/Óðinn, then who is it
and why is it placed so prominently in the public assembly space of
the church?

SKOG TAPESTRY FRAGMENTS

This medieval wall-hanging was discovered in the church at Skog,
Hälsingland, Sweden in 1912 and was sent to Historiska Museet in
Stockholm for conservation (Dimand, 1923; Ellis Davidson, 1969,

p.127). It is made from wool and linen by the soumak technique, and dates from the period 1240–1410 AD, established by radiocarbon dating. The imagery includes a procession (like those on the Oseberg tapestry, the Överhogdal textiles and other finds) with human figures, horses and other animals.

One of the scenes depicts three facing figures wearing headdresses, long tunics and narrow leggings, unlike those on the Oseberg textiles, and with their arms raised, one holding an axe and another with a small cruciform implement. These were quickly identified as the three primary gods (Óðinn, Þórr, Freyr) on the basis that the leftmost figure was missing an eye and the next figure was holding a hammer (Mannering, 2017). On detailed investigation, it was realised that the first figure was made with both eyes present, but one has been lost due to wear-and-tear, and the 'hammer' is more likely a processional cross. Another scene on the tapestry shows a church with bell-ringers inside, which clearly makes the context more probably Christian.

An image of these three characters was chosen for the cover of the paperback edition of H.R. Ellis Davidson's *Gods and Myths of Northern Europe* (1964).

Bergen Runic Wand

There is some archaeological-epigraphic evidence for Óðinn as a bringer of health (e.g., the *Nine Herbs Charm*). A wooden stick found at Søndre Søstergården, Bergen, Norway (reference N B380 M) and dated to circa 1185 AD bears text on two prepared faces (Liestol, 1964, p.37):

hæil ❖ se þu : ok : i : huhum : goþom

þor : þik : þig ❖ gi : oþen : þik ❖ æihi

'May you be hale and in good [frame of] mind. May Þórr receive you, may Óðinn own you.'

The runes are intended to confer good physical and mental health on the bearer through the supervision of both Þórr and Óðinn. The late date of the inscription implies that the empowering phrase 'may Óðinn have you!' no longer entailed a grisly death (as for example when King Eiríkr used it) and was now a kind of benediction (Grundy, 2014, p.13).

PASSIO ET VITA WALDEVI COMITIS

This anonymous 12th-13th c. Latin work relates the life of Waldef (or Waltheof), the son of Sigeward (or Siward) earl of Northumbria. He fought against the Normans in 1066, survived the turmoil of the following years and took part in the rebellion of 1075, after which he sought pardon from William I but this was refused; he was imprisoned and subsequently beheaded. A cult grew up around him in which he was portrayed as a patriot, martyred by the cruel foreign oppressors.

His father, Siward, was an almost mythic figure who, on one occasion while on his way to fight a dragon, received a magical banner from a mysterious old man standing on a rock, which could bring its bearer victory. It is likely that stories of the historical Siward have been conflated with those concerning Sigurðr (the legendary dragonslayer), and that the magical banner episode is drawn from the cycle of tales surrounding Sigurðr and his patron, Óðinn (Turville-Petre, 1964, pp.59-60).

SYMEON OF DURHAM: LIBELLUS DE PRIMO SAXONUM UEL NORMANNORUM ADVENTU

The manuscript BL Cotton Caligula A.viii, with a title meaning 'A small book about the first arrival of the Saxons or Northmen', shows on folio 29 recto an illustration of Woden crowned as a king. The surrounding text cites the royal lineages of the kingdoms of Kent, Mercia, Deira, Bernicia and Wessex and traces the royal line of each back to Woden.

HENRY OF HUNTINGDON: HISTORIA ANGLORUM

The manuscript of Henry's 'History of the English' Cambridge Corpus Christi College MS 66 folio 69 shows a facing full-length figure of a crowned and bearded man wearing ankle-length robes and a gold crown. The surrounding genealogies all begin with 'Voden' and small crowned heads peek out from the border.

WALTER MAP: DE NUGIS CURIALIUM

This work was completed in the late 12th c. by the Anglo-Welsh courtier, Gualterius Mappus or 'Walter Map', who became Archdeacon of Oxford in 1196 AD; he died at some point between May 1208 and September 1210. The title means 'On the Trifles of Courtiers' and the book is, at its heart, a collection of anecdotes and trivia, containing a small amount of verifiable history. In section 11 of *Distinctio Prima*, the first of five sections, Map writes of the Wild Hunt and its legendary leader, King Herla, who later went on to great fame and popularity under the French name 'Harlequin'. The same figure appears in the Italian Renaissance *Commedia dell'Arte* and in medieval French literature as the leader of the *familia Hellequini* (medieval Latin title) or Old French *la maisnie Hellequin* 'the Hellequin household', but these characters are both apparently derived from the traditional tales which also underlie Walter Map's compendium of ancient tales, where the name appears as *Herla rex antiquissimorum Britonum* 'Herla, king of the most ancient Britons'. Harlequin's Italian version traditionally speaks in the dialect of Bergamo, the northern stronghold of the Lombards (Langobards), which may be relevant if Lombard tradition preserved a memory of the Wild Hunt that had been lost elsewhere. According to Kemp Malone in *Herlekin and Herlewin*, 'all the occurrences of the term, until we come to the thirteenth century, have English connexions' (Malone, 1959, p.195). The character's adventures include some common folktale motifs, such as his three-day visit to a mysterious subterranean kingdom during which two centuries passed in the mortal world. His men were compelled to ride on ceaselessly henceforth, since if they were to dismount and touch the earth, they would turn to dust. In the days of King Henry I, the Host was observed sinking into the River Wye at Hereford, never to be seen again.

In folklore, Herla's ghostly cohort occasionally appears to mankind and its background derives ultimately from the Wild Hunt tradition. The name *Herla* is not recorded as a simplex in OE onomastics but it does occur as the prototheme in, e.g., *Herlebeald, Herlebeorht, Herlemund, Herleva, Herleweald, Herlewine, Herlewulf;* the extended 'tribal' form *Herlingas* probably underlies the names of two Norfolk villages, East and West Harling, as well as the *Herelingas* tribe of *Widsith* v.112 (Searle, 1897, p.295; Chambers, 1912, p.218). *Her(e)la* is a variant with formative *-il-a* of *Here-* as in *Herjann* 'Warlord', an *Óðinsheiti* (Malone, 1962, p.170; Kershaw, 2000, pp.39-40). The deuterotheme in 'Harlequin' appears to by OE *cyng*, i.e., 'king', so that the name develops from *herla cy(ni)ng* 'King Herle'.

German folklore recognises a character called the *Erlkönig* or 'Erlking' who lurks in the woods and snatches children. His name is also plausibly derived from *(H)Erlking* and he may have begun as a variant of 'Herla [the] King', the lord of the Otherworld and of the elves (Malone, 1959, pp.193-6). It corresponds to the plural form *Harlungen* found in *Þiðrekssaga* (Malone, 1962, p.170) – two kinsmen who are known in legend as the Gothic champions, Emerca and Fridla.

Malone concludes (1959, p.196): '...*herlekin(g)* was an English word to start with and was applied to Woden in his capacity as leader of the Wild Host, while *herlewin(e)* was applied to the Wild Host itself.'

Saxo Grammaticus: Gesta Danorum

The Danish writer Saxo Grammaticus composed a history of the Danes in Latin, probably while studying in Reims, France, using an array of traditional tales and folklore material; its poetry is in classical hexameters, indicating the literary aspirations of Saxo, and the distance of his retellings from the vernacular tradition (Fisher, 1979;

Ellis Davidson, 1998; Lassen, 2022, p.123). The work was commissioned by Archbishop Absalon during the reign of King Valdemar I (1131-1182 AD) and offers a commentary on Danish kings and kingship (Sawyer, 2015; Lassen, 2022, p.123.).[144] It is the oldest Scandinavian work on the subject of Norse mythology, though it still postdates the conversion by around two centuries and is forced to accommodate its narrative to the slightly clumsy Latin in which it is written (Lassen, 2022, pp.2-3).

That Saxo attempted to create a record of the rise of the Danes to prominence is no great surprise – an emergent nation needs a body of national myth and legend on which to call for inspiration. But he was a less gifted storyteller than Snorri and chose to write in the prevalent medium of medieval Latin instead of the vernacular - the reputation of his work has suffered because of this. The one full manuscript of the text was produced in Paris in 1514 AD, although other fragments are known; the Angers fragment may even be Saxo's own draft (Lassen, 2022, p.123). Saxo's sources included some Danish traditional lore but much of his work follows classical Latin models, and its composition predates most of the Icelandic saga material. He claimed to have used runic inscriptions as a source, but this has been shown to be highly unlikely since he showed no proficiency in that area (Lassen, 2022, p.124). Perhaps he felt that his work should make a claim to an authority embedded in local Danish culture.

Saxo's narrative often presents an alternative version of a tale known from elsewhere in Norse tradition, and with a different flavour (Lindow & Schjødt, 2020, p.978). He is quite clear that the

---

[144] Traditionally, the work is seen as propagandist support for the king and archbishop, glorifying the deeds of the rulers of old. Sawyer's interpretation casts a rather different light in which the archbishop often outshines the monarch, and the secular values of kingship are critiqued. Absalon died in 1201, before the work was finished.

gods of the north were originally men skilled in sorcery and deception who dazzled their benighted contemporaries (Ellis Davidson, 1998; Lindow, 2016, p.118):

> Olim enim quidam magice artis imbuti, Thor uidelicet et Othinus aliique complures miranda prestigiorum machinatione callentes, obtentis simplicium animis diuinitatis sibi fastigium arrogare coeperunt.

> *Gesta Danorum*, Book VI

> 'At one time certain persons imbued with sorcerous arts – that is Thor and Othinus and several others who were skilled at performing marvellous illusions – misled the minds of the simple and adopted the rank of deities.'

The gods are fully euhemerised in the *Gesta* and lack anything of the mystery and latent power which they retain in vernacular poems and tales. Óðinn's appearances are confined to the first nine chapters dealing with the pre-Christian past (Lassen, 2022, pp.126-31). A similar attempt to bring a familiar body of ancient myth into line with later Christian sensibilities can also be found in the inclusion of ancestral figures such as Beow and Scyld among the ancestors of the West Saxon kings (Cronan, 2014; Lassen, 2022, pp.123-48).

The text includes figures familiar from other tales: for example, *Starcatherus* for *Starkaðr*, *Wicarus* for *Víkarr*, *Hotherus* for *Hǫðr*, and so on. Again, these are all presented as human nobles and adventurers (Schlauch, 1931, p.971). Names such as *Uggerus* for *Yggr* and *Gestiblindus* for *Gestumblindi* are elsewhere bynames (*heiti*) for Óðinn but they appear as separate characters in Saxo's account. Lassen (2022, p.143) doubts that he understood them to be derived from or related to the god, although their status as recognised *Óðinsheiti* makes this unlikely. In Saxo's tales, the god interacts with human beings – he adopts a particular chief or warrior as his protégé for a while, then abandons him – so that the focus is away from the myths of Ásgarð and firmly in the world of men, of legend rather than myth in the narrow sense (Schjødt, 2020b, p.1143).

STURLA ÞÓRÐARSON: STURLUNGA SAGA

The text of *Sturlunga saga* (Saga of the Sturlung Family) was composed in part by Snorri Sturluson's nephew, Sturla Þórðarson (1214-1284), and deals with the period 1117-1264 AD during which the proto-republic of Iceland came increasingly under the sway of the Norwegian crown (Lassen, 2022, pp.78-80; Lindow & Andrén, 2020, p.905). The main text is *Íslendinga Saga* 'The Saga of the Icelanders'. Óðinn is mentioned here always as a figure to be feared and spurned. The first instance occurs during a stand-off between a farmer's wife called Þorbjǫrg and Hvamm-Sturla; she thrusts a knife at his face with the intention of putting out one of his eyes, shouting '*Hví skal ek eigi gera þik þeim líkastan er þú vilt líkastr vera, en þat er Óðinn*' ('Why shall I not make you like the one you most want to be like, and that is Odin?') (Lassen, 2022, p.78). The intention is both to disfigure Hvamm-Sturla and mark him out as a despised follower of the deprecated god.

Sturla composed a strophe (dated to 1261 AD) which appears in *Íslendinga saga*, relating to his enemy, Gizurr, who had promised Sturla his support and then betrayed and rejected him (Lassen, 2022, p.79). The verse accuses Gizurr in Odinic terms, that the god frequently broke his word to a champion in all that he had vowed, and *slægr jarl* 'the sly earl' has turned his back on Sturla because he really wants only strife (i.e., just as Óðinn brings down the heroes to whom he has previously offered his support). Gizurr 'he who guesses well' is attested as an *Óðinsheiti* in *Málsháttakvæði*.

EGILS SAGA SKALLA-GRÍMSSONAR

Egils saga Skalla-Grímssonar is 13th c. in date, perhaps ca. 1240 AD; it is the oldest surviving saga dealing with Icelanders and their deeds (Lassen, 2022, pp.71-6). The author of *Egils saga* is anonymous, but attribution to Snorri is often made (Thorgeirsson, 2014). Once Egill left Iceland and began to mix with nobles and magnates, using his skills as a warrior and a poet, he learnt of the worship of Óðinn (Tur-ville-Petre, 1964, p.69). His colourful life is recounted at length, although it is not considered a reliable source in detail: 'The narrative of *Egils saga* is practically useless as an historical document; but it may still preserve some genuine facts, and some genuine poems of a tenth-century, first-generation Icelandic *skáld*' as Hines put it (Hines, 1997, p.84). The chronology of important events is muddled: for example, Egil left Norway in 936 AD but the saga puts it *after* his involvement at *Brunanburh* in 937, Eiríkr was probably not king in York until 947, his famed verse in praise of the king composed in 948 (Gordon, 1957, p.107).

Two of his poems which stand out are quoted at length in certain redactions: *Hǫfuðlausn* and *Arinbjarnarkviða*. The first was composed when Egill suffered shipwreck off the Northumbrian coast and jour-neyed to his friend Arinbjǫrn at York, where he fell into the hands of his long-term enemy, Eiríkr Blood-axe. He had arrived one evening and gone to the lodgings of his friend, who then took him to the king's hall and asked that the traveller who had come so far to sit with him should be granted an audience. Eiríkr and his queen, Gunnhildr, were annoyed to see Egill's ugly face in their company but Arinbjǫrn managed to persuade them that to kill Egill at night-time would be an unworthy deed (*níðingsverk*) *því at náttvíg eru morðvíg* 'because kill-ings at night are murders'. The two men were bidden to return in the morning. They went to the lodging and sat up all night composing a remarkably intricate and end-rhymed praise-verse for Eiríkr, with which the poet hoped to be rewarded with his life. The poem includes occasional references to Egill's patron-god, e.g., l.176 (text from Gor-don, 1957):

> Berk Óðins mjǫð á Engla bjǫð
>
> 'I bear Óðinn's mead to the fields of the English'

where the 'mead' reference is to the winning of the mead of inspira-tion, so 'poetry'; or l.200:

Óðins eiki í járnleiki

'Óðinn's oaks [= warriors] in iron-play [= hand-to-hand combat]'

or l.238:

Óðins ægi of jǫru fægi.

'Óðinn's sea [= poetry] about the polisher of battle [= warrior]'

The god is also called Viðrir (l.182):

En Viðrir sá hvar valr of lá

'and Viðrir saw where the slain men lay'

The poem is a virtuoso piece with subtle aural patterning, sometimes across pairs of lines, and several rhymed refrains. The king was suitably impressed - or feared the damage to his reputation that killing Egill would entail after receiving so lavish a gift.

The other poem *Arinbjarnarkviða* was composed in praise of his close friend, Arinbjǫrn, who had returned to Norway to regain estates which he had been forced to abandon while Hákon was king. In this poem he refers to poetry as *Yggs full* 'the drink of Yggr' and *Yggjar miði* 'Yggr's mead'.

Egill is depicted as a fierce adherent of the cult of Óðinn: a warrior, adventurer, rune-magician and poet. His devotion to the wargod serves him well in terms of renown and reputation, but the accidental and tragic drowning of one of his sons (Bǫðvarr) he ascribes to the fickleness of his patron; another, younger son called Gunnarr had recently died from a fever. Egill was by this time about fifty years old and not likely to produce more heirs (Harris, 2007, pp.156-7). The poem which Egill composed to console himself for his sons' loss – *Sonatorrek* – is included only in the C redaction of the saga (Kershaw, 1922; Price, 2019, p.56; Lassen, 2022, p.74). It uses some familiar kennings to specify the god: *bróður vilis* 'Vili's brother', *mímis vinr* 'Mímir's friend'. It is plausible that the C-version of the saga's text (in which the poem appears) draws on additional information unavailable to the composer of the prose saga.

The opening stanza gives a flavour of the poem's tenderness and overwhelming grief, expressed in characteristically muscular terms (text from Jónsson, 1912):

Mjǫk erum tregt

tungu at hrœra

með loptvætt

ljóðpundara;

esa nú vænt

of Viðurs þýfi,

né hógdrœgt

ór hugar fylgsni

'Greatly am I grieved to move my tongue with the weight of the song-pounder; now there is a lack of Viður's theft, nor is it easy to bring it from my mind's hiding place'

The 'song-pounder' is the poet's tongue, Viðurr is a name of Óðinn and his 'theft' is the gift of verse-making in reference to the winning of the mead from Suttungr (Dronke, 1996). Egill finds strong images to show his difficulty in expressing the extent of his emotions; these are often drawn from myth, especially the cycle of tales relating to Óðinn. One recurrent theme is that of sacrifice and bloodshed, a tally of dead family members whose loss cannot be mended. In the closing sections (verse 22 onwards) Egill reproaches himself for trusting the god whom he knew to be full of deceit, and yet is thankful for the talents the god brought him which have allowed him to outwit foes and prepared him for warfare with immense defiant courage. The final verse (25) runs (text from Jónsson, 1912):

Nú erum torvelt,

Tveggja bága

njǫrva nipt

á nesi stendr,

skalk þó glaðr

góðum vilja

ok óhryggr

heljar bíða.

'Now I am troubled: Tveggi's enemy's sister stands on the headland, yet I shall await death gladly, with a good will and undaunted.'

'Tveggi's enemy's sister' is a kenning – Tveggi is Óðinn and his enemy is the wolf who finally devours him, Fenrir; the sister of Fenrir is Hel, queen of the land of the dead. Thus, the sentiment is 'death awaits me' (Price, 2019, p.56).

Egill is a significant Icelandic devotee of Óðinn in the saga literature, but his career mirrors in some ways that of the Icelander Víga-Glúmr, who grew up in a community which honoured Freyr. As a young man he visited his mother's family in Norway and met his maternal grandfather, Vigfúss, a renowned fighter and follower of Óðinn. As a parting gift, Glúm received a sword, spear and cloak from the old man with the advice that he would keep his good reputation as long as he kept those items; on Vígfúss's death, his *hamingja* or protective spirit travelled to Iceland to look out for Glúm henceforth. It is surely relevant that the cloak and spear were among the prized gifts, both of which appear often in descriptions of Óðinn (Turville-Petre, 1964, p.69).

The god is interested only in noblemen and kings; men of farmer-stock like Egill and Glúm usually have no business with the aristocrat's patron, and the god does not figure prominently in Icelandic folklore. In sagas and tales, Icelanders might still encounter him on their travels, especially in the liminal areas of Scandinavia. The paucity of references to Óðinn in Norse tales (as opposed to the strong traditions regarding Þórr and Freyr) implies that he was not considered an active threat to Christianity in the (quasi-)egalitarian society of Iceland (Lassen, 2022, pp.75-6).

LAXDÆLA SAGA

'The Saga of the Men of Laxdale' dating to the later 13th c. and of unknown authorship, deals with the deeds of some of the early inhabitants of this Icelandic valley, including Kjartan Ólafsson who visited Norway and was willingly converted to Christianity because, as he told King Ólaf Tryggvason, his countrymen *eiga meira traust undir afli sínu ok vápnum heldr en þar sem er Þórr ok Óðinn* 'have more faith in their own strength and weapons rather than in Thor and Odin' (Lassen, 2022, p.74). This supports the medieval notion that belief in the old gods was obsolescent in Iceland and that wise men already had a form of faith consistent with Christian values (Sigurðsson, 2020).

ORKNEYINGA SAGA

The 'Saga of the Men of Orkney' was apparently compiled in the late 12th c. (perhaps around 1200 AD) but the earliest extant version was created in the following century, probably at Oddi in Iceland (Sigurðsson, 2020, p.1653, 1687). The central characters are the various Norwegian *jarlar* 'earls' and other nobles, their military supporters and some leading female figures of the period roughly contemporary with the rule of Harald Fairhair in Norway. Feuds and killings are the main dramatic actions, often instigated by ferocious and implacable female characters. The tale of settlement appears to be broadly reliable, but the details are often embroidered, such as a poison-soaked shirt which brought about the death of an earl, and the notorious 'blood eagle' episode.

In chapter 8, Einar sacrifices his enemy Halvdan Haaleg (Palsson & Edwards, 1978, p.30; Grundy, 2014, p.17):

Þar fundu þeir Hálfdan hálegg, ok lét Einarr rísta ǫrn á baki honum með sverði, ok skera rifin ǫll frá hrygginum ok draga þar út lúngun, ok gaf hann Óðni til sigrs sèr

'They found Halvdan Long-Leg there and Einar had an eagle carved on his back with a sword and all the ribs sliced away from the spine and the lungs pulled out to give him to Óðinn for his [own] victory'

This is one of the two reports of the 'blood eagle' and, although it is frequently repeated in the more lurid accounts of Viking period history, it is of doubtful historicity (Hutton, 1991, p.282; Einarsson, 1993, pp.80-111). The other quasi-historical instance concerns the killing of King Ælla of Northumbria in a similar manner.

BÁRÐAR SAGA SNÆFELLSÁSS

This minor saga (*The Saga of Bárðr, God of Snow-Fell*) is probably a compilation of at least two sources, dating from the later 14th century AD combining folk-tale and historical elements. Bárðr was a settler with partly supernatural parentage who established himself in Iceland and late in life became a guardian-spirit helping travellers and seamen in need.

A character named Rauðgrani (Red-moustache) arrives mysteriously onboard a ship and begins to discuss the old religion with his messmates. He is one-eyed and wears a large mottled blue cloak. A Christian priest in the ship's complement takes exception to him and strikes him with a cross, at which he falls overboard. The crew believe that he may have been Odin in disguise (Lassen, 2022, p.74).

ODDR SNORRASON: ÓLAFS SAGA TRYGGVASONAR

A saga concerning Ólafr Tryggvason was composed in Latin in the late 1100s by Oddr Snorrason, a Benedictine monk at the Þingeyrar monastic house. It formed the basis of the vernacular *Ólafs saga Tryggvasonar* as well as some Latin works (Gunnell, 2020a, p.203). Óðinn is represented as an emanation or disguise of Satan, who wishes to subvert the successes of the Norwegian court in bringing Christianity to the north.

This story is an interesting commentary on kingship in the later 10th-early 11th century. Olaf's rise to power was opposed by most of the wealthy and important men of Norway, and he used a variety of methods to induce them to change their allegiance from the old gods to the Christian religion which he supported: these included deceit, intimidation and direct violence. Indeed, the king is shown to have few personal virtues (he was shrewd rather than wise, disrespectful of laws and customs, selfish and acquisitive, cruel to his enemies, ruthless and unpopular among his subjects) and his imposition of Christianity in Norway was a mere religious pretext for his political domination of all who opposed him.

In one incident (*Olafssaga Tryggvasonar* ch.71), the king was at a feast and listened with great interest to tales about the god Óðinn related by an old wayfarer wearing a broad-brimmed hat. The traveller's knowledge and lively speech beguiled the king, who sat up late into the night deep in conversation – until the bishop intervened to prevent Ólaf learning more (Sawyer, 2015, pp.60-1; Lassen, 2022, p.84). It is likely enough that Ólaf's interest in Óðinn was, in popular understanding, due to the king's personal moral outlook in which violence and deception figured prominently. Ólaf's arrogance eventually cost him his life: his kingdom was then divided up among his enemies, Svein Forkbeard and the sons of Earl Håkon.

QRVAR-ODDS SAGA

The text is found in three versions, the oldest probably written around 1300 AD. The hero is presented as an example of a heathen who intuitively behaves according to Christian ideas of morality and undertakes a pilgrimage to the Holy Land in order to bathe in the River Jordan. Once he was baptised, Qrvar-Odd encounters a character called Rauðgrani (Red-moustache) [145] wearing the customary blue cloak but of pleasing appearance, who is later identified as Óðinn (Lassen, 2022, pp.105-6). Rauðgrani swears friendship to the hero but tries to dissuade him from taking vengeance on his enemy, Qgmundr, and is always absent when danger is present; in this he is

---

[145] This name also appears in *Bárðar Saga Snæfellsáss;* the name denoting a 'red-beard' is more naturally associated with Þórr.

little more than a negative caricature of Óðinn who normally incites his protégés to battle.

In two recensions of the tale, a mysterious character called Jólfr offers the hero three magical arrows, from which his soubriquet 'Arrow-Odd' derives; he is not identified directly as Óðinn, and may not have been introduced with the god in mind. The tone of the story is very clearly anti–heathen, and the author's depiction of foolish pagans is contrasted with Ǫrvar-Odd's courage and good sense.

ÓLAFS SAGA TRYGGVASONAR EN MESTA

The 'longer saga of King Olaf' is probably 14th c. in date and is extant in multiple 14th century manuscripts. The saga is a compilation of sources which depict the conflict between the Christian champion, King Ólafr, and the adherents of the old religion (Du Bois, 2020, p.362; Lassen, 2022, p.74). It contains inserted incidental material (*þættir* 'short stories') not found in *Ólafs saga Tryggvasonar* (Lassen, 2022, p.83). The general presentation of the heathens is that they are foolish, simple and gullible; tellingly, the better sort of heathen is not fooled by such nonsense, and so refrains from any worship at all until the light of Christianity is brought to his attention.

The version of the saga in *Flateyjarbók* includes incidents not in other manuscripts, including one where Ólaf is having a new and very large ship built but no suitable timber can be found for the keel, until a huge, surly one-eyed man called Forni produces just the right piece of wood (Lassen, 2022, p.87). When Ólaf hears of this, he orders the plank split open and a dangerous snake is found inside which would have endangered the king's life, whereupon the bishop sanctifies the timber and the ship is named *Ormrinn inn langi* 'The Long Serpent' in recognition of this lucky escape.

SNORRI STURLUSON: HEIMSKRINGLA

Heimskringla is a summary account of the history of Norway set down by Snorri as a compendium of traditions regarding the great men and rulers of old, as told in various sagas. The name *Heimskringla* derives from the opening words *Kringla heimsins* 'the orb of the world'. A manuscript of the work dating to ca.1260 was lost in a fire in 1728, but a single leaf survived and is now in the National University Library of Iceland in Reykjavík (Lbs fragm. 82). To what extent Snorri should be credited with the authorship of the whole text is a moot point, since there are stylistic and other differences between the *Edda* sections and the *Ynglingatal* suggesting multiple sources.[146] Snorri probably worked with the stories in several existing manuscripts supplemented by skaldic poems (Hermann, 2020, p.49; Lindow, 2020, pp.77, 86, 89-92).

The text was apparently compiled in the 1230s and encapsulates several previous works with a similar subject matter: Norwegian history down to 1177 AD (Sawyer, 2015, pp.1-16). Many of the kings are shown in a less than favourable light, while the jarls and chieftains often appear as upholders of virtue and traditional values. Snorri's outlook and presentation of the stories are consistent with his medieval cultural milieu, but the information he records is crucial to modern understanding of the mythology (Schjødt, 2020b, p.1141).

YNGLINGA SAGA

The *Ynglinga saga* constitutes the earlier part of Snorri's *Heimskringla* text and includes the *Ynglingatal* or 'List of Yng's Descendants', the early rulers of the Scandinavian territories. The *Ynglingatal* is usually considered to be very much older than Snorri's text - possibly as early as the 9th c. - and does not share his preoccupation with showing the kings as weak or foolish while the magnates are generally shrewd and upstanding.

---

[146] For example, the author of the saga knew both Snorri's *Edda* and *Gylfaginning*.

The *Ynglinga saga* narrates the arrival of the Norse gods in Scandinavia from Asia, with emphasis on Óðinn's role as the *pater familias* and a sorcerer, and how Freyr founded the Swedish Yngling dynasty (Lindow, 2020, p.91; Lassen, 2022, pp.149-68). The account is dominated by Snorri's understanding that the name of the family of gods known as the *Æsir* must mean 'men of Asia' (Lassen, 2022, pp.150-1). It describes the descent of Swedish kings from the legendary past as far as Ingjald then turns to the line which settled in Norway and became the ancestors of the Norwegian king, Harald Fairhair. The extent to which Snorri or his sources invented explanations to account for incongruous names and motives has been much discussed, but it is no longer considered wise to dismiss all that the text has to say about the early history of the Scandinavian dynasties (Rausing, 1985; Du Bois, 2020, p.363; Lassen, 2022, p.149; Shippey, 2022).

The text survives in three medieval manuscripts, of which two were badly damaged by fire in 1728, but copies of both had been made which have been preserved. Its sources include the *Ynglingatal* proper and other works concerning the legendary early rulers (*Ragnarsdrápa, Skjǫldunga Saga, Háleygjatal* and others) by various poets (Lassen, 2022, p.150; Schjødt, 2020b).

The gods are presented as a tribe of human wizards with unusual abilities for deception and persuasion, euhemerized in order to demonstrate a proper Christian disdain for inconvenient local traditions. There are several early parts which tell of Óðinn and his exploits where 'we probably get information genuinely belonging to the pagan Óðinn discourse: he is wise, but often unreliable' (Schjødt, 2020b, p.1142).

These are the principal sections (text from Aðalbjarnarson, 1979):

(III.) Óðinn átti tvá brœðr. Hét annarr Vé, en annarr Vílir. Þeir brœðr hans stýrðu ríkinu, þá er hann var í brottu. Þat var eitt sinn, þá er Óðinn var farinn langt í brott ok hafði lengi dvalzk, at Ásum þótti ørvænt hans heim. Þá tóku brœðr hans at skipta arfi hans, en konu hans Frigg, gengu þeir báðir at eiga. En litlu síðar kom Óðinn heim. Tók hann þá við konu sinni.

'(3) Óðinn had two brothers, one called Vé and the other Vili. These brothers ruled the kingdom when he was away. One time when Óðinn had been travelling afar and dwelt abroad a long time, the Æsir lost hope of his return; his brothers began sharing out his wealth, and both took his wife Frigg for themselves. But a little later, Óðinn came home and took back his wife.'

(IV.) Óðinn fór með her á hendr Vǫnum, en þeir urðu vel við ok vǫrðu land sitt, ok hǫfðu ymsir sigr. Herjuðu hvárir land annarra ok gerðu skaða. En er þat leiddist hvárumtveggjum, lǫgðu þeir milli sín sættarstefnu, ok gerðu frið ok seldust gíslar. Fengu Vanir sína hina ágæztu menn, Njǫrd hinn auðga ok son hans Frey, en Æsir þar í mót þann, er Hœnir hét, ok kǫlluðu hann allvel til hǫfðingja fallinn. Hann var mikill maðr ok hinn vænsti. Með honum sendu Æsir þann, er Mímir hét, inn vitrasti maðr, en Vanir fengu þar í mót þann, er spakastr var í þeira flokki. Sá hét Kvásir. En er Hœnir kom í Vanaheim, þá var hann þegar hǫfðingi gǫrr. Mímir kenndi honum ráð ǫll. En er Hœnir var staddr á þingum eða stefnum, svá at Mímir var eigi nær, ok kœmi nǫkkur vandamál fyrir hann, þá svaraði hann æ inu sama: 'ráði aðrir', kvað hann. Þá grunaði Vani, at Æsir myndi hafa falsat þá í mannaskiptinu. Þá tóku þeir Mími ok hálshjoggu ok sendu hǫfuðit Ásum. Óðinn tók hǫfuðit ok smurði urtum þeim, er eigi mátti fúna, ok kvað þar yfir galdra ok magnaði svá, at þat mælti við hann ok sagði honum marga leynda hluti. Njǫrð ok Frey setti Óðinn blótgoða, ok váru þeir díar með Ásum. Dóttir Njarðar var Freyja. Hon var blótgyðja. Hon kenndi fyrst með Ásum seið, sem Vǫnum var títt. Þá er Njǫrðr var með Vǫnum, þá hafði hann átta systur sína, því at þat váru þar lǫg. Váru þeira bǫrn Freyr ok Freyja. En þat var bannat með Ásum at byggva svá náit at frændsemi.

'(4) Óðinn set off with a troop against the Vanir but they were well prepared and defended their lands, and they [both] had changeable fortunes; they each harried the lands of the others and did harm. In the end they wearied of it, and both sides set a meeting and made a truce and exchanged hostages. The Vanir took along their best men, Njǫrðr the blessed and his son Freyr, and the Æsir sent him who is called Hœnir, whom they said to be suitable for the rank of chieftain: he was a great man and the most handsome. With him the Æsir sent the one who is called Mímir, who was the most learned of men. The Vanir took along him who was the wisest of their group, who is called Kvasir. When Hœnir came to Vanaheim, he was made a chieftain and Mímir gave him all good counsel. But when Hœnir stood to speak at a *þing* or meeting while Mímir was not nearby, and any contentious issue came before him, he always answered in the same way: he said 'others should judge'. Once the Vanir began to suspect that the Æsir had been false in the exchange of men, they took Mímir and beheaded him and sent the head to the Æsir. Óðinn took the head and smeared it with herbs so that it should not rot, and spoke spells over it, and empowered it so that it spoke with him and disclosed to him many secrets. Óðinn set Njorðr and Freyr as sacrifice-priests, and they were the priests of the Æsir. Freyja, daughter of Njǫrðr, was the sacrifice-priestess and first taught *seiðr* to the Æsir as it was used by the Vanir. When Njǫrðr was with the Vanir he had his own sister as his wife, because such was the law there; their children were Freyr and Freyja. But it was banned among the Æsir to marry such near kinsmen.'

(V.) Fjallgarðr mikill gengr af landnorðri til útsuðrs. Sá skilr Svíþjóð ina miklu ok ǫnnur ríki. Fyrir sunnan fjallit er eigi langt til Tyrklands. Þar átti Óðinn eignir stórar. Í þann tíma fóru Rúmverjahǫfðingjar víða um heiminn ok brutu undir sik allar þjóðir, en margir hǫfðingjar flýðu fyrir þeim ófriði af eignum sínum. En fyrir því at Óðinn var forspár ok fjǫlkunnigr, þá vissi hann, at hans afkvæmi mundi um norðrhálfu heimsins byggja. Þá

setti hann brœðr sína, Vé ok Víla, yfir Ásgarð, en hann fór ok
díar allir með honum ok mikit folk annat. Fór hann fyrst vestr í
Garðaríki ok þá suðr í Saxland. Hann átti marga sonu. Hann
eignaðist ríki víða um Saxland, ok setti þar sonu sína til
landsgæzlu. Þá fór hann norðr til sjávar ok tók sér bústað í ey
einni. Þar heitir nú Óðinsey í Fjóni. Þá sendi hann Gefjun norðr
yfir sundit í landaleitan. Þá kom hon til Gylfa, ok gaf hann henni
eitt plógsland. Þá fór hon í Jǫtunheima ok gat þar fjóra sonu við
jǫtni nǫkkurum. Hon brá þeim í yxnalíki ok fœrði þá fyrir
plóginn ok dró landit út á hafit ok vestr gegnt Óðinsey, ok er þat
kǫlluð Selund. Þar byggði hon síðan. Hennar fekk Skjǫldr, sonr
Óðins. Þau bjoggu at Hleiðru. Þar er vatn eða sjár eptir. Þat er
kallat Lǫgrinn. Svá liggja firðir í Leginum sem nes í Selundi. Svá
kvað Bragi hinn gamli:

'Gefjon dró frá Gylfa

glǫð, djúprǫðuls ǫðla,

svát af rennirauknum

rauk, Danmarkar auka.

Bǫru øxn ok átta

ennitungl, þars gingu

fyr vineyjar víðri

valrauf, fjogur haufuð.'

En er Óðinn spurði, at góðir landskostir váru austr at Gylfa, fór
hann þannok, ok gerðu þeir Gylfi sætt sína, því at Gylfi þóttisk
engi krapt til hafa til mótstǫðu við Ásuna. Mart áttust þeir Óðinn
við ok Gylfi í brǫgðum ok sjónhverfingum, ok urðu Æsir jafnan
ríkri. Óðinn tók sér bústað við Lǫginn, þar sem nú eru kallaðar
fornu Sigtúnir, ok gerði þar mikit hof ok blót eptir siðvenju Ásanna.
Hann eignaðist þar lǫnd svá vítt sem hann lét heita Sigtúnir. Hann
gaf bústaði hofgoðunum. Njǫrðr bjó í Nóatúnum, en Freyr at

Uppsǫlum, Heimdallr at Himinbjǫrgum, Þórr á Þrúðvangi, Baldr á
Breiðabliki. Ǫllum fekk hann þeim góða bólstaði.

'(5) A great mountain range runs from north-east to south-west
which separates Great Sweden from other kingdoms. South of this
range it is not far to Tyrkland where Óðinn had great landholdings.
In those times the chieftains of Rome went widely across the
world and brought all peoples under them, and many chiefs fled
from their lands due to hostility. But Óðinn, having foresight and
foreknowledge, knew that his scions would dwell in the northern
part of the world. Then he set his brothers, Vé and Vili, over
Ásgarð and he set off with all the Díar and a great following of
men. He first went west into Garðaríki [eastern Europe] and then
south to Saxland. He had many sons, and when he had taken a
wide territory in Saxland he set his sons there as land-chiefs. He
then went north to the sea and made there a settlement on an
island which is called Óðinsey [Odense] on Funen. He then sent
Gefjon north across the sound on a reconnaissance. Then she came
to Gylfi who gave her one plough-land. Then she went into
Jotunheim, and bore four sons to a certain giant, and turned them
into a yoked team of oxen. She yoked them to the plough and
ploughed out the land into the sea west across from Óðinsey, and
that is called 'Zealand'. She dwelt there afterwards. Skjold son of
Óðinn took her to wife and they dwelt at Hleiðre. Where the
ploughland had been became a lake afterwards, called Lǫgrinn. So
the fjords of Lǫgrinn lie across from the headlands of Zealand.
Thus said Bragi the Old:

"Gefjon drew away from Gylfi / happily the freehold of the wave-
treasure / so that from the running beasts / sweat steamed off,
Denmark's increase / the oxen bore eight eyes also / stars of the
forehead, there they went / before the field's wide / spoils, four
heads."

When Óðinn learnt that good lands were to the east around Gylfi,
he went there and the two of them made a treaty, because Gylfi

thought that he had not the strength to withstand the Æsir. Óðinn and Gylfi each used many ploys and spells against each other, but the Æsir were always the stronger. Óðinn took for himself a dwelling place beside Lǫginn which is now called Sigtúnir, and he made a great hall-temple there and sacrifices according to the custom of the Æsir. He seized lands for himself which he called Sigtúnir. He gave settlements to the priests of the temple. Njǫrðr dwelt at Nóatún and Freyr at Uppsala, Heimdallr at Himinbjorg, Þórr at Þrúðvangi, Baldr at Breiðablik; to all of them he gave good landholdings.'

(VI.) Þá er Ása-Óðinn kom á Norðrlǫnd, ok með honum díar, er þat sagt með sannendum, at þeir hófu ok kenndu íþróttir þær, er menn hafa lengi síðan með farit. Óðinn var gǫfgastr af ǫllum, ok af honum námu þeir allir íþróttirnar, því at hann kunni fyrst allar ok þó flestar. En þat er at segja, fyrir hverja sǫk hann var svá mjǫk tígnaðr, þá báru þessir hlutir til: Hann var svá fagr ok gǫfugligr álitum, þá er hann sat með sínum vinum, at ǫllum hló hugr við. En þá er hann var í her, þá sýndisk hann grimmligr sínum óvinum. En þat bar til þess, at hann kunni þær íþróttir, at hann skipti litum ok líkjum á hverja lund, er hann vildi. Ǫnnur var sú, at hann talaði svá snjalt ok slétt, at ǫllum, er á heyrðu, þótti þat eina satt. Mælti hann allt hendingum, svá sem nú er þat kveðit, er skáldskapr heitir. Hann ok hofgoðar hans heita ljóðasmiðir, því at sú íþrótt hófst af þeim í Norðrlǫndum. Óðinn kunni svá gera, at í orrostum urðu óvinir hans blindir eða daufir eða óttafullir, en vápn þeira bitu eigi heldr en vendir, en hans menn fóru brynjulausir ok váru galnir sem hundar eða vargar, bitu í skjǫldu sína, váru sterkir sem birnir eða griðungar. Þeir drápu mannfólkit, en hvártki eldr né járn orti á þá. Þat er kallaðr berserksgangr.

'(6) When Æsir-Óðinn came into the northlands, and with him the priests, it is truly said that they brought and taught to others the skills which men have long since used. Óðinn was the most skilful of them all, and from him they all learnt their skills because he knew them first of all and many more than others knew. And it is now to be told for what reason he was so honoured, and which matters had bearing on that: he was so fair and so dignified in appearance when he sat among his own friends that it was a joy to all, but when he was in warlike mood he then seemed fearsome to his enemies. That came about from this cause, that he knew the skill whereby he could change his shape and form in whatever way he wished. Another reason was that he spoke so smoothly and cleverly that what he said seemed true to those who heard it. He said everything in verses, such as are now composed, which is called "poetry". He and his temple-priests were called 'song-makers' because from them that skill was brought into the northlands. Óðinn could work it so that in battle his foes became blind or deaf or awe-struck and their weapons did not bite more than a twig. Moreover, his men rushed forward unarmoured and were as mad as hounds or wolves, they bit their own shields, were as strong as bears or bulls. They killed menfolk but neither fire nor iron harmed them. That is called "berserkergang".'

(VII.) Óðinn skipti hǫmum. Lá þá búkrinn sem sofinn eða dauðr, en hann var þá fugl eða dýr, fiskr eða ormr ok fór á einni svipstund á fjarlæg lǫnd at sínum ørendum eða annarra manna. Þat kunni hann enn at gera með orðum einum at sløkkva eld ok kyrra sjá ok snúa vindum hverja leið, er hann vildi, ok hann átti skip, er Skíðblaðnir hét, er hann fór á yfir hǫf stór, en þat mátti vefja saman sem dúk. Óðinn hafði með sér hǫfuð Mímis, ok sagði þat honum mǫrg tíðendi ór ǫðrum heimum, en stundum vakði hann upp dauða menn ór jǫrðu, eða settisk undir hanga. Fyrir því var hann kallaðr draugadróttinn eða hangadróttinn. Hann átti hrafna tvá, er hann hafði tamit við mál. Flugu þeir víða um lǫnd ok sǫgðu honum mǫrg tíðendi. Af þessum hlutum varð hann stórliga fróðr. Allar þessar íþróttir kenndi hann með rúnum ok ljóðum þeim, er galdrar heita. Fyrir því eru Æsir kallaðir galdrasmiðir. Óðinn kunni þá íþrótt, svá at mestr máttr fylgði, ok framði sjálfr, er seiðr heitir, en af því mátti hann vita ørlǫg

manna ok óorðna hluti, svá ok at gera mǫnnum bana eða
óhamingju eða vanheilendi, svá ok at taka frá mǫnnum vit eða
afl ok gefa ǫðrum. En þessi fjǫlkynngi, er framið er, fylgir svá
mikil ergi, at eigi þótti karlmǫnnum skammlaust við at fara, ok
var gyðjunum kennd sú íþrótt. Óðinn vissi um allt jarðfé, hvar
fólgit var, ok hann kunni þau ljóð, er upp lauksk fyrir honum
jǫrðin, ok bjǫrg ok steinar, ok haugarnir, ok batt hann með
orðum einum þá, er fyrir bjoggu, ok gekk inn ok tók þar slíkt er
hann vildi. Af þessum krǫptum varð hann mjǫk frægr. Óvinir
hans óttuðust hann, en vinir hans treystusk honum ok trúðu á
krapt hans ok á sjálfan hann. En hann kenndi flestar íþróttir sínar
blótgoðunum. Váru þeir næst honum um allan fróðleik ok
fjǫlkyngi. Margir aðrir námu þó mikit af, ok hefir þaðan af
dreifzk fjǫlkyngin víða ok haldizk lengi. En Óðin ok þá hǫfðingja
tólf blótuðu menn ok kǫlluðu goð sín ok trúðu á lengi síðan.
Eptir Óðins nafni var kallaðr Auðun, ok hétu menn svá sonu sína,
en af Þórs nafni er kallaðr Þórir eða Þórarinn eða dregit af ǫðrum
heitum til, svá sem Steinþórr eða Hafþórr, eða enn breytt á fleiri
vega.

'(7) Óðinn could change his form; his body then lay as if asleep or
dead, and he then became a bird or beast, fish or serpent, and he
went swiftly through distant lands on his own business or that of
others. He knew how to make things happen with words alone,
to quench fire and to calm the sea, and to turn the wind to
whichever way he wished. Óðinn owned a ship which is called
Skíðblaðnir in which he travelled over great seas, and which he
could furl like a banner. Óðinn kept with him the head of Mímir,
and it spoke to him of great events in other lands. At times he
raised dead men out of the earth or sat himself down under hanged
men, whence he was called "Lord of the Undead" or "Lord of the
Hanged". He owned two ravens which he had taught to speak,
they flew widely over the lands and told him many tidings. From
these he became very wise. All these skills he taught with runes
and songs which are called *'galdrar'* [charms], whence the Æsir

were called "charm-makers". Óðinn understood the skill in which
the greatest power resides, which is called "*seiðr*". From this he
could know men's futures or their lot to come, and bring death
or bad luck to men, or poor health, or take the strength and wit
from one man and give them to another. But after this sorcery,
when it was done, followed such great '*ergi*' [shame] that no male
thought it honourable to undertake it, and it was taught to the
priestesses as a skill. Óðinn knew where all earthly wealth had
come to rest and understood the songs by which the soil, the hills,
the stones, and mounds were opened to him, and he bound those
who dwell in them with words alone, and [then] he went in and
took whatever he wanted. Through these abilities he became very
famed, his enemies dreaded him and his friends trusted in him, and
they relied on his power and on himself. But he taught most of
his skills to the blood-priestesses, and they came nearest to him in
all wisdom and sorcery. Many others took it up to great effect and
from then sorcery has spread widely and has long been practised.
To Óðinn and the twelve chiefs men offered sacrifice and called
them their gods, and trusted in them long afterwards. Auðun was
called after Óðinn's name, and men named their sons for him, and
after Þórr's name are called Þorir and Þoririnn, and also
augmented by other terms such as Steinþór or Hafþór, or changed
in many ways.'

(VIII.) Óðinn setti lǫg í landi sínu, þau er gengit hǫfðu fyrr með
Ásum. Svá setti hann, at alla dauða menn skyldi brenna ok bera
á bál með þeim eign þeira. Sagði hann svá, at með þvílíkum
auðœfum skyldi hverr koma til Valhallar sem hann hafði á bál,
þess skyldi hann ok njóta, er hann sjálfr hafði í jǫrð grafit. En
ǫskuna skyldi bera út á sjá eða grafa niðr í jǫrð, en eptir gǫfga
menn skyldi haug gera til minningar, en eptir alla þá menn, er
nǫkkut manns mót var at, skyldi reisa bautasteina, ok hélzt sjá
siðr lengi síðan. Þá skyldi blóta í móti vetri til árs, en at miðjum
vetri blóta til gróðrar, it þriðja at sumri, þat var sigrblót. Um alla

Svíþjóð guldu menn Óðni skatt, penning fyrir nef hvert, en hann skyldi verja land þeirra fyrir ófriði ok blóta þeim til árs.

'(8) Óðinn set down the law in his land as it had been before among the Æsir [in Asia]. He established it thus, that all dead men should be burnt and should take their belongings onto the balefire with them. He said that anyone should come to Valhǫll with such possessions as he had on the balefire; also, he could have use of whatever he had buried in the earth for himself; and the ashes should be taken out to sea or buried deep in the earth. A mound should be built after leading men as a memorial, while for all those men who held a certain status a standing stone should be raised – and this custom was held long after. Then a sacrifice would be made on Winter Day[147] for a good harvest and at midwinter for the crop, the third one at midsummer which was the victory-sacrifice. All men throughout Sweden gave tribute to Óðinn, a penny for each head, so he should ward their land against war and bless them with the harvest.'

[The passage next tells of the marriage of Njǫrðr and Skaði. Óðinn is referenced only in the phrase '*Njǫrðr fékk konu þeirrar, er Skaði hét. Hon vildi ekki við hann samfarar ok giptist síðan Óðni.*' 'Njǫrðr took a wife who was called Skaði. She did not wish to dwell with him and later married Óðinn.']

(IX.) Óðinn varð sóttdauðr í Svíþjóð. Ok er hann var at kominn dauða, lét hann marka sik geirsoddi ok eignaði sér alla vápndauða men. Sagði hann sik mundu fara í Goðheim ok fagna þar vinum sínum. Nú hugðu Svíar, at hann væri kominn í hinn forna Ásgarð ok myndi þar lifa at eilífu. Hófsk þá at nýju átrúnaðr við Óðin ok áheit. Opt þótti Svíum hann vitrast sér, áðr stórar orrostur yrði. Gaf hann þá sumum sigr, en sumum bauð hann til sín. Þótti hvárrtveggi kostr góðr. Óðinn var brenndr dauðr, ok var sú brenna gǫr allveglig. Þat var trúa þeira, at því hæra sem reykinn

---

[147] The day of the onset of winter, 1st November.

lagði í loptit upp, at því háleitari væri sá í himninum, er brennuna
átti, ok þess auðgari, er meira fé brann með honum.

'(9) Óðinn died of illness in Sweden, and when he was on the
point of death, he commanded himself to be marked with a
spearpoint and thus he took ownership of all men killed by
weapons. He said that he would have to pass to Goðheim [land
of the gods] and remain there among his friends. Now the
Swedes believed that he had reached the old Ásgarð [the gods'
former land in Asia] and would live there forever. Then trust in
Óðinn began, and calling on him. It seemed to the Swedes that
he often showed himself when a great fight was at hand; he then
gave victory to some, and others he called to himself, and they
reckoned both these outcomes good. Óðinn was burnt and his
cremation was splendid. It was their belief that the higher the
smoke [from the pyre] rose into the sky, the higher would he be
placed in the heavens who had such a burning, and so much
more blessed would he be, the more property was burnt with
him.'

In these passages, the god appears as a founder, a *ver sacrum*, a leader
and establisher of social order (Lassen, 2022, pp.156-7). His future
military exploits are foreshadowed here in chapter 4, his antipathy
towards but final acceptance of the Vanir, and his creation of magical
arts which will serve him and his followers. His position as 'priest' is
affirmed through his special skills and his leadership is founded on
his dignity and eloquence. The rite for the disposal of the dead and
the importance of a splendid show at the cremation are also established. In all, the god behaves here as an exemplary model for a
medieval king without any of the trickery and deceit which he displays elsewhere.

The author is careful to ascribe faith in Óðinn to Svíþjóð 'the
Swedish folk' (Lassen, 2022, pp.162-3). Sweden was the last bastion
of heathen belief and culture and, in the eyes of Christian Europe,
the people there were credulous and ignorant. Óðinn does not claim

divine status, but his foolish followers assign it to him because they know no better.

SNORRI STURLUSON: PROSE EDDA

The *Prose Edda* (or *Younger Edda*, or *Snorri's Edda*) was probably written or compiled by Snorri around 1220 AD. It provides the most detailed surviving sources for knowledge of Norse mythology (Hultgård, 2020, p.1017). The text comprises a series of separate works, most if not all of which probably existed independently before Snorri brought all the material together in the *Edda* to form a textbook with which to enable Icelandic poets and readers to understand the nuances of Norse alliterative verse, and the meanings of the many allusive kennings used in skaldic poetry (Hermann, 2020, pp.51-2). Only Manuscript U (*Codex Upsaliensis*) explicitly attributes the text to its author: *Bók þessi heitir Edda; hana hefir saman setta Snorri Sturluson eptir þeim hætti sem hér er skipat* 'This book is called Edda; Snorri Sturluson has put it together in the way in which it is set out here' (Lassen, 2022, p.169).

The manuscript features a Christian-themed *Prologue* which provides a disclaimer about the truthfulness of the accounts which follow, and a summary of contemporary (Icelandic) opinion about the creation of the world and the beings which inhabit it (Hermann, 2020, p.53). Three separate works follow: *Gylfaginning* (about 20,000 words), *Skáldskaparmál* (about 50,000 words), and *Háttatal* (about 20,000 words). The collection appears in seven manuscripts, dating from c. 1300 to the latest, post-medieval version of about 1600 AD.

Snorri compiled his tales from pre-existing fragments of myth and verse, but he seems to have worked according to his own plan using (mainly, if not exclusively) native Norse resources; his writing style is not obviously affected by the contemporary scholastic traditions of western Europe. These facts strengthen the case for accepting what he wrote as genuinely his own work within vernacular tradition – a rationalisation and synthesis of the materials he had to hand (Faulkes, 1993, p.16; Schjødt, 2020b, p.1141). The poems he quotes at length informed him of the overall narrative of the tales included. There is no firm agreement as to whether Snorri actually wrote the *Prologue* himself, and it is possible that Bede's *Expositio Actuum Apostolorum* was the model (Lassen, 2022, pp.171-3). In his lifetime, Snorri's reputation was built on his poetic accomplishments (Faulkes, 2007, p.xix).

The narrative thrust of the text is broadly chronological, and Óðinn features prominently in the first three sections (*Gylfaginning, Skáldskaparmál, Háttatal*), and little afterwards (Hultgård, 2020, p.1018).

GYLFAGINNING

Gylfaginning ('the tricking of Gylfi') deals with the story of the creation and destruction of the world of the gods with many allusions to tales known from other sources. It is written in prose with quotes from Eddic poetry. As a narrative frame, it introduces the tale of Gylfi, a king of Sweden, who wishes to determine whether the tales of the Æsir are all inflated conjuring tricks. Gylfi sets off to find their homeland and eventually comes to a great hall, where he names himself Gangleri (Wayfarer). He is led into the presence of three imposing figures who call themselves Hár, Jafnhár and Þriði. Gangleri questions the three about the creation and destruction of the world and the tales of the gods and goddesses. Once the information has been imparted, the hall and its inhabitants vanish, leaving Gylfi standing alone on empty waste ground. The king returns to Sweden and recounts his experiences – a neat means by which Snorri can set down a lot of information without in any way endorsing it: these may be 'just travellers' tales' or a record of Scandinavian oral tradition within a Christianizing context (Hermann, 2020, pp.55-6). This 'deluding of Gylfi' is thus the source of the whole of Norse mythology as Snorri recorded it (Lindow, 2016, p.119; Schjødt, 2020b, p.1141).

It is usually assumed that the three imposing figures in the hall are all emanations of Óðinn in his role as *dróttinn* 'lord' and as master of trickery; otherwise, the figures might be seen as three Æsir gods. They quote verses from the Eddic poems, thus implying that the myths were originally encoded and passed on in poetry. The following is a sample of a stanza with the accompanying prose (text from Faulkes, 2005):

36. Enn eru þær aðrar er þjóna skulu í Valhǫll, bera drykkju ok gæta borðbúnaðar ok ǫlgagna. Svá eru þær nefndar í Grímnismálum:

> Hrist ok Mist,
>
> vil ek, at mér horn beri,
>
> Skeggjǫld ok Skǫgul,
>
> Hildr ok Þrúðr,
>
> Hlǫkk ok Herfjǫtur,
>
> Gǫll ok Geirahǫð,
>
> Randgríðr ok Ráðgríðr
>
> ok Reginleif,
>
> þær bera einherjum ǫl.

Þessar heita valkyrjur. Þær sendir Óðinn til hverrar orrustu. Þær kjósa feigð á menn ok ráða sigri. Guðr ok Róta ok norn in yngsta er Skuld heitir ríða jafnan at kjósa val ok ráða vígum. Jǫrð, móðir Þórs, ok Rindr, móðir Vála, eru taldar með Ásynjum.

'36. There are others whose task is to serve in Valhǫll, to carry drink and mind the table-settings and ale-cups. They are named thus in *Grímnismál*:

Hrist and Mist, I wish that they bear a horn to me, Skeggjǫld and Skǫgull; Hildr and Thrúdr, / Hlǫkk and Herfjǫtur, Gǫll and Geirahǫd, Randgríðr and Ráðgríðr and Reginleif / they bear ale to the Einherjar.

These are called 'Valkyries'. Óðinn sends them to every battle; they determine men's fates and award victory. Guðr and Róta and the youngest Norn, who is called Skuld, always ride to choose the slain and decide clashes. Jǫrd, the mother of Thor, and Rindr, Váli's mother, are reckoned among the Ásynjur [goddesses].'

The single reference to the god Óðr appears in chapter 35 of this manuscript (text from Faulkes, 2005):

Freyja er tignust með Frigg. Hon giptisk þeim manni er Óðr heitir. Dóttir þeira er Hnoss. Hon er svá fǫgr at af hennar nafni ero hnossir kallaðar þat er fagrt er ok gersemligt. Óðr fór í braut langar leiðir, en Freyja grætr eptir, en tár hennar er gull rautt. Freyja á mǫrg nǫfn, en sú er sǫk til þess at hon gaf sér ýmis heiti er hon fór með ókunnum þjóðum at leita Óðs. Hon heitir Mardǫll ok Hǫrn, Gefn, Sýr.

'Freyja is the most honoured, beside Frigg. She was given in marriage to the man called Óðr. Their daughter is Hnoss. She is so beautiful that from her name all things that are fair and precious are called *hnossir* [jewels]. Óðr travelled abroad on long voyages and Freyja weeps after him, and her tears are red gold. Freyja has many names and the cause of this is that she gave herself bynames when she journeyed among foreign peoples looking for Óðr. She is called Mardǫll, and Hǫrn, Gefn [and] Sýr.'

The two pairs of deities with related names (Óðinn: Frigg, Óðr: Freyja) might be taken to indicate an original duo joined in sacred marriage has been multiplied in narratives which require Frigg to be virtuous and maternal just as Freyja is wilful and dissolute; perhaps a similar relationship existed between (guileful and untrustworthy) Óðinn and (upright and dutiful) Óðr (Schjødt, 2020b, pp.1144-5). Yet the god's many sexual liaisons and attempts at seduction should caution us to treat these adventures as 'dynamic' rather than fixed, part of a developing cadre of tales: 'there was no stable tradition about these relations, nor should we expect that' (Schjødt, 2020b, p.1145).

The journey of Hermóðr to Hel is only related in *Gylfaginning*; references to the death of Baldr elsewhere do not include this story. The early death of Baldr, son of Óðinn, was foretold to Frigg in a dream and she took pains to avert it; but it came about that the god was unexpectedly killed by his blind brother, Hǫðr. Another son of Óðinn called Hermóðr[148] undertook the journey to the land of the dead in order to secure Baldr's release. Óðinn's ring, Draupnir, which dropped eight copies of itself every ninth night, had been placed on the pyre; it was handed to Hermóðr as a return-gift for their father as he prepared to leave with the message that Baldr would indeed be allowed to return if all things would weep for him (text from Faulkes, 2005):

> Þá stóð Hermóðr upp en Baldr leiðir hann út ór hǫllinni ok tók hringinn Draupni ok sendi Óðni til minja, en Nanna sendi Frigg ripti ok enn fleiri gjafar, Fullu fingrgull. Þá reið Hermóðr aptr leið sína ok kom í Ásgarð ok sagði ǫll tíðindi þau er hann hafði sét ok heyrt.

> 'Then Hermóðr stood up and Baldr led him out from the hall and took the ring Draupnir and sent it [with Hermóðr] to Óðinn as a memento, and Nanna [Baldr's wife] sent to Frigg a shift and many other gifts, and to Fulla [their maidservant] a gold finger-ring. Then Hermóðr rode back on his travels and came into Ásgarð and told all the tidings which he had seen and heard.'

The goddess Fulla (whose name means 'abundance' or 'bounty') may be identical with the character named Volla in the *Second Merseburg Charm* above (p.198). Likewise, Draupnir's power of regeneration is

---

[148] This name is cognate with Heremod, the legendary king of the Danes whose rejection caused the interregnum and anarchy which allowed Scyld to come to power at the opening of *Beowulf*. Did Norse tradition regard Heremod as a special champion of Óðinn, similar to Erik Blood-axe celebrated in *Eiríkmál*?

surely connected to fertility, abundance and prosperity (Schjødt, 2020b, p.1145).

SKÁLDSKAPARMÁL

Skáldskaparmál ('the language of poetry') offers a dialogue between Ægir, the sea-god, and Bragi, a god of verse. It ranges over aspects of both mythology and poetic 'good practice' (Faulkes, 1993; Lindow, 2020, p.84; Lassen, 2022, pp.111-21). The origins of some kennings are given and Bragi provides a list for specific people, places, and things, discussing poetic language and *heiti*, the words found in verse which were no longer part of the usual vocabulary of Norse-speakers. The tales recounted at length include: the abduction of Iðunn and her apples of youth; the gods' slaying of the giant Þjazi and the compensation paid to his daughter, Skaði; Þórr's contests with Geirrøðr and Hrungnir.

In skaldic verse a range of kennings may be used with reference to Óðinn, employing his many bynames (Yggr, Hár, etc.) according to the metrical context (Lassen, 2022, p.114): *sóknar Yggr* 'the Yggr of attacks' = 'warrior', *sverðs leik Þundr* 'the Þundr of sword-play' = 'warrior', *Yggs él* 'shower of Yggr' = 'battle', *Hnikars veðr* 'weather of Hnikar' = 'battle'. Military themes dominate, of course, as well as terms for 'poetry' based on the view of verse as an (alcoholic) drink: *Yggs full* "cup of Yggr", *Yggs lið* "beer of Yggr', *mjǫð burar Bors* 'mead of Bor's son'. Many of these allusions entail a wide knowledge of the corpus of myth and legend in order that the listener may 'untangle the thread' and deduce what the poet intends: *Míms vinr* 'friend of Mímir' must refer to the relationship between the two gods which is central to the episode where the god's eye is surrendered.[149]

---

[149] Lassen (2022, p.115) notes that there are no obvious references in the kennings to myths or motifs which are *not* recorded somewhere in the corpus; this in turn implies that the material which has come down to us is the sum-total of all that was understood about the god in pre-Christian times. More likely in my view is that references to tales unknown to us remain as opaque allusions

The lengthy Óðinn references in *Skáldskaparmál* include the story of the creation, loss, transformation and regaining of the mead of inspiration (Lindow, 2016, p.119) which agree for the most part with the version given in the verse, of which this is the section where Óðinn eliminates Suttungr's workmen (text from Faulkes, 1998):

Þá mælir Ægir: 'Myrkt þykkir mér þat mælt at kalla skáldskap með þessum heitum, en hvernig kómu þeir Æsir at Suttunga miði?'

Bragi svarar: 'Sjá saga er til þess at Óðinn fór heiman ok kom þar er þrælar níu slógu hey. Hann spyrr ef þeir vili at hann brýni ljá þeira. Þeir játa því. Þá tekr hann hein af belti sér ok brýndi, en þeim þótti bíta ljárnir myklu betr ok fǫluðu heinina. En hann mat svá at sá er kaupa vildi skyldi gefa við hóf, en allir kváðusk vilja ok báðu hann sér selja, en hann kastaði heininni í lopt upp. En er allir vildu henda þá skiptusk þeir svá við at hverr brá ljánum a háls ǫðrum. Óðinn sótti til náttstaðar til jǫtuns þess er Baugi hét, bróðir Suttungs. Baugi kallaði ilt fjárhald sitt ok sagði at þrælar hans níu hǫfðu drepizk, en talðisk eigi vita sér ván verkmanna. En Óðinn nefndisk fyrir honum Bǫlverkr.

'Then Ægir says: "It seems obscure to me to call poetry by these names, but by what means did the Æsir come by Suttungr's mead?"

Bragi answers: "That tale is like this – that Óðinn went from his home and came to where nine thralls were cutting hay. He asked if they wanted him to sharpen their scythes. They answered 'yes' to this. When he took a hone from his belt and sharpened [the scythes], it seemed to them that the scythes cut much better, and they asked to buy the hone. He said he prized it so much that

---

which may still be interpreted in a loose manner, e.g., *Yggs él* 'the shower of the terrifying one' might refer to a specific spear-casting or arrow-shooting incident, but we can still capture the broad meaning 'battle' without knowing the specifics.

whoever wanted to buy it must pay well [for it], and they all said
that they would do so and asked him to sell it, but he cast the
hone up into the air. But when they all tried to catch [it] they
acted so that each [of them] put his blade across another's neck.
Óðinn sought a night-stay with the giant called Baugi, the
brother of Suttungr. Baugi called his luck bad and said that his
nine thralls had killed each other and said he did not know how
to mend his lack of workmen. Óðinn called himself 'Bale-
worker' in front of Baugi.'

The story is continued below (p.340).

HÁTTATAL

Háttatal ('list of verse-types') was compiled by Snorri using his own
poetic compositions supplemented by existing verses, noting where
older poets diverged from best practice (as he understood it). It forms
the last section of the *Prose Edda* (Faulkes, 2007; Clunies Ross, 2016,
p.18, 27) which exists in four manuscript versions, all copies of varying accuracy. The *Codex Regius* in Reykjavík is complete (but
slightly damaged) and dates from the 14th c. Similar is the *Codex
Trajectinus* in Utrecht which was written about 1595 but is a copy
of a lost 13th c. original, with some errors and omissions and the last
few pages absent. The mid-14th c. *Codex Wormianus* is in Copenhagen; large parts of the middle section were lost and subsequently
replaced by manuscript copies on paper in the 17th c. The earliest
document is the *Uppsala Manuscript*, dating to 1300-1315 AD; it is
incomplete and contains headings and phrases not found in other
copies, which has been taken to support the idea that it was transcribed directly from Snorri's own original (Faulkes, 2007, pp.xxi-
xxii). The processes of triangulation (comparing the oldest version
with the others to work out what the original text may have said)
has proved very difficult since all the surviving documents contain
errors, some shared and some unique.

The aim of the skalds was composition of praise-poems for their
patrons. Snorri used this as his frame of reference, focussing on verses

about Hákon Hákonarson, who was king of Norway 1217-1163, and Jarl Skúli who was his co-ruler and father-in-law. He composed his text in Iceland following a visit to Norway in 1218-20 and transmitted it in written form to be read aloud before the rulers – this was a departure from the centuries-old practice of composing and memorising the stanzas and was only possible due to an increased reliance on writing (Faulkes, 2007, p.vii). Whether this departure was approved of by the king and jarl is not known. It is perhaps unlikely that the old oral composition techniques continued for long after the time when Snorri wrote, although his nephew Sturla Þórðarson and a few others did maintain them. Prose narrative had become the ascendent medium for courtly entertainment and royal propaganda (Faulkes, 2007, p.xvii).

Snorri's treatise is the earliest attempt to describe vernacular poetic practice in a Germanic language: before this, it had been attempted in Irish (Faulkes, 2007, p.xxi). The work is in a sense the last glimmer of the centuries-old poetic tradition and, while it incorporates a quantity of ancient verses, it adds almost nothing to our knowledge of pre-Christian religion in any way (but see Lindow, 2020b, p.1042 for discussion of Mímir in this connection).

THE POETIC EDDA

The *Poetic Edda* text appears in the *Codex Regius* manuscript now in Reykjavík, Iceland and the *AM748 I 4to* fragment held in the Arnamagnæan Institute in Copenhagen (Lassen, 2022, p.169). The poems in the latter document all have a strong mythological element, e.g., *Hymiskviða, Baldrs draumar, Vǫlundarkviða* and others. The verse has been broadly dated to the later 10th c. but the prose elements, which are largely explanatory narrative frames for the poems, are probably contemporary with the manuscript's composition in the 12th-13th century.

From comparison of this medieval Scandinavian material with older records (albeit mainly still of Christian date) it is generally accepted that some of the alliterative poetry found in the *Poetic Edda* and elsewhere is of pre-Christian origin, dating from the Viking Age if not before (Lindow, 2016, p.115). The skaldic metre of the earlier verse appears to date to 9th c. Norway, and to come from an élite cultural milieu where complex verse was performed for wealthy patrons (Lindow, 2016, p.117). Although each performance of an oral poem involves an element of recomposition, the complex metre ensured that these poems were performed very consistently over long periods of transmission. The poetic medium has prevented wholesale adaptation to Christian didactic ends far better than is the case for the corresponding prose (Lassen, 2022, pp.2-3).

VǪLUSPÁ

This long poem forms part of the source from which Snorri composed the prose *Gylfaginning* (p.266). It is found in the *Codex Regius* and in a slightly different version in the *Hauksbók* manuscript which appears to be later; attempts to reconstruct the original text have met with many objections, and it may be wiser to treat the two poems as separate texts (Lindow, 2020, p.72, 81). Its date of composition is sometimes put at ca. 1000 AD due to its author's familiarity with pre-Christian lore alongside the apocalyptic themes which are typical of the Christian millennial period. The poem describes the history of the world from creation to destruction, with a continued theme of the development of the World Tree which parallels the unfolding history of creation. The verses are spoken by a reanimated *vǫlva* in reply to questions put to her by Óðinn, who seeks knowledge of the fates of the gods. The sections directly relating to Óðinn are given below, beginning with verses 17-18 (Schjødt, 2020b, p.1139; text from Dronke, 1997):

> Unz þrír kvómo
>
> ór því líði
>
> ǫflgir ok ástgir
>
> æsir at húsi.

Fundo á landi

lítt megandi

Ask ok Emblo,

ørlǫglausa.

'Until three mighty gods came out of the host to a house. On the land they found Askr and Embla having little strength, lacking power.'

Ǫnd þau ne átto,

óð þau ne hǫfðo,

lá né læti

né lito góða.

Ǫnd gaf Óðinn,

óð gaf Hœnir,

lá gaf Lóðurr

ok lito góða.[150]

'Breath they owned not, inspiration they had not, [nor] life nor voice nor good hues. Óðinn gave breath, Hœnir gave inspiration, Lóðurr gave voice and good hues.'

The World Tree is the hiding place of 'Heimdall's hearing' and 'Óðinn's pledge' in v.27-28:

Veit hón Heimdal[l]ar

hlióð um fólgit

---

[150] The English translation of *lito* is disputed; 'good colours' is a frequent choice. Libermann (2016, ch.8) argues for 'genitals; sexual power' and *lita góða* 'genitals ready for use' since the gods' act of creation is otherwise pointless: 'To infuse life into two inanimate objects and prevent them from multiplying seems to be an unfortunate plan.'

undir heiðvǫnom

helgom baðmi.

Á sér hon ausaz

augum forsi

af veði Valfǫðrs.

Vitoð ér enn, eða hvat?

'She knows that Heimdall's hearing is hidden beneath the holy tree, accustomed to bright mead. A tree she sees growing with the loamy waters, from the pledge of the Father of the Slain. Do you want to know more, and what? '[151]

Ein sat hon úti,

þá er inn aldni kom,

Yggiungr ása,

ok í augo leit:

'Hvers fregnið mik?

Hví freistið mín?

Alt veit ek, Óðinn,

hvar þú auga falt:

í enom mæra

Mímis brunni!

Drekkr miǫð Mímir

morgin hverian

af veði Valfǫðrs!

Vitoð ér enn, eða hvat?'

---

[151] ON *heið* more often means 'radiance, the brightness of the sky' but here the reference to gushing mead is preferred (Tolley, 2009, p.95)

She was sitting out alone[152] when the old [one] came and looked into her eyes, Yggiungr [the Fearsome One] of the Æsir. "What do you ask of me? Why do you test me? I know it all, Óðinn, where you hid your eye – in the famous well of Mímir. Every morning Mímir drinks mead from the pledge of the father of the slain. Do you know yet, and what?"

As the prelude to the final battle of gods and men against the giants, verse 45 shows Óðinn seeking knowledge from Mímir:

> Leika Míms synir,
>
> en miǫtuðr kyndiz
>
> at en[o] galla
>
> Giallarhorni.
>
> Hátt blæss Heimdallr
>
> – horn er á lopti –
>
> mælir Óðinn
>
> við Míms hǫfuð.
>
> Skelfr Yggdrasils
>
> askr standandi,
>
> ymr it aldna tré,
>
> en iǫtunn losnar.

'Mímir's sons are at play but the tree[153] is burning at the booming of the Gjallarhorn. Heimdall blows hard – the horn is in the air – Óðinn speaks with the head of Mímir. The ash-tree of Yggdrasill

---

[152] The reference here is to *úti sitja*, the solitary practice of magic.

[153] The word *miǫtuðr* in the text means 'fate' but the reference must surely be to *mjǫtviðr* the 'tree of measuring' (Yggdrasill) which is mentioned below (Tolley, 2009, p.96).

shudders [while] standing, the old tree shivers as the giants break free.'

HÁVAMÁL

The 'words of the high one' is the second part of the *Poetic Edda*, although it seems to have been a separate work originally and may only have been included with the *Edda* for the first time in the compilation of that manuscript (Sundqvist, 2009, p.649; Kay, 2013, p.12; Schjødt, 2020b, pp.1139-40). The present text is apparently a second generation (or later) written version of the oral original composition. There is some evidence for its completion in a Norwegian speech community, rather than a specifically Icelandic one (Kay, 2013, p.13).

Hávamál purports to be a set of verse tales about mainly mythical matters, embodying precepts for living in the harsh environment of northern Europe in the Viking age. It is poorly structured, compiled from several separate pre-existing poems with amendments and additions (Birkett, 2019, p.154).[154] Much of the verse is terse and pithy, with a gnomic quality which belongs to the long-lived tradition of 'wisdom literature'. The individual verses do not form a coherent – or even consistent – narrative, which argues for a recent (13th c.) origin for the work as we now have it, an arrangement of scraps and longer passages of traditional lore into a single narrative:[155] it is a collection of pre-existing stanzas of unknown antiquity.[156] The uniting factor is that the main character or the speaker in each stanza is Óðinn.

The section dealing with Óðinn's theft of the mead of inspiration from Suttungr (verses 104-110) is highly allusive and would be

---

[154] Sundqvist (2009, p.649) notes quotations from the poem in the works of several skalds of the Viking period, such as *Hákonarmál* by Eyvindr Skáldaspillr composed around 960 AD; these include epithets such as *hangaguð* or *hangatýr* (hanging god), *galga farmr* (burden of the gallows) and others.

[155] Sundqvist (2009, p.650) notes that scholars disagree as to the number of components, from three to seven.

[156] Sundqvist (2009) assigns a later 10th c. date to at least some of the stanzas.

difficult to resolve into a consistent narrative if we did not have access to the corresponding prose text in *Skáldskaparmál*. The relevant *Hávamál* verses are (text from Dronke, 2011):

> 104 Inn aldna iǫtun ek sótta,
>
> nú em ec aptr kominn –
>
> fátt gat ec þegiandi þar!
>
> Mǫrgom orðom
>
> mælta ek í minn frama
>
> í Suttungs sǫlom.

'I sought the old jǫtunn, now I have come back - little would I get there [if I were] being silent: I spoke to my advantage with many words in Suttungr's halls.'

> 105 Gunnlǫð mér um gaf
>
> gullnum stóli á,
>
> drykk ins dýra miaðar.
>
> Ill iðgiǫld
>
> lét ek hana eptir hafa
>
> síns ins heila hugar,
>
> síns ins svára sefa.

'On a golden seat Gunnlǫð gave me a drink of the dear mead; a poor reward did I let her have later for her kind thoughts, for her heavy heart.'

> 106 Rata munn
>
> létomk rúms um fá
>
> ok um griót gnaga;
>
> yfir ok undir
>
> stóðomk iǫtna vegir –

svá hætta ek hǫfði til!

'I made Rati's mouth ream a gap for me and gnaw through the stone; over and under me stood the jǫtunns' way, thus did I chance my head.'

107 Vélkeyptz [h]l[u]tar

hefi ec vel notit,

fás er fróðum vant:

þvíat Óðrerir

er nú upp kominn

á alda vés iaðar

'Well did I use the fraud-bought fortune: little is lacking for the wise, since Óðrerir has now come up to the edges of men's hallowed ground.'

108 Ifi er mér á,

at ek væra enn kominn

iǫtna gǫrðum ór,

ef ek Gunnlaðar né nytak,

ennar góðo kono,

þeirar er lǫgðomk arm yfir

'I have doubt that I might have come out of the jǫtunns' home if I had not used Gunnlǫð, that fine woman, and laid my arms about her.'

109 Ens hindra dags

gengo Hrímþursar

Háva ráðs at fregna

Háva hǫllo í.

At Bǫlverki þeir spurðo,

ef hann væri með bǫndum kominn

eða hefði hánom Suttungr of sóit?

'The next day the Frost-giants went to ask the advice of the High One in the hall of the High One. They asked after Bǫlverkr, whether he had come among the gods or Suttungr had slain him.'

110 Baugeið Óðinn,

hygg ek at unnit hafi;

hvat skal hans trygðom trúa!

Suttungr svikinn

hann lét sumbli frá

ok grœtta Gunnlǫðo

'I believe Óðinn to have sworn a ring-oath: what must his pledge be worth? He left Suttungr betrayed at the feast and Gunnlǫð weeping.'

There is a previous reference to the story in verses 13-14 where the dangers of strong drink are mentioned (text from Dronke, 2011):

13 Óminnis hegri heitir

sá er yfir ǫlðrom þrumir,

hann stelr geði guma.

Þess fugls fiǫðrom

ek fiǫtraðr vark

í garði Gunnlauðar.

14 Ǫlr ek varð,

varð ofrǫlvi,

at ins fróða Fialars.

Því er ǫlðr bazt,

at aptr uf heimtir

hverr sitt geð gumi.

'"Forgetfulness" is the name of the heron which hovers over the ale-drinking, [and] steals a man's wits. I was fettered with this bird's feathers in Gunnlǫð's home. Drunken I became, too drunken, at [the home of] wise Fjalar. Ale-drinking is best in this way – so that every man comes back to his senses.'

RÚNATAL

The section of *Hávamál* (stanzas 138-44) now called *Rúnatalsþáttr* 'list of rune-verses' deals with the acquisition of the knowledge of the runes by *Hár* 'the High One', a *nom de guerre* of Óðinn (p.50) (Polomé, 1991, p.430; Spurkland, 2005, pp.13-16; Birkett, 2019, pp.151-4). Verses 138-141 relate to the gaining of the runes on the World Tree and 142-5 discuss further runic matters (Sundqvist, 2009, p.650). This passage is sometimes called the *Ljóðatal,* a list of magic chants or spells which may be linked to the runes 'discovered' or 'won' in the previous section. In verses 142 and 144 the narrator addresses another person (*þú* 'you') with an instruction to find the powerful runes and for the making of sacrifices (Bremmer, 1991; Tolley, 2009, pp.109-111; Sundqvist, 2009, p.650; Liberman, 2016, pp.51-75; Birkett, 2019, p.153; Sundqvist, 2020, p.752). The relevant verses run (text from Dronke, 2011):

138 Veit ek, at ek hekk

vindga meiði á

nætr allar nío,

geiri undaðr

ok gefinn Óðni,

siálfr siálfom mér,

á þeim meiði,

er manngi veit,

hvers hann af rótom renn.

'I know that I hung on a wind-swept tree for nine nights in all, wounded by a spear and given to Óðinn - myself to myself - on that tree of which none knows whence its roots run.'

139 Við hleifi mik sældo

né við hornigi.

Nýsta ek niðr.

Nam ek upp rúnar,

œpandi nam.

Fell ek aptr[a]ð[r ú]tan

'They gave me no bread nor any [drinking] horn. I peered downwards. I took up runes - exulting [I] took [them]. I fell back from beyond.'

140 Fimbullióð níu

nam ek af inum frægja syni

Bolþor[n]s, Bestlo fǫður,

ok ek drykk of gat

ins dýra miaðar,

ausinn Óðreri!

'I took nine mighty spells from the famed son of Bolþor, Bestla's father, and I got a drink of the dear mead poured from Óðrerir.'

141 Þá nam ek frævask

ok fróðr vera

ok vaxa ok vel hafask.

Orð mér af orði

orðs leitaði,

verk mér af verki

verks leitaði.

'Then I began to be fruitful and wise and to grow and thrive. A word led me from a word to a word, a deed led me from a deed to a deed.'

142 Rúnar munt þú finna

ok ráðna stafi,

mjǫk stóra stafi,

mjǫk stinna stafi,

er fáði fimbulþulr

ok gørðu ginnregin

ok reist Hroptr rǫgna:

'Runes you must find and take advice from the staves - very great staves, very firm staves – which the one mighty in speech coloured and the great gods made and Hroptr of the gods carved.'

143 Óðinn með ásom,

en fyr álfum Dáinn,

ok Dvalinn dvergum fyrir,

Ásviðr iǫtnum fyrir –

ek reist sjálfr sumar!

'Óðinn among the Æsir and Dáinn for the elves and Dvalinn for the dwarves, Ásviðr for the jǫtunns. I myself carved some.'

144 Veiztu hvé rísta skal?

Veiztu hvé ráða skal?

Veiztu hvé fá skal?

Veiztu hvé freista skal?

Veiztu hvé bidia skal?

Veiztu hvé blóta skal?

Veiztu hvé senda skal?

Veiztu hvé sóa skal?

'Do you know how you must write? Do you know how you must read? Do you know how you must colour? Do you know how you must test? Do you know how you must ask? Do you know how you must sacrifice? Do you know how you must send [your soul]? Do you know how you must smother[157]?'

145 Betra er óbeðit

en sé ofblótit –

ey sér til gildis gjǫf.

Betra er ósent

en sé ofsóit.

Svá Þundr um reist

fyr þjóða rǫk,

þar hann upp um reis

er hann aptr of kom.

'It is better not to have bidden than to have offered too much, a gift always entails a payment; it is better not to have sent than to have over-smothered. Thus Þundr carved [that] before the folks' ending, in the place where he rose up when he came back.'

The ordeal through which the god had to pass to gain the runes can be viewed as self-sacrifice through hanging and stabbing with a spear (both Odinic rites) (Page [1964], 1995, p.107). The tableau of the

---

[157] The sense here seems to be 'hold one's breath' during the rune-carving, but from the following stanza the meaning must be 'stifle, smother, choke' in the act of sacrifice.

sacrificial god, wounded with a spear while hanging on a tree, has been taken as evidence for Christian influence on the poem (Bremmer, 1991, pp.409-10; Tolley, 2009, pp.110-1). [158] Scandinavian traders and wayfarers may well have become familiar with representations of the crucifixion of Jesus from their visits to western European lands, and it is possible that the image of a god sacrificed in this way was striking enough to enter their worldview, mediated through their own cultural assumptions about ritual sacrifice.

However, the familiar image of the Corpus Christi may mislead us (Birkett, 2019, pp.154-5). [159] The notion of a spiritual leader (the High One) undergoing physical torture and sacrifice in order to attain enlightenment is known across Europe and Asia, and indeed further afield, [160] so that the influence of Christian iconography can easily be overstated (Bremmer, 1991, p.411). The notion of a leader undertaking a quest which results in his death and resurrection (disappearance into the Otherworld and re-emergence) in order to gain supernatural power is at the heart of many myths (Sundqvist, 2009, p.652). The *Rúnatal* verses can be seen as a 'dramatisation of ritual bound up in an initiation into the written word' (Birkett, 2019, p.154). The acquisition of literacy was a key accomplishment in the transformation of

---

[158] Sundqvist (2009, p.650) offers a discussion of the parallels between traditions while refuting the notion that ritual sacrifice *can only be* an imitation of Christian practice.

[159] The purpose of the god's suffering is initiation and personal enlightenment, not the salvation of mankind. With the centrality of literacy to formal Christian authority, the Germanic use of imagery reflecting the acquisition of this technology underscores the very different aims and world-views of the two societies.

[160] Bishop (2007, p.11) cites the Egyptian Thoth, Chinese Huang Di and Mayan Itzam Na (Hunab Ku) as parallel cases of gods who create the world and instigate magical secrets through writing. In the case of the Egyptian *Nefer-ka-ptah*, knowledge of writing was acquired through rinsing Thoth's magical papyrus in beer, then drinking the beer in order to gain the esoteric knowledge of the god. Drinking beer and reading runes form central parts of the rites of Óðinn, possibly correlating with rites of initiation from Neolithic times (Kershaw, 2000; Tolley, 2009, p.108-9; Hornsey, 2012).

'youth' into 'man', and indeed mastery of the written word was one of the means by which Germanic societies transformed themselves from Iron Age chiefdoms into fully-fledged medieval kingdoms (Pollington, 2016, pp.251-3).

The equation of the Christian cross with a wondrous tree in the forest is a familiar *topos* of the Anglo-Saxon Christian tradition dating at least as far back as the 8th c. when the poem now called *The Dream of the Rood* was carved into the stone preaching cross at Ruthwell (Dumfriesshire, Scotland), suggesting a pre-existing familiarity with the notion of the 'tree of sacrifice'. The tree (*beam, treow*) in the poem is explicitly called a *rod* 'rood, cross, pole, gallows' as well as *gealga* 'gallows' and *gealgtreow* 'gallows-tree' (Orel, 2003, s.v. *róðó(n)*). Equation of the 'splendid tree' with a gallows on which a god met and defeated physical death is thus common to both traditions.

The poem deals with the acquisition through self-sacrifice of *rúnar* which must mean 'great mysteries' or 'mighty secrets'. That these secrets were revealed through physical forms (e.g., runestaves) is implied by the statement that Óðinn 'peered downwards' and took them. Having gained the *rúnar*, Óðinn grew in confidence, gained new spells and was able to draw on the power of Óðrerir, the powerful cauldron of inspiration, which led him to new knowledge (words) and power (deeds) (Spurkland, 2005, p.14).

The *regin* are the originating beings which create the world and set time in motion: they are most often identified with Óðinn, Vili and Vé but also sometimes include all the Æsir. Perhaps an even wider community of Otherworld beings is intended, since the following verse names one among the Æsir, elves, dwarves and etinns (giants) as using the *rúnar*.

The speaker of the *Hávamál* interrogates the hearer with a series of questions, all of which appear to relate to the use of carved runestaves for magical purposes (verse 144) (Spurkland, 2005, p.14; Bishop, 2007, p.37). This interrogation indicates that runes are powerful and dangerous, and only a skilled user should handle them.

The subsequent series of charms and spells includes one explicit runic reference, in the later verse 157 (Elliott, 1958, pp.66-7; text from Dronke, 2011):

> 157 Þat kann ek it tólpta,
>
> ef ek sé á tré uppi
>
> váfa virgilná,
>
> svá ek ríst
>
> ok í rúnom fák,
>
> at sá gengr gumi
>
> ok mælir við mik.

'The twelfth [spell] I know: if I see a dangling corpse upon a tree, thus I carve and I colour in runes so that that man goes and speaks with me.'

This verse explicitly links the carving and painting of runes to necromancy. It is surely no accident that the corpse (*virgilná*) which was forcibly reanimated had met its death through hanging, the means by which Óðinn himself gained his knowledge of the *rúnar*. It is therefore likely that, starved and deprived of drink, hanged on a windy tree and pierced with a spear, the god was the victim of a 'threefold death'. Having overcome his own death through this experience, he was able to share his victory with others who had been similarly executed.

An association with the dead and the Otherworld is echoed in some examples of runic usage, such as the word **ræginku[n]du** on the probably 7[th] c. Sparlösa stone, a Swedish runic monument, i.e., the same word as the later Norse *ræginkunnr* '[having] the nature of the *regin* powers' and thus 'divine, godly' (Bishop, 2007, p.15, 20; Birkett, 2019, p.154).[161] Earlier in *Hávamál*, the text reads:

---

[161] The same word occurs on a stone originally set inside a grave at Noleby in Västergötland. Its use in an early (7th c.) epigraphic context indicates that the god-given nature of the runes was not a medieval Icelandic fiction.

80 Þat er þá reynt

er þú at rúnum spyrr

inum reginkunnum,[162]

þeim er gørðu ginnregin

ok fáði fimbulþulr.

þá hefir hann bazt ef hann þegir.

- 'It is then proven when you ask of the runes [which were] originated by the powers - those which the *ginnregin* made and the one mighty in speech coloured - that he shall do best if he will keep silent.'

The *ginnregin* here are the *regin* (holy powers) who originate and create the world (*ginn* is cognate with 'begin', i.e., start, set off, initiate) (Pollington, 2011, pp.74, 333-4). The text shows that the *rúnar* are a gift of the *ginnregin*.

VAFÞRÚÐNISMÁL

The third poem in the *Poetic Edda* has the modern title *Vafþrúðnismál* 'Lay of Vafþrúðnir' which takes the form of successive conversations: initially Óðinn asks Frigg whether it is wise for him to visit the giant Vafþrúðnir's hall and she advises against it (Schjødt, 2020b, p.1139; text from Neckel, 1983):

1. 'Ráð þú mér nú, Frigg,

allz mic fara tíðir

at vitia Vafþrúðnis;

forvitni micla

qveð ek mér á fornum stǫfum

við þann inn alsvinna iǫtun.'

---

[162] Birkett, 2019, p.151: 'derived from the gods' is the acknowledged origin of the runes.

'(Óðinn said) "Advise me now, Frigg, [for] I long to travel to visit Vafþrúðnir; out of great curiosity, I will speak of ancient matters with him, the all-wise giant".'

2. 'Heima letia

ec mynda Herjafǫðr

í gǫrðum goða,

þvíat engi iǫtun

ec hugða iafnramman

sem Vafþrúðni vera.'

'(Frigg said:) "I remind the Father of Battle to stay at home in the halls of the gods; for I believe no giant to be of equal learning to Vafþrúðnir".'

But the god persists with his quest and on reaching the hall undertakes a wisdom-contest with the host, under the pseudonym Gagnráðr; once the giant thinks he has the measure of his guest, he agrees to continue on condition that the guest may only leave if he proves the wiser of the two, and if not he forfeits his head (McGillivray, 2018, p.105). Such contests are known elsewhere in Norse literature (e.g., *Alvíssmál, Hárbarðsljóð*) and in early Germanic poetry, e.g., the OE *Dialogues of Solomon and Saturn* (Larrington, 2002, pp.59-65). The text takes the form of a series of questions concerning cosmogony, history and the fates of the world, each contestant drawing on his own specific expertise; some of these topics are also referred to in *Vǫluspá*. The exchanges provide an overview of the cosmogony and ultimate fate of the world.

The giant asks about *inter alia* the names of the horse which brings the day, the river which separates the gods and giants, the field where gods and giants will fight – and Gagnráðr is able to answer in full; the god asks about the origins of earth and sky, moon and sun, day and night, etc. before moving onto the origin of the winds, who are the Einherjar and other general matters, as well as asking Vafþrúðnir how he knows these things when he provides good answers (Lindow & Andrén, 2020, p.909). Discussion turns to the ending of the world in the last few exchanges, and the god finally asks the question (verse 54) which must assure him of victory in the contest:

'Fiǫld ec fór,

fiǫld ec freistaðac,

fiǫld ec reynda regin:

Hvat mælti Óðinn,

áðr á bál stigi,

sialfr í eyra syni?'

'Much I travelled, much I learnt, much I got from the gods. What did Óðinn say into his son's ear before he burnt on the pyre?'

at which the giant realises the identity of his opponent and replies (verse 55):

'Ey manni þat veit,

hvat þú í árdaga

sagðir í eyra syni;

feigom munni

mælta ec mína forna stafi

oc um ragna rǫk.

Nú ec við Óðin

deildac mína orðspeki,

þú ert æ vísastr vera.'

'No man knows that – what in the ancient days you said into your son's ear; I have told old tales of the fall of the gods with fated words. Now I have striven against Óðinn in words of wisdom: you are ever the wisest of beings.'

At the end of the exchange, Óðinn learns of his own impending doom in the jaws of Fenrir when the gods and giants ride out to war for the last time. The recent 'god v. giant' contest is a foretaste of the final battle to come, but here the god contrives to win the contest; the poet makes it clear that in the end the gods and men alike must fail, to be replaced by a new order of both groups (a subject also treated in *Voluspá*) (Larrington, 2002, p.68).

GRÍMNISMÁL

This text, the 'sayings of the masked one', comprises an extensive prose introduction and a long (54 verse) poem composed in the *ljóðaháttr* metre, generally used for wisdom verse, followed by a prose epilogue. It appears in both the *Codex Regius* manuscript and the *Arnamagnæan Codex* fragment (Larrington, 2002; Schjødt, 2020b, pp.1139-40).

The story opens with the two sons of King Hrauðungr setting out to fish from their boat. In a stormy night the boat foundered and the boys came ashore and took shelter with a nameless crofter and his wife who harboured them over winter. The crofter took care of the elder boy, Geirrøðr, and his wife of the younger, Agnar. In the spring, the boys were provided with a boat for the return voyage, but before they set off the old man whispered secretly to Geirrøðr. The journey passed quickly with a fair wind, but as the boat neared the shore the elder brother leapt out onto the beach and shoved it back out to sea before Agnar could get out. Geirrøðr went up to his ancestral hall where he was welcomed because his father had died during the boys' absence; Geirrøðr was hailed as the new king.

Óðinn and Frigg sat surveying the world from *Hliðskjálfi* and spied the hall of Geirrøðr. Óðinn remarked that his fosterling was now a king while his brother, Agnar, was living in a cave with a troll-wife. Frigg retorted that the king was cruel and miserly, given to killing his guests if he thought there were too many of them. Óðinn denied this as a lie and they agreed to set a wager on the matter. Secretly, Frigg sent her handmaid, Fulla, to the hall to warn the king that a wizard was in the land meaning him harm, and that the stranger could be recognised because no dog would attack him. The king accordingly gave orders that any strangers whom the dogs shunned should be seized, and in due course a wayfarer arrived wearing a blue cloak, calling himself Grímnir. The visitor would not reveal any more about himself than his name, so the king had him tied between two posts set between fierce fires and left thus for eight nights. Presently, Geirrøðr's young son – named Agnar, after his uncle – took pity on the wretch and gave him a horn full of drink, saying that it was an evil thing to treat guests so. Grímnir emptied the horn and he was so close to the flames that the clothes on his back were smouldering. He then proceeded to utter the verses, the central point of the narrative, which includes a verbal tour of the homes of the gods and their special features. For example, verses 8-10 (text from Dronke, 2011):

8 Glaðsheimr heitir inn fimti,

þars en gullbjarta

Valhǫll víð of þrumir;

en þar Hroftr kýss

hverjan dag

vápndauða vera.

9 Mjǫk er auðkent,

þeim er til Óðins koma

salkynni at siá:

skiǫptum er rann rept,

skjǫldum er salr þakiðr,

bryniom um bekki strát.

10 Mjǫk er auðkent,

þeim er til Óðins koma

salkynni at siá:

vargr hangir

fyr vestan dyrr,

ok drúpir ǫrn yfir.

'8. The fifth [dwelling] is called Glaðsheimr [home of joy] where gold-bright Valhǫll stands broad, and there each day Hroftr chooses the weapon-dead men.

9. It is easy to recognise for those who come to see Óðinn's hall: it is raftered with spear-shafts, it is thatched with shields, the benches are strewn with byrnies.

10. It is easy to recognise for those who come to see Óðinn's hall: a wolf hangs above the western door and an eagle hovers above it.'

His recitation ends with more ominous sentiments (verses 51-4):

51 Ǫlr ertu, Geirrøðr,

hefr þú of drukkit!

Miklu ertu hnugginn,

er þú ert míno gengi!

52 Fjǫlð ek þér sagða,

en þú fátt of mant:

'of þik véla vinir.'

Mæki liggia

ek sé míns vinar

allan í dreyra drifinn.

53 Eggmóðan val

nú mun Yggr hafa!

Þitt veit ek líf um lifit.

Úfar ro dísir –

nú knáttu Óðin siá!

Nálgaztu mik, ef þú megir!

54 Óðinn ek nú heiti,

Yggr ek áðan hét,

hétumk Þundr fyr þat,

Vakr ok Skilfingr,

Váfuðr ok Hroftatýr,

Gautr ok Iálkr með goðum,

Ófnir ok Sváfnir –

er ek hygg at orðnir sé

allir af einum mér!

'51. You are drunken Geirrøðr, you have drunk too much, you have lost much now that you have forgone the help of Óðinn and all the Einherjar.

52. I told you much but you heed little, false are friends' words; I see the sword of my friend laid all wet with blood.

53. Yggr must now have a blade-hacked corpse, I know your life is spent; the *dísir* are unfriendly, now let Óðinn see, come to me if you can.

54. I am now called Óðinn, I once was called Yggr, I was called Þundr before that, Vakr and Skilfingr, Váfuðr and Hroftatýr, Gautr and Jalkr among the gods, Ófnir and Sváfnir, as I recall, are all words for me alone.'

When the king heard the last verse and realised that his guest was none other than Óðinn, he rose from his seat to release him but the sword which had been resting on his knees fell pommel-downwards to the floor and Geirrøðr stumbled forwards, impaling himself on the point. After this untimely death, young Agnar came to rule in his father's place.

Some features of the story remain puzzling, such as the identity of King Hrauðungr who is otherwise unknown. The name *Grímnismál* means 'the sayings of the hooded one' (or 'the masked one', or 'the disguised one'), which neatly refers to one aspect of Óðinn's personality, his taste for disguise and trickery. In verse 46 the traveller says *heto mek Grímr* 'I am called 'Mask'' (Price & Mortimer, 2014, p.12).

The poem contains many stanzas of general description relating to the layout of the heavens and its inhabitants, for example (concerning the god's hall in Ásgarð):

> 23 Fimm hundrað dura
>
> ok of fiórum tøgum,
>
> svá hygg ek á Valhǫllo vera;
>
> átta hundruð einheria
>
> ganga [senn] ór einom durom,
>
> þá er þeir fara at vitni at vega.

"I believe there are in Valhall five hundred and forty doors. Eight hundred Einherjar may pass together through each door when they go out to face the wolf."

Verse 19 states:

> Gera ok Freka
>
> seður gunntamiður,
>
> hróðigur Heriafǫður.
>
> en við vín eitt
>
> vápngǫfugr
>
> Óðinn æ lifir.

'The war-tamed [one] feeds Geri and Freki, the host-father of ancient fame. But on wine alone Óðinn lives always, bedecked with weapons.'

HÁRBARÐSLJÓÐ

This poem in the *Poetic Edda* manuscript is an example of a challenge-verse or flyting – or perhaps a parody on the flyting style - between Þórr and a surly ferryman called Hárbarðr (grey-beard). The 'true' identity of Hárbarðr has been the subject of some speculation, and either Loki or Óðinn is usually cited as the most likely: in *Grímnismál*, 'Hárbarðr' is given as one of Óðinn's bynames.

LOKASENNA

The verse called *Lokasenna* ('Loki's flyting') is composed in the *ljóðaháttr* metre, typically used for recording traditional wisdom. The accusations which Loki makes against the gods have to be seen in the light of the tradition of verbal challenges (*flyting*) which were customary in the meadhall culture of Northern Europe. Exaggeration and hyperbole were used to cast the addressee in a poor light, but outright lies were deprecated since the point of the game was to 'frame' the truth to make a point, not to invent falsehoods (Frakes, 2002, p.166).

A feast is in process when the poem opens, hosted by the sea god Ægir (also called Gymir), with ale brewed for the Æsir in a great cauldron; the gaining of this vessel is related in the poem *Hymiskviða* in the same manuscript. The participants are Æsir (including Óðinn, Týr, Sif, Bragi, Viðar, Gefjon and others), Vanir (Njorð, Skaði, Freyr, Freyja, Iðunn) and some *álfar* (elves). Ægir himself has *jotunn* ancestry, as does his wife Rán and Loki likewise. The gods had been warmly welcomed to the feast by Ægir's servants, Fimafeng and Eldir, and the praise they received for this angers Loki who then kills the former. The gathering turns against Loki for this breach of faith and drives him out of the hall. Loki later returns to learn from Eldir what the gods have been saying; on learning that they are discussing their various great deeds, and that he (Loki) is not welcome, the trickster forces his way into the hall and invokes the rules of guest-hosting which entitle him to a seat at the table and a measure of ale.

Bragi rises to repeat that his presence among them is not welcome, but Loki reminds Óðinn that they had sworn to drink together.

Viðar makes way for Loki at Óðinn's request and pours a drink for him. Loki toasts the assembly with his draught of ale but pointedly omits Bragi from the blessing. Bragi, wishing to keep the peace of the gathering, offers Loki a horse, a ring and a sword to appease him but Loki insults the god by questioning his courage. Bragi answers that it is not right for guests to fight within a hosts' hall, but it would be different if they were in Ásgarð. Bragi's wife, Iðunn, restrains her husband but Loki then insults her too, calling her a whore. Gefjon, Freyja, Njord, Týr, Freyr and Byggvir all try to calm him down and all receive an insult for their trouble. The exchange between Óðinn and Loki is especially bitter (Neckel, 1983):

> 22 'Þegi þú, Óðinn! þú kunnir aldregi
>
> deila víg með verom;
>
> opt þú gaft, þeim er þú gefa scyldira,
>
> inom slævorom, sigr.'

'Be quiet, Óðinn you never know how to apportion warfare among men; often you gave victory to the weak-willed, which you should not give.'

At last, Þórr comes late to the meal and receives insulting words, for which he threatens to kill Loki; this he does take seriously and leaves. The story ends with a short reference to the binding of Loki, which is told at greater length in the *Prose Edda*.

The interesting aspect of the tale – apart from the slurs and accusations which Loki feels able to level at his tormentors – lies in the duty which Loki invokes concerning the oaths of blood-brotherhood he swore to Óðinn.[163]

---

[163] See Paxson, 2017, p.102 for a discussion of this detail.

BALDRS DRAUMAR

This short narrative poem 'The Dreams of Baldr' also called *Vegtamskviða* comprises 14 verses and dates from the 10th c. It is found only in the *Arnamagnæan Codex* and in some late printed compendia. It derives from the story related in *Gylfaginning* concerning the death of Baldr, and may have been composed by the same poet as produced *Vǫluspá* as there are some verses shared between both texts.

The story concerns the god Baldr but the protagonist is Óðinn; indeed, Baldr is seldom mentioned in any stories except in the context of his untimely death (Schjødt, 2020b, p.1140; Lindow, 2020c, p.1303). At the outset, Baldr's portentous dreams have disturbed him and his father, Óðinn, decides to find out what they mean. He rides in disguise to the land of Hel and summons the spirit of a dead *vǫlva* whom he interrogates to discover the future, but in the course of their exchange he discloses his identity and she refuses to say more.

The opening stanza presupposes that the dreams have already been made known to the gods and that a meeting has been called to discuss them (Schjødt, 2020b, p.1151; text from Neckel, 1983):

> 1. Senn vóro æsir
>
> allir á þingi
>
> oc ásynior
>
> allar á máli,
>
> oc um þat réðo,
>
> ríkir tívar,
>
> hví væri Baldri
>
> ballir draumar.

'Once all the Æsir were at a meeting and all the Ásynjur [goddesses] in discussion, then the mighty gods exchanged views as to why baleful dreams had come to Baldr.'

2. Upp reis Óðinn,

alda gautr,

oc hann á Sleipni

sǫðul um lagði;

reið hann niðr þaðan

Niflheliar til,

mœtti hann hvelpi,

þeim er ór helio kóm.

'Óðinn, the Gautr of men, stood up and placed a saddle on Sleipnir; from there he rode downwards to [the land of] Niflhel and met the hound which came from Hel.'

The god passes the fearsome guard-dog and rides to the eastern door of Hel's hall beside which a barrow stands in which a seeress is buried. He speaks charms to raise her from the mound and she asks him:

5. Hvat er manna þat,

mér ókunnra,

er mér hefir aukit

erfit sinni?

Var ec snivin snióvi

oc sleginn regni

oc drifin dǫggu,

dauð var ec lengi'

"Who is this of men unknown to me, who has made the path harder for me? I have been snowed upon with snow and pelted with rain and drenched with dew – long have I been dead."

6. 'Vegtamr ec heiti,

sonr em ec Valtams;

segðu mér ór helio

– ec man ór heimi –:

hveim ero beccir

baugom sánir,

flet fagrliga

flóð gulli?'

"I am called Vegtamr son of Valtamr. I call on you from earth, tell me from hell for whom those benches are strewn with rings? [For whom] are the fair settles covered with gold?"

7. 'Hér stendr Baldri

of brugginn mioðr,

scírar veigar,

liggr scioldr yfir,

enn ásmegir

í ofvæni.

Nauðug sagðac,

nú mun ec þegia.'

"Mead stands here [ready] brewed for Baldr [and] a shield has been laid over the fair chalice [while] the mighty gods [are] waiting expectantly. I have been forced to speak, now I shall be silent."

Vegtamr insists that she continue to answer his questions: first, who is to be the killer of Baldr – to which she replies that it will be Hǫðr; and then who will avenge his death - to which she replies that Rindr, a giantess, will bear a son, Váli, who will slay Hǫðr while still one night old and will not wash his hands or comb his hair until he has achieved this. He then asks the identity of the three maidens who will weep for Baldur, and the vǫlva realises who she is dealing with:

13. 'Ertattu Vegtamr,

sem ec hugða,

heldr ertu Óðinn,

aldinn gautr.'

"You are not Vegtamr as I believed, rather you are Óðinn, the lord of men."

'Ertattu vǫlva,

né vís kona,

heldr es þriggja

þursa móðir.'

"You are not a *vǫlva* nor a wise woman, rather you are the mother of three giants."

14. 'Heim ríð Óðinn,

oc ver hróðigr!

Svá komit manna

meirr aptr á vit,

er lauss Loki

líðr ór bǫndum

oc ragna rǫk

riúfendr koma.'

"Ride home, Óðinn and be proud, [since] no more men shall come to me until Loki slips from his bonds and the downfall of the *regin* comes with destruction."

The implication of the last verse is that the seeress is none other than Loki himself, feeding false information to Óðinn in order to mislead him.

Hyndliuljóð

This poem is often taken to belong to the same tradition as the *Poetic Edda* although it appears only in the *Flateyjarbók* manuscript. Its background relates to the transmission of mythological information and 'lore', and parts of it are cited in the *Prose Edda*, attributed to the *Shorter Vǫluspá* (Schjødt, 2020a, p.843).

Hyndla, a *vǫlva* after whom the poem is named, meets Freyja and they ride together to Valhǫll in order to determine the ancestry of a hero named Ottarr who has been transformed into the boar on which the goddess is riding, in order that he should be able to claim his rightful inheritance. The seeress provides a large number of names of heroes, of which only a few have any tale attached known to modern readers. *Herjafǫðr* (father of armies = Óðinn) is mentioned in verse 2 as having provided a helm and mailcoat to Hermóðr (one of his 'sons' or heroes) and a sword to Sigmundr (text from Neckel, 1983):

> 2 Biðiom Heriafǫðr
>
> í hugom sitia!
>
> hann geldr oc gefr
>
> gull verðugom;
>
> gaf hann Hermóði
>
> hiálm oc brynio,
>
> enn Sigmundi
>
> sverð at þiggia.

'We ask the Father of Troops for favour; he yields and gives gold to worthy men: to Hermóðr he gave a helm and mailcoat and to Sigmund a sword to keep.'

ÚLFR UGGASON: HÚSDRAPA

This poem, 'House Verse', is mentioned in *Laxdæla Saga* and describes a wall-hanging, tapestry or (carved?) panel in a hall; it features mythological scenes including an image of Óðinn riding to Baldr's funeral, but the verses are not inserted continuously as a single poem (Hermann, 2020, p.50; Sigurðsson, 2020, p.1653). The poet is named as Úlfr Uggason, of whom little is known for sure. *Landnámabók* gives the lineage of his wife, Járngerðr, and he appears twice in *Brennu-Njáls saga*. In chapter 60, he is challenged to a duel by the noted warrior-farmer, Njál's friend Gunnar of Hlíðarendi.

EIRÍKSMÁL

This anonymous poem, 'The Song of Eiríkr', is a fragment of a longer work describing the arrival of Eiríkr Blóðøx in Valhǫll (Kershaw, 1922, pp.93-102; Schjødt, 2020b, pp.1138-9). It is structured as a dialogue between Bragi and Óðinn, with comment from the hero Sigmundr. The war-god awakes from a premonitory dream in which he prepares his hall for the coming of a great hero. Óðinn anticipates his coming because he has spilt so much blood in his time on earth, and he hopes Eirík's skills in war will help him in the forthcoming battle.

The poem is classed as 'skaldic' (i.e., courtly) because its subject is a historical figure, Eiríkr Blóðøx, a 10th century ruler in Norway who had a varied career, earning the enmity of many of the noblemen whose support he should have relied on. He fled to England and became the effective 'king' of Jórvík and Northumbria; eventually he was ousted and exiled, betrayed and killed on Stainmore (Yorkshire) in 954 AD. This gives a useful point of departure for dating the poem, which is composed in *fornyrðislag* metre, a more straightforward medium than the *dróttkvætt* of much other skaldic verse.

EYVINDR FINNSSON : HÁKONARMÁL

This poem, 'The Song of Hákon', was composed by the Norwegian poet Eyvindr Finnsson *Skáldaspillir* [despoiler of poets] in which Óðinn prepares to receive King Hákon after the fierce fighting at Fitjar, Norway, in 961 AD. The battle was fought between Hákon 'the Good' and his nephews, the three sons of Eiríkr Blóðøx. Hákon's military victory cost him his life (Kershaw, 1922, pp.101-110; Schjødt, 2020b, p.1138).

The verse is modelled on the form of *Eiríksmál* with Óðinn welcoming the dead king to his hall, but Hákon was Christian and very displeased at the idea of going to Valhǫll after death. The poet includes terms which stress that a man's honour can never die, unlike wealth and kinsmen – the same sentiment as can be found in *Hávamál*.

ÞJÓÐOLFR OF HVINIR : HAUSTLǪNG

This poem, meaning 'harvest-long', is probably 9th c. in date and is framed as a description of mythological scenes painted on a shield. It relates the stories of Idunn's abduction and of Þórr's fight with Hrungnir (Lindow, 2020d, p.1346). The matter relating to Óðinn (he is with Loki and Hoenir when they meet the giant Þjazi in eagleform) describes him in 'heroic' terms but he is nevertheless powerless to cook a meal due to the greater magical abilities of the giant.

ÁGRIP AF NÓREGSKONUNGASǪGUM

The *Ágrip* is a short Norse text dealing with the history of the kings of Norway, preserved in a 13th c. Icelandic manuscript, AM325 II 4to in the Arnamagnæan Institute, Copenhagen. Its sole reference to the god occurs in the first chapter where we read (text from Driscoll [ed.], 1995, p.1.):

Heiðnir menn gerðu sér samkundu ok í tígn við Óðin, en Óðinn heitir mørgum nøfnum. Hann heitir Viðrir ok hann heitir Hør ok Þriði ok Jólnir, ok var af Jólni jól kalluð.

'Heathen people made a ceremony for themselves in honour of Óðinn, and Óðinn is called by many names. He is called Viðrir and he is called Hár and Þriði and Jólnir, and "Yule" is named for Jólnir.'

The information is provided merely in explanation of the name of the heathen midwinter festival, 'Yule'.

ÍSLENDINGABÓK

The *Book of Icelanders* purports to tell the story of the conversion of the Icelanders to Christianity in the year 1000 AD (Benediktsson, 1968). It has little to say directly about the previous religion of the inhabitants.

HERVARAR SAGA OK HEIÐREKS

An early 14th c. composition drawing on folklore motifs and (presumably) some genuine traditions (Schjødt, 2020d, p.541; Egeler, 2020, p.303; Lassen, 2022, pp.95-6). The god appears in the guise of Gestr ('guest') or Gestumblindi ('blind-guest' or possibly 'unblind guest'). King Heiðrekr has been a successful ruler but sadly killed his own brother while following Óðinn, so later switched allegiance to Freyr. He wriggled out of a freely-given oath and condemned his father-in-law and his followers to death rather than face the consequences of his own dishonesty. The king challenged his enemy, Gestumblindi, to a riddle contest but the latter's place was taken by an old man of the same name who, it turned out, had an encyclopaedic knowledge of lore which Heiðrek could not match. Guessing that he had been deceived, the king tried to hack his challenger with his sword, but the guest escaped by changing into a falcon, while cursing the king to an ignominious death at the hands of his servants.

Having shifted from the worship of Óðinn to that of Freyr, the king had put himself outside Óðinn's protection and likely earnt his ill-will.

HLǪÐSKVIÐA

This poem appears in the *Hervarar saga*, where it is evidently anachronistic and was probably worked into the tale piecemeal from its originally independent form (Sundqvist, 2020, p.752). It relates to a plausible historical episode otherwise known in English as *The Battle of the Goths and Huns* (Tolkien, 1960). The action – insofar as it is historical – takes place in the 4th or 5th c. AD somewhere in central or eastern Europe;[164] some of the Norse names in the text may date back to the 8th c.[165] and are considerably older than the Icelandic manuscripts in which they were recorded: mainly *Hauksbók* ('H') of the early 14th c. and a separate 15th c. parchment copy with the reference letter 'R', and some 17th c. printed versions which record verses missing from the older manuscripts.

The story concerns Hlǫðr, the offspring of King Heiðrekr and his Hunnish mistress Sifka. Seeking to gain his portion of paternal inheritance, Hlǫðr made representation to his half-brother Angantýr, who was reluctant to divide his hereditary lands but made a handsome alternative proposal. Hlǫðr was giving consideration to the

---

[164] The battle may possibly be that of the Catalaunian Plains in 451 AD in which the Hunnish invasion of the Roman Empire was halted by an alliance of Roman, Germanic and other peoples; some details make a location in eastern Poland or Ukraine possible, but no independent account survives of these events. The generally confused nature of the text makes certainty impossible.

[165] One such is a verse reference to the death of King Heiðrek *und Harvaða-fjǫllum* 'beneath the Harfath mountains' which early modern scholars realised must be the Carpathians, and that the original name *karpat-* for this range had been transformed by the First Sound Shift to *xarfaþ-*, which underlies the Norse *Harfað-* of the poem. This name is otherwise unrecorded. The operation of the First Sound Shift must be dated to the last centuries BC, implying that the name is both genuine and ancient.

offer when a courtier called Gizurr Grýtingaliði[166] taunted him about his low birth, saying that a third of Angantýr's property was too generous a gift for the bastard son of a bondswoman. Hlǫðr left in anger for the Hunnish court where the king, Humli, agreed to support his cause. The following spring a huge army of Huns passed through the *Myrkviðr* 'murky woods' which divided the lands of the Huns from those of the Goths (called *Gautar*, 'Geats' in the poem's opening section). Angantýr's (and Hlǫðr's) sister, Hervǫrr, was over-whelmed in the first attack and her husband, Ormarr, rode to the Gothic court with word of the advancing Hunnish threat.

When news of Hervǫrr's brave defiance and death reached him, Angantýr was dismayed at the small group of followers who were available to take to the field with him, observing that there were plenty of men around when there was mead to be drunk, 'but when more are needed, the number is smaller' (1.20). The aged retainer, Gizurr, leapt on his horse and rode out to challenge the Huns, shout-ing (text from Jónsson, 1956; Kershaw, 1922, p.158, stanzas 25-6):

> Felmtr es yðru fylki, geigr es yðarr vísir,
>
> gnæfar yðr gunnfani, gramt es yðr Óðinn

'Your army is frightened, your warlord is fated to die, war-banners are raised against you, Óðinn is angry with you'

> ...Hræse yður at há hvorju
>
> ok láti svá Óðinn flein fljúga sem ek fyrir mæli'

'...may your corpses lie [unburied] on every battlefield and may Óðinn let the spear fly as I say it'

Battle was joined at *Dúnheiði* and many warriors rushed to An-gantýr's aid so that eventually he was able to overcome Hlǫðr and slay him with the sword, Tyrfing, which had belonged to their father.

---

[166] This name has been related to the name *Greuthungi* applied to one compo-nent of the Gothic nation; perhaps 'warrior of the Greutingas' is the meaning.

The historicity of the episode is supported by evidence from an unlikely source for events which happened in central Europe. A few names from the same event occur together in the OE poem *Widsith* in line 116 (text from Chambers, 1912):

Heaþoric ond Sifecan   Hliþe ond Incgenþeow.

'[I sought] Heaþoric and Sifeca[167], Hliþe and Incgenþeow.'

and ll.119-22:

Wulfhere sohte ic ond Wyrmhere: ful oft þær wig ne alæg,

þonne Hræda here   heardum sweordum

ymb Wistlawudu   wergan scoldon

ealdne eþelstol   ...

'I sought Wulfhere and Wyrmhere; seldom did warfare subside there when the military might of the Hrædas[168] had to defend [their] ancient homeland with hard swords.'

Heaþoric in the OE poem is *Heiðrekr* in the Norse version, *Sifeca* may be *Sifka*, *Hliþe* is *Hlǫðr*, *Incgenþeow* is *Angantýr* and *Ormarr* is *Wyrmhere* (Tolkien, 1960a, p.xxvi).

The behaviour of Gizurr is quite remarkable: he is an old man in apparently poor health who nevertheless manages to prevent Angantýr and his half-brother from making a peaceful and mutually beneficial arrangement and is quick to ride off to taunt and curse the Huns. His imprecations end with the revelation that 'Óðinn is angry with you' and his intention that they must all die is backed up by the wish that Óðinn should let the spear fly according to his words.

---

[167] *Sifeca* is formally identical with the Norse *Sifka*, the Hunnish concubine of Heiðrekr, but the OE name is masculine in gender. A man of this name (OHG Sibich) was believed to have been involved in the downfall of Ermanaric of the Goths (Chambers, 1912, p.34 fn2).

[168] The *Hrædas* are elsewhere identified as the Goths (Chambers, 1912, pp.252-3).

Gizurr is an *Óðinsheiti* and the old man may have been the war-god himself or one of his chosen heroes, like Starkaðr.

VǪLSUNGA SAGA

This story was written around 1260-70 AD, based on the author's knowledge of complete poems which only appear elsewhere in defective or partial versions, and sources such as *Reginsmál, Fáfnismál* and *Sigrdrífumál* (Jónsson, 1905; Kershaw, 2000, pp.59-62; Lassen, 2022, pp.96-9). Óðinn appears as an ancestor of the Vǫlsung family who takes a benevolent interest in their success, appearing occasionally in disguise to order events in their favour. The founder, Vǫlsung, was the product of the god providing his mother with an enchanted apple which kindled him in her womb; the father, Rerir, died before the son was born. Vǫlsung later married the valkyrie who brought the apple to his mother, and they went on to have eleven children, of whom the eldest was Sigmund. Sigmund and his son went on to live wild lives in the forest, taking what they wanted from farmers or catching prey for themselves (Kershaw, 2000, pp.59-60; Schjødt, 2020e, pp.560, 579-80)[169]. At the wedding of Signy, a sister, a one-eyed cloaked stranger entered the hall and thrust a sword into the stock of the tree which supported the hall's frame, announcing that whoever could draw the sword from the tree trunk could have it; Sigmund claimed the weapon and it served him well until, in one combat, he clashed his blade against the spear of his foe and it shattered – the foe being an old one-eyed man in a blue cloak and broad hat. Sigmund's wife tried to heal his wounds, but the king knew that his patron had betrayed him and his days were over. Carrying his dead son, Sinfjǫtli, Sigmund reached a river-crossing where a boatman offered to transport them over the water one at a time, but once the corpse of Sinfjǫtli was on the boat, they both disappeared. A surviving brother called Sigurð came to bear the god's favour and

---

[169] The two men underwent various forms of ritual initiation including a period in which they wore wolfskins.

was helped in various ways by a mysterious stranger; Sigurð went on to have an illustrious career as a dragonslayer using a sword called Gram, forged for him by the dwarves and his adventures are related in *Fáfnismál*, the story of the slaying of Fáfnir the dragon. The later history and fall of the Vǫlsung clan is entwined with that of King Jǫrmunrekr (i.e., Eormanric, the king of the Goths) and the collapse of the Gothic kingdom after the king's death.

SKJǪLDUNGA SAGA

The *Saga of the Skjoldungs* is usually considered one of the 'sagas of the kings' even though the dynasty itself is of great antiquity (its name appears in the opening of *Beowulf*) and the stories it tells concern the early history of the Danes and their struggles with their neighbours (Swedes, Heaðobeardan, Frisians, Geatas and others). It – or an earlier version of it – was probably known to Saxo Grammaticus (Lassen, 2022, pp.99-101). A Latin translation was made in the later 16th century by Arngrímur Jónsson, called *Rerum Danicarum Fragmenta* 'Fragments of Danish History' covering events down to the matters narrated in *Ólafs Saga Tryggvasonar en Mesta*.

From Jónsson's account, the legendary kings of the Danes are descended from Skjold, a son of Óðinn who also established the line of Swedish kings from Ingi (Yngr). Conflict between the two kingdoms was inevitable. Among the Danes a noble youth came to power called Hrólfr Kraki, who was determined to end the strife by destroying the seat of Swedish power at Uppsala. On their way there, Hrólfr and his men stayed overnight on a farm where they were offered a cloak and some mailcoats by the landowner, which the king refused, whereupon both farm and farmer vanished – a sure sign that this was Óðinn, and that their luck was about to change. After all-out warfare had been avoided for many years, eventually an attack was launched by his sister's husband with the supernatural aid of a mysterious figure who walked among the corpses reviving those of the Danes' enemies.

The story breaks off here, and when it resumes it is with King Harald Hilditǫnn (War-tooth) who had been taught the secret of the wedge-shaped battle-array called the *svínafylking* by his patron, Óðinn, and was successful with it until he took the field at Brávellir against the Swedish Sigurð Hring, who had also learnt of it and used it against him. (This story appears in a slightly different form in *Gesta Danorum* where Othinus causes the strife between the two kings and pits them against each other.)

HRÓLFS SAGA KRAKA

Legends of this Danish king probably go back to the 6th c. when the events of his reign may have happened, but the form of the present text took shape in the 15th c. and the surviving manuscripts are all post-medieval (Schjødt, 2020e, p.575; Lassen, 2022, pp.101-2). The storyline is enmeshed with that of *Skjǫldunga saga* and both Saxo and Snorri were familiar with the tale. Here, Hrólfr is a Danish king with a long-standing feud against the Swedish King Aðils. The incident with the farmer and his vanishing homestead is recounted in more detail, giving his name as Hrani. He advised Hrólfr to go on only with the men who slept well even without coverings in the bitterly cold night, and to send the others home. Hrólfr continued on his journey and curiously met the same Hrani further on his route, stayed overnight with him and received the advice that he should send home those men who could not resist thirst during the night. A second night under Hrani's roof resulted in a great fire being lit in the hall which was too much for all but the twelve picked champions of Hrolfr's army, so he decided to carry on with this small force. Hrólfr attacked Aðils successfully and on his return journey met Hrani again, who offered him a gift of weapons but the king refused them. This sent the farmer into a rage. Bjarki, chief of Hrólfr's men, sensed that refusing the gift was a mistake, and suspected that the one-eyed farmer may have been their patron, Óðinn. The king therefore avoided open warfare for some years since he knew that his rejection of the god's offering meant he would no longer be victorious.

This tale is first found in a 17th c. manuscript but the text shows evidence of copying errors, and a date of composition in the 14th c. is usually considered likely. There are 44 individual manuscripts. The events related refer to the rise and fall of the Skjǫldung dynasty in Denmark, the very same historical milieu as for the action of *Beowulf* composed nearly a thousand years before. The multitude of copies and long period of active interest show that this 'Matter of Denmark' was considered crucial to the rise of a central power in that area (Byock, 1998).

STYRBJARNAR ÞÁTTR SVÍAKAPPA

The 'tale of Styrbjǫrn, Champion of the Swedes' is recorded in *Flateyjarbók* and dates to perhaps the last decade of the 14th c. (Schjødt, 2020g, p.617). The hero is a legendary claimant to the throne of the Swedes whose legend is linked to with that of the Jómsvikings. His rival for the Swedish throne, the aged King Eiríkr, sacrificed to Óðinn for victory while Styrbjǫrn sacrificed to Þórr; at a crucial point in the battle, Styrbjǫrn's luck failed him and Eiríkr gained the victory. Eiríkr was believed to have agreed to go to Óðinn in return for ten years of military success.

GAUTREKS SAGA

This story is set in the 'legendary' land of Scandinavia before the exodus to Iceland when the kings and heroes of old were on earth; the stories often have the form of fable or legend. An episode called *Víkars þáttr* (Tale of Víkar) occurs in one redaction of the saga, in which the famed and feared warrior, Starkaðr, was travelling with his friend King Víkar. A similar tale appears in the *Gesta Danorum* using the latinised forms of the names: Starcatherus and Wicarus (Schlauch, 1931; Schjødt, 2020d, p.546). The saga is usually dated to the 13th century although the two versions in which it survives (called 'shorter' and 'longer') are in manuscripts from some centuries later.

The king's ship was becalmed, and it was decided that the gods should be consulted to determine the best course of action (Schjødt, 2020g, p.638). Starkaðr learnt from his foster-father, Hrosshárs Grani, a redoubtable warrior and leader, that a sacrifice to Óðinn was required in order to provide fair sailing weather (Kershaw, 2000, p.32). Lots were drawn for this purpose and the chosen victim was revealed to be the king himself. Hrosshárs Grani woke Starkaðr that night (text from Garmonsway, 1928):[170]

> Um nóttina nær miðri nótt vakti Hrosshárs Grani Starkað, fóstra sinn, ok bað hann fara með sér. Þeir taka bát ein lítinn ok reru til eyjar einna inn frá hólminum. Þeir gengu upp til skógar ok fundu þár rjóðr eitt í skóginum; í rjóðrinu var fjǫlmenni mikit ok var þar þing sett. Þar satu xi men á stólum er hinn tólfti var auðr. Þeir gengu fram á þingit ok settist Hrosshárs-Grani á stólinn hinn tólfta. Þeir heilsuðu allir Óðni.

> 'In the night, about midnight, Hrosshárs-Grani woke Starkaðr, his foster-son, and bade him leave with him. They took a certain small boat and rowed out to an island inland from the islet. They went up to a wood and found a clearing in that wood; in the clearing was a great gathering, and a formal meeting was established there. Eleven men sat on seats there but the twelfth [seat] was empty. They went forward to the meeting and Hrosshárs-Grani settled on the twelfth seat. They all greeted Óðinn.'

Hrosshárs-Grani was thus revealed to be Óðinn in one of his many disguises. Starkaðr knew that the king would not submit to sacrifice willingly, but the lives of the whole company depended on their being able to sail home. He persuaded Víkar that they should trick the gods by staging a mock-sacrifice: the king should stand on a

---

[170] The name *Víkarr* may mean 'sacred hair', while Starkaðr's foster-father is 'horsehair-moustache'. Emblems of status expressed through hairstyles seem to be reflected in these names.

block of wood, with a calf's intestine round his neck attached to a fir tree's branch while Starkaðr prodded him with a wand - thus mimicking the rites of death by hanging and stabbing which the god required (Pollington, 2002, pp.197-8; Lassen, 2022, pp.102-3; Tolley, 2009, pp.106-7; text from Garmonsway, 1928).[171]

Þá mælti Starkaðr til konungs: 'Nú er hér búinn þér gálgi, konungr, ok mun sýnask eigi allmannhættlígr. Nú gakktu hingat, ok mun ek leggja snǫru á hals þér.'

Konungr mælti: 'Sé þessi umbúð ekki mér hættuligri en mér sýnisk, þá vænti ek, at mik skaði þetta ekki, en ef ǫðruvís er, þá mun auðna ráða hvat at gerisk.'

Síðan steig hann upp á stofninn, ok lagði virgulinn um háls honum ok steig síðan ofan af stofninum.

Þá stakk Starkaðr sprotanum á konungi ok mælti: 'Nú gef ek þik Óðni!' Þá lét Starkaðr lausan furukvistinn. Reyrsprotinn varð at geir ok stóð í gegnum koninginn. Stofninn fell undan fótum honum en kálfsþarmarnir urðu at viðu sterkri en kvistrinn reis upp ok hóf upp konunginn við limar, ok dó hann þár.

Then Starkaðr said to the king: 'Now the gallows is prepared for you, king, and it seems not too dangerous. Come here now and I will place the snare around your neck.'

The king said: 'If this should be no more dangerous to me than it appears to me, then I expect that it will not harm me – but if it is otherwise, then the gods will determine what shall happen.'

---

[171] Liberman (2016, p.210-2) notes that the motif of the mock-killing with a reed which tragically and unexpectedly becomes a real murder is also found in Snorri's tale of the death of Baldr at the hands of his 'brother' Hǫðr and the mistletoe dart, but not in Saxo's version in which they are both human warriors competing for the affections of the same female. An origin in England has been considered for the detail of the mistletoe, *mistill* perhaps replacing another plant-name (*þistill* 'thistle'?) in the original tale. This substitution does not explain the motif.

[Starkaðr] then mounted the block, placed the halter round his neck and climbed back down from the block.

Then Starkaðr thrust at the king with the wand and said: 'Now I give thee to Óðinn!' Then Starkaðr let go of the fir bough. The wand became a spear and pierced through the king. The block slipped from beneath his feet and the calf's intestines became strong as wood and the bough sprang up and lifted the king up among the branches, and there he died.

It seems evident that Óðinn used his fondness for disguise and deceit to trick the king into thinking he could outwit the gods, while at the same time leading him willingly to his certain death. This was a double-death of simultaneous stabbing and hanging, of a type known from other evidence to have been associated with the Óðinn cult. Yet there is no suggestion that King Víkar was a criminal whose death was a legal requirement; it seems to have been a case of Óðinn favouring certain prominent men with victories for a while, then withdrawing his favour and exacting a terrible price for his former support (Lassen, 2022, pp.102-3).

The central character of Starkaðr is ambivalent, being both a proficient and brave fighter and the perpetrator of many terrible crimes. He was beloved of Óðinn but hated by Þórr because his ancestry was among the þursar, giant enemies of the gods and mankind (Kershaw, 2000, pp.44-6). Óðinn supported his protégé in debate with Þórr over the hero's future (text from Garmonsway, 1928):

Óðinn svaraði 'Þat skapa ek honum at hann skal lifa mannsaldra þrjá', Þórr mælti 'Hann skal vinna níðingsverk á hverjum mannsaldri' ... Óðinn svaraði 'Ek gef honum sigr ok snild at hverju vígi', Þórr svaraði 'Þat legg ek á hann at hann fái í hverju vígi meiðslasár'...

Gautreks saga, ch.7

'Óðinn said "I shape it for him that he shall live for three men's lifespans", Þórr declared "He shall do a disgraceful deed in each lifespan" … Óðinn said "I give him victory and strength in every battle", Þórr said "I lay it on him that he shall receive a deadly wound in each battle"…'

The support of Óðinn and the enmity of Þórr are used to explain the conflicting aspects of the hero, whose greatest achievements he is doomed never to enjoy, and whose long and violent life provides the northern tales with one of their more useful and memorable characters.

15ᵀᴴ-16ᵀᴴ CENTURY AD

The late medieval and post-medieval traditions concerning the god are generally routine and he often appears only to point up a moral: anyone who accepts help from Óðinn is doomed to regret it as the god is unreliable and false.

HARÐAR SAGA OK HÓLMVERJA

The manuscript for this tale, 'The Saga of Hǫrðr and the Men of Hólm', dates to ca.1475–1500 but it may have existed in written form up to a century before this; it overlaps Bárðar Saga to some extent (Lassen, 2022, pp.74-5). Hǫrðr, the hero, sets off with a group of fellows intending to open a barrow belonging to an old Viking called Sóti; on the way he meets a man wearing a blue-striped cloak standing outside his impressive house. The stranger introduces himself as Bjǫrn, a friend of Hǫrðr's kindred, and offers to help him in his task. Hǫrðr declines and sets his men to work digging the mound, but each morning when they awake the previous day's hole has disappeared; Bjǫrn's offer of help is then accepted and his advice is to place a sword in the hole which has the effect of preventing it from closing up overnight. The men then remove the treasure from the mound but cannot find Bjǫrn or his dwelling to thank him, and from this they conclude that he must have been the old trickster-god himself. Unknown to Hǫrðr, the treasure includes a cursed ring which brings bad luck to its owner, so the apparent benefit of gaining the gold is offset by the ill fortune which ensues – a Christian comment which points up the danger of accepting help from the old gods.

HÁLFS SAGA OK HÁLFSREKKA

The manuscript in which the saga is preserved dates from the mid-15th century, while the tale itself may have taken literary form up to a century earlier. The god appears in one story under the pseudonym Hǫttr, who arranges for his supplicant, Geirhildr, to marry King Alrekr; the king already has a wife, Signý, and the two females are soon in competition. Alrekr decides to choose whichever of them can brew the better ale, whereby Signý asks Freyja for help and Geirhildr calls on Hǫttr/Óðinn. The god introduces some of his spittle into the brew, and its superior fermentation affords him the victory, for which he demands payment of whatever lies between the lady and the vessel – her unborn child, who is later known as King Víkarr (as described in *Gautreks saga*) (Lassen, 2022, p.104).[172] The ale provokes a prescient vision in Alrekr, who sees his son hanged on the gallows (Lassen, 2022, p.104).[173] Later in the saga, a pair of brothers named Innsteinn and Útsteinn compose verses respectively blaming and praising the god for his choices in dealing victory.

The saga is unusual in not condemning the god for his capriciousness and bad faith; indeed, the 'domestic' ambience of the tale is closer to Paul the Deacon's story of Godan allocating victory.

ICELANDIC RUNE POEM

The *Icelandic Rune Poem* appears in two manuscripts: (i) AM 687d 4°, now in the Stofnun Árna Magnússonar, Reykjavík, dated to circa 1500AD and (ii) AM 461 12° in the same location, dated to 1539-58 AD (Pollington, 2016, p.216). There are two or more later

---

[172] This ruse is a well-known motif in folktales.

[173] The ale provides the king with the power of prophecy, in which it resembles the mead of inspiration which Óðinn covets. The mother of the brothers is called Gunnlǫð, the same as the daughter of Suttungr in the *Hávamál* episode.

manuscript copies and several citations in 17th c. printed books (Halsall, 1981, p.36; Page, 1999a). Each version comprises a sixteen-stanza poem, each stanza dedicated to one of the Younger Fuþark runes and consists of three paraphrases or kennings.

The *Icelandic Rune Poem* is based on the same traditional body of lore as the older *Norwegian Rune Poem*, dating from the 13th c. The sole medieval manuscript in which it was recorded was destroyed by fire in Copenhagen in 1728; three transcripts had been made, which vary in detail (Halsall, 1981, p.35; Neuner, 2006; Pollington, 2016, p.114, 216, 411).

The *Norwegian Rune Poem* contains no explicit reference to Óðinn by that name. The fourth strophe of the *IRP* with the title *óss* (god) cites *aldingautr ok ásgarðs jǫfurr ok valhallar vísi* 'old Gautr (sacrifice) and Ásgarð's prince (boar) and Valhǫll's wise-one (guide)' (Polomé, 1991, p.430; Page, 1998; Pollington, 1995, p.54). The allusion here is to Óðinn, specified by his frequent byname 'Gautr'.

DISCUSSION

CHAPTER 4

LORD OF THE MEAD HALL

Forgeaf þā Bēowulfe   brand Healfdenes

segen gyldenne   sigores tō lēane,

hroden hildecumbor,   helm ond byrnan.

Mǣre māðþumsweord   manige gesāwon

beforan beorn beran.   Bēowulf geþāh

ful on flette,   nō hē þǣre feohgyfte

for sc[ē]oten[d]um   scamigan ðorfte.

Ne gefraægn ic frēondlicor   fēower mādmas

golde gegyrede   gummanna fela

in ealobence   ōðrum gesellan.

'Then Healfdene's son gave to Beowulf a golden standard as a reward for victory, an ornamented war-banner, a helm and mailcoat; many saw a famed ancient sword brought before the warrior. Beowulf received a cup on the hall-floor - he had no cause to be ashamed of that gift of wealth before the warriors. I have never heard of four treasures decorated with gold being given more nobly by many men to another on the ale-bench.'

Beowulf, ll.1020–9

The origins of the Northern European 'meadhall' institution lie ultimately in the Neolithic period (Pollington, 2003; Gautier, 2006; Hornsey, 2012, p.341). The 'hall' – a high building with space inside to gather and hold a community – comes to the fore with the adoption of agriculture and the establishment of fixed settlements with defined boundaries and resources. The ritual consumption of alcoholic drinks, the giving of public rewards and the praise and promotion of individuals within an established hierarchy are all aspects of communal life which can barely have existed before the Neolithic revolution in food production and associated technological developments (Nelson, 2005; Jones, 2007; Hornsey, 2012; Hayden, 2014).

It was perhaps in the early Iron Age that the meadhall developed its special characteristics, founded on competition between communities for resources which might include food, land, slaves, mineral and other wealth. The value of artisans – especially weapon-makers and jewellers – to these communities was immense since their output enabled societies to express their political and material successes, and thus the implicit favour of the gods.[174] The feast as a public expression of solidarity (or exclusion) and an opportunity for reward-giving (or -withholding) became of central importance (Kershaw, 2000, pp.16-9). The feast-giver was conceived in OE sources as *goldwine* (gold-friend), *beaggiefa* (ring-giver) etc. in recognition of the leader's central role in the economy of prestige and public reward. Feasts could be seasonal (midwinter or harvest), or *ad hoc* events intended to seal an alliance, to solemnise a marriage, or offer thanks to the gods for success.

Versions of the meadhall sprang up across northern, western and central Europe among groups speaking related languages: Germanic ones, of course, but also Celtic, Baltic and Slavonic and probably others (Nelson, 2005, pp.45-66). While the details of each group's own traditions varied, the institution appears to have been broadly consistent and recognisable across boundaries (Nelson, 2005, pp.78-114). The splendid medieval character of mythical Valhǫll derives

---

[174] Lincoln (2018, p.30-3) argues that in *Beowulf* the enmity of Grendel towards King Hroþgar is 'an all-too-human envy' whereby the splendour of the hall reflects directly and proportionately the favour the king enjoys bestowed by God/the gods; Grendel's relative poverty and misery expresses itself in anger and violence. Yet Grendel's part in the tale presented by the poet is clearly drawn from folklore where characters' motives are not based on sound reasoning.

from its real-world Iron Age ancestor, which must have been conceived as a haven of warmth and friendship for the lord and his followers.

LORDSHIP

Woden was in certain respects the idealised lord of the meadhall for the Anglo-Saxons, stemming from the Iron Age traditions of feasting, worshipping and hosting guests (Jones, 2007, pp.233-49; Anthony & Ringe, 2015). Turville-Petre (1964, p.72) summarised the Anglo-Saxon evidence thus:

> ...the English records suggest that, among the pagan English, Woden had filled a place similar to that which he filled in Scandinavia as late as the tenth century. This implies that already the north German ancestors of the English, *Saxones*, *Angli* and *Iutae*, has seen him in a similar light; he was god of princes, victory, death and magic, perhaps also of runes, speech, poetry. It is not insignificant that the English came chiefly from north Germany and Denmark, where the cult of Óðinn seems to be old and particularly firmly established.

The position of Woden as 'king of the gods' (in the manner of Jupiter or Zeus) among the Anglo-Saxons is not directly supported by the evidence, but he was certainly an important deity linked closely to kingship, dynasty-foundation and military leadership. In the myths, Óðinn appears as a rather wilful and deceptive figure whose behaviour is 'transgressive' (i.e., challenging, disruptive and often immoral) in much the same way as Zeus appears in the Greek myths (Franks, 2019). Solli observes that 'Odin thus constitutes a paradox: he is the *manliest* god of warriors, but he is also the *unmanly* master of seid [*seiðr*]' (Solli, 2008, p.195). There is no direct evidence that the Anglo-Saxons viewed Woden in this way - nor any reason to doubt that they may have.

It is likely that Woden was the god of the intellect, of the strategic mind: he was the brain to set beside the brawn of Þunor. In battle, the furious rage that drove men on to unimaginable deeds of courage derived from the rites associated with this god; as Adam of Bremen put it *Uuoden, id est furor* 'Woden, that is, frenzy". Yet the worshipper of Woden - the *folctoga* 'army-leader', the *drihten* 'lord', the *heorra* 'warlord' - had to be more focussed and clear-thinking than the men he led.

DIVINE ANCESTORS

The notion that certain prominent persons were marked out as 'divine' or the offspring of the gods could apply to leaders who chose to emphasise this aspect of their role. Placing Woden at the head of a family line can be interpreted in two ways: either (i) biological descent from the god via a human ancestor, or (ii) divine patronage of the 'foster-father' type (Faulkes, 1978, pp.1-2). The first of these appears to have been the common heritage of mankind, since Tacitus recounts that the three great tribes of the Germanic peoples in his day (Ingævones, Istævones and Herminiones) were all descended from divine ancestors - presumably ancestral forms of the gods who appear in OE sources named *Ingwe* in the first case and *Eormen* in the latter. The Norse tale of Heimdallr in *Rígsþula* impregnating various women (and in so doing setting up the social structure) entails a similar notion.[175] All humanity thus shares a divine origin.

The Gothic tradition of descent from a demi-god named Ansis was mentioned above (p.127). The Ansis-god (from Germanic **ansiz/*ansaz/*ansuz*) is held to be only a half-god, because it would not be appropriate for living mortals to attain full divinity until they had passed into the Otherworld and become ancestors (cf. Polomé, 1991, pp.430-1; Pollington, 2011, p.78; Levin, 2020, p.42). The elevation of mortal leaders to semi-divine status was due to their (Latin) *fortuna*, their 'luck' or 'divine favour'. This agrees with later Germanic notions of the king's *hæl* or favour and also points to ideas

---

[175] It has been suggested (Schjødt, 2020b, p.1145) that the protagonist in this tale is really Óðinn the *Alfǫðr* 'father of all', although the text specifically contradicts this.

about the ancestor Hengest and the Woden-sprung kingship of the Angles. As we shall see, the initiates of the Woden-cult had access to secrets which brought them victory. We shall return to the name *Gaut* below (p.384).

The affiliation need not have been based on bloodlines, and it seems that some men were selected for divine favour due to their personal qualities alone. In these cases, the relationship is presented as 'fosterage'. The role of Óðinn as foster-father is exemplified in the tale of Hross-hárs-Grani and Starkaðr in *Gautreks saga* where the god is called specifically *fóstra sinn* 'his fosterfather' and takes charge of inducting the hero into his role as warrior champion. But Frigg took a similar patronage role and thwarted her husband's plans in the tale in *Griminsmál* concerning the foundling brothers Geirrøðr and Agnar, where the favoured king was deceived into ill-treating Óðinn and then paid for this with his life.

LORD AND LADY

The close connection between political leaders (Tacitus's *reges*) and military leaders (*duces*) became increasingly blurred in the Roman Iron Age. The rise of the warrior-king at the expense of the priest-king in Germanic societies of the early centuries AD has been extensively documented (e.g., Enright, 1996; Green, 1998). These new rulers, with the backing of respectable military forces, were able to transform the later Roman world in Western Europe and to create the successor states which arose from the ashes of the Western Roman Empire (Effros, 2002). This process led to the conversion of Iron Age 'chiefdoms' into medieval 'kingdoms', equipped with the full mechanism of statehood including literacy (a cadre of literate specialists), bureaucracy, rules of succession and inheritance, and a tax-based economy.

'Lordship' was the secret to success in the post-Roman world, in military, economic and dynastic terms. The foundation of the lords' power lay in the close bond between warrior and leader, a bond fostered in the meadhall and based upon reciprocation, an economy of prestige and honour, and the ritualised circulation of valuables (Enright, 1996; Pollington, 2003; Spurkland, 2005, p.15; Pollington, 2011). The *drihten* 'lord' at the head of his *gedriht* 'warband' supported by his *hlafdige* 'lady' was the central pillar of this social phenomenon, which entailed the formal and public bestowing of honours by the lord and giving oaths of service by his followers. Many of the 'honours', i.e., badges of prestige and social status, took the form of Mediterranean tableware including dishes and utensils of silver and glass (Grane, 2008, p.37). Items of this kind can be traced in Danish graves as far back as the 1st century BC, but they became prominent during the Roman Iron Age and the following Germanic Iron Age, i.e., from the 1st to 6th century AD (Grane, 2008, p.38). Roman tableware sometimes betokens direct diplomatic links with the Empire, but more often the archaeologically-detected dispersal patterns suggest re-distribution, i.e., goods entering *Germania Libera* as diplomatic gifts, and then being handed on within local exchange systems as prestige items which were not commonly available. Bronze tableware was a popular, if slightly less impressive, alternative to silver, while the ceramic *terra sigillata* wares were barely used (Grane, 2008, p.37). Roman coins are only found in limited numbers in Scandinavia, mainly *denarii* issues, but are relatively common within the former empire and its satellites.

The political and economic centre at Himlingøje (Denmark) was a powerbase from the 2nd c. onwards, having emerged in the context of the Marcomannic Wars; it became pre-eminent in the early 3rd c. perhaps through a monopoly on Roman contacts, expressed through displays of diplomatic tableware. The Himlingøje chieftain may have been courted by the emperor as a counterbalance to the power of the Marcomanni in the upper Rhineland, an ally to the rear of the Marcomannic territory who could be persuaded to support Roman interests. The successors to Himlingøje may have included the Hassleben-Leuna culture group in central Germany which benefitted from a political re-alignment in 260 AD under the Emperor Postumus, resulting in an increase in the importance and power of Cologne (Grane, 2008, p.38).

Although promoted as a means of building networks of influence among the military élite, the role of women in creating and maintaining such networks is often undervalued.[176] Due to the partiality of the records, women are seldom foregrounded in the secular narratives. Nevertheless, females played a number of central roles in establishing (male and female) leadership, supporting the hierarchical nature of the institution, reinforcing bonds of internal loyalty, influencing policy through guidance and prophecy (Enright, 1996; Franks, 2019; Sundqvist, 2020, p.747). The presence of noble and sumptuously dressed women remains a key feature of feasting scenes as presented in *Beowulf* and elsewhere. King Hroþgar's queen, Wealhþeo, was present on one important occasion as we learn when Beowulf tells of the feast the king and queen laid on in his honour to his own lord, Hygelac, on his return to Geatland.

The community presented in the feasting imagery demonstrates a tiered social structure. One purpose of the ritual feast – the *symbel* – was to demonstrate and re-affirm the hierarchical structure of the group, the position of the leader and the various grades of followers, supported by the community's females (Franks, 2019). Opportunities for display of access to resources were never missed: the lavish horns, glassware and tableware from the mounds at Sutton Hoo, Taplow, Prittlewell, Broomfield and elsewhere show this (Pollington, 2008; Blackmore et al., 2019). The feast was just one of the available *seledreamas* 'hall-joys', and both musical instruments and gaming pieces feature in the more lavishly furnished tombs (Sutton Hoo Mound 1, Taplow, Prittlewell, Asthall and others).

The presence of weapons and tableware displayed male authority, both in *Beowulf* and in the chamber tombs. Female authority was displayed through a variety of symbolic items, some relating to costume and others with a background in female-associated crafts such as textile production. The weaving-slay from a female grave at Shudy

---

[176] This issue was addressed in Enright's 1996 study *Lady with a Mead Cup: Ritual, Prophecy and Lordship in the European Warband from La Tène to the Viking Age.*

Camps (Cambridgeshire) made from a reused spearhead is a good candidate for an item of female 'regalia' displaying both mastery of an important skill and access to wealth and resources. Similarly, the ceremonial *vǫlva* rods with a writhen four-bar cage, found in Scandinavia, are very probably to be connected to aspects of female authority.[177] In Anglian contexts, the ornate forms of cruciform brooch have been interpreted as both ethnic and status markers, but may equally hold clues to initiation and arcane knowledge which conferred authority.[178] A fine example was excavated at West Heslerton (Yorkshire) with a runic text – sadly, an enigmatic four-rune sequence **neim** which has not been satisfactorily interpreted (Looijenga, 2003, p.279; Martin, 2013).

THE DRINK OF TRANSFORMATION

The *comitatus* warband was more than a loose association of warriors drawn from a range of societies, some not even sharing a common language. As with military regiments today, a range of complex social rituals developed in order to underscore differences between insiders and outsiders, leaders and followers, new recruits and old hands; likewise, the solidarity of the group was emphasised through sharing food and drink and undergoing common hardships.

Aspects of 'priestly' status fell into the hands of the warlords who benefitted from the opportunity to demonstrate their acquired wealth and access to power, implying that they had the favour of the gods. The idea of the 'sacral king' arose – the leader who intercedes with the powers of the Otherworld on behalf of his people, and who at times represents the Otherworld powers to those people

---

[177] Ullén, 2012, p.14; Price, 2019, pp.166–8.

[178] Martin (2013, p.13) suggests that the use of Style I ornament found on cruciform brooches and elsewhere was confined to persons who had reached 'adult' status and thus had gained wisdom and a social position which could be displayed through the intricate details of the art-style.

(Sundqvist, 2012, p.225ff).[179] Needless to say, the leader who donned the mask of Woden when placing the Sutton Hoo helmet on his head undertook a form of transformation – one might almost say 'transubstantiation'. The helmet is not a mere protective item, but actually a device which enabled the wearer to transfer into 'the liminal zone between nature and supernature, between power and the divine right of kings' (Price & Mortimer, 2014, p.12).

Access to the Otherworld was not available to everyone. Some had to undergo challenging rites of self-denial and alarming psychotropic experiences to achieve initiation into the religious mysteries of the warband's god (usually Woden) (Pollington, 2011, p.249).[180] Those who attained the status of 'initiate' were among the most privileged members of their societies, with access to secret knowledge which the uninitiated could neither understand nor share (e.g., literacy, military strategy, commercial negotiation skills).

A male initiate's inclusion in the warband (gedriht) was signalled publicly by the offering and acceptance of a draught of strong drink in a formal, communal setting (meduseld, the meadhall) in which the offer was made by the primary female of the group (hlafdige). The female role as producer of food, drink and textiles was the counterpart of the male role as the provider of the raw materials with which these females worked. The offered drink conveyed a formal message of prospective social inclusion, and its acceptance completed the rite. The drink – and the status it conveyed - had been earnt by military activity, whether solid battlefield performance or sound leadership (Pollington, 2010).

---

[179] Price & Mortimer (2014, p.2) note that the notion of sacral kingship has been controversial. Anglo-Saxon sources are often used to reject the idea of a priestly role for the king, and this view was generally accepted in Scandinavia until the turn of the 21st c., since when it has regained favour.

[180] The core of the god's mysteries was evidently common to many Germanic peoples, even though the name was adapted. In Norse tradition, he has many bynames, but Grímr 'the masked one' may be identical with Grim, a divine name found in some Saxon contexts.

There is a further dimension to the background of the use of formal rites of commensality. It is likely that the early English used psychotropic vegetable substances medically as anaesthetics, as well as ritually to heighten the sense of mystery and the awe of the divine power which surrounded them. Here we may recall the derivation of the word 'giddy' meaning 'dizzy, vertiginous, swooning' from OE *gidig* (for **gydig*), from a Germanic **guðigaz*, i.e., 'god-y, possessed by a god' (Orel, 2003, s.v. *guðz, guðaz*). If being possessed by a god meant dizziness, vertigo and loss of balance, this sensation might well have been induced by drinking a strong alcoholic brew spiked with some additional narcotic substance.

Drink was an important factor in the acquisition and retention of knowledge, especially the formal lore which was the preserve of the élite, the secrets which were only available to Woden's nominees. Larrington noted that 'internal mood states are equally relevant to memory tasks: what is learned [sic] drunk is better recalled drunk than sober' (Larrington, 2006, p.258 citing research by Goodwin et al.). Thus Óðinn was able to encode and memorise information with the help of ale, which he could only access later having drunk more ale.

There are two further terms of a similar nature which point to intoxicants or narcotics: 'dizzy' and 'woozy'. The modern word 'dizzy' is derived from OE *dysig*, an adjective meaning 'foolish, erroneous', perhaps originally 'confused, disorientated'. The etymology appears to include a cognate noun OE *dust* 'dust, powder, mist, smoke'. It is difficult to resist the obvious link to inhaled smoke affecting the concentration. In this connection the word *hænep, henep* 'hemp' invites speculation, derived from the (pre-Germanic?) root **kanib-* which provides the Greek cognate κανναβις 'cannabis' (Kroonen, 2013, s.v. *hanipa*). Another interesting word is modern 'woozy' meaning 'muddled, befuddled, dazed' probably derived from a form such as **wósæg* from the noun *wós* 'liquid, drink, juice' (Orel, 2003, s.v. *wósaz* –

wósan).[181] This term gives rise to OE *wésa* 'drunkard' and the verb *wésan* 'feast, make merry' (<*wósjan) which also means 'soak, seep'. The central idea here is of a liquid intoxicant, an alcoholic drink used in special circumstances such as feasts.

Perhaps the close connection of Woden to mead and ale is central to the puzzle: like the Indian *soma*, which is viewed as both a substance and a god, **woð-* may have been originally a quality of these alcoholic drinks, i.e., a form of intoxication releasing loquacity, rage, libido, prophecy and inspiration (Kershaw, 2000, p.80; West, 2007, pp.157-60). Its personification as *woð-an-az 'lord of intoxication' marked the change in attitude of its users as the drink assumed a central importance.

SHARING OF THE DRINK

References to the consumption of strong drink sit at the heart of many tales relating to Woden, including the early Lombard and Frankish sources. The later Norse traditions share this theme and expand it to explore the mythic significance of the mead, and the convoluted tale of its creation, loss, recovery and accidental sharing with men.

The real-world instances of mead-sharing were central to social life in the Iron Age and probably long before (Hornsey, 2012). A formal gathering at which food and drink were distributed in a highly public manner reinforced community, hierarchy and status. Enright suggests that the evolution of this social convention, which was common to many Iron Age Celtic and Germanic societies, involved a few key elements (Enright, 1996; Pollington, 2020, pp.43-48): (i) the lady (apical female) enters the hall (ritual space), finely dressed and in a formal manner befitting a priestess; (ii) she offers the

---

[181] The standard derived adjective should be *wésig with i-mutation of the root vowel. The retention of -*ó*- can be accounted for by assuming that the adjectival suffix is -*æg* or -*eg* rather than -*ig* (Lass, 1994, p.202). A small group of OE adjectives is formed in this way. The word *wósig* occurs in OE texts meaning 'juicy, succulent' and its related derivative *ealowosa* 'intemperate drinker of ale'.

first drink to the lord (apical male); (iii) she makes a formal greeting and names the lord before the community; (iv) she speaks publicly with advice for the lord; (v) she proceeds around the hall offering to those present a draught of the same drink from the same vessel, in a sequence determined by rank, standing and worth; (vi) the lord makes a formal speech of welcome. The ritual is both a bonding rite between the males, and a reinforcement of hierarchy through the public enactment of social rituals.

Mythic instances of this ritual are recalled in some of the *Edda* poems, particularly the initiation stories. The drink – typically characterised as 'mead' – is represented there as a source of inspiration, enhanced abilities, knowledge, wisdom and spells to the aspiring member of the group. The *Hávamál* deals with this in verse 140, where Óðinn learns the use of nine spells from his father-in-law and then gains a drink of mead from Óðhrérir (Kvilhaug, 2004, pp.43-4). The drink is served to the initiands by a richly-clad female but only after they have met challenges in the realm of death. Consuming the drink is the consummation of their transformation. The female is herself associated with supernatural skills, prophecy and hidden knowledge. The rite formalises the transformation of the youths to the status of 'companion' (OE *gesiþ*) with full membership of the élite community. A version of this process probably preceded the transformation of a 'noble' (OE *æþeling*) to 'lord' or 'king' (OE *drihten, cyning*).

LEADERS OF THE RITES

The ritual specialists who oversaw the ceremonies during which drink was shared and insight was gained have names which occur in some early runic texts (Sundqvist, 2015, pp.125-138; Sundqvist, 2020, p.740). In some cases they appear to have had some political or economic authority alongside (or derived from) their role in religious observances (Sundqvist, 2020, pp.739-40) which gives rise to the question as to whether there was ever a dedicated priesthood among the Germanic peoples. Aside from the terminological problem (Can a priest have any secular or practical functions, or must he or she be solely dedicated to religious observances?), there is the matter of distinguishing the differences between various names for the functionaries (Is an *erilaz* necessarily different from a *wiwaz*? If so, how?). The matter is made less clear by our reliance on Icelandic evidence, since Icelandic society was rather different from Scandinavian society generally, having no kings or earls, and investing political authority in the religious leaders (*goðar*). The relevant terms include:

Erilaz – there are nine certain (and one more possible) instances of this name in early runic texts including rune-stones, a spearshaft, bracteates and other small personal items. It appears to mean 'priest, ritual specialist' as well as 'master of runes'. The early form of the name *⋆erilaz* developed (slightly irregularly) to the ON *jarl* with the meaning 'leader, nobleman, warlord' while the OE equivalent *eorl* rather means 'active young man, champion, hero'. A link to the name *(H)Eruli*, a Baltic tribe who took part in military campaigns in the Mediterranean in the Roman period, is also possible (Levin, 2020, p.51; Shippey, 2022, p.23). In all, the attestations point to the *⋆erilaz* as a 'leader of a type of secret and bellicose group ... [that] denoted a military function' (Sundqvist, 2015, p.125) and 'the by-names used by the *erilaR* sometimes have connections to the names, functions or attributes of Wodan-Óðinn' (Sundqvist, 2015, p.127). A broken spearshaft found in a bog-sacrifice at Kragehul (Denmark) points firmly to the god's association with sacrifice and with spears.

Gudija – this term appears in a 5th c. inscription at Nordhuglo (Norway) where it occurs in the sequence **ekgudijaungandizih** 'ek gudija ungandiz ih' (I, the priest, immune to sorcery...). Parallel terms occur in both Gothic *gudija* which appears in Wulfila's biblical translation as 'priest, leader of sacrifice' (Sundqvist, 2020, p.745) and Old Icelandic *goði* 'secular chieftain, leader of sacrifice' (Sundqvist, 2015, pp.129-31). The Icelandic office was both secular (political mastery of a district) and religious (keeper of a sanctuary) and this may have been the case for the *gudija* of earlier times. Óðinn is called *hrafnablóts goði* 'priest of the raven-sacrifice' in a 10th c. *lausavísa* (Jónsson, 1931, p.164).

Wiwaz – A 5th c. inscription at Tune (Norway) opens with the sequence **ekwiwazafter. woduri/dewitadahalaiban: worahto**... 'I, Wiwaz, made [these runes] after Woduridaz provider of bread...' (Sundqvist, 2015, p.131). The name is derived from the verb **wei-han* and is found in Gothic as *weiha* 'high priest, he who consecrates' (Sundqvist, 2020, p.745). The connection of the 'one who consecrates' with Woduridaz the 'wild rider' (inspired by **wod* 'rage, frenzy') has suggested to some scholars that this is really a reference to Woden (an *Óðinsheiti*).

Þulaz – The ON term *þulR* (from an earlier form **þulaz*) is used to mean 'one who chants' with reference to the ritual speech acts that formed part of the priest's practice (Sundqvist, 2015, pp.133-4). The word appears in Younger Fuþark runes on a stone at Snoldelev (Denmark) in the sequence **kunuAltstAin sunaR / ruHalts þulaR osalHauku[m]** 'Gunvald's stone, son of Roald, *þulR* in Salhaugum'. It seems probable that the *þulaz* was responsible for the induction of young men into the warband and to worship of the god(s). Ritual speech-acts included a wealth of information which had to be memorised by the initiate, including genealogies, myths of the gods, legends of the ancestors. The OE term *þyle*, used to describe Unferþ in *Beowulf*, is evidently based on the same root but shows derivation from **þuliz* rather than **þulaz*.

Þewaz – A word which often designates a high-ranking person who serves a deity, e.g., **owlþuþewaz** (for **wulþuþewaz*) on the Thorsberg (Denmark) scabbard chape 'servant of Wuldor' and in *Widsith* the name Incgentheow (l.116) 'servant of Ingwe' (Sundqvist, 2015, pp.134-5). The name of Hroþgar's queen is given as Wealhþeo[w], which is best rendered as 'beloved devotee' without specifying the deity (Neidorf, 2017a).

In all, it must be admitted that the evidence for a dedicated (non-secular) Germanic priesthood is vague and sometimes contradictory, as might be expected when it is drawn from a variety of societies and time-periods. In the 1st c. AD, Tacitus is explicit about the presence of priests in the societies about which he had good information, mainly located in the northern parts of western Europe (Sundqvist, 2020, p.743), e.g., *Germania*, ch.7.1 where he notes that no warriors may be punished except by the priests (*sacerdotes*), or ch.10.1 where priests oversee the casting of lots in public (Rives, 1999, pp.80-81).[182] A century earlier, Caesar specifically says that the Germani do not have druids to take care of religious affairs (*de Bello Gallico*, ch.6) but in this he may be drawing a distinction between them and the Galli for the purpose of his treatise (Rives, 1999, p.81; Sundqvist, 2020, pp.743-4). The 4th c. text of Ammianus Marcellinus mentions a *sacerdos omnium maximus* (high priest) among the Burgundians of his day (Sundqvist, 2020, p.744). In the 7th c., Bede's tale of King Edwin's conversion and the pragmatic attitude of his high priest (*primus pontificum*) is probably not pure invention, although Coifi's motives appear rather venal for a dedicated religious specialist. Adam of Bremen specified that each of the three gods in the Uppsala temple had a priest devoted to his worship. The notion of a lack of 'priests' stems from Caesar's remark and the exceptional social conditions in Iceland, it seems.

ALE, BEER, MEAD

The drink which is shared among celebrants is conventionally referred to as *medu* 'mead', but it is likely that this honey-based brew was often substituted by a cereal-based fermented drink. The latter might be referred to as *beor* 'beer' or as *ealu* 'ale'. In this connection, the runic term **alu** has relevance.

Formally **alu** appears to be a cognate of OE *ealu, ealoþ* 'ale' referring to the intoxicating and empowering effects of alcohol on those celebrating and trying to contact the gods and ancestors through ritual drinking (Makaev, 1996, p.101; Pollington, 2003; Flowers, 2006, p.75; MacLeod, 2006, p.195; Pollington, 2016,

---

[182] Rives (1999, p.151) notes that the Germanic term may be represented in OHG *ewarto*, OE *æweweard*, with a meaning of 'keeper of the law (or custom)' and need not reflect purely religious authority (Sundqvist, 2020, p.745-6).

p.317-25). The ecstatic state achieved with the assistance of alcohol and other intoxicants was a powerful cultural phenomenon with great symbolic meaning. Larrington has suggested that ale may have been especially important for the recollection of knowledge which was otherwise inaccessible to the conscious mind, and if so this would add a further dimension to the important place it held in Germanic society (Larrington, 2006a). Raudvere stresses the importance of fluids in the creation myth encoded in the Norse text *Vǫluspá* in which the 'sea or the well under the tree and the dew falling on it … appear to be an image of the transformative nature of fluid: something which makes the tropes useful for visualising the acquisition, application and communication of the knowledge received' (Raudvere, 2012, p.106). Mees (MacLeod & Mees, 2006, pp.24-7) argues that the runic word **alu** functions much like Latin *sacer* 'set apart' whereby objects so described are 'holy, set apart for the gods' while persons bearing that description are 'accursed'. In other words, **alu** renders a text 'empowered' and those who gainsay it are owned or dominated by the gods.

Antonsen follows Polomé in regarding **alu** as a word with ritual significance, but instead of framing the semantic development as 'ale' = 'strong drink' giving rise to 'cultic substance', he reverses the principle so that *aluþ* was originally any substance used in ritual worship, whose meaning was later narrowed in scope in Germanic to 'strong drink' (Antonsen, 1988, pp.51-2; Antonsen, 2002, pp.198-9; Looijenga, 2003, p.195). Thus *aluþ* was originally the Germanic word for any entheogen, any substance which could offer altered states of consciousness used in ritual or religious contexts (Antonsen, 2002, p.214; Hornsey, 2012, p.134).[183] That 'ale' and 'beer' are not physically different substances is supported by the statement in the Icelandic *Alvíssmál* where we read *ɔl heitir með mɔnnum enn með ásom*

---

[183] Aside from strong-brewed beer and fortified beer (in which most of the water is removed), there were many vegetable substances known in the ancient world which could induce hysteria, narcosis, hallucination, etc. including fungi and plants such as henbane. Ergot in grain is another possible source of psychotropic chemicals.

bióm ('Ale' it is called among men, and among the Æsir 'beer'). The difference lies in the taxonomy of the languages, not in the properties of the physical substance, in the same way that 'calcium carbonate' is a chemical description and 'chalk' a prosaic one (Zimmerman, 2014).

The vessel in which the ale (or mead) is served is called in OE (*ealo*)*wæg* (ON *veig*), based on the root **waig-* 'set aside' and possibly referring to the special drink and its container used in ceremonies, contrasted with the mundane tableware used at normal mealtimes (Mees, 2009, p.115).

Finally, we read in *Grímnismál* that Óðinn does not need to eat food since he subsists on wine alone. West (2007, p.159) regarded this as an adaptation of an earlier tradition in which he consumed only ale or mead, the kind of diet necessary to fuel the god of the intellect. Neidorf (2019) showed that in early OE verse (e.g., *Widsith*) the use of *wīn-* in compounds is related specifically to the customs of the Roman Empire and so is regarded as exotic and 'other'.

THE DRINK OF INSPIRATION I: THEFT & DECEIT

The story of the 'mead of inspiration' and Óðinn's part in its distribution is particularly interesting. It is presented piecemeal in several verses in *Hávamál* and in a fuller prose form in *Skáldskaparmál* in *Snorra Edda* (Dronke, 2011; Knight, 2012; Kozák, 2021). Parts of the *Hávamál* have been dated to the 10th c. on stylistic grounds (Knight, 2012, p.22; Kay, 2013, p.12; Kozák, 2021). The verses in *Hávamál* relating to this story are nos.104-110. In *Skáldskaparmál* the later part of the story concerning the god's attempted acquisition of the mead is given in narrative form.

The mead had a complex history before the episode in the *Edda* took place. It began with the war in heaven between the Æsir and the Vanir, and the subsequent peace-treaty meeting at which each of the gods from both sides was required to spit into a spittoon. From the liquid in the vessel a being was created, called Kvasir, who possessed great knowledge. Kvasir travelled in Miðgarðr spreading his knowledge among men until eventually he encountered two dwarfs, Fjalar and Galar, who slew him and drained his blood into a vat, then mixed honey with it and fermented it into a mead. This mead was kept in the three containers named in the story: *Óðhrerir*, *Boðn* and *Són*. The two dwarfs were forced to surrender the mead to the giant Suttungr as a wergild, because they had killed his father, Gilling. Suttungr stored the mead beneath the mountain, Hnitbjörg, and told his daughter, Gunnlǫð, to guard it (Kvilhaug, 2004, p.42). Óðinn learnt of the mead's location and devised a plan to acquire it. He first turned up at the estate of a *jǫtunn* called Baugi where nine workmen were mowing in a field and demonstrated the miraculous sharpening power of the whetstone he owned. Each of the mowers wanted to buy the whetstone from him, but Óðinn threw it into the air saying that the one who caught it could keep it. They all rushed forward to seize it and their scythes cut each other into pieces. Óðinn then proceeded to the hall of Baugi in the guise of an itinerant workman, Bǫlverkr (text from Faulkes, 1998).

Óðinn sótti til náttstaðar til jǫtuns þess er Baugi hét, bróðir Suttungs. Baugi kallaði ilt fjárhald sitt ok sagði at þrælar hans níu hǫfðu drepizk, en talðiz eigi vita sér ván verkmanna. En Óðinn nefndisk fyrir honum Bǫlverkr. Hann bauð at taka upp níu manna verk fyrir Bauga, en mælir sér til kaups einn drykk af Suttunga miði. Baugi kvazk enskis ráð eiga at miðinum, sagði at Suttungr vildi einn hafa, en fara kvezk hann mundu með Bǫlverki of freista ef þeir fengi mjǫðinn.

Bǫlverkr vann um sumarit níu mannsverk fyrir Bauga, en at vetri beiddisk hann Bauga leigu sinnar. Þá fara þeir báðir til Suttungs. Baugi segir Suttungi bróður sínum kaup þeira Bǫlverks, en Suttungr synjar þverliga hvers dropa af miðinum. Þá mælir Bǫlverkr til Bauga, at þeir skyldu freista véla nǫkkvorra, ef þeir megi ná miðinum, en Baugi lætr þat vel vera. Þá dregr Bǫlverkr fram nafar þann er Rati heitir ok mælir at Baugi skal bora bjargit ef nafarinn bítr. Hann gerir svá. Þá segir Baugi at gǫgnum er borat bjargit, en Bǫlverkr blæss í nafars raufina ok hrjóta

spænirnir upp í móti honum. Þá fann hann at Baugi vildi svíkja
hann, ok bað bora gǫgnum bjargit. Baugi boraði enn. En er
Bǫlverkr blés annat sinn, þá fuku inn spæninir. Þá brást Bǫlverkr
í orms líki ok skreið í nafars raufina, en Baugi stakk eptir honum
nafrinum ok misti hans. Fór Bǫlverkr þar til sem Gunnlǫð var ok
lá hjá henni þrjár nætr, ok þá lofaði hon honum at drekka af
miðinum þrjá drykki. Í inum fyrsta drykk drakk hann alt ór
Óðreri, en í ǫðrum ór Boðn, í inum þriðja ór Són, ok hafði hann
þá allan mjǫðinn. Þá brásk hann í arnarham ok flaug sem ákafast.
En er Suttungr sá flug arnarins, tók hann sér arnarham ok flaug
eptir honum. En er Æsir sá hvar Óðinn flaug þá settu þeir út í
garðinn ker sín, en er Óðinn kom inn of Ásgarð þá spýtti hann
upp miðinum í kerin, en honum var þá svá nær komit at
Suttungr mundi ná honum at hann sendi aptr suman mjǫðinn,
ok var þess ekki gætt. Hafði þat hverr er vildi, ok kǫllum vér þat
skáldfífla hlut. En Suttunga mjǫð gaf Óðinn Ásunum ok þeim
mǫnnum, er yrkja kunnu. Því kǫllum vér skáldskapinn feng
Óðins ok fund ok drykk hans ok gjǫf hans ok drykk Ásanna.

'Óðinn sought a night's lodging from the jǫtunn called Baugi,
Suttungr's brother. Baugi reckoned his luck with property was bad
and said his nine thralls had killed each other, and [said] he did not
know how to mend his lack of workmen. Óðinn named himself
as Bǫlverk [bale-worker, evil-doer] before him. He offered to take
over the nine men's work for Baugi and named his price as one
drink of Suttungr's mead. Baugi said that he had no say in the
matter of the mead, that Suttungr wanted to have it all for himself,
but he said he would go with Bǫlverk to see if they might get the
mead.

Bǫlverk did nine men's work for Baugi over the summer, and
when winter came he asked for his payment from Baugi. Then
they both went to Suttungr. Baugi told his brother Suttungr of the
agreement with Bǫlverk, but Suttungr refused him even a drop of

the mead. Then Bǫlverk told Baugi that they would have to try a ruse to get the mead and Baugi agreed to that. Then Bǫlverk took out an auger called Rati [rat] and told Baugi to bore into the mountain if the auger would bite. He did so. Then Baugi said that the mountain had been bored through, but Bǫlverk blew into the auger's hole and the dust flew back towards him. Thus he found out that Baugi wanted to deceive him, and told him to bore through the mountain [again]. Baugi bored again. But when Bǫlverk blew a second time, the dust flew inside. Then Bǫlverk changed into a snake's likeness and slithered into the auger's hole, and Baugi poked after him with the auger but missed him.

Bǫlverk went to where Gunnlǫð was and lay with her for three nights, and she let him drink three draughts from the mead. In the first draught he drank all the mead from Óðrerir and in the second from Boðn and in the third from Són, and then he had got all the mead. Then he changed into his eagle-shape and flew eagerly away. But when Suttungr saw the flight of the eagle, he took on his own eagle-shape and flew after him. When the Æsir saw where Óðinn was flying they set up their own vessel in their courtyard and when Óðinn came into Ásgarð he spewed the mead up into the vessel – but it was so close that Suttungr might have caught him, so that he sent some of the mead backwards and this was not noticed. Any who wanted it might have it, and we call it the 'skald's lot'. Óðinn gave Suttungr's mead to the Æsir and to those men who know how to make verse. Therefore we call skald-craft 'Óðinn's catch' and his 'find' and his 'drink' and his 'gift' and the 'drink of the Æsir'.'

The mead was won for the Æsir but only through multiple instances of deceit and betrayal, and some loss of life. Baugi made a deal with Bǫlverkr which entailed his handing over property which he did not own; he tried to trick Óðinn into entering the bore-hole before it was finished, and then tried to skewer him with the augur. Bǫlverkr treacherously caused the nine workmen to kill each other, but he fulfilled his agreed contract of labouring throughout the summer.

Óðinn deceived the giant maiden into surrendering the drink, which he had earnt through his labours.

The two versions of the tale presented in the sources – *Hávamál* and *Skáldskaparmál* – do not agree completely, which may reflect different retellings of the myth, but they leave us with several problems of interpretation. For example, in *Hávamál* verse 104 Óðinn claims to have visited an old *jǫtunn* and to have used many words to get what he wanted, but in the prose version the god's visit to Suttungr is unsuccessful. Perhaps this is a reference to his powers of persuasion, mentioned in *Hávamál*, which he used on Gunnlǫð so that she would let him drink from the forbidden liquid. But Gunnlǫð cannot be both *inn aldna iǫtun* 'the old giant' and *góðo kono* 'a good woman' and it is surely more likely that the first character is the hall's owner, Suttungr, whose name means 'sated with drink' (Kvilhaug, 2004, p.50). Similarly, the subject of *gullnum stóli á* '[seated] on the golden throne' in verse 105 is not specified – is this Gunnlǫð seated on her golden chair while offering a drink to Óðinn, or is it the god in the position of honour in the guest-chair while the noble maiden offers him the mead? If the latter, then Gunnlǫð is shown acting as a noblewoman was expected to, welcoming an important guest into the hall, resting on a seat of honour and served with a horn of strong drink.

Did Óðinn charm the maiden with smooth words and ask her for the drink whilst wooing her? Or was there a more formal arrangement, a 'wedding' or betrothal with a holy oath (*baugeið*, 'oath sworn on a ring')? (Kvilhaug, 2004, p.30; Knight, 2012, p.26) If so, this might explain Óðinn's use of his 'many words' (verse 104) during the ceremony in which the union was sanctified. It would also explain the meaning of verse 110 where the god admits he has violated a solemn oath, left his father-in-law betrayed at the wedding feast and his bride in tears. Likewise in verse 109 the frost-giants come looking for Bǫlverkr *ins hindra dags* 'the next day', a term often used for the morning after a wedding. In one reading of the myth, the mead needed to be held in the Underworld by a female in order to activate its latent power fully before being returned to the world of gods and men (Lassen, 2000, p.225).

It would be difficult to understand the *Hávamál* verses without the frame of reference provided by the Eddic tale. It must be assumed *à priori* that the audience who heard the poet(s) declaim *Hávamál* was sufficiently familiar with the background narrative to understand the references.

THE DRINK OF INSPIRATION II: EXCHANGE & PLEDGE

Another set of tales exists to explain the god's acquisition of a drink which confers knowledge upon the partaker. This time, Óðinn behaves as a humble supplicant because the keeper of the liquid is imbued with an ancient and revered authority which he must respect.

According to the tales recorded by Snorri, Óðinn was one-eyed, having either (i) willingly exchanged one of his eyes for a draught of the mead of inspiration; or else (ii) passed the eye to Mímir who placed it in the well bearing his name – *Mímis brunnr* - which was sited at the roots of Yggdrasill (Kershaw, 2000, pp.1-9; Birkett, 2019, p.155; Lindow, 2020a, p.506). Mímir is descended from the *þursar* 'giants', as is Óðinn who has such beings in his ancestry. Both traditions – the drink and the pledge – seek to explain the god's exceptional knowledge but, as with the motif of the theft of the giant's mead, again the accounts cannot be reconciled into a single, coherent narrative. We shall return to the motif of the 'god with one eye' below (p.418).

Knowledge and insight were gained, but how was this achieved? Did the god give an eye and take a drink which enlightened him? Or did the placing of the eye in the well provide him with a unique vantage point from which to view space and time? The rationale behind the surrendering of the eye seems confused.

When Óðinn offered an eye to Mímir, it was afterwards called *veðr valfǫðrs* 'the pledge of the father of the slain' (Lassen, 2000, p.225; Hermann, 2020, p.58). But why does the severed head of Mímir want or need an additional eye? There is plainly another narrative strand at work here which recounts that Óðinn acquired his wisdom in two ways: one involved the pledging of his eye to a being who kept it in the well at the roots of Yggdrasill, and the other involved drinking the mead made from the blood of Kvasir (guarded by Suttungr and his daughter) (Lindow & Schjødt, 2020, p.956). How did Mímir acquire this mead from Suttungr? The tales are not consistent here.

The drink that Óðinn took from Mímir was a powerful and insight-conferring draft, deemed worth the price of an eye – and the placing of the eye among the roots of Yggdrasill provided the god with further insight.

MÍMIR, THE SENTIENT HEAD

Óðinn had taken Mímir's severed head and preserved it with powerful herbs, after which he was able to chant spells over it and force it to reveal its secrets (Armit, 2012, p.31). This tradition may be related to the god's claim in *Hávamál* that he knows a twelfth spell which could force a dead man to speak with him (Lassen, 2022, p.159).[184] The god consults the dismembered head before the last battle, in *Vǫluspá* verse 45. The motif of the 'symbolic severed head' is of great antiquity (Pollington, 2011, pp.151-4; Armit, 2012). Indeed, presenting the head of an enemy to a warlord seems to be an ancient custom in Indo-European military society, recorded as far back as ancient Greece (Ustinova, 2002, p.109, 114).[185]

A further consideration regarding the posthumous potency of a severed head is the Norse tradition of the *níðstǫng* or 'scorn-pole': a horse's head set on a rune-carved stake, used as a symbol of defiance and disdain for the authority of the ruler (Ellis Davidson, 1988, p.105).[186] Such a

---

[184] William of Malmesbury recounts a tale of Gerbert of Aurillac (later Pope Sylvester II) who had a mechanical head which could reply 'yes' or 'no' to any question put to it. There are other instances of a similar nature. What bearing this idea may have on the matter of Mímir's severed head is discussed by Lassen (2022, p.160-1).

[185] Kershaw, 2000, p.58 fn.29. One example is Dolon donning a wolfskin-coat to try to recover the head of Agamemnon in the siege of Troy. This scene appears painted on some Attic vases.

[186] McLeod & Mees (2006, p.236) doubt the historicity of this practice.

device was erected by Egil Skallagrímsson against King Eiríkr Blóðøx before leaving Norway (text from Garmonsway, 1928).

> Hann tók í hönd sér heslistöng ok gekk á bergsnös nökkura, þá er vissi til lands inn; þá tók hann hrosshöfuð ok setti upp á stöngina. Síðan veitti hann formála ok mælti svá: 'Hér set ek upp níðstöng, ok sný ek þessu níði á hönd Eiríki konungi ok Gunnhildi dróttningu,' – hann sneri hrosshöfðinu inn á land – 'sný ek þessu níði á landvættir þær, er land þetta byggva, svá at allar fari þær villar vega, engi hendi né hitti sitt inni, fyrr en þær reka Eirík konung ok Gunnhildi úr landi.' Síðan skýtr hann stönginni niðr í bjargrifu ok lét þar standa; hann sneri ok höfðinu inn á land, en hann reist rúnar á stönginni, ok segja þær formála þenna allan.

> *Egilssaga Skallagrimsonar*, ch.57

> 'He took a hazel-pole in his hand and went to a certain cliff which faced in towards the land; then he took a horse-head and set it up on the pole. After he uttered a curse and spoke thus: "Here I set up a scorn-pole and I direct this scorn towards King Eirik and Queen Gunnhild" – he turned the horse-head towards the land – "here I direct this scorn towards the land-spirits there, who dwell in that land, so that they may leave their dwellings and become lost, and may not find their homes, neither by chance nor through searching, until they have expelled King Eirík and Queen Gunnhild from the land." Then he fixed the pole in a crack of the rock and left it standing there; he then turned the head of the horse towards the mainland, and he scratched runes on the pole and spoke all that curse there.'

A head held aloft on a pole is a powerful image: it has been customary in many societies as the fate of traitors and defeated foes since ancient times (Armit, 2012). It seems plausible that in *Beowulf* the head of Hroþgar's friend Æschere was similarly arrayed to frighten and mock the search-party which Grendel's mother knew would track her to the lake where she dwelt (ll.1420-1):

...   syðþan Æscheres

on þām holmclife   hafelan mētton.

'...once they found Æschere's head on the sea-cliff'.

Grendel's head was used similarly as a trophy, carried back to Heorot on the tips of four spears (ll.1635-9)

from þǣm holmclife   hafelan bǣron

earfoðlice   heora ǣghwæþrum

felamōdigra;   fēower scoldon

on þǣm wælstenge   wǣrcum geferian

tō þǣm goldsele   Grendles hēafod

'from the sea-cliff they carried Grendel's head in high spirits, with much effort from each of them; four had to transport [it] with some pain on slaughter-poles to the gold-hall'

and brought into the hall (ll.1647-50):

Þa wæs be feaxe   on flet boren

Grendles hēafod,   þær guman druncon

egeslic for eorlum   ond þære idese mid

'Then Grendel's head was carried onto the floor of the hall where men were drinking, dreadful for the men and the lady with them.'

It seems that the custom of retaining a head as a trophy was still remembered when the *Beowulf* poet was active in the early 8th c. The dismembering of the corpse of King Oswald of Northumbria in 641 AD is also relevant here (Pollington, 2011, pp.141-3).

MÍMIS BRUNNR

The waters of Mímir's well rise from the Underworld, and are connected to the power of the Vanir, especially Freyja (Lassen, 2000, p.224). If Mímir's name means 'recollection, memory' then his well, the *Mímis brunnr*, is the 'well of remembrance' and it is this exceptional power of recall which is the secret of Mímir's wisdom (Kvilhaug, 2004, pp.50-1).[187] It is a draught from this well which Óðinn buys with one of his eyes: he used the horn *Gjallarhorn* for this purpose, (although this name elsewhere refers to the blast-horn which Heimdall uses to summon the gods at the Ragnarǫk).

Furthermore, the tradition of the god's missing eye has roots deep in prehistory. In *Vǫluspá*, verse 28, the seeress says (text from Dronke, 1997):

> Alt veit ek, Óðinn,
>
> hvar þú auga falt:
>
> í enom mæra
>
> Mímis brunni!

'I know it all, Óðinn, where you hid an eye: in that famed well of Mímir.'

Yet the poem continues:

> Drekkr miǫð Mímir
>
> morgin hverian
>
> af veði Valfǫðrs!

'Mímir drinks mead every morning from the Slaughter-father's pledge.'

This implies that the 'pledge' *veðr* (which must also be the eye) is a vessel from which mead may be drunk (Kershaw, 2000, p.2; Tolley, 2009, p.95).

It is of course possible that these various tales were never a unified, single story but were in origin told of different gods for varied

---

[187] The name appears in three slightly different forms: *Mímir*, *Mímr*, *Mími*. The first usually appears in connection with the well, and the second with the head alone while the third is confined to the World Tree (*Mímameiðr*) (Lindow, 2020b, p.1042)

reasons. Maimed or deficient gods are not unique to northern literature – here we think of one-eyed Óðinn, one-handed Týr, blind
Hǫðr, hamstrung Welund and possibly also Heimdall – but they are
a consistent feature of Germanic and Celtic myth and have also been
traced in Roman mythology (Dumézil, 1996): for example, Horatius Cocles, a noted warrior, received a debilitating wound to the
buttock which crippled him. The Roman authorities decided to offer him the honour of a bronze statue of himself which they placed
in the temple of Vulcan – the smith-god who was himself lame. The
relevance here lies in the underlying tales and analogues: Hephaistos
(Greek), Vulcanus (Roman), Vǫlundr (Norse) and Weland (Anglo-
Saxon) - each an artisan lamed by a monarch who sought to subju-
gate him (Lincoln, 1991, p.248). Relevant too is the Irish tale of Lug,
an artisan-god who assumed a one-eyed and one-legged stance as
part of his magical opposition to a foreign monarch, and who was
paired with Núadu Argetlám, a one-armed divine hero.[188]

ÓÐHRÉRIR

The name *Óðhrérir* is given to the mead that Óðinn stole (*Hávamál*,
v.107), and is also the name of one of the three vats in which the
mead was stored (Pollington, 2011, p.176).

The literal meaning of the term fits rather better with its application to the mead itself. The prototheme *óð-* is the word from
which Óðinn's name is derived. Its OE equivalent is *wód* which can
mean (i) rabid, raving; (ii) insane, mad; (iii) mad with anger, raging.
It has a Verner's Law variant *wóþ* which can mean 'lofty speech,
eloquence', or 'poetry, verse', or 'music, melodious noise'. These
words refer to the vital spark, the sentient mind. The deuterotheme
is an agent noun, derived from a Norse cognate of OE *hréran* 'stir,

---

[188] Liberman (2016, p.76) asserts that the correspondences between Woden and
Lug are superficial, supposed by people who were familiar with the iconography of worship but not the details of the myths.

move about, shake up, agitate'. The two elements in combination therefore mean 'that which stirs [the mind] [to anger, verse-making or music]'.

THE MEANING OF MEAD

'Mead', and intoxicating drink generally, played a crucial role in cementing social bonds in the Germanic societies of which we have record. To some extent, the acquisition of mead in the tales of Óðinn can be related to Indic tales of the wondrous substance *soma* which informs much of the older literature (Kershaw, 2000, p.80; Kvilhaug, 2004, pp.30-1). From the *soma* a drink is made called 'sweetness' *madhu*, cognate with OE *medu*, our word 'mead'.[189]

It is tempting to adduce here as a possible reflex of *soma* the reconstructed Germanic word **swampaz* attested as Gothic *swamms* 'sponge', OE *swamm* 'mushroom', etc., related more widely to Greek σομφός 'swampy, porous' and Latin *fungus* 'toadstool, mushroom' (from **sgᵘhongo-*) (Orel, 2004, s.v. **swampaz*; contra Kroonen, 2013, s.v. **swamb/ppan-*). Stimulants derived from fungi are a widespread phenomenon even today, and the link seems attractive (although the words are presumably not cognate).

Strong drink played a key role in the inauguration of kings and the induction of new members into the sworn brotherhoods of Iron Age and medieval Europe (Kvilhaug, 2004, p.29; Birkett, 2019, p.151). Its consumption was part of the traditional oath-swearing rites. That the mead was offered and delivered by a powerful female figure, and that it was prepared by the collective efforts of many (mainly female) members of the community, only serves to underscore the wide importance of the substance across the society. Indeed, the role of the leading female – the *hlafdige* in OE terms –

---

[189] In Greek tradition, a wise man should carry with him a special precious stone which had the virtue of preventing drunkenness. This stone was called *amethystos* 'amethyst' from the elements **ṇ* -- 'not' + *meth*- '[drunk on] mead'.

was to act as the fictive mother to the social group of which the *hlaford* was the fictive father – the leader – and in which the youthful warriors found a substitute family structure (Enright, 1996). Reliant as they were on these 'substitute parents' for their sustenance, guidance, wealth and wellbeing, the youths used the sharing of physical goods as a bonding mechanism. The *hlaford* and his consort nevertheless emphasised their role as social superiors through the enactment of these drinking rites within a hall, a fixed structure in which the owner was the all-important host and others were present as petitioners and guests.

THE SERVING AND DRINKING VESSELS

Mead was served in elaborate vessels such as glass beakers and drinking horns, some of which survive archaeologically – the English examples from Sutton Hoo Mound 1, Taplow, Broomfield and Prittlewell are the best attested (Blackmore et al., 2019). The drinking horn took on a significance as a symbol of solidarity, of oaths given and fulfilled, of inspiration and insight.

As mentioned above, in *Hávamál* the mead of inspiration was stored in three vessels, called Óðhrerir, Són and Boðn, and the first name is sometimes cited as the name of the mead itself: 'inspiration – stirrer', meaning the substance which kindles the drinker's poetic and imaginative qualities. Boðn may mean 'container' (cognate with OE *byden* 'barrel') and Són may mean 'reconciliation, atonement, sacrifice' (cognate with MLG *sone, swone* 'atonement', OHG *suona* 'reconciliation, atonement' and further related to Latin *sanus* 'healthy'). The image of three mead-filled containers may be reflected in the motif on the runestone at Snoldelev (Denmark) which is formed as three horns in a triskele formation (with runic text).

 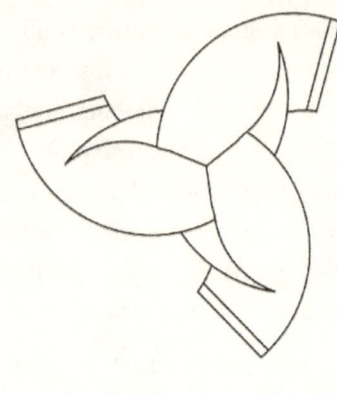

Fig. 23 The Snoldelev runestone (DR248) and the three-horns motif.

Another ON divine name with overtones of secret knowledge is *Bragi*, described in the sources as a poet and patron of verse-making; these are both aspects of Óðinn's persona. If Bragi's name is derived from the PIE root *$*b^hre\acute{g}^h$- which supplies the Vedic word *bráhman* 'priest', perhaps that god's expertise was part of the competence of a religious professional. The related noun *bragr* 'poetic skill, verbal dexterity' is among the attributes of Óðinn listed in *Hyndliuljóð* (Jackson, 2012, pp.58-9).

CHAPTER 5

LORD OF THE DEAD

> Fore thaem neidfaerae naenig uuiurthit
> thoncsnotturra than him tharf sie
> to ymbhycggannae aer his hiniongae
> huaet his gastae godaes aeththa yflaes
> aefter deothdaege doemid uueorthae.

'Before that unavoidable journey none becomes so wise in thought that he need not reflect before his going-forth as to what may be deemed to his soul of good or of evil after the day of his death.'

Bede's Death Song (from Hoad, 1978)

Óðinn is referred to as *Haptaguð* 'fetter-god' (*Gylfaginning* 20), *Fjall-Geiguðr* 'fell-dangler' (*Óðins nǫfn*), *Hangadróttinn* 'lord of hanged men' (*Ynglinga saga* 7), *Hangaguð* 'god of hanged men' (*Gylfaginning* 20 and elsewhere), *Hangatýr* 'god of hanged men' (*Skáldskaparmál* 1 and elsewhere), *Hangi* 'hanged man' (*Drápa* on Jarl Hákon), *Váfuðr* 'dangler' (*Grímnismál* 54), *Váfǫðr* 'dangler' (*Gylfaginning* 20), *Vingnir* 'swinger' (*Óðins nǫfn*), *Vǫfuðr* (*Óðins nǫfn*) (Price, 2019 p.63). What do all these references to hanging mean? And why should a god associated with warfare and victory be so closely connected to the inglorious death of the criminal rather than heroic death in battle?

We shall see that the god decided to undergo nine nights of painful torment hanging from the World Tree in order to win secret knowledge. This ritual death was intended to free his spirit from the mundane world, to open up new vistas of experience from which he could learn additional wisdom. The effect of gaining this mastery

over his physical body was to allow his mind to fly free to the Otherworld, and the trophy he won through his suffering and sojourn
in the Otherworld was the *fuþark*, literacy and accompanying spells.
But with this new set of skills he gained another competence: he
became the 'Lord of the Dead'. He took on the role of *psychopomp*,
whose function it was to lead the souls of the dead to the Otherworld. That he may always have included aspects of this role in his
cult is possible, given that the function of the Wild Hunt is to carry
away the souls of the living to the land of the dead.

There are other aspects to consider. State-sanctioned killing (or
sacrifice) of war-captives and criminals was an accepted and routine
practice in Europe and elsewhere until relatively recently. The last
judicial hanging in England took place in the mid-20th century (Peter Allen, 1964) but this took place away from the public gaze. Many
societies retain the right to terminate the lives of those they deem
offensive (e.g., for treason, repeated or brutal murder, espionage,
etc.) and often do so in a very public manner as a deterrent to others.

Homicide as an act of revenge, especially for murder, was not
considered exceptional in medieval Europe and the Icelandic sagas
are full of tales of killings by wronged kinsmen, often egged on by
their women. Mostly, these killings are presented in heroic terms
whereby the opponents engage in a deadly combat resulting in the
death of one or both participants. The rationale behind these hom-
icides was the restoration of balance: one kindred had lost a member,
so a corresponding member of the other kindred must perish. The
practice had the advantage of being equitable: it applied to all members of society, and those who committed murder knew in advance
the likely outcome for themselves and their families.

Killing could also be an act of religious observance, as the description of the Uppsala temple and grove reminds us. Tacitus knew
of the custom in the 1ˢᵗ century AD as he recorded in *Germania*
(ch.39):

Vetustissimos se nobilissimosque Sueborum Semnones memorant;
fides antiquitatis religione firmatur. Stato tempore in silvam auguriis

patrum et prisca formidine sacram omnes eiusdem sanguinis populi legationibus coeunt caesoque publice homine celebrant barbari ritus horrenda primordia. Est et alia luco reverentia: nemo nisi vinculo ligatus ingreditur, ut minor et potestatem numinis prae se ferens. Si forte prolapsus est, attolli et insurgere haud licitum: per humum evolvuntur. Eoque omnis superstitio respicit, tamquam inde initia gentis, ibi regnator omnium deus, cetera subiecta atque parentia.

'Of the Suebi, the Semnones believe themselves to be the most ancient and noblest; their belief is confirmed by religious faith. At a certain time, all the various peoples of the same stock gather in a wood, hallowed by the worship of their forefathers, and by religious awe in olden times. By publicly sacrificing a man in that place, they begin the fearsome observance of their worship. To this wood another sort of respect is paid. No-one may enter it otherwise than tied with bonds, admitting his service and low status, and the power of the god there. If he should fall down, he may not rise or be lifted, but must roll along upon the ground. Of all their beliefs, this is the understanding: that from this place, the whole folk began, that here a god, the supreme ruler of all, resides, and that all things are subject to him and bound to obey him.'

The notion of binding and applying boundaries is found frequently in Germanic culture, especially in relation to death (Bauschatz, 1982, ch.2).[190] Tacitus's text is the earliest known citation for Germanic sacrifice in a woodland setting.

The disposal of war-captives by summary execution was the expectation of Germanic troops serving in the Roman army according to Tacitus (Histories, IV; text from Church & Brodribb, 1887; see Grundy, 2014, p.16):

---

[190] The Angel of Death at the Rus funeral witnessed by Ibn Fadlan (Lund & Stone, 2012) causes the immolated slave girl to be strangled with a cord and stabbed with a dagger simultaneously.

tum Vitelliani, quos apud Bovillas in deditionem acceptos memoravimus, ceterique per urbem et urbi vicina conquisiti producuntur prope intecto corpore. eos Mucianus diduci et Germanicum Britannicumque militem, ac si qui aliorum exercituum, separatim adsistere iubet. illos primus statim aspectus obstupefecerat, cum ex diverso velut aciem telis et armis trucem, semet clausos nudosque et inluvie deformis aspicerent: ut vero huc illuc distrahi coepere, metus per omnis et praecipua Germanici militis formido, tamquam ea separatione ad caedem destinaretur.

'Then the supporters of Vitellius, whose capture at Bovillae we may recall, and the others of the group gathered from the town and its neighbourhood, were brought together with almost no coverings for their bodies. Mucianus ordered these men to be segregated, instructing the Britons, the Germans and troops from other armies to take up separate ranks. The first realization of their situation shocked them as they saw before them a hostile troop wielding spears and swords and they themselves were surrounded, weaponless, unwashed and miserable. Surely when they began to be split up, some to be sent to one place and some to another, fear overtook them all. Among the troops from Germania the apprehension was great, because they believed that such a separation consigned them to slaughter.'

The offering of a man's life may be interpreted as a re-enactment of the creation myth whereby a primordial being was slain and hacked apart to create the world (Tolley, 2009, p.352).[191] The religious dimension to the Semnones' belief in their pre-eminence is explained by Tacitus:

Eoque omnis superstitio respecit tamquam inde initia gentis ibi regnator omnium deus cetera subiecta atque parentia. Adicit

---

[191] The notion of a primordial being whose death gives rise to the world is of Indo-European antiquity.

auctoritatem fortuna Semnonum: centum pagi iis habitantur magnoque corpore efficitur ut se Sueborum caput credant.

Germania, ch.39

'All that superstition looks back to this, as if the source of the folk were there, where the god and ruler of all is, to whom everything else is subjected and devoted. The luck of the Semnones adds to their authority: they inhabit a hundred lands and due to this large size they believe themselves to be the head of the Suebi.'

Possession of the holy grove could bring the god's power and support to their cause, and they therefore enjoyed great luck, expressed in a swelling population which thus brought them prestige (Moisl, 1981, pp.218-9).[192] Notably, the emphasis is on common origins for the Swabian people in this one area where the god resided, as if the god were indeed an ancestor to every member of Swabian society (Tolley, 2009, pp.326-7, 337). We know also from Tacitus that, in his day, kings were chosen for their descent rather than any personal qualities: *reges ex nobilitate, duces ex virtute sumunt* 'they choose kings for their noble birth, leaders for their courage'.

As regards Óðinn, we have the evidence of *Ynglinga saga* that he was believed to have died, and that the rites he sanctioned for the disposal of his own body established a precedent for mortals to follow (Lassen, 2022, pp.164-5). His particular death ritual – marking with a spear's point, cremation with lavish goods – offered an opportunity for his followers to display their devotion, and for his mourners to display tangible evidence of the respect and affection in which they held him in life.

It is worth stating that the mere act of gaining the runes did not provide Óðinn with knowledge of the future: all it did was to give

---

[192] Similarly, there may be an association with possession of a sacred grove from which the race of men was believed to have sprung, and in which human ancestors (ON *Askr* and *Embla*) survived the destructive flood (Tolley, 2009, pp.94, 382-3).

him the means to awaken the dead and to ask them to share their knowledge (Kershaw, 2000, p.78 citing work by Arntz). The twelfth spell recalled in *Hávamál* explains this, in which the summoning of the hanged man is the occasion for the god to force him to speak.

CEMETERY EVIDENCE

The physical remains of worshippers identifying with the cult of Woden has been a contentious issue in archaeological thought, since religious belief can rarely be inferred from grave-goods unless these bear iconographic or epigraphic decoration (and even then, there is always room for interpretation). The so-called Weapon Burial Rite whereby adult males were accompanied in the grave by sets of weapons, has been considered emblematic of a 'warrior burial' and thus a likely candidate for a worshipper of the war-god. But more recent studies have shown that there are too many flaws in this simple association for it to be accepted generally (Härke, 1992; Sayer, 2023).

What constitutes a weapon in an Anglo-Saxon context? A spear can be used in hunting, as can a shield and a knife (*seax*) so the inclusion of these items cannot relate *directly* to 'warrior status' for the deceased. Hand-axes, large or small, may be considered more probably weapons than hunting equipment, but this is not certain as they can have domestic uses in woodworking, boat-building, etc. Swords are uncommon grave-goods[193] but far from unknown; helmets are rarer (only four certain examples interred in graves: Sutton Hoo Mound 1, Benty Grange, Wollaston, Shorwell) and there is only one mailcoat (Sutton Hoo Mound 1), so these items are unmistakeably extraordinary and thus likely to be exclusively military in nature (Pollington, 2002, pp.165-75).

---

[193] Mortimer & Bunker (2019) estimate that 1.7% of Anglo-Saxon graves contained swords, i.e., five swords for every 300 graves in their sample of nearly 1000 excavated.

But does the Weapon Burial Rite necessarily indicate worship of Woden – indeed, does it necessarily have any religious content at all? Despite the glamour of the later Norse ideas about the dead arriving in *Valhǫll* to sit feasting with Óðinn, the graves suggest rather a straight choice between inhumation and cremation, with occasional exuberances such as ship-burial forming an emphatic political and social statement on behalf of the bereaved kindred.

Infrequent oddities such as at Bogøvey (Denmark), grave P (a knife plunged into the grave beside a man buried prone and covered with some large stones) do require explanation. An expression of dedication to Óðinn by the mourner who created the burial is one possible explanation, but not the only one (Gardeła, 2014, pp.68-70). Thrusting a weapon certainly features in the myths attached to the god's name, such as the casting of his spear over the heads of the Vanir as an act of dedication before the two divine groups started fighting. But similar evidence occurs among the burials of Slavs, Balts and Finns where an association with the cult of Óðinn is very unlikely. Grave P at Bogøvej is more naturally interpreted as that of a feared or reviled individual – a sorcerer or *seiðsmaðr* for example – who suffered three 'deviant' burial rites of prone burial, burial beneath stones and burial with a naked knife.

Grave-goods have also been used to identify female 'cult practitioners', specifically with the inclusion of a specially-made staff with a writhen or helical metal cage to one end. In Scandinavian contexts, such devices are often taken to be examples of the 'wand' or *gǫndr* which was used in women's rituals (Gardeła, 2014, p.74). The females interred with these devices may have been priestesses in the cult of Freyja or some other deity, but it should not be overlooked that the traditional Germanic warband ideally included a female leader whose task it was to work magic for the warriors and to determine the outcome of battle in advance (cf. the tale of Gambara above).

Vandkilde wrote (2006, p.394):

'Personal equipment in burials can be understood in at least two different ways. First, as a direct metonymic statement of the

lived identity of the deceased; the warrior may not be interred
with full equipment but instead only those parts of the
equipment that have a certain symbolic meaning. Second, as a
symbolic metaphorical statement with a less direct bearing on the
lived identities (cf. Whitley, 1995). If, for example, a small,
exclusive group of mature males are [*sic*] interred with rich
weaponry, this is likely to reflect 'symbolic warriorhood' in the
sense of one or more of the following possibilities: a former
warrior identity, heroic status or ambition, political authority or
high social rank. Likewise, weapons accompanying small
children and young adolescents are unlikely to be actual signs of
practiced warriorhood but should rather be understood as
metaphors originating in warrior values.'

The element missing from this analysis is that all graves are conceptual constructs, the buried objects being incorporated by mourners
and family members whose motives for the inclusion of specific
items may have little or nothing to do with the actual 'lived identities' of the deceased. A kinship group wishing to stress its military
ascendence may have emphasised weapons and military equipment
in the funerary rites of its members, regardless of the real-world
achievements of such individuals.

DIVERSITY IN DEATH

It seems improbable that all the Anglo-Saxon kingdoms had identical traditions concerning their ancestral kings, and the likelihood is
that the 'authorised' Mercian version was imposed on (or adopted
by) both the West Saxons and the kingdom of Kent during the 8th
c. period of Mercian political supremacy (Welch, 2007).[194] However, there is a convergence of Woden-sprung Anglian kings and
the traditional Anglian burial rite of cremation, which is specifically

---

[194] It was perhaps in this context that the West Saxon kings adopted the Anglian
god *Woden* as their primal ancestor, abandoning their own god *Seaxneat*. See
Cronan, 2014.

linked to attainment of the noble afterlife in the Norse *Ynglinga saga*, where the rite was ordained by Óðinn (Du Bois, 1999, p.80) (text from Aðalbjarnarson, 1979):

> Svá setti hann, at alla dauða menn skyldi brenna ok bera á bál með þeim eign þeira. Sagði hann svá at með þvílíkum auðœfum skyldi hverr koma til Valhallar sem hann hafði á bál; þess skyldi hann ok njóta, er hann sjalfr hafði í jǫrð grafit.

> *Ynglinga saga* ch.8

> 'He established it thus, that all dead men should be burnt and bring their belongings onto the balefire with them. He said that anyone should come to Valhǫll with such possessions as he had [with him] on the balefire [and] he could also have use of whatever he had buried in the earth for himself.'

In respect of Óðinn it has been remarked that every aspect of his character can be attached either to his position as a magician or as sovereign (Schjødt, 2008, p.452 citing work by Renauld-Krantz). The worship of Woden as the god of kings and warlords was certainly a cult of blood and violence, in which the contest for supremacy in battle and in the meadhall was paramount: the god could give military advantage and persuasive, poetic fluency in support of his worshippers. In this connection one might note the ritual sacrifices of King Oswald of Northumbria – whose severed head and arms were displayed on a tree after his military defeat – and his predecessor, King Edwin, whose severed head was brought to York according to Bede (Meaney, 1966, p.111; Tolley, 1995a). Also relevant here is the execution of the last Wuffing king of East Anglia, Eadmund, and the story of his severed head guarded by a wolf.

KING EADMUND'S FATE

The fate of Eadmund, king of East Anglia. is recorded in a text by Ælfric the Homilist with the title XII. KAL. *Decembres, Passio Sancti*

Eadmvndi Regis Et Martyris (Twelfth Calends of December, the Passion of Saint Edmund, King and Martyr). The complete text survives in two manuscripts, with parts of it in three more.[195] The author claims that the story he has to tell was related by the king's own sword-bearer in his old age to King Æþelstan when Archbishop Dunstan was a young man, who later told the story to Abbo of Fleury who recorded it in a book, which came to the attention of Ælfric who translated it into English.

Eadmund, king of East Anglia, was regarded as a noble leader who refused to bow to the Danes when the Great Heathen Army overran eastern England in 864 AD. In Ælfric's eyes, the story concerns the head-on collision of heathen and Christian world-views:

> Eadmund se eadiga Eastengla cynincg wæs snotor and wurðfull, and wurðode symble mid æþelum þeawum þone ælmihtigan God

> 'Eadmund, the blessed king of the East Angles, was wise and honourable, and always worshipped the almighty God with noble behaviour.'

His kingdom was beset by the Danes, led by an arrogant warlord, called by the homilist Hinguar (possibly known to his men as Ívarr):

> Hinguar þa becom to eastenglum rowende, on þam geare þe ælfred æðelincg an and twentig geare wæs, se þe westsexena cynincg siþþan wearð mære. And se foresæda Hinguar færlice swa swa wulf on lande bestalcode, and þa leode sloh weras and wif, and þa ungewittigan cild, and to bysmore tucode þa bilewitan Cristenan. He sende ða sona syððan to þam cyninge

---

[195] Complete versions: MS A, British Library MS Cotton Junius E VII, early 11th c.; MS B, Bodleian MS 343 of the later 12th c. Partial versions in MS O British Library MS Cotton Otho B X, early 11th c; MS U, University Library Cambridge, MS Ii.I.33, later 12th c.; MS V British Library MS Cotton Vitellius D XVII, mid-11th c.

beotlic ærende, þæt he abugan sceolde to his manrædene gif he rohte his feores.

'Hinguar then came rowing to East Anglia in the year when Ælfred the prince was twenty-one years old, who later became the glorious king of the West Saxons. And the aforesaid Hinguar immediately stalked the land like a wolf and killed the people – the men and women and the innocent children – and afflicted the gentle Christians with humiliation. He then soon sent to the king a threatening message, that he should bow in submission if he cared for his life.'

Ignoring the advice of his bishop to save his life by offering homage to the invaders, Eadmund refused to become a puppet of the Danes, as the Mercian king had previously done. He said:

"... me nu leofre wære þæt ic on feohte feolle wið þam þe min folc moste heora eardes brucan."

"... It would be more acceptable to me now that I should fall in a fight in order that my people might be able to have the benefit of their homeland."

At the bishop's protestations, he continued:

"... Næs me næfre gewunelic þæt ic worhte fleames, ac ic wolde swiðor sweltan gif ic þorfte for minum agenum earde, and se ælmihtiga God wat þæt ic nelle abugan fram his biggengum æfre, ne fram his soþan lufe, swelte ic, lybbe ic."

"... It has never been my custom that I should take to flight, but I would rather die if I should have to for my own homeland, and the almighty God knows that I will not ever turn away from his worship, nor from the true love of him, whether I live or die."

Hinguar regarded Eadmund's proud stance as an affront and came to the hall where the king awaited him. Eadmund threw his weapons down and the Danes seized him.

Hwæt þa arleasan þa Eadmund gebundon, and gebysmrodon huxlice, and beoton mid saglum; and swa syððan læddon þone geleaffullan cyning to anum eorðfæstum treowe, and tigdon hine þærto mid heardum bendum, and hine eft swuncgon langlice mid swipum, and he symble clypode betwux þam swinglum mid soðan geleafan to Hælende Criste, and þa hæþenan þa for his geleafan wurdon wodlice yrre forþanþe he clypode Crist him to fultume.

'Lo, the wicked ones then bound Eadmund, and humiliated him shamefully, and beat him with cudgels, and then they led the pious king to an earth-fast tree and tied him to it with hard bonds, and whipped him at length with scourges, and he always called out between the blows with true faith to Christ the saviour, and because of his faith the heathens became very furiously angry because he called out to Christ for comfort.'

Eadmund's refusal to submit to Hinguar's will angered him:

Þa geseah Hingwar, se arlease flotman, þæt se æþela cyning nolde Criste wiðsacan, ac mid anrædum geleafan hine æfre clypode, het hine þa beheafdian and þa hæðenan swa dydon. Betwux þam þe he clypode to Criste þagit, þa tugon þa hæþenan þone halgan to slæge, and mid anum swencge slogon him of þæt heafod, and his sawl siþode gesælig to Criste.

'When Hingwar, the wicked seafarer, saw that the noble king would not forsake Christ but with single-minded faith called out to him still, he ordered him to be beheaded and the heathens did so. Between the times when he still called to Christ, the heathens led him to slaughter and with one blow struck the head off him, and his soul travelled blessed to Christ.'

Tiring of their sport, the Danes headed off:

Hwæt ða se flothere ferde eft to scipe, and behyddon þæt heafod þæs halgan Eadmundes on þam þiccum bremelum þæt hit bebyrged ne wurde.

'Lo, then the ship-army went back to their ship and hid the head of the holy Eadmund in thick brambles, so that it might not be buried.'

Þa æfter fyrste, syððan hi afarene wæron, com þæt landfolc to þe þær to lafe wæs þa, þær heora hlafordes lic læg butan heafde, and wurdon swiðe sarige for his slege on mode, and huru þæt hi næfdon þæt heafod to þam bodige.

'Then after a space of time, once they had left, the local folk who were then left there came to where their lord's body lay without a head and became very pained at heart for his slaying, and more so that they did not have the head for the body.'

Happily, a local man had been skulking nearby and had seen the whole thing and told them that he believed that the Danes had hidden the head in a stand of trees, at which they all set off in search of it.

Wæs eac micel wundor þæt an wulf wearð asend, þurh Godes wissunge to bewerigenne þæt heafod wið þa oþre deor, ofer dæg and niht. Hi eodon þa secende, and symle clypigende, swa swa hit gewunelic is þam ðe on wuda gað oft, "Hwær eart þu nu gefera?" and him andwyrde þæt heafod, "Her, her, her"; and swa gelome clypode andswarigende him eallum, swa oft swa heora ænig clypode, oþþæt hi ealle becomen þurh ða clypunga him to. Þa læg se græga wulf þe bewiste þæt heafod, and mid his twam fotum hæfde þæt heafod beclypped, grædig and hungrig, and for Gode ne dorste þæs heafdes abyrian, and heold hit wið deor. Þa wurdon hi ofwundrode þæs wulfes hyrdrædenne, and þæt halige heafod ham feredon mid him, þancigende þam ælmihtigan ealra his wundra; ac se wulf folgode forð mid þam heafde oþþæt hi to tune comon, swylce he tam wære, and gewende eft siþþan to wuda ongean.

'It was likewise a miracle that a wolf was sent through God's guidance to guard the head against other animals, by day and night. They then went looking and always calling out – as is the custom of those who often go into the woods – "Where are you now, fellow?" and the head answered him "Here, here, here!" and called out thus often answering them all, as often as any of them called out, until they all came to him due to the calling. Then the grey wolf that guarded the head lay down, and held the head clasped with his two paws, and though hungry and with a strong appetite, he dared not eat the head because of God, but kept it safe against animals. Then they were amazed at the wolf's guardianship and carried the holy head home with them, thanking the almighty one for all his wonders; but the wolf followed the head as if he were tame, until they came to the estate, and he then went back to the wood again.'

The head was treated with great reverence and was housed in a small chapel which was endowed with many gifts once the story became widely known and the relics were found not to become corrupt. Tales of miracles quickly spread, and the holy king's help was sought by pilgrims and pious people in need.

The wolf was the tutelary spirit of the East Anglian kings, descended from Woden through Wuffa ('wolf'). Lupine imagery appears on their coins and in the royal treasures from Mound I at Sutton Hoo – for example, the small gold figure on the 'wand' (Bruce-Mitford, 1978, pp.398-9).

The king's adherence to his perception of his own honour, even at the cost of his life, typifies the 'heroic' ethic seen also in the defiance of Hadubrand against his father Hildebrand, or Ealdorman Byrhtnoþ against the Vikings. The point is that Eadmund had the courage and willpower to choose for himself and did not allow himself to be swept along by the course of events (Neidorf, 2022c, pp.33-4).

GOD-POSTS

Bede relates that the East Saxons turned their backs on Christianity under the stress of an outbreak of plague and were re-converted by King Sigeberht who denounced the worship of idols made from wood or stone (*Historia Ecclesiastica Gentis Anglorum*, III.30). No earth-fast stone idols have yet been recognised in England, but the imagery of the Sutton Hoo stone suggests that the idea of carved stone idols may not be entirely due to Bede's imagination or his classical training (MacLean, 1997, p.83; Mortimer & Pollington, 2013).

Wooden posts played a major part in building construction and in marking important sites. Among the Anglo-Saxons, marker posts are evidenced in the archaeological record as well as four-post structures, perhaps some form of canopy or covering, especially where cremations are subsequently buried in urns (Hedges & Buckley, 1985, p.5; Arnold, 1997, pp.156-9; Glasswell, 2002, p.26). Both a marker post and a possibly temporary structure were suggested from the excavations at Swallowcliffe Down (Wiltshire) (Speake, 1989, p.105; Williams, 2006a, pp.27-35). At Gamlingay (Cambridgeshire), there were several anomalous features which may have been the postholes for grave-markers or other mortuary structures (Murray & McDonald, 2006, p.211).

Wooden posts were used as grave-markers by some Germanic tribes on the Continent: for example, when Queen Rodelinde of the Lombards ordered a church built outside the walls at Pavia, Italy, the foundation was known as *Santa Maria ad Perticas* 'Holy Mary at the Stakes', these being the grave-markers for fallen warriors (Schutz, 2001, p.125; Todd, 2004, p.236).[196] Decoration of the post in some manner to identify the deceased seems likely, although this may have been no more than a simple inscription of the name; such may have

---

[196] The presence of such posts was a great help to tomb-robbers who were thus able to target their efforts more effectively. Bruce-Mitford (1978, p.363) illustrates a stone 'bar' placed vertically at the foot of a grave in the Anglian cemetery at Uncleby (Yorkshire).

been the inspiration for the pillow-stones of Hartlepool and else-where in north-east England, bearing the occupant's name in runic or Roman script, or a mixture of both (Page, 1995, pp.322-5). However, in Merovingian Francia it is noticeable that grave-robbers knew where in the grave to dig for the items they were seeking, which varied according to sex and status of the deceased: this strongly suggests that the visible grave markers conveyed something more than just the position of a burial. One estimate puts the figure at 30% of burials having been selectively robbed (i.e., targeted in the grave's area) within a generation of interment (Effros, 2003, p.134; Klevnäs, 2013). Also, there are many cases of multiple interment at different times, which implies that the location of the grave was visible above ground.

At Frénouville (France) traces were found of stone steles and wooden posts which are assumed to have served a similar purpose (Effros, 2003, p.144). There are several examples of wooden stakes modified to resemble human figures, for example the pair from Braak (Schleswig-Holstein, Germany), and the phallic males from Njutanger (Sweden) and Broddenbjerg (Denmark) (Hachmann, 1971). These are thought to be images of deities, but against this we have Tacitus's testimony that the Germani did not think it appro-priate to reduce the gods to mere likenesses (e.g., the reference to the Alcis). This may explain the rather rudimentary modifications to the basic form of the stake shown on these figures – they were not intended as accurate portrayals in the Graeco-Roman manner.

Even in later Christian societies the tradition of the wooden marker was not entirely forgotten, as this incident in the settlement of Greenland shows (Du Bois, 1999, p.87):

> Skyldi setja staur upp of brjósti hínum dauða en síðann er kennimenn kómu til þá skyldi upp kippa saturinum ok hella þar í vigðu vatni

> 'A post would be set up from the breast of the dead man and then, when clerics later came by, they had to pull the posts up and pour water into the space.'

The purpose here was to sanctify the dead with holy water in Greenland, where proper Christian facilities such as consecrated ground were not available, but the apparently mundane nature of the posts argues for such objects forming part of the standard range of burial rites.

Yet archaeology and other literary sources agree that Germanic 'totems' or figural images could be carved into stakes or posts.[197] The Old Saxons are recorded as worshipping a large post made from a tree-trunk, known as the *Irminsul* 'great pillar' (Simek, 1993, s.v. *Irminsul, pole gods*). It may have had nails driven into it, for use in a fire-striking ceremony (Simek, 1993, s.v. *reginnaglar*; Hachmann, 1971, plates 89-95; Ellis Davidson, 1988, p.15).[198] A structure consisting of four such poles erected for worship was called in ON a *stallr* or *stalli*; presumably sacrifice or offerings took place on the frame (Simek, 1993, s.v. *altar*).[199] Such carved stakes may be the counterparts of the commemorative posts set up at the grave, and reflect an aspect of ancestor-worship in Germanic tradition which surfaces again and again – for example, the Norse notion of the ancestor asleep within his mound but still able to intercede in the affairs of men (e.g., Angantyr in *Hervarar saga*) or the admonition by Ælfric in *De auguriis* ('On Auguries') (Pope, 1967) against seeking healing at a grave-mound where demons would appear in the guise of the dead person (Pollington, 2000, p.53):

Gyt farað wiccan to wega gelæton and to hæþenum byrgelsum mid heora gedwimore and clipiað to ðam deofle, and he cymð

---

[197] van der Sanden & Capelle, 2001; Grigsby, 2005, p.159. Maclean (1997) notes that the tradition of free-standing crosses in Anglo-Saxon England may have its origins in the heathen tradition of wooden posts as objects of veneration. Ellis Davidson (1988, p.18) recalls the observation of Ibn Fadlan that Rus merchants used to make offerings to images and wooden stakes carved with the likeness of a human face.

[198] However, Motz (1995, p.56) suggests that Þórr's association with fire may be based on the lightning and also on the 'northern lights', the *aurora borealis*.

[199] The structure of stakes or poles erected beneath the horse's body on the Lärbro runestone would seem to be an example of a *stallr*.

hym to on þæs mannes gelicnysse þe þær lið bebyrged swylce he
of deaðe arise, ac heo ne mæg þæt don þæt se deada arise þurh
hire drycræft.

'Witches still travel to where roads meet and to heathen graves
with their illusory skill and call out to the devil, and he comes to
them in the guise of the person who lies buried there, as if he
might rise from the dead – but she cannot really make it happen,
that the dead man should arise through her wizardry.'

Perhaps Egil's *níðstǫng* forms part of a similar tradition, where it is
turned to negative use.

The wooden cross erected by King Oswald of Northumbria to
celebrate his victory at Heavenfield was partly commemorative and
partly an object of veneration in itself. The king may have been
inspired by the free-standing wooden pole at Yeavering, erected on
top of the eastern barrow between 300 and 500 AD, which led to
the replacement of a pre-existing stone circle by a wooden structure
(MacLean, 1997). It appears that the early Bernicians were replacing
stone with wood in their cult sites at this time, and free-standing
wooden posts were still part of the worship enacted there into the
later 500s: the 'grandstand' on this site had a wooden post as its focus,
with building D2 (the presumed *hof* or temple) behind the seating
area. When the post required replacement, another was erected almost next to it and the fill of the posthole contained sheeps' or goats'
teeth, suggesting that the severed heads of animals had been displayed there. It is notable that the West Saxon royal site at Cheddar
also featured a wooden post, usually interpreted as a flagpole but
potentially either a wooden preaching cross or a heathen pillar.

North further cites the episode in Saxo's *Gesta Danorum* where
Othinus (i.e., Woden, Óðinn) was able to restore a damaged statue
of himself and make it speak when touched by men (North, 1997,
p.90, 110). This resonates with the references in *Hávamál* where *Hár*
'the High One' claims to have given life to two wooden images of
men by clothing them, possibly linked to the tale of the first humans

Askr and *Embla*, Ash and Elm which is also recounted in *Vǫluspá* v.17-8 (Simek, 1993, s.v. *Embla*).[200]

GOD OF THE HANGED

One of Óðinn's more memorable names is *Hangatýr* 'god of the hanged' which presumably references the tale of his sacrifice on the World Tree and acquisition of the runes. Yet the notion of a sacrificial god may be considerably older than the dating of Snorri's text suggests.[201] There are echoes of a similar tale in the OE poem *The Dream of the Rood* which was recorded in the 10th c. in the *Vercelli Book* (Krapp, 1932), but parts of which appear on the 8th c. Ruthwell cross in Dumfriesshire, Scotland, on the western edge of Northumbrian territory (Kay, 2013, p.2; Neidorf, 2021). In this poem, the cross recounts its experiences to the poet in a dream-vision, from growing as a tree in the forest, being cut down to make the timbers for the cross used in the crucifixion, buried ignominiously then retrieved and covered in gold and jewels as an object of human veneration. Giving a voice and expression of sentiments to an inanimate object was a commonplace device of Anglo-Saxon riddling, and audiences familiar with this form of entertainment would have found nothing remarkable in its use in this context (Pollington, 2011, pp.215-9; Neidorf, 2021). The extensive runic text may be a physical manifestation of this same notion: a linguistic utterance directly connected to the cross itself. Likewise, the dream-manifestation or prophetic vision is a known *topos* of both Christian (e.g., Job's ladder) and heathen cultures (e.g., Baldr's death foreseen by Frigg in *Baldrs*

---

[200] The meaning of *Askr* is secure (ash) but *Embla* is only conjectured to mean 'elm'; van der Sanden & Capelle (2001, pp.90-2) note that male idols are consistently made from oak while alder is used for a female figure, and ash is used for figures guarding trackways. Perhaps 'Óðinn's clothing' is a kenning for 'armour and weapons', and in accepting these gifts men could become *Einherjar*, members of his elite troop.

[201] Sundqvist (2009, p.650) shows that the epithets *hangatýr* and *hangaguð* may date from the 10th c. or earlier.

draumar). The miraculous dream in which Cædmon learnt the art of verse-making bridges the gulf between the old and the new forms of spirituality (Pollington, 2011, pp.22-5).

The relationship between the West Saxon version recorded in the manuscript and the Northumbrian one written in runes has been explored on several occasions, but it should be stressed that since Anglo-Saxon verse was intended primarily for oral performance, the differences in vocabulary and phrasing are negligible and it is remarkable that both versions agree to the extent that they do. The older, Northumbrian version may be given priority on present evidence, but it is not necessary to conclude that the poem was first conceived in that kingdom, nor that the runes record the oldest form of the poem.

The Ruthwell cross's present location inside the church building is the result of the modern desire to preserve the detailed carving: it originally stood in the churchyard, and probably predated the church itself. In other words, the site of the church was chosen because it was close to the existing cross and the customary place of assembly, whether a traditional market-site or place of heathen worship. Elliott (1959, p.96) dated the cross's runes to ca. 650-750 AD, so plausibly carved at a time when elements of heathen belief were still part of the local tradition. The poem's image of an erect tree surrounded by death may call to mind the practice of hanging evil-doers, criminals and defeated enemies from beams.

Christ, in the poem, is described in terms evoking a successful Germanic leader with a small hearthtroop of loyal followers. Loyalty and determination to see through the mission entrusted to it inform the cross's decision not to waver when the doomed lord embraces it in death, nor to topple and crush the persecutors. The cross here is as much a faithful thane as any of Christ's human disciples (text from Krapp, 1932, p.62; ll.47-9):

> ...   Ne dorste ic hira ænigum sceððan.

> Bysmeredon hie unc butu ætgædere. Eall ic wæs mid blode bestemed,

begoten of þæs guman sidan   …

'I did not dare harm any of them [though] they shamed us both together. I was all smeared with blood which poured from the man's side.'

The impetus behind the ornamentation of standing monuments with Christian imagery may well lie in the tale of the 'finding of the true cross' which became a cult object in the early 7th c. (Kay, 2013, p.5). If heathen posts bore imagery, we have no direct record of this unless we assume that the Anglo-Saxon preaching-cross was derived from the pre-Christian *ós* or god-pole. We do however know that temples were decorated with zoomorphic imagery. Such a god-pole should have featured a 'human' face and an attribute of the god, if it resembles the statues that Adam of Bremen wrote about having stood in Uppsala in his day. A less secure comparandum might be the (so far undated) Zbruč pillar with its four facing theomorphs and the frieze of characters at the bottom of the stele (Mortimer & Pollington, 2013, p.134).

The association of Óðinn with death by hanging is explicit in *Gautreks saga* where it forms one of the three simultaneous deaths enacted upon King Víkarr, as well as the *Hávamál* episode of suffering and privation in order to gain spiritual power (Sundqvist, 2009, p.652). In the 13th c. *Orkneyinga saga*, offering a victim to Óðinn in exchange for victory is mentioned as if it were a common practice, although it may have been a mere literary convention by then.

In later Anglo-Saxon England it was seemingly the custom for a gallows to be erected at a site of known heathen veneration, such as a crossroads or a burial mound from the pre-Christian past, designated as *cwealmstowa* 'places of legal execution' (Pollington, 2008; Reynolds, 2009). There are several sites known as *Gally Hill* or *Gallows Hill* where gibbets stood into the 19th c. (e.g., Reigate, Surrey; Ballidon, Derbyshire; Eddlesborough, Buckinghamshire and others) and where Anglo-Saxon barrows serve as the focal point for a number of satellite burials from the later period. The flat burials at Sutton Hoo surrounding the mounds contained many examples of what appear to have been 'executions', where the head has been displaced due to decapitation. The reasons for these 'deviant' burials have been discussed at some length, but the practice is found across northern Europe from Poland to England and elsewhere and it is not to be expected that a single tradition explains them all (Klevnäs, 2013).

The corpse of a miscreant or defeated foe was often exposed on a prominent post or tree which is consistent with the record of King Oswald's grisly end, with the fate which King Ongenþeow proposes for his enemies (*Beowulf*, l.2940, text from Fulk et al., 2008) and with the 'hanged man' verse in *Beowulf* ll.2444-9 (Chadwick, 1899, pp.18-9; J. Wills, pers. comm.; Kay, 2013, p.20; Grundy, 2014, p.32).

> Swā bið geōmorlic   gomelum ceorle
>
> tō gebīdanne,   þæt his byre rīde
>
> giong on galgan.   Þonne hē gyd wrece,
>
> sārigne sang,   þonne his sunu hangað
>
> hrefne tō hrōðre,   ond hē him helpe ne mæg,
>
> eald ond infrōd,   ænige gefremman

Beowulf ll.2444-9

'So it must be grievous for an old man to endure that his youthful offspring should ride the gallows. Then he may make a lament, a sorrowful song, while his son is hanged as sport for a raven and, being himself old and weakened, he cannot offer any help to him…'

Into the 19th century the corpses of hanged criminals were displayed on the gibbet. It seems certain that similar gruesome displays did happen in Anglo-Saxon times since manuscript illustrations depict this, and the Sutton Hoo cemetery revealed an example in Burial 27 (Carver, 2005, p.322). The so-called 'sand bodies', human remains found between the barrows remain only as stains in the sandy soil of the site, many of whom appear to have had their hands and feet tied, and to have suffered trauma at death. They are usually classified as victims of penal killing, since hanging was a common way of carrying out a death sentence into modern times, and one body was buried with the remains of the gallows on which he met his end (the so-called 'ploughman' burial, no.27) (Carver, 2005, p.322). The usual assumption is that these people were executed in much later times, but there is little in the archaeology to support this and some few do appear to be roughly contemporary with the barrows. These sand-bodies may even have been the executed foes of the Anglian kings, offered up as hanged sacrifices to the gods (North, 1997, p.297).

Kay has suggested that there is a strong thematic link between the gallows and the horse. Both are a means of support for a journey, bear a man up from the ground and provide a vigorous 'ride'. *Yggdrasill* on which Óðinn suffered death and resurrection, was both a gallows and a *drasill* 'steed, horse' (Kay, 2013, p.20; cf. Liberman, 2016, pp.53-65). Horses were used for divination, according to Tacitus (*Germania*, ch.10.1), and their neighing and snorting could be interpreted by priests. Is it possible that the god suffered on the 'fearsome steed' *Yggdrasill* to gain his knowledge because there was already a cultural link between riding and gaining secret wisdom?

SUFFERING AND DEATH ON THE WORLD TREE

The association of a mighty god and a central tree or post was very strong in OE tradition: the fact that the cross is specifically imagined as a tree connects with other OE plant-lore and the association between Woden and the *wuldortanas* in the *Nine Herbs Charm* (Glosecki, 2007a, p.64). A similar tradition to that expressed in the *Dream of the Rood* is in the Old Saxon poem *Heliand*, which details a parallel attitude of veneration towards the wooden cross and to Christ as a young hero with a warband. That the Old Saxon poem may have been inspired by the Anglo-Saxon tradition should not be discounted, despite the many objections raised against this hypothesis: it was, after all, an Anglo-Saxon and Anglo-Irish missionary effort that brought Christianity to this part of Europe, coupled with the later political expansion of the Carolingian Franks (Kay, 2013, p.9). The Anglo-Saxon missionary Boniface, is recorded as having destroyed a holy tree at Geismar (Hesse, Germany) known as *rubor iovis* 'Jupiter's Oak', presumably dedicated to the thunder-god. The story of the missionary's attack on the *Irminsuul* is cited below (p.414).

Kendall noted that 'sacred trees were a ubiquitous feature of the pagan religions of northern and western Europe. Anglo-Saxon missionaries, both in the British Isles and on the Continent, prided themselves on felling these idolatrous objects. From a detached modern perspective, it may be doubted whether the missionaries ever really succeeded in eradicating the worship of trees. The veneration of the cross might be viewed from this standpoint as a 'displacement' from the worship of trees' (Kendall, 2006, p.134). The story of St. Martin's felling of the tree venerated by the Franks also bears witness to this tradition of reverence for trees. These objects of veneration may not always have been specific trees growing in the woods, but might rather be columns or posts carved in human likeness, such as the pair of wooden figures from Braak (Netherlands) (Pollington, 2013, p.93, 110, 114).

The correlation of Christ on the cross with Óðinn on Yggdrasill cannot be entirely fortuitous, although what it actually means has been much debated (Sundqvist, 2009; Kay, 2013, p.12ff.). It is possible that the (Bronze Age?) tale of the sacrificed god, which inspired and gave resonance to the Christian story, was developed in northern Europe into the tale of Óðinn on the World Tree[202] as a deliberate reaction to Christian imagery. Yet there is little in the Germanic tale that seems alien or invented – Óðinn appears in other stories where he suffers at the hands of his foes (e.g., the tale of Geirrøðr) and the god's associations with both writing and warfare also appear to be ancient.

---

[202] Liberman (2016, p.51) notes that the phrase *vindgameiði á* need not be read as 'on a windy tree' but could be 'on the windy gallows'; ibid., p.57, 68, the similarity of the crucified god and the hanged god is discussed.

Óðinn's tale of hanging in *Hávamál* reflects the period of 'nine nights' as the duration of the god's suffering, with parallels in the nine males hanged on the tree at Uppsala in Adam of Bremen's account and in the nine-year frequency of the major sacrifices. This emphasis on groups of nine has been variously interpreted, but it is worth pointing out here that any Christian-influenced tradition would surely reflect a three-day period during which the god was withdrawn from the world (Good Friday to Easter Sunday) or a longer seven-day sequence relating to the Judaeo-Christian week and its recurrent cycle of Sabbath days. The insistence on a period of nine nights has the feeling of a genuine pre-Christian tradition.

The purpose of Óðinn's ordeal was to gain knowledge and to increase his own 'divine power' (*ásmegin*), which enabled him to 'take up 'the runes (Sundqvist, 2009, pp.652-3). The god's hanging might therefore be in itself a prototype ritual sacrifice, which is confirmed by the use of the verb *gefa* 'give, offer'. The god on the tree is *gefinn Óðni* 'given/consecrated to Óðinn' while the sacrifice (simultaneous stabbing and hanging) of King Víkarr is accompanied by the speech-act *nú gef ek þik Óðni* 'now I give/consecrate thee to Óðinn' (Liberman, 2016, p.52).

There has been much debate concerning the meaning of the tree-hanging episode: is it a prototype for human sacrifice to be enacted in the here-and-now by worshippers of the god? Or is it perhaps a kind of initiation rite, whereby youths were brought to an advanced state of awareness through pain and deprivation? We shall explore this below.[203] The point is that secret knowledge could only be won from the inhabitants of the Otherworld at the point of death – whence the story of Óðinn bound between fires and revealing his

---

[203] Sundqvist (2009, p.654) shows that the fundamental character of sacrifice is the principle of *do ut des* (I give so that you may give) which does not apply to the 'hanged god' episode since Óðinn is at once the giver, the recipient and the sacrificial object (*vndaðr oc gefinn Óðni, siálfr siálfom mér* 'wounded and given to Óðinn, myself to myself' *Hávamál* v.138). The exchanged gift is the enlightenment necessary for a new social role, as in an initiation ceremony which transforms the status and competence of the giver.

secrets. Gaining knowledge required dedication and willpower, to overcome extreme discomfort and suffering. Elsewhere, the god himself had to ask the dead for their insights, e.g., the deceased *vǫlva* in *Vǫluspá*, and in *Baldrs draumar*.

In a context not linked to literacy or the gaining of knowledge, the practice of sacrificing powerful persons on trees is well-evidenced in Anglo-Saxon England in relation to the Viking wars – King Eadmund of East Anglia was one such victim and another was St. Ælfheah (Pollington, 2002, pp.198-9). In both cases the initial purpose was to break the victim's will through torture – to force Edmund to renounce his allegiance to Christianity and thus become a puppet of the Danes, and in Ælfheah's case to force him to hand over gold for his deliverance. In neither case was the procedure intended to kill the victim at the outset: from this it may be understood that tying the victim to a tree was a prelude to deprivation and severe torture, not to murder.

A mighty or prominent tree could be used as a vehicle to display the dead. Adam of Bremen mentions this in connection with the cult centre at Uppsala where the corpses of men and animals were suspended openly in the holy grove (Sundqvist, 2009, p.653). Likewise, we have the evidence of the fate of King Oswald of Northumbria after losing a battle against King Penda of Mercia.

A prominent tree or post is probably referred to in the literature as a *stapol*, which metamorphosed with the religious conversion into the Christian 'Tree of Life' or 'Cross of Victory' (Tolley, 1995a; Hooke, 2010, p.29). Oswald was himself connected with the erection of such a symbol before the battle of Heavenfield, which proved to be a great victory for the Bernicians. Bede contrasts King Oswald, newly enthroned and piously Christian, with his apostatised brother Eanfrið, and takes the opportunity to show the king acting with great reverence for the standing monument of the cross (text from Colgrave & Mynors, 1969).

Ostenditur autem usque hodie et in magna veneratione habetur locus ille, ubi venturus ad hanc pugnam Osuald signum sanctae crucis erexit, ac flexis genibus Dominum deprecates est, ut in tanta rerum necessitate suis cultoribus caelesti succurreret auxilio. Denique fertur quia facta citato opere cruce, ac fovea praeparata in qua statui deberet, ipse fide fervens hanc arripuerit, ac foveae imposuerit, atque utraque manu erectam tenuerit, donec adgesto a militibus pulvere terrae figeretur.

Historia Ecclesiastica Gentis Anglorum, ch. 3.2

'Even today that site is shown and held in great reverence where, when about to enter this battle, Oswald erected the sign of the holy cross and on bended knees prayed to God to rescue his worshippers with heavenly help in such need. It is said that once the cross was made by swift work, and a hole made ready to stand it in, with fervent faith he grasped it to himself and stood it in the hole, and with both hands held it erect until it was secured with the dirt of the earth piled up by the soldiers.'

The king's devotion resulted in the granting of divine favour and a magnificent victory over the British aggressor, Cadwallon. The site of the battle was later called *Hefenfelth* 'field of heaven' and the site of the cross erected by Oswald became a place of pilgrimage for the monks of Hexham abbey who made an annual visit to it, celebrating with a vigil and a mass.

The theme of the military victory in the shadow of a cross is a commonplace of religious tales (e.g., Emperor Constantine's revelation at the Milvian Bridge) used by Bede to show the superiority of Christian orthodoxy (represented by the Northumbrian Oswald) over the heretical British church (in the person of the Welsh Cadwallon) and resurgent heathenism (i.e., Oswald's brother, Eanfrið). The Hexham monks likewise used the story of the defeat of the British heretics and the erection of the cross to mark the beginning of their faith in Northumbria.

Tolley has argued that Oswald knew very well that his actions before the battle must inspire his entire army, which is likely to have

constituted both Christians from the Scottish court and local Northumbrian heathens (Eanfrið had been nominally Christian while in
exile among the Scots, but reverted to the old religion once he was
back in Northumbria) (Tolley, 1995a). Oswald, who does seem to
have been genuinely committed to Christianity, cannily took over
a heathen battle-rite and adapted it to the purposes of Christian
propaganda.

Ælfric offers another story concerning King Oswald (text from
Needham, 1984):

> Hwæt þa Oswold cyning his cynedom geheold hlisfullice for
> worulde 7 mid micclum geleafan 7 on eallum dædum his
> Drihten awurðode, oð þæt he ofslægen wearð for his folces ware
> on þa, nigoðan geare þe he rices geweold, þa þa he sylf wæs on
> ylde eahta 7 þrittig geare. Hit gewearð swa be þam þæt him wann
> on Penda, Myrcena cyning, þe æt his mæges slege ær, Eadwines
> cyninges, Cedwallan fylste; 7 se Penda ne cuðe be Criste nan
> þincg, 7 eall Myrcena folc wæs ungefullod þagit. Hi comon þa
> to gefeohte to Maserfelda begen 7 fengon togædere oð þæt þær
> feollon þa Cristenan 7 þa hæðenan genealæhton to þam halgan
> Oswolde. Þa geseah he genealecan his lifes geendunge 7 gebad
> for his folc þe þær feallende sweolt 7 betæhte heora sawla 7 hine
> sylfne. Gode, 7 þus clypode on his fylle: "God gemiltsa urum
> sawlum!" Þa het se hæþena cynincg his heafod of aslean 7 his
> swiðran earm, 7 settan hi to myrcelse. Þa æfter Oswoldes slege
> feng Oswig his broðor to Norðhymbra rice 7 rad mid werode to
> þær his broðor heafod stod on stacan gefæstnod, 7 genam þæt
> heafod 7 his swiðran hand 7 mid arwurðnysse ferode to
> Lindesfarena cyrcan. Þa wearð gefylled, swa we her foresædon,
> þæt his swiðre hand wunað hal mid þam flæsce butan ælcre
> brosnunge…

> From Ælfric's *Life of St. Oswald*

'Lo, then King Oswald held his kingdom gloriously before the world and with great faith and he praised his Lord in all his deeds, until he was slain in the defence of his people in the ninth year that he held power when he himself was thirty-eight years of age. It came about because Penda, strove against him, the king of Mercia who had helped Cedwalla in the slaying of his kinsman, King Eadwine. This Penda knew nothing about Christ and the whole Mercian nation was then unbaptized. They both came to fight at Maserfeld and closed together until the Christians fell there and the heathens drew near to the holy Oswald. Then he saw his life's end approaching and prayed for his men who were falling dead there and entrusted their souls and himself to God and called out thus at his death: "May God have mercy on our souls!" Then the heathen king had his head and his right arm struck off, and had them set up as a marker. Then, after Oswald's slaughter, Oswig came to power in Northumbria and rode with a troop to where his brother's head stood fastened to a stake, and he took the head and his right hand and carried them with honour to the church of Lindisfarne. Then it was fulfilled, as we said before, that his right hand remains whole with its flesh, without any corruption ...'

The interesting aspect of this tale is that Penda sought to display the physical remains of his defeated foe, much as the Danes did with the body of King Eadmund. While neither of these tales is presented as an example of 'human sacrifice' in the narrow sense, it is clear that the public execution of a defeated leader and the prominent display of his mutilated body were part of the military and religious culture of the period. The king's physical remains on the tree may have been a form of 'scorn pole' (ON *níðstǫng*) on which the dead king's power was shown to be ended (Tolley, 1995a). There is no suggestion that the defeated Northumbrian warriors were dealt with in this manner – indeed, most would have been despoiled, then bound and held for ransom – and it seems to have been reserved for kings whose presence embodied the 'luck' of their people.

The world-tree was conceived as a means of communication between the three levels of being: heaven, earth and hell (overworld, middle world, underworld). Trees were very important in pre-Christian Europe, and some special examples were objects of veneration in their own right. An 11th c. penitential mentions men who bring offerings to *eorðfæstum stane and eac to treowum and to wylspringum* 'an earth-fast stone, and also to trees and to wellsprings', a combination of objects of veneration which recurs through Anglo-Saxon history (North, 1997, p.276). Ælfric also tells a story about St. Martin who was active in Gaul in the 4th c. The saint intended to cut down a holy tree which the heathens worshipped; they agreed to allow this if Martin would lie beneath it while they cut, and he accepted, but when the tree began to topple he directed it back towards the crowd and crushed the men cutting it down (Griffiths, 1996, p.99). In Ælfric's version of the tale, there was little protest at the destruction of a heathen temple, but a great outcry at the cutting down of the associated tree (Hooke, 2010, pp.21-2):

> Se halga martinus towearp sum hæðengild on sumere tide on sumere stowe. Þa wæs an pintreow wið þæt templ gefriðed swiðe halig geteald on þa hæþenan wisan. Þa wolde he eac forceorfan eac swilce þæt treow ac ða hæðengildan þam halgan wiðcwædon, sædon þæt hi ne mihton on heora mode findan þæt he þæt treow forcurfe, þeah ðe he heora templ towurpe.

Ælfric's Life of St. Martin, ll.390-7

'The holy Martinus threw down a certain idol at a certain time in a certain place. A pinetree was by the temple, considered a very holy shrine in the heathen manner. Then he wanted also to cut down the tree but the heathens gainsaid the saint, [they] said they could not find it in their hearts that he should cut down that tree even though he might throw down their temple.'

Evidently the temple's *geteald* – a tent or temporary covered structure – could be easily substituted but the tree itself was irreplaceable.

Trees are not easy to trace in the archaeological evidence, but some exceptions have been commented upon. At Yeavering, the Western Ring Ditch enclosed a later square structure with a central post, around which burials were laid out in an arc; activity here was later replaced with a focus on building D2 (the presumed temple with the pile of ox-skulls by one of its walls) (Semple, 2010, pp.40-1).

The West Saxons were praised by Aldhelm for conducting Christian instruction on a site where the pagan idols of 'the snake and the stag' were once found on the pillars. This suggests that the site was one of those heathen sacred spaces newly rededicated to Christian worship, that it once held effigies of two cult animals, and that the *ermula* 'columns, posts, pillars' formed part of its structure (North, 1997, p.51 and cf. Carver, 2010, p.13, Semple, 2010, pp.39-40). Aldhelm died in 709, so the reference is to 7th c. practice. It is worth recalling that in *Beowulf* the hall of King Hroþgar was called *Heorot* 'hart', perhaps because of prominent hart's horns or some other imagery, while the 'snakes' may be the interlaced figures of Salin's Style II decoration. An *ermulum* was originally a small 'herm', a stele or small statue of the god Hermes erected at a boundary, showing just the god's face and genitals.

The association of the divine powers with the *axis mundi* was not swept away during Christianisation: in fact, the image of the god suffering on the wooden gallows became one of the more important symbols of the new religion. The 'holy rood' remained central to Christian worship, replacing the earlier XP (*chi-rho*, Christogram) and ἰχθύς (*ikhthis*, fish) symbols, and in many parts of Europe surpassing the rival 'Madonna and Child' icon. It is probable that the *Dream of the Rood*, an 8th c. poem concerning the crucifixion, recalls heathen-period phrasing when it refers to the cross in such terms as *syllicre treow* 'wondrous tree' (1.4) and *wuldres treow* 'tree of glory' (1.14)(Branston, 1957, p.108; Glosecki, 1989, pp.92-3; North, 1997, p.273ff). [204] Unusually, the *rod* 'rood' in this poem is able to talk,

---

[204] The latter phrase can also be rendered as 'tree of Wuldor'.

which may have some basis in Germanic beliefs about the sentient nature of large, old trees (North, 1997, pp.276-7, 286-7).[205]

Glosecki noted that the association of a powerful god and a central tree was very strong in OE tradition: the fact that the rood or cross is specifically imagined as a tree connects it with other OE plant-lore such as the association between Woden and the *wuldortanas* in the *Nine Herbs Charm* (Glosecki, 2007a, p.64). The *syllicre treow* motif also recalls both the Norse *barnstokkr* or 'protective tree' for the household, and the role of Yggdrasill in sheltering and protecting mankind and the gods (Tolley, 1995a; 2009, p.279, 375). It was replaced by the Holy Cross in Christian cosmology, standing at the pivotal point of the world and offering protection (and redemption) to all (Foster, 2007-8).

GAUT, GAPT, GEAT

A figure called *Geat* was known in OE legend or myth, and his associations made him suitable for inclusion among the noble forebears of living rulers. A character of the same name is found in *Deor* where he is linked to a lady named Mæþhild (Simek, 1993, s.v. *Gautr, Geat*; North, 1997, pp.257-8). The name *Geat* or *Geot* (and compounds such as *Angengeot*) appears in several Anglo-Saxon royal genealogies among the upper levels where the names may be those of tribal gods (Cronan, 2014).

It is plausible that the name *Geat* was applied to a god of victory and warfare by one or more of the Germanic-speaking peoples from early on, which spread with his worship. While the god named 'Woden' may not have a pedigree stretching back much further than the Iron Age, or Late Bronze Age perhaps, the name **Gautaz* is proposed by Kershaw (2000, p.8) as a possible progenitor of the Goths and with a more extensive backstory.

The etymological background of the name *Geat* may shed some light. The associations are with the verb *geotan* 'pour' and *getan* 'make

---

[205] Both ON *Heimdallr* and OE *Æsc* may be tree-spirits.

blood pour; kill, eviscerate' but the exact sense is debated.[206] It may be that the liquid 'poured out' is blood, and that the name denotes a victim whose blood is spilt at the time of sacrifice (Moisl, 1981, p.221; North, 1997, pp.140-3, 301; Pollington, 2011, p.238). The ON form *Gautr* means 'a person who is to be sacrificed', a name associated with Óðinn and his cult in Viking times (North, 1997, pp.84, 133-71).[207]

The homonym *Geat* in its plural *Geatas* is borne by the people to whom Beowulf belongs – also called *Wederas* and *Weder-Geatas*. This word is phonetically equivalent to the *Gautar*, a people of southern Sweden; more distantly and less certainly, the people of Gotland may be involved, as well as the Goths, who called themselves the *Gutans* (Orel, 2003, s.v. *gautaz*).[208] A location for the Geatas in the western Baltic or Oslofjord seems justified, although there is little agreement among specialists as to details (Shippey, 2022, pp.57-8). The Lombards also looked back to a founder with the name *Gausus*, which is probably a version of the same name, *Gaut* (Moisl, 1981, p.221; North, 1997, p.135).[209] The name *Geta* occurs in Asser's Latin *Life of King Alfred* at the end of a list of West Saxon noble ancestors (text from Acomb Leake, 1967):

> quem Getam iamdudum pagani pro deo venerabantur cuius Sedulius poeta mentionem facit in Paschali metrico carmine

> 'Geta, whom the pagans used to worship as a god, of whom the poet [Coelius] Sedulius makes mention in a Paschal verse song.'

---

[206] See discussion in Kroonen, 2013 s.v. *geutan* for the PIE root *gheu- 'pour a libation'.

[207] Shaw (2002, p.179) notes that in skaldic verse, *Gautr* is the commonest by-name for Óðinn with 18 instances, followed by *Yggr* (14). *Gautr* may originally have referred to a sacrificial offering to Yngvi/Ingwe.

[208] North (1997, pp.160-6) has argued for a political dimension to the insertion of Geat into the West Saxon dynastic records after King Æþelwulf's visit to Rome and connection to the Gothic tradition; *Geat* may have been an OE term which fitted his purpose in establishing a putative family connection. See Cronan, 2014, for a different view.

[209] The word has undergone characteristic Second Sound Shift of *-t-* to *-s-* .

The Goths are said to have made special ritual sacrifices, and perhaps their name (*Gutans*, from *geut- 'pour'*) was originally a reference to their practice of shedding blood, as recorded by Jordanes in the *Getica* (text from van Nuffelen & van Hoof, 2020):

> Quem Martem Gothi semper asperima placavere cultura, nam victimae eius mortes fuere captorum, opinantes bellorum praesulem apte humani sanguinis effusione placandum. Huic praede primordia vovebantur, huic truncis suspendebantur exubiae, eratque illis religionis preter ceteros insinuatis affectus eum parenti devotio numinis videretur impendi.

> 'This Mars the Goths have always placated with cruel practices, since his dead victims were prisoners, thinking that the governor of warfare would be properly pleased by the shedding of men's blood. To him they offered the first booty, for him weapons were hung from trees, and more than any others they had a stronger sense of religion since the worship of the god they regarded as bestowed upon their ancestor.'

For Jordanes, *Gapt/Gaut* seems to have been a hero or legendary progenitor (Schjødt, 2019, p.67).[210] Orel (2003, s.v.*3eutanan*) links the name of the 'Goths' *Gutans, Gutþiuda* to the same root (*3autaz, *3autōn*). Indeed, North has argued that Gaut was not merely an ancestor but a mortal hero who attained the status of *ansis* – half-god – and was regarded as divine while still alive (North, 1997, p.137ff).

Sacrifice, especially of enemy warriors, seems to have played an important role in the military and religious culture of the period. Sacrificial sites such as Alken Enge (Søe et al., 2017), Nydam (Bemmann, 1998) or Illerup (Ilkjaer, 2001), all in Denmark, indicate that large-scale destruction of defeated enemies was a recognised (perhaps even a common) practice. This is borne out by the near-contemporary description of the Cimbri and the defeat of Varus by

---

[210] A notable fact about the Goths is their propensity for human sacrifice, according to Jordanes (*Getica* 5),

Arminius (Murdoch, 2006; McNally & Dennis, 2011; Abdale, 2016). Display of the mutilated body of a defeated foe is also evidenced in the story of King Oswald (Meaney, 1966, p.111) and the display of the bones of King Hygelac at the mouth of the Rhine after his slaughter there (Chambers, 1963, pp.2-13; Shippey, 2022, p.8).

If we set aside for the moment the possible link of the name *Geat* / *Gautr* to bloodletting, another area of activity suggests itself of which 'pouring out' is a characteristic part. The role of alcoholic drink in religious observance has been discussed above. It forms one of the central elements of ritual in which female involvement was central – both in the production of the drink itself and in its formal distribution in a ritual setting. There is great appeal in the image of the well-dressed and beautiful 'lady' passing among the mead-benches with her companions, offering the drinking horn to each guest in turn and refilling it from the cauldron in which the brew is stored. Beguiling as this notion is, it should not blind us to the fact that drink could also be offered by males, albeit perhaps not on such important occasions. The role of the *byrele* in the Anglo-Saxon hall was presumably male (if the masculine gender of the noun is any guide), whose duties included keeping the cup of the lord full.[211]

Given the traditional association of strong drink with both oratory and warfare, it seems plausible that some divine power was held to reside in and be transmitted by the beer or mead: it is this factor which made the celebratory drinking festivals so objectionable to the Christian missionary in the story of St. Columbanus among the Swabians. May the name Geat, with its links to 'pouring', be cited here as such a supernatural power?

---

[211] Orel, 2003, s.v. *burilon*; the cognate ON term is *byrli*. It is tempting to adduce the Burgundian word *berils* 'bearer' and its associated medieval Latin form *barillus* which gives rise to the word *barrel* 'container for drink' (Orel, 2003, s.v. *berilaz*).

CHOOSERS OF THE SLAIN

Female emissaries of the war-god were understood to enjoy a special place in the warriors' hall. As we read in *Gylfaginning* (text from Faulkes, 2005):

> Þessar heita valkyrjur. Þær sendir Óðinn til hverrar orrostu. Þær kjósa feigð á men ok ráða sigri.

> 'these [maidens] are called *valkyrjur*. Óðinn sends them to every battle. They choose those men approaching death and they decide victory.'

The *valkyrjur* have a specifically Scandinavian flavour, but a cognate term is found in OE *wælcyrige*, both words meaning 'chooser of the slain'. They were believed to preside over battle and to mark out certain heroes and champions for an afterlife in the hall of Óðinn. These graceful damsels belong to Snorri's medieval world and derive from 'maids of battle' or female attendants of the warband, whether bearing arms alongside the men or taking part in rituals of divination which could foretell the outcome of any engagement (Branston, 1957, p.100, 106; Ellis Davidson, 1964, pp.61-6; Meaney, 1990, p.162ff; Tolley, 2009, pp.225-6; Grundy, 2014, pp.45-9). The OE tradition does not seem to have been based on the Scandinavian, and is perhaps older (North, 1997, p.106).

A class of plate-brooch, mainly bronze but occasionally silver-gilt, appears in the 9th c. depicting in profile a figure on horseback approaching a standing figure; the rider has long hair worn in a loop, and the standing figure wears a helmet and carries a shield (Holst et al., 2017, items 12a, 12b, 12c; Gardeła, Pentz & Price, 2022). Another type of brooch (or perhaps a mere variant?) shows a long-haired, probably female figure brandishing a sword and holding a shield underarm (e.g., the examples from Galgebakken, Denmark and Wickham Market, Suffolk [Gardeła, Pentz & Price, 2022, nos. 4, 30]). These figures are often interpreted as 'valkyries' because they mix male and female attributes, straddling the classes of warriors and those of hall-maidens. In almost every case, the weapons are displayed but do not appear to be deployed for combat: are they being used, for example, to be brandished in an act of assent as exemplified by the ON phrase *vapnaták* 'seizing of weapons' to show public agreement? Or did the wearing of such a brooch merely signify membership of a religious group? We do not have any examples from graves, so we cannot be sure that they were worn by females (although this has often been the presumption).

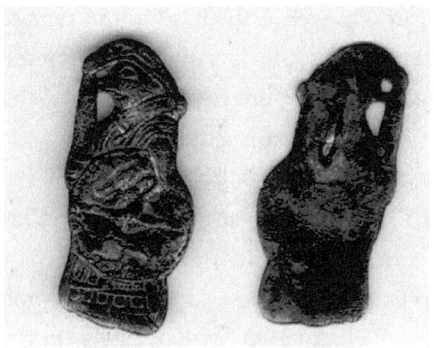

Fig. 24 Silver Valkyrie pendant from Wickham Market, Suffolk, England. Length: 40mm. 9th century. (PAS Reference: SF9305)

The word *valkyrjur* is Norse; the OE cognate word *wælcyrge* appears in some glosses where it refers to the Furies and to Bellona, goddess of war (Ellis Davidson, 1988, p.93, 96). One description of *Gorgons* in the Anglo-Saxon manuscript *The Wonders of the East* in the Nowell Codex describes them thus: *Ða deor habbaþ eahta fet ond wælkyrian eagan* 'those beasts have eight feet and valkyries' eyes' while a similar description of the *Gorgones* is found in the text *Narratiunculae Anglice Conscriptae* (Damico, 1990, p.177; Fulk, 2010, p.21). The OE adjective *wælceasigea* 'slain-choosing' in the poem *Exodus* (l.164) describes a raven, recalling the 'beasts of battle' *topos* in OE literature (Hunt, 1902, p.18). The raven was viewed as an agent of the war-god and the two birds Huginn and Muninn were Óðinn's spies and informants on developments in the world of men (Meaney, 1966, p.112; Hermann, 2020, p.57). There is insufficient evidence to relate Woden directly to the *wælcyrigean*, but the inference seems reasonable in the light of the Scandinavian tradition.

Another class of supernatural female is called in OE *ides*, where the OHG form is *idisi* and the ON *dísir* (Meaney, 1990, pp.158-62; Pollington, 2011, pp.313-7). They all seem to be potent figures, perhaps imbued with powers of prophecy. In *Beowulf*, the term *ides* is used to describe both Wealhþeo (l.620) and Hildeburh (l.1075) – royal ladies of the court – as well as the bloody and capricious wife of Offa (ll.1940-3). Grendel's Mother is assigned this epithet in l.1259 alongside *aglæcwif* 'horrendous female opponent'. Schjødt (2008, p.294) notes that in early Germanic culture females were often regarded as having a two-fold aspect: on the one hand 'frail human' and on the other 'sacred', 'prophetic' and 'numinous'. Females were highly esteemed, it seems, and treated with reverence – perhaps the tale of Veleda encapsulates both these aspects. Wild, noisy warrior-females appear in the OE charm *Wið Færsticce* where they wield weapons, ride horses, threaten the living and are formidable opponents (Grundy, 2014, pp.52-4, 56). Similarly, a group of bloodthirsty female beings is seen weaving a grisly fabric from dead men's entrails in the poem *Darraðarljóð*.

The *valkyrjur*, it seems, were originally ferocious female battle spirits, bringers of bloodshed, slaughter and death, but their stories were adapted (perhaps in the later Iron Age) to a format which could be accommodated within the rigid structure of medieval Scandinavian society. They transformed from 'bringers of death' into 'bringers of mead' (Lionarons, 2005, pp.272-4).

LEADER OF THE WILD HUNT

In extant tales, one can sometimes recognize ancient gods demoted to devils and sorcerers or characters of little interest to a historian of religion. The folklore plot related to Wodan/Óðinn is that of the so-called wild hunt, or wild chase.

Liberman, *In Prayer and Laughter*

Relegation of ancient gods and supernatural figures to the margins of tradition – to folklore and fable – is a commonplace of cultural studies.

The 'Wild Hunt' is a generic name given to a host of supernatural riders who rush through the air on stormy nights with a pack of baying hounds before them. In Scandinavia, the leader of the Wild Hunt is often called *Oden* or the local variant of that name, while *Wode* is one German term for the huntsman (Kershaw, 2000, pp.20-4; Liberman, 2016, p.31, 33).[212] The etymon is reconstructed as *$w\bar{o}\eth u$-, a u-stem collective noun meaning 'band of ghosts, spirits, procession of the animated dead' or similar (Liberman, 2016, p.75). The sense development from *$w\bar{o}\eth u$- to ON *Óðr* and thence to *Óðinn* is difficult to follow. *Óðr* is mentioned (e.g., in *Gylfaginning*, v.34) as the name of the missing husband of Freyja, and already appears in an 11th c. verse by Einarr Skulason (Simek, 1993, s.v. *Óðr*; Libermann, 2016, pp.32-3). But the simple equation of this god with Óðinn raises more questions than it answers.[213]

The Hunt, as a collective, is not closely similar to the normal psychopomp role (e.g., Mercury or Charon) in any respect, though. The supernatural huntsmen often exist in this world and interact with the living; by the time of our most complete records, they do not reside in the Otherworld. It is likely that the ultimate origins of the stories of the Wild Hunt predate formal mythology entirely and relate to a period very early in man's development when the forces of nature were feared because of their perceived capacity for harm (disease, bad weather, bad luck), and were propitiated accordingly (Liberman, 2016, pp.31-3). These forces cannot be characterised as 'gods' since they do not have physical form, nor motives which humans could understand. They are abstract as well as collective in nature.

---

[212] Wode may be the huntsman deified, but this explanation cannot account for the complex figures of Woden, Godan and Óðinn.

[213] This would be on the principle that divine names may sometimes take more than one form, e.g., *Ullr* and *Ullinn*.

Over time, these supernatural forces were anthropomorphised, took on human forms and motivations, and came to be considered a multitude of entities following the example of a leader – the Wild Huntsman himself. This character could be identified with an important or impressive person drawn from history (e.g., Sir Francis Drake in England) as well as folktale figures such as Harlequin, but the association was always based on Wode, the personification of the band of ghosts (Kershaw, 2000, pp.30-4, 65-8).

The Hunt is constituted from the dead who ride in the air at great speed and furiously (and in this they resemble the valkyries, of course). In some traditions, the motivation is to catch unwary humans and carry them off to the Otherworld, while in others the riders are themselves pursued by a demonic figure (or even a demonic man-eating horse[214]) who tries to catch and devour them (Liberman, 2016, p.32, 45).

The riders of the *Wið Færstice* charm share some attributes with the Hunt – they are 'loud' (*hlude*), they launch their attacks while screaming or yelling (*gyllende garas sændan*) and they are armed (*seax, spere*). It was once considered plausible that Woden was originally a god of the wind, connected to the Vedic deity *Váta* 'the one who blows', associated with storms and the like (Liberman, 2016, pp.37-9, 44).[215] But the general trend in mythological studies away from explanations founded in the natural world has relegated this interpretation to the sidelines.

---

[214] Liberman (2016, p.62-3) suggests that the name of the fearsome horse was *Yggdrasill*, which later became associated with the World Tree; the second element of that name is *drasill* 'headstrong horse', subsequently renamed *Sleipnir* 'slippery one'.

[215] The Gothic verb **waian* 'to blow' is known, indicating that the root was in use among Germanic speakers. But *Váta* is not usually considered a god, rather a personification of the wind.

THE WARRIOR BROTHERHOOD

Tacitus's passage in *Germania* concerning the warbands of his day sum-
marises the nature of the military institution known today by the Latin
name *comitatus* or the German name *Gefolgschaft* (text from Anderson,
1997):

> Nihil autem neque publicae neque privatae rei, nisi armati agunt.
> Sed arma sumere non ante cuiquam moris, quam civitas
> suffecturum probaverit. Tum in ipso concilio, vel principum
> aliquis vel pater vel propinquus scuto frameaque juvenem ornant:
> haec apud illos toga, hic primus juventae honos: ante hoc domus
> pars videntur, mox reipublicae. Insignis nobilitas, aut magna
> patrum merita, principis dignationem etiam adolescentulis
> assignant: ceteris robustioribus ac jampridem probatis
> aggregantur; nec rubor, inter comites aspici. Gradus quin etiam
> et ipse comitatus habet judicio ejus, quem sectantur: magnaque
> et comitum aemulatio, quibus primus apud principem suum
> locus, et principum, cui plurimi et acerrimi comites. Haec
> dignitas, hae vires, magno semper electorum juvenum globo
> circumdari, in pace decus, in bello praesidium. Nec solum in sua
> gente cuique, sed apud finitimas quoque civitates id nomen, ea
> gloria est, si numero ac virtute comitatus emineat: expetuntur
> enim legationibus et muneribus ornantur et ipsa plerumque fama
> bella profligant.

> *Germania*, ch.13

'Neither public nor private business do they handle without
bearing weapons. But it is not the custom for anyone to bear arms
till his society has tested his skill with them. Then, at a meeting,
one of the leaders or the young man's father or some close kinsman
provides him with a shield and a spear; as the 'toga' is [with us],
this is the first honour for a youth, [because] until then he is seen
as [just] a member of the household, and afterwards as an adult.
The noble birth or great merit of the father secures rank for the
youths, and they attach themselves to elders of strength and

known courage. It is no shame to be seen amongst a band of fighters. Thus in the troop there are rankings according to the leader's judgement. The followers compete with each other as to who shall have first place with the leader, the leaders compete as to who has the largest and the bravest troop. It is an honour and a source of strength to be surrounded always with a body of chosen followers; it is an adornment in peace and a defence in war. It is the fame and splendour of a leader to be known for the number and strength of his followers not only among his own folk but also in the neighbouring tribes, since such a man is honoured by delegations, privileged with gifts, and the status of his fame often settles a war.'

Cum ventum in aciem, turpe principi virtute vinci, turpe comitatui, virtutem principis non adaequare. Jam vero infame in omnem vitam ac probrosum, superstitem principi suo ex acie recessisse. Illum defendere, tueri, sua quoque fortia facta gloriae ejus assignare, praecipuum sacramentum est. Principes pro victoria pugnant; comites pro principe. Si civitas, in qua orti sunt, longa pace et otio torpeat plerique nobilium adolescentium petunt ultro eas nationes, quae tum bellum aliquod gerunt; quia et ingrata genti quies, et facilius inter ancipitia clarescunt, magnumque comitatum non nisi vi belloque tuentur: exigunt enim principis sui liberalitate illum bellatorem equum, illam cruentam victricemque frameam. Nam epulae et, quanquam incompti, largi tamen apparatus pro stipendio cedunt: materia munificentiae per bella et raptus. Nec arare terram, aut expectare annum, tam facile persuaseris, quam vocare hostes et vulnera mereri. Pigrum quinimmo et iners videtur, sudore acquirere, quod possis sanguine parare.

Germania, ch.14

'Once engaged in a battle, it is a disgrace for the leader to be outshone in courage, and a disgrace for his followers not to match the courage of their chief. And it is a humiliation and a matter of lifelong blame to have outlived the leader [who died in battle] and returned from the battlefield. To defend and protect him, to ascribe one's own great deeds for his fame, is the greatest loyalty. The leader fights for victory, the men fight for their leader. If the tribe slumbers in long-lived peace, many of the noble youths willingly seek out those tribes which are waging war, both because inaction is hateful to their kind, and because they win fame more easily in danger. They cannot keep a large following except by violence and war; moreover, men look to the open-handedness of the leader for a war-horse and for a blood-stained and victorious spear. Feasting and entertainment are their only rewards which, though rough, are plentifully supplied; the source of this bounty is warfare and plunder. Nor can they be so easily persuaded to plough the earth and to wait for the year's crops as [they can] to call out an enemy and earn wounds. It is seen as tame and feeble to gain through sweat what can be won with blood.'

The crucial element in the relationships described by Tacitus is that of reciprocity between leader and followers. The leader surrounds himself with willing retainers (his *comitatus*) who protect and defend him and enforce his will. The retainers surrender their plunder to the leader and ascribe the glory of their brave deeds to him. In return, the leader ensures that their physical and other needs are met through housing, clothing and feasting them, and that a share of the tribute or plunder is distributed to them publicly in a show of grateful respect and honour commensurate with the sacrifices they have made (Green, 1998, pp.68-9).[216]

---

[216] The military application of the term *woþs* is connected by Kershaw (2000, p.71) with the antecedent of the Greek term *menos*, a quality which urges the warrior to act as the defender of his community; it is derived from the Olympian gods and fills the man and his weapons, so that all together are instruments of the gods. It is not a quality restricted to the simple dichotomy 'good/evil' but relates rather to proficiency with weapons and to danger.

The young men initially own nothing other than the clothes and weapons they bring with them, but if the leader is prudent and lucky, they stand to gain much in both wealth and social status from his success; all such warfare is little more than competition for resources, mainly livestock, women and thralls (Kershaw, 2000, pp.16-9). The system hinges on the integrity of both parties: leaders have to be honest and generous in their dealings with their followers, and the followers have to be bold and loyal to the leader.

Shared rites connected with eating and drinking characterised these groups, as well as protocols controlling who may speak and when, where each may sit in relation to the leader's seat, and so on. There were formal but negotiable rules regarding membership, leadership and behaviour. Since the young men were drawn from many different kinship groups and polities, probably speaking different languages, common standards had to be affirmed and maintained to prevent unnecessary friction. The collective term used for such youngsters is *geogoð* 'the youth', contrasted with the *duguð* or 'doughty elders'. The individual warrior may have been called a *hægsteald*, the owner or settler of a *hæg* or plot of land insufficient to support a family, which appears on the Kjølevik (Norway) runic inscription **hadulaikaz / ekhagustadaz** 'I am Hadulaikaz the bachelor' (Insley, 1991, p.326; Antonsen, 2002, p.204; Looijenga, 2003, p.344; Spurkland, 2005, p.43; Barnes, 2012, pp.180-3).

The purpose of the *comitatus* for the youngsters is to offer them opportunities for enrichment, to broaden their experience, to acquire fame and to prepare for life as an older man with the responsibilities of a household and territory. For the families from which they are drawn, the *comitatus* offers a means of tapping the excessive energy of their young men and putting it to good use, without having too many hormonal teenagers looking to prove themselves in pointless fights. The *comitatus* is one of the many types of male-only group known collectively as 'fraternal interest groups' or *Männerbunde*, which feature in the structure of many societies. The members form a closed set based on gender and age, which cut across the other dominant structure of Germanic society, the kindred.

EINHERJAR

The Einherjar are represented in a similar light in the verse, where they form the bodyguard of the war-god and his personal following of chosen warriors who will ride out to fight at his side in the last battle at the end of time (Lindow & Andrén, 2020, pp.909-10). The name – a collective plural – derives from *ein* + *heri* 'lone fighter' or 'uniquely good fighter' (Kershaw, 2000, pp.15-6, 19) and is evidently of great age since the singular *heri* is barely attested in any Germanic language:[217] it occurs in the plural describing 'raiding army', 'invasion forces' and the like (e.g., OE *here* '[attacking] army'). Óðinn was himself the personification of the 'leader of the *heri*', called in ON *Herjann*, an *Óðinsheiti*.

Their numbers are great, since Óðinn's hall has 540 doors and each can accommodate 800 men at a time according to *Grímnismál* v.23. In preparation for their last great test, these men indulge their martial appetites by fighting each other during the day, after which the dead are resurrected and they all sit together amiably at mealtime (*Vafþrúðnismál* v.41). *Gylfaginning* v.39 supplies further details concerning the magical provision of food and drink for these feasts. These elements have the feel of fanciful rationalisations and reworked scraps of tradition – a human warlord must have a sound economic base to support himself and his warband, but since Óðinn is a deity, such mundane matters can be brushed aside with tales of enchanted beasts who provide rivers of mead from their teats, and the like. None of this excess appears in *Vǫluspá*, where we hear only that (text from Dronke, 1997; cf. Kershaw, 2000, p.14):

Gól um ásom

Gullinkambi –

---

[217] Tacitus, *Germania* ch.43 mentions redoubtable warriors called *harii*, and the text on the Negau helmet is a dedication to a god called *Harigastiz*. The word has greater currency in personal names, e.g., OE Ælfhere, Wulfhere, etc. and ON Einarr, derived from **einheri*. The ON noun *einheri* appears once in *Lokasenna* v.60 meaning 'champion' and describing Þórr.

sá vekr hǫlða

at Heriafǫðrs –

'Gullinkambi [the cockerel] sang among the Æsir in order to wake the heroes at [the house] of the Father of Battle.'

The Einherjar appear to be uniquely Scandinavian realisation of the standard 'lord and followers' theme, given a major role in the story of the world's ending; the influence of the Wild Hunt may be suspected in this case. But the expectation that an accomplished warrior or leader could anticipate a martial afterlife is supported by poems such as *Hákonarmál* (plausibly mid-10th c. in date) in which the god's meadbenches are made ready to welcome the dead king.

The Einherjar have something of the status of 'sacred warriors' (German *Weihekrieger*) who are the favourites of Óðinn but there are other, better-attested fighters who fulfil that role: the *berserkir*.

BERSERKIR

The subject of the inspired berserk warriors is closely allied with that of the war-god who is their leader. Much of the background to these figures is murky but a few traits are common to the Norse tradition and some earlier accounts of frenzied warriors (Kershaw, 2000, pp.80-3; Samson, 2011). Tacitus's description of the warriors called *Harii* (*Germania*, ch.43) echoes something of the supernatural awe in which berserks were held including invulnerability to harm by fire or iron: in their case, by blackening their bodies and equipment and striking on the darkest nights in order to engender dread among their foes (Kershaw, 2000, pp.41-2).

Human *berserkir* are first mentioned by the poet Þorbjǫrn Hornklofi in a poem commemorating the battle of Hafrsfjǫrðr, fought in 872 AD, in which Harald Fairhair won a notable victory, in the phrase *grenioðo berserkir guðr var þeim a sinom emioðo úlfheðnar ok ísarn glumdo* 'the berserks roared, the battle was afoot, the wolfcoats howled and shook the irons' (Kershaw, 2000, p.44; Liberman, 2016, p.101). It is unclear from the context whether *berserkir* and *úlfheðnar* are to be re-garded as synonyms in apposition or as two separate (and potentially conflicting) sets of warriors. Snorri remarks in *Heimskringla* that *ber-serkergang* is a condition that comes upon warriors and makes them raving mad and impervious to the weapons of their foes. In *Hárbarðsljóð*, Þórr says that he has fought *brúðir berserkia* 'the brides of berserks', which appears from the context to mean 'troll-women' or something similar, implying a supernatural dimension for the term.

Notably, Harald Fairhair was himself a devotee of the war-god: in *Heimskringla*, Snorri tells us that Harald's amorous advances were rejected by a lady named Gyda who said that his landholding was too small and that he must conquer all Norway before she would consent to marry him. He then undertook a vow with these words (text from Aðalbjarnarson, 1979; cf. Kershaw, 2000):

'Þess strengi ek heit, ok því skýt til guðs, þess er mik skóp ok ǫllu ræðr, at aldri skal skera hár mitt né kamba, fyrr en ek hefi eignazk allan Nóreg með skǫttum ok skyldum ok forráði, en deyja at ǫðrum kosti.'

"This vow I make and to it I call witness the god who made me and rules all, that never shall I cut nor comb my hair before I have come to own all Norway with tribute and dues and rulership, or else die."

It took ten years for Harald – who was then known as *lúfu* 'shaggy' – to achieve his sworn aims, after which he bathed and trimmed his hair and received the new name *hárfagr* 'fair-hair'.[218] It seems that the denial of personal hygiene marked him out as 'consecrated' and thus under the god's protection, in the same way that *berserkir* were consecrated to him.

---

[218] Kershaw (2000, p.50-65) notes similar customs among the Greeks and in the coming-of-age ceremonies of many ancient European societies. The avenger of the slaying of Baldr – the enigmatic Váli – likewise must forego washing his hands or hair until his vengeance is taken (p.218).

The meaning of the word *berserkr* has been debated for more than a century, and ranges between two options: the *serkr* deutero-theme is transparently 'shirt, sark, tunic' and the prototheme *ber-* may be either (i) 'bare' (naked) or (ii) 'bear' (i.e., 'made from bear-skin')(Samson, 2011, pp.24-6). The role of ritual nudity in warrior-cults informs the first interpretation, while the Germanic (and older) bear-cult informs the second. Opinion is still divided as to the more likely meaning, although the parallel between 'wolf-coat' and 'bear-shirt' has often persuaded scholars that these are two categories of warrior inspired by cult animals, despite some reservations about the inadvisability of wearing a heavy fur garment in battle (Liberman, 2016, pp.105, 109-10). Needless to say, the advisability of wearing nothing at all seems even more questionable.

In legendary sagas, *berserkir* are the élite troops of various kings and warlords, demanding rich rewards for their service, but forming an effective and unstoppable military force and earning their pay in full. In the family saga literature, the *berserkr* has become the stock villain, a bully who uses threats and intimidation to take all he wants from a hapless farmer and his family – and is finally overpowered or outsmarted by a young visiting Icelander who thus wins the farmer's gratitude.[219] These berserks fear neither fire nor edged weapons, and are generally invulnerable to both, but can nevertheless be beaten with blunt-trauma weapons; they may also be overcome by Christian magic (Liberman, 2016, p.110). They apparently owe more to folktale than to myth, but are sufficiently well-evidenced in history to have been subject to outlawry in the 1012 AD lawcode of Jarl Eiríkr Hákonarson – it may even have been this change in legal status in Norway which caused them to disperse into Iceland and the North Atlantic colonies (Liberman, 2016, p.108). In Iceland they were subject to 'lesser outlawry' in the *Grágás* code.

---

[219] Liberman, 2016, pp.102-3; ibid, pp.108-9, he suggests that these plundering marauders may be closer in fact to the gangs of itinerant cut-throats of medieval society who made the lives of farmers and fishers almost unbearable.

Snorri (*Heimskringla*, ch.6) explained the *berserkergang* as the effect of a magic potion, from which remark the modern belief in hallucinogens (often fly agaric) as the stimulant for the berserk rage has often been accepted. The sagas do not mention drinks, mushrooms or other substances in relation to the berserks, who are presented as mere psychopaths who work themselves into a rage by their own will (Liberman, 2016, pp.108-9). Part of the berserk's preliminary performance included howling and biting the rim of his shield – displays of intimidating behaviour which would probably terrify anyone unfamiliar with them. Three of the carved ivory chessmen found on the Isle of Lewis are shown doing just this (Stratford, 1997).

The background to the Viking *berserkir* may indeed be found in the warrior traditions of an earlier age. Specifically, the *pressblech* dies from Torslunda, Öland, are relevant since one (denoted as 'D') depicts two human warriors, armed and advancing on foot, one wearing an animal-skin mantle which covers his body from the head to the knees and terminates in a tail at the rear (Samson, 2011, p.27; Pollington, 2011, p.380). Schjødt (2020e, p.577) remarks that the men described as *berserkir* in *Hrólfs saga Kráka* are elsewhere (e.g., *Skáldsaparmál*) called *kappar* 'champions, élite warriors' – the distinction is probably to be attributed to the opprobrium associated with *berserkir* in medieval texts.

It is likely enough that cultic societies were formed among the groups of young, landless men who formed the backbone of early military forces, for whom appropriate totems may have been the wolf, bear, eagle, raven or other symbolic beast. The war-gear of these warriors was often decorated with images of such animals. Whether these cult-groups actually formed the historical basis for the berserk-warriors of saga literature is debatable, but should not be dismissed from consideration. The historicity of such groups as the *Jómsvíkingar* is also highly dubious – if not entirely unfounded in the real world, they have at least been embellished into a 'Golden Age' society of blood-brothers.

Mythic *berserkir* are few: for example, four were present at the funeral of Baldr, where they failed to restrain the steed of Hyrokkin the giantess. They never form the bodyguard or servants of Óðinn, and generally seem unconnected with the war-god outside Snorri's statement in *Heimskringla* about *berserkergang*.

The dramatic or fanciful notion of the barely-human savage fighter has its place in the early history of warrior societies, as Tacitus describes them (*Germania*, ch.31; text from Anderson, 1997; cf. Kershaw, 2000; Rives, 1999, pp.90, 251-2):

> Omnium penes hos initia pugnarum, haec prima semper acies. Visu nova; nam ne in pace quidem vultu mitiore mansuescunt. Nulli domus aut ager aut aliqua cura; prout ad quemque venere, aluntur – prodigi alieni, contemptores sui – donec exsanguis senectus tam durae virtuti impares faciat.

> 'Every battle begins with them, they always form the front line. An alarming sight; nor do they appear milder even in peace. No house nor parcel of land nor property do they have, they are fed by whomever they may lodge with – they are wasteful with [their hosts'] property, scornful of their own – until [they are] weakened by old age and can no longer maintain such a harsh life.'

Much of this description would be applicable to the berserks of Norse legend, as well as to Starkaðr and some other favourites of the war-god.

The canine as a figurative warrior is surely founded in the notion of the *comitatus* or hearthtroop, whereby the warlord is the 'master of the house' and his followers are a pack of hounds or wolves who follow him, share his hall and his food and protect him when danger threatens.

CHAPTER 6

LORD OF INSPIRATION

> Enn Konr ungr
> kunni rúnar,
> ævinrúnar
> ok aldrrúnar.

'But Kon the Young knew the runes – everlasting runes and life-runes.'

Rígsþula, v.44

One interpretation of the name *Woden* is 'lord of inspiration'. As mentioned above, the *–en* is the Old English reflex of a suffix found in many Germanic languages meaning 'lord, leader, master', e.g., OE *þeoden* 'lord of a tribe (*þeod*)'; so also Gothic *kindins* 'leader of a family, adjudicator, judge', Norse *dróttin* 'lord of a warband' (Kershaw, 2000, pp.75-6). The lexical item on which the god's name is formed is the noun **wód-* with its derived adjective **wóda-* 'delirious, raving' found in Gothic *wods* 'possessed', ON *óðr* 'frantic, furious', OE *wōd* 'insane' as well as some obsolete words such as Dutch *woed* 'frantic, wild, crazy' and (early modern) English *wood* 'maddened, frantic' (Orel, 2003, s.v. *wóðanaz, wóðaz, wóðó*; Kroonen, 2013, s.v. *wóda*).

It is possible that Latin *vátes* 'prophet, seer' is a (Gallic) loanword, cognate with the plural term *ouateis* 'prophets' mentioned by Strabo as a class of Gallic priests who were adept in the study of nature (*Geographica*, ch.IV.4.4). Related is the Germanic root **wōþa, *wōþō* which gives rise to ON *óðr* 'mind; emotion, song; poetry' and OE *wōþ* 'song, voice; noise, music' as well as Gothic *woþeis* 'sweet, pleasing, charming', OE *wéðe* 'sweet, gentle' (Orel, 2003, s.v. *wóþjaz*). The group appears to be confined to the Germanic and Celtic language groups, assuming the Latin word is actually a loan. Koch

(2020, p.140) relates it to a shared Celto-Germanic theme *wātis 'inspired by a god'. The key indicator is that a person who is wōd is under the control of an exterior power, a deity (Kershaw, 2000, p.71).

The notion of a god whose spheres of influence include inspiration, intoxication, poetry, verbal dexterity, ecstasy and music is reminiscent of the Greek deity Dionysos who led groups of devoted revellers in binges of drinking alcohol and taking stimulants in order to help them experience 'the divine' (Mavromataki, 1997, pp.100-12). These associations with out-of-body experiences brought his worshippers into contact with prophecy (foretelling the future) and sorcery (influencing the future by magical means). Of course, the idea of 'the future' would have had a different meaning in pre-Christian Germanic society where there were only 'fixed' and 'fluid' outcomes (Bauschatz, 1982). Nevertheless, gaining information about the likely course of events was one of the principal goals of Óðinn. In *Yngligasaga*, Snorri records that (text from Aðalbjarnarson, 1979):

Óðinn kunni þá íþrótt, svá at mestr máttr fylgði, ok framði sjálfr, er seiðr heitir

'Óðinn knew the mightiest [magical] craft, which is called *seiðr*, and performed it himself.'

Despite the great *ergi* 'shame, humiliation, degradation' for males associated with this kind of magical activity, Óðinn became a master in it and indeed, seems to have gained strength rather than weakness in the process (Lindow, 2020a, p.506). He was taught its secrets by the foremost female deity – Freyja – with whom he shared half the men slain on the battlefield: thus the leader of the gods compromised his 'alpha-male' position by practicing a kind of magic which could only demean and dishonour him. The god's close relations with the feminine extended to the battlefield where his emissaries were not the masculine *Einherjar*, but the unworldly *valkyrjur* – female choosers of the slain. Here the war-god's interest extended beyond the male sphere of feasting and fighting into more traditionally feminine territory.

Óðinn's patronage of poets is well known, although the Norse tradition of poetry did not preclude violence and frenzy. Men such as Egil Skallagrímsson were feared and respected, and it was Óðinn's inspiration that manifested itself in the warrior's ability to compose extempore verses. Óðinn's gifting of the mead to men was at least a little ignominious: human poets benefit from the residue which the god failed to regurgitate accurately into the targeted vats.

Poetry was the means by which important information was encoded and stored – in pre-literate societies, such mnemonic devices are crucial for the accurate retrieval of details (Kershaw, 2000, pp.77-9). Germanic verse was rhythmic, based on a metrical line of four stressed syllables, but it used alliteration rather than end-rhyme as the mechanism which governed the choice of words. Verse constructed according to the ordering principles of the medium could be highly resistant to change; equally, when linguistic and social changes did affect the vocabulary it is often possible to detect their effects. Instances would include: the loss of *v-* from the word *vreiðr* 'angry, wrath' in the manuscript version of *Þrymskviða* (1.1) which is spelled *reiðr* but needs *v-* to complete the alliteration (Gordon, 1957, p.136 and p.241 note XII [1]): *Vreiðr vas þá Ving-Þórr es vaknaði* 'Ving-Þórr was angry when he awoke'; the spellings *Rum* for *Rom* (Rome) and *Eatule* for *Italia* (Italy) found in the *Exeter Book* poem *Widsith* (Neidorf, 2014, p.45 citing Malone, 1962) or *Hunferþ* for *Unferþ* in *Beowulf*, lines 499, 530, 1165, 1488 (Neidorf, 2017a).

POETIC INSPIRATION IN THE HALL

An early English instance of poetic inspiration may show that Woden was similarly regarded as having power over eloquence, music, verse-making and persuasive storytelling. Indeed, the tale has long been regarded as the earliest instance of English verse-making, concerning a man called Cædmon, who was a humble member of the

Christian religious community at Whitby (Yorkshire). The story appears in Bede's *Historia Ecclesiastica Gentis Anglorum* and is included above (p.154).

The events narrated by Bede would have happened around 685 AD (Orchard, 2003, p.99; Pollington, 2011, pp.22-5).[220] Given that Cædmon was not proficient as an original songsmith, the creation story he declaimed must have been put together from existing vocabulary, metaphors and imagery from then-current tradition. Cædmon was not a trained cleric or student, but a humble brother of the monastic community who shared in all the menial tasks including looking after the cattle. It therefore seems most likely that the phrasing he used in his verse was already traditional and common to the community in which he grew up. His verse was drawn from a body of existing ideas, from 'popular culture'; for later 7th c. Anglo-Saxon England, which means that it was composed from phrases known and used in heathen times. In other words, Cædmon's marvellous song of creation drew on long-standing heathen tradition with imagery and phrasing which were already part of the standard source material for such a subject. The retelling of the Christian story of creation is thus a paraphrase of heathen Anglian myths concerning the creation of the world (Pollington, 2011, p.25).

Several phrases in his 'hymn' suggest heathen cosmology: heaven as a roof, the world of men (two different expressions), the middle-yard. Cædmon could not escape his grounding in heathen thought and consciousness, and indeed he seems to have revelled in carefully choosing language from the old tales which would be consistent (or at least, not obviously in conflict) with Christian cosmogonic notions. His use of verse to frame his tale was appropriate, because poetic language was one of the means by which inspiration could be manifested. Verse was the medium in which such important matters were normally conveyed. Indeed, the Anglo-Saxons' own gods may be considered as 'poetic truths', meaning that they were culturally-

---

[220] Niles (2007, p.23-5) relates a traditional Scots tale which follows much the same pattern.

determined beings whose primary function was to make natural and social phenomena meaningful, and to allow their worshippers to approach them as individuals, developing interpersonal relationships of trust and dependence.

Poetry was the customary vehicle used to express these ideas, and the public performance of it was central to the social bonding structures which the Anglo-Saxons used to form and maintain their communities. It may be that the source of Cædmon's inspiration was found in the beer which he consumed. If so, his *gebeorscipe* with its convivial consumption and musical performance parallels the Swabians' festival preparations in which a beer-vat was set up in preparation for worship of the god *Vodan*.

THE WHISPERING GOD

The vehicle for the inspiration which Woden lent to his followers was his *rúnó 'whisper, secret knowledge', a word or idea shared by means of an implanted thought, a sudden flash of insight, a 'divine inspiration' (Koch, 2020, p.137, s.v. *rūn*). It is likely that this inspiration was understood as the god's whispering of a powerful word into his follower's ear to provoke sudden understanding. The source of this whisper must have been the god himself, mediated through the ravens which accompanied and obeyed him.[221] Ravens are well known for their ability to mimic the human voice.

Wulf (1994, p.32) sees the avian image as a specifically Scandinavian phenomenon and states 'on the Continent and in England Wodan has nothing to do with the raven' which ignores a good deal of iconographic evidence for pairs of birds as icons outside their later Viking-age appearances: the 7th c. helmet from Sutton Hoo Mound

---

[221] Antonsen (2002, pp.192-4) rejects the runic texts at Noleby and Vånga (Gotland) as evidence for an early Scandinavian hawk-cult, since the forms **hakuþo** and **haukoþuz** cannot be derived from PGmc **habuk-* 'hawk'. This does not invalidate the archaeological and iconographic evidence for the importance of birds of prey in the cult of the war-god.

1 depicts a pair of sword-wielding warriors dressed in caps with crescentic horns above, each horn ending in a bird's head (Pollington, 2011, pp.416-7). [222] Similar imagery is found on the Torslunda (Sweden) *pressblech* die (D), the belt-buckle from Finglesham (Kent), *pressblech* plates from Valsgärde (Sweden) mound 8, the Caenby (Lincolnshire) *pressblech* foil, and a number of small amuletic figurines and pendants of 6th-7th c. date (Pollington, 2011, pp.137-44). These figures all have headgear with birds' heads attached.

An alternative icon is the facing mask of a bearded male with a bird on each shoulder, found in several locations in southern England and on the North Sea coast, on attachment fittings for a sword's chape (Pollington, 2011, p.199 and fig.22; cf. Menghin, 1983, p.154 item 91). The facing 'mask' was used to embody the tribal ancestors in ritual and ceremonial performances, where their presence was necessary for the completion of rites honouring the dead (Kershaw, 2000, p.26). This evidence, taken together, amounts to a good case for two birds' heads in association with a protective (probably amuletic) male mask.

QUEST FOR KNOWLEDGE

Óðinn had five principal means of gaining information: (i) his position on the *hásæti* 'high-seat' in Ásgarð which allowed him to survey the Nine Worlds; (ii) his two ravens, *Huginn* and *Muninn*; (iii) the gaining of the runes; (iv) the situation of his eye in Mímir's well; (v) access to Mímir's severed head. We shall consider these in turn.

---

[222] The substance of Wulf's rejection is the length of time between the 4th c. text **harabanaz** from Järsberg and the 13th c. Icelandic sources which call Óðinn *Hrafnáss* 'raven-god'. There is, of course, considerable evidence for a range of raven images from Anglo-Saxon England and the Merovingian Frankish lands in the form of brooches and other items, bridging the chronological gap between the 4th and 13th centuries.

HLIÐSKALF

The high-seat reflects the position of a mortal *drihten* in his own meadhall. It is an elevated position, and from this seat the whole gathering and its activities can be viewed (Herschend, 2009; Pollington, 2003, pp.83-5; Pollington, 2010, p.184). The *hásæti* is an extension of the lord's seat into the realm of the gods where the scope of the lord's view is at its widest. This seat is called *hliðskjálf* and is mentioned in several sources (*Grímnismál*, *Gylfaginning*, *Skírnismál*) but in *Gylfaginning* the name appears to refer to the entire hall or dwelling of Óðinn and in the *Prose Edda* it is also called *Valaskjálf*. In *Grímnismál*, both Óðinn and Frigg are both looking out from the seat when they see the fates of their protégés Agnar and Geirrøðr, suggesting that *hliðskjálf* was a raised dais with a bench, rather than the chair itself.

The high-seat was a position of power and advantage but it could be a perilous place: when Freyr assumed the seat, he saw the giantess Gerð and instantly fell in love with her, which led to his surrendering his sword as part of the marriage settlement, and ultimately to his inability to defend himself when the last battle took place.

HUGINN AND MUNINN

In *Grímnismál*, Grímnir explains that the god receives his knowledge of events from his two ravens, Huginn and Muninn, which fly out each morning and report to him at the evening meal (text from Dronke, 2011):

> Huginn oc Muninn
>
> fliúga hverian dag
>
> iǫrmungrund yfir.
>
> Óumk ek of Hugin,
>
> at hann aptr né komit,
>
> þó siámk meirr um Munin.

'Every day Huginn and Muninn fly over the wide earth; I fear for Huginn (thought) lest he should never come back, though I fear more for Muninn (memory).'

Similar information appears in *Gylfaginning*. In *Skáldskaparmál*, both names occur: Muninn as a poetic word for 'raven' and Huginn as part of a kenning for carrion. In the Old Norse *Third Grammatical Treatise*, the birds are associated with hanged men and slain warriors.

These two creatures are clearly intended to be personifications of mental processes, and their names appear to be traditional (Hermann, 2020, p.57). *Huginn* means 'thought' from the ON verb *hyggja* 'think', *hugga* 'comfort' (Orel, 2003, s.v. *xu3janan* 'think' and *xu3iz, xu3uz* 'mind, understanding'; Kroonen, 2013, s.v. *hugi*). *Muninn* means 'memory' from the verb *muna* 'remember, recall' (Orel, 2003, s.v. *mana*; Kroonen, 2013, s.v. *muna* 'recall', *mundi* 'memory', *mainan* 'mean, intend').[223] Their respective functions derive from the two-tense verbal structure of the Germanic language group in which the verbal state or activity is conceived in a binary opposition: past/non-past (Bauschatz, 1982). Whatever is marked as 'past' is fixed, static, an event; whatever is non-past is fluid, evolving, a process. Thus Huginn denotes 'thought', the active aspect – planning for today and tomorrow, while Muninn denotes 'recollection' or thought in and about the past. Both processes are necessary for a successful leader who uses his knowledge of history and the precedents it offers to shape his active planning in the here-and-now.

Norse poetry almost confines raven references to Óðinn and the valkyries (Grundy, 2014, p.25), and other birds of prey are largely excluded although *arnhǫfði* 'eagle-headed [one]' is used as an *Óðin-sheiti* in *Óðins nǫfn*. An association with carrion and violent death is implied.

Predecessors of these two birds are present in pre-Christian Germanic art in Scandinavia, the North Sea rim and Britain (Pollington,

---

[223] This Germanic preterite-present verb is related more widely to Sanskrit *mányate* 'to think', Greek μέμονα 'to think intensively', Latin *meminī* 'to think of, to remember'. MnE 'mind' is from the same verbal root.

2011, pp.198-9; Hilgner, 2015, fig.7). An example is the type of scabbard chape featuring a facing male mask flanked by birds. Such items are found mainly in southern England and the Netherlands, dating to the mid-5th to mid-6th c.

The relations between birds and humans, and the specifics of the use of birds in cremation funeral rites in the Viking period in Denmark and Norway has been studied by Klaudia Karpińska (Karpińska, 2023). Only a few species were chosen to be sacrificed, and they were used both during the main ceremony and during the cremation process, but they do not appear to have been treated as a food-offering (in the way that cattle had been). Perhaps they were included because of their monetary value (since trained birds were valuable) or used as offerings with symbolic meanings (speed, strength, keen sight, etc.). They may even have provided protection for the dead person during the journey to the Otherworld.

Fig. 25 Scabbard chape with mask and flanking birds, from Micheldever, Hampshire. (PAS ref. HAMP-4CBF82)

GERI AND FREKI

These are the names of two wolves associated with the god in *Grímnismál* verse 19 where the Herjafoðr 'father of armies' feeds them – implicitly by causing strife so that they can gorge on the corpses which it produces; however, since Óðinn subsists on wine alone, the wolf-hounds may perhaps have been envisioned as receiving food from their master's table. Both these names appear in verse as synonyms for 'wolf' (Grundy, 2014, pp.34-5); Geri is 'greedy' and Freki 'bold, fierce, dangerous' (the cognate OE *freca* is a synonym for 'warrior' in the sense of 'a daring, dangerous man').

Huge supernatural hounds are often associated with the Wild Hunt, and it may be that Geri and Freki were thought to recall this tradition as companions of the Erlking on his night-time riding. Hounds were always essential for any hunt where their ability to follow a trail invisible to humans made them invaluable. They are also a useful metaphor for death, since the devouring spirit strips flesh from the bone in the manner of a gnawing dog (Grundy, 2014, pp.38-9).

GAINING THE RUNES ON THE WORLD TREE

No Anglo-Saxon tradition survives of Woden winning the runes as Óðinn did, but the *OE Rune Poem's* verse for the fourth rune hints darkly at such an association. There is also the unusual exchange recorded in *The Dialogue of Solomon and Saturn*, where 'Mercurius the giant' is stated to be the inventor of writing (Anlezark, 2009; Pollington, 2011, p.471).

In Scandinavian tradition, Óðinn won the runes while enduring nine nights of pain hanging on the tree *Yggdrasil*. Gaining the runes offered the god access to secrets, charms and abilities, some of which are listed in the *Hávamál* verses called *Rúnatal* dealing with the various spells Óðinn knew and their effects; this tale is told allusively and only in this one text (Kozák, 2021). There is no strong evidence for a similar close association between Woden and the runes in Continental Germanic communities, nor in England. Literacy was the secret of a restricted élite group, passed on in the Iron Age as part of the initiation of leaders (Rausing, 1995; Pollington, 2016, pp.251-80; Birkett, 2019, p.155). A knowledge of writing may have had

greater impact on societies in Scandinavia where no previous de-
motic literacy tradition existed, while in other parts of northwest
Europe there was greater familiarity with the idea of script.

The place where the runes were won is remarkable: Yggdrasill
is the name of the central vertical axis which connects the various
worlds under the vault of the heavens. The notion of the 'World
Tree' or *axis mundi* is found widely across Eurasia. It survived into
the Christian period under a new guise – Calvary. That this should
be considered the most appropriate location for the gaining of arcane
and supernatural knowledge is not surprising. The Vedic term *yupa*
denotes such a post set up in the sacred area, which symbolizes both
the thunderbolt and the god Indra, who deals with protection of the
community (Birkett, 2019, p.157).[224] The post denotes the sacred
vertical boundary, but not the horizontal. It is, therefore, a *columna
mundi*, a post supporting the sky, and the worshipper who climbs to
the top of the column symbolically takes possession of all he can see
from that vantage point (Woodard, 2006, p.259ff).

The mythic background to the rune-gaining story is also interesting. *Yggdrasill* means 'terrible, frightening steed' and probably
referred originally to the gallows; if so, it may have been on such a
post that the predecessor deity to Óðinn (Woden, or another such
initiatory god) suffered in order to gain knowledge (Tolley, 2009,
pp.358-9; Kay, 2013, p.20; Birkett, 2019, p.155).[225] But vital and
culturally transformative knowledge must be acquired in a place outside space and time – at the very centre of the universe. The role of
Yggdrasill is therefore of central importance in the tale, since the
tree is the support of the heavens and the pivot around which they
revolve.

---

[224] Indra and Þórr share many mythic features and clearly derive from a common fund of myths and tales. Cf. Tolley, 2009, pp.287-8.

[225] The name *askr yggdrasils* does not mean 'the ash-tree called Yggdrasil' but
rather the 'ash-tree of the terrifying walker', i.e., Óðinn. Simek (2004, p.93)
dismisses the evidence for the great tree as the *axis mundi*, finding no such
allegorical thinking in Germanic religion.

The question posed by this episode is: if Óðinn seized the runes in his trance state, then they must have already existed – so who created them before the god won them? The answer appears to be that they were 'of divine origin' – *raginkunnr* as *Hávamál* specifies. The god grasped and ripped them from an external source – the Otherworld – and subjected them to his will (Birkett, 2019, p.157).

A 12th c. carved stave from Lödöse bears a sequence of runes interpreted as comprising 3 *þurs*-runes, 6 *ás*-runes and 6 *nauð*-runes – a composition of 'giant', 'god' and 'corpse'. It may be that such a use of the *nied* rune is referred to in the *Hávamál* verse where Óðinn claims to be able to converse with the dead.

The god sacrificed on the World Tree has been likened to a shaman undergoing the transformative psychological processes which will afford him mastery of the spirit-world (Liberman, 2016, pp.69-75). As with Christian, Hindu and other ascetics practising severe degrees of self-denial and resistance to suffering and pain, the experience was supposed to transform the individual and provide a degree of spiritual authority (Kvilhaug, 2004, pp.32-3).

The Indic *yupa* column mentioned above finds a parallel in the oak tree belonging to the thunder god, in western and northern Europe often called 'Jupiter's oak' (*robur iovis*) in the literature; the post and the tree are seemingly interchangeable in these tales (Tolley, 1995a; cf. Hooke, 2010, pp.4-5). The Old Saxon term for this pillar or post was *Hirminsuul* (or *Irminsul*)(North, 1997, p.51). The element *irmin*- means 'vast, great' while *sul* is a word for a 'column' or 'post' (Pollington, 2011, p.224). The name Irminsul is used to gloss *colossus* and other such terms; in later tradition, it became a common name for an obelisk (Tolley, 2009, p.277). The Pillars of Hercules are named *Ercoles syla* 'Hercules's posts' in Ælfred's translation of Orosius, where *syla* is the plural of *syl*, the OE cognate of OS *sul*.

Tolley (1995a; 2009, p.279) cites Hertlein's work on Germanic house structures and their cosmological influences. In the *Lex Baiuvariorum* the main supporting post of a house is called a *firstsul* 'roof-post' and in Notker's *Boethius* the column which sustains the heavens is called *magansul* 'strength-column'. The great pillar of Germanic worship was described in the 9th c by Rudolf of Fulda, who says (cf. Branston, 1957, p.176; Tolley, 1995a; text from West, 2007, p.346):

> Truncum quoque lignis non parvae magnitudinis in altum erectum sub divo colebant, patria eum lingua irminsul apellantes, quod latine dicitur universalis columna quasi sustinens omnia.

> 'They raised a trunk on high beneath the sky – although of wood, of no small size – called in the language of that country *Irminsul*, which in Latin is called 'universal column' as if it were sustaining everything.'

This 'column which sustains everything' has an obvious reference in the Norse *askr yggdrasils* which is also a support for the universe and for all life; it shelters the first human pair when the earth is engulfed by floods (Bauschatz, 1982; Tolley, 2009, pp.344-5). The column was said by Widukind of Corvey in *Res Gestae Saxonicae* 1.12 to be worshipped while facing to the east, and an eagle image was set up to the east of the pillar, i.e., beyond and behind it (Tolley, 2009, p.277; text from Waitz, 1839):

> Mane autem facto ad orientalem portam ponunt aquilam, aramque victoriae construentes secundum errorem paternum sacra sua propria veneratione venerati sunt; nomine Martem, effigie columpnarum imitantes Herculem, loco Solem, quen Graseci appellant Apollinem. Ex hoc apparet aestimationem illorum utcumque probabilem, qui Saxones orignem duxisse putant de Graecis, quia Hirmin vel Hermis Graece Mars discitur; quo caocabulo ad laudem vel ad vituperationem usque hodie etiam igorantes utimur.

> 'Morning having come, they place an eagle at the eastern gate and, building an altar to victory, they worship their own holy [objects] with appropriate reverence, following the folly of their forebears; they copy Mars in its name [and] Hercules in its shape of a column [and] the sun in its placement, whom the Greeks call Apollo. From this it seems that the opinion is probably true

of those who trace the origin of the Saxons to the Greeks, since *Hirmin* or *Hermes* is the name of Mars in Greek; we use this word today in praising or cursing, in our ignorance.'

WODEN AND THE OS RUNE

In the development of a phonemically relevant runic script, additional runes were created between the 4th and 6th c. in the region of the southern North Sea in line with linguistic changes. Three of the four new 'Anglo-Frisian' runes have names based on trees: ᚪ *ac* 'oak', ᚫ *æsc* 'ash', ᚣ *yr* 'yew-bow' while the fourth ᛠ *ear* may mean either 'grave' or 'sea' (Halsall, 1981).

The fourth rune in the standard fuþorc sequence, *os*, retained the name and meaning of the Elder Fuþark rune **ansuz* but adopted the new shape ᚩ. Likewise in Anglo-Saxon tradition, the name of the third rune ᚦ was changed from the original *þyrs* 'malevolent being' to *þorn* 'thorn', another term based on vegetation. The use of tree-names for the new runes derived from **ansuz* may appear odd given that, among the Elder Fuþark runes, only **eihwaz* 'yew' and **berkano* 'birch' specifically referred to trees. What may have inspired the Angles and Frisians to create new rune-names based on tree-names? It is possible that the answer to this riddle lies in the multiple meanings of the word **ansuz* itself. Aside from referring to 'a god', the word could also mean 'post, beam, stake, pole': these were the physical objects of veneration used by speakers of Germanic languages (Pollington, 2011, pp.86-7). Examples of these carved poles have been found archaeologically, e.g., the Broddebjerg god and the Braak posts (Pollington, 2011, p.101, 122). The physical expression of worship included the veneration and adornment of posts or stakes, whether free-standing examples placed prominently in the landscape, the load-bearing beams of the hall or the supporting pillars of the high-seat (Pollington, 2011, pp.118-

9).[226] The rune-name *ansuz* therefore encompassed the meaning 'wooden post carved into the likeness of a god' – and the new runes derived from it took names which reflected this facet of the word's meaning. (This process is paralleled with the adoption of the rune Þ into Anglo-Saxon bookhand.)

The significance of the name *ear* is less easy to pin down. The Bosworth & Toller dictionary offers several meanings: (i) the ocean (also spelt *ær*) with compounds *eargebland* 'the mingling of the waves, the surging sea' and *eargrund* 'the sea-bottom'; (ii) an ear [of corn]; (iii) the ground, and specifically the grave (based on the evidence of the *OE Rune Poem*). The only obvious link to vegetation here is meaning (ii). The poem's verse concerning this rune is very negative in its presentation, mentioning the cooling of the corpse (*hraw colian*) and the falling of a crop of fruit (*bleda gedreosaþ*).[227] It might be argued that in this verse we have an oblique reference to the preparation of a meal with the slaughter of an animal (*hraw*, the corpse) and the gathering of fallen fruit (*bled*, fruit), and that the whole verse is connected in some ill-defined way to rebirth and regeneration, consuming the substance of beasts and crops in order to continue life. But this does not explain why the new rune was given the name *ear* nor why the tone of the verse is so gloomy.

It is worth mentioning in this context that *bleda gedreosaþ* is not so straightforward an expression as it at first appears. The word *blæd*, *bled* has several overlapping meanings according to Bosworth & Toller: (i) a leaf, blade [of grass]; (ii) a cup, goblet; (iiia) a blast, act of blowing, breath; (iiib) prosperity, success, glory, honour, abundance; (iv) flower, blossom, fruit. The verb *gedreosan* can be taken as a perfective (with *ge-* prefix) of *dreosan* with the meanings 'rush', 'perish' and 'fall'; the Gothic cognate *driusan* just means 'fall' and that appears

---

[226] Here might be included the description of the veneration of posts by the Scandinavian Rus on the Volga in the account of Ibn Fadlan (Tolley, 2009, p.82-5; Lunde & Stone, 2012, p.47-8).

[227] Polomé (1991, p.429) notes that *ear* is an ancient word for 'mud', 'clay' with cognates in Norse *aurr* 'clay' and Gothic *aurahjons* 'tombs', suggesting an association with the type of soil selected for the burial of men.

to be the main sense from which the others developed. Thus *bleda gedreosaþ* has many shades of meaning which would include 'leaves (sense i) fall', 'fruits (sense iv) fall (from a tree)' and 'triumphs (sense iiib) pass away'. If *ear* is understood as 'the grave' then the senses might be restricted to 'the breath of life (sense iiia) fails' as well as 'successes (sense iiib) cease'. In common with much OE verse, the multiple meanings of the chosen words and the ambiguous phrasing allow – or invite, or require – very nuanced interpretations of even such a short passage.

ÓÐINN'S 'MISSING' EYE

The god is usually said to have just one eye, and indeed this characteristic almost defines his physical appearance. The single eye is a consistent feature which does not change when a disguise is adopted – this is why the god wears a large hat (*síðhǫttr*) to make his identity less obvious to men. Yet the depiction of the god in *Ynglinga saga* does not mention the defect; in Chapter 6 it specifically says:

> Hann var svá fagr ok gǫfugligr álitum, þá er hann sat með sínum vinum, at ǫllum hló hugr við. En þá er hann var í her, þá sýndisk hann grimligr sínum óvinum.

> 'He was so fair and so dignified in appearance when he sat among his own friends that it was a joy to all, but when he was in warlike mood he then seemed fearsome to his enemies.'

Saxo likewise portrays Othinus as a king and counsellor but does not mention any specific physical attributes. Perhaps less striking (but no less important) is the lack of any instance of a missing eye in, for example, the Anglo-Saxon images of Woden in manuscript genealogies, and also in the Langobard traditions regarding Godan.

It seems that the motif of the single eye is a development arising from just some of the tales associated with him. In other words, he starts out as a handsome divine youth and at some point undergoes a transformation which results in the loss – or better, displacement – of one of his eyes. The statue of Wodan standing in the temple at

Uppsala as described by Adam of Bremen (text from Waitz, 1876; cf. Kershaw, 2000, p.6) is telling: *Wodanem vero sculpunt armatum sicut nostri Martem solent* 'they depict Wodan as armed, just as our [artists] usually do Mars'. Indeed, in Saxo's and Snorri's works, the one-eyed feature appears *only* when the god is interacting with mankind, while in his celestial life he is 'fair and dignified' (Kershaw, 2000, p.6). This, I think, is the key to understanding the iconography of the god: the one-eyed feature is dependent on the context. Among the gods he appears in a resplendent guise, while he presents himself to humanity in a rather humble and disfigured form.

The 'missing' eye of the god is not easy to understand if it is assumed to be a lack, a disability, a shortfall from the full range of attributes. Yet the power of the god's eye is not negated by its removal, but rather enhanced (Liberman, 2016, p.82; Birkett, 2019, p.156).

One of the bynames of Óðinn is ON *Hár*, usually interpreted as 'the high one' (Orel, 2003, s.v. *xauxaz*; Kroonen, 2013, s.v.*hauha*) as in *Hávamál* 'high one's speech' but the same surface form may also derive from the PGmc adjective **haihaz* 'one-eyed', cognate with Latin *caecus* 'one-eyed, half-blind' and Sanskrit *kekera-* 'squinting' (Orel, 2003, s.v. *xaixaz*; Kroonen, 2013, s.v. **haiha*).[228] The notion that the god's vision is impaired stands behind the *heiti* Blindr, Bileygr and the like (Kershaw, 2000, p.3) This physical peculiarity is one of a series of divine 'impairments' including Hǫðr's blindness and Tyr's missing hand (Lincoln, 1991, pp.246-7; Birkett, 2019, pp.156-7). Just as Óðinn enjoys keen insight despite his lack of an eye, so Heimdallr has 'lost' his *hljóð*, his ear or his hearing but is able to hear the grass growing and can sound the great horn *gjallarhorn* (Birkett, 2019, p.156). A physical loss accompanies a corresponding physical enhancement: perhaps Tyr's surrender of a hand thus relates to his physical strength and military power?

---

[228] See Liberman (2016, p.206-7) for the association of one-eyed Óðinn with blind Hǫðr.

This lack should be seen in the context of Heimdallr's *hljóð* (hearing) which also resides in Yggdrasill, and Þórr's stern stare and sharp-sighted eyes. Þórr's fierce gaze was enough to terrify the giant Þrymr in *Þrymskviða* when he stole the god's hammer and demanded the hand of Freyja in marriage in exchange for it – Þórr dressed in a bridal gown to trick the giant, who lifted the bride's veil and asked: '*Hví eru ondótt augu Freyju? Þykki mér ór augum eldr of brenna*' 'Why are Freyja's eyes fearsome? It seems to me a fire blazes from her eyes' (Gordon, 1957, p.140).

Keen sight is another of the attributes of Heimdallr, whose hearing is also of supernatural acuity – perhaps the placing of his *hljóð* in the World Tree affords him access to all the sounds in the Nine Worlds. Heimdallr is associated strongly with the regulation and structure of human societies, initiation and the passing on of secret wisdom (Pollington, 2016, p.236).[229] Óðinn's eye, likewise, placed in the well at the root of Yggdrasill, was sited at the centre of the Nine Worlds and able to see all of them from this position.

Despite having just one eye when interacting with humans, there is no suggestion in the myths that the god was compromised by this defect (Kershaw, 2000, p.5). In fact, he showed an acuity beyond that of his fellow deities. From his high-seat, *Hliðskjálfr*, he could see over all he worlds – he even saw where Loki ran to hide after he had caused the death of Baldr.

An illuminating exception exists among the Æsir to the general rule that gods with a lack or disability in one area have a corresponding superability in another. The god Hǫðr, despite his blindness, appears to have no compensatory special strength; indeed the god is known almost exclusively from the tale of Baldr whose death at Hǫðr's hands induces the great battle at the end of the world. His only achievement is the unintentional killing of his beloved

---

[229] Liberman (2016, p.92) discusses but rejects any parallel between Heimdallr and Víðarr, the son of Óðinn who avenged his death.

brother.[230] Fratricide is *niðingsverk* 'an unmanly and dishonourable deed' and Hǫðr is evidently guilty of such inappropriate behaviour: Snorri uses the pretext of the god's blindness as a means of exculpation. Hǫðr's action renders him unworthy to stand with the Æsir, until the brothers are reunited after Ragnarǫk. In direct contrast to Snorri's tale, in *Gesta Danorum* Saxo treats the corresponding characters, Balderus and Hotherus, as mortal princes who contend for the hand of a maiden, Nanna.

The one-eyed attribute has been a tempting explanatory device, but often a misleading one. An early attempt at interpreting the Möjbro runestone's retrograde text **frawaradaz / ana hahai slagina / z** tried to force the reading *ana haha is (s)laginaz* 'Ane the one-eyed is slain' but this has been refuted by the linguistic difficulties and is more usually read *frawaradaz ana haŋhe slaginaz* 'Frawaradaz slain on [his] stallion' which matches the accompanying image of a sword-wielding warrior on his horse (Antonsen, 2002, p.13, 194; Looijenga, 2003, p.333). A one-eyed mounted warrior – an appealing image in the light of the Woden cult – proved not to be supported by better readings of the runic text.

The body's outer, physical form was considered a guide to inner, mental qualities. Having full control of oneself was not just admirable, but necessary to be a successful leader. In *Egils saga*, Egill and his followers were guests at a hall where the host served them very strong drink which they were obliged to consume, since to refuse it would be to offer a gross insult to the host and an admission of unmanliness on the part of the guests (Lassen, 2000, p.222). Egill's men grew drunk on the brew and eventually began to vomit so Egill, as their leader, was obliged to finish their drinks himself in order to save face. In the morning, he took his revenge on the host – he set about him while he was still in bed, cut off his beard and gouged out one of his eyes – a symbolic 'castration' or emasculation which

---

[230] Lassen (2000, p.223) notes the early attempts to link the blind god who accidentally kills Baldur to medieval traditions concerning the blind legionary, Longinus, and his piercing of the body of the crucified Christ with a spear.

countered the host's attempt to demean Egill's masculinity (Dronke, 1996, VIII, pp.56-7).

The loss of a physical or mental faculty could render a person ineligible for rule – there are echoes of this in the Irish tale of Nuada, the one-time king who lost an arm and the throne in the same fight (the First Battle of Mag Tuired), and in medieval legal injunctions against the *rex inutilis* 'ineffectual king' (Lincoln, 1991, p.249). In the tale of Offa of Angeln, as recounted by Saxo Grammaticus, Uffo (Offa) undertook the challenge of a duel on behalf of his blind father, because King Vermundus (OE Wærmund) had lost his sight through old age; his son's previous slackness had excluded him from leadership.

Blinding, maiming and gelding were traditional means of dealing with surplus (Anglo-Saxon and Scandinavian) royals whose threat to the incumbent had to be nullified – after such treatment, the victim would never be fit to rule (Lassen, 2000, p.221). Candidacy for kingship included full command of one's physical abilities and sexual power; blinding and gelding an enemy rendered him unfit for the role of leader or ruler. Yet Óðinn was not merely eligible to rule, he was in many respects the paragon of leadership, despite his physical disability. This paradox touches at the heart of the god's power which transgresses all boundaries – active/passive, male/female and living/dead.

ÓÐINN'S PLEDGE

The absence of the eye resulted from the god's quest for wisdom. The eye was offered to Mímir in exchange for a mind-expanding drink. It is called *veðr Valfǫðrs* the 'pledge of the father of the slain' (*Vǫluspá*, v.28). A *veðr* 'pledge' is a token of good faith in relation to an agreement or contract, and Óðinn's pledged eye was central to his power. In surrendering an eye – a symbol of his masculinity and fitness to rule – the god became partly emasculated, rendered partly non-masculine and thus perhaps given access to the Vanirs' powers of chthonic magic. Óðinn then symbolically united masculine and feminine aspects, the earth and the sky, the Vanir and the Æsir, and thus achieved greater wisdom and understanding than any other (Hermann, 2020, pp.58-9).

The 'missing' eye resided in the well where it saw all that happened in creation – but it was passive, an observer. Óðinn's remaining eye was active and especially powerful as his various nicknames attest: *Báleygr* 'flaming-eye', for example, expresses his ability to terrify enemies with his glance, to stop weapons in flight, to blind his opponents (Kershaw, 2000, p.5; Woodard, 2013, p.171, pp.181-99). Perhaps the god retained his active/masculine eye with which he preserved the role of leader, while the passive/feminine eye kept watch from the depths of the well. The 'debilitating gaze' of the god is a theme known from Iranian and Indic mythology with parallels in Italic and Celtic tradition (Woodard, 2013, pp.166-76).

The pairing of a god or hero with one eye and another with one hand is quite rare, and the meaning of the tradition has been examined by students of comparative mythology. A one-eyed hero who saves his people from enemy assault appears in the early Roman histories: Horatius Cocles (one-eyed) holds off alone an Etruscan attack over the Tiber; Mucius Scaevola tells the Etruscan king, Porsenna, that he is one of a large group of assassins sworn to take the king's life, and convinces him by thrusting his hand into a fire in support of this false oath. The parallels with Óðinn and Týr are obvious. They represent, in Lincoln's words (1991, pp.246-7)

> 'two complementary sides of sovereignty … (1) magic, as represented by a one-eyed visionary god able, *inter alia*, to render his enemies' weapons ineffective, and (2) legal, as represented by a one-handed deity given to absolute, if occasionally deceptive fidelity to the demands of oaths, pledges, contracts and the like.'

In this respect, Óðinn's eye is a token of good faith in the same way that Týr's hand was offered as surety for the honesty of the gods; in the latter case, it was a pledge given in utmost bad faith (Kershaw, 2000, pp.272-4). Both Óðinn's eye and Heimdallr's *Gjallarhorn* are said to remain in *Mímis brunnr* 'Mímir's well or stream'. Possibly, originally the eye itself was the source of water, the spring from which this stream rose up.

Fig. 26 Scabbard mount from Chessel Down, Isle of Wight. The central motif on the lower edge is a single 'eye'. © Trustees of the British Museum

JULIUS CIVILIS

Perhaps the most illuminating instance of a one-eyed leader in the Germanic world is the character known as Julius Civilis, the nobleman who incited the Batavian Rebellion of 69 AD. It has been suggested that some details of the cult of Woden can be traced directly to Civilis himself, who used existing traditions regarding a war-god figure to support and legitimatise his rise to power (Enright, 1994, p.217; Kershaw, 2000, pp.46-7).[231] The implication is that Civilis instituted a new form of military service based not on the tribal or family structure, but rather on the warlord as absolute ruler of a group of young men whose principal allegiances and loyalties were to each other and to the leader – this is the very heart of the 'warband tradition' (Latin *comitatus*, OE *gedriht*, *werod*, etc.) which drew on the ambitions of youngsters of various backgrounds and cut across previous ties of kindred and friendship (Kershaw, 2000,

---

[231] Enright implies that the god's cult was promoted deliberately in the Rhineland, drawing on a familiar local cult with a one-eyed Mercury figure as the focus of attention, known as *Vassocaletis* 'hard as a young warrior'. The Alemannic invasion under King Chrocus in 260 AD involved the plundering of the temple of this god, according to Gregory of Tours, *Historia Francorum*, book 1: 32.

pp.16-9). The leader's position was usually supported by a powerful and charismatic female who embodied the luck of the group, and who supervised and presided over ceremonial gatherings at which public expressions of honour and gratitude took place.

Tacitus, writing about the Batavi in *Historia*, Book IV, describes how the leadership of that people fell to Gaius Julius Civilis – a local whose family had been awarded Roman citizenship by either Augustus or Caligula. The Batavi had been Roman clients for some decades and were among the troops picked for the Claudian invasion of Britain. They paid no tribute to Rome but were obliged to supply a quantity of young men for military service – a contentious burden which had already caused some unrest, so that Julius had rebelled at least twice before the death of Nero in 68 AD presented him with a further opportunity: he recruited a cadre of armed followers on the pretext of supporting the ascendancy of Vespasian. Once he had resolved to take up arms, he made an oath not to cut his hair until he had overcome the legions, which he fulfilled with the slaughter of Legio V and Legio XV; he then cut off his hair, which he had dyed red with *minnium* (red lead) (Kershaw, 2000, p.47). Similar oath-customs are reported among the Alamanni and Saxons.

The subsequent revolt spread among such neighbouring tribes as the Tungri and the Roman garrisons along the lower Rhine were overwhelmed (Birley, 2011; Mees, 2023, p.114). Two legions were sent to quell the uprising; they were defeated, so the garrison of Castra Vetera (Xanten) then threw in its lot with the rebels. Further insurrection followed, involving troops across northern Gaul, but it soon came to nothing as the various warlords refused to settle. Civilis was advised to surrender but declined; a strong show of force by Quintus Petillius Cerialis led to a battle at Augusta Treverorum (Trier) and the withdrawal of Civilis to the Batavian heartland where he took a stand on an island in the River Waal and was offered favourable terms to surrender. Nothing further is heard of him from this time.

According to Tacitus, Civilis was one-eyed, and he used this to his advantage since it accorded with notions of wisdom and leadership among both Celtic and Germanic dwellers on the Lower Rhine, which allowed him to present himself as a new Sertorius or Hannibal to his Roman captors (*Historia*, Book IV. XII; text from Church & Brodribb, 1887):

> sed civilis ultra quam barbaris solitum ing enio sollers et sertorius se aut annibalem ferens simili oris dehonestamento ...

> 'But Civilis, who was more cunning than is usual for a barbarian, presented himself like Sertorius or Hannibal, because his face was disfigured like theirs ...'

It is possible that tales of Hannibal were still current among Roman servicemen, even though he had been dead for three centuries by the time Civilis came to power (Schjødt, 2020b, p.1182, 1186). The Carthaginian general had fought a long and successful campaign against Rome, which made him a figure to be feared as well as respected.

One aspect of Civilis's success was the sympathetic soothsaying of a prophetess called Veleda, who seemingly lived in a tower near the River Lippe and was widely regarded as a semi-divine authority (Tolley, 2009, p.126). Her pronouncements were mediated by messengers, which only served to increase the air of mystery surrounding her (text from Church & Brodribb, 1887; see Tolley, 2009):

> ...sed coram adire adloquique Veledam negatum: arcebantur adspectu, quo venerationis plus inesset, ipsa inedita in turre; delectus et propinquis consulta responsaque ut internuntius numinis portabat.

> 'But they were not allowed to reach or speak to Veleda herself: they were prevented from seeing her in her tower, which increased their respect for her; a chosen relative carried the questions and answers like the messenger of a deity.'

Possibly Veleda foresaw the rebellion, or incited it herself; her support induced other Romanised locals to join the cause, and the full-scale rebellion was soon underway. Once it collapsed, she was not punished but put to work serving Rome's interests by mediating in local tribal disputes until circa 84 AD. Tacitus mentioned her in *Germania* (ch.8) in 98 AD, by which time she was already dead.

It is perhaps unwise to read too much into the success of Civilis's military campaigns, his public display of dedication to the war-god through his unshorn hair, his tactful use of the prophecies of Veleda and his evident mastery of oratory, tactics and deception. Hannibal would have been an obvious historical example for any leader wanting to find a precedent for an uprising, and the harnessing of 'supernatural support' would be helpful in boosting morale (see discussion in Enright, 1994, pp.220-1, stressing the Celtiberian dimension of Sertorius's religious and military rebellion).

MODIFIED EYE MOTIFS

That the god's missing eye was not a newly-created fiction of the Viking age is evidenced by a series of finds from England and Scandinavia. As discussed above (p.95), the Sutton Hoo helmet, with its differential treatment of the eyebrows, is one piece of evidence for eye-modification in the 6th-7th century AD, and the treatment of Face B1 on the stone from the same chamber grave is another (Mortimer & Pollington, 2013, pp.133-53, 166-7). The deliberate modification of a single eye on a range of iconic images, including the dancing figure on the *pressblech* die from Torslunda (Öland, Sweden) betokens an interest in the phenomenon of the one-eyed god stretching back several centuries (Neiss, 2007, p.87).

There are several further instances of modified eyes known in the archaeological record (Price & Mortimer, 2014, p.525):

- A set of four dies for producing *pressblech* plates was found on the island of Öland at a site called Torslunda (Thor's grove) one with a modified eye (Kershaw, 2000, p.7).

- At the mouth of the Volga in northern Russia is the port of Staraja Ladoga which has close links to contemporary sites in Sweden and elsewhere in the Baltic. Among a cache of smith's tool dated to 750–800 AD was found a small bronze ferrule with a horned headdress; its left eye had been struck off with a chisel. It is similar to a horned figure from Uppåkra, similarly modified, of possibly 9th c. date.
- A 6th c. silver-gilt belt buckle tongue found at Elsfleth (Germany) is ornamented with a face; the fill of the left eye had been gouged out in antiquity.
- The belt buckle from the Taplow mound also has missing foils which might be interpreted as eyes (Price & Mortimer, 2014, p.530).
- A detector-find at Vandet in Thy (Denmark) comprises a gilt-bronze face-mask of probable Irish manufacture. Dating to the 8th c. and only 2cm long, it may have been a detail from a casket or similar piece. It had been removed and filled with lead for use as a trade-weight. The eyes had been inlaid with amber, but the left one was absent.
- Another small pendant head from Ribe (Denmark) of 'Viking Age' date, has a punched deformation to the right eye.

Finally, the social custom of 'winking' or closing one eye to indicate a shared secret might be relevant here: this appears to be largely confined to parts of Europe and Asia where it is considered a friendly gesture, an invitation to share a secret. Elsewhere it may be thought offensive, or at least improper.

CHAPTER 7

WORKER OF MAGIC, READER OF RUNES

> Initiation is a certain sequential structure – ritualistic or narrative – which makes use of a series of symbols that mark the difference and the transition between the initial and the final phases of the sequence.
>
> Schjødt, *Initiation Between Two Worlds. Structure and Symbolism in Pre-Christian Scandinavian Religion.*

In myth, runes were won from the Otherworld through Óðinn's suffering on the 'windy tree' (*Hávamál*, v.138 *vindga meiði á*); they were apprehended as a ready-made system and the god himself played no part in their creation. They therefore had a separate existence independent of the Æsir or mankind and were an emanation of some natural force or power; their making is ascribed to the *gin-negin* 'originating powers'. To harness and channel their potency, it was necessary to complete certain ritual acts or sing spells over them, as *Hávamál* v.157 tells us: *svá ek ríst / ok í rúnom fák* 'thus I carve and colour in runes' and v.142 *rúnar munt þú finna / ok ráðna stafi* 'you must find runes and take advice from the staves'.

Prosaically, the origins of the runic script lie in the fruitful cultural borderlands between the Roman Empire and *Germania Libera*; the adoption of literacy marked an important transition for northern European societies (Pollington, 2016, pp.220-2). It appears to have taken place at about the same time (circa 1st c. AD) that the cult of Wodanaz began to gain a new importance, which was itself probably driven by increased contact with the Central European Celtic-speaking communities and with the Roman Empire. The context for these contacts was often military and hostile, but sometimes commercial in nature:

wars between powerful tribes in northern and central Europe generated large numbers of prisoners-of-war who were traded into the slave-markets of Rome.

The original names of the runes have been reconstructed from a variety of sources including four 'rune poems', some manuscript tabulations and the names assigned to the letters devised by Bishop Wulfila for the writing of the Gothic language (Rauch, 2003; Pollington, 2016, pp.365-8). The reconstructed names which might be anticipated for gods connected to runes, such as 'woðanaz' or 'gautaz', are absent from the original series but there are enough clues to be sure that the rune-god was present. Why he was not named directly can only be surmised.

GODS IN THE RUNES

The *Icelandic Rune Poem* (*IRP*) offers a listing of the runes in the traditional fuþark sequence, each followed by a short two-line mnemonic verse. The fourth strophe with the vale /a/ and title *óss* (heathen god) cites *aldingautr ok ásgarðs jǫfurr ok valhallar vísi* 'old Gautr (sacrifice) and Ásgarð's prince (boar) and Valhǫll's wise-one (guide)' (Polomé, 1991, p.430; Pollington, 1995, p.54). The reference here is clearly to Óðinn, prince of the Æsir and lord of the hall of the slain. The reconstructed form which became *óss* in Norse is *ansuz*, which also became *ōs* in Old English.

The phoneme /t/ is represented by the rune **t** with the reconstructed name *tiwaz*, the same name as that of the Æsir war-god (ON *Týr*). This rune (in its Younger Fuþark form **↑**) stands at the beginning of the third *ætt* (set of eight runes) of the *IRP* in a position of prominence. In the *IRP* the verse runs:

(Týr) er einhendr áss ok úlfs leifar ok hofa hilmir

'(Tyr) is a one-handed god and [the] wolf's leavings and [the] temples' protector'

The phoneme /ŋ/ (the sound -*ng*-) has the reconstructed name *ingwaz* which appears in OE as *Ingui* and in ON as *Yngvi*. The rune ◊ represents this sound in the Elder Fuþark, and ᚸ in the Anglo-Saxon *fuþorc*. The Vanir god Freyr is sometimes referred to as *Yngvi-Freyr* and this name is perhaps a title 'Lord Yngvi', to refer to the god alone. The *OERP* verse mentions the god's appearance among the East-Danes in connection with a waggon – with intriguing links to the archaeology of the Baltic islands and Jutland, to Tacitus's statements about the worshippers of Nerthus and to archaeological finds such as the wheeled vehicle from Dejbjerg (Denmark) and others.

The word *ansuz* for 'deity' appears once spelt out in full, albeit in an oblique case (dative?) and with its nasal elided, on a buckle from Vimose (Denmark) from the 2nd c. with the runic text **asau:wija**, i.e., *ansau wija* 'to the Ans I dedicate [this]'; this is also the earliest known use of the term (Simek, 1993, s.v. *Æsir*). Orel notes the paired forms (*ansuz and *ansiz) and suggests that they are cognate with Sanskrit *ásu-* and Avestan *aŋhu-*'life, vital strength' and Venetic *ahsu* 'cult image' (Orel, 2003, s.v. *ansiz).[232] He also notes that a third variant *ansaz can be reconstructed 'in view of worship of pillars erected to Germanic gods' without elaborating further.

Aside from gaining runes from the Otherworld through a painful ordeal, Óðinn also learnt nine spells from Bǫlþór, a supernatural character who may have been the god's own grandfather, in a scene connected to Óðhrerir. This tale is related in *Hávamál* v.140. The spells, the runes and the mead are three core elements in the process of transformation – specifically, elements of induction and instruction (Birkett, 2019, p.157). The transfer of knowledge took place through speech (spells), writing (runes) and inspiration (via the magical mead). The transformation which these acquisitions entailed is, in essence, a mythic model for initiation into élite society. Then we learn that the god grew in stature:

> Þá nam ek frævask
>
> ok fróðr vera

---

[232] The form *ansiz is reconstructed on the basis of the i-mutated OE plural *ese*.

ok vaxa ok vel hafask.

"Then I began to be fruitful and wise and to grow and to thrive."

With literacy came wisdom, wellbeing and status. From the Æsir, knowledge of runes spread to other orders of being (elves, dwarves, etinns) who harnessed this new skill for themselves (*Hávamál* v.143; cf. Birkett, 2019, p.158).

INITIATION

The Norse evidence suggests that the deities most involved with initiation were Óðinn, Heimdallr and Freyja. The court poets have most to say about the two male divinities, but there is good evidence for female initiation into the practice of *seiðr* with all its attendant skills connected with charms, divination, control of the weather and other matters (Pollington, 2016, pp.235-51; Price, 2019).

The process of transformation for the initiated individual is usually understood to involve three stages: separation, transition, aggregation (Schjødt, 2008, pp.23-5). Each of these stages should be accompanied by an appropriate set of rituals, the forms of which vary with the culture and setting.

Initiation was an important process in the lives of those who were selected to be the future leaders of their communities; it involved the acquisition of the 'numinous potential', meaning an indefinable supernatural and charismatic quality which imbued the initiate with authority based on his or her special knowledge acquired through lengthy training (Schjødt, 2008, pp.13-5). This knowledge would be gained and prized for its own sake (not as a means of gaining, e.g., wealth, or a spouse), but its successful acquisition entailed a change of status for the learner.

'Initiation' in the broadest sense underlies a great many folktales where the hero must obtain knowledge or a special 'key' in order to complete a task. But initiatory knowledge is of permanent importance and not limited to an immediate problem: it is, in fact, 'wisdom', a body of knowledge and experience which can be applied to a great many situations. This may be acquired in myth and legend by many means – often the ingestion of a specific numinous drink (e.g., the mead of inspiration) or the recitation of specific words (e.g., charms) or use of a sigil (e.g., runes). The source of this numinous material is understood to be the Otherworld, and it is not accessible without great effort. It is 'transformative', in the sense that the person acquiring it takes on a new status and responsibility. The Otherworld can only be contacted though ritual, and while the actions undertaken in This World can be seen and recorded, the reaction of the Otherworld powers is a matter of conjecture and religious belief (Schjødt, 2008, pp.18-9).

We see the process of instruction at work in the poem *Rígsþula* in which the enigmatic traveller Rígr (identified with the god Heimdallr) wanders the earth establishing the classes of men and their roles. Having impregnated the wives of his various hosts to kindle a bondsman (verse 6, Þræl), a free man (verse 20, Karl), a nobleman (verse 33, Iarl) and finally a king (verse 42, Konr Ungr), Rígr takes the latter under his protection.

Iarl or 'Earl', the noblest of the freeborn, received instruction in warfare, weapon-handling and hunting (text from Dronke, 1997):

35. Svein ól Móðer,

silki vafði.

Iósu vatni,

Iarl létu heita.

'Mother gave birth to a son. She swathed him in silk and sprinkled him with water, gave him the name "Jarl".'

36. Upp óx þar

Jarl á fletjum –

lind nam at skelfa,

leggIa strengi,

álm at beygja,

ǫrvar skepta,

flein[um] at fleygia,

frǫkkur dýia,

hestum ríða,

hundum verpa,

sverðum bregða,

sund at fremia.

'Jarl grew up there in the halls, learnt to bear a shield, to set a bowstring, to bend a bow, to shaft an arrow, to cast a dart, to shake a spear, to ride a horse, to set hounds, to draw a sword, to swim a sound.'

37. Kom þar ór runni

Rígr gangandi,

Rígr gangandi,

rúnar kendi,

sitt gaf heiti –

son kveðz eiga.

Þann bað hann eignaz

óðalvǫllu –

óðalvǫllu,

aldnar byggðer.

'Then Rígr came striding from the thicket – Rígr striding taught [him] runes, gave him his own name [and] claimed him as his own son; then he bade him take charge of his ancestral lands – the ancestral lands and ancient dwellings.'

Jarl's achievements were great and he went on to have sons, of whom Konr Ungr (Kon the young) was the most promising:

42. ...Konr var hinn yngsti.

43. Upp óxu þar

Iarli bornir –

hesta tǫmðu,

hlífar bendu,

skeyti skófu,

skelfðu aska.

'... Konr was the youngest; Jarl's children grew up there, they tamed horses, bent shields, shaved arrow-shafts, shook spears.'

44. En Konr Ungr

kunni rúnar,

ævinrúnar

ok aldrrúnar.

Meirr kunni hann

mǫnnum bjarga,

eggiar deyfa,

ægi lægia.

'But Kon the Young knew runes – everlasting runes, runes of life; he knew more – how to protect men, to blunt swords, to calm the sea.'

45. Klǫk nam fugla,

kyrra eida,

sæva ok svefia,

sorger lægia ...

'He learnt the speech of birds, how to quench a flame, to soothe the mind, to heal sorrows.'

46. Hann við Ríg Iarl

rúnar deildi,

brǫgðum beitti

ok betr kunni.

Þá ǫðlaðiz

ok þá eiga gat

Rígr at heita,

rúnar kunna.

'Rígr shared secrets with Jarl, who outwitted him with wiles and had a deeper understanding so that he was able to gain his heritage, to be called 'Rígr' and to understand runes.'

Evidently, the process of initiation involved stages in which various skills were acquired, all the while preparing the youth through physical activity for the mental and spiritual transformation which would eventually make him a master.

THE SEPARABLE SOUL

Óðinn was a powerful figure, evidenced by his facility with key 'supernatural' skills including sorcery, poetry, warrior frenzy and smithcraft (Du Bois, 1999, pp.53-4; Price, 2003, p.97; Wallis, 2003, p.126; Hall, 2007, p.148). One aspect of his roles involved the 'spirit journey', in other words sending his soul out from his body in a host creature: most often, an eagle, as in the tale of Bǫlverkr and the winning of the mead. Other than the gods (Óðinn, Loki, Freyja), witches and sorceresses were known to be able to transform themselves and in various ON sources they are called *kaldríða* 'cold-rider', *þráþríða* 'thread-rider' and *túnríða* 'hedge-rider' (Price, 2003, pp.121-2). They were believed to have the supernatural ability to send out their spirits to attack others; probably relevant here is the OE *hægtesse* and OHG *hagusizza* 'hedge-sitter', one who works magic from a liminal location. The so-called 'riding' was a kind of aggressive intent and behaviour which could result in physical harm to the victim, and 'riding' – sending out the soul from the body – was fundamental to the successful quest for knowledge and power. This practice is founded on – indeed, is probably a variant of – the spirit-travelling tradition in shamanism (Du Bois, 1999, pp.53-4; Price, 2001; 2003; Hall, 2007, p.126; Liberman, 2016, pp.71-5). Within such societies, the shaman is understood to be able to commune with the dead, the spirits and other realms of being.

The centrality of Woden-Óðinn within such a system seems evident, and his name is specifically linked to the ecstatic trance, *wōþ-*. As mentioned above, the users of these powers were mainly female (*vǫlur*) but males are also known (*seiðmenn*), including one of the sons of King Harald Hárfagr, called Rognvaldr Rettilbeini ('straight-leg'), who was married to a Sámi woman and founded a 'college' of male sorcerers in 9th c. Norway (Price, 2019, pp.80-2). The king sent another of his sons, Eirík, to put a stop to this, so Eirík burned down the hall where the group met, killing all those inside including his brother. Eirík was praised for this deed, although in later life he fell into disfavour and was exiled, eventually becoming the famous Eirík Blóðøx (Eric Blood-axe), sometime ruler of a kingdom based on the city of York.

SEIÐR

The specifics of *seiðr* were learnt from the Vanir gods and goddesses, adopted by Óðinn and made available to his human devotees. It was a specifically female skill: the poles, shafts and staves used in the *seiðr* rites may have been used for simulated sexual acts, which would explain some of the sexualised names given to them, and also the ritual use of the *vǫlsi*, a preserved horse's penis (Price, 2003, p.216;

McLeod & Mees, 2006, p.53).[233] These practices were maintained where a household was in the charge of a female, a *vǫlva* or seeress, whose power was bound up within her staff (*vǫlr*).

The specifics of the *seiðr* included the creation of 'bonds', 'fetters' or 'ropes' which were both spiritual-magical and physical. Hyllested posits a group of words uniquely shared by the Celtic and Germanic language families, including Proto-Celtic **soito* 'sorcery' (e.g., Breton *hud* 'magic') and Proto-Germanic **saiða* 'charm' (e.g., ON *seiðr*), both derived from an earlier **soi̯-to* 'string, thong, rope' (from the root **seh₂i-* 'bind') (Hyllested, 2010; Koch, 2020, p.144). Other instances of the root are found in Lithuanian *saĩtas* 'sign, talisman' and *sietas* 'string, necklace'.

The practice of such magic could involve several incremental stages of preparation and performance: fasting for a defined period before consuming a ritual meal or drink; vigorous dancing, usually to a drum; adopting a ritual physical posture for a prolonged period; sending forth the practitioner's soul to gain knowledge from the spirit-world (Tolley, 1995; Price, 2003, p.121; Gardeła, 2014, p.65; see Lincoln, 2018, for a different view). For its human practitioners, *seiðr* was a means of directly achieving their ends without recourse to the high gods of *Ásgarð*.

Such magical activity was regarded as aberrant in Scandinavian society. The aspects of effeminacy and deviant sexuality associated with *seiðr* which received so much opprobrium may relate at least in part to the association of the *seiðsmaðr* (male *seiðr*-worker) with exclusively female matters such as childbirth, but an erotic element was present and it is likely that sexual energy and libido were among the forces harnessed to carry out the magic (Tolley, 1995, p.60; Price, 2003, p.108, 336).

OE evidence for *seiðr* is sparse. Aside from the noun *sada* 'bonds, halter' (from PGmc **saiða*) there is also the enigmatic term *ælfsiden*

---

[233] The word *gǫndull* can mean both 'staff' and 'penis'. It was dried and wrapped in linen, with preservative herbs applied. It is likely that the use of overtly sexual imagery was connected with the Vanir cult and its earthy eroticism.

used in three medical manuscripts and the nonce-word *sidsa* (Orel, 2003, s.v. *saiðaz, saiþaz*; Hall, 2007, pp.119-56; Kroonen, 2013, s.v. *saida-*).[234] The latter terms denote some kind of illness, associated with fever and with hallucination; the *ælf* was presumably the bringer of the *sidsa*, the trance state. Related to *ælfsiden* in the medical manuscripts are other terms, such as *leodrune* 'babbling speech, chanted secret, prophecy' and *mære* 'night visitor, succubus' which indicate that the *ælfadl* 'elf-sickness' manifested as a form of febrile delusion.

The practice of *seiðr* was taught to Óðinn by Freyja after the war between the Vanir and the Æsir, and may be connected with the ritual promiscuity and fertility aspects of the worship of these divine beings (Tolley, 1995, p.70; North, 1997, p.85; Price, 2003, p.69): Freyja herself was considered indiscriminate in her sexual adventures.

Óðinn was taunted by Loki about his use of *seiðr* in *Lokasenna* verse 24 (Price, 2003, p.69, 117, 174-5; Jakobsson, 2011; text from Dronke, 1997):[235]

> En þik síða kóðo
>
> Sámseyio í,
>
> ok draptu á vett sem vǫlor.
>
> Vitka líki
>
> fórtu verþióð yfir,

---

[234] Both *seiðr* and *-siden* are derived from the Germanic verb *síþanā 'work magic, bind'.

[235] A *vitka* was a 'cunning woman' and the *vett* was the equipment used for the performance, presumably a drum on which the rhythm was beaten out by the *volur* 'sorceresses'. However, no drum has ever been found in a Norse context, despite the many parallels in Sámi culture. Possibly, as Price notes, the drum's function could have been taken by a barrel or other hollow vessel; if so, the OE term for drum, *bydenbotm* 'barrel-end' may support this idea. Alternatively, the custom of Germanic warriors to amplify their war-cries by clashing their weapons against their shields may be relevant if they were also used as percussion instruments.

ok hugða ek þat args aðal.

'But you made 'seiðr' on Samsø, they say, and struck a drum like
the sorceresses. Like a witch you went over the race of men and
I thought that to be disgraceful conduct.'

It was regarded as women's magic, as unmanly, and it might have
involved taking the submissive, female role in a sexual act (Ström,
1974; Price, 2003, p.179, 210ff; Hall, 2007, p.147).[236] The reference
here to *arg* is telling. The negative aspect of *seiðr* is that it involved *ergi*
(the quality of being *argr*) which covered morally negative activities
and states, such as homosexuality, transvestitism, sloth, cowardice and
effeminacy, but the sexual element in the meaning of the word was
often prominent (Jakobsson, 2011, p.6).

Accusations of *ergi* were taken very seriously and were severely
punished in law, on a par with murder and rape; nevertheless, several
sagas recount how such implications could give rise to spirals of aggression and violence in revenge. An accusation of this kind was a
declaration of *níð*, 'scorn, public abuse', towards the person named
and could destroy his reputation and social standing if both the ac-
cuser and his scornful accusation were not dealt with effectively. The
implications of a charge of *ergi* were not simply sexual, but also that
the allegedly *argr* man was devoid of honour, was shameless (and so
worthless) in his behaviour.[237] When laid against a woman, a charge
of *ergi* implied that she was sexually insatiable or indiscriminate in

---

[236] Part of the opprobrium against males associated with *seiðr* may lie in the fact
that to enter the trance state involved loss of control. In a society where adult
males were responsible for their own acts and the safety of those who relied on
them, the trance-like, soporific state of the *seiðmann* would have been regarded
as dangerously inappropriate.

[237] Ström, 1974; Franks, 2019 with a critique of the most in-depth modern
treatment of the topic: Preben Meulengracht Sørensen's *The Unmanly Man:
Concepts of Sexual Defamation in Early Northern Society* (1983). A contrary view
(Kershaw, 2000, p.63 fn.40) regards the 'unwarlike' man as not necessarily in-
ept or cowardly but just unsuccessful, unable to gain initiation as a full warrior
because he lacked the means to maintain a family and household.

her choice of partners, which also meant she was without honour or a sense of shame (Ármann Jakobsson, 2011 cited in Franks, 2019).

Seiðr was connected with violence and battle-magic, but also with dreams; in a sense, Óðinn is the perfect performer of this magic since his dual nature straddles both the Æsir and Vanir cults, and is concerned with both the male activity of warfare and the female activity of revival through *seiðr*; these multiple roles may have been managed through a series of masks which the god (or his fictive substitute, the priest) was accustomed to wearing when going about his ceremonies (Kershaw, 2000, pp.26-30; Kajkowski, 2023, p.126). The *seið*-worker had to be seated on a special platform or raised seat, called a *seiðhallr*, which seems to have been specifically built for the occasion and therefore not the same as the high-seat of the leader (Price, 2003, p.163; Pollington, 2003, p.81-4).

Many of the god's gifts, talents and skills were gained through deliberate acts of deceit – especially the seduction of females (e.g., Suttungr's daughter) and assumption of a false identity (e.g., Bǫlverkr) - both qualities associated with the *ylfe* (elves) in Anglo-Saxon tradition. These multiple identities gave rise to the many bynames and epithets by which he was known – Price lists over two hundred (Price, 2003, pp.85, 91, 101-7, 214-6).[238] If the donning of the mask conferred 'fictive divinity' on the leader within the religious rite, then the songs of power used in the ceremony may well have been specialised forms of communication by which men's wishes and needs could be made known to the gods (Kershaw, 2000, pp.26-30; Price, 2003, pp.62-3, 94-5, 171-4).

As the prime practitioner of that deprecated type of magic, Óðinn could be viewed as transgressive. This impression is reinforced when we read, e.g., in *Gylfaginning* ch.9 that (text from Faulkes, 2005):

Jǫrðin var dóttir hans ok kona hans. Af henni gerði hann hinn fyrsta soninn, en þat er Ásaþórr.

---

[238] They fall into a few categories relating to wealth and wisdom, warfare, frenzy, death and the gallows, sorcery, trickery and disguise, wandering, shapeshifting and appearance. See Appendix II.

'Earth was his daughter and [also] his wife. With her he kindled his first son, and that is Þórr of the Æsir.'

There was a strong taboo against incest in Scandinavian society, yet the god was able to retain men's respect despite his breaches of the moral code (Jakobsson, 2011, pp.8-9).

INITIATION RITES

The *Hávamál* scene in which Óðinn suffers for nine nights on Yggdrasill can be interpreted, in the light of the god's close associations with the military and with social élites, as the model for induction into a mystery religion with antecedents stretching back into the Roman Iron Age or further (Kvilhaug, 2004, p.27; Sundqvist, 2009, pp.653-5; Liberman, 2016, p.74; Pollington, 2016, pp.251-70; Birkett, 2019, p.155). Such creeds were once a common aspect of service in the Roman military, which by the 4th c. AD was a largely Germanic-influenced institution in western Europe, and likewise in those Germanic warbands which interacted with the Roman state. Induction into such a group would form part of the training and preparation of young men for their later-life roles as community leaders (Schjødt, 2020a, p.841).

The rites of these religions (including the cults of Sol Invictus and Isis, Mithraism and Christianity in its earlier forms) usually involved performance of elaborate ceremonies enacting events from myth. It is tempting to equate the fact that the god was 'pierced and marked' by a spearpoint with the writer's use of a similar metal point to inscribe a message in runes (Birkett, 2019, pp.156-7).

Those who successfully completed these processes of induction then entered into a special relationship with a divinity (whether god or goddess), which promised the opportunity to overcome death (Sundqvist, 2009, pp.653-5). This 'mystical union' of mortal and immortal could be expressed as 'sacred marriage' where the deity was a female and the worshipper a male. A further manifestation might include the rites associated with the circulation of the drinking-horn during formal gatherings in the meadhall: as with the classical cults of Orpheus, Dionysus and Bacchus, ritual inebriation through strong drink was one of the central observances (Linforth, 1941). A further aspect to the process was self-denial and the prolonged endurance of privation and physical pain, during which the initiand underwent lack of sleep, food and drink. These intense physical hardships could cause changes in cognitive ability through light-headedness, inability to focus and slow reactions; the effects of such a procedure over several days could induce paranoiac hallucinations and severely impaired mental processes. On release, a draught of strong drink would doubtless have unleashed even more powerful hallucinatory effects. When Óðinn tells of Gunnlǫð offering him a drink while seated on her golden throne, this may be a reference to the feelings of pleasurable release and empowerment which the final ingestion of alcohol excited in him.

In *Hávamál* verse 139 Óðinn describes the effect of nine nights without food or drink, suffering on the tree (Birkett, 2019, p.152; text from Dronke, 2011):

Við hleifi mik sældu

né við hornigi.

'[None] refreshed me with a loaf nor with a drinking-horn'

immediately before acquiring the runes:

Nýsta ek niðr.

Nam ek upp rúnar,

œpandi nam.

Fell ek aptr[a]ð[r ú]tan

'I peered down, runes I took up, howling I took [them]. I fell back from beyond'

Similarly, in *Grímnismál*, the god was bound between two fires and denied food or drink in an ordeal of willpower.

Having seized the runes from the Otherworld, the god learns nine charms or spells from Bǫlþór, his maternal grandfather and a notable leader among the jǫtnar. He also receives a drink of the mead of poetry, so that the transmission of secret knowledge is threefold: runes, spells, mead (i.e., writing/reading, chanting/singing and the insight drawn from an alcoholic entheogen) (Birkett, 2019, p.157). At this point, Óðinn is able to state that he has begun to gain insight (*Hávamál* v.141).

Initiation ceremonies formed the culmination to a process of physical and mental preparation for a profound transformation - not simply from childhood to adulthood, but into a new relationship with the gods. From this, the role of the *drihten* or *cyning* as both political and religious leader could derive – drawing authority from having endured the toughest of all trials (Kvilhaug, 2004, p.35). Einar Haugen suggested that the name for this initiate was ON *þulr*, OE *þyle* but, while possible, this is not clear from the scant references to such a status. The *þyle* in *Beowulf*, Unferþ, is a confidante of the king, a spokesman, a famous warrior and high-ranking member of the community, commanding authority and respect.[239] The cognate ON word *þulr* occurs in conjunction with runic knowledge in *Hávamál* (v.142): *miǫk stinna stafi, / er fáði fimbulþulr/ ok gǫrðu ginnregin* 'very firm staves which *fimbulþulr* [one mighty in speech] coloured and *ginnregin* [originating powers] made'. The *fimbulþulr* 'one mighty in speech' coloured the runes while the *ginnregin* 'creator-god' 'made' them. The implication is that Óðinn becomes 'mighty in speech' due to his acquisition of the runes.

---

[239] See Neidorf, 2017a, 2022. Unferþ does not emerge with much credit from the exchange with Beowulf. He accuses the hero of failing to make good his promise to outswim his rival, Breca, but Beowulf dismisses the adventure as youthful folly, then reveals that Unferþ had slain his own brothers. If the *þyle* was a person of authority within pre-Christian religion, as seems most likely, then it may have been the Christian poet's intention to show Unferþ in as poor a light as possible.

BOY

The aim of a boy of moderate status – in Anglo-Saxon England he had to be freeborn and have the right physical and mental qualities – was to develop into the normative adult male through various processes of transformation (Pollington, 2002, p.79; Sundquist, 2012, p.4). The concept of a 'boy' (OE *cnapa*) does not correspond to the modern view: a baby (*cradolcild* 'cradle-child') had little social identity but, by the age of about seven, one who was chosen for military service began the process of acquiring strength, stamina and skill with weapons. Still legally a child, a *cnapa* might serve as a craftsman's or labourer's assistant or apprentice. This is suggested by the passage in Ælfric's *Colloquy on the Occupations* in which the ploughman discloses that he has an assistant (text from Garmonsway, 1978):

> '... ic hæbbe sumne cnapan þywende oxan mid gadisene, þe eac swilce nu has is for cielde ond hreame...'

> "... I have a boy driving the oxen with a goad, who is likewise now hoarse because of the cold and the shouting..."

In the lawcode of King Ine, clause 7 reads (text from Liebermann, 1903, p.92):

> Be stale. Gif hwa stalie swa his wif nyte ond his bearn, geselle LX scillinga to wite. Gif he ðonne stalie on gewitnesse ealles his hiredes, gongen hie ealle on ðeowot. X winter cniht mæg bion ðiefðe gewita.

> 'Concerning theft. If anyone shall steal so that his wife and child[ren] do not know [of it], let him give 60 shillings as a fine. [But] then if he should steal with the knowledge of all his household, let them all go into servitude. A ten-year-old child may be witness to a theft.'

This code was issued in 694 AD - its later amendment under Alfred raised the age of responsibility to twelve years old.

YOUTH

At about 14 years of age, the *cnapa* 'boy' became a *cniht* 'youth'. While not yet a fully adult member of society, he could take part in military activities in a supporting role, and in so doing he learnt the basics of tactics and survival (Kershaw, 2000, pp.59-60). The process of initiation and transformation involved his separation from his family and familiar surroundings, spending time with a mentor who guided his development and instructed him in the lore and customs which he would need to have mastered by the time he became an adult (Kershaw, 2000, pp.24-6). He would also be introduced to sexuality (Schjødt, 2008, p.30).

'Initiation' among the warrior class and the élite was a process culminating in a transformative event. The process began before the onset of adolescence, when the youngster was provided with a carefully limited exposure to new ideas and attitudes. As Larrington put it: 'Adolescence ... is a time when learning is occurring and social roles are being restructured; although the young man remains subordinate to community elders, he is preparing for adulthood and manifestly no longer a child' (Larrington, 2010, p.145 and references there). The transition from child to adolescent to adult was protracted, and the end of the process was typically marked with a rite of passage (Kershaw, 2000, p.58; Schjødt, 2008, pp.30-2).

The transformational phase of the youth's passage to manhood involved living in a wild (but not entirely lawless) state for a period: the process typically involved the foregoing of sexual relations, of sleeping in a bed, of bathing, of combing the hair and beard or shaving; this period in which social norms were set aside formed the prelude to the emergence of the adult. The unkempt appearance was a social signal regarding the liminal status of the youth, paralleled in the process by which Haraldr Lúfa ('the shaggy') refused to wash or comb his hair until he had fulfilled his oath. A similar ritual element seems to have informed the development of the *berserkir* as devotees of the war-god (Kershaw, 2000, p.63).

The phase associated with the pre-adult or pubescent stage is 'liminal' - a threshold which must be crossed in order to progress to adulthood. During this phase, skills must be acquired and tests passed to demonstrate the youth's suitability for leadership. References to the liminal phase in the later literature include the period in *Vǫlsunga saga* where Sigmundr and Sinfjǫtli, his nephew, live as outlaws in the wild; another example might be Þórr's visit to Útgarðr in *Gylfaginning* where he is assessed by his host (Schjødt, 2008, p.50). For those who were trained for a prominent role, learning the use of runestaves was an important accomplishment, one of the key attainments which could lead to political and social advancement. The 'youth' was effectively both landless and homeless; he had to earn his social position through service. Such a person would attach himself to a leader from outside his own kinship group and take himself away in order to broaden his experience and 'win his spurs'. In OE a person of this status is called a *hæggesteald*, a 'bachelor' who had no property other than what he could earn from the favour of his *hlaford* 'lord, leader'.

MAN

A fully-grown (*fullweaxen*) freeman was expected to participate in the administration of justice, the pursuit of offenders, the prosecution of military campaigns, the administration and protection of his own property, the financial support of the shrine, temple or church and also of his social superiors through a tax-payment.

The freeman had to rely on the support of family, neighbours and friends – and to provide such support himself when necessary. The kindred was the basis of the social structure and was predicated on the participation of all its members: those who refused effectively stepped outside the network of protection and help that the family provided. Families extended on both sides – through both parents to sisters, brothers, fathers and mothers – and the goodwill of both the maternal and paternal elements was expected.

The burden on a female was no less onerous. On marriage, she was expected to live with her husband in a house which might be a new building, and to create a household in which to manage a range of resources from which to provide the means for the raising of a family; if she were wealthy, she would bring some maids and servants with her, but the estate would already have a workforce. She would find it very important to be on good terms with her husband's blood-relations since she and her offspring would be dependent on them if her husband were absent or died.

The wider community seemingly gathered periodically mainly to take part in religious rites and to administer the law: in pre-Christian times, this seems to have been seasonal, with a more extensive celebration every nine years. Such gatherings transformed into seasonal fairs and markets in Christian times.

ELDER

'Lordship' or 'leadership' was a quality acquired through long practice rather than a natural gift: a leader was expected to have a set of skills which would serve him in specific situations, and which were not available to everyone. In the pre-Christian period, these qualities derived from the gods, primarily Woden. The elders of the community were expected to take charge of the processes of initiation whereby tradition was handed on to the succeeding generations.

LOKI

Óðinn's oath-brother, Loki, appears in an even more negative light than the god himself, as if he were in some sense an embodiment of the 'dark side' of Óðinn, emphasising the god's negative and deviant qualities (Ström, 1956; Frakes, 2002, p.166). Transgression appears to be the defining trait of both Óðinn and Loki: they commit various prohibited acts: incest (Óðinn in *Gylfaginning* ch.9, where Jorð is both his wife and his daughter), gender-transgression (Loki gave birth to Sleipnir; he disguised himself as a woman in order to trick

Frigg into revealing the secret weakness of Baldr; he assumed the identity of the giantess Þǫkk who refused to weep for Baldr) and violations of the guest-host relationship (he kills Ægir's servant Fimafengr while a guest)(Schjødt, 2020f, pp.1255-6); they use guile, fraud and deceit to achieve their ends (Schjødt, 2020f, p.1254). Just as the gods transcend the limitations of their physical bodies – transforming into snake, bird, mare (and in Loki's case, giving birth to viable offspring) at will – they also transcend human moral limitations (Callahan, 2013). They deviate markedly at times from the norms of acceptable behaviour, but they are gods and thus not subject to the same regimen of proper conduct as applies to members of human society.

Loki appears in a good many tales: his ambition, deceptiveness and malice are the mainspring for many of the most memorable narratives (Liberman, 2016, p.172; Schjødt. 2020f, pp.1247-9). Elsewhere, he appears in some *Poetic Edda* sources, as well as being portrayed iconographically, e.g., on a carved hearthstone from Snaptun (Denmark) which shows a male face with vertical lines across the lips, related to the *Skáldsapannál* tale whereby the god's lips were sewn shut by the sons of Ivaldi (Madsen, 1990). One may probably discount the name **logaþore** on the Nordendorf fibula, although not without regret since this citation leads to other words with overtones of deceit and trickery. Saxo certainly knew of the character 'Ugarthilocus',[240] Snorri's *Utgarðaloki*, yet opinion is divided as to the relationship between this lord of an extra-liminal realm and 'Ása-Loki', the blood-brother of Óðinn (Liberman, 2016, pp.155-7, 174, 192-3 and sources cited there).

Loki's background is surely among the trolls and etinns, and his offspring comprise the fiercest enemies of the gods. He is the particular foe of Heimdallr and of Skaði, yet he dwells among the Æsir as if on equal terms. Various interpretations of his 'true' nature have been offered – a personification of fire; a chthonian deity; a god of

---

[240] He was said to be worshipped by seafarers and to require offerings from those who wanted to gain information from him.

water or air; a raven-god;[241] a spider-god; a pagan equivalent of Lu-
cifer, the fallen angel; a culture-hero; a trickster – yet none captures
adequately the full character of Loki in the Norse tales (Price, 2019,
p.267). He is a marginal figure in the mythological system, not a
central deity demanding reverence, and in this sense he is both inside
and outside its structure, interacting with the great gods but not included in their number (Frakes, 2002, p.165, 170). He is not a 'god'
of anything specific, nor is there any evidence for his worship, no
place-names or cult-sites associated with him (Frakes, 2002, p.164;
Orton, 2005, p.304; Schjødt, 2020f, p.1248). This lack of independent verification might be taken to suggest that Snorri re-worked or
combined several pre-existing traditions and in doing so created a
new composite figure out of scraps of folktale and some partly understood verses, although this is far from certain (Price, 2019, p.268;
Schjødt, 2020f, p.1255).

'Trickster' is a name which appears often in discussion of Loki:
this figure is drawn from North American native lore but has counterparts among many cultures, often based on the character of some
animal ('Brer Rabbit' is a noted example). 'Socially-sanctioned devi-
ance' is another quality of the tales surrounding him (Price, 2019,
p.267): he fathered the monsters, Fenrir (wolf) and Miðgarðsormr
(serpent), and the queen of the underworld, Hel; he is the fierce opponent of Heimdallr, the watchman of Ásgarð;[242] he devises the death
of the god Baldr; he is credited with having invented the fishing net,
but not sharing the knowledge (Liberman, 2016, pp.169-75).[243] He

---

[241] Liberman (2016, p.176) based on the speculative equation Loki = *lugos*, the
Brythonic god *Lug*.

[242] Heimdallr is himself outside the tripartion scheme in as much as he shares
enhanced senses and knowledge with Óðinn, stands watch over the gods like
Þórr and is the progenitor of the classes of human society and can see the future
like the Vanir gods (Frakes, 2002, p.170-1). Perhaps Loki is as much a negative
version of Heimdallr as of Óðinn?

[243] The purpose of the net was deduced from its abandoned ashes by the god
Kvasir in the *Edda* story; this is Kvasir's only appearance outside the myths
surrounding the 'mead of inspiration' and is thus probably very ancient. The

is generally a disruptive personality, but his tricks and mischief form the driving force of many of the more entertaining tales. The poem *Lokasenna* with its unwelcome and often scandalous accusations against the gods (which are never refuted by the accused, it should be noted!) must be regarded as ancient since it contains many fragments of stories which are otherwise unrecorded or only exist as allusions (Libermann, 2016, pp.158-60). Loki plays the part of the 'court jester' in Ásgarð, providing opportunities for merriment and broad humour, but he also brings about the death of Baldr[244] and sets in train the events which will lead to the final battle in which the world perishes (Frakes, 2002, p.164). The tales regarding him do not form a coherent or easily categorised whole. And in the end, Óðinn is no less complex and multivalent in his deviousness but he receives social approval, whereas Loki is finally treated with outrage and disdain.

In sum, Loki fits the category of 'trickster' to a large degree, inasmuch as it is the function of the trickster to thwart the creator-gods, to spoil what they make and to undermine their grand schemes. He is transgressive (like Óðinn) and petulant. When he steals, it is usually in order to save his neck, not for his own profit. When cornered, he is ready to make amends – for example, to atone for cutting off Sif's hair by compelling the dwarf-smiths to replace it with a golden substitute. But his transgressive nature is such that he is always ready to commit further mischief when the opportunity presents itself. He 'embodies certain aspects of the (functional) gods to the extent necessary to caricature them; he undermines their functional roles' (Frakes, 2002, p.166).

---

underlying theme of the tale is that the god-hero is generally invulnerable to any weapon other than his own (his salmon-form can only be caught by the net of his own design).

[244] This is the case in the Icelandic material, but Saxo's account of the death of Baldr does not mention Loki – it is attributed to the rivalry of two noblemen, Balderus and Høtherus. Saxo's stories always present the gods as fallible humans, so perhaps there was no need for a supernatural enemy in 'East Norse' tradition (Schjødt, 2020f, p.1255).

ANIMAL TRANSFORMATIONS

In the tales of Óðinn related by Snorri, disguise and transformation often play a central part. That a god might disguise himself as a human is surely unremarkable – gods are, after all, conceived as humans without all the limitations of humanity. But animal transformation is a rather different prospect, involving an alteration of physical properties rather than mere outward appearance: when Óðinn becomes a serpent, he acquires the physical dimensions which allow him to slip into a narrow hole, and when he becomes a bird he acquires the means of flight. Transformation into an animal form is one of the characteristics of gods in Greek and Vedic myth, and is presumably of considerable antiquity.

ANIMAL MOTIFS

Animal and geometric forms constitute a major element in the 'ornament' of physical material in the Germanic world (Pollington, Kerr & Hammond, 2010, pp.388-421). Decoration of even humble objects (spoons, knife-handles, spear-shafts, tools, combs) is a consistent feature of Northern European and other societies from the Bronze Age onwards. This may have been a pragmatic effort to make each item distinct and thus to avoid disputes over ownership, but it may reflect a more deep-seated notion that each item had its own personality and character, its *animus*, and the surface detailing applied was an attempt to realise and solidify that unique quality.

Neiss has shown that some of the dense imagery found on Viking Age female brooches may refer to aspects of the cult of Óðinn, especially the god's adopted form as a serpent (Neiss, 2007, p.82). He considers a figure accompanied by two snakes to represent Óðinn, while another figure pulling at his hair is engaged in magical activity, or another with his legs in a dynamic pose is in a state of ecstasy. He follows Hauck in seeing bracteate imagery as representative of the Migration Period Woden in his various mythic roles, and the depiction of helmeted male figures as icons of the god.

The development and spread of more ambitious metal casting techniques in the Viking period enabled artists to produce figures modelled in the round or half-round, and to convey even more information to the viewer through raising the most important designs elements away from the flat surface, which had been the norm for Migration Period and Vendel Period art (Neiss, 2007, p.83). The gods may also be represented in the form of the anthropomorphic 'gripping beast' in Oseberg Style art, creating a thematic link between the earlier 'serpent' and 'band' motifs of Styles I, II and III and the various later Viking period styles.

It seems likely that Woden's cult animals included the raven and the wolf, which were likewise associated with Óðinn in later centuries. Certainly, both these creatures appear widely in heathen-period Anglo-Saxon art, although Meaney preferred to see an association with literary convention and battlefield scavenging rather than with memories of the god's cult (Meaney, 1966, p.112).

The bird (either a raven or eagle, but perhaps better viewed as an undifferentiated 'raptor') figures prominently on the equipment in Sutton Hoo Mound 1 – on the helmet, shield, purse-lid, great gold buckle and harp (Pollington, Kerr & Hammond, 2010; Sanmark, 2010, pp.164-5). The raven is certainly viewed negatively in the writings of Bede, but this may be due to its biblical reputation (the dark bird of death, contrasted with the white dove of peace) as much as its role in Germanic tradition. Northumbrian Christian artists avoided the depiction of the bird of prey The adjective *wælceasaga* 'corpse-choosing' is used attributively of the raven (*Exodus*, l.164); this term is derived from a noun cognate with the Norse *valkyrjur* the maidens of battle who serve the war-god.

The wolf is hard to discern with certainty, but early Anglo-Saxon art in both Style I and Style II is not easy to decipher and it may be that some of the disjointed and 'serpentine' quadrupeds on shield decorations and elsewhere are intended to be mythical wolves; the so-called 'Bamburgh Beast' would be an obvious candidate. The small plaque on the wand from Sutton Hoo Mound 1 is certainly a symbolic lupine animal, depicted in an active pose.

The horse was important as a means of transport in war and peace, and it may also have figured as an element in the god's cult as Sleipnir did for Óðinn (Ellis Davidson, 1969, pp.45-6; Schjødt, 2020b, p.1145). Indeed, the 'rider' figure on the Sutton Hoo helmet may represent the war-god himself, mounted on his steed and brandishing his spear. If so, the small bronze mounted figure from Bradwell, Norfolk, discovered in 2021 may have a similar symbolic meaning (PAS ref NMS-40A7A7).

CHAPTER 8

WARLORD

Ellen sceal on eorle...
'Courage belongs to a hero...'

Exeter Book Gnomic Verses, l.15

Þegi þú, Óðinn,
Þú kunnir aldregi
deila víg með verom.
Opt þú gaft,
þeim er þú gefa skyldíra
– enom slævorom! – sigr.
'Be quiet, Óðinn you never know how to apportion warfare among men; often you gave victory to the weak-willed, which you should not give.'

Lokasenna, v.22

By the late 6th c. AD in western Europe, the traditional 'chiefdom' model of society was in competition with, and giving way to, new ideas based around the 'state' and the 'royal kindred', offering institutions with increased stability in place of the naked rivalry and lack of permanent structure that characterised the earlier 'chiefdoms'. In reality, the leading families were as likely to carry out murderous purges as ever before, but medieval institutions were better equipped to deal with the effects of such activity (Shippey, 2022, pp.112-5, 123).

Woden was a product of the mentality of these times – a chieftain or warlord, but not a 'warrior' as such, present on the battlefield sometimes but not as an active participant in slaughter. Saxo's tales include his attempt to win the heart of the giantess Rindr, whereby he appeared as a battle-hardened hero (Book III, iv) but the disguise failed and he had to try another tack as a smith called Rotherus (Grundy, 2014). When he appeared on the human battlefield, his role was to initiate hostilities by casting the first spear, and to ensure the untimely death of his heroic worshippers. Indeed, his enmity towards the *jǫtnar* is mentioned several times but seldom results in actual combat or bloodshed – only the tale of his killing and dismembering Ymir seems to involve violence (Schjødt, 2020b, p.1149). His final combat at Ragnarǫk resulted in his being overcome and swallowed by Fenrir.

The story of his salvation by Víðar, his giantess-born son, is told by Snorri in the *Edda*, and has been identified iconographically on Viking-period monuments (Thorwald's Cross on the Isle of Man, for example). The possibility of conflation with a scene or motif drawn from Christian legend cannot be discounted (Simek, 1993, s.v. *Víðarr*).

WODEN'S OFFSPRING

In southern Scandinavia, a religious change was taking place which saw the replacement of lake sacrifice (offering to the gods below the water and beneath the earth) by hanging (offering to the gods in the heavens); a transformation which may have seen the deprecation of the old Vanir deities, such as Nerthus, and the elevation of the Æsir to prominence (Gunnell, 2020, p.259). If so, this religious schism would have been a more far-reaching break with previous long-standing traditions than the later acceptance of Christianity (Fabech, 1994, pp.174-6).[245] With the adoption of Christianity, there was still a focus on a heavenly father-god (*drihten, hælend*) and a special venerated post (preaching cross), both of which were familiar from the Woden cult.

These turbulent times, in which new identities formed around prominent leaders and families, are characterised as the 'Migration

---

[245] Hall (2007, p.27) suggests that the Vanir were not 'gods' in the sense that the Æsir were, but they were rather *álfar*, 'elves, nature-spirits'.

Period' (Kvilhaug, 2004, p.24). This is an unhelpful term, since it implies that all important social groups were permanently in transit while those who remained in the lands of their forefathers were re-calcitrant or unambitious. It was later considered a time of 'gold and feasting-halls' when viewed from the perspective of the medieval period (Simek, 2006, ch.2).

In Britain around 575 AD, as far as can be judged, the major Anglo-Saxon kingdoms of the existing historical records had come into being with their (sometimes Woden-based) royal mythology and their strong regional identities, divergent if not yet divorced from those of the Continental homelands (Hedeager, 1992, p.246). Parallel developments were underway in southern Scandinavia at around the same time (Shippey, 2022). Once political consolidation had taken place along the eastern seaboard of Britain, those Anglo-Saxon kingdoms with the opportunity to dominate neighbouring polities came to the fore in the later history of England (Charles-Edwards, 2003, pp.39-40). These kingdoms – Northumbria, Mercia and Wessex – were able to use the tribute (OE *gombe, gafol*) of their neighbours to support large military forces.

The early medieval aristocracy relied on social status and access to resources to achieve and maintain dominance. While ironworking typically took place on a small scale in even quite humble settlements, specialist ironworking centres located in 'central places' appeared - the estates of wealthy and influential families (Hjärthner-Holdar, Lamm & Magnus, 2001). These centres were associated with the production of weapons and other military equipment, with gold- and silversmith-ing and with impressive 'ritual' objects such as bracteates and guldgubber.

GAMES, LUCK AND STRATEGY

Woden could bestow victory and his followers trusted that he would support them in their struggles with their foes. But as Liberman suggests: 'Uncertainty in the outcome of battle explains why Óðinn was believed to be treacherous and even vicious. At one time, a myth was composed that Óðinn granted victory to weaker warriors because he wanted great ones in Valhǫll, ready for *Ragnarǫk* – an impressive example of rationalization with a poetic touch' (Liberman, 2016, p.85).

A link has been inferred between the cult of the war-god and the battle-tactic known as the 'boar's head' or *svínfylking*, a triangular array of heavy infantry troops whose impact on charging an enemy shieldwall was held to be unstoppable. It seems that some such tactic was indeed used by the Germani, as noted by Caesar (*de Bello Gallico* 1:52) and Tacitus (*Germania*, ch.6). The latter states (text from Anderson 1938; see Rives, 1999, p.79 and note p.143):

acies per cuneos componitur

'the battle-line is composed of wedges'

Tacitus describes this wedge formation as typical of the Germani and implies that they were poorly equipped due to their lack of iron, and relied on infantry rather than on cavalry. These infantry troops were lightly armed with javelins and lacked armour. Yet the regular employment of Germanic troops by the Roman authorities – for example, Batavians recruited for the Claudian invasion of Britain – argues against the assumption that they were inferior (Mees, 2023, p.109, 114). The preference for lightly-armed troops may then have been tactical – and the later reliance on skirmishers by such successful peoples as the Heruli supports this (Chadwick, 1899, pp.39-40).

Horsemanship was a noted military accomplishment. The role of Woden as 'lordly horseman' may be commemorated in the name on the Tune (Norway) stone **woduridaz**, i.e., **wódurídaz* 'furious rider' – prototheme **wód* 'ecstatic, maddened, inspired', deuterotheme **rídaz* 'rider, horseman' (Spurkland, 2005, pp.35-40). An alternative meaning for the name is 'rider of *wód*', i.e., inspiration (Liberman, 2016, p.44). However, the man named Woduridaz is specifically called a 'lord' (**witandahlaiban*) in the same inscription and it may be that the personal name comprises a divine name as its first element in much the same way as Anglo-Saxon kings could be called *Oshere, Oswiu, Oswald* or in Viking times names such as *Þórbjorn, Þórolfr, Þórstein, Ingvar*, etc. became popular.

Strategy and strategic thinking were part of the initiation for young leaders, which is shown by the presence of gaming counters in high-status male graves – the mounds at Taplow, Asthall, Sutton Hoo and Prittlewell are recorded examples (Pollington, 2008, p.86). These items could be made of glass or ceramic, while some partial remains indicate that bone was also used. They occur singly (e.g., Alfriston, Sussex, grave 28) (Griffith & Salzmann, 1914; Hines, 1997b, p.279; Lucy, 2000, p.63) but more usually in larger sets (e.g., the finds from Sutton Hoo Mound 1 and the Prittlewell chamber tomb). There is no consistency in the numbers of pieces deposited, but it is not clear whether this reflects different games to be played or different attitudes to burial (Geake, 1997, p.100). Decoration of the pieces is usually minimal, often just hatching or scoring, while the glass examples were made in contrasting-coloured materials. The larger sets are more common in male graves, while females tend to have just one or two pieces.

Three urns at Caistor-by-Norwich (Norfolk) held gaming-pieces and a fourth one was a stray find from the site (Green, 1973, pp.98-100). One vessel (no.N59) held what appears to be a full set of counters: twenty two white bone pieces and eleven darker ones made from shale. In the same urn were thirty-five sheep's astragali (knuckle-bones), plus a larger roe-deer astragalus with a short runic text which is considered to be among the earliest known English (Anglian) inscriptions. Astragali occur regularly in Roman military contexts where they were used as rudimentary dice.

The runic sequence reads **raihan** '[of a] roe-deer' (Green, 1973, p.98; Page, 1973).[246] The runes were neatly cut into one flat surface of the bone with a sharp pointed tool. The text is so early in date (mid-5th century) that the Germanic system of transliteration is used, rather than the Anglo-Saxon one (i.e., the second and fifth runes are rendered

---

[246] This interpretation assumes that *raihan* is the genitive singular of the noun, but formally it could be any of the oblique cases.

with 'a' not 'æ'). The third rune ∫ is transcribed here as 'i' although its exact value is uncertain (Pollington, 2016, pp.122-3). The **h** is of the early type **H** with a single cross-bar, which is rare but not unknown in England and is perhaps to be expected in the context of an Anglian soldier attached to a Roman military base (Pollington, 2016, pp.151-2). Other examples of single-bar **h** occur in Angeln (e.g., the Thorsberg shield boss) but finds from further south and elsewhere in England usually have the double-barred form: **ᚺ**. The grave goods in the Caistor-by-Norwich cemetery show many cultural links to the area of Fyn and southern Jutland, which merely underscores the likely ethnic background of the people buried there.

BATTLE-MAGIC

Tactics can win a battle for those who understand how to use them, but in warfare a positive mental attitude is of paramount importance. Confidence-boosting measures included the deployment of supernatural help, whether this involved chanting spells over one's weapons, carving runes and *þwengas* on to the shaft of a spear, blessing a weapon to enhance its abilities. Magical thinking served to both promote confidence in one's own unit and to sow doubt and fear among the enemy; magical acts of empowerment thus had positive and negative aspects (based on Price, 2019, p.294):

Effect on Self and Friends	Effect on Foe
+ instill courage and clarity of thought	– instill doubt, fear and confusion
+ confer physical strength and stamina	– instill fatigue and weakness
+ confer invulnerability	– (magically) hinder movement[247]
+ confer protection from foe's magic	– make weapons fail

---

[247] See below '*Binding and Loosing*' for more on this.

+ confer efficiency and accuracy of weapons	

A specific benefit of battlefield sorcery mentioned in the Scandinavian sources is the resurrection or reanimation by means of powerful charms of warriors who had already been killed. This is confined to the 'legendary' and mythic tales, of course, although belief in the possibility of such a process may have been prevalent (for example, when a battle had been in process for a long time but the numbers of the enemy did not appear to reduce).

Spells for use on the battlefield form the natural domain of Óðinn, who combines the roles of shaman / wizard / spell-caster with warlord / warrior. One section of *Hávamál* is called *Ljóðatal* 'the tally of charms' which lists the various spells which the speaker (Óðinn) knows, many of which relate to warfare, the inflicting and healing of wounds, charming of weapons, etc. (based on Price, 2019, pp.294-7; texts from Dronke, 2011):

1. Ljóð ek þau kann

   er kannat þióðans kona

   ok mannskis mǫgr.

   Hiálp heitir eitt,

   en þat þér hiálpa mun

   við sǫkum ok sorgum

   ok sútum gǫrvǫllum.

'I know those charms which [even] a lord's wife does not know, nor a child of mankind. One is called 'Help' which must help you against strife and sorrows and all distress.'

2. Þat kann ek annat

   er þurfu ýta synir,

   þeir er vilia læknar lifa.

'A second one I know which those sons of men need who wish to live as healers.'

3. Þat kann ek þriðja:

ef mér verðr þǫrf mikil

hapts við mína heiptmǫgu,

eggiar ek deyfi

minna andskota —

bítat þeim vápn né veler.

'A third one I know: if a great need comes on me for a fetter against my attacker, I blunt the blades of my opponents [so that] neither their weapons nor their staves will harm [me].'

4. Þat kann ek it fiórða:

ef mér fyrðar bera

bǫnd at bóglimum,

svá ek gel

at ek ganga má —

sprettr mér af fótum fiǫturr,

en af hǫndum hapt.

'A fourth one I know: if foes bring bonds for my limbs [then] I chant so that I can go [free], the fetter springs from my feet and the shackle from my hands.'

5. Þat kann ek it fimmta:

ef ek sé af fári skotinn

flein í folki vaða,

flýgra hann svá stinnt,

at ek stǫðvigak,

ef ek hann siónum of sék.

'A fifth one I know: if I see a shot from a foe flying into the ranks
it will not soar so forcefully that I may not stop it - if I see it with
my own eyes.'

7. Þat kann ek it siaunda,

ef ek sé [sofenda] loga

sal um sessmǫgum,

brennrat svá breitt

at ek hánom biargigak

þann kann ek galdr at gala.

'A seventh one I know: if I see a hall of sleepers burning around
its bench-sitters, not so greatly does it burn that I cannot save it
– I know how to sing that charm.'

8. Þat kann ek it átta –

er ǫllum er

nytsamlikt at nema:

hvars hatr vex

með hildings sonom,

þat má ek bœta brátt.

'An eighth one I know which it is helpful for all to keep: where
hatred grows among the sons of a chief, I can quell it soon.'

11. Þat kann ek it ellipta,

ef ek skal til orrosto

leiða langvini,

undir randir ek gel,

en þeir með ríki fara

heilir hildar til,

heilir hildi frá,

koma þeir heilir hvaðan.

'An eleventh I know: if I must lead long-term friends into battle, beneath my shield I chant and they pass victorious – safe into the fight, safe away from the fight, they come away safe from anywhere.'

These charms form part of the kinds of magic that an able warrior might trust in when his life was at risk – the ability to quell disputes (8), to lead followers safely through danger (11), to prevent weapons from doing harm (5), to induce fear in his foes (3) and to shed it from his own men (4), to prevent a 'burning-in' (7), a particular kind of attack in which the enemy's house was surrounded and set ablaze, and any of those inside who managed to get out were cut down. This tactic was used in *Hrólfs saga Kraka* and is paralleled by the hall-burning episode commemorated in the fragmentary OE poem *The Fight at Finnsburg* and the corresponding summary in *Beowulf* ll.1063-1155 (Tolkien, 1982). It was also the fate of the *seiðmenn* led by *Rǫgnvaldr rettilbeini* when King Háraldr decided to put a stop to their magical practices.

BINDING AND LOOSING

The notions of binding and unbinding recur throughout Germanic Iron Age art, often in places of great prominence and importance. The motif in masculine contexts is applied to weapons and appears to have been a specifically military and Woden-based notion. The feminine aspects of binding appear rather to be connected with the traditional female crafts of spinning, weaving and the working of spells and enchantments.

Óðinn is said to have the power of the *herfjǫturr* 'army-fetter' which enabled him to render his foes impotent and immobile (Ellis Davidson, 1988, p.70; Kershaw, 2000, p.80) and *Ljóðatal* verse 4 refers to the god's power to defeat all restraints. It is likely that this notion derives from hunting, where nets and snares are used to immobilise even terrifyingly powerful opponents. The motif of capturing an animal opponent of great power was recalled in the mythic binding of the great wolf, Fenrir, in the *Eddas* and *Heimskringla*. As well as an aspect of the warrior initiation rite, the motif relates to hunting customs and mastery over the animal kingdom.

Binding could encompass more than the huntsman's prey, though. The Norse gods were able to bind the fates of men and were known collectively as *hǫpt* 'those who capture' and *bǫnd* 'those who bind', both words associated with confining and containing (Ellis Davidson, 1988, p.202). The interlaced, knotted, braided and woven artistic designs on weapons and wargear symbolise the gods' power to subdue, to take captives, to render others helpless, to enmesh foes in charms and keep them 'spellbound'.

One of the legendary kings in *Helgakvida Hundingsbana II* called Dagr ('day') sacrifices to Óðinn and receives the loan of a spear with which he means to kill his brother-in-law. He meets his opponent, Helgi ('holy one'), in a woodland spot called *fjǫturlundr* 'fetter-grove' and slays him there. The association of violent death, a forest grove and the binding of a foe raises the possibility that Helgi's death was a ritual act of sacrifice on Dagr's part, perhaps related to what Tacitus tells of the grove of the Semnones where sacrificial slaughter took place (Turville-Petre, 1964, p.51; Kay, 2013, p.22).

FIRST MERSEBURG CHARM

Alongside the motif of 'binding' is that of 'loosing' or 'freeing': a god who can apply a magical restraint must be able to undo the charm. A rare survival in Continental Germanic tradition is a spell in Old High German called the *First Merseburg Charm* which refers to just this process (text from Steinmeyer, 1916; Simek, 1993, s.v. *Idisi*; Pollington, 2011, p.317 following Tolley's amended text; Grundy, 2014, p.55; Price, 2019, p.295):

Eiris sâzun idisi

sâzun hera duoder

suma hapt heptidun

suma heri lezidun

suma clûbôdun

umbi cuoniouuidi:

insprinc haptbandun,

invar vîgandun.

'Once the ladies were sitting – they sat here and there; some braided fetters, some hindered a foe, some cleaved the bonds: leap free of the fetters, escape the foemen.'

The identity of the *idisi* 'ladies' is disputed: the OE cognate *idesa* usually refers to a high-born and dignified female of some status, while the Norse form *dísir* has a more overt supernatural quality, perhaps played down in the Christian Anglo-Saxon tradition (Storms, 1948, p.145; Lionarons, 2005, pp.273, 275-282).

Fetters and bonds are evident in Germanic art – Salin's Style I, II and III at the least, but even some of the later Viking period material in such traditions as Ringerike Style and Urnes Style show very clearly their derivation from the earlier formats. Dense bands and panels of linear ornament in 'interlace' or 'knotwork' form are typical of Northern European decoration from the Iron Age onwards. The evidence from e.g., shafts of spears is largely lacking in English contexts due to the poor preservation of both the metal and the wooden components, but the Iron Age parallels from Danish bog-deposits are decorated with a knotwork design which closely resembles the construction of braided thongs, and similarly suggests a notion of something bound or constrained: a weapon decorated in this way might have been magically 'charged' or 'empowered', since the tying of special knots was one of the means used to effect a charm. This was known as *þweng* 'knot, thong' in OE and is mentioned in several of the magical texts (Pollington, 2000, p.422; McLeod & Mees, 2006; Hall, 2007, p.119). The complex, dense interlace on items such as the Icklingham die or the Sutton Hoo belt buckle should certainly be considered in this light.

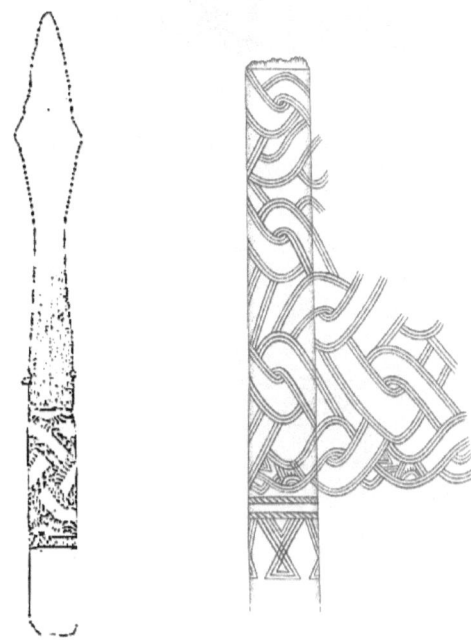

Fig. 27 Spearshafts with incised knotwork designs carved into the wooden surface. (Image: Lindsay Kerr)

Fig. 28 Strap-end from Würtemburg, Germany, with zoomorphic knotwork motifs. (Image: Lindsay Kerr)

Fig. 29 Bronze pressblech die from Icklingham, Suffolk England. (Image: Lindsay Kerr)

Reconstruction of the rectangular interlace panel from the Sutton Hoo shield
Source: Bruce-Milford vol. II, fig. 64, page 81.

Fig. 30 Reconstruction of the dense interlace panel from the outer face of the shield, Sutton Hoo Mound 1. (Image: Lindsay Kerr)

The binding imagery is not confined to weapons, but also occurs on other high-status items connected with the world of gift-exchange and feasting. The drinking horn vandykes from Taplow (Berkshire) show an open-mouthed male with his hands bound by a cord or rope; both the hands and their binding are prominently displayed, as if they are an important element in the iconography (Pollington, 2010, fig.13.47). Both Bauschatz and Lynn note the use of containers, vessels and feasting equipment in the display of power from various societies across ancient Europe (Bauschatz, 1982; Lynn, 2006, pp.118-21).

GUNGNIR – SPEAR OF VICTORY

Óðinn always uses a spear as his primary weapon, and marking with the tip of a spear was probably one of the initiatory rites associated with his cult. It is usually called in Norse *geirr* which is perhaps a throwing-spear rather than a thrusting-spear, although they are to some extent interchangeable. The preferred weapon of the military élite was the sword (e.g., Beowulf's *Nægling* and several other named weapons such as *Hrunting, Gramr, Balmung,* etc.) but we have Tacitus's testimony (*Germania,* ch.6.1) that, in the Iron Age, the weapons of Germanic tribesmen were short spears which could be used at close range or at a distance (text from Anderson, 1997):

> Hastas vel ipsorum vocabulo frameas gerunt angusto et brevi ferro
>
> 'They carry spears or, to use their own name, 'frameas', narrow and with a short blade'

and he notes (*Germania,* 13.1) that the emblems which a youth received when he achieved adulthood were the spear and shield. It is presumably in this context that we should regard Gungnir – a symbolically male weapon, an outward show of full membership of society. Graves of the pre-Christian period across northern Europe frequently contain a spearhead and knife; these were tokens of masculine identity.[248]

The god's spear is foregrounded in some descriptions, as when Egill calls him *geirs dróttin* 'lord of the spear' (*Egils saga Skallagrímsonnar,* ch.93). It is called Gungnir 'Shaker' or 'Swayer', and it is likely enough that when the god hung on the World Tree wounded with a spear, it was his own weapon which was used in this act of sacrifice. Óðinn received it from the dwarf-smiths, Brokk and Sindri, who made it in answer to Loki's challenge, according to the story presented in *Skáldskaparmál* (text from Faulkes, 1998, p.41):

---

[248] There is a danger of circular reasoning here because skeletal evidence does not always allow for an independent marker for the deceased's sex.

Eptir þat fór Loki til þeira dverga er heita Ívalda synir, ok gerðu þeir haddinn ok Skíðblaðni ok geirinn er Óðinn átti er Gungnir heitir. Þá veðjaði Loki hǫfði sínu við þann dverg er Brokkr heitir ...

'After that Loki went to those dwarfs who are called the sons of Ívaldi and they had made a [golden] head of hair and Skíðblaðnir [a collapsible boat] and the spear that Óðinn owned, which is called Gungnir. Then Loki pledged his own head with the dwarf who is called Brokk ...'

Loki was trying to avoid paying the dwarfs for their work, by challenging each of the brothers to outdo the other in the workmanship of the gifts he made for the gods.

The enigmatic *Sigrdrífumál* verse 17 gives a listing of places where runes should be carved, including the tip of the god's spear (text from Neckel, 1983):

> á gleri ok á gulli
>
> oc á gumna heillom,
>
> í víni oc í virtri
>
> oc vilisessi,
>
> 5 á Gungnis oddi
>
> oc á Grana bríósti,
>
> á nornar nagli
>
> oc á nefi uglo.

'On glass and on gold and on heroes' amulets; in wine and in wort, and beloved seats, on Gungnir's point and on Grani's breast, on the Norns' nails and on the beak of an owl.'

The *virtri* in l.3 is 'wort', a sweet-tasting liquid obtained from grain, one of the early stages in the production of beer and other alcoholic drinks. In l.6, 'Grani' is the horse ridden by Sigurðr, one of Óðinn's champions. Spearheads bearing runic text and sigils are known from archaeology (Pollington, 2016, pp.268-70).

In *Styrbjarnar þáttr Svíakappa* before the great battle to be fought outside the holy site of Uppsala in the late 10th c., King Eiríkr of the Swedes is handed a reed by a mysterious stranger wearing a broad-brimmed hat with the instruction to hurl it over the approaching army of his enemy, Styrbjǫrn, chanting the enabling phrase *Óðinn á yðr alla* 'May Óðinn have you all'. In flight, the reed becomes a spear and the attackers are engulfed in a landslide (Price, 2019, p.294). This motif – a humble and innocuous rod becoming a deadly spear – recurs in the *Gautreks saga* incident concerning the death of King Víkarr.

A spear thrown as an act of ceremonial destruction forms part of the tale of the priest Coifi in the *Historia Ecclesiastica Gentis Anglorum* tale regarding Northumbrian conversion. The spear-cast motif occurs considerably earlier in *The Battle of the Goths and Huns* in *Hloðskviða* where the trouble-making counseller, Gizurr – an old spear-fighter like the one among the Heaðobeardan in *Beowulf* – curses the Hunnish army and asks that 'May Óðinn let the spear fly according to my words'. Likewise, in *Eyrbyggja saga* (ch.44) a fight is opened with the throw of a spear, although this may have been regarded simply as a customary and symbolic act by the 13th c. with the meaning long forgotten.

As an aside, spear-imagery forms the principal motif of the poem *Darraðarljóð* 'Lay of Darts') which relates to the battle fought between the Irish High-King Brían Borumh and an alliance of Norse challengers led by Sigurðr, Earl of Orkney (Kershaw, 1922, pp.111-25). The poem appears in *Njáls saga* (ch.157).

CHAPTER 9

HEALER

'Were such things here as we do speak about? Or have we eaten on the insane root that takes the reason prisoner?'

Shakespeare, *Macbeth* I.iii

Other than occasional observations such as *Woden worhte weos* 'Woden made sanctuaries' in the *Exeter Book* verse *Maxims I*, the god features by name in only one OE narrative – part of a lengthy charm against diseases invoking the powers of various plants to assist the healer. The verse is normally referred to as the *Nine Herbs Charm*, part of the *Lacnunga* manuscript of medical and curative literature (London, British Library Harley MS 585). It is numbered as sections 79 to 83 in modern editions (Cockayne, 1864; Watkins, 1995, pp.424-6; Lindow, 2016, pp.114-5). The text was probably originally performative, involving a rehearsal of myth occurring in sacred time in order to effect a cure in quotidian time.

This aspect of Woden bearing arms against the *wyrm* (serpent), here portrayed as the disease-bringing enemy of man, displays the god's protective role where he is associated with healing and the prevention of illnesses (Grendon, 1909; Branston, 1957, p.97; Meaney, 1966, pp.110-1; Bremmer, 1991, p.412; Pollington, 2000, pp.501-2). In the charm, the healer fights against *onflyge* 'flying matter, flying venom' which has been linked to the flying spears of the elves, gods and witches of the *Wið Færstice* charm (Glosecki, 1989). There are other parallels between these two works – for example, the *wuldortanas* 'rods of wonder' may be thematically linked to the spears shot by the gods, elves and witch; or the 'dreadful enemy which roams the land' may reflect the loud riders thundering over the burial mound. Likewise the *wuldergeflogenum* of line 45 – 'wondrous things which fly' – may also denote the flying spears of the riders. The *onflyge* itself is

closely linked with the nine *attor* 'venoms' and with the snake, which
may be a poetic description (like *hildenædre* 'snake of war') of an arrow
or an unseen attacker.

CONTRA VERMES

A parallel case to that of the attack of the *wyrm* in *Lacnunga* above is an
Old Saxon charm 'Against Snakes', against a similar enemy (text from
Gallée, 1864, p.208; Glosecki, 1989; Tolley, 2009, p.449; Pollington,
2011, p.351):

> Gang ut, nesso mid nigun nessiklinon
>
> Ut fana themo marge an that ben,
>
> Fan themo bene and that flesg,
>
> Ut fan themo flesgke and this hud
>
> Ut fan thera hud and thesea strala.
>
> Drohtin, uuerthe so.

'Against a serpent. Go out, worm, with nine small worms, out from
the marrow into the bone, from the bone into the flesh, out from
the flesh into the skin, out from the skin into this arrow. Lord, may
it be so!'

While the charm does not specify the next step in the worm's removal,
it seems probable that the arrow would be shot into the wilderness, or
perhaps into a body of water, so that the serpent could not find its way
back to the patient or the healer.

In the *Ljóðatal* section of *Hávamál*, Óðinn claims that he has the
knowledge which healers need and furthermore that he is able to protect a warrior in battle (text from Dronke, 2011):

> 13. Þat kann ek it þrettánda,
>
> ef ek skal þegn ungan
>
> verpa vatni á,

munat hann falla,

þótt hannn í fólk komi,

hnígra sá halr fyr hiǫrum.

'A thirteenth I know: if I should drip water onto a young thane, he shall not fall even though he may come into a fight – that hero does not bow before swords.'

The god is of course highly competent in the use of runes and spells to further his own ends. This aspect is also emphasised in the *Second Merseburg Charm* where the damaged foot of a foal is enchanted by Sinthgunt and Frija in turn, presumably without success, but (third time lucky) finally *thu biguol en uuodan, so he uuola conda* 'then Wodan charmed it, as well he knew how'.

WULDORTANAS

It is significant that Woden bears *wuldortanas* 'rods (or twigs) of glory'. He uses them as a weapon against nine illnesses, and the rods are drawn from the nine powerful and magical plants which the god had previously charmed (Glosecki, 1989, p.121).[249] These rods may be the prototype of the staff or spear, *Gungnir*, which the Norse Óðinn carries on his travels. *Gungnir* is mainly used to foment strife and bad feeling among men, and the (admittedly fragmentary) Anglo-Saxon tradition is less apt to foreground this aspect of the god's character although Neidorf has detected elements of such disruptive behaviour in several texts (see Neidorf, 2022c).

The word *wuldortanas* is a compound of two elements: *wuldor* means 'splendour, glory' and is cognate with the Norse divine name *Ullr*, while *tanas* (plural of *tan*) are slips or slivers of wood, twigs or shoots. The word *tan* occurs in a passage in the poem *Andreas* where

---

[249] Page (1995, p.117) asserts that the text does not refer explicitly to rune-magic and should not be used to support speculation about the topic.

warriors cast lots by means of marks on slips of wood.[250] This in turn corresponds to the practice of lot-casting referenced in the *OE Rune Poem* verse 1 (text from Halsall, 1981):

ᚠ (Feoh) byþ frofur   fira gehwylcum

sceal ðeah manna gehwylc   miclun hit dælan

gif he wile for drihtne   domes hleotan.

'Wealth is a comfort to any man yet each person must share it readily if he should wish to be assigned a good name before his lord.'

The ambiguous *drihtne* reference here may mean a secular leader or 'the Lord' in the Christian religious sense. The verb *hleotan* carries the meaning 'gain by lots, acquire by chance or divine will' as well as 'be assigned'.

The god's role as healer is not foregrounded in the Scandinavian tradition which emphasises his position as leader of the Æsir, receiver of dead warriors, champion of warlords and trickster-god. Yet the Ribe skull fragment includes runic **uþin** (Óðinn) in its charm to cure pain. This text confirms the early association of Óðinn/Woden with healing and supports the idea that the god was able to bring health as well as death. The Bergen runic wand is much later but appears to derive from the same tradition.

GANDR

One Scandinavian Phase I text may be connected to the *wuldortanas* or 'glory-rods'. The Nordhuglo stone is carved with the retrograde

---

[250] Bremmer (1991, p.413-5) notes that compounds with *tan* fall into two groups: those descriptive of the wood (*actan* 'oak-twig', *misteltan* 'mistletoe') and those in which the sliver's purpose is emphasised (*hearmtanas* 'harm-twigs'). In *Beowulf* a sword is said to be *atertanum fah* (l.1459) 'ornamented with venom-twigs' which may be a reference to the pattern-welded 'herringbone' surface of the blade. A poetic association between words for 'sword' and *teinn* 'twig' (cognate with OE *tan*) is common in Icelandic tradition, e.g., *undateinn* 'wounding-twig'.

text **ekgudijaungandiz///**, i.e., *ek gudija ungandiz* 'I, a priest' followed by the adjective *ungandiz*, evidently formed with the privative or negative prefix *un-* and the root *gand-* which connotes 'something achieved through magic' or an 'object used in magical rites' as for example in *gandrekr* 'storm brought about by witchcraft', *gandreið* 'riding aloft by means of magic', *spágandr* 'spirits of foresight'. The phrase in *Þíðrekssaga: fór Ostracia út ok rœrði gand sinn*, 'Ostracia (a witch) went out and raised her magical power', shows that *gandr* might refer to the magical might of the wielder. The term *ungandiz* thus probably means 'not-bewitched, immune to sorcery' (Spurkland, 2005, pp.48-9).

Antonsen, on the other hand, takes the prosaic meaning of *gandr* as 'rod, stick' and translates the word *ungandiz* as 'not beaten, unvanquished' (Antonsen, 2002, p.225). The original meaning of *gandr* appears to relate to a staff or wand with which rites were enacted, and which was believed to confer power on the holder. It may be that the *gandr* is depicted on the Scandinavian *guldgubbar*, where male figures are shown with a staff with a splayed top like a sprouting plant (Tolley, 1995, p.70; Simek, 1993, s.v. *gandr, gondul*; Hupfauf, 2003, p.12; Price, 2003, pp.177-9; Watt, 2004, pp.167-222).[251] Such a wand was used by Skirnir to tame Freyr's reluctant bride, Gerðr; on it were written three words of power in runes: *ergi ok œði ok óþola* '[sexual] depravity and frenzy and unsated longing' (Hupfauf, 2003, p.127; Price, 2003, pp.177-80).[252] The spell could be reversed by erasing the runes.

Price noted the prohibition against using such magical devices in the Norwegian law-code *Eiðsivaþingslov* (1:24) (Price, 2003, p.175):

---

[251] North (1997, p.38) notes the Norse use of the word *gambanteinn* 'wand, twig with buds' in a magical context, which he associates with the Ingui cult of fertility and regrowth. The *gamban-* prefix refers to 'majesty' or the gods, and the *-teinn* is a twig or rod (cognate with OE *tan* as in the *wuldortanas*); the purpose of such a rod was to provoke delirium and sexual longing in the victim.
[252] The 'wand' was called both a *gambanteinn* 'rod of power' and a *tamsvǫndr* 'taming-wand' which Skirnir was able to use to break the lady's will. Both these terms have sexual overtones, and the three evils with which she is threatened all have a sexual element.

Engi maðr skal hafa í húsi sínu staf eða stalla, vítt eða blot eða þat er til heiðins siðar veit

'No man shall have in his house a staff or altar, sorcery-device or blood-sacrifice or whatever belongs to the customs of a heathen.'

The range of possible meanings extends further since ON *gandr* also referred to the spirit or supernatural being which assisted the magician: a bird, fish or even a werewolf. The magician's soul was able to ride such a spirit-animal, while in the physical world he or she bestrode a wooden staff (Spurkland, 2005, pp.35-40).[253] This practice was part of the *seiðr* tradition, which was specifically a female form of magic (Pollington, 2011, pp.393-5).[254] Not only small spirit-animals were involved though: Tolley noted that the Great Beast of the sea's depths was called *Jormungandr* 'vast *gandr*'.

The *gandr* spirit-animal was summoned using a special staff called a *vǫlr*, from which the ON word *vǫlva* 'she of the staff, seeress' was formed; the staff itself could also be called a *gǫndull* (Tolley, 1995, p.71; Mallory& Mair, 2000, p.150; Price, 2003, p.177).[255] Price related the references to the *gandr* in the form of a rod or staff to the presence of heavy iron staves in some female Scandinavian graves (e.g., the Oseberg ship-burial), each with a curious writhen basketwork handle. Similar examples of iron basketwork were found on iron chains, handles of spits and meat hooks, handles of keys – all symbolic roles associated with the world of women (Price, 2007).

All the above references relate to the use of a staff or rod which conferred power, with resonances in the Otherworld. It is surely no coincidence that Woden is involved in a tale of overcoming a serpent (a spirit of disease) using *wuldortanas*, rods of power.

---

[253] The male personal name *Woduridaz* 'frenzied rider' may be connected to this idea.

[254] Kvilhaug (2004, p.25) argues for more general male involvement in *seiðr* alongside a degree of opprobrium attached to those who used it.

[255] Another derivative of *vǫlr* is *vǫlsi*, an object of veneration in the form of a pickled horse's penis. Stakes and staves were sometimes used as representations of the gods (Pollington, 2011, p.87), as well as of humans.

HEALER ICONOGRAPHY

The designs impressed into the surface of bracteates were evidently of great significance to the societies which produced them. They serve no utilitarian purpose, unlike other highly decorated items such as brooches and clasps, and therefore 'may be considered a vehicle used primarily to convey status and belief' (Wicker, 2005, p.57). A single bracteate would be prominently displayed on a woman's costume, worn high on the chest alongside swags of glass and amber beads. Only close inspection would reveal the iconography and only those who were initiated into the religious and social rites would be able to read the messages encoded: perhaps ethnicity, status and identity as well as a religious affiliation.

Gaimster suggested that bracteates may have been used in ceremonies where they acted as symbolic payments, such as the taking of wergeld or a dowry (Gaimster, 1992, pp.13-5) while Abramson (2006, p.ix) noted that a form of stored value (i.e., a coinage) would be needed for symbolic purposes such as wergeld payments. If so, bracteates correspond symbolically to ritual objects such as arm-rings, which formed part of the gift-exchange system and the display of symbolic power in the Scandinavian, Anglo-Saxon and Merovingian worlds. The bracteate 'coins' were not 'money' in the commercial sense but 'donatives', symbolic gifts from a leader or ruler which indicated the initiation of a personal relationship with the recipient – a bond of mutual trust and loyalty. The use of bracteates as grave-goods probably expresses their status as personal belongings, carrying a declaration of the owner's power and worth, which was being 'stored' for the afterlife.

Bracteates may also have been used as symbolic gifts to the gods, made of the most precious metal – gold – and bearing imagery drawn from tales of the gods themselves. The iconography of Roman donatives (which are the source of the Germanic re-interpretations) often shows the Emperor as a divine figure. This symbol was adopted in the post-Roman Scandinavian cultural context, where the religious aspects were emphasised: the icon of the 'Emperor-God' became that of the 'King of the Gods' (Hauck, 1994; Franceschi, Jorn & Magnus, 2005a, p.46). Bracteates perhaps continued to function as items given in settlement of particular forms of debt – not mundane tribute to a landowner, but symbolic debts whose payment marked a rite of passage (i.e., wergeld, dowry, etc.). They formed part of a cultural assemblage which was used to bind together communities on the eastern, western and southern edges of the North Sea into a single cultural continuum, with a magical figure, 'Woden the healer', at its centre (Franceschi, Jorn & Magnus, 2005a, p.50).

The cultural background in which bracteates developed is that of southern Scandinavia, and the continuity of cultural tradition which bracteates demonstrate is that of the axis from the western Baltic to the southern North Sea, although they occur on the Continent (mainly northern Germany) and occasionally as far away as Hungary and Russia (Bakka, 1981; Hatch Wicker, 1992, p.149; Gaimster, 1992, p.2, 17). The Hungarian finds have been plausibly linked to the Langobards, who looked back to a legendary Scandinavian beginning and maintained a cultural connection with their former neighbours – here we may recall the practices of fosterage and of military service with a foreign leader, as well as diplomatic marriages. Local production within cultural groupings is suggested by the markedly regionalised distribution patterns, including such local features as the lack of a rim which is not usual in Scandinavia but occurs regularly on English finds.

Bracteates developed a rich iconographic tradition of their own, which included 'mythological' scenes and stylised animal designs. References to the Balder myth and to the *Miðgarðsormr* (Great Serpent which encircles the earth) appear on various bracteate types (Franceschi, Jorn & Magnus, 2005a, pp.48-9). The bracteate's imagery may have acted partly as a badge of rank for important females, such as the mead-offerers and priestesses known to have been associated with the rise of the warband and its male leadership (Hauck, 1994, pp.79-84).

A central figure in the presumed guise of a healer is a theme on many bracteates; this is often interpreted as 'Woden' based on English and German tradition, e.g., the *Lacnunga* section now called *The Nine Herbs Charm*, or the *Second Merseburg Charm* where *Uuodan* (Woden) is the last of several gods and goddesses to attempt the healing of a foal's lamed leg (Simek, 1993, s.v. *Second Merseburg Charm*; Hauck, 1994; North, 1997, p.83; Price, 2003, p.99). In this connection, the bracteate from Raflunda (Sweden) is among many which show the motif of the 'horse-whispering god' in which a large human head is poised above a quadruped with his mouth placed at the creature's ear, often interpreted as depicting the healing of the horse's foot, as recounted in the *Second Merseburg Charm*. The scene is surrounded by a double-headed serpent with gaping jaws and sharp teeth, strongly reminiscent of the creature on the crest of the Sutton Hoo helmet.

CHAPTER 10

CONCLUSION

'Le doute n'est pas une condition agréable, mais la certitude est absurde.'
(Doubt is an uncomfortable condition, but certainty is a ridiculous one.)
Letter from Voltaire to Frédéric II, King of Prussia, 6 April 1767

We have seen that the study of Woden in his various guises encompasses a wide range of evidence – literary, of course, but also runic epigraphy and iconographic. That aside, the vast range of nicknames and pseudonyms which can refer to him introduces an element of uncertainty: is Gautr the 'same' as Óðinn? And if he is, does that make Geat the 'same' as Woden? How can we tell?

Despite the general feeling that there is little more to be said for sure about the god and his cult – he is never named directly by classical sources, and the physical iconography is necessarily ambivalent – I believe that the investigation presented in these pages has opened up several possibilities for further investigation.

'THE ROMAN INTERPRETATION'?

How should we understand the many literary references to the god in our medieval sources? What do the early runic texts have to say? What do the archaeological finds tell us about the worship of Woden, his cult and his mysteries? What can we infer about his origins from these data? As is usually the case when discussing medieval Europe, the 'Romans' have to be invoked as initiators and originators. Of course, 'Romans' can mean vastly different things according to context. Does it mean Republic or Empire, Eastern or Western Empire, pagan or Christian, Arian or Catholic?

How many 'Romans' were involved in the Claudian invasion of Britain? The bulk of the military personnel – the front-line troops – were drawn from subject peoples such as the Tungri and Batavi tribes (settled in the modern Netherlands) according to Tacitus (*Historia*, Book IV); the officers were perhaps veterans of the Gallic campaigns and drawn from across the Empire. How many of these putative 'Romans' had ever even visited the city of Rome, we may wonder? While we can characterise them as 'politically Roman', i.e., servants of the state centred on Rome, it may be that their diverse origins intruded into their daily lives in ways that we cannot begin to capture. Invoking 'Roman' origins may therefore involve making assumptions about the loyalties and outlook of the 'Roman' community that are not warranted.

As regards the cult of Woden – which is to say, the praxis, the details of his worship and the appropriate kinds of devotion shown to him – we have to begin with three areas of evidence: (i) the cults of Mercurius, especially in the context of the Roman *limes*, with all its military and commercial dimensions; (ii) the Roman military machine and the place of Germanic recruits within it; (iii) the glamour of the Emperor as a remote and fabled figure with power over lesser kings and chiefs.

Mercury was not one of the principal deities of classical Rome, although his worship does seem to have been popular with the military. We may broadly characterise the main area of his devotion as northern Gaul, the Rhineland and Britain – all outlying or border areas with a strong military presence, which manifested itself in the material culture and in the epigraphic remains. Whether we follow Enright in inferring an ultimately Gaulish origin for the god or not, we must allow that a number of shared or compatible elements combined to result in a religious tradition that possesses some striking characteristics: notably an emphasis on the art of negotiation; on fluent and persuasive speech; on oracular wisdom couched in verse; on the acquisition of a form of literacy from a supernatural source; on the curing of and protection from disease; on military strategy; on initiation and transformation; on a reliance on secrecy resulting in disguise, dissimulation, deception.

Halamarðus and Hranno may be examples of local gods whose worship shared enough points of similarity with those of Mercury to enable an equation to be made; we cannot know exactly which features were selected for this purpose. But these figures – the one who hosts dead warriors in his hall and the other who is associated with aggressive speech – perhaps played some part in the development of the persona of the later god. Such features persisted as far as the Middle Ages in aspects of the cult of Óðinn.

Perhaps the Hellvi helmet with its mask and its modified eyes will prove to be a crucial piece of evidence here (Price & Mortimer, 2014, p.12). The helmet is undoubtedly the product of an official 'Roman' workshop (perhaps one situated in the Rhineland) and it was most likely brought to Gotland in one of two ways: either as part of the equipment of a Scandinavian man retiring home after years of service in the Roman military, or else as an item of booty captured in some local military expedition against Roman forces – and here it is difficult to resist the parallel of the 6th c. Geatish King Hygelac who mounted a raid on Frankish territory at the mouth of the Rhine in the early 6th c. (Chambers, 1963, pp.2-13). Once brought safely to Gotland, the helmet was modified by a local metalworker before being mounted prominently on a post in the hall of a regional potentate, where it seemingly formed the focus of that community's religious observances before being roughly handled in the later destruction of that building.

MASKS AND ICONOGRAPHY

The initial veneration of the helmet and mask demonstrates a respect for the power and authority it embodied, subject to the later physical modifications which made it appropriate for the specific local religious use to which it was then to be put. The mask of the helmet incorporated – perhaps embodied – the essence of *imperium*, of an eerie otherworldliness, of an impassive and highly ornate countenance which was both impressive and unsettling. The glamour of the Caesar – the Emperor – was captured in this highly-prized item of wargear.

Representation of the 'divine mask' in two dimensions later came to convey wealth, military might and arcane secrets which might be harnessed and shared by the leaders of successive communities through religious rituals and ceremonies. The anthropomorphic figures reproduced so carefully on bracteates bear witness to a similar adaptation of Roman imperial imagery to local religious conventions (Hauck, 1985–9; Price & Mortimer, 2014, p.13; Imer & Vasshus, 2023). The Undley example is especially pertinent here, as it shows elements of the design of both the obverse and reverse of the *Urbs Roma* coin type on which it is based, but again modified with an extensive and enigmatic runic text (Pollington, 2016, pp.170-6). The bracteate displays clearly the political aspiration of the group which used it, for whom the Emperor was a remote, 'otherworldly' and quasi-divine figure with power over luck, health, wealth and magic. Although he was only presented as a profile bust, the symbols of power surround him and encompass him: the emblematic headgear, the Woden-won runic script, and the others of which the meaning is still unclear.

Does the symbolic and supernatural 'disembodied head' of the bracteate tradition give rise to the later notion of Mímir, companion and confidante of Óðinn, as a superannuated severed head with prophetic powers? The motif of the protective 'severed head' – itself an ancient device which manifested itself in the Greek *Gorgoneion* and elsewhere – is represented persistently in the traditions of Iron Age Europe (Armit, 2012), for example, in Bran the Blessed (Bendigeid Vran) of the *Mabinogion*. It became a symbol of mastery over death, and of the owner's access to the knowledge which made this possible.

The 'head' or 'mask' motif eventually appeared on coins and elsewhere, deepening the association between 'ruler', 'deity' and 'wealth'. Moreover, the Vindelev example, with its specific naming of the god *Wodanaz*, sheds a light on the early representation of his worship: the image there is of the dutiful worshipper, perhaps fulfilling his oath of loyalty to the god.

Fig. 31 The Undley bracteate with helmeted head, wolf-and-twins motif and runic text. (Image: Lindsay Kerr)

Masks and disguises allowed Woden-Óðinn to move easily through-out human society, passing among his victims and enemies without arousing suspicion, maintaining an unassuming and unobtrusive appear-ance. Deception and cunning were much prized by the military and its strategist-leaders, whose successes promoted the worship of the patron-god. The deceit extends into our modern understanding, whereby it is often difficult to be sure of motives and meanings. Price stated the situa-tion clearly (Price & Mortimer, 2014, p.13):

> '…although an Odinnic symbolism seems clear to us, at the time it may have meant something subtly different … the trajectory of storytelling and myth-making may have come very far indeed from the mid-sixth century to the thirteenth when most of our sources were written down … The meaning of these narrative objects may best be understood as a web of connections, intersections and implications. Within its tangles we can discern the importance of border-crossing and liminality, masking and drama, the role of ritual warfare, leadership and sacrifice.'

Schjødt (2020b, p.1144) likewise cautions against the imposition of a predetermined 'meaning' on the ancient material:

'these sources can probably not be taken to relate mythic ideas that were necessarily common throughout Scandinavia because traditions about the relations and structures within the world of the gods are likely to have varied substantially from one area to another.'

Regional and local preferences must have played a far greater part in the lived experience of religion and worship than our sources can convey.

SUCCESSOR STATES

Literary (not epigraphic) references naming Woden begin in the early medieval period as he develops from a numinous and remote figure (perhaps the leader of the Wild Hunt) into a more approachable – if still untrustworthy – character.

The largest group of references to Woden in *early* medieval literature is probably in the OE kinglists, where his name usually figures near the end (i.e., chronologically removed from the time of the text's composition), meaning that he was considered an ancestral figure from the distant past (North, 1997, pp.12-3, 111ff; Shaw, 2002, p.101; Pollington, 2011, p.189). Of the surviving Anglo-Saxon royal lines, only the East Saxon kings resisted citation of Woden as royal ancestor. It is nevertheless probable that successful kings and leaders of the 5th-7th centuries saw themselves as heirs and kinsmen of the gods, and so likely to benefit from access to their wisdom and advice.

The incidence of Woden-based imagery on the royal wargear from Sutton Hoo Mound 1 shows that already in the early 7th c. tales were being told relating to the mead of inspiration and the complex string of shameful and ignoble incidents which brought it into the realm of the gods. (In Norse tradition these include the betrayal and killing of Kvasir; facilitated killing of the hay-cutters by Bölverkr; attempted killing of Óðinn by Baugi; deception and seduction of Gunnlöð, and others). A strong link to alcohol and its ceremonial consumption by human society appears at this time – probably always an essential factor in the rituals of the military, but now given a greater prominence with the evolution of 'kingship' and the rise of new forms of social structure which included a central role for resplendently dressed females with the combined status of bearers of tradition (displayed in the rich symbolism of their dress and jewellery) and bestowers of worth and rank. A large gathering-space in which these ceremonies could be conducted formed an essential part of the structure of governance.

Elsewhere, the Lombard sources depict the god as a beneficent patron, able to bestow military success according to his changeable wishes, but nonetheless capable of being out-manoeuvred by his spouse. This vision of Woden relates him directly to the power structures of the post-Roman world, and to the god's role as 'political leader' which entailed the trappings of a human chief (hall, bedchamber, etc.).

Public enactment of religious ceremonies (ON *blót*) figures in many discussions of the god's worship: the gathering of countryfolk whom Columbanus interrupted in their sharing of ale, the cult-house which King Edwin's priest tore down, the *triclinium* at Uppsala where figures of the gods were housed. If human leaders needed to demonstrate their power by showing themselves among their people (the medieval king's *iter* or ceremonial journey among his supporters being the obvious example), then it follows that a demonstration of power by the gods would need to be similarly public. Worship appears to have been a communal experience, an occasion when community bonds and hierarchies could be strengthened; this would apply equally to the various rites of initiation undergone by youths on the path to adulthood and leadership.

But with the adoption of Christianity as the dominant ideology across western Europe, the god retreated somewhat into the shadows: he might appear as a 'mysterious stranger' who changed the fortunes of a favoured nobleman at a crucial point in his career (Edwin) or as the patron of a long-lived troublemaker who managed to disrupt the political geography of Europe (Widsith) and topple ruler after ruler according to the plan of his protector deity. He was recalled for his military exploits and his creation of sanctuaries (*Woden worhte weos*) which remained on the edge of memory, but perhaps he no longer commanded respect, only fear.

A SCANDINAVIAN VIEW

On the outer edge of northern Europe, Scandinavia retained many traditions which elsewhere had already fallen into disuse. Its unique position enabled its inhabitants to straddle the twin traditions of the classical and pagan worlds. The value of Scandinavian evidence to the enquiry into Woden-Óðinn is immeasurable, if not always easy to evaluate. Lindow (2003) has argued that the early texts can be read as descriptions of a human 'performer' who had acquired shamanic skills among the Sámi, but Schjødt (202b, p.1148) cautions that 'Snorri probably knew other sources on Óðinn, which were in accordance with this picture [*Ynglinga saga*] … the Óðinn figure, whom Snorri presents here, seems to accord with what we know about the god from other sources, although many details may be of dubious value' and (p.1149) 'The main point here, however, is that these abilities all conform to what other evidence leads us to expect of a guardian god of chieftains and kings in a religious society such as that of pre-Christian Scandinavia: he should be able to manipulate both nature and culture for the benefit of land and people by supernatural or numinous means.'

Óðinn was considered treacherous, changeable, wilful – qualities which made him a dangerous ally. Perhaps his use of *seiðr* likewise made him unpredictable and volatile. It seems that both Loki and Óðinn shared a lack of respect for the normal standards of conduct, and both accepted an accusation of 'effeminacy' or undertaking a female role (*Lokasenna*, stanzas 23-24). The fact that they became blood brothers probably denotes an exchange of attributes, a blending of their qualities and the associated negative qualities (Schjødt, 2020b, pp.1152-3).

If, as Schjødt implies, Saxo and Snorri were largely correct in their presentations of the Æsir as a group and of Óðinn in particular, what relevance does this have for the study of pre-Christian religion?

To answer such a question, it is necessary first to specify which period and place is under discussion, since there is no doubt at all that the notions and expectations of an Iron Age farmer in 4th c. Jutland would be very different from those of an 11th century warlord in Dublin.

The trajectory of development began with the god as an elemental force, be it as the hunter of souls, the bearer of inspiration and enlightenment, the arbiter of victory. The success of military campaigns, indeed the survival of a whole people, rested on his continued favour. However, by the end of the medieval period, as social expectations and religious notions developed, he became little more than a stock figure from folktale – the 'sage', the 'wise old man' who provides the hero with advice, a warning, an implement which will help him fulfil his quest: far from a terrifying and revelatory figure, he became Merlin, Gandalf or Obi-Wan Kenobi – a mere facilitator. Yet those who spurned his help learnt to rue their choices.

DARK LIGHT IN A BRIGHT AGE

> Odin's sacrifice is appropriate to his roles as god of Wōd who has become High God: he bestows poetic vision, he transfixes the enemy army; but he also sees all the worlds from his high seat. It is also fully in character for this god who underwent self-torture to compel the runes to his service: he is emerging as a god who is obsessed with acquiring the power of knowledge.
>
> Kershaw, *The One-Eyed God*

Woden brought his worshippers and favourites a brilliant career and immense success - but always accompanied by the inescapable fact of his guile and his treachery. In fact, the god is almost defined by his wilful and transgressive nature, his willingness to step beyond the boundaries of what is normally considered acceptable, fair or reasonable. He represents and typifies the arrogant and 'aristocratic' nature of his followers who were larger-than-life characters in many ways, always willing to think the unthinkable, to perform deeds beyond the normal compass of man's behaviour. Kings and nobles were supposed to be law-makers and upholders of order, but the followers of Woden just as often broke those laws as they observed them.

Scandinavian contact with Anglo-Saxon England and Western Europe encouraged development of an adapted Western European style social model including stable states, efficient bureaucratic and fiscal machinery, and an attempt at orderly succession in the office of 'king'. It may have been this recognition – that the 'chiefdom' social model, which persisted in Scandinavia longer than in Western Europe, was doomed to fail when confronted by better-organised opposition – which led to the development and settlement of trading communities: a first step towards emulating medieval European societies in the north. The largest and most successful of these were under the control of ecclesiastical authorities – Copenhagen in Sealand (Denmark) and Sigtuna on Lake Mälaren (Sweden) (Sawyer, 1994, p.163). These sites were intended from the outset to be royal-sponsored mercantile centres, with political and ideological control over a large area. They were also centres from which Christianity could be imposed on the local population.

But these medieval mercantile sites were preceded by similar complex settlements, as modern archaeology is revealing – Uppakra, Gudme, Lejre, Ribe and several others in southern Scandinavia, with contemporary equivalents along the North Sea coasts in the Netherlands and Britain (Grundvad, pers. comm.). The principal buildings and enclosures are often of huge proportions – a recent (2023) discovery of a hall at Rendlesham, Suffolk, is estimated at 10 metres long and 5 metres wide set in a compound of about 15 hectares with a perimeter of 1.5km, large enough to accommodate a community of worshippers which perhaps encompassed a broad territory along the east coast of Britain (reported in the national press on 22nd November 2023 – e.g., *Heritage Daily, Daily Telegraph* and elsewhere).

This find has a particular relevance since it is likely the 'temple' or 'cult-house' associated with the kingly family whose mounds and ship-burials were created at nearby Sutton Hoo, above the River

Deben. This structure may be the same building as the one in which Edwin was to lodge before the mysterious stranger approached him – or even the very temple which Bede mentioned, in which King Rædwald erected an altar to Christ alongside the existing ones to the traditional gods of the Angles. As a polytheist, the king probably saw no difficulty in practicing different forms of worship in the same sacred space – although Bede disagreed on this point.

This indeed was a turning point. Followers of the old war-god did not fit easily into the new, classically-inspired Judaeo-Christian mould (Neidorf, 2022c, ch.1). The decisive actions of the heroes of earlier times – Ingeld of the Heaðobeardan would be a good example, or Hengest of the *Finnesburh* episode – were not easily accommodated to the new ways of thinking. These men lived in an age dominated by the imperative of 'duty', of behaving well according to the moral code of the day which comprised two main directives: (i) do not kill members of your own family, and (ii) do not break your freely-given word. Needless to say, in the beloved old tales the 'hero' was put in a position where he could not fulfil both these obligations.

As already discussed, Ingeld's father, King Froda, had been killed in a war against the Danes but later the Danish king, Hroþgar, offered Ingeld the hand of his own daughter *tō bōte* 'in compensation' as the law-codes might have put it: a means of creating a new and peaceful relationship between bitter enemies with many a grievance on both sides. Ingeld accepted the generous offer and was betrothed to the princess; at the wedding celebration, an old warrior from the Heaðo-bard warband incited a youngster to attack one of the Danish guests, at which fighting broke out and the Dane was slain but the killer es-caped and Ingeld was drawn into the fray. He then had to choose: should he keep his word to his bride and his father-in-law, and impose a cessation of hostilities to avoid kin-slaying? Or should he obey his sworn duty to avenge his father's death on the man who had brought it about: his father-in-law, King Hroþgar? In the end, at the insistence of the *eald æscwiga* 'old spear-fighter' Ingeld could not bear to leave his father's death unavenged and his family thus shamed. He broke faith with the Danes and led an attack on their stronghold which saw their mighty hall burnt down, but it cost him and his men their lives.

This tale (and probably many others like it) was evidently popular among the Anglo-Saxon élite in the 8th c. In a letter to Bishop Unwona of Leicester, datable to 797 AD, Alcuin fulminated against its recitation in monastic halls where uplifting bible stories should have been told instead (text from Malone, 1959, p.1):

> Verba Dei legantur in sacerdotali convivio. Ibi decet lectorem audiri, no citharistam; sermones patrum, no carmina gentilium. Quid enim Hinieldus cum Christo? Angusta est domus; utrosque tenere non poterit ... Non vult rex coelestis cum paganis et perditis nominetenus regibus communionem habere ...

> 'The words of God should be read at a communal meal for clerics. It is fitting to hear there a reader, not a harp-player; sermons of the Fathers [of the church], not songs of the heathens. What has Ingeld to do with Christ? The house is narrow: it cannot hold both ... the king of heaven will not be associated with pagans and lost so-called kings ...'

However, from a Christian perspective, what lesson can be drawn from Ingeld's story? It is not a simple tale of 'good versus evil', of moral rectitude opposed to villainous iniquity, of heroic St. George and the inimical Dragon. Rather, it is a complex and tragic tale of a man who wishes to behave well, but in his special circumstances he finds he cannot – he must disobey one or other of the principal obligations of his society. To attempt to evade the decision would be doubly unacceptable, since it would satisfy neither imperative.

Such is the fate of the 'migration period' hero who precedes the medieval knight: he does not fight for Christ, nor even for his liege-lord, but rather for his and his kindred's good name at no matter what personal cost. His patron might be any of the old gods, but the instigator of the action is Woden, stirrer of strife.

Strife – bloody and inherently unresolvable – defines those long centuries when the old world of 'antiquity' was shaken, taken apart and re-shaped into a new order following a different set of ethical imperatives, but no less violent and turbulent in any case. It took the leadership of men following Woden and striving for *ealdorlang tir* 'life-long glory' to build new, purposeful and confident societies which could deal with the challenges to come.

THE WAY AHEAD

Future research may be taken in new directions by archaeological finds – for instance, the Vindelev bracteate may prove to be one of many with a similar image and text and each new find will add another clue to the puzzle. Furthermore, the (supposed) Anglian cult-house at Rendlesham which served the élite of East Anglia buried at Sutton Hoo (revealed by excavation in 2023) may disclose features which will aid our understanding of the praxis of Woden's worship. Buildings of a similar nature are under excavation in eastern Jutland at the time of writing, which may in turn shed new light on the relations between 6th c. Denmark and East Anglia. Physical objects have a story to tell.

Research into the literary records is perhaps unlikely to produce more new texts to study – although undiscovered or neglected Latin summaries of known works are always a possibility. So also is the establishment of the locations of cult-sites through toponymy and cartographic studies. More promising is the re-evaluation of known texts in the light of fresh ideas and insights.

The old one-eyed god was always thought wily and wilful, but in the end his riddles could be solved. That work continues.

Appendix I: Divine Threes

Note: In the following tabulation, where a name appears to correspond etymologically or by character to *Woden*, I have included it in the first column regardless of where it appears in the source's order.

Source	Origin	Date	1	2	3
Nordendorf brooch	WGmc	7ᵗʰ c.?	wodan	logaþore	wigiþonar
Ribe skull fragment	NGmc	8ᵗʰ c. or earlier	uþin	ulfr 'wolf'	hótýR 'high god'
Old Saxon Baptismal Vow	WGmc	9ᵗʰ c.?	Uoden	Thunaer 'thunder'	Saxnot 'sword-friend'
Gesta Hammaburgensis Ecclesiae Pontificum	NGmc	11ᵗʰ c.	Wodan	Thor 'thunder'	Fricco 'beloved'
Lokasenna (Poetic Edda)	ON	13ᵗʰ c. or earlier	Óðinn	Vili 'will'	Vé 'holy one'
Gylfaginning	ON	13ᵗʰ c. or earlier	Hár 'high'	Jafnhár 'just as high'	Þriði 'third'
Vǫluspá	ON	13ᵗʰ c. or earlier	Óðinn	Lóðurr	Hœnir
Prose Edda	ON	13ᵗʰ c. or earlier	fyrsti 'first'²⁵⁶	annarr 'second'	þriði 'third'

---

[256] These are not necessarily proper names, and are used in the narrative to distinguish the three deities who give life and form to the first human beings.

APPENDIX II: *ÓÐINSHEITI* – THE BYNAMES OF ÓÐINN

In Scandinavian myth as they have come down to us from various sources, Óðinn bears a truly prodigious quantity of bynames; Price (2019) lists 204 based on research into the *Edda*, skaldic verse, *þula* lists and traditional tales, ignoring alternative readings and possible copying errors.[257] Some of these names reflect aspects of his many mythic adventures, others describe his appearance and his association with magic, wayfaring, necromancy, military success, deep thought; others (e.g., *Yggr* 'the fearsome one') are perhaps tabu names given to refer to the god without invoking him (cf. 'Old Nick' used for Satan in English folklore) (Kershaw, 2000, pp.1-9; Jakobsson, 2011, p.7).

The multitude of names attributable to Óðinn was a puzzle even to Viking period skalds and their medieval counterparts. The price of gaining such a breadth of information could be hard to bear, as Egill says in his poem *Sonatorrek*, verse 24, composed on the accidental death of his sons (for which no reciprocal vengeance could be taken): *Gáfumk íþrótt ulfs of bági vígi vanr vammi firða* 'The wolf's foe, hardy in battle, dealt a spotless skill to me' (Kershaw, 1922, p.140; Jackson, 2012, p.58). Here Egill uses the poetic kenning device to call his patron-god Óðinn 'the wolf's foe', in reference to the monstrous beast which will finally devour him.

The god's propensity for transformation and deceit lies behind many of these names: for example, in the tale of the gaining of the mead, he appears as a nobleman, a vagrant farmhand (*Bǫlverkr*), a snake, a handsome young man and an eagle (Jakobsson, 2011, p.8). Two specific and much-referenced areas of activity are warfare and magic (Schjødt, 2020b, p.1149). Some of the names understood to refer to Óðinn may be plausibly assigned to other deities (e.g., *Þórr*); or they may have been given to originally separate divinities whose legends and worship became blended with those of the dominant god.

Below is a summary of the principal names attributed to Óðinn and a specimen citation for each (Falk, 1924; Simek, 1993; Kershaw, 2000; Price, 2019, pp.63-9). The list is not exhaustive, so that a few very obscure names have been

---

[257] See Price, 2019, pp.62-8 for a full discussion of the topic, based on the work of Hjalmar Falk (*Odensheite*, 1924) supplemented by subsequent scholarship (Schjødt, 2020b, p.1149). A handful of names are ambiguous, or still unexplained and Kershaw (2000) offers alternative explanations for some. Many are referenced in *Óðins nǫfn*, a versified list of names for Óðinn preserved in certain manuscripts of *Skáldskaparmál*.

omitted (e.g., *Eylúðr* 'island-crock', which defies explanation). Many names have more than one meaning (*Gautr*, for example) which makes a dependable interpretation impossible.

Aldafǫðr 'Father of men', so 'progenitor' or 'ancestor of all [people]'. *Vafþrúðnismál* 4.

Aldagautr 'Gautr of men' where *Gautr* may mean 'sacrifice' but elsewhere 'man from Gotland' or 'father, ancestor'. *Baldrs draumar* 2. The form *Aldingautr* appears in the *IRP* where the sense is 'father from old times', so 'originator'.

Alfǫðr The term *alfǫðr* 'all-father' appears to derive from an ancient theonym, perhaps of Late Bronze Age date, shared by Germanic- and Celtic-speakers (Koch, 2020, p.139). The hypothetical proto-form **olo-patēr* gives rise to the Norse term and to the Middle Irish (*Eochu*) Ollathair, a designation of the Dagda who himself also has many bynames. *Helgakviða Hundingsbana I* 38, *Grímnismál* 48.

Arnhǫfði '[He with the] eagle-head', probably a reference to the myth of the theft of the mead in which the god transforms into a bird of prey. Elsewhere (*Grettis saga* 38), he is called *Ǫrn* 'eagle'. This is also one of his shape-shifting or disguise names, like *Bjǫrn* 'bear' and others. *Óðins nǫfn*.

Atríðr 'Attack-rider' emphasizing the god's military skill and aggression; sometimes the weak form *Atríði* is used. *Grímnismál* 48.

Auðun(n) 'Wealth-friend' in reference to the god's ability to create prosperity for his worshippers, in much the same way as in *Beowulf* (l.2584) the king is called *goldwine* 'gold-friend'. *Óðins nǫfn*.

Báleygr 'Flame-eyed' with specific reference to the *bál* or cremation fire, so emphasizing the god's role in the death-rites. This name may give rise to the figure called *Bolwisus* in Saxo's account of the hero Hagbardus (ch.VII). *Hákonardrápa* 6.

Biflindi 'Shield-shaker' or 'he who has a painted shield' or 'he who makes shields tremble', so a terrifying enemy. *Grímnismál* 49.

Bileygr 'Weak-eyed', a counterpart to *Báleygr* emphasising the god's lack of binocular vision. This name probably appears as the character *Bilwisus* in Saxo. *Grímnismál* 47.

Bjarki 'Little bear' and *Bjǫrn* 'bear', both referring to shapeshifting and to the *berserkir* warriors who follow the god. *Harðar Saga* 15.

Blindr 'Blind one' (also *Blindi*) referring to the god's lack of an eye. *Helgakviða Hundingsbana II*.

Bragi 'Poet' or 'Skilful Speaker', perhaps originally 'lord, leader'; the OE form *brego* appears in *Beowulf* (1.427, 609, 1954) without obvious supernatural meaning. The name is borne by a hero in *Valhǫll* in *Eiríksmál* and the notion of a separate god of poetry may have arisen from there. Only in *Hǫfuðlausn* is there a clear connection to Óðinn.

Brúni 'Brown one' referring to the bear – see *Bjarki*. Possibly a reference to the god's bushy eyebrows which hide his eyes from men.

Bǫlverkr 'Bale-worker, evil-doer' the *nom de voyage* that the god uses when posing as an agricultural labourer with a magical whetstone, in an episode relating to the gaining of the mead in *Skáldskaparmál* 58

Draugadróttinn 'Lord of the undead' or 'chieftain of ghosts', in reference to the god's ownership of *Valhǫll* and role as a psychopomp. *Ynglinga saga*, ch.7.

Dresvarpr 'Proud and wild' or perhaps 'he who casts [a weapon] incautiously'. *Óðins nǫfn*.

Dǫrruðr 'Spear-fighter' from **darr-hǫðr* 'dart-warrior' or *darraðr* 'throwing-spear, dart', in reference to the god's use of the spear as his weapon. *Darraðarljóð*.

Farmaguð 'Cargo-god', in reference to the god's connection to wealth and prosperity in *Gylfaginning* 10. Also found as *Farmatýr* in *Grímnismál* 48 with much the same meaning. The phrase *farmr Óðins* 'Óðinn's burden' appears in reference to the theft of the mead of inspiration.

Farmǫgnuðr 'He who travels with power' referring to his escape from *Hnitborg* with the mead of inspiration in his belly. *Háleygjatal* 2.

Fengr 'He who seizes' perhaps in reference to the god's taking souls after death; but possibly like OE *fengel* 'prince' meaning 'he who takes [booty]'. *Reginsmál* 18

Fimbultýr 'Great god' or 'mighty power'; The OE cognate of the proto-theme is *fifel* used in *Beowulf* (1.104 *fifelcynnes eard*) to describe a kind of sea-monster (Holthausen. 1974, s.v. *fifel*). *Vǫluspá* 60.

Fimbulþulr 'Mighty speaker' or 'one with great prophetic power'; the *þulr* was the speaker on religious occasions. *Hávamál* 80.

Fjallgeiguðr 'Mountain-dangler' or 'fell-traveller' in reference to the god's wandering in remote places. *Óðins nǫfn*.

Fjǫlnir 'Very wise (one)' or perhaps 'he who hides things' in reference to the mead of inspiration. *Grímnismál* 47.

Fjǫlsviðr 'Very wise' in reference to his depth of knowledge. *Grímnismál* 47.

Fráríðr 'From-rider' perhaps 'he who rides away in victory', if not 'he who rides off (to war)'; a counterpart to *Atríðr*. *Skáldskaparmál*.

Fundinn 'He who has been found', in a 14th c. kenning by Einarr Gilsson.

Gagnráðr 'He who countermands' or 'he who advises against' or 'opponent (in a discussion)'. *Vafþrúðnismál* 8.

Gangleri 'Wanderer' or 'one who is tired from walking' in reference to his wayfaring. *Grímnismál* 46.

Gangráðr 'Way-adviser' or 'he who knows the path'; possibly a misspelling of *Gagnráðr*. *Vafþrúðnismál* 8.

Gautr 'Man of Gotland' or 'Man of the Gautar' or 'Goth' or 'sacrifice'. In most senses 'a tribal leader', but since *gautr* can also refer to a corpse, the meaning may be 'sacrifice'. Also found in the weak form *Gauti*. *Óðins nǫfn*.

Gautatýr 'God of the Gotlanders' or 'of sacrifices', etc. see *Gautr* above. *Hákonarmál* 1.

Geiguðr 'Dangler' or 'hanged man' in *Ynglinga saga* ch.22.

Geirlǫðnir 'He who invites [men] to the spear-fight' in reference to the god's role in warfare and his characteristic weapon. *Óðins nǫfn*.

Geirǫlnir 'Spear-charger' or 'he who rushes out with a spear' also found as a valkyrie-name *Geirǫnul* in *Grímnismál* 36.

Geirtýr 'Spear-god' in *Hákonarkviða* 21.

Geirvaldr 'Spear-wielder' or 'master of the spear' in *Stjǫrnu-Oddadraumr* 7.

Gestr 'Guest, stranger' in reference to the god's wayfaring, the name by which he introduces himself in *Ólafs saga hins helga*.

Gestumblindi Blind guest (= 'guest with impaired vision') The name the god assumes in *Hervarar Saga* when he undertakes a wisdom-contest with King Heiðrek. Saxo (ch.VI) has *Gestiblindus* as a king of Gotland.

Ginnarr 'Deceiver' or 'bewitcher' (or 'originator'). *Óðins nǫfn*.

Gizurr 'Guesser' i.e, he who guesses correctly in a game of wits. Similar in this respect to *Sanngetall*. *Málsháttakvæði* 22.

Goðjaðarr 'Protector the gods' in Egill's *Sonatorrek* 23.

Glapsviðr 'Seducer' or 'he who seduces with ease' relating to the god's many attempts at wooing the daughters of the giants. *Grímnismál* 47.

Grímnir 'Masked (one)' also *Grímr* 'mask', referring to the god's many disguises and concealments; possibly an allusion to the face-covering worn by his worshippers in processions and ritual drama. *Grímnismál* 49.

Gunnblindi 'Battle-blinder', he who disables his foes in battle, so similar to *Herblindi*. *Óðins nǫfn*.

Gǫllnir 'Clasher' or 'shrieker, screamer' also *Gǫllor, Gǫllungr* based on *gǫll* 'din of battle'. *Óðins nǫfn*.

Gǫndlir 'Wand-bearer' from *gǫndull* 'magician's staff' or 'penis', from *gandr* 'item used in magic-working'. *Grímnismál* 49.

Hagvirkr 'Skilful, useful worker', an antonym to *Bǫlverkr*. *Óðins nǫfn*.

Hangadróttinn 'Lord of the hanged' in relation to his own hanging on the world-tree, and the multiple deaths (hanging and stabbing) of those offered to him; also *Hangi* 'hanged man', *Hangaguð* and *Hangatýr* 'god of the hanged'. *Ynglinga saga* 7.

Haptaguð 'God of fetters' referring to the god's power to bind and free his foes; the word *hǫpt* 'bindings, shackles' is used to refer to the gods as a group – perhaps because they constrain their followers' behaviour through divine laws. *Gylfaginning* 19.

Hár 'High one' or 'half-blind one'. Stories of a deity with just one eye must belong to an early period, since an ancient adjective for 'one-eyed' or 'half-blind' is **káikos* which gives rise to Proto-Celtic **kaiko* 'blind in one eye', from which comes Old Irish *cáech* 'blind in one eye, squinting' and other terms; in Germanic, the root becomes **xaixa*, **haiha* and in Gothic *haihs* 'one-eyed'. The Latin equivalent *caecus* is less specific: 'blind', 'dark', 'invisible' (Koch, 2020, p.140). The reference may be to the closing of one eye in a ritual (said of the god Lug) while Óðinn surrenders his eye in order to gain knowledge. One-eyed destructive characters are found in early Irish tradition, such as Balor and Ingcél Cáech.

In *Gylfaginning*, the wayfarer Gangleri asks three wise beings (*Hárr, Jafnhárr* and *Þriði* – 'High', 'Just-as-high' and 'Third') by what names the god Óðinn should be called in poetry. They proceed to offer some obscure references (text from Faulkes, 2005):

> Þá mælir Gangleri: 'Geysi mǫrg heiti hafi þér gefit honum. Ok þat veit trúa mín, at þat mun vera mikill fróðleikr sá er hér kann skyn ok dœmi, hverir atburðir hafa orðit sér til hvers þessa nafns.'

> Þá segir Hárr: 'Mikil skynsemi er at rifja vandliga þat upp. En þó er þér þat skjótast at segja at flest heiti hafa verit gefin af þeim atburð at svá margar sem eru greinir tungnanna í verǫldunni, þá þykkjask allar þjóðir þurfa at breyta nafni hans til sinnar tungu til ákalls ok bœna fyrir sjálfum sér, en sumir atburðir til þessa heita hafa gerzt í ferðum hans ok er þat fært í frásagnir, ok muntu eigi mega fróðr maðr heita ef þú skalt eigi kunna segja frá þeim stórtíðendum.'

Then Gangleri said: "Very many names have you given him, and this I trust I know, that he must be very retentive who is to know all the causes and events from which each of these names arises."

Then Harr said: "Great knowledge is to be gained to explain them, so it is shortest to say that most names have been given to him because there are many kinds of language in the world, so that all the peoples thought to change his name to their own tongue to call out and pray to him themselves. Some of the events these names came from happened on his travels and these are recorded in tales, and you cannot be called a wise man if you cannot tell of these great events."

Hárr 'Grey-haired' is distinct from the previous entry and is elsewhere the name of a dwarf. *Gylfaginning* 17 (unless this is a reference to the dwarf of the same name).

Hárbarðr 'Grey-beard' relating to the god's disguise as an old man. *Hárbarðsljóð.*

Hávi 'The high one', the name on which is formed the title of the poem *Hávamál* 'Sayings of the High One'.

Helblindi 'Hell-blind' in reference to his single eye and his association with death. Another character of the same name is a brother of Loki in *Gylfaginning* 32. *Grímnismál* 46.

Hengikeptr 'He with the drooping jaw', also *Hengikjǫptr*, in reference to his long beard. *Skáldskaparmál* 40.

Heráss 'God of the army' appearing on the Eggjum runestone (Sogne, Norway), and probably in reference to the god's role as a military leader and psychopomp (Simek, 1993, s.v. *Heráss*). The stone features the image of a horse which may be intended to convey the dead person to the Otherworld. The alternative name *Hertýr* appears in *Vellekla* 3.

Herblindi 'He who blinds the enemy army', similar to *Helblindi* and referring to the god's power to disable his foes. *Óðins nǫfn*.

Herfǫðr 'Father of the army' meaning 'elder' or 'leader'; also *Herjafǫðr* with the same meaning. *Vǫluspá* 29.

Herjann 'Warlord', a derivative of **harja* 'group of raiders, invading army', describing the leader of such a group or its personification (Kershaw, 2000, p.74); also *Herann*. *Vǫluspá* 30.

Herteitr 'Happy with the army' so 'rejoicing in battle', an appropriate name for the *Hertýr* 'god of the army'. *Grímnismál* 47.

Hildólfr 'Battle-wolf' or 'ravager in war', such as the *ulfheðnar* 'wolf-coats'. *Hárbarðsljóð* 8.

Hjálmberi 'Helm-bearer' or 'he who wears a helmet', referring to the magnificent war-helms such as those from Vendel, Valsgårde, Sutton Hoo, Benty Low and elsewhere which were the mark of leadership in peace and war. *Grímnismál* 46.

Hjarrendi 'Screamer' or 'rattler'. *Ragnarsdrápa* 11.

Hléfreyr 'Lord of the burial mound' or 'lord of renown'; the prototheme may be ON *hlé* 'barrow' or derived from the prototheme found in the name **Hlewagastiz** on the Gallehus runic horn, where it means 'fame, renown'. *Óðins nǫfn*.

Hnikarr 'Instigator (of conflict)' in reference to the god's habit of stirring up strife among men; also *Hnikuðr* with the same meaning. *Reginsmál* 18.

Hrafnáss 'Raven-god' referring to the birds which feast on the bodies of slain men; also *Hrafnaguð* 'god of ravens' which may be more specifically his own avian informants, *Huginn* and *Muninn*. *Haustlǫng* 4.

Hrafnfreistuðr 'Tester of ravens' in reference to the god's consultations with his two ravens. *Húsdrápa* 10.

Hrammi 'Binder' or perhaps 'he who tears open' with reference to the bear-form of the berserkir. *Óðins nǫfn*.

Hrani 'Blusterer' or 'rough person', a name used of farmers, labourers and unsophisticated people. *Hrólfs saga kraka* 26.

Hrjótr 'Roarer' or 'growler' with reference to the savage nature of the god. *Óðins nǫfn.*

Hrosshárs Grani '(He with a) horse-hair beard', the pseudonym the god uses in *Gautreks saga* where he appears as Starkað's foster-father. 'Grani' can mean 'moustache' or 'beard' or refer to the facial hair on a horse. The connection here may be with the horse-cult, or a reference to prolific facial hair also seen in the name *Langbarðr*.

Hroptr 'Secret (one)', also *Hroptatýr* 'god of the hidden ones' or 'of hidden (things)', a name which occurs frequently but is never explained. A link to the etymologically-related Greek word *kryptos* 'hidden, secret' seems likely. Óðinn is a master of riddles, secrets and cryptic lore of all kinds. This name seems to have been foregrounded when Christianity became a serious threat *Grímnismál* 54.

Hvatmóðr '(He with a) bold heart', a suitable name for the god who instigates turmoil, hostility and warfare wherever he goes. *Óðins nǫfn.*

Hveðrungr 'Roarer' in reference to the god's link to anger, rage and raving. *Óðins nǫfn.*

Hǫttr '(He with a) hood, cowl, coif', referring to the god's fondness for disguise and concealment. *Hálfs saga.*

Ítrekr 'Splendid ruler', in a list of the god's offspring. *Hervarar saga* 37

Jafnhár 'Just as high', grouped with *Hár* and *Þriði* in *Gylfaginning.*

Jalkr 'Gelding' another name associating the god with an animal. *Grímnismál* 49.

Jǫlfuðr '(He with the) yellow-brown back', a reference to the bear. *Ǫrvar-Odds saga* 35.

Jólfr 'Bear', a disguise by which the god provides Oddr with magical arrows in *Ǫrvar-Odds saga.*

Jólnir 'Yule-man' whose feast was celebrated at midwinter. *Þorsdrápa* 12.

Jǫrmunr 'Great one' or *Jǫrundr*, cognate with OE *eormen* 'vast, great, powerful'. *Óðins nǫfn.*

Karl 'Old man' especially with reference to his offspring, Baldr. *Gylfaginning* 49.

Kjalarr 'Nourisher (of ravens), with reference to his promoting warfare. *Grímnsimál* 49.

Langbarðr 'Long-beard', another 'disguise' name like *Síðhǫttr* or *Hárbarðr*. The name may also be a reference to the Lombards, who were his worshippers and from whom they received their name. *Óðins nǫfn.*

Loðungr '(He with the) shaggy cloak', as he is a traveller dressed for bad weather. *Óðins nǫfn.*

Njótr 'User' in reference to the god's appetite for enjoyment and manipulation. *Óðins nǫfn.*

Óðr 'Frenzy' or 'poetic inspiration'; also the name of the lost husband for whom Freyja weeps. *Vǫluspá 25.*

Ófr 'Inciter', also *Ófnir*, due to the god's practice of fomenting trouble. *Grímnismál 54.*

Olgr 'Roarer, bellower' or 'protector'. *Óðins nǫfn.*

Ómi 'Boomer, bellower', in reference to his loud or resonant voice. *Gylfaginning.*

Óski 'Wish-giver' or 'granter of wishes' from whom the valkyries are called *óskmeyjar* 'wish-maidens'. *Grímnismál 49.*

Rauðgrani '(He with the) red moustache', perhaps parallel to *Hrosshárs Grani*, another disguise name. *Bárðar saga.*

Reginn 'Adviser', referring to the god's wisdom and initiatory function. *Óðins nǫfn.*

Reiðatýr 'Waggon-god', referring to the cult-waggons in which idols were paraded among their worshippers. *Skáldskaparmál 1.*

Rǫgni 'Adviser' also *Rǫgnir*, in reference to the god's leadership of the *regin* 'Otherworld powers'. *Hyndluljóð 35.*

Sangetall 'Truth-teller', in reference to his ability to solve riddles and gain wisdom thereby. *Grímnismál 47.*

Saðr 'Truth', perhaps because the god's understanding of reality surpasses that of his worshippers. Given that he uses deception and guile so frequently in the myths, this seems an unlikely or ironic description of the god. *Grímnismál 47.*

Síðgrani '(He with the) broad moustache', another disguise reference like *Langbarðr, Rauðgrani,* etc. *Alvíssmál 6*

Síðhǫttr '(He with the) broad-hat or hood', in reference to the headgear which conceals his face. *Gylfaginning 20.*

Síðskeggr '(He with the) broad beard', a reference to one of his disguises. *Gylfaginning 20.*

Sigfǫðr 'Father of victory' in reference to his ability to bestow or withdraw success on the battlefield. *Vǫluspá 55.*

Siggautr 'Victory-sacrifice' or 'the powerful one who brings victory'. The OE form *Sigegeat* appears in kinglists. *Óðins nǫfn.*

Sigmundr 'Protection in victory', also the name of a human protégé of the god (*Sigemund*) in *Beowulf* 1.884, 875. *Óðins nǫfn*.

Sighǫfundr 'Victory-judge' referring to his power to award military success. *Óðins nǫfn*.

Sigrunnr 'Tree of victory', or possibly 'granter of victory' if the deutero-theme is from the verb *unna* 'grant'. *Húsdrápa* 9.

Sigtryggr 'Trustworthy for victory' or 'reliable in victory', an unlikely epithet for so fickle a god. *Óðins nǫfn*.

Sigtýr 'God of victory', bringer of victory to his followers. *Skáldskaparmál* 34.

Sigþrór '(He who) thrives in victory', a military epithet. *Óðins nǫfn*.

Skilfingr 'Crag-dweller' or 'mountain-dweller', the OE name for the royal line of the Swedes is the cognate term *Scilfingas* (*gomela Scilfing*, *Beowulf*, l.2968); also, *Fjallgeiguðr* is another name with a 'mountain' reference, as is the vantage point *Hliðskjálf* which may be related to the prototheme here. *Grímnismál* 54.

Skollvaldr 'Ruler of treachery' in reference to his guile and deceit. *Óðins nǫfn*.

Sváfnir '(He who) causes men to sleep' so 'death-bringer'. *Grímnismál* 54.

Sveigðir 'Branch-servant', the 'branch' being the horizontal support of the gallows as in the story of *Hrosshárs Grani* in *Gautreks saga*.

Sviðurr 'Spear-god' also *Sviðuðr*, relating to the god's iconic weapon, Gungnir. *Grímnismál* 50.

Svipall 'Changeable' in reference to the god's propensity to change his appearance. *Grímnismál* 47.

Svipdagr Blindi 'Blind Dawning-day', called *Svibdavus* (i.e *Svipdaf*) in Saxo's tale (*Gesta Danorum* VI; Ellis Davidson, 1998, p.173). Svipdagr is also the name of one of Óðinn's emissaries. The name means '(the day which) dawns swiftly' with obvious cosmological reference, and presumably the epithet *blindi* was added to the name since, in *Hrólfs saga kraka*, this character loses one of his eyes. *Ynglinga saga*.

Svǫlnir 'Shield-bearer' from *svǫl*, the name for the disc which is held before the sun conceived as a shield protecting the earth from the radiance. *Óðins nǫfn* .

Tveggi 'Double, two-fold', perhaps in reference to his dual nature as both benefactor and traitor, or to his duplicitousness. *Sonatorrek* 25.

Tvíblindi 'Double-blind', the blind god who inflicts blindness on others. *Óðins nǫfn.*

Þekkr 'Well-liked', an attribute of the god perhaps related to *Óski. Grímnismál* 46.

Þrasarr 'Furious (one)', in reference to the god's association with raving anger. *Óðins nǫfn.*

Þriði 'Third', one of the enigmatic beings who confront Gylfi in *Gylfaginning.*

Þriggi 'Triple, threefold' parallel to *Tveggi.* Gods and heroes in groups of three are a common feature of European myth and folktale. *Sonatorrek* 23.

Þrór 'Thriver', more likely an epithet for Freyr as the lord of plentifulness, but it is used occasionally in reference to Óðinn. *Grímnismál* 49.

Þróttr 'Power', often used to refer to the god's magical abilities. (Several instances in skaldic verse.)

Þunnr '(The) pale (one) or *Þuðr*, in reference to the god's suffering in order to earn wisdom. *Gylfaginning* 20.

Þundr ''Swollen' or perhaps '(he who) swells', perhaps in reference to the god being able to put forth his might. *Grímnismál* 21.

Unnr 'Beloved' or *Uðr*, referring to his status as 'benefactor, friend' to his chosen champions. *Grímnismál* 46.

Váfuðr 'Wind', in reference to his time on the windswept tree in *Hávamál. Grímnismál* 54.

Vakr 'Watchful, (the) awakened (one)', in reference to his vigilance and constant seeking new information. *Gylfaginning* 20.

Valfǫðr 'Father of the slain', in reference to his welcoming heroes who have died on the battlefield into his heavenly hall, *Valhǫll. Vǫluspá* 27.

Valgautr 'Gautr of the slain', an extended form of *Gautr. Óðins nǫfn.*

Valkjósandi 'Slain-chooser', referring to the god's status as *Valfǫðr* and to his leadership of the host of *valkyrjur. Lausavísa* 21.

Valtamr 'Accustomed to the slain', in reference to his status as *Valfǫðr. Baldrs draumar* 6.

Valtýr 'God of the slain', in reference to his status as *Valfǫðr. Háleygjatal* 15.

Valþǫgnir 'Receiver of the slain', in reference to his status as *Valfǫðr. Lausavísa* 8.

Vegtamr 'Accustomed to the road', the pseudonym the god uses on his journey to the kingdom of Hel in *Baldrs draumar* 6.

Veratýr 'God of men', in reference to his patronage of mankind, thus similar to *Aldaföðr*. *Grímnismál* 3.

Viðhrimnir '(He who) screams at his prey', so a reference to his eagle-form also seen in *Arnhöfði*. *Óðins nöfn*.

Viðrir 'Weather-maker', in reference to his power over storms and fine weather. *Lokasenna* 26.

Viðurr 'Killer', a common reference to the god's power of the life and death of men. *Óðins nöfn*.

Yggjungr 'Son of the terrible one' or 'descendant of Yggr'. *Völuspá* 28.

Yggr 'Terrifying one', in reference to the god's association with violent death. *Hávamál* 3.

Ýrungr 'Stormy', perhaps in relation to his power over the weather; a link to the name *Iring* has been suggested, after whom the Milky Way is named *iringaes uueg* 'Iring's path' in the *Épinal Glossary* (Pheifer, 1974, p.55). *Óðins nöfn*.

Even in this condensed and non-comprehensive listing, there is room for multivalence and ambiguity: the name *Siðhöttr* 'broad-hat' or 'droopy-hat' refers to the god's customary appearance, but the garment itself is the kind of broadbrimmed headgear used by travellers to protect them from both sun and rain, and therefore might fall within the 'wandering' category, while its broad, concealing brim also provides for 'deceit' and 'disguise'. Indeed, the concealing hat has been taken to be a version of the folktale *Tarnkappe* 'cap of invisibility' which is won by the hero in order to enable him to accomplish his tasks. The cap appears in medieval tales as a hat or as a hooded cape, both of which offer the opportunity for disguise and concealment (Kershaw, 2000, p.260).

A statistical analysis of the incidence of pre-Christian names in the literature has been used to show that there was a sharp increase in the use of kennings in the later 10th c., and a corresponding fall in the early 11th c. with a small rise after ca. 1150 AD. This has been interpreted as the effect of Christianisation producing a reluctance to rehearse the old myths, and a later resurgence in interest when such tales were no longer considered a threat to society but retained 'antiquarian interest' (Lassen, 2022, pp.116-7).[258] Equally, a few of the kennings for Óðinn appear to be inspired by Christian ideas of the 'ruler of heaven'.

---

[258] A parallel with Graeco-Roman notions concerning Jupiter or Mars might be invoked, whereby the characters were still familiar after the introduction of Christianity, and over time no longer carried any tabu.

BIBLIOGRAPHY

ABAG   *Amsterdamer Beiträge zur Älteren Germanistik*

AJ   *Antiquaries' Journal*

ANF   *Arkiv för nordisk filologi*

Arch. Cant.   *Archaeologia Cantiana*

ASE   *Anglo-Saxon England*

ASSAH   *Anglo-Saxon Studies in Archaeology & History*

AWLSK   Mededelingen van de Koninklijke Academie voor Wetenschappen, Letteren en Schone Kunsten van België

BAR   British Archaeological Reports

BMP   British Museum Publications

CUP   Cambridge University Press

EETS   *Early English Text Society*

EUP   Exeter University Press

JEGP   *Journal of English and Germanic Philology*

JIES   *Journal of Indo-European Studies*

JMH   *Journal of Medieval History*

Med. Arch.   *Medieval Archaeology*

MGH   *Monumenta Germaniae Historica*

MUP   Manchester University Press

NOWELE   *North West European Language Evolution*

OUP   Oxford University Press

PMLA   *Publications of the Modern Language Association*

RGA   *Reallexikon der Germanischen Altertumskunde*

Scandia   *Journal of Medieval Norse Studies*

TPAPA   *Transactions and Proceedings of the American*
               Philological Association

Abdale, J. *Four Days in September. The Battle of the Teutoburg.* (Barnsley: Pen
    & Sword Books, 2016)
Abramson, T. *Sceattas. An Illustrated Guide. Anglo-Saxon Coins and Icons.*
    (King's Lynn: Heritage Publications, 2006)
Acker, P. & Larrington, C. *The Poetic Edda. Essays on Old Norse Mythology.*
    (London: Routledge, 2002)
Agnarsson, V.L. (ed.) *The Cleasby-Vigfusson Old Norse to English Dictionary.*
    Reprint. (Scotts Valley: CreateSpace, 2009)
Aldhouse Green, M. *Cosmovision and Metaphor: Monsters and Shamans in*
    Gallo-British Cult Expression in *European Journal of Archaeology*, vol. 4.
    (London: CUP, 2001: 203-231)
Alkemade, M. *A History of Vendel Period Archaeology. Observation on the Re-*
    lationship Between Written Sources and Archaeological Interpretation in
    Roymans, N. & Theuws, F. *Images of the Past: Studies on Ancient Soci-*
    eties in Northwestern Europe. (Amsterdam: Amsterdam University Press,
    1991: 267-298)
Ament, H. *The Germanic Tribes in Europe* in Wilson, D.M. (ed.) *The North-*
    ern World. The History and Heritage of Northern Europe. AD 400-1100.
    (London: Thames & Hudson, 1980: 47-70)
Anderson, J.G.C. (trans.) *Tacitus - Germania.* (Oxford: Bristol Classic Press
    / OUP: 1997)
Andersson, K. *Det Förflutnas Ansikten. Öga met öga med Forntiden.* (Stock-
    holm: Atlantisbok, 2020)
Andrén, A., Jennbert, K. & Raudvere, C. (eds.) *Old Norse Religion in Long-*
    Term Perspectives, Origins, Changes and Interactions. (Lund: *Vägar til*
    Midgard 8, 2006)

Anlezark, D. *The Old English Dialogues of Solomon and Saturn.* Anglo-Saxon Texts 7, (Cambridge: OUP, 2009)

Antonsen, E.H. *Runes and Germanic Linguistics.* Trends in Linguistics Studies 140. (New York: Mouton de Gruyter, 2002)

Arent, A.M. *The Heroic Pattern: Old Germanic Helmets, Beowulf and Grettis-saga* in Polomé, E. *Old Norse Literature and Mythology: A Symposium in Honour of Lee M. Hollander.* (Austin: University of Texas, 1969: 130-199)

Armit, I. *Headhunting and the Body in Iron Age Europe.* (Cambridge: CUP, 2012)

Arnold, C.J. *An Archaeology of the Early Anglo-Saxon Kingdoms.* (London: Routledge, 1997)

Arnold, M. & Finlay, A. (eds.) *Making History. Essays on the Fornaldarsögur,* (London: Viking Society for Northern Research, 2010)

Arrhenius, B. *Merovingian Garnet Jewellery: Emergence and Social Implications.* (Stockholm: Almqvist & Wiksell, 1985)

Aðalbjarnarson, B. (ed.) *Heimskringla,* vol. 1. 3rd. ed. (Reykjavik: Hið Íslenzka Fornritafélag, 1979)

Ausenda, G. (ed.) *After Empire. Towards and Ethnology of Europe's Barbarians.* (Woodbridge: Boydell Press, 1995)

Ausenda, G., Delogu, P. & Wickham, C. (eds.) *The Langobards Before the Frankish Conquest: An Ethnographic Perspective.* (Woodbridge: Boydell Press, 2009)

Axboe, M. *Gudme and the Gold Bracteates* in Nielsen, P.O., Randsborg, K. & Thrane, H. (eds.), *The Archaeology of Gudme and Lundeborg. Papers presented at a Conference in Svendborg, October 1991.* (Copenhagen: Akademisk Forlag Universitetsforlaget i København, 1992)

- *The Year 536 and the Scandinavian Gold Hoards* in *Med. Arch.,* vol. XLIII. (1999: 186-188)

- *Amulet Pendants and a Darkened Sun: On the Function of the Gold Bracteates and a Possible Motivation for the Large Gold Hoards* in Magnus, B. (ed.) *Roman Gold and the Development of the Early Germanic Kingdoms. Aspects of Technical, Socio-Political, Socio-Economic, Artistic and Intellectual Development A.D. 1-550.* (Stockholm: Almqvist & Wiksell Intl, 2001)

- *Guld og Guder* in Capelle, T. & Fischer, C. (eds.) *Ragnarok. Odins Verden.* (Silkeborg: Silkeborg Museum Press, 2005)

Axboe, M. & Källström, M. *Guldbrakteater fra Trollhättan – 1844 og 2009* in *Fornvännen*. (2013: 153-171)

Bakka, E. *On the Beginnings of Salin's Style I in England*. (Bergen: Historisk-antikvarisk rekke no. 3, 1958)

- *Scandinavian-Type Gold Bracteates in Kentish and Continental Grave Finds* in Evison, V. (ed.) *Angles, Saxons and Jutes. Essays Presented to J.N.L. Myres*. (Oxford: OUP, 1981: 11-38)

Bammesberger, A. (ed.) *Old English Runes and Their Continental Background*. (Heidelberg: Brill, 1991)

Bammesberger, A. & Waxenberger, G. (eds.) *Das Fuþark und seine Einzelsprachlichen Weiterentwicklungen*. RGA vol. 51 (Berlin: Mouton de Gruyter, 2006)

Bammesberger, A. & Wollmann, A. (eds.) *Britain 400-600: Language and History*. Anglistische Forschungen, Heft 205. (Heidelberg: Carl Winter Verlag, 1990)

Banghard, K. & Stauch, E. *Ein frühmittelalterliches Pressblech aus Obrigheim (Rheinland-Pfalz). Ursprung, Wirkungsgeschichte und Entzerrungsversuch einer politischen Bilderzählung*. (Internationale Archäologie Studia Honoraria, Band 40, Rahden, 2021: 239-254)

Barley, N.F. *Anglo-Saxon Magico-Medicine*, in *Journal of the Anthropological Society of Oxford*. (Oxford: 1973)

Barnes, M.P. *Runes. A Handbook*. (Woodbridge: Boydell Press, 2012)

Bately, J & Englert, A. *Ohthere's Voyages*. (Roskilde: Viking Ship Museum, 2007)

Bauschatz, P. *The Well and the Tree – World and Time in Early Germanic Culture*. (Amherst: University of Massachusetts Press, 1982

Beck, H. A *Das Fuþark und Probleme der Verschriftung/Verschriftlichung* in Bammesberger, A. & Waxenberger, G. (eds.) *Das Fuþark und seine Einzelsprachlichen Weiterentwicklungen*. RGA vol. 51. (Berlin: Mouton de Gruyter, 2006: 61-79)

Becker, A. *Franks Casket. Zu den Bildern und Inschriften des Runenkästchens von Auzon*. Regensburger Arbeiten zur Anglistik und Amerikansitik, Band 5. (Regensburg: Peter Lang, 1973)

Bedyński, W. & Povedák, I. *Landscape as a Factor in Creating Identity. Papers from the Conference held in Jarosław, Poland 22-24 June 2012*. (Warsaw: Państwowa Wyższa Szkoła Ekonomiczna w Jarosławiu, 2014)

Bemmann, G. & J. *Der Opferplatz von Nydam. Die Funde aus den alteren Grabungen: Nydam-I und Nydam-II.* (Neumünster: Wachholtz, 1998)

Benediktsson, J.(ed.) *Íslendingabók. Landnámabók.* (Íslenzk fornrit, 1. Reykjavík: Hið íslenzka fornritafélag, 1968)

Benjamin, W. et al. *Theses on the Philosophy of History. Illuminations, Essays and Reflections 1.* (New York: Schocken Books, 2012)

Bessinger, J.B. & Creed, R.P. (eds.) *Medieval and Linguistic Studies in Honor of Francis Peabody Magoun.* (London: George, Allen & Unwin, 1965)

Bierce, A. *The Devil's Dictionary.* (London: Folio Society, 2007)

Biggam, C. *Blue in Old English.* (Amsterdam: Rodopi, 1997)

- *Grey In Old English.* (London: Runetree Press, 1998)

Birley, A. *Garrison Life at Vindolanda. A Band of Brothers.* (Stroud: History Press, 2011)

Bishop, C.R. *Runic Magic,* M.A. dissertation. (University of Maryland, 2007)

Bitterli, D. *Say What I Am Called. The Old English Riddles of the Exeter Book and the Anglo-Latin Riddle Tradition.* (Toronto: Toronto Old English Studies, 2009)

Blackmore, L., Hirst, S. & Scull, C. *The Prittlewell Princely Burial. Excavations at Priory Crescent, Southend-on-Sea, Essex 2003.* (London: Museum of London Archaeology Monograph,73, 2019)

Blomfield, J. *Runes and the Gothic Alphabet* in *Saga-Book of the Viking Society for Northern Research,* vol. XII (Kendal: University College London, 1945: 177-194)

Bloomfield, M.W. *Patristics and Old English Literature* in Nicholson, L.E. (ed.) *An Anthology of Beowulf Criticism.* (Notre Dame: Notre Dame University Press, 1963: 36-43)

Bóna, I. *The Dawn of the Dark Ages. The Gepids and the Lombards in the Carpathian Basin.* (Budapest: Corvina, 1976)

Bosworth, J. & Toller, T. N. *An Anglo-Saxon Dictionary.* (Oxford: OUP, 1898; reprint, 1991)

Branston, B. *The Lost Gods of England.* (London: Thames & Hudson, 1957)

Brandt, J.R., Ingvaldsen, I & Prusac, M. (eds.) *Death and Changing Rituals: Function and Meaning in Ancient Funerary Practices.* (Oxford: OUP, 2014)

Bremmer, R.H. *Hermes-Mercury and Woden-Odin as Inventors of Alphabets: A Neglected Parallel* in Bammesberger, A. (ed.) *Old English Runes and Their Continental Background.* (Heidelberg: Brill, 1991: 409-419)

Brink, S. *Political and Social Structures in Early Scandinavia – a Settlement-Historical Pre-Study of the Central Place. Tor*, vol. 28. (Uppsala: University of Uppsala, 1996: 235-281)

Bruce-Mitford, R. *Aspects of Anglo-Saxon Archaeology. Sutton Hoo and Other Discoveries.* (London: BMP, 1974)

- *The Sutton Hoo Ship-Burial. Volume 1. Excavations, Background, The Ship, Dating and Inventory,* (London: BMP, 1975)

- (ed) *Recent Archaeological Excavations in Europe.* (London: BMP, 1975a)

- *The Sutton Hoo Ship-Burial. Volume 2. Arms, Armour and Regalia.* (London: BMP, 1978)

- *The Sutton Hoo Ship-Burial. Volume 3. Late Roman and Byzantine Silver, Hanging Bowls, Drinking Vessels, Cauldrons and Other Containers, Textiles, The Lyre, Pottery Bottle and Other Items.* (London: BMP, 1983)

Buchholz, P. *Perspectives for Historical Research in Germanic Religion* in *History of Religions*, vol. 8. (Chicago: University of Chicago Press,1968)

Bullough, D.A. *What has Ingeld to do with Lindisfarne?* in *ASE*, vol. 22 (1993: 93-125)

Bursche, A. *Contact Between the Late Roman Empire and North-Central Europe* in *AJ*, vol. 76, (London: 1996: 31-50)

- *Roman Gold Medallions as Power Symbols of the Germanic Elite* in Magnus, B. (ed.), *Roman Gold and the Development of the Early Germanic Kingdoms* (Stockholm: Kungl. Vitterhets Historie och Antikvitets Akadamien, 2001: 128-164)

Byock, J. *The Saga of King Hrolf Kraki.* (London: Penguin, 1998)

Cabaniss, A. *Beowulf and the Liturgy* in Nicholson, L.E. (ed.) *An Anthology of Beowulf Criticism.* (Notre Dame: Notre Dame University Press, 1963: 223-232)

Calder, D.G. & Christy, T.C. (eds.), *Germania. Comparative Studies in the Old Germanic Languages and Literatures.* (Berkeley: D.S. Brewer, 1988)

Callahan, M. *Magic beyond the Binary: Magic and Gender in the Poetic Edda.* (Ph.D. thesis, University of St Andrews, 2013/2014)

Campbell, A. *Old English Grammar.* (Oxford: OUP, 1959 reprinted 1987)

Capelle, T. & Fischer, C. (eds.) *Ragnarok. Odins Verden.* (Silkeborg: Solkeborg Museum Press, 2005)

Cartlidge, N. (ed.) *The Owl and the Nightingale.* (Exeter: University of Exeter Press: 2001)

Caruthers, L. (ed.) *Anges et Démons dans la littérature anglaise au Moyen Âge*. (Paris: PU Paris-Sorbonne, 2002)

Carver, M.O.H. (ed.) *The Age of Sutton Hoo: The Seventh Century in North-Western Europe*. (Woodbridge: Boydell Press, 1992)

- *Sutton Hoo. A Seventh-Century Princely Burial Ground and its Context*. Report of the Research Committee of the Society of Antiquaries of London, no.69. (London: BMP, 2005)

- *The Sutton Hoo Story. Encounters with Early England*. (Woodbridge: Boydell Press, 2017)

Chadwick, H.M. *The Cult of Othin. An Essay in the Ancient Religion of the North*. (Cambridge: CUP, 1899; reprinted 2013)

- *The Origin of the English Nation*. (Cambridge: CUP, 1924)

Chadwick Hawkes, S. (ed.) *Weapons and Warfare in Anglo-Saxon England*. Oxford University Committee for Archaeology Monograph no.21. (Oxford: OUP, 1989)

Chambers, R.W. *Widsith: A Study in Old English Heroic Legend*. (Cambridge: CUP, 1912)

- *Beowulf. An Introduction to the Study of the Poem with a Discussion of the Stories of Offa and Finn*. 3rd edition (Cambridge: CUP, 1963)

Charles-Edwards, T. *After Rome*. (Oxford: OUP, 2003)

Chase, C. *The Dating of Beowulf*. (Toronto: University of Toronto Press, 1981)

Church, A.J. & Brodribb, W.J. *The Works of Tacitus*. (London: Macmillan & Co., 1887)

Christensen, A.E., Ingstad, A.S. & Myhre, B. *Osebergdronningens grav: vår arkaeologiske nasjonalskatt i nytt lys*. (Oslo: Schibsted, 1992)

Clackson, J & Olsen, B.A. *Indo-European Word Formation*. (Copenhagen: Museum Tusculanum Press, 2004)

Clemoes, P. (ed.) *Ælfric's Catholic Homilies. First Series. Text*. (Oxford: EETS, 1997)

Clunies Ross, M. *The Anglo-Saxon and Norse Rune Poems: A Comparative Study in ASE*, vol. 19. (1990: 23-39)

- *The Transmission and Preservation of Eddic Poetry* in Larrington, C., Quinn, J. & Schorn, B. *A Handbook of Eddic Poetry. Myths and Legends of Early Scandinavia*. (Cambridge: CUP, 2016: 12-32)

Colgrave, B. & Mynors, R.A.B. *Bede's Ecclesiastical History of the English People*. (Oxford: Clarendon Press, 1969)

Collins, R. *Die Fredegar-Chroniken. Monumenta Germaniae Historica*, vol. 44. (Hannover: Hahnsche Buchhandlung, 2007)

Cockayne, T.O. *Leechdoms, Wortcunning and Starcraft of Early England.* 3 vols. (London: Longman, Green, Longman, Roberts and Green, 1864)

Cronan, D. *Beowulf and the Containment of Scyld in West Saxon Royal Genealogy* in Neidorf, L. *The Dating of Beowulf – A Re-Assessment.* (Cambridge: D.S. Brewer, 2014: 112-137)

Cross, J.E. & Hill, T.D. (eds.) *The Prose Solomon and Saturn and Adrian and Ritheus.* (Toronto: University of Toronto Press, 1982)

Dalton, M.O. (trans.) *Sidonius Apollinaris: Letters.* (Cambridge: Cambridge University Press, 1915)

Damico, H. *The Valkyrie Reflex in Old English Literature* in Damico, H. & Olsen, A.H. (eds.) *New Readings on Women in Old English Literature.* (Bloomington: Indiana University Press, 1990: 177-190)

Davis, N. & Wrenn, C.L. (eds.) *English and Medieval Studies Presented to J.R.R. Tolkien.* (London: Allen & Unwin, 1962)

Day, C.L. *Knots and Knot Lore* in *Western Folklore*, vol. 9, no.3. (1950: 229-256)

De Vries, J. *Some Contributions to the Study of Othin Especially in his Relation to Agricultural Practices in Modern Popular Lore.* Folklore Fellowship Communications no.94. (1931: 3-79)

Dickens, B. *Runic Rings and Old English Charms* in *Archiv für das Studium der Neueren Sprachen*, vol. 167. (1935: 252)

Diekamp, W. *Die Vitae Sancti Liudgeri.* (Münster: Theissing, 1881)

Dillmann, F-X. *Georges Dumézil et la religion Germanique. L'interprétation du dieu Odhinn* in J.-C. Rivière (ed.), *Georges Dumézil. à la découverte des Indo-Européens*, (Paris: Copernic, 1979)

- *Le Mâitre-des-Runes: Essai de Determination Socio-Anthropologique: Quelques Reflexions Methodologiques* in Thompson, C.W. (ed.) *Proceedings of the First International Symposium on Runes and Runic Inscriptions. Michigan Germanic Studies*, vol. VII no.1 (Michigan: University of Michigan, 1981)

Dimand, M.S. *Mediæval Textiles of Sweden. The Art Bulletin*, vol. 6, no.1. (1923: 11-16)

Driscoll, M.J. *Ágrip af Nóregskonungasǫgum.* (Viking Society for Northern Research: London, 1995)

Dronke, U. *Myth and Fiction in Early Norse Lands*. (Aldershot: Variorum, 1996)
- (ed.) *The Poetic Edda. Volume I Heroic Poems*. (Oxford: OUP, 1969)
- (ed.) *The Poetic Edda. Volume II Mythological Poems*. (Oxford: OUP, 1997)
- (ed.) *The Poetic Edda. Volume III Mythological Poems II*. (Oxford: OUP, 2011)

Du Bois, T.A. *Encounters: Sámi* in Schjødt, Lindow & Andrén *The Pre-Christian Religions of the North*. (Turnhout: Brepols, 2020: 353-372)

Dumézil, G. (trans. D. Coltman) *From Myth to Fiction. The Saga of Hadingus*. (London: Chicago University Press, 1973)
- *Gods of the Ancient Northmen*, (ed. and trans. Einar Haugen et al.). (Berkeley: University of California Press, 1973)
- *The Stakes of the Warrior*. (Berkeley: University of California Press, 1983)
- *Archaic Roman Religion*. 2 vols. (London: Johns Hopkins University, 1996)

Dümmler, E. (ed.) *XIV Versus Pauli Diaconi*. (Berlin: MGH, 1881, p. 51-52)

Dumville, D.N. (ed.) *Nennius. The Historia Brittonum: The Vatican Recension, vol.3*. (Cambridge: D.S. Brewer, 1985)
- *Histories and Pseudo-histories of the Insular Middle Ages*. (Aldershot: Variorum, 1990)

Düwel, K., Marold, E. & Zimmermann, C. (eds.), *Von Thorsberg nach Schleswig*. (Berlin: Mouton de Gruyter, 2000)

Ebbinghaus, A. (ed.) *Althochdeutsches Lesebuch*. 17th Auflage. (Tübingen: Max Niemeyer Verlag, 1994)

Effros, B. *Skeletal Sex and Gender in Merovingian Mortuary Archaeology* in *Antiquity*, vol. 74. (2000: 632-639)
- *Creating Community with Food and Drink in Merovingian Gaul*. (New York: Palgrave Macmillan, 2002)
- *Merovingian Mortuary Archaeology and the Making of the Early Middle Ages*. (Berkeley: University of California Press, 2003)

Egeler, M. *Encounters: Celtic* in Schjødt, Lindow & Andrén *The Pre-Christian Religions of the North*. (Turnhout: Brepols, 2020: 289-318)

Einarsson, B. *The Blood-Eagle Once More: Two Notes* in *Saga-Book of the Viking Society XXIII* (1990-1993: 80-111)

- (ed. Hermannsdóttir, S.) *Egils saga*. (Reykjavík: Stofnun Árna Magnússonar á Íslandi, 2003)

Elliott, R.W.V. *Runes, Yews, and Magic* in *Speculum*, vol. 32, no.2, (1957: 250-261)

- *Runes. An Introduction*. (Manchester: MUP, 1959)

Ellis Davidson, H.R. *The Sword in Anglo-Saxon England*. (Woodbridge: Boydell & Brewer, 1962, reprinted 1994)

- *Gods and Myths of Northern Europe*. (Harmondsworth: Penguin Books, 1964)

- *The Finglesham Man: The Significance of the Man in the Horned Helmet*. (*Antiquity*, vol. 34, 1965: 17-32)
  Scandinavian Mythology. (London: Hamlyn, 1969)

- *The Battle God of the Vikings*. (York: University of York Medieval Monograph 1, 1972)

- *Myths and Symbols in Pagan Europe*. (New York: Syracuse University Press, 1988)

- *Myths and Symbols in Religion and Folklore. Folklore*, vol. 100. (1989: 131-142)

- *The Lost Beliefs of Northern Europe*. (London: Routledge, 1993)

- *Saxo Grammaticus: The History of the Danes Books I-IX*. (Woodbridge: D.S. Brewer, 1998)

Ellis Davidson, H.R. & Webster, L. *The Anglo-Saxon Burial at Coombe (Woodnesborough), Kent* in *Med.Arch.*, vol. 11. (1967: 1–41)

Engelhardt, C. *Sønderjyske og Fynske Mosefund, Bind I-III. Thorsbjerg Mosefund. Nydam Mosefund. Kragehul og Vimosefundene*, (1863 reprinted Copenhagen: Forlaget ZAC, 1969)

Enright, M.J. *Lady With a Mead Cup: Ritual, Prophecy and Lordship in the European Warband from La Tène to the Viking Age*. (Dublin: Four Courts Press, 1996)

Eriksen, M.H. *Between the Real and Ideal. Ordering, Controlling and Utilising Space in Power Negotiations – Hall Buildings in Scandinavia, 250-1050 CE*. (University of Leicester MA Thesis, 2010)

Evison, V.I. *An Anglo-Saxon Cemetery at Holborough, Kent* in *Arch.Cant.*, vol. LXX, (1956: 84-141)

- (ed.) *Angles, Saxons and Jutes. Essays Presented to J.N.L. Myres*. (Oxford: OUP, 1981)

- *Dover Buckland Anglo-Saxon Cemetery*. Historic Buildings & Monuments Commission for England Archaeological Report no.3, (London: English Heritage, 1987)

Fabech, C. *Reading Society from the Cultural Landscape: South Scandinavia between Sacral and Political Power* in Nielsen, P.O., Randsborg, K. & Thrane, H. *The Archaeology of Gudme and Lundeborg. Papers Presented at a Conference in Svendborg, October 1991.* (Copenhagen: Akademisk Forlag, 1994)

Falk, H. *Odensheite.* (Kristiania: Dybwad, 1924)

Farrell, R. & Neuman de Vegvar, C. (eds.) *Sutton Hoo: Fifty Years After.* (Oxford: American Early Medieval Studies, 1992)

Faulkes, A. *Descent from the Gods* in *Medieval Scandinavia* 11 (1978: 92-125)

- *Sources of Skáldskaparmál* in Wolf, A. (ed.) *Snorri Sturluson. Kolloquium anläßlich der 750. Wiederkehr seines Todestages.* (Tübingen: Gunter Narr Verlag, 1993: 59-76)

- (ed.) *Snorri Sturluson. Edda. Skáldsaparmál. 2 vols.* (London: Viking Society for Northern Research, 1998)

- (ed.) *Snorri Sturluson. Edda. Prologue and Gylfaginning.* (London: Viking Society for Northern Research, 2005)

- (ed.) *Snorri Sturluson. Edda. Háttatal.* (London: Viking Society for Northern Research, 2007)

Fern, C., Dickinson, T. & Webster, L. *The Staffordshire Hoard, An Anglo-Saxon Treasure.* (London: Society of Antiquaries, 2019)

Fischer, O., van Kemenade, A., Koopman, W. & van der Wurff, W. *The Syntax of Early English.* (Cambridge: CUP, 2004)

Fischer, S. & Soulat, M. *Runic Swords & Raw Materials – Anglo-Saxon Interaction with Northern Gaul.* Proceedings of the 58th Sachsensymposium. (Trondheim: Tapir, 2009)

Fisher, C.D. *Tacitus – Annales.* (Oxford: OUP, 1963)

Fisher, P. & Ellis Davisdon, H.R. *Saxo Grammaticus – The History of the Danes*, vol. 1. (Cambridge: CUP, 1979)

Frakes, J.C. *Loki's Mythological Function in the Tripartite System [Lokasenna]* in Acker, P. & Larrington, C. *The Poetic Edda. Essays on Old Norse Mythology.* (London: Routledge, 2002: 159-175)

Franceschi, G., Jorn, A. & Magnus, B. *Ten Thousand Years of Folk Art in the North*: vol. 1, *Men, Gods and Masks in Nordic Iron Age Art.* (Köln: Verlag Walther König, 2005a)

- vol. 2 *Bird, Beast and Man in Nordic Iron Age Art*. (Köln: Verlag Walther König, 2005b)

Fransson, U. et al. (eds.) *Cultural Interaction between East and West Archaeology, Artefacts and Human Contacts in Northern Europe*. (Stockholm: Department of Archaeology and Classical Studies; Stockholm University, 2007)

Fulk, R.D. (ed. & trans.) *The Beowulf Manuscript*. (London: Harvard University Press, 2020)

Fulk, R.D., Bjork, R.E. & Niles, J.D. *Klaeber's Beowulf*. Fourth Edition. (London: University of Toronto Press, 2008)

Furneaux, H. (ed.) *Cornelii Taciti Annalium Libri I-IV*. (Oxford: Clarendon Press, 1904)

Gaimster, M. *Scandinavian Gold Bracteates in Britain. Money and Media in the Dark Ages*. (*Med. Arch*., vol. XXXVI, 1992: 1-28)

- *Vendel Period Bracteates on Gotland: On the Significance of Germanic Art*. (Lund: Acta Archaeologica Lundensia, Series in 8o no. 27, 1998)

- *Gold Bracteates and Necklaces: Political Ideals in the 6th Century* in Magnus, B. (ed.) *Roman Gold and the Development of the Early Germanic Kingdoms. Aspects of Technical, Socio-Political, Socio-Economic, Artistic and Intellectual Development A.D. 1-550*. (Stockholm: Almqvist & Wiksell Intl, 2001)

Gallée, J.H (ed.) *Old Saxon Texts*. (Leiden: Brill, 1864)

Gannon, A. *The Iconography of Early Anglo-Saxon Coinage: Sixth to Eighth Centuries*. Medieval History and Archaeology (Oxford: OUP, 2003)

García Losquiño, I., Sundqvist, O. & Taggart, D. *Making the Profane Sacred in the Viking Age. Essays in Honour of Stefan Brink*. (Turnhout: Brepols, 2020)

Gardeła, L. *Death in the Margin. The Landscape Context of Viking-Age Deviant Burials* in Bedyński, W. & Povedák, I. *Landscape as a Factor in Creating Identity. Papers from the Conference held in Jarosław, Poland 22-24 June 2012*. (Warsaw: Państwowa Wyższa Szkoła Ekonomiczna w Jarosławiu, 2014: 63-76)

- *Women and Weapons in the Viking World. Amazons of the North*. (Oxford: Oxbow Books, 2021)

Gardeła, L., Pentz, P. & Price, N. *Revisiting the 'Valkyries'*. (*Current Swedish Archaeology*, vol. 10. 2022: 95-147)

Gardenstone, *The Mercury-Woden Complex: A Proposal*. (Norderstedt: Books on Demand, 2011)

Gardner, J. *Guilt and the World's Complexity: The Murder of Ongentheow and the Slaying of the Dragon* in Nicolson, L. & Frese, D.W. (eds), *Anglo-Saxon Poetry: Essays in Appreciation*. (Notre Dame: University of Notre Dame Press, 1975: 14-22)

Garmonsway, G.N. *An Early Norse Reader*. (Cambridge: CUP, 1928)

- (ed.) *Ælfric's Colloquy*. (Exeter: EUP, 1978)

Gautier, A. *Le Festin dans l'Angleterre anglo-saxonne (Ve-XIe siècle)*. (Rennes: Presses Universitaires de Rennes, 2006)

Geake, H. *The Use of Grave-Goods in Conversion Period England, c.600-850*. (Oxford: B.A.R. British Series, no. 261, 1997)

Glasswell, S. *The Earliest English: Living and Dying in Early Anglo-Saxon England*. (Stroud: Tempus, 2002)

Glob. P.V. (trans Bruce-Mitford, R.) *The Bog People. Iron Age Man Preserved*. (London: Faber & Faber, 1969)

Glosecki, S.O. *Shamanism and Old English Poetry*. (New York: Garland Reference Library of the Humanities, 1989

Godden, M. *Ælfric's Catholic Homilies. Introduction, Commentary and Glossary*. (Oxford: EETS, 2000)

Gordon, E.V. *Introduction to Old Norse*. 2nd Edition (Oxford: OUP, 1957)

Graham-Campbell, J. *The Vikings in England*. (London: Anglo-Danish Viking Project, 1981)

- *Viking Art*. (London: Thames & Hudson, 2013)

Grane, T. (ed.) *Beyond the Roman Frontier: Roman influences on the Northern Barbaricum*. (Rome: Edizioni Quasar, 2007)

Grattan, J. H. G. & Singer, C. *Anglo-Saxon Magic and Medicine*. Publications of the Wellcome Historical Medical Museum, New Series, No. 3 (London: OUP, 1952)

Green, B. *The Grave Goods from the Cremations* in Myres, J.N.L. & Green, B. *The Anglo-Saxon Cemeteries of Caistor-by-Norwich and Markshall, Norfolk*. (London: Society of Antiquaries Occasional Papers no. 30, 1973)

Green, D.H. *Language and History in the Early Germanic World*. (Cambridge: CUP, 1998)

- *Linguistic and Literary Traces of the Langobards* in Ausenda, G., Delogu, P. & Wickham, C. *The Langobards Before the Frankish Conquest. An Ethnographic Perspective.* (Woodbridge: Boydell Press, 2009: 174-194)

Grendon, F. *The Anglo-Saxon Charms* in *Journal of American Folk-Lore* (22). (1909: 105-237)

Griffith, A. & Salzmann, L. *An Anglo-Saxon Cemetery at Alfriston, Sussex.* (Sussex Archaeological Collections, vol. 56, 1914: 16-53)

Griffiths, B. *Meet the Dragon: An Introduction to Beowulf's Adversary.* (Loughborough: Heart of Albion Press, 1996)

Grigsby, J. *Warriors of the Wasteland.* (London: Watkins Publishing, 2002)
- *Beowulf and Grendel.* (London: Watkins Publishing, 2005)

Grimm, W.C. *Deutsche Mythologie.* (Göttingen: Dietrich Verlag, 1835)

Grundvad, L. et al. *Fæstedskatten – Danmarks Største Guldskat fra Vikingetiden.* (Sønderskov: Museet på Sønderskov, 2017)

Grundy, S. *The Cult of Óðinn: God of Death?* (New Haven: Troth, 2014)

Guber, S. *Die Bildsteine Gotlands der Völkerwanderungs- und Vendelzeit als Spiegel frühgescichtlicher Lebenswelten.* B.A.R. International Series 2257. (Oxford: British Archaeology Reports, 2011)

Gunnell, T. *The Origins of Drama in Scandinavia.* (Woodbridge: D.S. Brewer, 1995)
- *Eddic Performances and Eddic Audiences* in Larrington, C., Quinn, J. & Schorn, B. *A Handbook of Eddic Poetry. Myths and Legends of Early Scandinavia.* (Cambridge: CUP, 2016: 92-113)
- *The Goddesses in the Dark Waters* in García Losqino et al., (eds.) *Making the Profane Sacred in the Viking Age.* (Amsterdam: Brepols, 2020: 243-265)
- *Folklore* in Schjødt, Lindow & Andrén *The Pre-Christian Religions of the North.* (Turnhout: Brepols, 2020: 195-204)

Gustavson, H. & Swantesson, J.O.H. *Strängnäs, Skramle och Tomteboda: tre urnordiska runinskrifter* in *Fornvännen* (Stockholm: Kungl. Vitterhets Historie och Antikvitets Akademien, vol. 106, no.4 (2011: 306-321)

Hachmann, R. *The Ancient Civilization of the Germanic Peoples.* (London: Barrie & Jankins, 1971)

Hagen, A. *A Handbook of Anglo-Saxon Food – Processing and Consumption.* (Pinner: Anglo-Saxon Books, 1992)
- *A Second Handbook of Anglo-Saxon Food & Drink – Production & Distribution.* (Hockwold-cum-Wilton: Anglo-Saxon Books, 1995)

Hagen, S.N. *The Skodborg Runic Inscription* (*Acta Philologica Scandinavica*, vol. 20, 1949: 339-344)

Haggman, B. *Eruli Influence in South Scandinavia – Migration and Remigration* in *Migracijske teme*, vol. 15. (1999: 215-227)

Hall, A. *Elves in Anglo-Saxon England. Matters of Belief, Health, Gender and Identity.* (Woodbridge: Boydell Press, 2007)

Halsall, G. *Social Change Around AD 600: an Austrasian Perspective* in Carver, M. *The Age of Sutton Hoo.* (Woodbridge: Boydell Press, 1992: 265-278)

- (ed.) *Violence and Society in the Early Medieval West.* (Woodbridge: Boydell & Brewer, 1998)

- *Warfare and Society in the Barbarian West, 450-900.* (London: Routledge, 2003)

Halsall, M. *The Old English Rune Poem: A Critical Edition.* (Toronto: Toronto University Press, 1981)

Hårdh, B. *Uppåkra – A Centre in Southern Sweden in the 1st Millennium AD* in *Antiquity*, vol. 74 (2000: 640-648)

- *The Uppakra Beaker. A Discussion of the Figure Representation* in Andrén et al. *Old Norse religion in long-term perspectives. Origins, changes and interactions.* (Lund: Lund University Press, 2006: 254-258)

Hårdh, B. & Larsson, L. *Uppåkra – Lund Före Lund.* (Lund: Föreningen Gamla Lund, 2007)

Harhoiu, R. *The Treasure from Pietroasa, Romania.* B.A.R. Supplementary Series 24. (Oxford: B.A.R., 1977)

Härke, H. *Angelsächsische Waffengräber des 5. Bis 7. Jahrhunderts.* (Köln, Rheinland Verlag, 1992)

Härke, H. & Belinksij, A. *Causes and Contexts of Long-Term Ritual Change: The Iron Age to Early Medieval Cemetery of Klin-Yar (North Caucasus, Russia)* in Brandt, J.R., Ingvaldsen, I & Prusac, M. (eds) *Death and Changing Rituals: Function and Meaning in Ancient Funerary Practices.* (Oxford: Oxbow Books, 2014: 93-104)

Harris, J. *Hadubrand's Lament: On the Origin and Age of Elegy in Germanic* in Beck, H. *Heldensage und Heldendichtung im Germanischen.* Ergänzungsbände zum Reallexikon der Germanischen Altertumskunde, Bd. 2. (Berlin: de Gruyter, 1988: 81-114)

- *Homo Necans Borealis: Fatherhood and Sacrifice in Sonatorrek* in Glosecki, S. (ed) *Myth in Early Northwest Europe*. (Turnhout: Brepols, 2007: 153-174)
- *Myth and Meaning in the Rök Inscription* in *Viking and Medieval Scandinavia*, vol. 2. (Turnhout: Brepols, 2020: 45-109)

Haseloff, G. *Bild und Motiv im Nydam-Stil und Stil I* in Roth, H. (ed.), *Zum Problem der Deutung frühmittelalterlicher Bildinhalte*. Akten des 1. Internationalen Kolloquiums in Marburg a.d. Lahn, 15. bis 19. Februar 1983, vol. 1. (Sigmaringen, 1986: 67-110)

Hatch Wicker, N.L. *Swedish-Anglian Contacts Antedating Sutton Hoo: The Testimony of the Scandinavian Gold Bracteates* in Farrell, R. & Neuman de Vegvar, C. (eds.) *Sutton Hoo: Fifty Years After*. (Oxford: American Early Medieval Studies, 1992: 149-171)

Hattatt, R. *Iron Age and Roman Brooches. A second selection of brooches from the author's collection*. (Oxford: Oxbow Books, 1985)

Hauck, K. *Methodenfragen der Brakteatendeutung. Erprobung eines Interpretationsmusters für die Bildzeugnisse aus einer oralen Kultur (Zur Ikonologie der Goldbrakteaten, XXVI)* in Roth, H. (ed.) *Zum Problem der Deutung frühmittelalterlicher Bildinhalte*. Akten des 1. Internationalen Kolloquiums in Marburg a.d. Lahn, 15. bis 19. Februar 1983, vol. 1. (Sigmaringen: Phillipps Universität, 1986)

- *Gudme als Kultort und seine Rolle beim Austausch von Bildformularen der Goldbrakteaten (Zur Ikonologie der Goldbrakteaten, L)* in Nielsen, P.O., Randsborg, K. & Thrane, H. (eds.), *The Archaeology of Gudme and Lundeborg. Papers presented at a Conference in Svendborg, October 1991*. (Copenhagen: Akademisk Forlag Universitetsforlaget i København, 1994)

Hauck. K. et al. *Die Goldbrakteaten der Völkerwanderungszeit,* vol. 1.1 *Einleitung*. (Munich, 1985)

- vol. 1.2, *Ikonographischer Katalog*. (Munich: de Gruyter, 1985a)
- vol. 1.3, *Ikonographischer Katalog*, IK1-*Tafeln*. (Munich: de Gruyter, 1985b)
- vol. 2.1, *Ikonographischer Katalog*, IK1-*Text*. (Munich: de Gruyter, 1986)
- vol. 2.2, *Ikonographischer Katalog*, IK2-*Tafeln*. (Munich: de Gruyter, 1986a)

- vol. 3.1, *Ikonographischer Katalog*, IK3-*Text*. (Munich: de Gruyter, 1989)

- vol. 3.2, *Ikonographischer Katalog*, IK3-*Tafeln*. (Munich: de Gruyter, 1989a)

Hawkes, S.C. *The Finglesham Man: The Find and its Archaeological Setting*. (*Antiquity*, vol. 34, 1965: 17-32)

- (ed. Cameron, E. & Hamerow, H.) T*he Anglo-Saxon Cemetery of Bifrons, in the Parish of Patrixbourne, East Kent* in *ASSAH*, vol. 11, (Oxford, 2000: 1-94)

Hawkes, S.C. & Grainger, G. (et al.) *The Anglo-Saxon Cemetery at Worthy Park, Kingsworthy near Winchester, Hampshire*. Oxford University School of Archaeology Monograph 59. (Oxford: OUP, 2003)

Hawkes, S.C. & Page, R.I. *Swords and Runes in South-East England* in *AJ*, vol. 47. (1967: 1-26)

Hawkes, J. & Mills, S. *Northumbria's Golden Age*. (Stroud: Sutton Publishing, 1999)

Hayden, B. *The Power of Feasts from Prehistory to the Present*. (Cambridge: CUP, 2014)

Heanley, R.M. *Lincolnshire Superstitions* in *Folklore*, vol. 9. (1898: 186-189)

Hedeager, L. *Kingdoms, Ethnicity and Material Culture: Denmark in a European Perspective* in Carver, M. *The Age of Sutton Hoo*. (Woodbridge: Boydell Press, 1992: 265-278)

- *Iron Age Myth and Materiality. An Archaeology of Scandinavia AD 400-1000*. (London: Routledge, 2011)

Hedges, J.D. & Buckley, D.G. *Anglo-Saxon Burials and Later Features Excavated at Orsett, Essex, 1975* in *Med. Arch.*, vol. XXIX (1985: 1-24)

Helgesson, B. *Tributes to be Spoken. Sacrifice and Warriors at Uppåkra* in Larsson, L. (ed.*) Continuity for Centuries. A Ceremonial Building and its Context at Uppåkra, Southern Sweden*. Uppåkrastudier 10. (Stockholm: Almqvist & Wiksell, 2004: 223-239)

Helm, K. *Wodan. Ausbreitung und Wanderung seines Kultes*. (Giessen: *Giessener Beiträge zur deutschen Philologie*, 85, 1946)

Helmbrecht, M. *Figures with horned headgear: a case study of context analysis and social significance of pictures in Vendel and Viking Age Scandinavia*. (Lund Archaeological Review, 13-14, 2008: 31-53)

Henson, D. *The Origins of the Anglo-Saxons*. (Hockwold-cum-Wilton: Anglo-Saxon Books, 2006)

Hermann, P. et al. *Old Norse Mythology – Comparative Perspectives*. (Cambridge: Harvard University Press, 2017)

- *Memory, Oral Tradition and Sources* in Schjødt, Lindow & Andrén *The Pre-Christian Religions of the North*. (Turnhout: Brepols, 2020: 41-62)

Herschend, F. *The Early Iron Age on South Scandinavia. Social Order in Settlement and Landscape*. (Uppsala: Uppsala University, 2009)

Hilgner, A. *Eine kommunikative Bilderwelt? Anmerkungen zu einer angelsächsischen Gürtelschnalle aus Burwell (Cambridgeshire/GB)*. (*Archäologisches Korrespondenzblatt*, 2015: 403-416)

Hill, J. *Old English Minor Heroic Poems*. (Durham: Durham Medieval Texts, 2009)

Hill, T.D. *Woden as 'Ninth Father': Numerical Patterning in Some Old English Royal Genealogies* in Calder, D.G. & Christy, T.C. (eds.), *Germania. Comparative Studies in the Old Germanic Languages and Literatures*. (Berkeley: D.S. Brewer, 1988: 161-174)

Hills, C. *The Anglo-Saxon Cemetery at Spong Hill, North Elmham. Part I. Catalogue of Cremations nos. 20-64 and 1000-1690* East Anglian Archaeology Report no.6. (Gressenhall: East Anglian Archaeology, 1977)

Hines, J. *The Scandinavian Character of Anglian England in the pre-Viking Period*. (Oxford: B.A.R. British Series, 1984)

- *Ritual Hoarding in Migration-Period Scandinavia: A Review of Recent Interpretations* in *Proceedings of the Prehistoric Society*, vol. 55. (1989: 193-206)

- *Philology, Archaeology and the Adventus Saxonum vel Anglorum*, in Bammesberger, A. & Wollmann, A. (eds.) *Britain 400-600: Language and History*, Anglistische Forschungen, Heft 205. (Heidelberg: Carl Winter Verlag, 1990: 17-36)

- *The Scandinavian Character of Anglian England: An Update* in Carver, M. *The Age of Sutton Hoo*. (Woodbridge: Boydell Press, 1992: 315-329)

- *The Becoming of the English: Identity, Material Culture and Language in Early Anglo-Saxon England* in *ASSAH*, vol. 7. (1994: 49-59)

- (ed.) *The Anglo-Saxons From the Migration Period to the Eighth Century: An Ethnographic Perspective*. (Woodbridge: Boydell Press, 1997)

- *Religion: The Limits of Knowledge* in Hines, (ed.), *The Anglo-Saxons From the Migration Period to the Eighth Century: An Ethnographic Perspective*. (Woodbridge: Boydell Press, 1997: 375-401)

- *Egill's Hǫfuðlausn in Time and Place* in *Saga-Book of the Viking Society*, vol. XXIV 1994-1997. (London: University College, 1997: 83-104)
- *A New Corpus of Anglo-Saxon Great Square-Headed Brooches*. (Woodbridge: Boydell Press, 1997
- (ed.) *The Pace of Change: Studies in Early Medieval Chronology*. (Oxford: OUP, 1999)
- *The Sixth Century Transition in Anglian England: an Analysis of Female Graves from Cambridgeshire* in (ed.) *The Pace of Change: Studies in Early Medieval Chronology*. (Oxford: OUP, 1999: 65-79)

Hinton, D. *Catalogue of the Anglo-Saxon Ornamental Metalwork 700-1100 in the Department of Antiquities, Ashmolean Museum*. (Oxford: OUP, 1974)
- *The Fifth and Sixth Centuries: Reorganization Among the Ruins* in Karkov, C.E. *The Archaeology of Anglo-Saxon England: Basic Readings*. (London: Routledge, 1999: 53-78)
- *A Smith in Lindsey. The Anglo-Saxon Grave at Tattershall Thorpe*, Lincolnshire, Society for Medieval Archaeology, Monograph no. 16. (London: Routledge, 2000)
- *Gold and Gilt, Pots and Pins: Possessions and People in Medieval Britain*. (Oxford: OUP, 2005)

Hjärthner-Holdar, E., Lamm, K. & Magnus, B. *Metalworking and Central Places* in *Central Places in the Migration and Merovingian Periods: papers from the 52nd Sachsensymposium*. (Lund: Almqvist & Wiksel, 2001)

Hoad, T.F. (ed.) *Sweet's Second Anglo-Saxon Reader: Archaic & Dialectal*. (Oxford: OUP, 1978)

Holmberg, P., Gräslund, B. & Williams, H. *The Rök Runestone and the End of the World. Futhark* vols. 9-10 (2018: 7-38)

Holmqvist, W. *Germanic Art During the First Millennium A.D.* (Stockholm: Almqvist & Wiksells Boktryckeri, 1955)
- *Vår Tidinga Konst*. (Stockholm: Statens historiska museum, 1977)

Holst, S., Jørgensen, L. & Wamers, E. *Odin, Thor und Freyja. Skandinavishe Kultplätze des 1. Jahrtausends n. Chr. und das Frankenreich*. (Regensburg: Schnell & Steiner, 2017)

Hornsey, I.S. *Alcohol and its Role in the Evolution of Human Society*. (Cambridge: Royal Society of Chemistry, 2012)

Holthausen, F. *Altenglisches Etymologisches Wörterbuch*. (Heidelberg: Carl Winter Verlag, 1974)

Holtzmann, R. et al. *Die Chronik des Thietmar von Merseburg* (Halle: Mitteldeutscher Verlag, 2007)

Hooke, D. *Trees in Anglo-Saxon England*. (Woodbridge: Boydell Press, 2010)

Hultgård, A. *Cosmic Eschatology: Ragnarøk* in Schjødt, Lindow & Andrén, *The Pre-Christian Religions of the North*. (Turnhout: Brepols, 2020: 1017-1032)

Hunt, T.W. *Cædmon's Exodus and Daniel, Edited from Grein*. (Boston: Ginn & Company, 1902)

Hutterer, C.J. *Die Germanischen Sprachen: ihre Geschichte in Grundzügen*. (Wiesbaden: Drei Lilien Verlag, 1975)

Hutton, R. *The Pagan Religions of the Ancient British Isles: Their Nature and Legacy*. (Oxford: Blackwell, 1991)

Hyllested, A. *The Precursors of Celtic and Germanic* in Jamieson, S.W, Melchert, H.C. & Vine, B. (eds.) *Proceedings of the 21st Annual UCLA Indo-European Conference*. (Bremen: Hempen Verlag, 2010)

Ilkjær, J. *Illerup Ådal. Die Lanzen und Speeren*, Jutland Archaeological Society Publications, XXV, vols. 1 & 2. (Højbjerg, 1990)

- *Illerup Ådal – Archaeology as a Magic Mirror*. (Moesgård: Moesgård Museum Press, 2001)

Imer, L.M. & Vasshus, K.S.K. *Lost in Transition: The runic bracteates from the Vindelev hoard*. NOWELE 76: 1. (Amsterdam: John Benjamins Publishing, 2023)

Insley, J. *The Scandinavian Runic Inscriptions of the Older Fuþark and Old English Personal Names* in Bammesberger (ed.), *Old English Runes and Their Continental Background*. (Heidelberg: Brill, 1991: 309-334)

Iversen, R.B. *Kragehul Mose. Ein Kriegsbeuteopfer auf Südwestfünen*, Jernalderen in Nordeuropa. (Moesgård: Moesgård Museum Press, 2010)

Jackson, P. *The Merits and Limits of Comparative Philology. Old Norse Religious Vocabulary in a Long-Term Perspective* in Raudvere & Schjødt (eds) *More than mythology. Narratives, ritual practices and regional distribution*. (Lund: Nordic Academic Press, 2012: 47-64)

Jakobsson, Á. *Óðinn as Mother. The Old Norse Deviant Patriarch* in *ANF*, vol. 12. (2011: 5-16)

- *Vampires and Watchmen: Categorizing the Medieval Icelandic Undead* in *JEGP*, vol. 110. (2011: 281-300)

Jansson, S.B.F. *Runes in Sweden*. (Stockholm: Gidlunds, 1987)

Jensen, K. *Out of Chaos. Between the Roman Eagle and Odin's Ravens.* (Moesgaard: Moesgaard Museum, 2022)

Jesch, J. *Further Thoughts on E18 Saltfleetby* in Futhark vols. 9-10. (2020: 201-13)

Jolly, K. L. *Popular Religion in Late Saxon England: Elf Charms in Context.* (Chapel Hill: University of North Carolina Press, 1996)

Jones, M. *Feast. Why Humans Share Food.* (Oxford: OUP, 2007)

Jónsson, F. *Den norsk-islandske skjaldedigtning.* 4 vols. (Copenhagen: Gyldendal, 1912–15)

- *Edda Snorra Sturlusonar.* (Copenhagen: Gyldendal, 1931)
- (ed.) *Íslendingabók.* (Copenhagen: Jørgensen & Co., 1930)

Jónsson, G., ed. *"Hlöðskviða", Eddukvæði (Sæmundar-Edda).* (Reykjavík: Íslendingasagnaútgáfan, 1956)

Jónsson, G. *Eddukvæði: Sæmundar-Edda.* (Reykjavík: Kristjánsson, 1947)

Jørgensen, L. *The Find Material from the Settlement of Gudme II – Composition and Interpretation* in Nielsen, P.O., Randsborg, K. & Thrane, H. *The Archaeology of Gudme and Lundeborg. Papers Presented at a Conference in Svendborg, October 1991.* (Copenhagen: Akademisk Forlag, 1994: 53-63)

- *The "Warriors, Soldiers & Conscripts" of the Anthropology in Late Roman and Migration Period Archaeology* in Storgaard, B. (ed.) *Military Aspects of the Aristocracy in Barbaricum in the Roman and Early Migration Periods.* Publications from the National Museum, Studies in Archaeology & History, vol. 5. (Copenhagen, 2001: 9-20)

Jørgensen, L., Storgaard, B. & Thomsen, L.G. (eds.) *The Spoils of Victory – The North in the Shadow of the Roman Empire.* (Copenhagen: Nationalmuseet, 2003)

Kajkowski, K. *Masks from Opole in the Context of the Medieval Slavic Rites* in Laloje, P. & Zochios, S. (eds.) *New Researches on the Religion and Mythology of the Pagan Slavs.* (Lisieux: Lingva, 2023: 115-158)

Kaliff, A. & Sundqvist, O. *Oden och Mithraskulten. Religiös ackulturation under romersk järnålder och folkvandringstid.* (Occasional papers in archaeology, 35. Uppsala, 2004)

Karkov, Farrell & Ryan, (eds), *The Insular Tradition.* (Albany: SUNY Medieval Studies, 1999)

Karkov, C.E. *The Archaeology of Anglo-Saxon England: Basic Readings.* (London: Routledge, 1999)

Karnell, M.H. (ed.) *Gotland's Picture Stones. Bearers of an Enigmatic Legacy.* (Visby: Gotland Museum, 2012)

Kay, M.P. *The Hanged-God: The influence of pre-Christian literary motifs on the depictions of the crucifixion in The Dream of the Rood and Hêliand.* (Milton Keynes: Ph.D. dissertation, 2013; revised 2015)

Keller, E. *Odin's names in the Poetic Edda compared to Gods names in the Heliand.* (Oslo: Univerrsity of Oslo, 2012)

Kelly, S.E. *Charters of Barking Abbey and Waltham Holy Cross.* Anglo-Saxon Charters 20. (Oxford: OUP, 2021)

Kershaw, K. *The One-Eyed God. Odin and the (Indo-)Germanic Männerbünde.* (Washington: JIES Monograph, no. 36, 2000)

Kershaw, N.K. *Anglo-Saxon and Norse Poems.* (Cambridges: CUP, 1922)

Kitzler Åhfeldt, L., *Huggspårsanalys av ett runfragment från Strängnäs.* (Stockholm: *Arkeologiska Forskningslaboratoriet* 8, 2007)

Klevnäs, A.M. *Whodunnit? Grave Robbery in Anglo-Saxon England and the Merovingian Kingdoms.* British Archaeological Reports International Series 2582. (London: BAR, 2013)

Knirk, J.E. *Proceedings of the Third International Symposium on Runes and Runic Inscriptions. Grindaheim, Norway, 8-12 August 1990. Runrön,* vol. 9, (Uppsala: Uppsala universitet, 1994)

- *Runic inscription from Hogganvik, Mandal, Vest-Agder.* Revised Preliminary Report, 2009.
  (accessed online at: http://www.khm.uio.no/forskning/publikasjoner/runenews/ hogganvik/report-2.pdf)

Knüsel, C. & Ripley, K. *The Berdache or Man-Woman in Anglo-Saxon England and Early Medieval Europe* in Frazer, W.O & Tyrrell, A. (eds.) *Social Identity in Medieval Britain, Studies in the Early History of Britain.* (London: Bloomsbury, 2000: 157-191)

Koch, J.T. *Celto-Germanic Later Prehistory and Post-Proto-Indo-European Vocabulary in the North and West.* (Aberystwyth: University of Wales Centre for Advanced Welsh and Celtic Studies, 2020)

Kozák, J.A. *Óðinn and the Mead: The Two-Faced Myth* in *Viking and Medieval Scandinavia* 17. (Turnhout: Brepols, 2021: 135–164)

Kramer E. et al. *Nordsøens Konger, år 250-850.* (Den Haag: Fries Museum, 2000)

Krapp, G.P. & Dobbie, E. V. K. (eds.) *The Anglo-Saxon Poetic Records.* 6 vols. (New York: Columbia University Press, 1931-1953)

Kroonen, G. *Etymological Dictionary of Proto-Germanic*. Leiden Indo-European Etymological Dictionary, vol. II. (Leiden: Brill, 2013)

Kvilhaug, M. *The Maiden with the Mead. A Goddess of Initiation in Norse Mythology*. (M.A. dissertation, Oslo, 2004)

- *The Maiden with the Mead: A Goddess of Initiation Rituals in Old Norse Mythology?* (Riga: VDM Verlag, 2009)

Laloje, P. & Zochios, S. (eds.) *New Researches on the Religion and Mythology of the Pagan Slav.s* (Lisieux: Lingva, 2023: 115-158)

Lamm, J.P. & Nordström, H.-Å., *Vendel Period Studies. Transactions of the Boat-Grave Symposium in Stockholm, February 2-3, 1981*. (Stockholm: Statens Historiska Museum, 1983)

Lanz, N.G. *The Enigma of the Horned Figure. Horned Figures in Pre-Christian Germanic Societies of the Younger Iron Age*. (Reykjavík: Félagsvísindasvið Háskóla Íslands, 2021)

Larrington, C. *Vafþrúðnismál and Grímnismál: Cosmic History, Cosmic Geography* in Acker, P. & Larrington, C. (eds) *The Poetic Edda. Essays on Old Norse Mythology*. (London: Routledge, 2002: 59-77)

Larrington, C., Quinn, J. & Schorn, B. *A Handbook of Eddic Poetry. Myths and Legends of Early Scandinavia*. (Cambridge: CUP, 2016)

Larsson, L. *Kulthuset I Uppåkra* in Capelle, T. & Fischer, C. (eds) *Ragnarok. Odins Verden*. (Silkeborg: Silkeborg Museum, 2005: 107-118)

Larsson, L. & Lenntorp, K-M. *The Enigmatic House* in Larsson, L. (ed.) *Continuity for Centuries. A Ceremonial Building and its Context at Uppåkra, Southern Sweden*. Uppåkrastudier 10. (Stockholm: Almqvist & Wiksell, 2004: 3-48)

Lass, R. *Old English. A Historical Linguistic Companion*. (Cambridge: CUP, 1994)

Lassen, A. *Hoðr's Blindness and the Pledging of Óðinn's Eye: A Study of the Symbolic Value of the Eyes of Hoðr, Óðinn and Þórr*. Proceedings of the 11th Saga Conference. (Copenhagen: Museum Tusculanum Press, 2000)

- *Odin på kristent pergament. En teksthistorisk studie*. (Copenhagen: Museum Tusculanum Press, 2011)

- *Odin's Ways. A Guide to the Pagan God in Medieval Literature*. (Abingdon: Routledge, 2022)

László, G. *The Art of the Migration Period*. (London: Allen Lane, 1970)

Lavelle, R. *Alfred's Wars. Sources and Interpretations of Anglo-Saxon Warfare in the Viking Age.* (Woodbridge: Boydell & Brewer, 2010)

Leahy, K. *Anglo-Saxon Crafts.* (Stroud: Tempus Books, 2003)

- *P.A.S. Fen Drayton* in *Med. Arch.*, vol. 50. (2006: 279-80)

Lehmann, W.P. *A Gothic Etymological Dictionary.* (Leiden: Brill, 1986)

Liberman, A. *In Prayer and Laughter. Essays on Medieval Scandinavian and Germanic Mythology, Literature and Culture.* (Moscow: Palaeograph Press, 2016)

Liebermann, F. (ed.) *Die Gesetze der Angelsachsen*, vol.1. (Halle: Niemeyer, 1903)

Lincoln, B. *Myth, Cosmos and Society. Indo-European Themes of Creation and Destruction.* (Cambridge: Harvard University Press, 1986)

- *Death, War and Sacrifice. Studies in Ideology and Practice.* (Chicago: University of Chicago Press, 1991)

- *Apples and Oranges. Explorations In, On and With Comparison.* (Chicago: University of Chicago Press, 2018)

Linder, N. & Haggson, H.A. *Heimskringla.* (Uppsala: Schultz, 1869–72)

Lindow, J. *Murder and Vengeance Among the Gods. Baldr in Scandinavian Mythology.* (Helsinki: Academia Scientiarum Fennica, 1997)

- *Eddic Poetry and Mythology* in Larrington, C., Quinn, J. & Schorn, B. *A Handbook to Eddic Poetry.* (Cambridge: CUP, 2016:114-131)

- *Comparing Balto-Finnic and Nordic Mythologies* in Hermann, P. et al. *Old Norse Mythology – Comparative Perspectives.* (Cambridge: Harvard University Press, 2017: 223-239)

- *Written Sources* in Schjødt, Lindow & Andrén *The Pre-Christian Religions of the North.* (Turnhout: Brepols, 2020: 63-102)

- *Language Religious Vocabulary* in Schjødt, Lindow & Andrén *The Pre-Christian Religions of the North.* (Turnhout: Brepols, 2020: 103-114)

- *Ethics* in Schjødt, Lindow & Andrén *The Pre-Christian Religions of the North.* (Turnhout: Brepols, 2020a: 479-508)

- *Vanir & Æsir* in Schjødt, Lindow & Andrén *The Pre-Christian Religions of the North.* (Turnhout: Brepols, 2020b: 1033-1050)

- *Baldr* in Schjødt, Lindow & Andrén *The Pre-Christian Religions of the North.* (Turnhout: Brepols, 2020c: 1033-1330)

- *Týr* in iSchjødt, Lindow & Andrén *The Pre-Christian Religions of the North.* (Turnhout: Brepols, 2020d: 1345–1362)

Lindow, J. & Andrén, A. *Worlds of the Dead* in Schjødt, Lindow & Andrén *The Pre-Christian Religions of the North*. (Turnhout: Brepols, 2020a: 897-926)

Lindow, J. & Schjødt, J.P. *The Divine, the Human and In-Between* in Schjødt, Lindow & Andrén *The Pre-Christian Religions of the North*. (Turnhout: Brepols, 2020: 951-988)

Lionarons, J.T. *Dísir, Valkyries, Völur and Norns: the Weise Frauen* in in Shippey, T. (ed.) *The Shadow-Walkers. Jacob Grimm's Mythology of the Monstrous*. (Turnhout: Brepols, 2005: 271-297)

Ljungkvist, J. *The Birth of a Kingdom. Warrior Graves and Royal Residences in a Changeable World* in Jensen, K. *Out of Chaos. Between the Roman Eagle and Odin's Ravens*. (Moesgaard: Moesgaard Museum, 2022:125-135)

Looijenga, T. *Texts and Contexts of the Oldest Runic Inscriptions*. (Leiden: Brill, 2003)

Lunde, P. & Stone, C. (trans.) *Ibn Fadlan and the Land of Darkness*. (Harmondsworth: Penguin Classics, 2012)

Lundin, A. *The Advent of the Esteemed Horseman-Soverign. A Study of Rider-Motifs on Gotlandic Picture-Stones* in Andrén, A., Jennbert, K. et al. (eds.). *Old Norse Religion in Long-Term Perspectives: Origins, Changes, and Interactions*. (Lund: Nordic Academic Press, 2006: 369-74)

Lynn, C.J. *Suggested Archaeological and Architectural Examples of Tripart Structures*. (*JIES*, vol. 34, 2006: 111-142)

MacGregor, A. et al., *A Summary Catalogue of the Continental Archaeological Collections (Roman Iron Age, Migration Period, Early Medieval)*. (Oxford: OUP, 1997)

MacGregor, A. & Bolick, E. *A Summary Catalogue of the Anglo-Saxon Collections (Non-Ferrous Metals)*. (Oxford: B.A.R. British Series 230, 1993)

MacLean, D. *King Oswald's Wooden Cross at Heavenfield in Context* in Karkov, Farrell & Ryan, (eds), *The Insular Tradition*. (Albany: SUNY Medieval Studies, 1999: 79-97)

MacLeod, M. *Bind-Runes. An Investigation of Ligatures in Runic Epigraphy*. (Uppsala: Institutionen för Nordiska Språk, 2002)

MacLeod, M. & Mees, B. *Runic Amulets and Magic Objects*. (Woodbridge: Boydell & Brewer, 2006)

MacNamee, M.B. *Beowulf – An Allegory of Salvation?* in Nicholson, L.E. (ed.) *An Anthology of Beowulf Criticism.* (Notre Dame: Notre Dame University Press, 1963: 88-102)

Madsen, H.J. *Loke fra Snaptun* in Kjaerum, P. & Olsen, R.A. *Oldtidens Ansigt: Faces of the Past.* (Oslo: Det kongelige Nordiske Oldskriftselskab, 1990: 180)

Magennis, H. *Images of Community in Old English Poetry.* (Cambridge: CUP, 1996)

Magnus, B. *The Firebed of the Serpent: Myth and Religion in the Migration Period Mirrored Through Some Golden Objects* in Webster, L. & Brown, M. (ed.) *The Transformation of the Roman World AD 400-900.* (London: BMP, 1997)

- *Monsters and Birds of Prey. Some Reflections on Form and Style of the Migration Period* in *The Making of Kingdoms. ASSAH,* vol. 10. (Oxford, 1999: 161-172)

- (ed.) *Roman Gold and the Development of the Early Germanic Kingdoms. Aspects of Technical, Socio-Political, Socio-Economic, Artistic and Intellectual Development A.D. 1-550.* (Stockholm: Almqvist & Wiksell Intl, 2001)

- *The Enigmatic Brooches* in Magnus, (ed.). (2001a)

Makaev, E.A. (trans. Meredig, J.) *The Language of the Oldest Runic Inscriptions. A Linguistic and Historical-Philological Analysis.* (Stockholm: Almqvist & Wiksell, 1996)

Mallory, J.P & Adams, D.Q. *The Oxford Introduction to Proto-Indo-European and the Proto-Indo-European World.* (Oxford: OUP, 2006)

Mallory, J.P. & Mair, V.H. *The Tarim Mummies. Ancient China and the Mystery of the Earliest Peoples from the West.* (London: Thames & Hudson, 2000)

Malone, K. *Widsith and the Hervararsaga* in *PMLA,* vol. XL, 4. (1925: 769-813)

- *Studies in Heroic Legend and in Current Speech.* (Copenhagen: Rosenkilde & Bagger, 1959)

- *Widsith. Anglistica,* vol. XIII. (Copenhagen: Rosenkilde & Bagger, 1962)

- *The Literary History of Hamlet. The Early Tradition.* (New York: Haskell House, 1964)

Mannering, U. *Iconic Costumes. Scandinavian Late Iron Age Costume Iconography.* Ancient Textiles Series, vol. 25. (Oxford: Oxbow Books, 2017)

Marten, V.V. *The Magnate Farm of Åker. Past, present and future of a farm with central functions* in *Hierarchies in Rural Settlements*. Ruralia IX. 26th September-2nd October 2011, Götzis, Austria. (Turnhout: Brepols, 2013: 329-340)

Martin, J.S. *From Godan to Wotan: An Examination of Two Langobardic Mythological Texts*. The 11th International Saga Conference, 2000.

Martin, T. *Women, Knowledge and Power: The Iconography of Early Anglo-Saxon Cruciform Brooches* in *ASSAH*, vol. 18. (2013: 1-17)

Marzinzik, S. *Early Anglo-Saxon Belt Buckles (late 5th to early 8th centuries AD) Their Classification and Context*. (B.A.R. British Series 357). (Oxford: OUP, 2003)

- *Masterpieces of Medieval Art: The Sutton Hoo Helmet*. (London: BMP, 2014)

Matasovic, R. *Etymological Dictionary of Proto-Celtic*. (Leiden: Brill, 2009)

Matešić, S. *Das Thorseberger Moor; 3 Die militärischen Ausrüstungen*. (Schloss Gottorf: Schleswig-Holsteinische Landesmuseen Schloss Gottorf, 2015)

Mavromataki, M. *Greek Mythology and Religion*. (Athens: Editions Haitalis, 1997)

McGillivray. A.E. *Influences of Pre-Christian Mythology and Christianity on Old Norse Poetry: A Narrative Study of Vafþrúðnismál*. Northern Medieval World 2. (Kalamazoo: Western Michigan University Medieval Institute Publications, 2018)

McKinnell, J. & Simek, R. (with Düwel, K.) *Runes, Magic and Religion: A Sourcebook, Studia Medievalia Septentrionalia*, vol. 10. (Vienna: Fassbender, 2004)

McNally, M. & Dennis, P. *Teutoburg Forest AD 9 – The Destruction of Varus and his Legions*. (Oxford: Osprey Publishing, 2011)

Meaney, A.L. *Woden in England: A Reconsideration of the Evidence* in *Folklore*, vol. 77 no. 2 (1966: 105-15)

- *Women, Witchcraft and Magic in Anglo-Saxon England* in Scragg, D.G. (ed.), *Superstition and popular medicine in Anglo-Saxon England*. (Manchester: Manchester Centre for Anglo-Saxon Studies, 1989: 9-40)

- *The Ides of the Cotton Gnomic Poem* in Damico, H. & Olsen, A.H. (eds.) *New Readings on Women in Old English Literature*. (Bloomington: Indiana University Press, 1990: 158-175)

Mees, B. *The English Language Before England. An Epigraphic Account.* (Abingdon: Routledge, 2023)

Menghin, W. *Das Schwert im Frühen Mittelalter.* (Stuttgart: Theiss, 1983)

- (ed.) *Merowingerzeit. Die Altertümer im Museum für Vor- und Frühgeschichte – Berlin.* (Berlin; Wbg Philipp Von Zabern, 1995)

- *The Merovingian Period. Europe Without Borders.* (Berlin: Minerva, 2007)

Migne, J-P. et al., *Patrilogia cursus completus, series Latina,* vol. 87 (Paris: Migne, 1844-64)

Miller, A. *The Old English Rune Poem – Semantics, Structure and Symmetry* in *JIES,* vol. 34. (2006: 419-436)

Mitchell, S.A. *Heroic Legend and Onomastics: Hálfs saga, the Hildebrandslied and the Listerby Stones* in *A virtual birthday gift presented to Gregory Nagy on turning seventy by his students, colleagues, and friends.* (Washington, D.C., Center for Hellenic Studies, 2012)

- *Place-Names, Periphrasis and Popular Tradition: Odinic Toponyms on Samsø* in García Losquiño, I., Sundqvist, O. & Taggart, D. *Making the Profane Sacred in the Viking Age. Essays in Honour of Stefan Brink.* (Turnhout: Brepols, 2020: 284-293)

- *Myth, Magic and Memory in Early Scandinavian Narrative Culture.* (Amsterdam: Brepols, 2021)

Moisl, H. *Anglo-Saxon Royal Genealogies and Germanic Oral Tradition* in *Journal of Medieval History,* vol. 7. (1981: 215-248)

Mommsen, T. *Iordanis Romana et Getica.* (Berlin: Weidmann, 1882)

- *Historia Brittonum cum additamentis Nennii. Chronica Minora.* Monumenta Germaniae Historica, Auctorum Antiquissimi, vol. 3. (Berlin: Weidmann, 1898)

Mortimer, P. *Woden's Warriors. Warriors and Warfare in 6th-7th century Northern Europe.* (Ely: Anglo-Saxon Books, 2011)

- *What Colour a God's Eyes? An exploration of eye imagery on weapons, and ornaments mainly from 6th and 7th centuries in Northern Europe.* (Malmö: Historiska seminariet. 2018)

Mortimer, P. & Pollington, S. *Remaking the Sutton Hoo Stone: the Ansell-Roper Replica and its Context.* (Ely: Anglo-Saxon Books, 2013)

Motz, L. *The Wise One of the Mountain. Form, Function and Significance of the Subterranean Smith. A Study in Folklore.* (Göppinger: Arbeiten zur Germanistik, 1983)

- *The King, the Champion and the Sorceror: A Study in Germanic Myth.* (Vienna: *Studia Medievalia Septentrionalia* no.1, 1995)

Muir, B.J. (ed) *The Exeter Anthology of Old English Poetry. An Edition of Dean & Chapter MS 3501.* 2 vols. (Exeter: University of Exeter Press, 1994)

Murdoch, A. *Rome's Greatest Defeat. Massacre in the Teutoburg Forest.* (Stroud; Sutton Publishing, 2006)

Murdoch, B. & Read, M. (eds.), *Early Germanic Literature and Culture,* vol. 1. (Woodbridge: Boydell Press, 2004)

Murray, J. & McDonald, T. *Excavations at Station Road, Gamlingay, Cambridgeshire* in *ASSAH,* vol. 13. (2006: 173-330)

Myres, J.N.L. & Green, B. *The Anglo-Saxon Cemeteries of Caistor-by-Norwich and Markshall, Norfolk.* (London: Society of Antiquaries, 1973)

Neckel, Gustav, ed. *Edda: Die Lieder des Codex Regius nebst verwandten Denkmälern*: vol. 1, *Text,* revised by Hans Kuhn, 5th ed. (Heidelberg: Carl Winter, 1983)

Nedoma, R. *Die Inschrift auf dem Helm B von Negau. Möglichkeiten und Grenzen der Deutung norditalischer epigraphischer Denkmäler.* (Wien: Philologica Germanica, 1995)

Needham, G.I. *Ælfric: Lives of Three English Saints.* (Exeter: Exeter University Press, 1984)

Neidorf, L. *Scribal Errors of Proper Names in the Beowulf Manuscript.* (*ASE,* vol. 42, 2013: 249-69)

- *The Dating of Beowulf – A Reassessment.* (Cambridge: D.S. Brewer, 2014)
- *Unferth's Ambiguity and the Trivialization of Germanic Legend.* (*Neophilologus,* vol.101, 2017a: 439-454)
- *Wealhtheow and Her Name: Etymology, Characterization, and Textual Criticism.* (*Neophilologus,* vol. 102, 2017b: 75-89)
- *Caesar's Wine and the Dating of Widsith.* (*Medium Ævum,* vol. 88, 2019: 124-128)
- *Goths, Huns, and The Dream of the Rood.* (*The Review of English Studies,* vol. 72, 2021: 821-835)
- *Woden and Maxims I.* (*Traditio,* vol. 78, 2023, 79-104)
- *Woden and Widsith.* (*English Studies,* vol. 103, 2022a: 1-18)
- *Woden and the English Landscape: The Naming of Wansdyke Reconsidered.* (*Folklore,* vol. 133, 2022b: 378-398)

- *The Art and Thought of the Beowulf Poet.* (New York: Cornell University Press, 2022c)

Neidorf, L. & Xu, N. *Óðinn as Cargo-God: A Suggestion from Beowulf* in *Neophilologus.* (2023)

Neiss, M. *The Ornamental Echo of Óðinn's Cult. Kontinuitetsfrdgor i germansk djurornamentik II* in Fransson, U. et al. (ed*.), Cultural Interaction between East and West* (eds.). (2007: 82-89)

Nelson, M. *The Barbarian's Beverage. A History of Beer in Ancient Europe.* (London: Routledge, 2005)

Nerman, B. *Die Vendelzeit Gotlands* 2 vols. (Stockholm: Almqvist & Wiksell, 1969)

Neuman de Vegvar, C. *The Travelling Twins: Romulus and Remus in Anglo-Saxon England* in Hawkes, J. & Mills, S. *Northumbria's Golden Age.* (Stroud: Sutton Publishing, 1999: 256-267)

Newton, S. *The Origins of Beowulf and the Pre-Viking Kingdom of East Anglia.* (Woodbridge: D.S. Brewer, 1993)

- *The Reckoning of King Rædwald. The Story of the King Linked to the Sutton Hoo Ship-Burial.* (Colchester: Red Bird Press, 2008)

Nicolay, J.A.W. *Scandinavian influences in the southern North Sea area during the Migration and Early Merovingian Periods* in Eriksem, B.V., Abegg-Wigg, A., Bleile, R. & Ickerodt, U. (eds.) *Interaction Without Borders, vol. I.* (Schleswig: Stiftung Schleswig-Holsteinische Landesmuseen, 2017: 500-514)

Nicolson, L. & Frese, D.W. (eds), *Anglo-Saxon Poetry: Essays in Appreciation.* (Notre Dame: University of Notre Dame Press, 1975)

Nicholson, L.E. (ed.) *An Anthology of Beowulf Criticism.* (Notre Dame: Notre Dame University Press, 1963)

Nicolson, W. *Two Letters from Mr W. Nicolson, concerning Two Runic Inscriptions at Bewcastle and Bridekirk.* (*Philosophical Transactions (1683-1775)*, vol. 15, 1685)

Nielsen, H.F. *The Early Runic Language of Scandinavia. Studies in Germanic Dialect Geography.* (Heidelberg: Winter Verlag, 2000)

Nielsen, P.O. *The Gudme-Lundeborg Project – Interdisciplinary Research, 1988-91* in Nielsen, Randsborg & Thrane (eds.), 1994.

Nielsen, P.O., Randsborg, K. & Thrane, H. *The Archaeology of Gudme and Lundeborg. Papers Presented at a Conference in Svendborg, October 1991.* (Copenhagen: Akademisk Forlag, 1994)

Niles, J.D. *Beowulf and Lejre*. (Temple: Arizona Center for Medieval and Renaissance Studies, vol. 323, 2007)

Noble, T.F.X. (ed) *From Roman Provinces to Medieval Kingdoms*. (London: Routledge, 2006)

Nordberg, A. *Continuity, Change and Regional Variation in Old Norse Religion* in Raudvere, C. & Schjødt, J-P. (eds) *More than mythology. Narratives, ritual practices and regional distribution*. (Lund: Nordic Academic Press, 2012: 119-152)

Nordvig, M. *Cosmogony* in Schjødt, Lindow & Andrén *The Pre-Christian Religions of the North*. (Turnhout: Brill, 2020: 989-1000)

Norr, S. *To Rede and to Rown. Expressions of Early Scandinavian Kingship in Written Sources*. Occasional Papers in Archaeology 17. (Uppsala: Uppsala University, 2nd edition, 2008)

- *Valsgärde Studies: the Place and its People, Past and Present*. (Uppsala: Uppsala University, 2008)

North, R. *Heathen Gods in Old English Literature*, Cambridge Studies in Anglo-Saxon England, 22. (Cambridge: CUP, 1997)

Northcott, K. *An Interpretation of the Second Merseburg Charm* in *Modern Language Review*, vol. 54. (1959: 45-50)

Nylén, E. & Lamm, J.P. *Bildsteine auf Gotland*. (Neumünster: Karl Wachholtz Verlag, 1981)

- *Stones, Ships & Symbols*. (Stockhom: Gidlunds Bokförlag, 1988)

Oanță-Marghitu, R. *The Pietroasa Treasure. The Splendour of the Romans and the Barbarians* in Jensen, K. *Out of Chaos. Between the Roman Eagle and Odin's Ravens*. (Moesgaard: Moesgaard Museum, 2022: 43-55)

Odenstedt, B. *The Inscription on the Undley Bracteate and the Beginnings of English Runic Writing*. Umeå Papers in English no.5. (Umeå: Universitetet i Umeå, 1983)

- *On the Origin and Early History of the Runic Script. Typology and Graphic Variation in the Older Futhark*. (Uppsala: Uppsala University, 1990)

Oosten, J.G. *The War of the Gods. The Social Code in Indo-European Mythology*. (London: Routledge & Keegan Paul, 1985)

Orchard, A. *Pride and Prodigies. Studies in the Monsters of the Beowulf Manuscript*. (Cambridge: CUP, 1995)

- *A Critical Companion to Beowulf*. (Cambridge: CUP, 2003)

Orel, V. *A Handbook of Germanic Etymology*. (Leiden: Brill, 2003)

Orton, P. *Theriomorphism: Jacob Grimm, Old Norse Mythology, German Fairy Tales, and English Folklore* in Shippey, T. (ed.) *The Shadow-Walkers. Jacob Grimm's Mythology of the Monstrous.* (Turnhout: Brepols, 2005: 299-334)

Ovenden, R. & McIlwaine, C. *The Great Tales Never End.* (Oxford: Bodleian Library, 2022)

Owen Crocker, G.R. *Dress in Anglo-Saxon England.* (Woodbridge: Boydell & Brewer, 2004)

Page, R.I. *Runes and Runic Inscriptions.* (Woodbridge: Boydell Press, 1995)
- *The Icelandic Rune Poem.* (London: Viking Society for Northern Research, 1998)
- *An Introduction to English Runes.* (Woodbridge: Boydell Press, 1999)

Pálsson, H. & Edwards, P. *Orkneyinga Saga. The History of the Earls of Orkney.* (Harmondsworth: Penguin Books, 1978)

Papahagi, A. *The Anglo-Saxon Hero: Angel or Demon? A Reading of Beowulf* in Caruthers, L. (ed.) *Anges et Démons dans la littérature anglaise au Moyen Âge.* (Paris: PU Paris-Sorbonne, 2002: 75-100)

Parker Pearson, M. *The Archaeology of Death and Burial.* (Stroud: History Press, 1999)

Paxson, D. *Odin. Ecstasy, Runes & Norse Magic.* (Newburyport: Weiser Books, 2017)

Pertz, G.H. *Capitilaria Regum Francorum. Monumenta Germaniae Historica,* vol. 1. (Hannover: Hahnsche Buchhandlung, 1835: 19-20)

Pesch, A. *Uppåkra im Licht der Formular-Familien der Völkerwanderungszeitlichen Goldbrakteaten* in Hardh, B. & Larsson, L. (eds.) *Central Places in the Migration and the Merovingian Periods, Papers from the Sachsensymposium, Lund, 2001.* (Uppåkrastudier 6) (Lund: Lund University Press, 2002: 55-78)
- *Blodoffer, Drikkelag og Frække Sange...?* in Capelle, T. & Fischer, C. (eds) *Ragnarok. Odins Verden.* (Silkeborg: Silkeborg Museum, 2005: 119-130)
- *Die Goldbrakteaten der Völkerwanderungszeit – Thema und Variation,* RGA, vol. 36. (Berlin, 2007)

Petersen, P.V. *Odins Fugle, Valkyrier og Bersærker* in Capelle, T. & Fischer, C. (eds) *Ragnarok. Odins Verden.* (Silkeborg: Silkeborg Museum, 2005: 57-86)

Pheifer, J. *Old English Glosses in the Épinal-Erfurt Glossary.* (Oxford: OUP, 1974)

Pinault, G-J. *Védique Damunas- Vedic, Latin Dominus and the origin of the Hoffmann suffix.* (Paris: Bulletin de la société de linguistique de Paris, 2000: 61-118)

Plunkett, S.J. *Guardians of the Gipping. Anglo-Saxon Treasures from Hadleigh Road, Ipswich.* (Ipswich: Ipswich Borough Council, 1994)

Pollington, S. *Rudiments of Runelore.* (Hockwold-cum-Wilton: Anglo-Saxon Books, 1995, revised 2008)

- *Leechcraft. Early English Charms, Plantlore and Healing.* (Hockwold-cum-Wilton: Anglo-Saxon Books, 2000)

- *The English Warrior from Earliest Times till 1066*, 2nd edition. (Hockwold-cum-Wilton: Anglo-Saxon Books, 2002; 3rd edition, (forthcoming))

- *Anglo-Saxon Burial Mounds.* (Swaffham: Anglo-Saxon Books, 2008)

- *The Mead-Hall – Feasting in Anglo-Saxon England.* (Hockwold-cum-Wilton: Anglo-Saxon Books, 2003; 2nd edition, Ely: Anglo-Saxon Books, 2010)

- *Elder Gods. The Otherworld in Early England.* (Ely: Anglo-Saxon Books, 2011)

- *Runes: Literacy in the Germanic Iron Age.* (Ely: Anglo-Saxon Books, 2016)

Pollington, S., Kerr, L. & Hammond, B. *Wayland's Work – Early English Art and Material Culture From the 4th to the 7th Century.* (Ely: Anglo-Saxon Books, 2010)

Polomé, E. (ed.) *Old Norse Literature and Mythology: A Symposium in Honour of Lee M. Hollander* (Austin: University of Texas, 1969)

- *Essays on Germanic Religion*, JIES monograph 6. (Washington: Institute for the Study of Man, 1989)

- *Beer, Runes and Magic* in *JIES*, vol. 24. (1996: 99-106)

Poole, R.G. *Viking Poems on War and Peace.* (Toronto: University of Toronto Press, 1991)

Pope, J.C. *Homilies of Ælfric: A Supplementary Collection*, 2 vols. *EETS* 259, 260. (London: Early English Text Society, 1967).

Price, N. *The Viking Way. Religion and War in Late Iron Age Scandinavia*, AUN 31. (Uppsala: Uppsala University Press, 2003; 2nd edition. Oxford: Oxbow Books, 2019)

Price, N. & Mortimer, P. *An Eye for Odin? Divine Role-Playing in the Age of Sutton Hoo.* (*European Journal of Archaeology* 17, 2014: 130-199, 517-538)

Prokosch, E. *A Comparative Germanic Grammar.* (Philadelphia: University of Pennsylvania, 1939)

Quast, D. (ed.) *Weibliche Eliten in der Frühgeschichte.* (Mainz: Romisch-Germanisches Zentralmuseum, 2011)

Quirk, R. & Wrenn, C.L. *An Old English Grammar.* (Cambridge: Routledge, 1955)

Ramqvist, P.H. *Högom.* (Stockholm: Riksantikvarieämbetet, 1988)

- *Högom. The Excavations 1949–1984.* (Umeå: University of Umeå, 1991)

Rau, A. & Nedoma, R. *Eine Herstellerinschrift in Zierrunen auf einem Holzschaft aus dem Moor von Nydam. Die Sprache,* vol. 50,1, (2012/2013: 63-82)

Ravn, M. *Death Ritual and Germanic Social Structure (c. AD 200–600),* B.A.R. International Series 1164. (Oxford: OUP, 2003)

Rauch, I. *The Gothic Language. Grammar, Genetic Provenance and Typology, Readings.* (New York: Peter Lang, 2003)

Raudvere, C. *Fictive Rituals in Vǫluspá. Mythological Narration Between Agency and Structure in the Representation of Reality* in Raudvere & Schjødt, (eds.), *More than mythology. Narratives, ritual practices and regional distribution.* (Lund: Nordic Academic Press, 2012: 97-118)

Raudvere, C. & Schjødt, J-P. (eds) *More than Mythology. Narratives, Ritual Practices and Regional Distribution.* (Lund: Nordic Academic Press, 2012)

Rausing, G. *The Days of the Week and Dark* Age *Politics* in *Fornvännen,* vol. 90. (Stockholm: Vitterhetsakademin, 1995: 229-239)

Redin, M. *Studies in Uncompounded Personal Names in Old English.* (Uppsala: Uppsala, A.-b. Akademiska bokhandeln, 1919)

Reynolds, A. *Anglo-Saxon Deviant Burial Customs.* (Oxford: OUP, 2009)

Richards, J.D. *The Significance of Form and Decoration of Anglo-Saxon Cremation Urns.* B.A.R. British Series 166. (Oxford: B.A.R., 1987)

- *Anglo-Saxon Symbolism* in Carver, M. *The Age of Sutton Hoo.* (Woodbridge: Boydell Press, 1992: 131-147)

Ringe, D. *From Proto-Indo-European to Proto-Germanic. A Linguistic History of English,* vol. I. (Oxford: OUP, 2006)

Ringe, F. & Taylor, A. *The Development of Old English. A Linguistic History of English*, vol. II. (Oxford: OUP, 2017)

Rives, J.B. (trans.) *Tacitus – Germania.* (Oxford: OUP, 1999)

Robinson, O.W. *Old English and its Closest Relatives: A Survey of the Earliest Germanic Languages.* (London: Routledge, 1992)

Roth, H. *Kunst der Völkerwanderungszeit.* (Frankfurt-am-Main, 1979)

- (ed.) *Zum Problem der Deutung frühmittelalterlicher Bildinhalte.* (Sigmaringen: Helmut Roth, 1986)

Roymans, N. & Theuws, F. *Images of the Past: Studies on Ancient Societies in Northwestern Europe.* (Amsterdam: Amsterdam University Press, 1991)

Ryan, J.S. *Othin in England Evidence from the Poetry for a Cult of Woden in Anglo-Saxon England.* (*Folklore*, vol. 74, 1963: 460-80)

Salin, B. *Die Altgermanische Thierornamentik. Typologische Studie Über Germanische Metallgegenstände aus dem IV bis IX Jahrhundert, Nebst Einer Studie über Irische Ornamentik.* (Stockholm: Fourier Verlag, 1904 reprinted 1935)

Samson, V. *Les Berserkir. Les Guerriers-Fauves dans la Scandinavie Ancienne, de l'Age de Vendel aux Vikings, (Vie-XIe Siècle).* (Villeneuve d'Ascq: Septentrion Presses Universitaires, 2011)

Sawyer, P. *Textus Roffensis: Parts I and II. Early English Manuscripts in Facsimile.* (Copenhagen: Rosenkilde and Bagger, 1962)

Sayer, D. *Early Anglo-Saxon Cemeteries. Kinship, Community and Identity.* (Manchester: MUP, 2023)

Schjødt, J.P. *Initiation Between Two Worlds. Structure and Symbolism in Pre-Christian Scandinavian Religion. The Viking Collection*, vol. 17. (Odense: University Press of Southern Denmark, 2008)

- *Mercury – Wotan – Óðinn: One or Many?* in Wickstrom et al. *Myth, Materiality, and Lived Religion: In Merovingian and Viking Scandinavia.* (Stockholm: Stockholm University Press, 2019: 59-88)

- *Passage Rituals* in Schjødt, Lindow & Andrén *The Pre-Christian Religions of the North.* (Turnhout: Brepols, 2020a: 823-852)

- *Óðinn* in Schjødt, Lindow & Andrén *The Pre-Christian Religions of the North.* (Turnhout: Brepols, 2020b: 1123-94)

- *Continuity and Break: Germanic* in Schjødt, Lindow & Andrén *The Pre-Christian Religions of the North.* (Turnhout: Brepols, 2020c: 248-268)

- *Kings & Rulers* in Schjødt, Lindow & Andrén *The Pre-Christian Religions of the North.* (Turnhout: Brepols, 2020d: 529-558)

- *Warrior Bands* in Schjødt, Lindow & Andrén *The Pre-Christian Religions of the North*. (Turnhout: Brepols, 2020e: 559-588)
- *Loki* in Schjødt, Lindow & Andrén *The Pre-Christian Religions of the North*. (Turnhout: Brepols, 2020f: 1247-1272)
- *Various Ways of Communicating* in Schjødt, Lindow & Andrén *The Pre-Christian Religions of the North*. (Turnhout: Brepols, 2020g: 589-642)

Schlauch, M. *Widsith, Vithförull and Some Other Analogues. PMLA*, vol. 46. (1931: 969-987)

Schutz, H. *Tools, Weapons and Ornaments. Germanic Material Culture in Pre-Carolingian Central Europe 400-750*. (Leiden: Brill, 2001)

Schwab, U. *The Inscription of the Nordendorf Brooch I: A Double Reading in Line III?* in Thompson, C.W. (ed.) *Proceedings of the First International Symposium on Runes and Runic Inscriptions*. Michigan Germanic Studies, vol. VII, no.1. (Michigan: University of Michigan, (1981: 38-49)

Scragg, D.G. (ed.) *The Battle of Maldon*. (Manchester: MUP, 1981)
- *Superstition and Popular Medicine in Anglo-Saxon England*. (Manchester: MUP, 1989)
- *The Battle of Maldon, AD 991*. (Oxford: OUP, 1991)

Seeck, O. *Notitia Dignitatum: Accedunt Notitia Urbis Constantinopolitanae et Laterculi Provinciarum*. Cambridge Library Collection Reprint. (Cambridge: CUP, 2019)

Shaw, P. *The Uses of Wodan – The Development of his Cult and of Medieval Literary Responses to It* (Ph.D. thesis, Leeds, 2002)
- *The Origins of the Theophoric Week in the Germanic Languages*. (*Early Medieval Europe*, vol. 15, 2007: 386-401)
- *Pagan Goddesses in the Early Germanic World: Eostre, Hreda and the Cult of Matrons*. (London: *Studies in Early Medieval History*, 2011)

Shepherd, C. *A Study of the Relationship Between Style I Art and Socio-Political Change in Early Medieval Europe*. (Oxford: B.A.R. International Series 745, 1998)

Sherley-Price, L. (trans.) *Bede. A History of the English Church and People*. (Harmondsworth: Penguin Classics, 1955)

Shippey, T.A. *Old English Verse*. (London: Routledge, 1972)
- *Names in Beowulf and Anglo-Saxon England* in Neidorf, L. *The Dating of Beowulf – A Re-Assessment*. (Cambridge: D.S. Brewer, 2014: 58-78)

- *'King Sheave' and 'The Lost Road'* in Ovenden, R. & McIlwaine, C. *The Great Tales Never End.* (Oxford: Bodleian Library, 2022a: 166-180)
- *Beowulf and the North Before the Vikings.* (Leeds: ARC Humanities Press, 2022)

Sigurðsson, J.V. *The Christianization of the North Atlantic* in Schjødt, Lindow & Andrén *The Pre-Christian Religions of the North.* (Turnhout: Brepols, 2020: 1649-1694)

Simek, R. *Dictionary of Northern Mythology.* (Cambridge: D.S. Brewer, 1993)
- *Germanic Religion and the Conversion to Christianity* in Murdoch, B. & Read, M. (eds.), *Early Germanic Literature and Culture*, vol. 1. (Woodbridge: Boydell Press, 2004: 73-101)
- *Götter und Kulte der Germanen.* 2nd edition. (Munich: Theiss Verlag, 2006)
- *Religion und Mythologie der Germanen.* (Darmstadt: Konrad Theiss Verlag, 2014)

Simpson, J. *Some Scandinavian Sacrifices* in *Folklore*, vol. 78. (1967: 190-202)

Smith, R. *British Museum Guide to Anglo-Saxon Antiquities.* (London: BMP, 1923, reprinted 1993)

Søe, N. E., Odgaard, B. V., Nielsen, A. B., Olsen, J. & Kristiansen, S. M. *Late Holocene landscape development around a Roman Iron Age mass grave, Alken Enge, Denmark. Vegetation History and Archaeobotany,* 26(3). (2017: 277-292)

Sørensen, P.Ø. *Gudme. Iron Age Settlement and Central Halls.* (Oxford: Oxbow Books, 2022)

Speake, G. *Anglo-Saxon Animal Art and its Germanic Background.* (Oxford: OUP, 1980)

Spears, K.H. The Picture Stones of Gotland: Type C D Stones as Death memorials. (PhD Thesis, University of Houston, 2016)

Spurkland, T. *Norwegian Runes and Runic Inscriptions* (trans. B. van der Hoek). (Woodbridge: Boydell Press, 2005)

Speidel, M.P. *Ancient Germanic Warriors – Warrior Styles from Trajan's Column to Icelandic Sagas.* (London: Routledge, 2004)

Staecker, J. *Heroes, King and Gods* in Andrén, A., Jennbert, K. et al. (eds.). *Old Norse Religion in Long-Term Perspectives: Origins, Changes, and Interactions.* (Lund: Nordic Academic Press, 2006: 363-8)

Stanley, E.G. *The Search for Anglo-Saxon Paganism.* (Cambridge: CUP, 1964, reprinted 1975)

- *Hæþenra Hyht in Beowulf* in *A Collection of Papers with Emphasis on Old English Literature.* (Toronto: Pontifical Institute of Medieval Studies, 1987: 192-208)

Starkey, K. *Imagining an Early Odin - Gold Bracteates as Visual Evidence?* (*Scandinavian Studies*, vol. 71, 1999: 373-392)

Steinmeyer, E. *Die Kleineren Althochdeutscen Sprachdenkmäler.* (Berlin: Weidmann, 1916)

Stoklund, M. *The Ribe Cranium Inscription and the Scandinavian Transition to the Younger Reduced Futhark* in Looijenga, T. & Quak, A. *Frisian Runes and Neighbouring Traditions. Proceedings of the First International Symposium on Frisian Runes at the Fries Museum, Leeuwarden 26-29 January, 1994.* (Amsterdam: Rodopi, 1996: 199-210)

Stone, A. *Ymir's Flesh. Northern European Creation Mythologies.* (Loughborough: Heart of Albion Press, 1997)

Storgaard, B. *The Årslev Grave and Connections between Funen and the Continent at the End of the Later Roman Iron Age* in Nielsen, P.O., Randsborg, K. & Thrane, H. *The Archaeology of Gudme and Lundeborg. Papers Presented at a Conference in Svendborg, October 1991.* (Copenhagen: Akademisk Forlag, 1994: 160-168)

- *Himlingøje: Barbarian Empire or Roman Implantation?* in Storgaard, (ed.), *Military Aspects of the Aristocracy in Barbaricum in the Roman and Early Migration Periods*, Publications from the National Museum, Studies in Archaeology & History, vol. 5. (Copenhagen: National Museum, 2001: 95-112)

- (ed.) *Military Aspects of the Aristocracy in Barbaricum in the Roman and Early Migration Periods*, Publications from the National Museum, Studies in Archaeology & History, vol. 5. (Copenhagen: National Museum, 2001)

- *Cosmopolitan Aristocrats* in Jørgensen, L., Storgaard, B. & Thomsen, L.G. (eds.) *The Spoils of Victory – The North in the Shadow of the Roman Empire.* (Copenhagen: Nationalmuseet, 2003: 106-125)

Strassmeir, A. & Gagelmann, A. *Das Heer des Arminius,* Heere & Waffen 11. (Berlin: Zeughaus Verlag, 2009)

Stratford, N. *The Lewis Chessmen and the Enigma of the Hoard.* (London: British Museum Press, 1997)

Ström, F. *Loki. Ein mythologisches Problem.* (Göteborg: Elander, 1956)

- *Níð, Ergi and Old Norse Moral Attitudes*. (London: University College, 1974)

Sundqvist, O. *"Religious Ruler Ideology" in Pre-Christian Scandinavia: A Contextual Approach* in Raudvere & Schjødt (eds.), *More than Mythology. Narratives, ritual practices and regional distribution*. (Lund: Nordic Academic Press 2012: 225-262)

- *Custodian of the sanctuary: protecting sacred space as a ritual strategy for gaining legitimacy and power in pre-christian Scandinavia* in Jezierski, W. [ed] et al. *Rituals, performatives, and political order in Northern Europe, c. 650-1350*. (Turnhout: Brepols, 2015: 113-137)

- *Freyr's Offspring: Rulers and Religion in Ancient Svea Society*. (Uppsala: Uppsala Universitet, 2000)

- *Contributions of the Oldest Runic Inscriptions to the Reconstruction of Ancient Scandinavian Religion. Some Methodological Reflections with Reference to an Example of the Phenomenological Category of "Ritual Specialists"* in Grimm, O. & Pesch, A. (eds.) *Archäologie und Runen. Fallstudien zu Inschriften im älterne Futhark*. Schriften des Archäologischen Landesmuseums. Band 11. (Schloss Gottorf: Schleswig-Holsteinische Landesmuseen, 2015)

- *Cultic Leaders and Religious Specialists* in Schjødt, Lindow & Andrén *The Pre-Christian Religions of the North*. (Turnhout: Brepols, 2020: 739-779)

Suzuki, S. *The Quoit Brooch Style and Anglo-Saxon Settlement – A Casting and Recasting of Cultural Identity Symbols*. (Woodbridge: Boydell Press, 2000)

- *The Undley Bracteate Reconsidered: Archaeological, Linguistic and Runological Perspectives*. (Oxford: *ASSAH*, vol. 13, 2006: 31-49)

Sweet, H. (revised Hoad, T.F.) *A Second Anglo-Saxon Reader: Archaic and Dialectal*. (Oxford: OUP, 1978)

Tanner, G.H. *Rune Stones and Magnate Farms: The Viking Age in Vadsbo Hundred*. (Master's Essay, Stockholm University, 2011)

Tatar, M. *Enchantments, Spells and Curses: The Sorcery of Stories and the Magic in Them* in Mitchell, S. *Myth, Magic and Memory in Early Scandinavian Narrative Culture*. (Amsterdam, 2021: 113-127)

Taylor, M. *The Etymology of the Germanic Tribal Name 'Eruli'*. (*General Linguistics*, vol. 30, 1990: 108-125)

Taylor, R.L. *Deviant Burials in Viking-Age Scandinavia.* (M.Phil dissertation, London: UCL, 2014)

Thomsen, P.O. *Lundeborg – An Early Port of Trade in South-East Funen* in Nielsen, P.O., Randsborg, K. & Thrane, H. *The Archaeology of Gudme and Lundeborg. Papers Presented at a Conference in Svendborg, October 1991.* (Copenhagen: Akademisk Forlag, 1994: 23-29)

Thorgeirsson, H. *Snorri versus the Copyists: An Investigation of a Stylistic Trait in the Manuscript Traditions of Egils Saga, Heimskringla, and the Prosa Edda.* (*Saga-Book*, vol. 38, 2014: 61-74).

Thorpe, B. *The Anglo-Saxon Chronicle.* (2 vols). (London: Longman, Green, Longman and Roberts, 1861)

Thorpe, L. (trans.) *Gregory of Tours. The History of the Franks.* (Harmondsworth: Penguin Classics, 1974)

Thrane, H. *Guld, Guder og Godtfolk – at Magtcentrum fra Jernalderen ved Gudme og Lundeborg,* (Copenhagen: National Museum, 1993)

- *Gudme – A Focus of Archaeological Research 1833–1987* in Nielsen, P.O., Randsborg, K. & Thrane, H. *The Archaeology of Gudme and Lundeborg. Papers Presented at a Conference in Svendborg, October 1991.* (Copenhagen: Akademisk Forlag, 1994: 8-15)

Thurston, T.L. *Landscapes of Power, Landscapes of Conflict. State Formation in the South Scandinavian Iron Age.* (New York: Kluwer Academic, 2001)

Todd, M. *The Early Germans,* 2nd edition. (Oxford: OUP, 2004)

Tolkien, C. *The Battle of the Goths and Huns.* Saga-Book, vol. XIV. 1953–1957 (London: UCL, 1960)

- *The Saga of King Heidrek the Wise.* (London: Thomas Nelson & Sons, 1960a)

Tolkien, J.R.R. (ed. A. Bliss) *Finn and Hengest – the Fragment and the Episode.* (London: Allen & Unwin, 1982)

- (ed. C. Tolkien) *Beowulf. A Translation and Commentary together with Sellic Spell.* (London: Harper Colins, 2016)

Tolley, C. *Vörðr and Gandr: Helping Spirits in Norse Magic. Arkiv för Nordisk Filologi,* vol. 110. (1995: 57-68)

- *Shamanism in Norse Myth and Magic,* 2 vols. (Helsinki: Folklore Fellows' Communications, 2009)

Ton, O., Thrane, H. & Vandkilde, H. (eds.) *Warfare and Society. Archaeological and Social Anthropological Perspectives.* (Århus: University Press, 2006)

Tosi, M. *L'Edictus Rotharu nei Manoscritti Bobiensi.* (*Archivum Bobiense*, vol. 4, 1982: 11-71)

Travis, H. & Travis, J.R. *Roman Helmets.* (Stroud: Amberley Publishing, 2016)

Turville-Petre, E.O.G. *Myth and Religion of the North. The Religion of Ancient Scandinavia.* (London: Weidenfeld and Nicolson, 1964)

- *Scaldic Poetry.* (Oxford: Clarendon Press, 1976)

Unwerth, W. von, *Óðinn und Rota.* (*Beiträge zur Gescichte der deutschen Sprache und Literatur*, 1914: 213-21)

Ustinova, Y. *Lycanthropy in Sarmatian Warrior Societies: The Kobyakovo Torque.* Ancient West and East, vol. 1. (Leiden: Brill, 2002: 102-123)

van der Sanden, W & Capelle, T. *Immortal Images: Ancient Anthropomorphic Wood Carvings from Northern and Northwest Europe.* (Silkeborg: Silkeborg Museum, 2001)

van Nuffelen, P. & van Hoof, L. *Jordanes – Romana and Getica.* (Liverpool: Liverpool University Press, 2020)

Vang Petersen, P. *Excavations at Sites of Treasure Trove Finds at Gudme* in Nielsen, P.O., Randsborg, K. & Thrane, H. *The Archaeology of Gudme and Lundeborg. Papers Presented at a Conference in Svendborg, October 1991.* (Copenhagen: Akademisk Forlag, 1994: 30-40)

von See, K. *Das Alter der Rígsþula* in *Acta Philologica Scandinavica*, vol. 24 (Copenhagen, 1961: 1-12)

Voyles, J.B. *Early Germanic Grammar – Pre-, Proto- and Post-Germanic Languages.* (London: Academic Press, 1992)

Waitz, G. *Widukindi Res Gestae Saxonicae. Monumenta Germaniae Historica*, vol. 60. (Hannover: Hahnsche Buchhandlung, 1861)

- *Historia Langobardorum Codicis Gothani. Monumenta Germaniae Historica: Scriptores rerum Langobardorum.* (Hannover: Hahnsche Buchhandlung, 1878)

Wallis, R.J. *Shamans and Neo-Shamans. Ecstasy, Alternative Archaeologies and Contemporary Pagans.* (London: Routledge, 2003)

Wamser, L. *Karfunkelstein und Seide. Neue Schätze aus Bayerns Frühzeit.* (München: Archaeologisce Stattssammlung, 2010

Ward, D. *The Divine Twins: An Indo-European Myth in Germanic Tradition. Folklore Studies*, 19. (London: University of California Press, 1968)

Watkins, C. *How to Kill a Dragon. Aspects of Indo-European Poetics.* (Oxford: OUP, 1995)

Watt, M. *The Gold-Figure Foils (Guldgubbar) from Uppåkra* in in Larsson, L. (ed.) *Continuity for Centuries. A Ceremonial Building and its Context at Uppåkra, Southern Sweden.* Uppåkrastudier 10. (Stockholm: Almqvist & Wiksell, 2004: 167-222)

Webster, L. & Backhouse, J. *The Making of England. Anglo-Saxon Art and Culture AD 600-900.* (London: BMP, 1991)

Webster, L. & Brown, M. (ed.) *The Transformation of the Roman World AD 400-900.* (London: BMP, 1997

Welch, M. *Anglo-Saxon Kent to AD 800* in Williams, J.H. *The Archaeology of Kent to AD 800.* (Woodbridge: Boydell Press, 2007)

West, M.L. *Indo-European Poetry and Myth.* (Oxford: OUP, 2007)

Wicker, N.L. *Bracteate Workshops and Runic Literacy. Testimony from the Distribution of Inscriptions* in Knirk, J.E. *Proceedings of the Third International Symposium on Runes and Runic Inscriptions. Grindaheim, Norway, 8-12 August 1990. Runrön*, vol. 9. (Uppsala: Uppsala universitet, 1994: 59-81)

Willemsen, A. *Gouden Middeleeuwen. Nederland in de Merovingische Wereld, 400-700 na Chr.* (Leiden: WalburgPers Algemeen, 2014)

Williams, H. *Heathen Graves and Victorian Anglo-Saxonism: Assessing the Archaeology of John Mitchell Kemble* in *ASSAH*, vol. 13. (Oxford, 2006: 1-18)

Williamson, T. *Sutton Hoo and its Landscape. The Context of Monuments.* (Oxford: Oxbow Books, 2008)

Wilson, D. *A Note on OE hearg and weoh as Place-Name Elements Representing Different Types of Pagan Saxon Worship Sites* in *ASSAH*, vol. 4. (1985: 179-184)

- *Anglo-Saxon Paganism.* (London: Routledge, 1992)

Wilson, D.M. (ed.) *The Northern World. The History and Heritage of Northern Europe. AD 400-1100.* (London: Thames & Hudson, 1980)

Wissowa, G. *Interpretatio Romana. Romische Götter im Barbarenlande.* (Archiv für Religionswissenschaft 19, 1916: 1-49)

Wood, I. *Pagan Religions and Superstitions East of the Rhine From the Fifth to the Ninth Century* in Ausenda, G. (ed.) *After Empire. Towards and Ethnology of Europe's Barbarians*. (Woodbridge: Boydell Press, 1995: 253-267)

- *The Pagans and the Other: Varying Presentations in the Early Middle Ages*. Network & Neighbours 1.1. (2013:1-22)

Woodard, R. *Myth, Ritual and the Warrior in Roman and Indo-European Antiquity*. (Cambridge: CUP, 2013)

Wyatt, A.J. & Chambers, R.W. *Beowulf with the Finnsburg Fragment*. (Cambridge: CUP, 1920)

Yorke, B. *The Fate of Otherworldly Beings After the Conversion of the Anglo-Saxons* in Ruhmann & Brieske (eds) *Dying Gods. Religious Belief in Northern and Eastern Europe in the Time of the Christianisation*. (*Neue Studien zur Sachsenforschung* 5. Hannover: Niedersachsische Landesmuseum Hannover, 2015: 167-175)

Zachrisson, T. *Ritual Space and Territorial Boundaries in Scandinavia* in García Losquiño, I., Sundqvist, O. & Taggart, D. *Making the Profane Sacred in the Viking Age. Essays in Honour of Stefan Brink*. (Turnhout: Brepols, 2020: 85-98)

INDEX

Aðalsteinsfóstri, 5

Adam of Bremen, 34, 35, 40, 54, 201, 228, 233, 326, 337, 373, 377, 378, 419

Adam's Grave, 27

Aðils, King of Sweden, 312, 313

Ælfred, King of Wessex, 362, 414

Ælfric, 44, 361, 362, 369, 380, 382

Ælfric of Eynsham, 205

Ælle, 71

Æsir, 8, 49, 53, 84, 112, 201, 212, 220, 228, 254, 255, 256, 257, 259, 260, 261, 263, 266, 267, 271, 277, 284, 287, 296, 299, 339, 342, 398, 420, 421, 423, 429, 430, 431, 432, 439, 441, 442, 449, 456, 476, 490

Æþelberht, King, 56, 135, 149, 192, 197

Æþelfriþ, king of Northumbria, 135, 136, 138, 139, 197

Æþelstan, King, 362

Agio, 174

Agnar, 292, 293, 295, 327, 409

Ágrip, 305

Åker, 110

Alaisiagae, 79

Alcis, 56

Alcuin, 31, 146, 494

Aldhelm, 214, 383

Alrekr, 318

altar, 69, 145, 146, 415, 478, 493

Alvíssmál, 225, 290, 338, 506

Ambri, 174

Anderida, 71

Angantýr, 307, 308, 309

Angles, 18, 50, 53, 55, 57, 88, 132, 135, 152, 154, 327, 416, 493

Anses, 127

Arminius, 69, 387

ASC, 57, 71, 167, 190

Asdingi, 150

Ásgarð, 10, 228, 243, 257, 258, 263, 264, 269, 296, 298, 319, 341, 342, 408, 430, 438, 450, 451

astragalus, 459

Attila, 10, 127, 128, 208, 209

Augusta Treverorum, 425

Augustus, 73, 80, 425

Bacchus, 443

Balder, 198, 199, 421, 451, 480

balefire, 263, 361

Baltic, 15, 23, 63, 77, 96, 106, 107, 113, 120, 178, 324, 335, 385, 428, 431, 480

Bamburgh Beast, 453

banner, 211, 239, 261, 308, 323

Bárðar Saga, 250, 251, 317

barnstokkr, 384

Battle of Maldon, 6, 7, 223

Battle of the Goths and Huns, 307, 471

Baugi, 272, 340, 341, 342

Beardan, 132, 160, 161

Bede, 5, 45, 55, 56, 135, 136, 141, 146, 147, 148, 149, 152, 153, 154, 157, 190, 192, 195, 266, 337, 353, 361, 366, 367, 378, 379, 406, 453, 493

Beow, 243

Beowulf, 5, 7, 14, 22, 30, 31, 64,

76, 77, 88, 130, 132, 158, 162, 164, 166, 167, 170, 171, 210, 212, 269, 311, 313, 323, 324, 329, 336, 346, 347, 374, 383, 385, 390, 405, 444, 464, 469, 471, 476

binding, 53, 65, 177, 298, 355, 464, 465, 468, 502

Birka, 121

Boniface, 171, 376

bracteate, 2, 15, 18, 24, 42, 43, 81, 87, 101, 106, 107, 182, 202, 228, 335, 452, 457, 479, 481, 486, 487, 495

Bragi, 258, 270, 271, 297, 298, 304, 352, 500

Brávellir, 187, 312

Brennu-Njáls saga, 304

Broa, 110

Brynhild, 181

Busta Gallorum, 46, 100

Cadwallon, 379

Cædmon, 141, 154, 155, 156, 169, 372, 405, 406, 407

Canterbury, 43, 54

Charlemagne, 51, 171, 177

chessmen, 401

Christ, 14, 26, 130, 144, 192, 206, 219, 364, 375, 376, 381, 421, 493

Christmas, 73

Cimbri, 62, 69, 78, 212, 386

Coifi, 141, 144, 146, 147, 148, 149, 337, 471

columna mundi, 413

comitatus, 13, 81, 330, 393, 395, 396, 402, 424

Contra Vermes, 474

Cornuti, 123

cosmology, 384, 406

cremation, 264, 357, 359, 360, 367, 411, 499

de Bello Gallico, 62, 66, 337, 458

Deor, 206, 384

deuterotheme, 52, 53, 89, 199, 241, 349, 400, 458, 507

Dionysos/Dionysus, 34, 220, 404, 443

disease, 215, 218, 219, 224, 391, 473, 478, 484

dísir, 110, 224, 294, 295, 390, 466

Divine Twins, 55, 56

donatives, 22, 479

Draupnir, 8, 269

Dream of the Rood, 287, 371, 375, 383

drihten, 36, 224, 326, 328, 334, 409, 444, 456

duel, 57, 109, 110, 133, 168, 304, 422

Eadmund, king of the East Angles, 361, 362, 363, 364, 366, 378, 381

Eadwine, 193, 381

eagle, 12, 60, 100, 111, 112, 181, 185, 249, 250, 294, 305, 342, 401, 410, 415, 436, 453, 498, 499, 509

Eanfrið, 378, 379, 380

East Saxons, 52, 53, 56, 191, 192, 366

Edwin, king of Northumbria, 135, 136, 138, 139, 140, 141, 147, 148, 156, 337, 361, 489, 493

Eggja stone, 124

Egil Skallagrímsson, 5, 346, 405

Eiðsivaþingslov, 477

Einherjar, 211, 267, 290, 295, 296, 371, 397, 398, 404

Eiríkr Blóðøx, 5, 304, 305, 346, 437
Ekhammar, 121
elves, 26, 222, 223, 241, 284, 287, 473
Eote, 19
Épinal, 156
Essex, 6, 27, 53, 122, 212, 237
Exeter Book, 4, 31, 206, 211, 213, 214, 226, 405, 455, 473
Exodus, 389, 453
Exogamy, 5
Fen Drayton, 99, 114, 119, 120, 175, 534
Fenrir, 109, 115, 202, 203, 237, 248, 292, 450, 456, 465
feverfew, 221, 222
Finglesham, 117, 118, 119, 121, 408
Finn, 18
First Merseburg Charm, 465
Fjǫlnir, 195, 501
Flateyjarbók, 252, 303, 313
Francia, 6, 95, 177, 367
fratricide, 167, 421
Frea, 52, 173, 174
Frealaf, 191, 194
Freawaru, 161, 162
Fredegar, 87, 134
Freki, 296, 411, 412
Freyja, 18, 37, 189, 201, 256, 268, 297, 298, 303, 318, 347, 359, 391, 404, 420, 432, 436, 439, 506
Freyr, 28, 32, 51, 53, 148, 190, 212, 238, 248, 254, 256, 259, 297, 298, 306, 307, 409, 431, 477, 508
Frigg, 40, 189, 255, 268, 269, 290, 292, 327, 371, 409, 449

Frija, 199, 475
Froda, 160, 162, 210, 493
fuþark, 43, 83, 90, 124, 186, 204, 228, 319, 336, 354, 416, 430, 431
Gagnráðr, 290, 501
Gambara, 134, 173, 174, 359
Gapt, 175, 384, 386
Gårdlösa, 34
Gaut, 16, 327, 385, 386
Gautr, 133, 175, 295, 319, 385, 483
Gautreks saga, 207, 313, 316, 318, 327, 373, 471, 505, 507
Gauzo, 133
Geat, 133, 175, 384, 385, 387, 483
Geirhildr, 318
Geirrøðr, 174, 270, 292, 293, 294, 295, 327, 376, 409
Gepids, 6, 10
Gerðr, 53, 477
Geri, 296, 411, 412
Germania, 56, 60, 62, 63, 64, 73, 76, 80, 123, 131, 150, 175, 176, 177, 328, 337, 354, 356, 375, 393, 394, 397, 398, 402, 427, 429, 458, 469
Germany, 3, 20, 21, 51, 73, 96, 114, 233, 325, 328
Gesta Hammaburgensis Ecclesiae Pontificum, 54, 228, 229, 230
Gestr, 207, 208, 306, 501
Gestumblindi, 243, 306, 501
Getica, 54, 126, 127, 386
Gizurr Grýtingaliði, 308
Glasbacka Mount, 60
Godan, 1, 2, 66, 68, 70, 131, 135, 173, 174, 175, 176, 177, 318, 391, 418

Goðheim, 264

gǫndull, 438, 478, 502

Gosforth, 203

Gothic Horizon, 192, 193

Goths, 10, 73, 88, 104, 126, 127, 207, 208, 210, 307, 308, 311, 384, 385, 386, 471

Gotland, 20, 23, 106, 178, 185, 385, 485, 499, 501

Grani, 181, 470

grave-goods, 3, 20, 21, 89, 118, 151, 200, 201, 358, 359, 479

Gregory of Tours, 5, 149, 167, 424

Grendel, 166, 324, 346, 347, 390

Grim, 1, 44, 331

Grímnismál, 296, 327, 339, 353, 397, 411, 499, 500, 501, 502, 503, 504, 505, 506, 508, 509

Gualchelm, 234

Gudme, 18, 125, 492

Gungnir, 67, 72, 220, 469, 470, 475, 507

Gunnlǫð, 105, 279, 280, 281, 282, 318, 340, 342, 343, 443

Gylfaginning, 37, 40, 48, 49, 85, 232, 253, 265, 266, 269, 274, 299, 353, 388, 391, 397, 409, 410, 441, 447, 448

Hærik, 5

hairstyle, 84, 150, 314

Hákon I, 5

Halamarðus, 79, 80, 485

Halga, 160

hamingja, 112, 248

Hangatýr, 353, 371, 502

Harald Hárfagr, 437

Háraldr Harðráða, King, 110

Háraldr Hilditǫnn, 187

Haraldr Lúfa, 446

harigasti teiwa, 61

Harii, 194, 398

Harlequin, 240, 241, 392

Harold Godwineson, 167

Hassleben-Leuna, 328

Hávamál, 188, 223, 278, 279, 282, 287, 288, 305, 318, 334, 339, 343, 344, 345, 349, 351, 358, 370, 373, 377, 412, 414, 419, 429, 431, 432, 442, 443, 444, 461, 474, 500, 503, 508, 509

headdress, 117, 149, 150, 238, 428

Healfdene, 160, 323

Hefenfelth, 379

Hegge, 24, 236

Heiðrekr, 306, 307, 309

Heimdallr, 61, 204, 258, 259, 326, 384, 419, 420, 423, 432, 433, 449, 450

Heimskringla, 32, 253, 399, 401, 402, 465

Hel, 269, 299, 508

Helgi, 465

Heliand, 146, 375

Hellvi, 3, 81, 96, 106, 107, 485

helmet, 57, 61, 81, 94, 105, 106, 109, 114, 118, 119, 122, 125, 150, 331, 388, 397, 407, 454, 485

Hengest, 55, 57, 152, 153, 196, 327, 493

Heorot, 132, 161, 165, 347, 383

Hercules, 30, 31, 77, 81, 107, 414, 415

Hercules Magusanus, 77, 81

herfjǫturr, 53, 172, 267, 464

Herlewin, 235, 240, 241

Herminiones, 64, 326

Heruli, 458

Hildaland, 26
Hildebrandslied, 167
Himlingøje, 328
Hinguar, 362, 363, 364
Historia Ecclesiastica Gentis Anglorum, 45, 55, 56, 135, 136, 192, 195, 366, 379, 406, 471
Historia Francorum, 167, 424
Historia Langobardorum, 134, 173
hlafdige, 328, 331, 350
Hliðskjálf, 189, 292, 409, 420, 507
Hlǫðr, 307, 308, 309
Hloðskviða, 471
Högom, 102
hood, 146, 147, 201, 296, 505, 506, 509
horn, 20, 56, 180, 184, 185, 267, 277, 293, 343, 348, 351, 387, 408, 419, 468
horned dancer, 98
Horsa, 55, 57, 152, 153, 196
hostage, 6, 7, 50, 256
Hǫttr, 318, 505
Hranno, 75, 76, 77, 78, 90, 485
Hroðgar, king of the Danes, 5, 64, 160, 161, 162, 165, 166, 167, 168, 210, 324, 329, 336, 346, 383, 493
Hrólfr Kraki, 311, 312
Huns, 5, 134, 208, 210, 307, 308, 309, 471
Hygelac, 31, 161, 329, 387, 485
Hyndliuljóð, 203, 352
Iceland, 28, 81, 150, 244, 248, 249, 250, 253, 273, 313, 400
Icelandic Rune Poem, 318, 319, 430
idol, 103, 145, 146, 147, 150, 157, 189, 211, 212, 213, 230, 366, 367, 371, 376, 382, 383, 506

Indiculus Superstitionum et Paganiarum, 50, 170
Indra, 413
Ingævones, 64, 326
Ingeld, 30, 31, 160, 161, 164, 165, 210, 493, 494
Ingwe, 52, 64, 88, 103, 197, 326, 336, 385
inhumation, 93, 118, 359
Irmingot, 52
Irminsul, 369, 414, 415
Isle of Lewis, 401
Íslendingabók, 44, 306
Istaevones, 64, 326
Italy, 2, 3, 46, 114, 128, 130, 131, 133, 176, 177, 193, 206, 367, 405
jaundice, 215
Jelling, 24, 42, 43, 81, 82, 83
Jonas of Bobbio, 66, 89, 128, 205
Jordanes, 54, 126, 193, 386
Jormungandr, 237, 478
jǫtnar, 8, 444, 456
Julius Civilis, 77, 424, 425
Jupiter, 9, 40, 64, 149, 172, 325, 376, 414
Kent, 6, 18, 53, 54, 56, 121, 135, 136, 149, 152, 192, 239, 360
King Eiríkr of the Swedes, 471
Kirklevington, 203
knot, 149, 172, 201, 466
knotwork, 108, 178, 180, 203, 466
Lacnunga, 199, 215, 219, 473, 474, 480
Landnámabók, 304
Langobard, 6, 131, 133, 134, 135, 173, 174, 175, 176, 193, 207, 209, 240, 367, 385, 418, 480, 505

Ledberg, 203

Life of St., 128, 157, 380, 382

Lincolnshire, 204, 212, 408

Lindisfarne, 381

Lokasenna, 40, 297, 397, 439, 451, 455, 490, 497, 509

Loki, 8, 10, 40, 47, 50, 89, 90, 151, 297, 298, 302, 305, 420, 436, 439, 448, 449, 450, 451, 469, 470, 490, 503

Mannus, 62, 63, 64

Mars, 69, 70, 415, 416, 509

Mars Halamarðus, 79, 80

Matronae, 74, 81

Maxims I, 4, 211, 473

mead, 8, 67, 100, 105, 130, 185, 245, 247, 270, 271, 277, 278, 283, 301, 308, 319, 323, 330, 333, 334, 339, 340, 342, 344, 345, 348, 349, 350, 351, 397, 405, 431, 433, 444, 453, 488, 499, 500, 501

Mellitus, bishop, 192

Mercurius, 66, 68, 74, 128, 129, 130, 175, 205, 412, 484

Mercurius [Fr]iausus, 78

Mercurius Arvernorix,, 78

Mercurius Cimbrianus, 78

Mercurius Dumatius, 78

Mercurius Gebrinius, 78

Mercurius Leud[isius], 79

Mercurius Mercator, 79

Mercurius Nundinator, 79

Mercurius Rex, 79

metrical charm, 222

Miðgarðsormr, 450, 480

Milvian Bridge, 379

Mithras, 10, 14

mythology, 1, 8, 10, 11, 14, 39, 113, 223, 242, 253, 265, 266, 270, 349, 391, 423, 457

Naharvali, 56, 150

Negau Helmet B, 61

Nennius, 196, 198

Neptunus, 37

níðstǫng, 345, 370, 381

Nine Herbs Charm, 13, 32, 90, 199, 215, 220, 238, 375, 384, 473, 480

Nordendorf, 42, 50, 87, 88, 90, 198, 449, 497

Nordhuglo, 335, 476

Nornir, 208, 224, 232

North Sea, 15, 17, 20, 21, 22, 43, 44, 50, 73, 408, 410, 416, 480, 492

Northumbria, 135, 153, 157, 191

Norway, 5, 251, 253, 254, 273, 305, 399, 400

oath, 26, 50, 51, 70, 131, 147, 164, 167, 170, 281, 298, 306, 328, 343, 350, 351, 423, 425, 446, 486

Obrigheim, 114, 115

Odense, 25, 83, 258

Óðhrérir, 334, 340, 349, 351, 431

Óðins nǫfn, 353, 410, 499, 500, 501, 502, 504, 505, 506, 507, 508, 509

Óðinsheiti, 1, 76, 125, 208, 241, 243, 244, 310, 336, 397, 410, 498

Óðr, 37, 268, 391, 506

Oisc, 55

Ólafs saga Tryggvasonar, 207, 250, 252, 311

Öland, 98, 113, 123, 401, 427

Old English Rune Poem, 222, 226, 412, 417, 476

Old Saxon Baptismal Vow, 43, 50, 170

Origo Gentis Langobardum, 133, 174

Orkney, 26, 249, 471

Ormrinn inn langi, 252

Orosius, 63, 414

Orpheus, 443

os, 222, 227

Oseberg, 121, 200, 201, 238, 453, 478

Oswald, King of Northumbria, 347, 361, 370, 374, 378, 379, 380, 381, 387, 459

Oswig, King of Northumbria, 381

otherworld, 71, 74, 99, 105, 152, 181, 201, 223, 224, 235, 241, 286, 288, 326, 330, 331, 353, 354, 377, 391, 392, 411, 414, 429, 431, 433, 444, 478, 485, 486, 504, 506

Ouranos, 37

Paul the Deacon, 66, 88, 133, 134, 173, 318

Paulinus, bishop, 141, 143, 145, 147

Penda, King of Mercia, 27, 191, 378, 380, 381

Play o' de Lathie Odivere, 26

Poetic Edda, 232, 273, 278, 289, 297, 303

pole, 170, 287, 345, 346, 369, 370, 373, 381, 416, 437

pressblech, 20, 97, 100, 108, 110, 113, 115, 119, 121, 401, 408, 427

priesthood, 147, 148, 149, 334, 336

Prittlewell, 6, 111, 329, 351, 459

procession, 88, 98, 108, 110, 113, 201, 238, 391, 502

Prose Edda, 32, 39, 40, 49, 204, 265, 272, 298, 303, 409

prototheme, 27, 45, 46, 133, 241, 349, 400, 458, 500, 504, 507

psychopomp, 16, 74, 75, 99, 354, 391, 500, 504

Quintus Petillius Cerialis, 425

Rædwald, 45, 46, 93, 135, 137, 138, 139, 140, 192, 493

Ragnarǫk, 115, 202, 237, 348, 421, 456, 458

Rauðgrani, 250, 251, 506

rheumatism, 223

Rhine, 13, 14, 62, 74, 78, 177, 328, 387, 424, 425, 426, 484, 485

Ribe, 42, 43, 47, 54, 135, 428, 476, 492

riddling, 186, 227, 371

Ringerike Style, 185, 466

Rognvaldr Rettilbeini, 437

Rome, 59, 60, 72, 73, 77, 126, 188, 258, 385, 405, 425, 426, 427, 430, 484

Roseberry Topping, 29

Rothari, 87, 133

Rudolf of Fulda, 415

runes, 2, 8, 18, 30, 42, 43, 83, 87, 90, 124, 185, 187, 202, 204, 211, 226, 227, 238, 261, 282, 285, 287, 289, 319, 325, 335, 336, 346, 351, 352, 357, 371, 372, 377, 403, 408, 412, 414, 416, 417, 421, 429, 436, 442, 447, 459, 460, 470, 475, 477, 491, 504

Sæberht, king of the East Saxons, 56, 191, 192

Sámi, 437, 439, 490

Sarmatian, 113

Saxo Grammaticus, 44, 187, 235, 241, 311, 422

Saxons, 40, 44, 50, 51, 52, 70, 71, 123, 153, 160, 170, 239, 369, 416, 425

sceattas, 19

scop, 169, 206

Scyld, 64, 130, 243

Seaxneat, 51, 52, 53, 192

Second Merseburg Charm, 13, 23, 189, 198, 219, 269, 475, 480, 481

seiðr, 151, 201, 256, 262, 325, 404, 432, 437, 438, 439, 440, 441, 478, 490

Semnones, 65, 66, 172, 177, 355, 356, 357, 465

shaman, shamanism, 122, 150, 152, 414, 437, 490

shield, 20, 93, 95, 104, 110, 111, 117, 119, 123, 125, 164, 183, 221, 260, 294, 301, 305, 358, 388, 393, 401, 434, 439, 453, 458, 460, 464, 468, 469, 499, 507

Sigifrid, King of the Danes, 177

Sigmundr, 303, 304, 447, 507

Signý, 318

Sigrdrífumál, 310, 470

Sigurðr, 181, 187, 208, 239, 470, 471

Sinfjǫtli, 310, 447

Sinthgunt, 198, 199, 475

Sir Francis Drake, 392

Skáldskaparmál, 47, 265, 266, 270, 271, 279, 339, 343, 353, 410, 469, 498, 500

Skírnir, 53

Sleipnir, 181, 182, 300, 392, 448, 454

smith, 221, 222, 223, 349, 428, 436, 451, 456, 457, 469

snake, 67, 90, 101, 105, 185, 252, 342, 383, 449, 452, 474, 498

Snorri Sturluson, 3, 5, 14, 40, 41, 91, 208, 235, 242, 244, 253, 254, 265, 266, 272, 273, 274, 312, 399, 401, 404, 421, 450, 456, 490

Solomon and Saturn, 225, 290, 412

sorcery, 151, 243, 262, 335, 404, 436, 438, 441, 461, 477, 478, 549

spear, 24, 63, 67, 72, 75, 99, 100, 101, 108, 109, 110, 113, 115, 116, 117, 119, 120, 121, 122, 124, 125, 128, 133, 146, 148, 160, 162, 183, 201, 203, 210, 222, 223, 224, 248, 283, 285, 286, 308, 309, 310, 316, 358, 359, 452, 454, 456, 465, 469, 470, 471, 500

St. Columba, 157

St. Columbanus, 128, 387

St. Cuthbert, 157

St. Martin, 376, 382

stabbing, 285, 315, 316, 377, 502

staff, 60, 67, 74, 121, 170, 201, 220, 359, 475, 477, 478, 502

stag, 231, 383

Starkaðr, 115, 165, 187, 207, 210, 243, 310, 313, 314, 315, 316, 327, 402

Stephen of Ripon, 157

Strängnäs, 87, 90, 185

Sturla Þórðarson, 244, 273

Sturlunga saga, 244

Style I art, 18, 23, 98, 330, 453

Style II art, 23, 98, 100, 118, 383, 453

Styrbjǫrn, 313, 471

Suebi, 62, 64, 65, 66, 131, 355, 357

Sutton Hoo, 3, 20, 46, 57, 91, 92, 95, 97, 98, 99, 100, 102, 103, 106, 108, 111, 112, 114, 118, 119, 121, 123, 125, 150, 213, 329, 331, 351, 358, 366, 367, 373, 374, 407, 427, 453, 454, 459, 467, 468, 481, 488, 492, 495, 504

Suttungr, 33, 67, 105, 156, 184, 247, 271, 272, 278, 279, 281, 340, 341, 342, 343, 345, 441

Sweden, 21, 54, 90, 160, 186, 212, 258, 264, 428

sword, 52, 99, 109, 114, 119, 123, 146, 159, 164, 166, 183, 201, 248, 270, 298, 303, 306, 308, 310, 317, 323, 356, 358, 408, 421, 434, 469, 497

Tacitus, 52, 56, 62, 63, 64, 65, 66, 68, 69, 70, 73, 88, 114, 123, 131, 135, 150, 151, 172, 326, 327, 336, 354, 355, 356, 357, 368, 375, 393, 395, 397, 398, 402, 425, 426, 427, 431, 458, 465, 469, 484

tapestries, 121, 200, 201

Taplow, 329, 428, 459, 468

Textus Roffensis, 43, 44, 46, 135, 236

The Wonders of the East, 389

Þórr, Thor, 28, 32, 40, 84, 89, 90, 110, 113, 150, 165, 172, 187, 204, 205, 207, 212, 229, 237, 238, 248, 243, 249, 251, 258, 259, 261, 262, 270, 297, 298, 305, 313, 316, 317, 369, 397, 399, 405, 413, 420, 441, 442, 447

Þorwald's cross, 202

þulr, 336, 444

Þunor, 51, 84, 89, 90, 172, 325

þyle, 166, 168, 169, 336, 444

Tissø, 6, 190

Tiw, 52, 172, 430

Tjängvide, 178, 180

Torpo, 237

Torslunda, 98, 99, 103, 113, 114, 116, 119, 120, 121, 123, 175, 202, 401, 408, 427

transgressive hero, 168, 207

tripartite structure, 8, 11

Tuisco, 62, 63, 64

Týr, 47, 53, 109, 172, 190, 228, 297, 298, 349, 423, 430

Ullr, 190, 212, 391, 475

Unferþ, 166, 167, 168, 336, 405, 444

Unwona, Bishop, 494

Uppåkra, 125, 428

Uppland, 50, 93, 108, 187

Uppsala, 26, 28, 40, 54, 76, 93, 201, 230, 259, 272, 311, 337, 354, 373, 377, 378, 419, 471, 489

Vafþrúðnismál, 225, 289, 397, 499, 501

Valhǫll, 75, 181, 228, 263, 267, 294, 303, 304, 305, 319, 324, 359, 361, 430, 458, 500, 508

valkyrie, valkyrjur, 75, 101, 181, 182, 199, 220, 223, 224, 267, 268, 310, 388, 389, 390, 392, 404, 410, 501, 506, 508

Valsgärde, 20, 93, 99, 100, 101, 108, 114, 121, 125, 408

Vandals, 10, 150, 173

Vanir, 50, 51, 53, 84, 112, 149,

174, 202, 256, 264, 297, 339,
347, 359, 422, 423, 431, 437,
438, 439, 441, 450, 456
Varus, 80, 386
Vé, 40, 48, 49, 187, 255, 258,
287, 497
Vegtamskviða, 299
Veleda, 63, 390, 426, 427
Vémóðr, 187
Vendel, 20, 57, 93, 95, 97, 108,
109, 114, 116, 121, 125, 178,
453, 504
venom, 473, 474, 476
Versus Pauli ad Carolum, 177
Víðarr, 203, 298, 420, 456
Víkarr, King, 243, 313, 314, 316,
318, 373, 377, 471
Vili, 40, 41, 47, 48, 49, 64, 255,
258, 287
Vindelev, 2, 3, 22, 42, 43, 81, 82,
83, 85, 86, 101, 202, 486, 495
Vitlyckehäll stone, 24
Volla, 198, 199, 269
vǫlr, 438, 478
vǫlsi, 437, 478
Vǫlsunga saga, 310, 447
Vǫluspá, 48, 49, 50, 148, 188,
232, 274, 290, 299, 338, 345,
348, 371, 378, 397, 422
vǫlva, 189, 201, 202, 274, 299,
301, 302, 303, 330, 378, 438,
478
Vortigern, 57, 196
Waldere, 5
Wansdyke, 27, 29, 196
war-god, 53, 81, 88, 100, 168, 175,
176, 208, 209, 211, 246, 304,
310, 358, 388, 389, 397, 398,
399, 402, 404, 407, 424, 427,
430, 446, 453, 454, 458, 493

Waten, 177
Wednesbury, 26, 92
Wednesfield, 26
Weland, 223, 349
Wensley, 26, 27
Wenslow, 26, 27
wergeld, 133, 479, 480
Whitby, 157, 406
Wið Færsticce, 32, 215, 220, 222,
390, 392, 473
Widsith, 3, 31, 76, 77, 123, 131,
132, 165, 193, 206, 207, 208,
211, 241, 309, 336, 339, 405,
489
Wihtgils, 55, 153, 154
Wild Hunt, 34, 37, 57, 193, 194,
198, 223, 234, 240, 241, 354,
390, 391, 392, 398, 412, 488
Wilfrid, St., 157
Winniles, 70, 134, 173, 174, 175
witch, 152, 221, 222, 223, 224,
370, 436, 440, 473, 477
Wodden Stone, 26
Wode, 391
Wodnesdæg, 72, 226
Wodnesdic, 29
Woduridaz, 336, 458, 478
wolf, 12, 45, 47, 53, 98, 102,
113, 114, 115, 116, 119, 120,
175, 202, 203, 248, 294, 296,
310, 345, 361, 363, 365, 366,
398, 400, 401, 412, 430, 450,
453, 465, 478, 487, 497
Woodnesborough, 26, 27
wuldortanas, 220, 375, 384, 473,
475, 476, 477, 478
Wulfhere, King of Mercia, 192,
309
wyrm, 219, 473, 474
Ybor, 174

Yeavering, 370, 383

Yggdrasill, 232, 233, 277, 344, 345, 375, 376, 384, 392, 413, 420, 442

Yggr, 1, 29, 243, 246, 270, 295, 385, 498, 509

ylfa, 223

Ynglinga saga, 5, 7, 30, 40, 50, 191, 253, 254, 353, 357, 360, 361, 418, 490, 500, 501, 502, 507

Ynglingatal, 40, 195, 253, 254

York, 146, 147, 245, 361, 437

yupa, 413, 414